EAST ANGLIAN ARCHAEOLOGY

Frontispiece
Area A under excavation with the presumed site of the ship mound behind in the garden
and with scheduled tumulus in the background to the south (right) of the road

In Memoriam Mary Harrison, 1912—1999
Sine qua non.

Snape Anglo-Saxon Cemetery: Excavations and Surveys 1824–1992

by William Filmer-Sankey and Tim Pestell

with contributions from
Sue Anderson, Harry Appleyard,
Teresa Briscoe, Esther Cameron,
Shirley Carnegie, Elisabeth Crowfoot,
Simon Davis, Vanessa Fell, Rowena Gale,
Graeme Lawson, Peter Marsden,
Simon Mays, Carol Neuman de Vegvar,
Mark Robinson, James Steele,
Penelope Walton Rogers,
Jacqui Watson and Stanley West

illustrations by
Rebecca Archer, Rupert Cook,
Simon Pressey, Hoste Spalding,
Gordon Turner-Walker, Donna Wreathall

East Anglian Archaeology
Report No.95, 2001

Archaeological Service
Suffolk County Council

EAST ANGLIAN ARCHAEOLOGY
REPORT NO. 95

Published by
Environment and Transport
Suffolk County Council
St Edmund House
Rope Walk
Ipswich
Suffolk IP4 1LZ

in conjunction with
The Scole Archaeological Committee

Editor: Stanley West
EAA Managing Editor: Jenny Glazebrook

Scole Editorial Sub-Committee:
Brian Ayers, Archaeology and Environment Officer, Norfolk Museums Service
David Buckley, County Archaeological Officer, EssexPlanning Department
Keith Wade, Archaeological Service Manager, Suffolk County Council
Peter Wade-Martins
Stanley West

Set in Times Roman by Joan Daniells and Jenny Glazebrook using Corel Ventura Publisher ™
Printed by Geerings of Ashford Ltd., Ashford, Kent

ISBN 0 86055 264 0

For details of *East Anglian Archaeology* see last page

This volume was published with the aid of a grant from English Heritage

Cover illustrations
(front) Grave 47 shield boss laid over bow of logboat.
(back) Grave 47 showing stain of logboat.
Photos: Tim Pestell

Contents

List of Plates

List of Figures

List of Tables

Contributors

Sue Anderson
Suffolk Archaeological Unit (human bone)

the late Harry Appleyard
Consultant microscopist (plant fibres)

the late Teresa Briscoe
Archive of Anglo-Saxon Pottery Stamps

Esther Cameron
Institute of Archaeology, Oxford (conservation)

Shirley Carnegie
formerly Principal Project Assistant, Suffolk
Archaeological Unit

Elisabeth Crowfoot
Consultant on textiles

Simon Davis
Instituto Português de Arqueologia, Lisboa, Portugal
(horse skull)

Vanessa Fell
Institute of Archaeology, Oxford (conservation)

William Filmer-Sankey
Alan Baxter and Associates

Rowena Gale
Consultant on charcoal

Graeme Lawson
Cambridge Music-Archaeological Survey (lyre)

Peter Marsden
Director, Shipwreck Heritage Centre, Hastings
(dugout boat)

Simon Mays
Centre for Archaeology, English Heritage, Fort
Cumberland, Portsmouth (cremated bone)

Carol Neuman de Vegvar
Dept. of Fine Arts, Ohio Wesleyan University

Tim Pestell
Centre of East Anglian Studies, University of East
Anglia

Mark Robinson
Environmental Laboratory, University Museum, Oxford
(insect remains)

James Steele
Dept. of Archaeology, University of Southampton
(cremated bone)

Penelope Walton Rogers
Manager, Textile Research in Archaeology, York (dyes)

Jacqui Watson
Centre for Archaeology, English Heritage, Fort
Cumberland, Portsmouth (wood remains)

Stanley West
formerly Suffolk County Archaeologist
(beads, brooches)

Acknowledgements

The excavations of the Snape Anglo-Saxon cemetery were a combined effort, which could not have taken place without the help, goodwill and support of an enormous number of people. The principal thanks must go to the late Mrs Vernon-Wentworth who, as landowner, allowed us to excavate her fields, and to John Stigwood and Bill Rix who, as tenants, tolerated the disruption caused by our presence with constant good humour. More generally, the excavation would never have taken place without the wonderfully infectious enthusiasm of Mrs Mary Harrison, under the spell of which WFS fell at the age of seven. Other members of the Snape Historical Trust, notably Ken Baird and Stanley West, have all given limitless amounts of free advice and encouragement. The excavation, especially in its early days, was an heroic effort in which Ken Brown, Shirley Carnegie, Charles Foster, Debbie and Julian Stannard and Sue Balls deserve particular mention.

Many institutions, friends, colleagues and employers deserve special thanks. English Heritage principally, but also the Society of Antiquaries, the Moncrief Trust, the Scarfe Trust, the Francis Coales Charitable Trust and the Marc Fitch Fund all contributed towards the costs of

excavation and writing up. Dr Simon Collcutt of Oxford Archaeological Associates gave WFS the time to carry out and write up the excavation; Professor Roberta Gilchrist and the Centre for East Anglian Studies at the University of East Anglia allowed TP intercalation from his PhD course. Dr Steven Plunkett of Ipswich Museum helped to locate material from former excavations and provided information on the 1862 excavators. Clare Foss at Aldeburgh Museum allowed access to their collections of 1862 material for examination and drawing, while Leslie Webster at the British Museum arranged for the 1862 ring to be drawn. The Swedish Central Board of Antiquities and Margareta Nockert provided plates XLVIII and XLIX of the textiles from Högom; other photographs in the report were taken by Stuart Boulter, Esther Cameron, Bob Carr, Simon Davis, Vanessa Fell, Graeme Lawson, Tim Pestell and Bob Wilkins. Diana Briscoe finalised the pottery stamp report after the death of her mother, Teresa Briscoe. Catherine Hills and Kenneth Penn allowed access to unpublished material from Spong Hill and Harford Farm, whilst Trevor Ashwin and Andrew Reynolds both provided helpful discussion on certain points of interpretation. Philip Walker, as English Heritage Inspector, and Pete Wilson, as our project monitor, did their best to keep us on target. Of the many colleagues with whom we discussed our findings, Sam Newton will always stand out.

Esther Cameron and Vanessa Fell would like to thank Karen Wardley for conservation of the finds from 1985–9 and for the use of her records. They would also like to thank Jacqui Watson (English Heritage) for wood species and antler identifications, and for inspired interpretation of some of the more complex items; Dr B. Juniper (Department of Plant Sciences, University of Oxford) for commenting on the condition of the wood; Justine Bayley (English Heritage) for advice on non-ferrous alloys and other material; Malcolm Ward (English Heritage) for X-ray diffraction analysis; Wendy Hills (John Radcliffe Infirmary, Oxford) for tomography; and Susan Hardman (University of Wales, Cardiff) for FTIR microscopy.

Esther Cameron would like to thank Glynis Edwards (English Heritage) for leather identifications, Anna Cselik (English Heritage) for animal fibre identifications, and Professor C. Perrins (Department of Zoology, University of Oxford) for examining feather remains. We are also grateful to R.V. Davis, who made the petrological identification of the quern fragment from grave 20 and to David Buckley (Essex Archaeology Section) who provided a discussion of it. Jean Cook kindly examined and described the bucket from grave 47.

TP and WFS owe a particular debt to Keith Wade, Bob Carr, and all the staff of the Suffolk Archaeological Unit, for providing space and for constant help towards the project. Shirley Carnegie carried out much of both the excavation and the initial post-excavation work that made this report possible.

Finally, WFS wishes to record his undying gratitude to his father, Patrick, for his ceaseless interest and encouragement. Would that he had lived to see this report published.

Summary

The Snape Anglo-Saxon cemetery stands in the Sandlings area of east Suffolk. The first recorded excavations on the site were conducted in 1862–3 by the landowner, Septimus Davidson and some friends. In trenching the largest barrow they encountered rivets, and by careful excavation were able to reveal the remains of a complete Anglo-Saxon ship burial, the first to be found in England. Although already robbed, they recovered a number of items including a gold Germanic finger-ring, now in the British Museum, which showed that the burial had been of the highest status. Their excavations also revealed a large number of Anglo-Saxon cremation burials. Subsequently the site was almost forgotten until in 1970 a dowser found an Anglo-Saxon urn in the field to the north of the road, and in 1972 a sewer trench excavated along the road yielded a further nine cremations, one in a bronze bowl (published by West and Owles, 1973).

In 1985 a research project was initiated under the aegis of the Snape Historical Trust. Excavations have shown the site to be a mixed cremation and inhumation cemetery. Amongst the inhumations, a wide variety of burial practices has been noted, including the use of two, and possibly three, dugout logboats as burial containers. Other graves made extensive use of organics, in some instances of textile, including the first observed use of *Rippenköper* weave in England (grave 37). The grave-goods were within the normal range of material to be expected in an Anglo-Saxon cemetery, more exotic finds including a lyre (grave 32) and a horse's head with tack (grave 47). Finds show the cremation burials to date from the late 5th to 7th centuries, and the inhumations to date from the mid 6th to 7th centuries. Other features excavated included ring-ditches, some associated with inhumations, and six burnt stone features, apparently surrounding mound 4.

This report attempts to publish all the material known to have been excavated from the cemetery although the urns and their contents from the 1862–3 excavations have become dispersed over the years and many undoubtedly lost. The 1970 and 1972 finds have also been re-examined, re-drawn and are here republished.

The final draft of the text was submitted by the authors in May 1998.

Résumé

Le cimetière anglo-saxon de Snape est situé dans la région des Sandlings à l'est du Suffolk. Les premières fouilles attestées du site datent des années 1862–63 et furent dirigées par le propriétaire Septimus Davidson aidé par quelques amis. En creusant le plus grand tumulus, ils trouvèrent des rivets et, en procédant avec précaution, ils parvinrent à dégager les vestiges d'une sépulture déposée dans un navire anglo-saxon. Il s'agissait d'un ensemble complet qui constitua la première découverte de ce type en Angleterre. Ils réussirent également à entrer en possession de plusieurs objets qui avaient été dérobés auparavant, comme une bague germanique en or. Ce bijou, qui est à l'heure actuelle exposé au British Museum, prouve que le défunt avait une position sociale très élevée. Les fouilles entreprises révélèrent également la présence d'un grand nombre de sépultures anglo-saxonnes par crémation. Par la suite, le site sortit presque complétement des mémoires jusqu'à la découverte en 1970 par un radiesthésiste d'une urne anglo-saxonne enfouie dans un champ au nord de la route. Enfin, en 1972, le creusement d'une tranchée pour les égouts permit de mettre à jour neuf nouvelles crémations, dont l'une était placée dans un vase en bronze (voir la publication de West et Owles, 1973).

En 1985, un projet de recherche fut lancé sous l'égide du Snape Historical Trust. Des fouilles révélèrent que nous avions affaire à un cimetière où avaient licu à la fois des inhumations et des crémations. Dans le cas des inhumations, on peut noter la grande variété des pratiques funéraires: ainsi, deux, voire trois barques en rondins servaient à accueillir le corps du défunt. D'autres sépultures contenaient également en abondance des éléments naturels tels que des textiles; on trouve par exemple dans la tombe 37 le premier tissu *Rippenköper* dont on ait trouvé la trace en Angleterre. Les objets funéraires mis à jour correspondent à ce qu'on trouve habituellement dans un cimetière anglo-saxon, à l'exception de quelques découvertes originales, telles qu'une lyre (tombe 32) ou une tête de cheval accompagnée de la sellerie (tombe 47). Les éléments rassemblés permettent de dater les crémations de la fin du cinquième au septième siècle, et les inhumations du milieu du sixième au septième siècle. Des fouilles ont également menées dans des fossés circulaires dont certains étaient associés à des inhumations, et six pierres brûlés, qui apparemment entouraient le tertre 4, ont été exhumées.

Le présent rapport s'efforce de rendre compte de tous les objets qui ont été trouvés dans le cimetière, même si les urnes mises à jour lors des fouilles de 1862–63 ont été dispersées ainsi que leur contenu au fil des années et que beaucoup sont désormais perdues. Les découvertes de 1970 et dc 1972 ont également fait l'objet d'un nouvel examen; elles ont été redessinées et sont présentées dans la publication.

La version définitive du présent texte fut proposée par les auteurs en mai 1998.

Zusammenfassung

Der angelsächsische Friedhof von Snape liegt im Sandlings-Gebiet von Ost-Suffolk. Die ersten verzeichneten, 1862–63 durchgeführten Grabungen dort gehen auf den Landbesitzer Septimus Davidson und einige seiner Freunde zurück. Beim Ausheben des größten Grabhügels stießen sie auf Nieten. Durch vorsichtiges Weitergraben gelang es ihnen, die Überreste eines vollständigen angelsächsischen Schiffsgrabs freizulegen, dem ersten in England gefundenen. Obwohl bereits geplündert, kam eine Reihe von Objekten zum Vorschein, die deutlich machten, dass hier eine Person von höchstem Rang begraben lag – darunter ein goldener germanischer Fingerring, der nun im British Museum aufbewahrt wird. Ihre Grabung förderte außerdem eine Vielzahl angelsächsischer Urnengräber zutage. In der Folgezeit geriet die Stätte in Vergessenheit, bis 1970 ein Rutengänger im Feld nördlich der Straße auf eine angelsächsische Urne stieß und 1972 beim Ausheben eines Abwasserkanals entlang der Straße Überreste von neun weiteren Feuerbestattungen auftauchten, eine davon in einem Bronzegefäß (1973 von West and Owles veröffentlicht).

Wie ein 1985 unter der Schirmherrschaft des Snape Historical Trust begonnenes Grabungsprojekt zeigte, beherbergt die Stätte eine Mischung aus Urnen- und Erdgräbern. Die Erdgräber wiesen auf eine Vielzahl von Bestattungssitten hin; unter anderem kamen zwei, vielleicht sogar drei ausgehöhlte Baumstämme (Einbäume) als Grabbehältnisse zum Vorschein. In anderen Gräbern fand sich viel organisches Material, in einigen Fällen Textilien, darunter der in England erstmals verzeichnete Gebrauch von Rippenköpergewebe (Grab 37). Als Grabbeigaben wurden die für einen angelsächsischen Friedhof typischen Materialien festgestellt. Zu den exotischeren Funden zählten eine Leier (Grab 32) und ein Pferdekopf mit Sattel- und Zaumzeug (Grab 47). Die Feuerbestattungen konnten auf die Zeit des späten 5. bis 7. Jahrhunderts, die Erdbestattungen auf die Zeit zwischen der Mitte des 6. und dem 7. Jahrhundert datiert werden. Des Weiteren förderte die Ausgrabung Kreisgräben zutage, von denen einige mit Erdgräbern in Verbindung standen, und sechs Feuerstellen, die Steinfunde mit Brandspuren enthielten, offenbar um Hügel Nummer 4.

Der vorliegende Bericht versucht, alles bekannte Material aus den verschiedenen Grabungen zu dokumentieren, auch wenn die 1862–63 freigelegten Urnen und ihr Inhalt über die Jahre hinweg verstreut wurden und viele zweifelsohne verloren gegangen sind. Auch die 1970 und 1972 gemachten Funde wurden neu untersucht, neu gezeichnet und im vorliegenden Band neu veröffentlicht.

Die endgültige Textfassung der Autoren stammt vom Mai 1998.

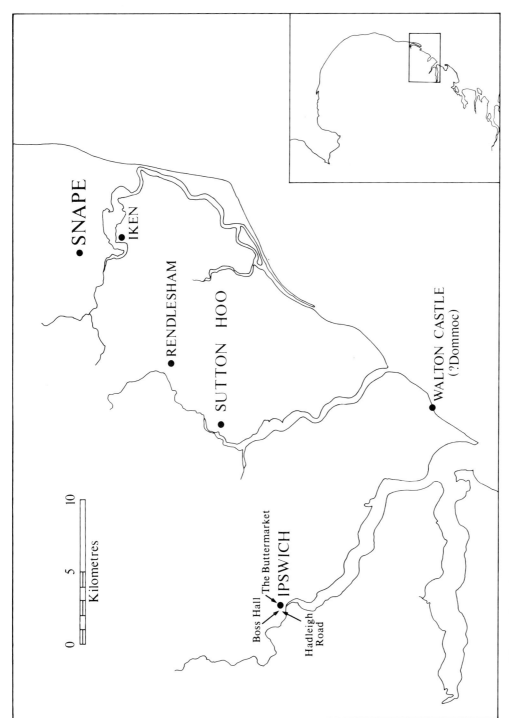

Figure 1 Location map, showing important Anglo-Saxon sites in the area, including cemetery sites in Ipswich

SNAPE

●IKEN

●RENDLESHAM

SUTTON HOO
●

WALTON CASTLE
(?Dommoc)

Boss Hall
The Buttermarket
●IPSWICH
Hadleigh
Road

0   5   10
Kilometres

Chapter 1. Introduction
by William Filmer-Sankey

I. Introduction

The present project on the Snape Anglo-Saxon cemetery began in 1984. Its overall aim initially was to bring together all existing information on the site, which was widely scattered, and to suggest areas where current *lacunae* could be filled by judicious excavation. The project was conceived at the same time as the renewed work at Sutton Hoo and its aims were always seen as contributing to the wider context of Sutton Hoo and the emergence of the East Anglian kingdom. In particular, it was thought to be important to provide information on such matters as the cemetery's size, nature and state of preservation, which could be compared with that from Sutton Hoo, so as to put both sites in their wider context.

Inevitably, the Research Strategy changed as the project evolved. In particular, as information on the seriously damaged parts of the cemetery became available, it was decided that excavation on a larger scale than originally envisaged was necessary to record those areas in imminent danger of total destruction by ploughing.

This report is not just an account of the excavations which took place from 1986–1992. It attempts to assemble all the available evidence for the cemetery into a coherent whole. In line with current English Heritage guidelines and with previous practice in *East Anglian Archaeology*, it begins by outlining the history of investigation and excavation on the site, from 1827–1992 (Chapters 2 and 3). It then brings together all the available evidence in the form of a catalogue (Chapter 4). Finally, in Chapters 5, 6 and 7, we have selected for interpretation and discussion those areas where we believe that the site has provided new information, whether on the detail of Anglo-Saxon burial rite, on the mechanics of organic survival, or on the emergence of the Anglo-Saxon kingdom of East Anglia.

Inevitably, this report contains only a highly edited and selective version of the total information available in the site archive, which has been deposited with the Suffolk Archaeological Unit at Bury St Edmunds, where the SMR number is SNP 007.

II. Location

The Snape Anglo-Saxon Cemetery lies at TM 402593, in the north-east corner of the present parish of Snape, some 550m from the parish boundary with Friston (Figs 1 and 2). Although some individual houses stand either on or close to the site, it is generally remote from modern settlement, with the villages of Snape and Friston 1.5km and 1.25km distant respectively. Snape church, itself isolated from modern settlement, is 800m to the west. The A1094 road to Aldeburgh, which cannot be traced back earlier than the 19th century (Mary Harrison, pers. comm.), runs broadly through the middle of the site. The wide estuary of the river Alde is 2.5km to the south, and the North Sea at Aldeburgh is 7km to the east.

Although part of the site lies beneath the rough garden of a house called St Margaret's, today's landscape is predominantly agricultural, and rather featureless. Until the agricultural clearances of the 1940s and 50s, however, the site lay within a huge area of acid heathland which stretched from Snape to Aldeburgh and which was used predominantly as sheep walks. Its characteristic 'Sandling' vegetation of heather, gorse and grass reflects the area's underlying geology. The largely stone-free glacial sand of the area is very free-draining, so that the present cultivation of rape, linseed, potatoes and rye is only possible through extensive irrigation during the growing season.

Native English trees do not grow well in such an environment and it is probable that, before the extensive, predominantly pine plantations of the 20th century, the site would have been visible both from the river Alde to the south and from the North Sea to the east (Figs 2 and 3). That such long views were possible is hard to believe today, when the site appears totally remote from the sea. That they could be is proved by an extract from a long poem of indifferent quality which appeared in the *East Anglian Daily Press* in 1912:

> *At last, passing Snape Church, on Snape Common, believe me,*
> *A Friend in the coach, with intent to deceive me,*
> *To a number of sticks my attention directed*
> *Which for May-poles, she said, had been lately erected.*
> *But that this was mere joking, I very well know*
> *For presently many tall ships passed in view:*
> *And you cannot but guess how my heart was in motion,*
> *When at length we obtained a full view of the Ocean.*

Although it is clear from this that the sea could be seen from a point very close to Snape church, calculation of the exact extent to which the site would have been visible from the sea in the 6th century is difficult. We have no way of knowing either how much coastline has been lost to coastal erosion in the subsequent years or, of even greater importance, where exactly the Alde flowed into the sea at the time. A map of 1588 shows that Aldeburgh extended considerably further to the east, with six streets parallel to the sea, where today there are only two (Arnott 1961, 9). Cartographic evidence from *c*.1530 onwards charts the gradual southward elongation of the gravel spit, with the consequent movement of the river mouth to the south (Anon 1966). It is undeniably tempting to suggest that the 6th-century Alde flowed out at Slaughden Quay, where the present shingle spit (breached by the 1953 floods) is only *c*.70 metres wide and where the earliest maps show a creek that might well be a relict entrance. However, this cannot be proved. Fig. 3 thus shows the situation today.

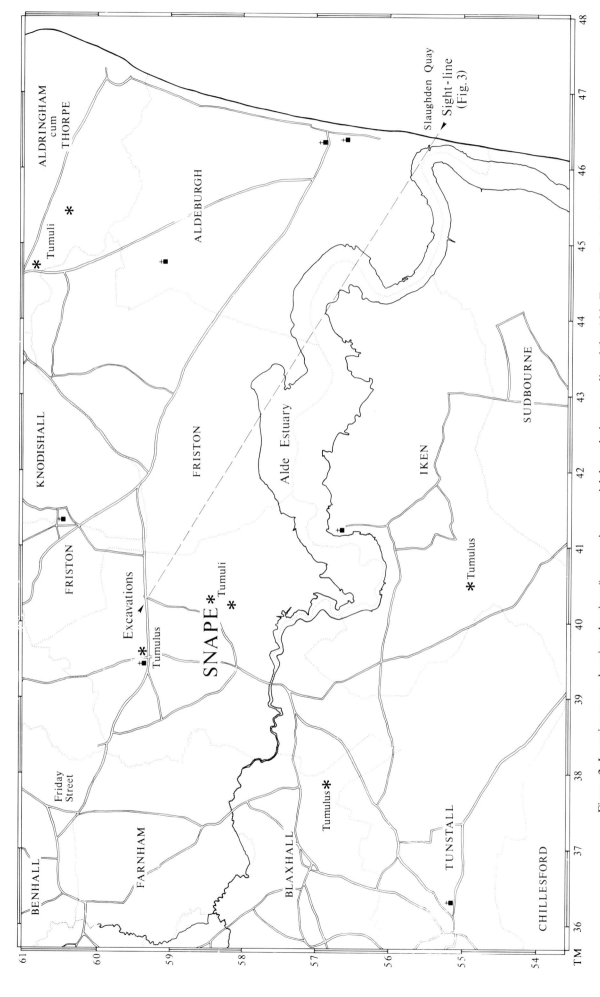

Figure 2 Location map, showing the site of excavations, parish boundaries, tumuli and the Alde Estuary. Scale 1:50,000

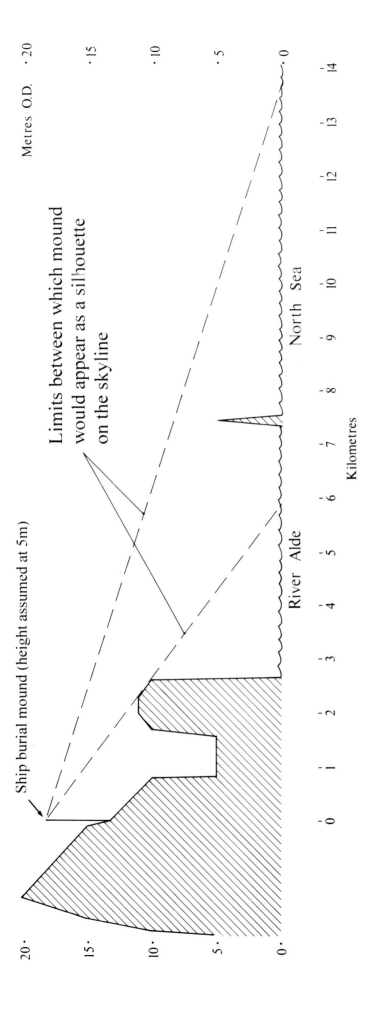

Figure 3 Line of sight from the excavation to the North Sea, illustrating how the ship burial mound could have been visible out to sea

3

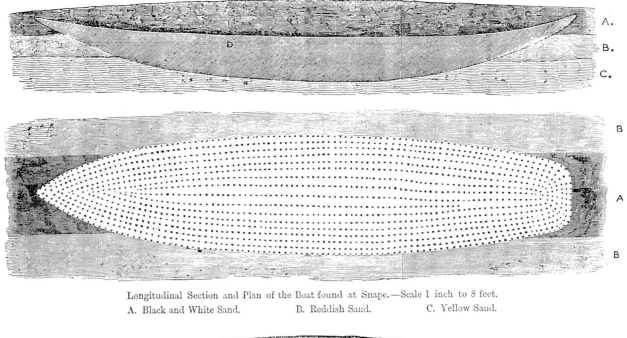

Longitudinal Section and Plan of the Boat found at Snape.—Scale 1 inch to 8 feet.

A. Black and White Sand.   B. Reddish Sand.   C. Yellow Sand.

Transverse section of boat.   Scale, 1 inch to 8 feet.
AA. Black and white sand.
B. Reddish sand.   C. Yellow sand.

Figure 4 Engraving of the ship burial as published in the *Proceedings of the Society of Antiquaries*, 1863 (*c.f.* Plate I)

Chapter 2. Excavations and Surveys
1827–1984

I. Excavations and Surveys 1827–1984
by William Filmer-Sankey

The first recorded excavation on the site of the cemetery took place in 1827. In this year, according to a letter published in *The Field* in March 1863 written by an unidentified man who had been a boy in Snape at the time, a group of 'seven or eight gentlemen', reported to be Londoners, opened several barrows and found 'quantities of gold rings, brooches, chains, *etc.*'. From Snape, the group moved across the Alde to open a tumulus on Blaxhall Common (SMR No. BLX 001), where the legend 'Roman Urns found 1827' given on the old 6-inch OS map provides confirmation of their visit. Thereafter unfortunately they disappear along with their finds.

The mounds were probably opened again by the Ordnance Survey around the middle of the century, though no records of this investigation have been traced (Davidson 1863, 177). In 1862 an excavation of much higher calibre took place. It was initiated by the owner of the land to the north of the present A1094 road, Septimus Davidson. Septimus Davidson was a city solicitor and one time legal adviser to the Ottoman Government (according to his obituary in the *Solicitors' Journal* of 7 February 1885). He does not seem to have had any special training or interest in archaeology, but was simply curious to know what lay beneath the three mounds in his possession. He was assisted by Dr Nicholas Hele, a local surgeon whose writings show a lively curiosity in the area's history, and who went on to excavate (with less success) a group of tumuli at Aldringham; by Francis Francis, whose epitaph in Winchester Cathedral does not mention any special antiquarian interests (he was keen on fishing!); and an enigmatic character known only as 'Mr C'.[1]

Although none of the excavators appear to have had any previous excavation experience, or indeed special knowledge of archaeology, they nevertheless carried out the excavation in an exemplary way, for which we owe them a great debt. In the first place, they were not treasure hunters; they were aware of the previous excavations and thus had 'little expectation of gathering any results' (Davidson 1863, 177). The reason for the excavation was their own intellectual curiosity. Their techniques were typical for the period: they started with a pit at the centre of each mound, and then dug outwards. Frequently there were accidents: 'We came upon an urn and crush went the spade through a portion of it, fracturing the rim seriously', but generally they were careful: 'We [...] conducted the digging with the greatest caution, and rather under-digging and mining so as to let the upper mass of the earth, in which the remains might be supposed to lie, to fall in' (Francis 1863a, 61). They were clearly aware of the fragile nature of the evidence and of the need to record *in situ* features such as the rivets of the ship, which they revealed by 'scraping and sweeping with the hands only'.

Our greatest debt to Septimus Davidson and his friends is owed for the prompt and detailed way in which they published the excavation. Very shortly after its completion all the principal parties (with the exception of Mr C) had published accounts. Septimus Davidson had his account read to the meeting of the Society of Antiquaries in January of 1863 (Davidson 1863); Francis Francis wrote two lively articles in *The Field* in January and March 1863, and a paper for the *Archaeological Journal* (Francis 1863a and 1863b); and Dr Hele devoted a chapter of his book *Notes and Jottings about Aldeburgh* to the excavation (Hele 1870). The three authors all give slightly differing perspectives on the excavation, reflecting their particular interests, but all are remarkable for their consistency and for the detail that they give.

From these three accounts, it is possible to form a reasonably accurate view in the first place of what the site looked like, and (in the absence of any cartographic evidence) of how it was laid out.

A group of nine or ten mounds, 'a matter of wonderment to the simple peasant — who in these latitudes is remarkably simple indeed' (Francis 1863a, 61), stood in a group on either side of the Aldeburgh road. Of these nine or ten mounds, five or six are described as 'large' and lay in two lines on either side of and close to the road. The road had indeed 'run so close that it had cut off a considerable slice of one of them' (Francis 1863a, 61). The largest of the mounds, which lay to the south of the road and was thus not excavated in 1862, was 84 feet (25.58m) in diameter and stood 7 to 8 feet (2.13–2.44m) tall. To the north of the road, the central mound was 60–70 feet (18.27–21.3m) in diameter and stood 4½ feet (1.37m) tall. The westernmost was the largest, being 72 feet (21.93m) in diameter and 4½ feet (1.37m) tall. We are not given the dimensions of the easternmost mound, though it was the smallest. It was clear to the excavators that the mounds had originally been much taller, but that their height had been reduced by previous excavation.

Although it is possible to locate these mounds in relation to each other, the lack of any site plan accompanying the accounts, and the subsequent damage to the site (see below, p. 11) make it much harder to relate the mounds to the current topography. Not surprisingly, Septimus Davidson and his friends did not believe it possible for such dominant mounds to be wholly destroyed. We must assume, however, that the two tumuli which appear to the south of the road on the 25-inch OS map correspond to two of them. Those to the north of the road do not appear on any map, and have left no obvious trace on the surface. If we assume that they were broadly across the road from those to the south, they must have lain within the current garden of St Margaret's. We know furthermore that they must have been very close to the road line, since part of one (the westernmost) had been sliced off by the road.

In addition to the five or six large mounds, the excavators also noted the presence of some smaller mounds (by implication, four or five in number), "some of no more than 6–7 feet in diameter" (1.83–2.13m; Davidson 1863, 177). No attempt is made to relate these to the larger mounds, so there is no clue from the accounts as to where they lay.

As already noted, the 1862 excavations were confined to the area north of the A1094 road, which was in Septimus Davidson's possession. They began with the centre of the three mounds, which was 60–70 feet in diameter and stood 4½ feet tall. Trenching into the centre, they noted that the soil of the mound was composed of 'a black thin, light, sandy earth, and the surface enriched by the decay of vegetable fibre' (Davidson 1863, 178). With the excavation base clearly well into undisturbed natural soil, trenches were then cut out from the centre, so as to form a continuous east-west cutting through the mound. At about 'half the radius' 'a fragment of a sepulchral urn' was found (cremation grave 53).

No further finds were made, so they then turned their attention to the easternmost mound, the smallest of the three north of the road. Francis Francis describes the make-up of the mound thus:

> One very noticeable fact was evident, viz., the traces of large fires which were abundantly visible. The soil was sandy (a sort of peaty sand), and as we cut down through it layers of black matter of a charred appearance and soft greasy feel, were as distinctly visible as are small seams of coal or flint in some formations. In some places (the immediate locality of the fire itself as we supposed them to be) the soil was black and caked as though baked with some other substance which had caused the caking, and this substance I make little doubt in my own mind was neither more nor less originally than human flesh; the bones appertaining to which had been collected and placed in the urns within the barrow. These hard core-like places frequently (though not always by any means) indicated the neighbourhood of an urn. [...] These traces of fire and strata of charred matter occurred everywhere — in all parts of the barrows, apparently without method or regularity. (Francis 1863a, 61).

Francis' implied interpretation, that these are the remains of pyres, is not mentioned by the others, and is hard to evaluate. Nothing similar was encountered in the recent excavations, where the possible pyre was of a quite different nature (see below, p. 252–5). The black and caked nature of the soil might well have been produced by iron-panning, since a broadly similar phenomenon was noted in the natural sand elsewhere on the site. An alternative explanation, suggested by a correspondent to a subsequent issue of *The Field* (in March 1863, 75), is that the black lines reflect the remains of turves, of which the mound was constructed.

Despite the failure to find any further urns or other finds in the easternmost mound, the excavators were not put off. Instead, they began to dig into the westernmost mound, the one which was so close to the road as to have been partially cut away by it. It was 22m in diameter and stood 1.7m tall. Rather than beginning in the middle, they cut in to it 'from margin to margin, so as to make a trench from 6 to 8 feet wide clear through it; the depth of the trench of course varied from the margin to the centre and thence again to the opposite margin, inasmuch as the base of the cutting was kept to the level of the natural soil on which the tumulus was raised' (Davidson 1863, 178). During this work, five 'mutilated vases' containing 'calcined bones' were encountered. Four were identified as Anglo-Saxon (they include the swastika decorated urn of cremation grave 51). The fifth, which was intact, stood apart both by reason of the fact that it was found upside down, and for its form and size (cremation grave 48, Fig. 111). Though Septimus Davidson thought it 'British', it is in fact a Bronze Age collared urn, which from its intact state must have come from an undisturbed burial which had been incorporated into the Anglo-Saxon mound (see below, p. 233, 265). Septimus Davidson said that it was empty, but Hele (a surgeon) reports that it contained burnt bone, 'the femur or thighbone and part of the pelvis being perfect' (Hele 1870, 26). They also found the remains of two iron spearheads (Fig. 78, *Fi* and *Fii*), in the general vicinity of the Bronze Age urn. They then dug deeper:

> They trenched deeply down below [the mound]: the soil here lost all appearance of the black burnt strata or the peaty colour and consisted of a pure bright-yellow or golden sand. While digging in this, they came upon the remains of some woodwork. The wood was of course perfectly decayed though retaining its form and fibre. Carrying the excavation further, the woodwork seemed to form a flooring of some kind. [...] We traced the pieces of iron from one end of the trench to the other, without removing the pieces; the result was this: I think we have most clearly and satisfactorily established that the pieces of iron were large rivets. On either side of the trench there were six rows exactly corresponding, having the appearance of so many steps; in fact they were the ribs of a boat, for the wood between them had all gone to decay. The rivets were horizontal. Proceeding with our investigations, we came to the flooring, where the rivets were vertical, and also to the ends [...] the clear outlines of a vessel were apparent. The boat was 46 to 48 ft long and about 9ft 9ins or 10ft amidships. [...] Subsequently the spot was visited by a naval gentleman who quite confirmed all that remained doubtful as to the woodwork being that of a vessel. (Francis 1863a, 62–3).

Although ship burials had been recognised in Scandinavia prior to this date, this was the first time that one had been identified in England (Müller-Wille 1970, 9). Only two years before, at Sutton Hoo, incompetent excavators seem to have dug through a ship burial without the slightest appreciation of what they had found (Hoppitt 1985). Once again, we must be grateful that the Snape excavators' painstaking technique, combined with their intellectual curiosity, enabled them to uncover the full length of the ship, and to identify it correctly. They also took the trouble to collect many rivets, which survive today in Aldeburgh Museum.

Septimus Davidson's account of the excavation is accompanied by a plan (also reproduced by Hele; here Fig. 4), the first of a boat grave to be published in European archaeology (Müller-Wille 1970, 9). The plan is an edited version of a watercolour drawing, now in the library of the Society of Antiquaries (MS *Primaeval Antiquities*, p. 115) (Pl. I). This drawing, which must have been done either during or very shortly after the excavation, gives far more

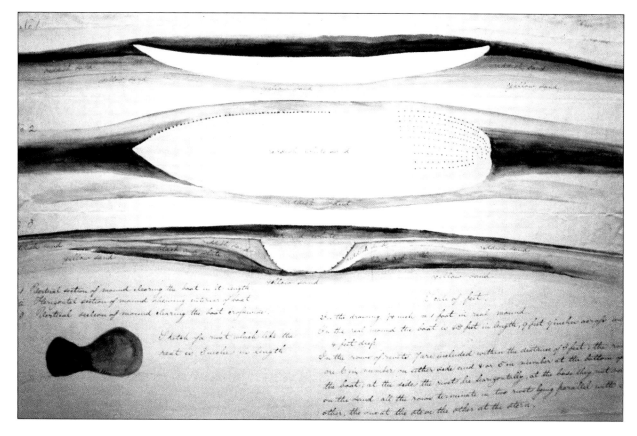

Plate I Watercolour plan of the ship burial. *Copyright the Society of Antiquaries of London*

detail and includes a complete section through the boat and tumulus and pencil annotations of the various soil layers. The watercolour also makes clear that the confusingly illogical pattern of rivets shown on the engraving was filled in by the engraver, and does not represent the original pattern as seen by the excavators. For details of this, we need to refer to the original accounts.

It was clear to the excavators that the boat grave had been plundered already. An element of luck, however, combined with their painstaking approach enabled them to recover some objects missed by earlier diggers.

In the first place, above the level of the ship, somewhere in the vicinity of the Bronze Age urn, two iron spearheads were found. Missing when Rupert Bruce-Mitford wrote his paper (Bruce-Mitford 1952), they have now been identified among the mass of rivets in Aldeburgh Museum. It is probable that they derive from the primary inhumation, but were disturbed by the previous digging.

The remaining finds were in a group from the very base of the ship, probably from amidships, though the accounts are not completely clear on this point. The first and finest is a gold ring, which 'slipped out of the sand' and was 'pounced upon' by Mr C (Pls II and III, Fig. 78). There were also the shattered remains of a glass claw beaker (Pl. IV and Fig. 78). Close by, the excavators were intrigued by 'a mass of human hair, about the covering for one head. It was dark dirty red. This hair, or the head upon which it formerly grew (but of which no trace was found), had been wrapped up in a cloth of some kind, for though the fabric had been entirely destroyed by decay, its texture and the warp and woof could be distinctly seen; about four feet

from it was found another, but smaller mass of hair' (Francis 1863a, 62). In the same general area were some fragments thought to be of jasper, and a single fragment of blue glass, which is mentioned only by Francis Francis (Francis 1863a, 63). The interpretation of this grave is considered in Chapter 5 section I, below.

The triumphant conclusion to the first season's excavation prompted Septimus Davidson to return in the following year, though with less spectacular results. The *Archaeological Journal* reported that 'Stimulated by the success of the explorations during the previous summer, Mr Davidson had directed the field in its whole length east and west, next the side of the road from Snape to Aldeburgh, by a breadth of more than twelve yards north and south, to be double trenched. By this arrangement the whole circumference of the base of the largest tumulus was included. [...] More than forty vases, mostly fragments, have been exhumed; but the most remarkable circumstance is the fact that by far the greater number have been found in the level between the two largest tumuli, and much outside the extreme base of either of them' (Proc. at Meetings 1863, 373–4). Finds were sparse: 'The only relics or ornaments found were two small pieces of ivory (as supposed), mounted with a serrated margin of metal, and showing the remains of a rivet in the centre [a bone comb?]; a portion of a convex plate of copper, having the appearance of part of a helmet [still in Aldeburgh Museum; a bowl?]; an oblong copper ring, evidently the remains of a buckle [from an inhumation?]; an iron spearhead 10 inches in length, joined in the centre by a rivet [also from an inhumation?]; and a human tooth'.

Plate II Intaglio finger ring; detail of gemstone

Plate III Intaglio finger ring; side view of granulated shoulders

Despite the lack of spectacular discoveries, the *Archaeological Journal* congratulated Septimus Davidson on 'having thrown fresh light on the obscure sepulchral vestiges in this district'.

Septimus Davidson's excavations caused huge interest. As already noted, accounts of the excavation were published within a year of the completion. Interpretation was hampered by the then infant state of Anglo-Saxon archaeology. Septimus Davidson realised that the ring, the claw beaker and most of the urns were Anglo-Saxon, but he was confused (not surprisingly) by the Bronze Age urn, which he labelled 'British'. His final conclusion was that 'the largest urn is British, the others Anglo-Saxon; that the interment in the boat was that of a Dane, or other Northern person' (Davidson 1863, 181–2). Francis Francis was less scholarly in his article in *The Field*, but after ranging widely through the Druids and the last battle between Boadicea and the Romans, he eventually reached much the same conclusion (Francis 1863a, 75).

The level of interest generated by the find is best seen in *The Field*, which received a large number of letters following the publication of Francis Francis' articles. Among them was the one quoted above, which gave information both on the Gentlemen from London, and on what appears to have been the plundering of another rich burial mound, 900m to the south, by one Nathan Licence, its rather shady early 19th-century owner (SMR No. SNP 020).

In the years following, however, interest in the site waned, and legends began to accumulate. In the 1920s, the owner of the adjacent house was telling visiting schoolgirls that the ship had contained a seven foot Viking in full armour, and a servant (Swinburne n.d., 239)! Also in the 1920s a house, St Margaret's, was built immediately

to the north of the three mounds excavated by Septimus Davidson (Fig. 5). Its garden, carved out of the common but never landscaped, included the mounds and was ringed with a line of pines. It is said that numerous urns were found when these were planted, though no record was made (Mary Harrison, pers. comm.).

Urns were also found during the construction of the house, but again no record was made. The source for our knowledge is the son of the house's builder, who recalled in his old age his father telling him of finding 'old wine jars', some of which 'still had wine in them'! (Mary Harrison, pers. comm.).

Despite the absence of interest in the finds of the 1920s, memory of the ship burial remained alive. In 1938, Mrs Pretty's chauffeur drove Basil Brown over to Aldeburgh Museum to view the rivets from the ship, and Bruce-Mitford has observed how he appears to have been influenced by the 'transom stern' of the Snape ship in his interpretation of the boat from mound 2 at Sutton Hoo (Bruce Mitford 1974, 141–69).

Ploughing up of the heathland began during the Second World War, when the field to the north of the road (then the village football pitch) was cultivated. It is curious that, despite the damage which must have been done by this first ploughing (comparable to that at the Lackford cemetery), no one appears to have noticed anything untoward. The field south of the road (containing the mounds not touched by Septimus Davidson) was first ploughed in 1951, again without record of any finds. On both sides of the road, a 'gyrotiller' was also used. This machine is said to have comprised two First World War submarine engines mounted vertically on a caterpillar tractor, to drive blades designed to stir up the soil, and

Plate IV Claw beaker from mound 1 ship

break up roots to a depth of *c.*1 yard. Its popularity was, fortunately for archaeology, brief! Nevertheless, erosion of the surviving mounds in the field south of the road was rapid. In 1862 the largest mound on the site was 25.5m in diameter and 2m tall. By *c.*1950 it had shrunk to 9.1m in diameter and 0.3m in height (report in SMR). In 1990 a detailed contour survey revealed it as an irregular circle, with a diameter of 10m and a height of 50mm (*sic*). It was fortunate that one mound, right in the north-east corner of the field, was excluded from the field and has thus survived intact. Another smaller mound immediately to the south was bisected by the field edge and was only identified as a mound in 1991, when excavations picked up the ditch surrounding it.

In 1970 a dowser called Major-General Scott-Elliott found a single urn, some 40m to the west of the garden (cremation grave 67). According to reports in the *Proceedings of the Suffolk Institute of Archaeology*, the Major-General also found and excavated a 'sterile pit' and a 'palisade trench' (Owles 1970, 103). In the light of experience from later excavations, it seems probable that the former is either natural or a tree pit, and that the latter is a plough furrow.

Two years later, a sewer trench was dug along the northern side of the road. Ipswich Museum was alerted by a local resident that urns were being found in the area of the cemetery. As a result, the digging of the remainder of the trench was archaeologically observed and a total of nine cremations was recovered. Of these, seven were urned and one was unurned. The ninth was in a thin-walled bronze bowl (West and Owles 1973). Also noted was a segment of a ring-ditch, close to the assumed site of the ship burial.

A year later a further trench was put along the road through the cemetery. Forewarned this time, archaeological supervision was at hand, but (remarkably) only one sherd of pottery was recovered.

Endnotes:

1. Dr Steven Plunkett has suggested two possible candidates for identification with 'Mr C'. The first, Edward Charlesworth, was active in the 1840s and 1850s, mainly as a geologist but with antiquarian leanings. The second and more likely is Edward Clod, an important and active citizen of Aldeburgh in the 1870s and 1880s. He wrote books and organised meetings on evolution and was a Rationalist. Since the Rationalists objected to inhumation burial, and had a strong interest in cremation, Septimus Davidson's excavation would have been of particular interest to him.

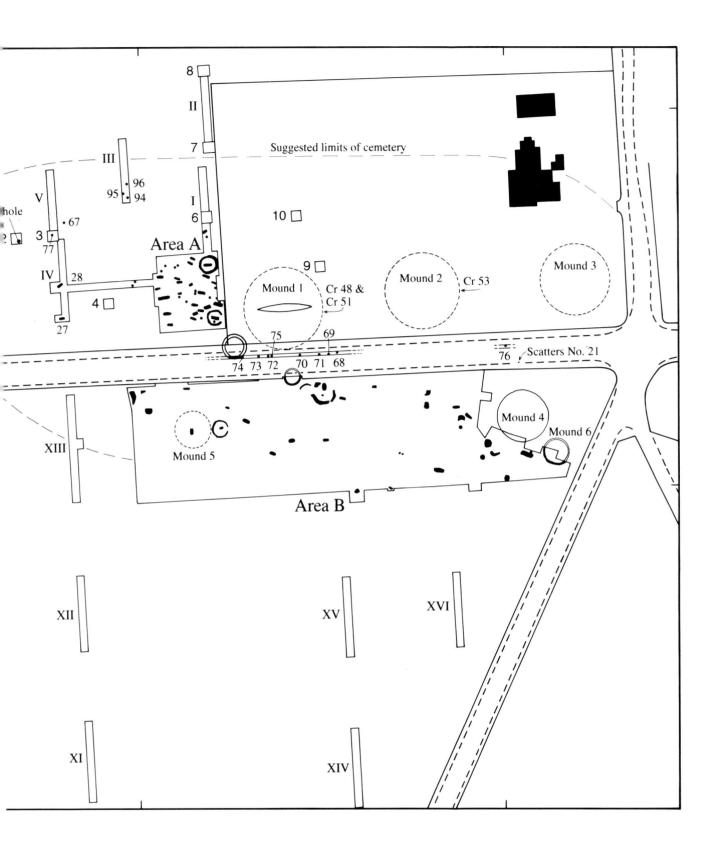

Figure 5 Overall plan of the site showing location of 1972 sewer trench, 1985 trial boxes, 1989–90 trial trenches and main excavation areas. Features and graves not in the main excavation areas are also located and numbered. Scale 1:1000

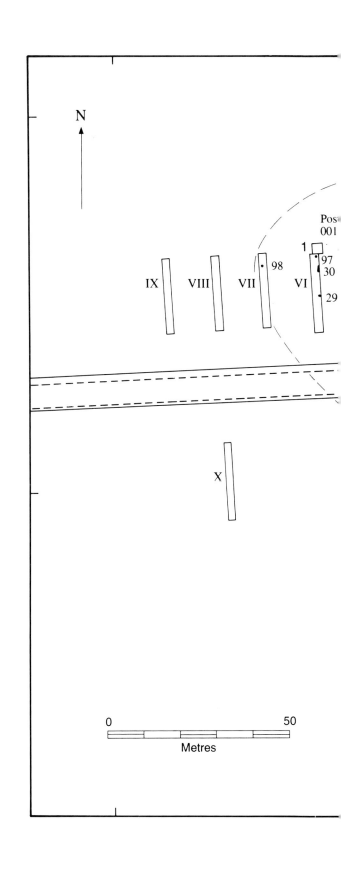

Chapter 3. Excavations and Surveys 1985–92

I. Excavations and Surveys 1985–92
by William Filmer-Sankey

During the 120 years from 1862 to 1985, when the present project began, the appearance of the Snape Anglo-Saxon cemetery altered beyond recognition. The heathland had been ploughed up; a house (St Margaret's) had been constructed; most fundamentally perhaps, all but one of the nine or ten mounds visible in 1862 had been ploughed flat or otherwise destroyed. Repeated fieldwalking by local residents and the author produced not a single find, even in areas where urns (like that discovered by Major-General Scott-Elliott) were known to exist. Only two parts of the site survived in anything like its former condition. The first was the mound in the north-east corner of the field south of the road. The second was the western part of the garden of St Margaret's, which was never seriously cultivated and thus retained its heathland vegetation of rough grass and gorse. Even here, however, the only evidence for the existence of large mounds were the possible spoil heaps from the ship burial excavation (below, p. 193).

Academically, too, the site had lost its importance, being eclipsed by the 1939 excavation of the great Sutton Hoo mound 1 ship. In 1948 the Swedish archaeologist Birger Nerman wrote of the 'rather uncertain boat grave' and doubted the association between it and the ring and claw beaker (Nerman 1949, 89, n.29).

In 1952 Rupert Bruce-Mitford began the site's rehabilitation with an important paper in the *Proceedings of the Suffolk Institute of Archaeology*, in which he firmly rebutted Nerman's scepticism, and gave a comprehensive summary of knowledge of the site, the 1862 excavation and the ship burial (Bruce-Mitford 1952). He was also able for the first time to publish a full description and photographs of the ring, which had miraculously reappeared in 1950. Although many aspects of Bruce-Mitford's paper, particularly on the provenance and dating of the ring, need revision with the benefit of hindsight (see below, pp. 195–6), his paper was a brilliant synthesis of what was then known.

If Rupert Bruce-Mitford's paper kept knowledge of the site alive, it did little to stimulate any desire for further work, except among a small group of local archaeologists. It was the commencement in 1983 of Martin Carver's work at Sutton Hoo, with its emphasis on the need to see that site in its wider, East Anglian, context, that once more focused attention on Snape as the best, indeed the only parallel to the mound 1 ship burial. This attention brought in its turn the realisation that really very little was known about the site. The location of all but one of the mounds had been lost, and although finds of urns indicated a number of places where the cemetery definitely was, there was no idea of its size or state of preservation.

Since fieldwalking produced no finds at all, an initial attempt to fix the size of the cemetery was made by geophysical survey. In 1982 two trial areas of magnetometry and resistivity were surveyed by Stephen Dockrill of the School of Archaeological Science at Bradford University. The former produced no results, but the latter appeared to show what might be the base and surrounding ring-ditch of a ploughed out tumulus. During the next three years, a total of some 13,000m^2 were covered by resistivity survey, initially by Bradford, but latterly by Dr Roger Walker of Geoscan Research (report in site archive). The initial promise was not fulfilled, however, and with the exception of a pair of parallel ditches (subsequently shown to be of relatively recent origin) no features could be detected against the strongly variable geological background.

Accordingly, it was decided that a more coherent approach was required. This took two forms. The first was the bringing together and analysis of all the existing information on the site. This exercise underlined the cemetery's crucial importance as a point of comparison for Sutton Hoo. It also indicated that the site was predominantly a cremation cemetery, with densely packed urns. All the evidence from the earlier excavations appeared to show that the use of inhumation in the ship burial was exceptional and a parallel with the Spong Hill cemetery seemed obvious (Filmer-Sankey 1984). This conclusion on the character of the cemetery was then used to plan the second stage, a sampling strategy, directed at finding its size and its state of preservation. Since neither fieldwalking nor geophysical survey had produced any results, it was clear that this sampling strategy would have to involve excavation.

The excavation began in 1985, and involved the hand excavation of fourteen 3 × 3 metre boxes. The size of the boxes was based on the assumption that the cemetery was like Spong Hill, with an equivalent density of urns. A statistician confirmed that an empty box would give a 99.7% chance that it was outside the limits of the cemetery.

In the event, only two of the fourteen boxes contained urns, both damaged by ploughing, and it was clear either that the cemetery had been largely destroyed by ploughing or that the theoretical basis of the sampling strategy was wrong. In the closing days of the excavation, the latter was shown to be the case when one box, close to the presumed site of the 1862 ship burial, was enlarged to 6 × 6 metres and produced not only two more urns, but an inhumation burial (grave 17).

The indication that the cemetery might contain a significant proportion of inhumations prompted a revision of the sampling strategy. Before any attempt could be made to work out the size of the cemetery, it was necessary to establish its character. Unless the proportion of inhumation to cremation burials was known, together with an indication of grave density, it would not be possible to

Plate V Cremation 95 smashed and smeared across the bottom of a plough furrow

Plate VI Cremation 79, intact with rim collapsed in on itself

produce a sampling strategy which would give reliable results.

Accordingly, it was decided to excavate a larger part of the cemetery, in order to define its character. An area of 17 × 20 metres was selected, centred on the known inhumation grave, and immediately to the west of the garden of St Margaret's and the supposed site of the 1862 ship. The excavation took 20 weeks, spread over three seasons (1986–8) (Area A; Fig. 6).

At the same time, the opportunity was taken to put a 2m wide trench across the possible ring-ditch and tumulus base located by the resistivity survey. Removal of the topsoil showed that the anomaly had in fact been caused by an area of natural sand rising particularly close to the surface.

The result of this excavation was for the first time an accurate idea of the character of the cemetery, which was shown to consist of inhumations and cremations in roughly equal numbers (24:15 in the 1986–8 excavation). The graves were reasonably scattered, with an average density of one cremation per $21.45m^2$ and one inhumation per $16.3m^2$.

The nature of archaeological survival was similar to that being encountered at the same time at Sutton Hoo. Most striking was the parallel occurrence of sand silhouettes, where the acidic soil conditions had all but totally destroyed skeletons but had replaced the bone with a curious greasy brown organic stain. This made it possible in many cases to reconstruct body positions, though sexing of bodies (other than by accompanying grave-goods) was of course impossible. For reasons still not wholly understood (see below, pp. 204–7) the soil conditions had also in some cases produced unusually good organic preservation of such objects as horn (grave 4) and actual textile (grave 37). Pottery by contrast survived poorly; fabrics were very friable when first exposed and were badly penetrated by roots. Iron survived in a very corroded, frequently totally mineralised, state, while objects of thin copper alloy were very fragile indeed.

Armed at last with accurate information on the cemetery's character and on the nature of archaeological survival, it was possible to produce a sampling strategy which would be able to define its limits. After extensive consultation it was decided that this would best be achieved by excavating a series of trenches 2m wide and at least 20m long, positioned north-south to be across the normal line of inhumation grave orientation. Two empty trenches in a row would mean that the edge of the site had been reached.

In 1989 and 1990 a total of eighteen of these trenches were excavated, and the limits of the site were fixed (Fig. 5). It is worth noting that although the suggested limits to the north of the road have not been tested by excavation, those to the south were, and were found to be accurate. No trenches were placed in the garden of St Margaret's, where hand excavation from the surface would have been necessary. Nor were any trenches excavated to the east of St Margaret's. The field here was ploughed to the depth of 36 inches as an experiment in the 1950s (information from John Stigwood, farmer) and it was thought very unlikely that any remains would survive. In any case, the pattern of finds in the 1972 sewer trench indicated that the cemetery did not extend any further to the east.

All seasons of excavation had provided information on the cemetery's state of preservation. In the first place, no finds at all were made in the ploughsoil, even in areas immediately on top of plough-damaged cremations. It would appear that the pottery is so fragile that it totally disintegrates when hit by the plough, a fact which may account for the apparent absence of finds when the fields were first ploughed (see above, p. 11). More generally, the state of preservation was found to vary widely.

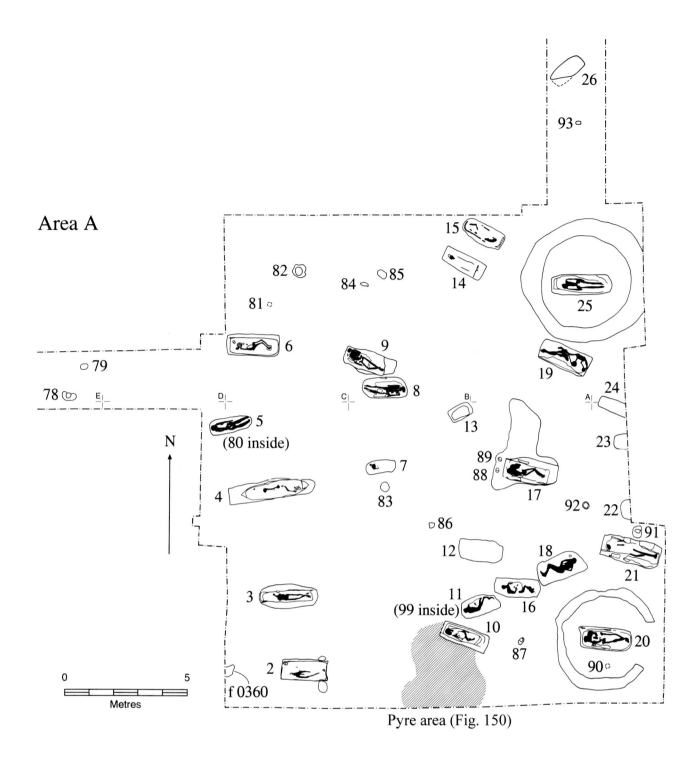

Area A

N

0   5
Metres

Figure 6 Plan of all graves and associated features, Area A. Scale 1:150

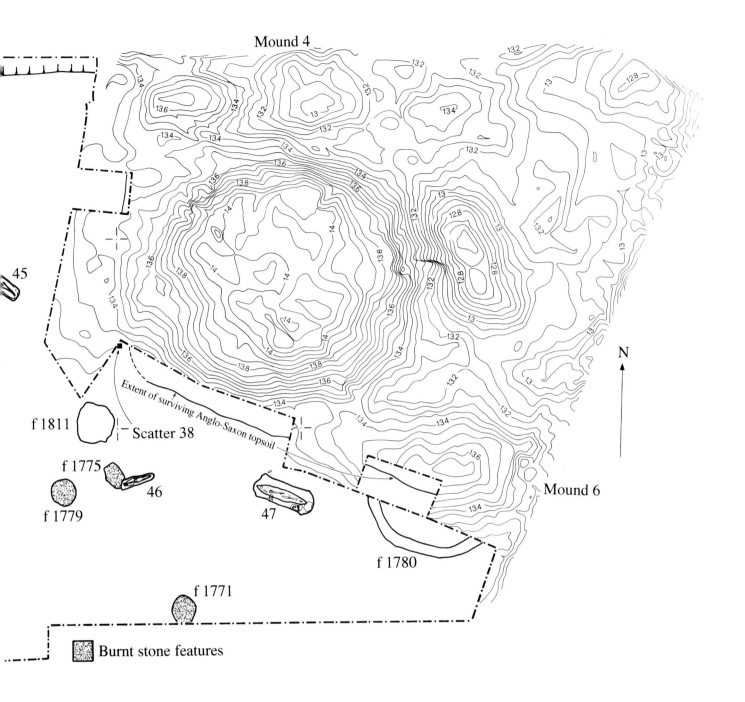

Figure 7 Plan of all graves and associated features, Area B, and contour plan of scheduled area enclosing mound 4. Scale 1:200

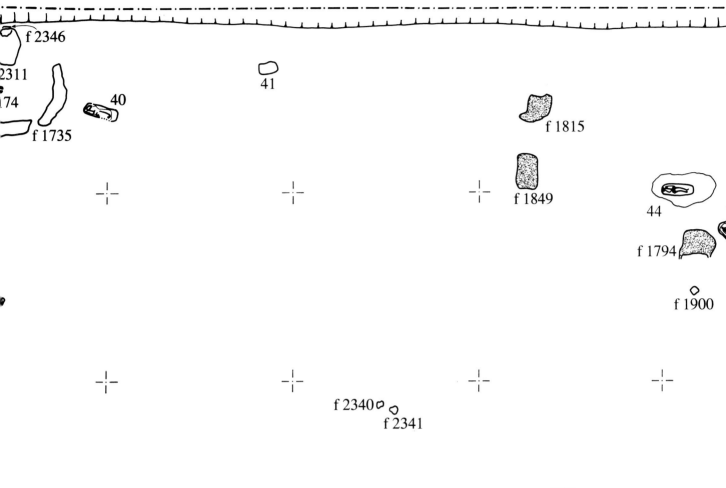

Area B

f 2346

2311

74

f 1735

40

41

f 1815

f 1849

44

f 1794

f 1900

f 2340

f 2341

43

42

f 2251

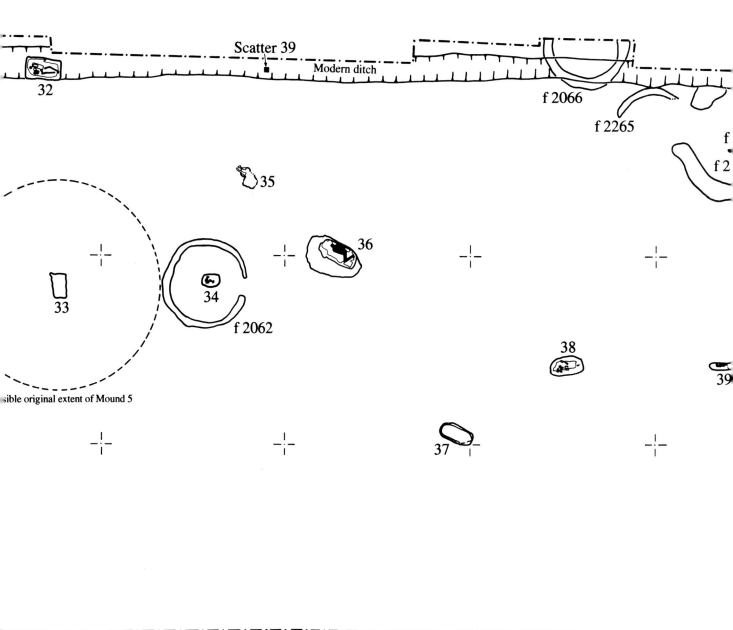

Scatter 39

Modern ditch

32

f 2066

f 2265

f

f 2

35

36

33

34

f 2062

38

39

sible original extent of Mound 5

37

0   5   10

Metres

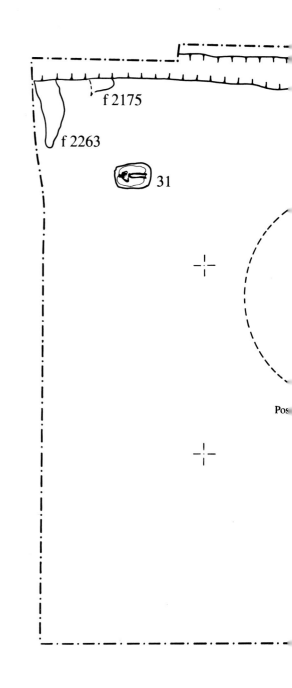

f 2175

f 2263

31

Pos

The cremation burials were the most vulnerable to plough damage, since they were less deeply buried than the inhumations. Their state of survival varied from the totally intact to the all but destroyed (Pls V and VI). The crucial factor was the variable existence of a layer of pale grey sand, sandwiched between the base of the 300mm thick ploughsoil and the top of the orange natural sand. The cremation burials (and other features such as the pyre) were all found within this layer, and the inhumation graves had been cut through it. It was therefore clearly the remains of the truncated Anglo-Saxon topsoil. Its thickness was greatest in Area A, where it was up to 300mm, but even in Area A there were significant parts where it had been totally destroyed. This variation could be accounted for by undulations in the underlying natural. Before ploughing, these undulations would have been reflected in the surface topography. Fifty years of constant cultivation had, however, completely flattened the surface and had thus destroyed the Anglo-Saxon topsoil layer in all but the deeper hollows.

Damage to the site had been compounded by soil erosion. The light land of the Sandlings is notorious for its 'sand blows', particularly in the autumn and spring before crops have taken hold. Soil erosion was at its worst away from the protection of hedge lines (where the blown sand tends to accumulate). It was particularly serious in the field south of the road, where no traces of the Anglo-Saxon topsoil layer were found. A few fragments of cremated bone from rabbit burrows and the fills of two inhumation graves indicate that cremation burials had formerly existed south of the road, but that they had been totally ploughed away.

The relatively gradual rate of this type of soil erosion (no more than a few millimetres each year) makes it even less likely that finds, whether of bone or pottery, will survive in the ploughsoil.

It was not only cremation burials that had suffered in the field south of the road. An inhumation grave (40) located in a 2 × 20m trench in 1990 had had the top of its head sliced off by ploughing, so that only 200mm of the grave remained (Fig. 66).

One important aim of the project (which never envisaged the total excavation of the site) was to define the differing states of preservation, so that decisions could be made about the need for future protection, whether by management agreements to restrict particularly damaging types of agricultural activity, or by extending the Scheduled Area.

By 1990 it was possible to map the differing 'zones' of preservation, following the technique which had been used at Sutton Hoo (Carver 1986, 33–9, fig. 25). Four such zones could be identified. The first was the garden of St Margaret's and the area of the surviving tumulus, which had been damaged by past excavation, but were otherwise intact. The second was the area of the present road, where preservation (as demonstrated by the intact urns found in the 1972 sewer trench) was excellent. The third was the field north of the road, where ploughing and subsoiling had caused considerable damage, but where cremations and inhumations nevertheless survived. The fourth was the field south of the road, where all cremation burials had been destroyed and where the inhumation graves were also threatened by destruction within the next five or so years.

In consultation with English Heritage it was decided that the level of preservation in this fourth zone was too poor to merit scheduling or a management agreement to control ploughing. At the same time, the area undoubtedly contained important evidence which should be recorded before it was destroyed. Accordingly the decision was taken to excavate the entire area of the cemetery within the field, and English Heritage agreed to fund the work.

The excavation took place in two 10 week seasons in 1991 and 1992 and covered an area of 100 × 30m. Preservation was found to be if anything worse than expected, with some inhumation graves surviving to a depth of only 100mm. Most striking was the fate of the largest tumulus visible on the site in 1862, when it was 25.5m in diameter and stood up to 2m tall. Although a Scheduled Ancient Monument since the 1950s, its erosion had continued until it was invisible on the surface, but it was assumed that it would leave some subsurface traces. In the event, the only feature which could possibly be linked to it was a 420mm deep pit, containing a number of sherds of pottery, which lay in the approximate centre of the mound, as marked on the 1973 edition of the OS 25-inch map (grave 33). It is therefore interpreted as either the robbed remains of a central burial or a 19th-century excavation trench. Apart from this, however, the mound (which presumably had no ditch) had left no traces whatsoever.

II. Excavation Techniques
by Tim Pestell

The method of excavation remained substantially unchanged throughout the project. Whilst the 1985 3 × 3m trial boxes were all excavated by hand, the other areas examined were machine-stripped of ploughsoil using a JCB with a 2m wide toothless bucket. Fieldwalking and the first season's excavation had shown the ploughsoil to be devoid of finds and it was therefore removed with no further examination down to the top of the Anglo-Saxon topsoil layer, where it existed, or to the top of the natural sand.

The revealed surface was given a light shovel scrape before being trowelled over. All cremation burials and other spreads of material surviving in the topsoil layer were plotted mostly as detailed 1:10 or 1:20 plans with finds being individually numbered and levelled. Scatters consisted predominantly of pottery sherds or cremated bone, but also included a few metal objects, charcoal and burnt flint. Following the plotting and removal of all such material and the cremation burials (see below), the topsoil layer was removed by hand, to reveal the natural sand. It was at this stage that the inhumation grave cuts normally became visible. The whole excavation area was re-trowelled, often several times, to ensure that all inhumation grave cuts had been located. The need for this was demonstrated by the discovery of several graves rendered almost invisible by their fills of redeposited natural. As a final check, c.0.15m of natural sand was removed by shovel over the entire area.

Excavation of cremation graves and surface scatters

Cremation burials, except when contained within the fill of an inhumation grave (graves 88 and 89), were typically severely damaged and some survived as only a scatter of material, either wholly in the topsoil layer or cut slightly into the underlying natural sand.

In a very few cases cut marks for the burial pit were observed. Excavation was undertaken in quadrants, bone being hand recovered and sieved later for specialist examination. Hand collection, usually with a fine paintbrush, ensured that no bone or small-finds were missed, as sand could be brushed off the cremated material.

Surface spreads were excavated as part of the overall removal of the topsoil layer. Individual components were plotted in three dimensions on detailed plans.

Excavation of inhumation graves

Inhumation grave cuts generally appeared at the top of the natural sand level, although several from Area A were seen in the original topsoil layer. As soon as the outline of the grave was clear, gridpoints were established at each end of the grave and then tied into the overall site grid. These two points became the fixed reference points for all plans of the grave.

One of the most important factors governing the excavation of the graves was the lack of surviving skeletal material, bone having been destroyed by the high acidity of the natural heathland soil, producing a soil 'stain' of the body (Pls XI, XIV, XIV and XXII). Similarly, it rapidly became clear that many graves contained the remains of organics, also preserved as sand stains. To enable the recognition and recording of both these types in their entirety, excavation was undertaken 'in plan', with spits at 50mm intervals. Plans were drawn every 100mm in the upper levels and every 50mm lower down, or when container stains first appeared. All recording was at 1:10 scale with certain worthy features, typically grave-good groups, drawn in more detail, usually at 1:1 or 1:2. At the bottom of each grave the remaining fill was emptied to reveal the three-dimensional stain of the body and the base of any container or fitting for the final grave plan. Profiles and sections were made, often in a series of running quadrants. Sections were drawn at 1:10. As a result, plans could be 'stacked' and combined with sections to reconstruct the graves and their contents in the three-dimensional way shown in the catalogue (Chapter 4). This method often projects the location of objects onto the sections generated, rather than portraying the actual situation in the ground along every section line.

Initially, graves were excavated by removing only the fill. Experimentation showed that excavating the surrounding natural sand as part of the spit showed the grave edges better throughout. Excavating a 'box' around the cut also enabled planning frames to be placed immediately above the surface being recorded, thus improving the accuracy of the plans. This technique also ensured that grave edges could not be accidentally over- or under-cut.

Sampling

Body stains were extensively sampled in all inhumation graves excavated, originally to provide supporting material for the Sutton Hoo Research Project's study of 'sand burials' (Bethell and Carver 1987). Samples were taken from each component of the body and bagged individually. Any remaining stained soil was reburied in the grave following the completion of excavation. Samples of stains from containers or other objects were taken where they survived well and in all cases where there was any charcoal present. Burnt flint fragments were also present in many graves but they were only recorded systematically in the later years of the project. On the advice of Peter Murphy (pers. comm.), it was not considered worth taking samples for pollen analysis as this was unlikely to have survived in the prevailing soil conditions.

Extraction of finds

It rapidly became apparent that metal objects within graves were associated with the very good survival of organic remains such as textile. A technique was therefore evolved (in conjunction with Esther Cameron at the Institute of Archaeology, Oxford) which enabled the maximum amount of associated organic material to be raised with the object for laboratory examination, while still allowing the object to be accurately plotted onto the grave plans.

Following location, finds were only lightly cleaned for recording before being lifted. The aim, where possible, was to extract objects still in their surrounding matrix of earth. The area surrounding an object was left upstanding as a pedestal. Depending on the size of the block being extracted, a wooden frame and expanding two part polyurethane foam, plastic container or bandages were used to support the soil while a steel sheet was slid beneath. Pins in the soil block marked its orientation and were planned relative to the grave grid points. Soil blocks were then taken to the laboratory for X-radiography and excavation. As a result many tiny and fragile details were identified, the relationship between organic remains and the metal object could be explored, while the pins, showing up on the X-ray, could be used for accurate location of the object on the overall grave plan. The success of this method owed much to the absence of bone and to the pure, almost stone-free, sand of the site which made the creation and extraction of blocks relatively easy.

Other features

All other features encountered were planned at 1:10 or 1:20 at the surface level. Burnt stone features were excavated in spits of 100mm, with new plans at each spit level, in an effort to define them better due to their agricultural damage. The remaining features from the site were planned at surface level and sectioned. All features were fully excavated and in Area B, the fills were 100% sieved.

Chapter 4. Catalogue of Inhumations, Cremations and Other Features

I. Introduction
by Tim Pestell

Numbering
All contexts, samples and small-finds were numbered on site in a single numerical sequence according to the Suffolk Archaeological Unit's 'OP' context system. For publication, the inhumations and cremations have been re-numbered in a single continuous series, cremations beginning at grave 48. A few inhumation graves have more than one plan or section, and these are distinguished by upper case roman numerals. Grave-goods are distinguished by upper case letters whilst organic materials have, where necessary, been given lower case roman numerals. Different textile weaves are indicated by lower case letters in brackets. Other assorted objects or contexts have generally been left under their original site numbers, italicised within the text. For the ease of those wishing to use the site archive, all original OP numbers for finds are given in square brackets at the end of each catalogue entry.

Inhumations

Sex/age
In the absence of any skeletal material, graves have been sexed on the basis of grave-goods alone. This method has been questioned by some as it can lead to assumptions of gender (Henderson 1989) but work by Brush (1993) suggests that there are only a minority of probable exceptions to these traditional equations.

Assessment of age cannot be made with any accuracy for most burials due to the destruction of bone in the acid sand, although the size of cut provides a clue in some cases, for instance graves 7, 13 and 42. Because body stain is generally poor or non-existent for infants or children, whilst full-size graves usually have good stains, juvenile burials might arguably be present where only a poor or partial stain is observed. However, a large number of other organic stains in a grave also seems to lead to a poor or less distinct body stain, so that burials need not have contained juveniles even where they have been tentatively suggested (as for instance in grave 47). Similarly, the survival of bone in grave 12 suggests a middle-aged adult even though no body stain survived.

Grave containers
The containers and other organic inclusions in the inhumations are generally shown at their highest outline, although at times staining seen at different levels has been joined together in plan for clarity. Stains are shown in their entirety if they appeared as a layer at the bottom of a grave rather than with edges higher up (for instance Fig. 55). Wood stains are, where thick or large in number, shown in outline only. In a handful of cases pieces have been removed from some of the sections for clarity, but in all

such cases this is noted in the accompanying catalogue entry.

Ring-ditches
Three graves (20, 25 and 34) were surrounded by ring-ditches. They are described in the text of the relevant grave catalogue entries, but for ease of comparison, the ditches themselves are illustrated with the other ring-ditches (Chapter 4 section VI).

Grave-goods
For convenience, all objects of copper alloy are abbreviated as Ae. All drawings are ordered by grave and are published at the following scales: copper alloy, gold, silver and beads 1:1; iron objects and glass 1:2; pottery 1:3 with stamps at 1:1. Exceptions to this are iron objects such as buckles and dress pins which are at 1:1 for comparison with copper alloy counterparts; the sword and bucket from grave 47 at 1:4, and the copper alloy bowl from cremation 68 at 1:3. Scales of all illustrations are given in the captions. The poor condition of some objects due to decuprification (the leaching out of a metal's copper content in the acidic conditions) has meant that they could only be drawn from X-ray plates. A few others are too badly corroded for any illustration. Objects found within the fill of graves, but not obviously 'grave-goods', are illustrated with the other objects from the grave.

Artefact classification
Despite the problems with many classification systems, the following have been used: spearheads, Swanton (1973); shield bosses, Dickinson and Härke (1992); wrist clasps, Hines (1984); glass claw beakers, Evison (1982); florid cruciform brooches, Leeds and Pocock (1971) and Hines (1997).

Cremations
The catalogue includes all those urns known to have been recovered from Snape. There are a number of problems associated with this, notably the very limited information available for most of those urns found in the 1862–3 excavations. Consistency of terms is at times difficult and a number of descriptions have been used to characterise the state of the cremations. In some cases, 1862–3 urns are noted as containing concreted cremated bone which was not examined. This is because the bone was truly solid and could not be removed without danger of breaking up either the urn or its contents. For present purposes, the 1862–3 urns are all presumed to have originally contained complete single cremations although most bone has been lost since their recovery. The mixing of what bone survives in all but a handful means that they are regarded as 'incomplete', since they were possibly intact in the ground. Otherwise, where possible, cremations are listed as intact or truncated. A distinction is made between 'no

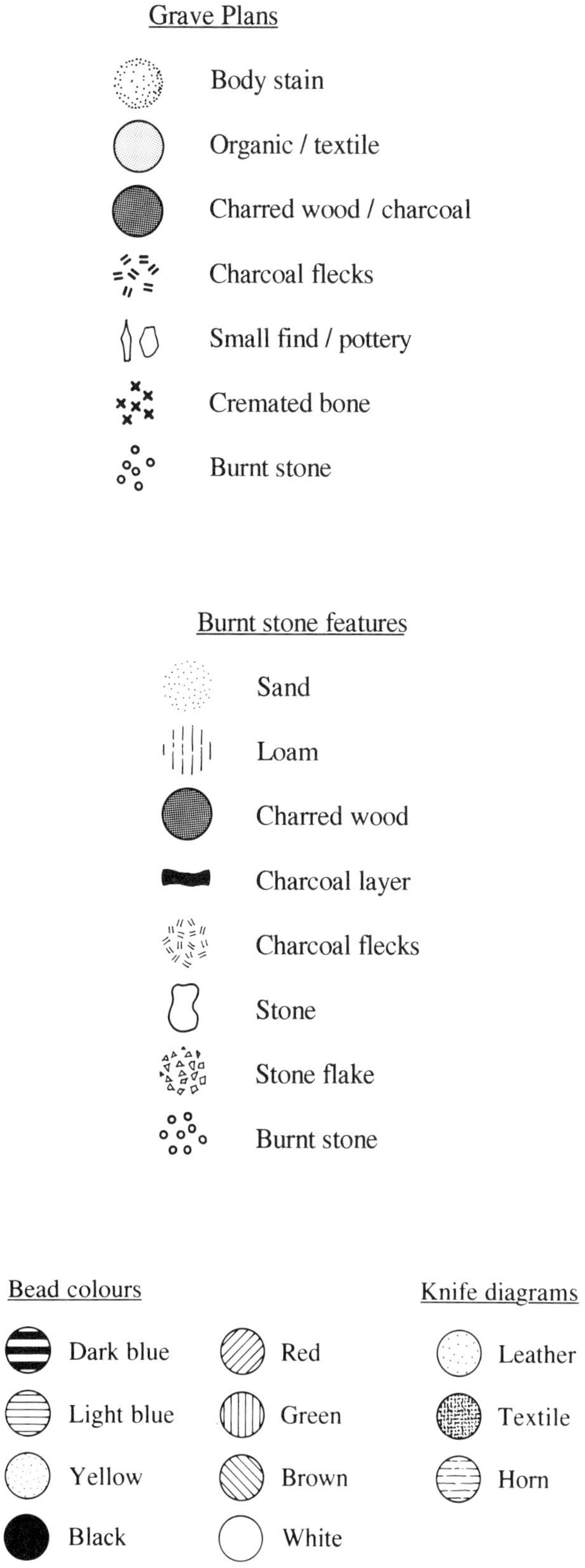

Grave Plans

Body stain

Organic / textile

Charred wood / charcoal

Charcoal flecks

Small find / pottery

Cremated bone

Burnt stone

Burnt stone features

 Sand

 Loam

 Charred wood

 Charcoal layer

 Charcoal flecks

 Stone

 Stone flake

Burnt stone

Bead colours

Dark blue

Light blue

Yellow

Black

Red

Green

Brown

White

Knife diagrams

Leather

Textile

Horn

Figure 8 Conventions used in the inhumation grave
plans and for grave-goods

cut observed' (as there may have been one which was not
seen) and 'unknown' where there are no records. That cuts
may exist but not be observable is a result of the difficult
soil conditions, especially in the 'buried topsoil' layer
within which most cremations were interred.

The 1972 material has already been published (West
and Owles 1973) and is incorporated here. However, direct
comparisons are not always possible since bone weights,
for instance, were not noted. Moreover, the 1972 material
was collected more in a spirit of salvage than excavation,
often from the spoil heap running parallel with the sewer
trench, causing other difficulties. It is likely that much was
missed and the bone samples are incomplete. In addition,
a few bags of bone with uncertain locations and laconic
identifications (for instance, 'bone' and 'manhole bone')
exist in Ipswich Museum. There has been no incorporation
of these contexts into the catalogue although a small iron
rivet in a bag marked 'manhole bone' is listed as scatters
No. 40 (section IV).

Decoration
Those urns decorated with stamps have been classified
according to the system developed by Teresa Briscoe for
the Archive of Anglo-Saxon Pottery Stamps. The
implications of these stamp types are discussed by her in
Chapter 5 section X.

Urn numbers
All urns have been included within the single sequence of
context numbers used in the excavations at Snape. For
publication, these contexts have been used within each
catalogue entry. Those urns now in museum collections
also have, at the end of each catalogue entry, their museum
accession numbers given. The following abbreviations are
used:

Ald	Aldeburgh Moot Hall Museum, Suffolk
Ash	Ashmolean Museum, Oxford
BM	British Museum
Ips	Ipswich Museum
Ver	Verulamium Museum

Those urns contained in Myres' *Corpus of Anglo-Saxon
Pottery of the Pagan Period* (1977) have been noted and
his corpus number given. The urns have been redrawn in
all cases, many having been inaccurately represented in
previous illustrations, with one exception (cremation 50).
This has had to be redrawn from the illustration in Myres
(1977) because the urn is now missing.

Radiocarbon dates
Throughout this report, radiocarbon results have been
calibrated using CALIB v.2.1 (Stuiver and Reimer 1986)
and data from Stuiver and Pearson (1986). The ranges
cited are those for 95% confidence (2σ) unless otherwise
stated.

II. Catalogue of Inhumations

By Tim Pestell, incorporating specialist contributions by Harry Appleyard (fibre analysis), Sue Anderson (human bone) Teresa Briscoe (pot stamps), Esther Cameron (knives, sword and conservation), Elisabeth Crowfoot (textiles), Shirley Carnegie (pottery), Simon Davis (horse head), Vanessa Fell (conservation), Rowena Gale (charcoal), Graeme Lawson (lyre), Simon Mays (cremated bone), Carol Neuman de Vegvar (rim binding), Mark Robinson (insect remains), Penelope Walton Rogers (textile dyes), James Steele (cremated bone), Jacqui Watson (wood) and Stanley West (beads and brooches).

Grave 1 (probable inhumation) (Pl. I, Figs 4 and 78)
Dimensions: Tumulus; diam. approx. 22m, height approx. 1.7m.
Orientation: Ship in trench beneath tumulus E–W.
Container for body: Clinker-built ship.
Sex/age: Male, unknown.
Body position: Unknown.

Description: A robbed tumulus presumed to have contained the inhumation burial of a male within a ship. The burial probably re-used a Bronze Age barrow, judging by the presence of the collared urn encountered in the 1862 excavation (grave 48). The mound also contained several Anglo-Saxon cremations, including grave 51, but their stratigraphic relationships with the ship burial deposit are unclear (Chapter 5 section I, pp.193–4).

There are several remains of metalwork from the ship itself, variously held by the Aldeburgh, Ipswich and National Maritime museums. Most appear to be of partial or complete rivets, although other fittings are present, notably Fe strip *1660*, discussed further below (Chapter 5 section I, pp. 194–5). All pieces have been X-radiographed and allocated individual context numbers, records of which are held in the site archive. Examination of mineralised wood attached to some of the rivets in the Aldeburgh museum showed the boat's strakes to have been made of slow-grown oak heartwood (*Quercus* sp.). The burial and its contents are discussed in detail in Chapter 5 section I.

Grave-goods:
A: Incomplete glass **claw beaker** (Evison 3c) (Pl. IV). Many fragments survive including seven claws and most of the rim; the foot is missing. The glass is a bubbly olive-green, with wisps of a rich brown in the claws. It originally consisted of eight broad-lobed claws arranged in two tiers. Each claw has a vertical overtrail covering the central hook-channel; six of the surviving claws have the trail notch-tooled, with the seventh plain. The horizontal trail at the rim is of 23 turns, that at the foot of 13 turns. Estimated original height was 175mm, the irregular oval mouth diameter approx. 100mm. [0557]
B: Au **finger ring** with a Roman onyx intaglio depicting the standing figure of *Bonus Eventus* (Happy Outcome) (Pls II and III). This gemstone is set within a massive hoop whose wide shoulders are decorated with granules and beaded and twisted wire. Granules and hook-and-eye decoration on the shoulders has been combined to give a zoomorphic effect. See Chapter 5 section I for a detailed consideration of the ring. Drawing by James Farrant. [0556]
C: Unknown **object** described as being of a few pieces of jasper (a type of quartz). Now missing (*not illus.*). [0767]
D: Small fragment of **opaque blue glass** considered by Francis Francis to have been from another vessel (Francis 1863a, 75), although it might also possibly have derived from a cremation burial. Now missing (*not illus.*). [0768]
E: A mass of 'dark dirty red' hair with a smaller amount four feet away, wrapped in 'sailcloth'. Originally, they probably formed a shaggy **woollen cloak**. Now missing (*not illus.*). [0765, 0766]
F: Two **spears**, the Fe heads of which were found apparently in the upper levels of the robber trench backfill, described by Francis Francis (1863a) thus: 'one or two spearheads were found, the only weapons that were discovered. They were of iron, but the metal was almost entirely oxidised... a portion of the wooden shaft of the spear still remained perfect in form and appearance, imbedded in the socket of the weapon'. (i) survives in two fragments which suggest Swanton H2 type. (ii) survives as only badly corroded fragments, the base of which can be recognised and illustrated from X-rays. Lengths: i. *c.*110mm, ii. *c.*135mm. [i: 1650 and 1670. ii: 1655 and 1669]

Grave 2 (inhumation) (Figs 9, 10, 11, 79 and 80)
Dimensions: 1.94 × 0.88m
Orientation: 269°
Container for body: Organic lined chamber with posts at each corner and a possible post-built structure above.
Sex/age: Female.
Body position: Supine extended, legs probably crossed. Head to west.

Description: A regular rectangular cut with uneven vertical sides, undercutting in places. It contained a fill of yellow-brown and grey sands. The fill was stony throughout, as the grave cut through a band of ironpanned gravel. The grey sand was delineated from the yellow-brown along an east-west line on the north side of the grave, probably reflecting the circumstances of the grave's backfilling (Pl. VII and p. 242). A small lump of charcoal, i, of oak stem (*Quercus* sp.) emerged at 14.16mOD.

The dark brown organic stain of a liner showed clearly throughout excavation. At 14.07mOD the east end began to hollow in, a process increasing in subsequent layers to show bulges at the corners. A similar process began at the west end from 13.98mOD. A quadrant was left upstanding in the south-west corner; a pot obscured any such possible bulging in the north-west corner. These bulges seem to represent stake or post-holes used to support the organic chamber within which the body was laid. These post-holes showed well in section but are difficult to reconstruct accurately from spit plans. They are superimposed on the eastern cross-section grave cut (Fig. 11, I–J); the post-holes shown on the long section are from the grave south side. Two lumps of clay, *0358* and *0359*, encountered whilst shovelling off the bottom of the ploughsoil proved to lie almost directly over the two eastern corners of the grave. They possibly represent the clay packing or pads of post-holes for a structure above

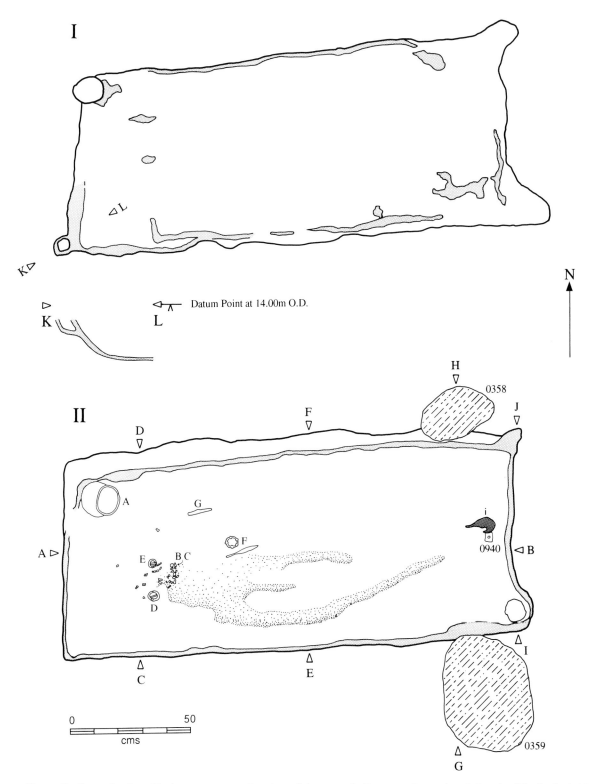

Figure 9 Grave 2, plan. (I) shows a composite plan of the organic liner at a lower level than in (II). Scale 1:15

the grave. They were only sectioned along a north-south axis so they are shown only on the long section.

The body stain was very poorly preserved and definition was made more difficult because the organic lining on which the body was laid was of a similar colour. The chest area was removed in a block for laboratory excavation. The areas defined suggest a body laid supine extended, slightly to the south of the chamber. A central line suggests the backbone whilst the lines continuing on from the legs imply arms laid alongside the body. Metal salts from annular brooch *E* preserved a number of teeth and bone fragments by mineralisation, as well as fragments of fine thread (the best 10×8mm, Z and S, but the weave was unclear and no dye was detected). A fragment of textile (a) was also recovered, *1261*; 13×9mm, wool, ?pigment, no dye detected, spin Z/S, loose, 2/2 twill, count 10/10.

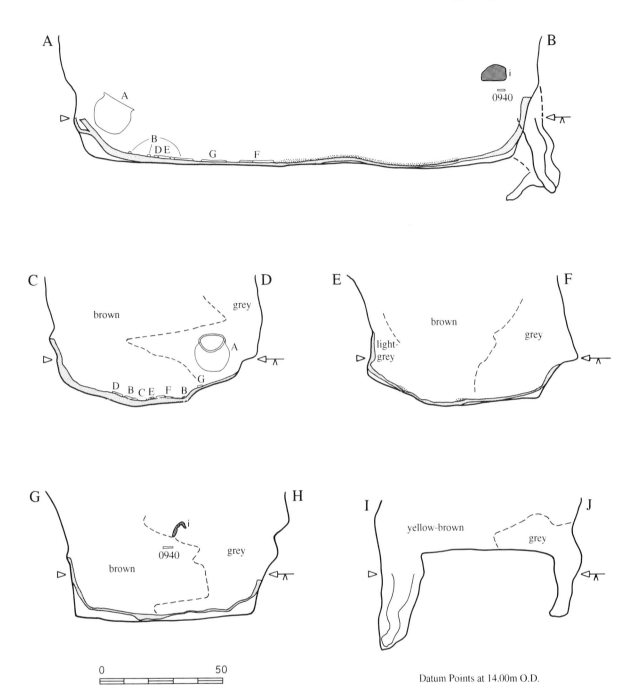

Figure 10 Grave 2, long and cross-sections. Scale 1:15

A sherd of pottery, *0275*, found in the topsoil immediately above the grave before the cut was clear derives from pot *0930* from the 'cremation pyre' area (**scatters No. 12** and pp. 244–6). A fragment of Ae, *0940*, possibly from a brooch and decorated with dots, was found within the upper grave fill at 14.10mOD. It has mineralised threads around it, Z-spun or fine Z-ply, but cannot be specifically linked with the pyre scatter.

Grave-goods:

A: Complete globular **pot** with short upright rim and slightly hollowed base. Decoration consists of three horizontal lines above a double incised chevron decoration at the shoulder showing an overlap where the pattern was started and finished. The fine sandy fabric has some grit, is grey internally and brown externally, with grey reduced areas. It has been smoothed inside and out. The pot was placed left of the head. Height 126mm. [0944]

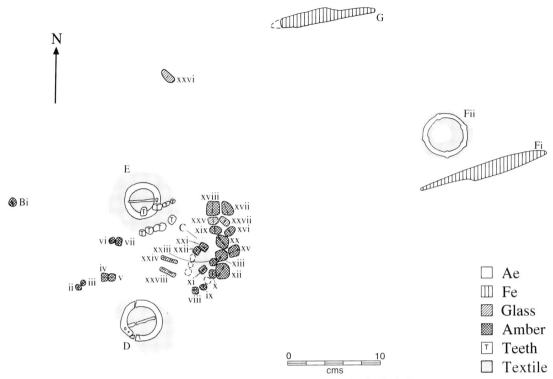

Figure 11 Grave 2, detail of grave-goods. Scale 1:4

□ Ae
▥ Fe
▨ Glass
▩ Amber
T Teeth
□ Textile

B: String of 28 **beads**, of which 23 are amber and 5 are glass. Amber: Small; flattened (i, v–vii, xxiii. Bead i has an Fe link or mineralised thread protruding); globular (ii, x, xxii); roughly shaped (iii, iv, viii, ix, xi, xvi. Bead iv has a mineralised thread): Large; roughly shaped (xiii, xiv, xvii, xviii, xx); wedge (xii, xix); disc (xvi). Glass: disc (xxv, xxvii. Pale yellow translucent); cylindrical, drawn and twisted (xxiv, xxviii. Dark blue; xxiv has both ends smoothed, xxviii one end smoothed, the other snapped); disc (xxvi. Black opaque with broad white zig-zag trail). The block from which the beads were excavated also contained 4 cavities, perhaps formerly containing beads. Amber bead xiv is now missing (*not illus.*). [1226–1253; 1260–64]

C: Fe **fastening**, ?for garment, with small patches of mineralised textile (fine, Z-spun, weave unclear; no dye detected). The concreted lump contained amber bead *Bxxii*, now detached. Length 38mm. [1262]

D: Ae **annular brooch**. Thin flat flange decorated with two rows of 'arrowhead' stamps. Fe pin, possibly attached through a central hole in the flange. It is covered in organic material including two weaves. (a), on the upper surface of the ring is dark brown and very deteriorated, spin probably Z/S. (b), beneath, clear for *c.*10 × 10mm, is lighter brown with very deteriorated threads; spin Z/Z, 2/2 twill, count estimated *c.*13/10 on 10mm. No fibres were found and no dye was detected. Another blackened area near the pin may belong to this. (c), of coarse Z, S-ply threads lying for 20mm along the pin may be associated with bead string *B*. Brooch diameter *c.*44mm. [1267]

E: Ae **annular brooch** with Fe pin. The brooch, broken, has a stamped dot design around the inner and outer edges. Diameter *c.*40mm. Associated are patches of textile (a) and (b). (a), above, is dark brown with Z/S spin, loose twist, a fragment only 6–7 (Z)/5–6 (S) on 5mm twill being preserved. (b) on the under side, over 18 × 10mm, is Z/Z twill, with fine threads, medium twist, count *c.*10/12. There is another mineralised patch of similar weave also present on a small folded strip detached in cleaning. Corrosion products have preserved some bone. [1268]

F: Fe **knife** (i) and cast Ae **ring** (ii). The knife, length 143mm, has the remains of a horn handle. A mineralised layer 1–1.5mm thick lies at the blade tip, centre blade and handle junction which it overlaps by 5mm. No grain surface survives but SEM examination confirms it as leather. A small patch of wood over the leather is preserved, as are traces suggestive of textile (a). A double layer, 25mm wide of very similar weave, a Z/S-spun twill, with thread count 15/12 on 10mm, lies across half of the ring. The fibres are degraded, reddish-brown in some areas and give only slight evidence for scale structure, but what there is suggests wool. A scrap 15 × 10mm of ?(b) lies near the ring. The ring, diameter 45mm, of oval section with five irregularly spaced three-dimensional knobs, narrows in width by 2mm to the bottom right of the figure. A leather attachment loop 5.5mm wide survives over the ring which suggests that it might be part of a sheepskin bag with a twill lining. Another twisted strip of leather suggests a leather band from the ring; fragments of textile, probably from the other side of the ring, including a 20mm length of Z, S-ply thread, perhaps suggest that the knife was originally contained in the bag (Pl. XXXVI). A sample (c) from under the ring has a mass of fibres that look like hair but are too fine for this; the fine medium non-medullated fibres have no

22

Plate VIII Grave 3. Outline of the burial container with the shield boss leaning against the inside edge

Plate VII Grave 2, showing differential colouring of backfill

pigmentation. What scale structure there is indicates wool. No dye was detected. [1272, 1274]

G: Fe **knife** with broken tip, length 106mm. There are traces of horn on the tang and a 1mm thick compact layer, probably from a leather sheath, curves over the blade back. It extends a little beyond the cutting edge and overlaps the handle junction by 11mm. The weave of the associated textile is unclear and partly infested with insect pupae which are too degraded for identification. A small textile patch appears to have coarse Z/S-spun threads. A 13 × 12mm patch on the sheath fragment is of (d). It has Z/Z spinning and a very even 2/2 twill weave, thread count *c.*15/13 on 10mm. Its coarse-fibred threads suggest flax. [1280]

Grave 3 (inhumation) (Figs 12, 13, 80 and 81)
Dimensions: 2.44 × 0.98m
Orientation: 270°
Container for body: Charred container — part of a boat?
Sex/age: Male.
Body position: Extended supine, right leg crossed over left.

Description: A large apsidal-ended cut with near vertical sides. The cut was very difficult to observe at the surface as it was set within a mottled area of grey sand and natural. The fill was a stone-free, heavily mottled, mix of orange-brown redeposited natural with some mid grey sand throughout. Within the uppermost levels the remains of wood lumps were observed and although samples were taken the remains were too poor to be identified.

The charred stain of a container appeared at 14.23mOD with a flat blunt end to the west. The stain was

always quite distinct due to being charred and in places was seen as two thin parallel lines, suggesting that it had been burnt on both surfaces of the wood. Samples show the wood to have been of oak heartwood (*Quercus* sp.).

The original form of the container is of interest since it was open on the eastern edge (the long section in Fig. 13 shows the extent of the stain on the north side), whilst the western end sloped down to a flat bottom where the body was actually laid. A possible interpretation is that the container was a part of a boat with the west end bow point and the eastern half or end third removed. This identification is tentative but would accord well with the slope shown on the long section, the rounded bottom seen in the cross-sections and the container being made of oak heartwood. The width of the container is also similar to that of the well-preserved boat stain in grave 47. Against this interpretation is the fact that there is no significant widening of the stain to the east and the lack of narrowing at the west. However, if the bow had been cut off at the west end (as a bow is argued to have been, for burial on its own in grave 10) the ensuing lack of rigidity in the boat sides may have caused a flattening, and therefore widening of the stain at this point. Parts of boats are known to have been used as burial containers at Slusegård (Crumlin-Pedersen 1991) and this may be a parallel to the practice employed there.

The body stain was very poorly preserved and was frequently only a smear on the bottom of the container, although the feet were reasonably well preserved.

Grave-goods:
A: **Spear** with (i) Fe **head** (Swanton H2), length 292mm, lying with the blade flat, the base tipped with (ii) an Fe **ferrule**, length 90mm. Approximate length of spear from these (tip to tip) was 2.1m. Mineral preserved wood in the sockets of both head and ferrule is of ash (*Fraxinus* sp.), from mature timber. Patches of mineralised textile on the ferrule, the best 20x9mm, are Z/Z spin, 2/2 twill, count *c.*7/6–7, thread diameter *c.*1mm; damaged, threads missing. The spear appears to have been laid on the top of the container. [0668, 0777]
B: Fe **knife** with horn handle fragmented by corrosion, length *c.*130mm. The blade is encased in a compact 1mm layer confirmed as leather by SEM with traces

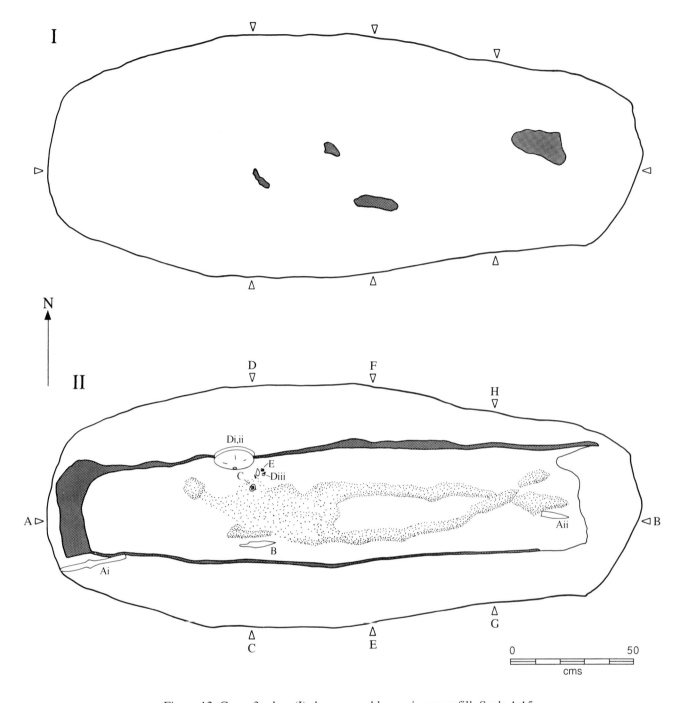

I

N

II

Figure 12 Grave 3, plan. (I) shows wood lumps in upper fill. Scale 1:15

of textile (unidentifiable) overlying it. Could only be drawn from X-ray. [0952]

C: Ae **buckle**. Heavy loop with narrowed bar for strap. Stout Ae tongue curved to fit the loop, width 23mm. Found lying on carbonised wood of ash (*Fraxinus* sp.), with a tangential surface. Two textiles are preserved: (a) adhering under the buckle in a fold over an area 30 × 38mm, is dark brown, spin Z/Z, loose with fine threads; the twill weave has *c*.8 threads on 5mm in one system; the fibres are probably wool. (b), in a layer next to the buckle, 32 × 22mm, is very clear but deteriorated. Z/Z, very even 2/2 twill, no reverses, thread count 12–14/12–14 on 10mm. Lying across is a coarse Z-spun thread, similar to (a) and probably of wool. No dye was detected. [0954]

D: **Shield** with (i) Fe **boss** (Dickinson and Härke Group 3) and (ii) **grip**, apparently placed leaning against the inside of the body container (Pl. VIII). Boss diameter *c*.180mm, height 72mm; grip length 144mm. The grip appears to have slipped out of place after burial and fragmented in the ground. Mineralisation preserves a thin layer of leather between the boss rim and shield board, but there is possibly no leather between the board and an Ae **washer**. The shield board, made of birch (*Betula* sp.) has a radial surface at the centre and a tangential one at the side (depth of wood at the rim is 4–5.6mm). On the grip there is a thin layer of leather between the iron and the wood. Only a sliver remains of the wood, whose grain lies along the length of the grip which may indicate that it was an inserted type.

24

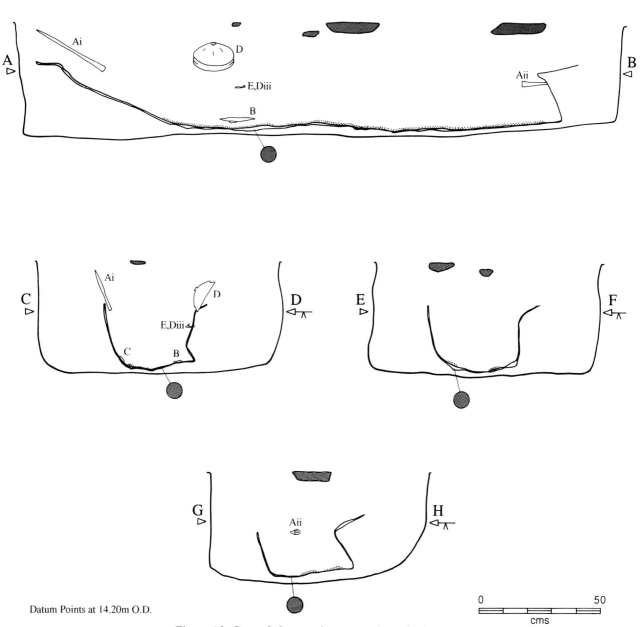

Figure 13 Grave 3, long and cross-sections. Scale 1:15

Datum Points at 14.20m O.D.

0   50

cms

The outer part of the grip was bound with two strips of leather, approximately 2mm wide. A **shield stud** (iii) found with the grip and buckle *E* preserves traces of the shield board; at this point it is 6.6mm thick with an oblique transverse surface and covered with leather on both sides. Leather on the front of the shield board is a third of the thickness of the back and the complete shield thickness at this point is 13mm; it is possible that the edge of the board has been trimmed to a tapered shape. The boss front also preserves mineralised plant stems and other random organic material; ash wood (*Fraxinus* sp.) is preserved on the head of the stud. [0678, 0732]

E: Fe **buckle** with wrap around Fe tongue; width of loop *c*.18mm. Found adjacent to the shield grip which preserves a fragment of ash (*Fraxinus* sp.) on the front, with a tangential surface possibly belonging to another artefact. There are traces of possible strap remains (not textile) on the pin loop. [0594]

Grave 4 (inhumation) (Figs 14, 15 and 82)
Dimensions: 3.68 × 0.82m
Orientation: 263°
Container for body: Small logboat.
Sex/age: Unknown, juvenile?
Body position: Flexed to right, head to west?

Description: A long rectangular grave cut with a rounded west end, containing a small logboat. The grave was first seen as an area of light grey sand between patches of mid brown sand at each end. Their positions were maintained throughout the fill. This seems to reflect the grey topsoil being backfilled into the centre of the grave whilst the orange lower fill was put in at the same time at each end. The fill had several small peagrit stones deriving from a band of ironpanned gravel sand through which the grave was cut.

The upper fill contained several small patches of charcoal, only some of which were planned, and a few sherds of pottery. Charcoal patches i (*not illus.*) and ii were

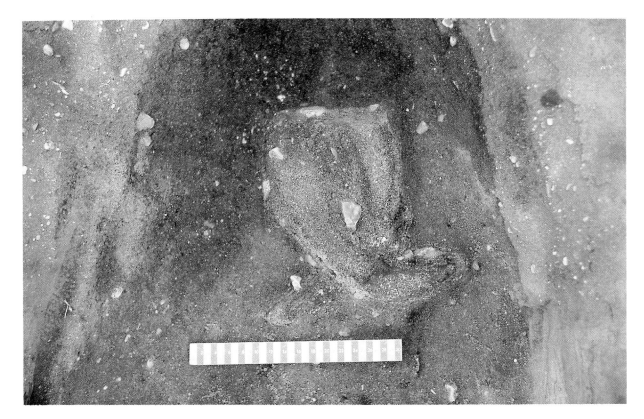

Plate IX Drinking horns arranged at the feet in the eastern bow of grave 4

seen after initial site clearance before the grave cut was properly defined. i was of oak stem (*Quercus* sp.) but ii could not be identified. Midway down the fill was iii, in three smaller patches (unidentified), and a burnt flint fragment, *0917*. Tiny fragments of *?Rosaceae/Ericaceae* ?root were also found at this level (*0931*). A mass of very small charcoal fragments (*0945*) found in the logboat's eastern bow stain at 14.05mOD were of oak (*Quercus* sp.), possibly softwood, but did not derive from the boat. Several small patches of charcoal appeared at the boat bottom close to the body stain: iv, v and vi. The latter two are of oak (*Quercus* sp.), v being softwood.

Three sherds of pottery were found in the fill. One, *0919*, derives from vessel *0408*, an open bowl with a dark grey sandy fabric (Fig. 82). Grey-brown on both surfaces, it had a smoothed outer surface and roughly scraped inner face. The other two sherds, *0918* and *0946*, of a soft dark-brown fabric with angular grit and pitted surfaces derive from vessel *1152*. Other sherds from this vessel were found within urn *0073* in grave 78 and loose in topsoil layer *0273*, including a sherd directly above the inhumation before the cut was located (catalogued as scatters No. 20). They show the vessel to have originally been an open bowl (*illus.* under grave 78, Fig. 119). Finally, a small fragment of fused iron, *0915*, was found midway down the grave fill (Fig. 82). It possibly derives from a cremation elsewhere on the site.

The logboat from this grave has already been published (Filmer-Sankey 1990a), but is discussed further with that from grave 47 in Chapter 5 section II. The distinctive V-shaped bow stain first appeared at the east end at 14.22mOD and the stain, always thin and patchy, gradually extended west. The plan shows the stain at its various highest surviving points throughout the grave. The

length of the boat as revealed was 2.96m although it was undoubtedly originally longer since the western bow only survived from 14.02mOD. The boat had a beam of approximately 0.70m, only slightly narrower than the grave cut, and a depth of about 0.4m. The force of the earth had distorted the stain and flattened the base, making it more difficult to reconstruct the boat's original shape compared to that in grave 47.

The bow changed from its V-shape to develop a pointed 'fin' at its lower levels (Pl. XXXIII). At 14.03mOD a curved stain appeared within both bow ends, but most clearly at the east end (Pl. XXXIV). These appear to represent solid blocks inserted into the bow spaces to act as thwarts or bulkheads, perhaps to help hold the sides of the boat apart if it had been expanded. Two samples of greasy organic material (*1019* and *1135*) were recovered from within the stain and possibly represent a caulking material, used to patch holes or cracks in the logboat.

The body stain barely survived and was located as only thin smears. These are best interpreted as representing a flexed burial, possibly of a juvenile, as the approximate body height is 1.40m.

Grave-goods:
A: **Knife** with a short Fe blade and the remains of horn on the handle. It has no other organic remains. It comes from beyond the suggested head, at the west end of the boat. Length 104mm. [0959]
B: 'D' shaped Fe **buckle** and tongue, width 20mm. Found lying tongue-side down, at the suggested waist of the body stain, covered in mineralised textile obscured by sand grains. Inside the ring is a damaged area *c*.9 × 9mm, with Z/S spinning, of very fine twill. [0960]

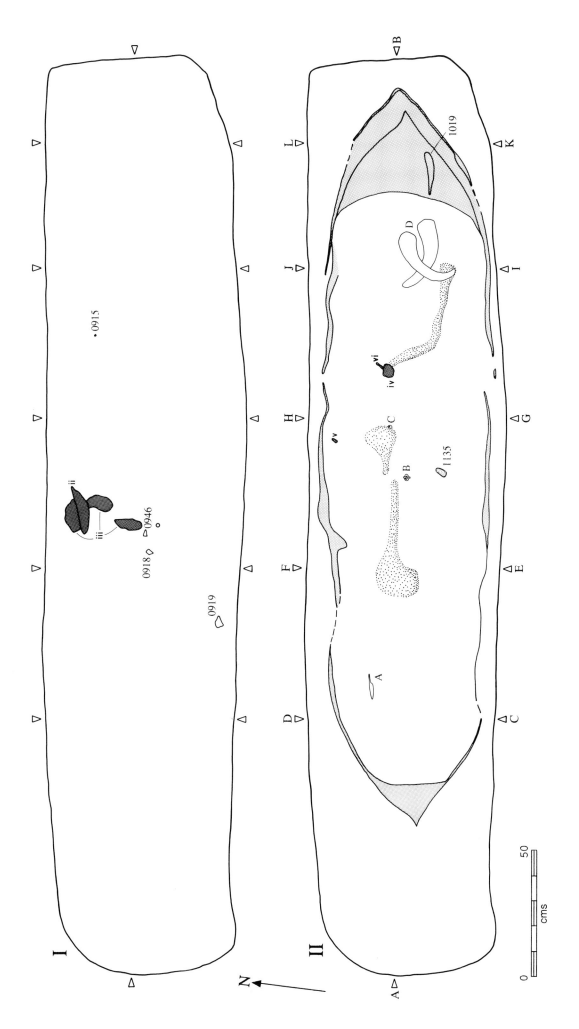

Figure 14 Grave 4, plan. (I) shows wood and pottery in upper fill. Scale 1:15

27

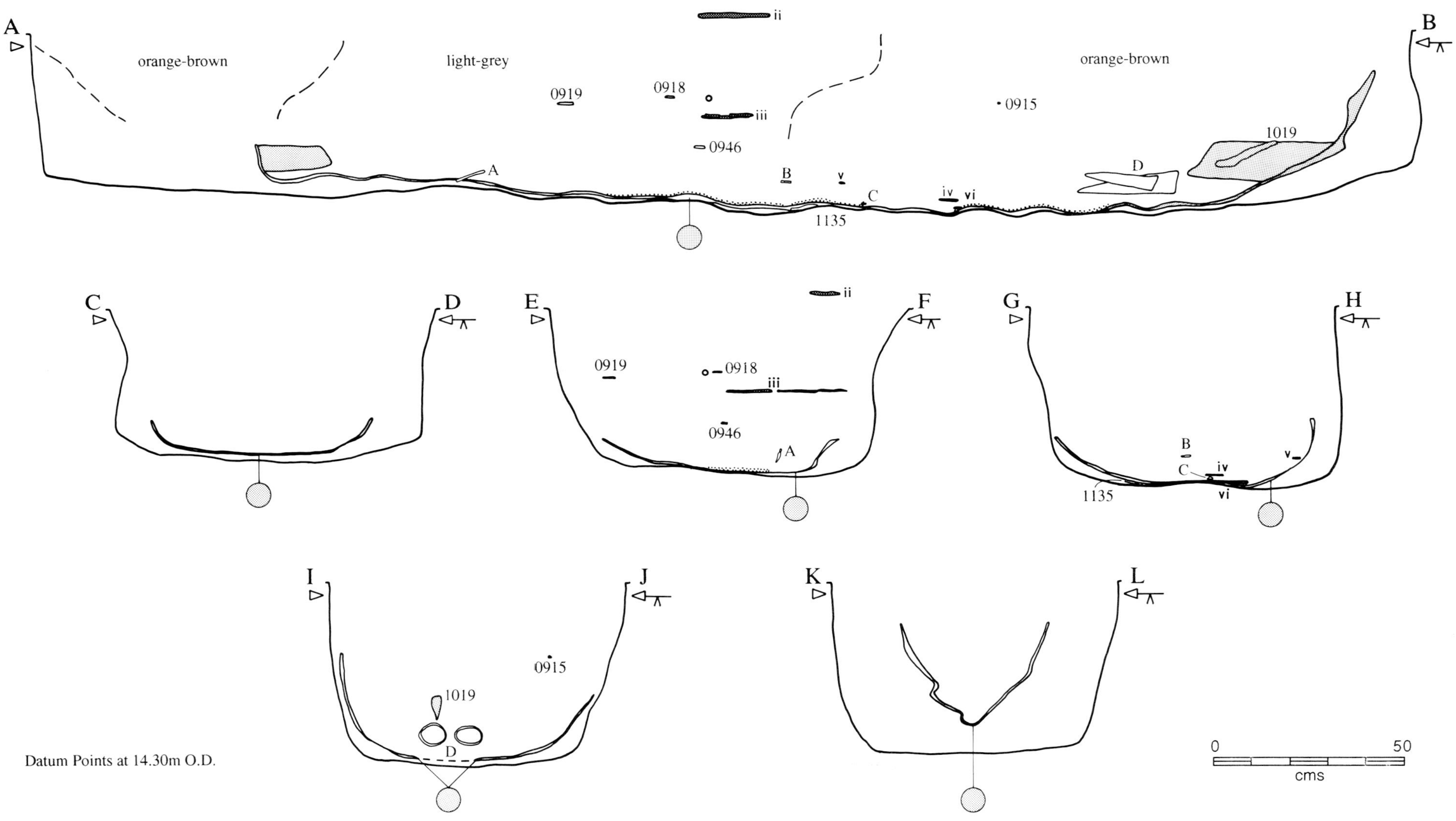

Figure 15 Grave 4, long and cross-sections. Scale 1:15

Datum Points at 14.30m O.D.

28

C: Fe **stud** or **tack** at the grave base, possibly beneath the body stain. There are traces of leather on the head and mineralised textile beneath, perhaps from a belt; weave damaged, Z-spun. Diameter of head *c*.18mm. [1001]

D: Pair of **drinking horns** arranged symmetrically by the body's feet at the east end of the grave. Both are apparently cattle horns. The shorter, (i), lays over the longer, (ii). The horns survived at their bases despite the absence of any metal fittings. The original extent of both could be discerned from dark stains of their upper parts (Pl. IX). See also Chapter 5 section III. [0963, 0987]

Grave 5 (inhumation) (Figs 16, 82 and 83)
Dimensions: 1.69 × 0.61m
Orientation: 259°
Container for body: None.
Sex/age: Female.
Body position: Extended, right arm laid over waist. Head to west.

Description: This grave was originally seen as a scatter of pottery fragments with some cremated bone and metalwork, thought to be a smashed cremation. Ploughmarks could be seen running through the scatter in its highest layer. The grave cut could be vaguely seen at this height but was only clearly defined at 14.41mOD.

The fill consisted of a stone-free greyish-brown sand, quite light grey in the upper fill becoming increasingly darker brown. Several lumps of ironpan mixed in with the fill halfway down. More fragments of pottery and cremated bone were found within the fill and three thin lengths of charcoal were seen at 14.20mOD. Smaller charcoal flecks and lumps were found scattered more widely in the fill. Those identified were all of oak (*Quercus* sp.) of heartwood and possibly stem.

The 118 pottery fragments from the surface scatter and throughout the fill derive from decorated pot *0318*. They seem to be associated with scattered cremated bone and two metal finds, a burnt and twisted bronze buckle (*0165*) and an iron nailhead or tack (*0185*). This group is interpreted as a disturbed cremation and catalogued as grave 80. The plan and sections show only those fragments planned. No fragments of *0318* were found in the very bottom levels of the grave, although a few pieces of cremated bone were.

The body, showing as a very rounded, 'bloated' stain, was apparently laid directly in the grave. The remains of pot *H* were all found in the very bottom levels, concentrated in a dense cluster. They were placed immediately over the pelvic area of the body on the grave south side, apparently deliberately.

Grave-goods:
A: Ae **annular brooch** with Fe pin lying near-vertically over left shoulder. Traces of three transverse bars. Oval shape, max. diameter *c*.46mm. Two textiles are preserved, semi-mineralised: (a), round to the top of the brooch in three folds has clear areas of 13 × 10 and 30 × 13mm. The spinning is Z in both systems with a medium twist even thread; weave 2/2 twill with variable thread counts 10/10, 10/8–9 on 10mm. The threads are wool with medium fibres, some pigmented, dyed blue with indigotin. (b), beneath (a),

has a clear area 27 × 12mm visible. The threads are dark brown with Z spinning in warp and weft; the weave is a 2/2 twill with variable thread counts, estimated 10/8 on 10mm. On this wool weave, the surface fibres are slightly matted, possibly raised. A fragment of tubular selvedge is preserved for 27mm on one edge (Fig. 139.6). No dye was detected. Both brooch and pin are fragmented and are too fragile for a side view. [0696]

B: Ae **annular brooch** with Fe pin, lying over right shoulder, pair to *A*. Oval shape, max. diameter *c*.5mm. The textile beneath is probably of (a). The area *c*.55 × 35mm, in folds over the pin, is stained with Fe. Its spin is again Z/Z, the weave a wool 2/2 twill with thread count 10/10 on 10mm. An area *c*.15 × 10mm of (b) was present in folds under the pin. Here, it seems to be looser than (a), with a thread count of *c*.12/6–8. Of wool, it was probably dyed brown, grey or black from oak galls. [0753]

C: Fragmentary Ae **wrist clasp** (probably Hines B7). Elongated slit for fastening; decorated with single row of tiny annular stamps. Fragment length 23mm. The thin strip is fragmented within a wedge of mineralised textile. This shows two meeting edges from under the two pieces of the clasp with remains of the twill sleeve and the tablet-woven band (c) sewn to its edge: (i), 35 × 9mm, twill (a) or (b), *c*.30mm in length is turned under, with tablet warps protruding for 4mm, with no pattern wefts surviving. A damaged guilloche plait is sewn to the long edge. (ii), 13 × 30mm, a fragment from the other edge, with the guilloche plait of Z-spun thread (Fig. 139.4) sewn to it, is well-preserved for 22mm. This also has a 20mm wide fragment of the band (c), tablet-woven with warp threads Z-spun, showing part of the centre pattern area with stationary cords, 10–12 on 10mm. The wefts are also Z-spun, 12 on 10mm. The remains of a pattern, in fine horsehair, show two diagonal lines of wrapping ('soumak') surviving 6mm from the folded edge, and traces of other similar lines (Fig. 139.9, Pl. XLVI). The back of the braid is damaged and folded under, with untidy coarse S-ply threads that sewed it to the clasp, and a piece of the twill sleeve. The coarse fibres are very densely pigmented. No dye was detected. [0737]

D: Ae **wrist clasp** (i and ii), (Hines B7) paired with *C*, found over the left wrist of the body, in two pieces. Catch-plate decorated with single row of tiny annular stamps. As on *C*, a fragment of braid (c) (14 × 45mm) is preserved, with the end turned under. Again it is Z-spun, the tablet-weave protected by the broken metal of the clasp; braid width 30mm, in the centre area stationary cords 6 on 5mm, and on one edge S,Z,S,Z,S. The pattern on this piece shows square tapestry patches, weft wrapping over threads from two tablets, alternately chestnut and black horsehair (Fig. 139.9, Pl. XLV). A guilloche plait similar to that on *C* is sewn to the edge, with a fragment hanging loose at the corner, probably originally sewn along the edge of the cuff opening. Remains of Z-spun twill adhere to the underside of the braid and protrude 15mm from the braid end. Coarse S-ply sewing thread hangs from a hole in the clasp. [0667 and 0699]

E: Ae **belt buckle** with Fe tongue, drawn from X-ray. Obscured by traces of wool textile, ?(a) above; 38 ×

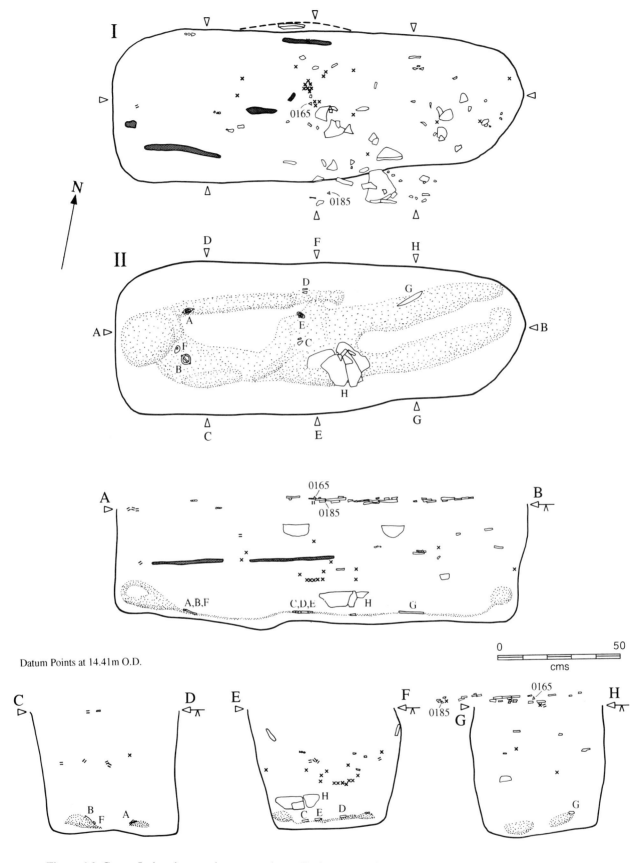

I

0165

0185

N

II

D   F   H

D
A
E
G
A   F   B
B   C
H
C   E   G

A   0165   B
0185
A,B,F   C,D,E   H   G

Datum Points at 14.41m O.D.

0   50
cms

C   D   E   F   0165   H
0185
G
B   H   C   G
F   A   E   D

Figure 16 Grave 5 plan, long and cross-sections. (I) shows wood, pottery and cremated bone in the upper fill.
Scale 1:15

35mm, Z/Z spin, 2/2 twill, of very even spin and weave, count *c*.8–9/8 on 5mm. No dye was detected. Also (d) below, a tiny fragment, 3 × 3mm, ?hair or silk, 3 (?warp) bundles/*c*.24(?weft), possibly tabby, on leather. On one surface is a thin layer of oak (*Quercus* sp.). [0751]

F: Large, flat amber **bead**, adjacent to annular brooch *B* at the throat. Length 29mm. [0754]

G: Fe **knife**, length 110mm, preserving traces of horn on the tang. Fragments of the leather sheath are preserved on one side of the blade. The sheath is folded over the blade back but eroded along the blade edge. It overlaps the handle junction by at least 7mm. The leather, 1mm thick, has a grain pattern on one surface identified as calf. Associated textile is in detached fragments, the best 13 × 5mm, twill, Z/Z. There are only a few clear threads, which could be (a) or (b). [0845]

H: Base and lower half of a **pot**, probably of a tall and open-mouthed shape. Of a dark brown sandy fabric with grey-brown vesiculated surfaces. None of the sherds have any decoration. The sherds were found crushed directly over the body stain. As reconstructed it has a hole in the base, but this may be due to a missing sherd rather than intention. Surviving height *c*.110mm. [0677]

Grave 6 (inhumation) (Figs 17, 83 and 84)
Dimensions: 2.1 × 0.86m
Orientation: 269°
Container for body: Coffin or ?organic lined grave
Sex/age: Male.
Body position: Flexed, knees to the body's left. Only fragmentary stains of backbone and skull. Head to west.

Description: The grave showed at top of natural as a regular rectangular cut with heavy black staining running along the grave north edge. The fill was primarily redeposited natural of mottled orange-brown sand, with light grey sand mixing in at the east end. The grave was excavated in very dry conditions which made locating the cut very difficult and it was seen best at the lower levels. The fill remained mottled orange-brown throughout, with patches of grey in the east end becoming more sparse deeper down. Within the fill were two fragments of cremated bone (*0613*) at the same level as the bottom lip of pot *A*. The large body sherd *E* lay at the grave bottom just east of the shield boss and seems to have been deliberately deposited. A few small flecks (*0780*) of oak (*Quercus* sp.) were found on the knees of the body stain.

The dense black humic stain of the body container retained moisture longer and was seen from the highest level of the grave. It began running along the grave north edge and lengthened from the west end until it showed as a complete rectangle at 14.07mOD. The western half of the stain was always the most dense. Its edges sloped inward and given the packing of the fill, this seems to accurately reflect the original container shape.

The bottom of the grave was a dense black semi-humic layer made up of a number of organic stains. The body stain was poor but showed the occupant to have been laid out supine with legs flexed.

Grave-goods:
A: Nearly complete **pot** of high shouldered form with a damaged eversion for a thin flaring rim. The fine brown fabric with rounded grit has a grey inner surface with an outer surface of reddish-brown and grey areas. Both surfaces are vesiculated and carefully burnished. Decoration consists of three horizontal lines above a row of circular rosette stamps with a central boss. Beneath are another three horizontal lines above a row of rosette stamps on the shoulder (Briscoe types A5fii and A5ai respectively). The one surviving rim fragment was found elsewhere, associated with grave 90 in the south-east corner of Area A (Fig. 147). Pot placed within upper fill of grave inside container. Height surviving *c*.120mm. [0462, 0605, 0606, 0607, 0608, 0614, 0618]

B: **Spear** with Fe head (Swanton H2), the blade laid vertically. The socket preserves mineralised wood of ash (*Fraxinus* sp.) from mature timber. Length 352mm. [0593].

C: **Shield** with button-tipped Fe boss (Dickinson and Härke Group 3). It was laid flat over the head and shoulders of the body. The boss preserves traces of various organic materials including a patch of horn. The wooden shield board was made from willow (*Salix* sp.) or poplar (*Populus* sp.) and has an oblique tangential surface. There is a thin layer of leather between the wood and boss rim. More unidentifiable wood was squashed onto the front of the boss, but was too poorly preserved to identify. Staining in the area of the boss within the grave fill possibly represented the remains of the shield board. Diameter *c*.190mm, height 94mm. [0627, 0703].

D: **Knife** with Fe blade and horn handle, length 102mm. Extensively mineralised covering leather is probably from a sheath and overlaps the handle by 40mm on the underside. It is folded over the blade back and joined along the blade edge where it forms a sinuous line but no stitching survives. Traces of mineralised textile adhere to the end of the blade (10 × 13mm) and near the handle (5 × 5mm); threads fine, spin not clear, twill weave. [0779]

E: Single body **sherd** from a sub-globular pot of a dense grey sandy fabric. It has a grey inner surface and brown exterior surface. The inner surface is heavily scored with tooling and the outer surface is roughly burnished. [0700]

Grave 7 (inhumation) (Figs 18 and 84)
Dimensions: 1.36 × 0.62m
Orientation: 271°
Container for body: None.
Sex/age: Uncertain, juvenile.
Body position: Unclear as little body stain left. Probably supine. Head to west.

Description: A shallow grave with rounded ends, with a stone-free fill of mixed grey and brown sands. A rectilinear patch of dark grey sand and charcoal about 2cms thick, within the fill, possibly represents a cut turf. A raising of the grave bottom at the west end possibly represents a 'pillow' of natural sand on which the head rested.

Several sherds from urn *0635*, of adjacent grave 83, were found directly above what was later seen as the grave

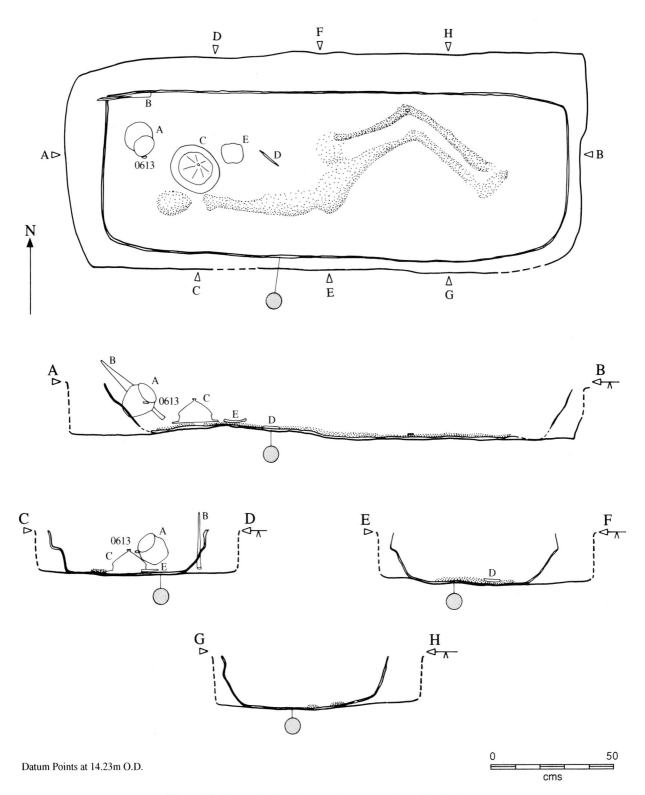

N

Datum Points at 14.23m O.D.

0 ⟵⟶ 50
cms

Figure 17 Grave 6, plan, long and cross-sections. Scale 1:15

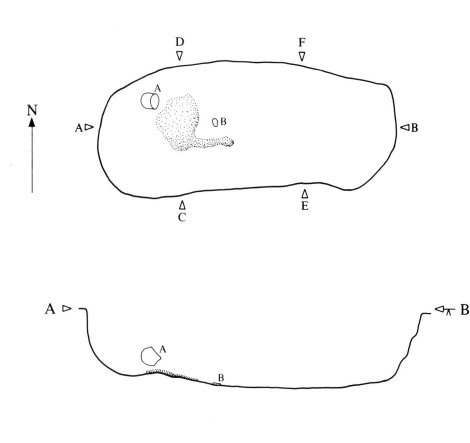

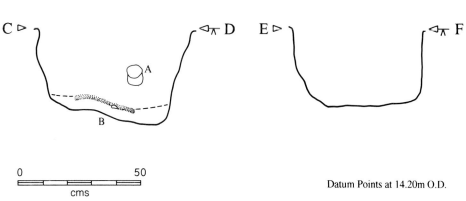

Figure 18 Grave 7, plan, long and cross-sections. Scale 1:15

fill but nowhere else outside the cremation's cut. This might represent their having been contained in the grave upper fill originally, but is probably by chance.

Grave-goods:
A: A complete small round-bottomed **pot** with vesiculated inner and outer surfaces. The fabric is not visible but is grey-brown on the inside and red-brown on the outer with reduced areas. Undecorated, it was placed slightly above the body in the grave fill. Height 63mm. [0991]
B: Ae **buckle** and tongue, width 13mm. A lump of mineralised textile 15 × 15mm adheres; spin Z/Z, even and rather loose. The weave is 2/2 twill, one clear patch 7 × 7mm giving a thread count of *c.*9/10. The same weave is present but damaged on the other side. The buckle could only be drawn from X-rays. [0990]

Grave 8 (inhumation) (Figs 19, 20 and 84)
Dimensions: (Top) 1.72 x 0.76m; (Base) 1.80 x 0.79m
Orientation: 269°
Container for body: Wood and organic base?
Sex/age: Female.
Body position: Supine extended, laid along south edge of grave, arms by the sides. Head to east.

Description: A sub-rectangular shape at the surface which undercut to produce a grave cut with neat rounded ends. The fill was a consistent stone-free dark reddish-brown with mottlings of light brown. Small lumps of ironpan were encountered halfway down the fill, as was coarser sand from 13.92mOD.

Three pieces of wood, (i)–(iii), were encountered in the eastern half of the grave mid-way down the fill; (i) was of oak stem (*Quercus* sp.). Another fragment, (iv), also of oak, probably sapwood but not from a narrow stem, appeared to overlie the face of the body. At the bottom of

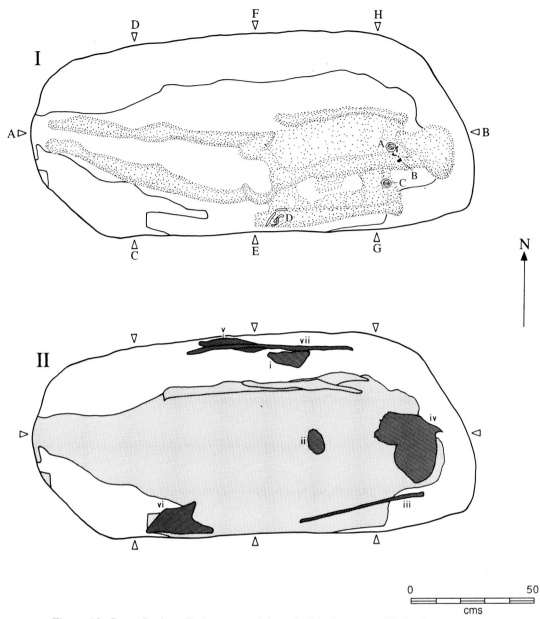

Figure 19 Grave 8, plan. (I) shows wood deposited in the upper fill. Scale 1:15

the grave there was a mixture of wood and staining. Three smaller pieces, (v, vi and viii) could be isolated; all were of oak (*Quercus* sp.). (vi) was of stem burnt at a high temperature and partially vitrified. Piece (vii) was seen as a very dark stain, elements of which were of oak (*Quercus* sp.) sapwood and heartwood. The piece is shown as an organic stain on plan as it could not be proved that the whole context was of wood although this is likely. (vii) was widest in the grave centre and tapered with the legs. In several areas the pieces retained traces of grain, all running E–W. The fragments were typically small and those on the floor of the grave possibly formed part of the same structure. Pieces v, vi and viii are omitted from the long section for clarity.

Sections across the body stain showed that it was laid on the organic base. The body was reasonably well defined and degraded fragments of bone survived at the left shoulder, perhaps under the influence of mineral salts deriving from brooch *C*.

Grave-goods:

A: Ae **annular brooch** with fragmentary Fe pin and mineralised textile adhering. Three groups of four transverse lines can be seen through the corrosion products and others probably exist on the other half of the circumference. A narrowed neck represents the seating for the pin. Diameter 40mm. On the front of the ring, an area of textile (a) 18 × 10mm was preserved, also mineralised for 10 × 6mm under the pin, spinning Z/Z, loose twist; weave 2/2 twill, thread count *c*.10/8. A fragment (b) of semi-mineralised whip-cord (Fig. 139.5) protruding from under the brooch, is fastened to the weave with one Z-spun thread. A black degraded spongy material on the underside with no apparent weave may have been leather. [0848]

B: String of 17 **beads**; 4 of amber, 13 of glass. Amber: small elongated (i, ii); roughly shaped (iii); globular (iv). Glass: drawn globular (v, vi); drawn double globular (vii–xi); drawn triple globular (xii–xvii). The glass beads are segmented and coloured either by

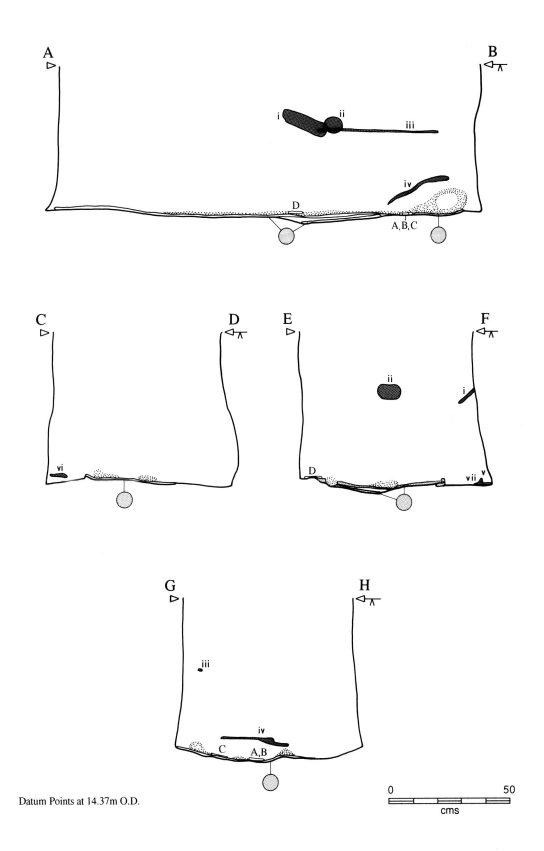

A B

C D E F

G H

iii

iv

C A,B

Datum Points at 14.37m O.D.

0 50

cms

Figure 20 Grave 8, long and cross-sections. Scale 1:15

Au/gilding (v–xii) or with Ag foil sandwiched between the glass (xiii–xvii). Together they form a cluster in the throat area, body right hand side. Three fragments of Z-spun, S-ply thread, (c), are preserved in the beads, the best length 19mm. Unfortunately there is not enough information for a detailed reconstruction as some beads became detached and orientations were lost. [0848 and 1000]

C: Ae **annular brooch**, flat flange with single rebate for seating the iron pin. Decorated with two rows of tiny annular stamps. Diameter 42mm. Partly mineralised wool textile of (a) above, with mineralised wood, over 26 × 23mm; twill, thread count 10/8, no dye detected. (a) is also partly mineralised on the pin for c.45 × 13mm. A mineralised fragment (d) lies under (a) over 5 × 6mm; it is a Z-spun tabby weave, thread count 7/8–9 on 5mm. This shows paired threads (Fig. 139.1), possibly a stripe. Overlying the brooch was a twig impregnated with Cu corrosion products. Original orientation of brooch unknown. [0851]

D: Fe **knife** (i) and **ring** (ii). The knife, length 112mm, has a horn handle but all other organic remains are of very degraded textile probably (a). This adheres along the ring visible for an area 30 × 15mm with another detached fragment 12 × 11mm. The ring, diameter c.50mm, is broken. [0849]

Grave 9 (inhumation) (Figs 21, 22 and 85)
Dimensions: (Top) 2.09 × 0.92m; (Bottom) 1.66 × 0.75m
Orientation: 289°
Container for body: None but upper body rested on an organic layer.
Sex/age: Unknown.
Body position: Supine extended, left arm crossed over chest, right arm next to body. Left leg crossed over the right at the ankles. Head to west, turned to face the north.

Description: A rectangular cut with a sharply defined west end at the surface with slight undercutting. The fill was a mix of fine and coarse sands with some small pebbles. The fill had two distinct colours of grey and brown sands at the surface which became increasingly mottled. At the bottom of the grave dirty orange natural probably represents trampled sand. A shelf in the east end of the cut reduced the bottom of the grave to a length corresponding to the body (Pl. XI).

The grave was notable for the large amount of charred wood contained within the fill, apparently from branches. The first pieces appeared near the top of the fill at 14.35mOD and in all eight pieces were located. All pieces except (iv) were identifiable, being of oak (*Quercus* sp.). (i) was of stem and sapwood; (ii; Pl. X) of sapwood and heartwood; (iii) of sapwood probably from a wide stem or narrow pole, fast grown; (v) of heartwood; (vi–viii) were all of stem, (viii) being almost vitrified. Pieces (i–iii) can be seen to have been arranged directly over the body and whilst not as clear, pieces (iv–viii) seem also to have been arranged with this aim in mind. The wood was exceptionally well preserved; the charring was typically 5–10mm thick and the grain and wood knots could be made out (Pl. LVII). The irregular shape of some pieces is best interpreted as a result of their having been crushed and flattened slightly as the unburnt interiors, characterised by light grey sand, rotted away.

Plate X Charred wood fragment ii from grave 9. Scale rod 1m

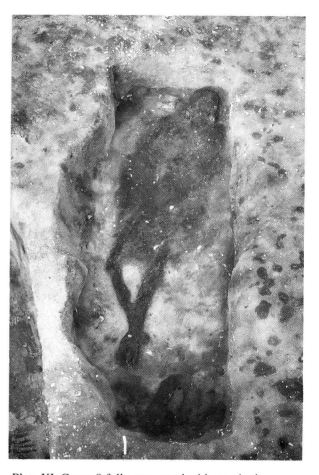

Plate XI Grave 9 fully excavated with step in the grave cut east end

The body stain was very well preserved and its upper half lay on an organic substance, probably of textile judging by the remains on the underside of the knife. An organic soil, similar to body stain, lay next to the right upper arm. Traces of degraded bone remained within the stain of the skull, but were too fragmentary for identification.

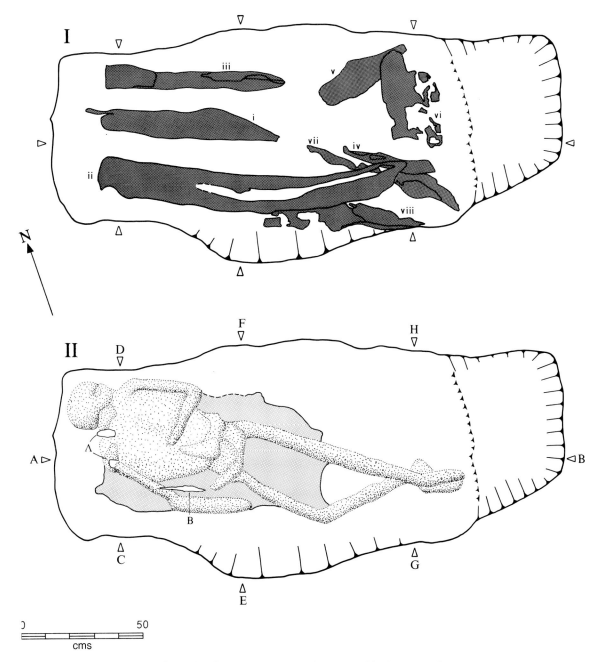

I

II

N

0   50
cms

Figure 21 Grave 9, plan. (I) shows wood deposited in the upper fill. Scale 1:15

Grave-goods:

A: Wooden **vessel** with Ae sheet and rivets (i and ii), forming mounts or repairs. The wood fragments seem to belong to a lathe-turned vessel probably made from walnut (*Juglans* sp.). From the thickness of the wood and rivets, the vessel appears to have been consistently 5.5–7mm thick for the base and sides, sharply tapering to 3mm at the rim. The base appears to have had a flat bottom with a diameter of around 70–80mm. The grain orientation suggests near vertical sides rather than the slight incline of a shallow bowl. There is no indication of the height of the vessel but it was possibly quite small. Fig. 85 gives two possible reconstructions. On the rim was a mineralised ?string, Z-spun. Deteriorated scraps from textile, perhaps originally covering the bowl, are preserved over an area *c.*20 × 18mm, with loose

fragments on metal 23 × 20mm, and on wood 40 × 40mm. The Z/Z loose spun threads were (1) light, with fine to medium wool fibres, no pigmentation or medullation 1.5–2mm diameter and (2) dark threads of medium diameter wool fibres with dark pigmentation, 1mm diameter. They represent a 2/2 striped twill weave (Fig. 139.2); no dye was detected. [0661, 0840, 0847]

B: Fe **knife**, length 186mm, with traces of horn on the tang. Corrosion products lie on one side of the blade but do not extend over the handle junction and offer no features, apart from proximity to the blade, to suggest being from a sheath. Overlying it and on the other side of the blade are the remains of textile (unidentified). [0900]

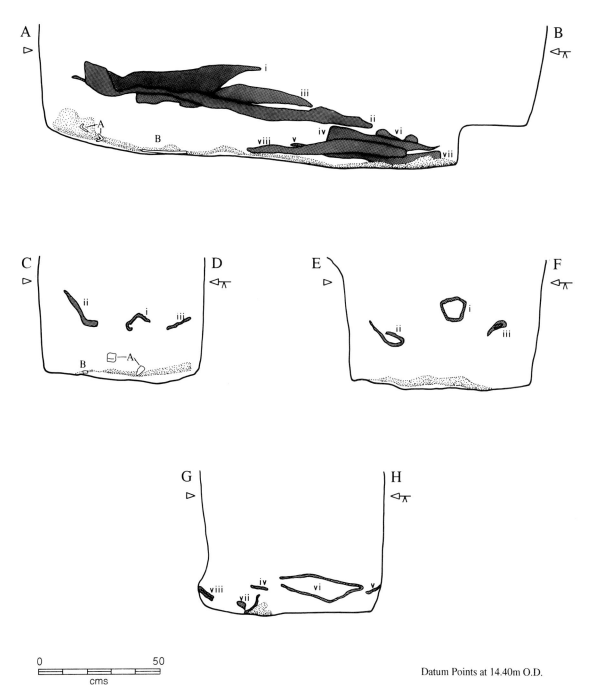

A ▷   B ◁⊼

C ▷   D ◁⊼   E ▷   F ◁⊼

G ▷   H ◁⊼

0   50
cms

Datum Points at 14.40m O.D.

Figure 22 Grave 9, long and cross-sections. Scale 1:15

Grave 10 (inhumation) (Figs 23, 24, 25, 85, 86, 87 and 88)

Dimensions: (Top) 1.96 x 0.71m; (Base) 2.00 x 0.72m

Orientation: 290°

Container for body: Coffin or ?textile lining.

Sex/age: Female.

Body position: Flexed, lying on right hand side. Position of wrist clasps suggests that left arm bent so hand lay on right shoulder, right arm by side of body. Head to west.

Description: A regular rectangular cut maintaining its edges to the bottom of the grave, with a slight undercutting. The fill was a mix of fine mid and light brown sand with occasional grit and small stones up to 10mm diameter. There were small ironpan lumps and occasional patches of grey sand in the upper fill.

Contained in the fill of the grave were two scatters of pottery, sherds of which can be identified as deriving from vessels found in a surface spread around the grave. These are catalogued and illustrated elsewhere (Scatters, section IV, below pp. 175–9) and are suggested as having derived from a cremation pyre, discussed more fully in Chapter 6 (pp. 252–5). The first scatter was in the uppermost layers of the grave at about 14.35mOD, contained within a lens of pale grey sand; the second, at 14.15mOD, was a far more distinctive irregularly-shaped deposit of dark grey-brown earth, similar to one encountered in grave 12. This contained a small amount of cremated bone, charcoal and the Ae fragments of a strap end and a burnt buckle in addition to the pottery. Another sherd also relating to the 'pyre' spreads was found in the fill at this level but outside the main concentration. Together, this material all seems likely to be redeposited from a topsoil scatter cut through during the digging of the inhumation grave. The uppermost scatter seems to represent pottery from the topsoil which was dug through first and would have been backfilled last; the dense scatter probably represents a spadeful of topsoil redeposited lower down in the grave fill. Its central position within the grave is suggestive of a deliberate redeposition but this can only be speculation. The sherds recovered derive from vessels *0406, 0616, 0617, 0930* and *1588* (catalogued as scatters Nos 7, 8, 9, 12 and 14, where they are described more fully). Since the metalwork is argued to derive from the 'cremation pyre' spread, it is listed as scatters Nos 22 and 24. One sherd of pottery, *0317* (*not illus.*), could not be identified with any of the other component vessels.

At 13.98mOD a curious dark greyish-brown stain was seen at the west end. The pronounced 'beak' shape resembles the bow of a boat (Pl. XII). At 13.92mOD the stain was V-shaped with a mix of dark grey-brown and light grey to its east narrowing to form an elegant 'tail' of dark grey-brown. The overall length of the stain conforms well to that of the body as laid out beneath it in the grave. In addition, the main 'beak' portion lay almost directly over the head of the body. A small area of wood stain was found within the mix of sand.

The body container was first seen at 13.83mOD, most pronounced in the south-west corner as a black line 10–15mm wide. The stain continued running in a westerly direction towards the grave edge beyond its south-west corner. This running line had disappeared by 13.76mOD, and the container assumed a regular rectangular shape. The bottom appeared at 13.70mOD, with the centre sagging slightly. The material of the container is unclear. Along its upper edges the dark dense stain has the appearance of degraded wood but was thinner at the base of the grave and similar to the general organic stains elsewhere on the site. The stain perhaps suggests a textile running around onto itself. The body stain traces were poor but enough survived to demonstrate the flexed body position.

Grave-goods:
A: Ae **cruciform brooch**, length 94mm, forming a pair with *C*. Found beneath *B*, with face up and 'foot' towards the head of the grave. Narrow head-plate outlined with crescentic stamps, the narrow rectangular wings having a single row of crescent stamps. Integral top and side knobs slightly hollowed behind. Short plain bow and faceted catch-plate; animal-head terminal with protruding eyes within distinctive cross shape. Unusual squared muzzle bearing crescent stamps and broken loop for spangle. Remains of iron pin and spring, and large catch. Mineralised textile is preserved for 52 × 35mm on the front of the head and passing round behind, probably twill (b), thread count 12 × 12 on 10mm. [0817]
B: Large Ae **cruciform brooch**, length 132mm, found face up between brooches *A* and *C*, under textile patch. Rectangular head-plate outlined with tiny annular stamps. Plain narrow side wings with notches above and below. The side knobs are moulded separately, with grooves to fit the wings, and are held in place by

Plate XII Possible bow stain in mid fill of grave 10

an Fe pin for the spring. The top knob, with distinct finial, is deeply hollowed behind. Faceted bow with central groove worn smooth in the middle. Catch-plate has annular stamps and narrow lappets. Strong triple moulding above animal-head terminal which has protruding eyes within a distinctive cross shape similar to *A* and *C*. The same cross-shape defines the upstanding, rounded nostrils. The muzzle is flattened and expanded, the whole of the animal head being strongly hollowed behind. Remains of the Fe spring survive.
Tucked inside the brooch under the front is an area 25 × 23mm of mineralised textile (d) with tight Z spin; tabby weave, thread count 8/7–8 on 5mm, tightly pleated. A fragment 35 × 18mm of Z-spun twill is probably (b). On top of a detached knob is an area of mineralised weave (d), 20 × 18mm and a scrap of twill (b), 34 × 30mm. A detached fragment of mineralised textile seems to be (d). It is an even pleated tabby weave, with very even fine threads, diam. 0.3mm with a thread count of 17–18/16 on 10mm. The appearance suggests flax. [0816, 0820]
C: Ae **cruciform brooch**, length 96mm, found face up beneath *B* and forming a matching pair with *A*. In this case, the loop at the end of the muzzle is complete. The two brooches *A* and *C* are unusual in having such distinctive squared nostrils. A close parallel is Morning Thorpe grave 131 with squared nostrils and protruding eyes and a similar overall squat appearance. On the front ?twill (b) is of animal fibre, over an area 40 × 40mm, thread count 12–14/12, and again partly mineralised on the back. No dye detected. [0818]
D: String of 25 **beads**, 3 of crystal, 12 of glass and 10 of amber. All except xv, found beneath a brooch during conservation, were planned at 1:1 during excavation (see 1:2 detail plan, Fig. 25). Amber: large flat (xxiii–xxv); wedge (xxi); roughly shaped (xvi–xix); long cylinder (xx, xxii). Glass: globular (v, vii; opaque white with translucent brown crossing trails and dots. vi, xv; opaque white with irregular, scattered green dots and brown part-trails. viii, x; reticella, ropes of green and yellow with red blobs); barrel (xii; reticella, grey with ropes of red and yellow. xiv; reticella ropes of green and yellow); cylinder (xiii; reticella, ropes of

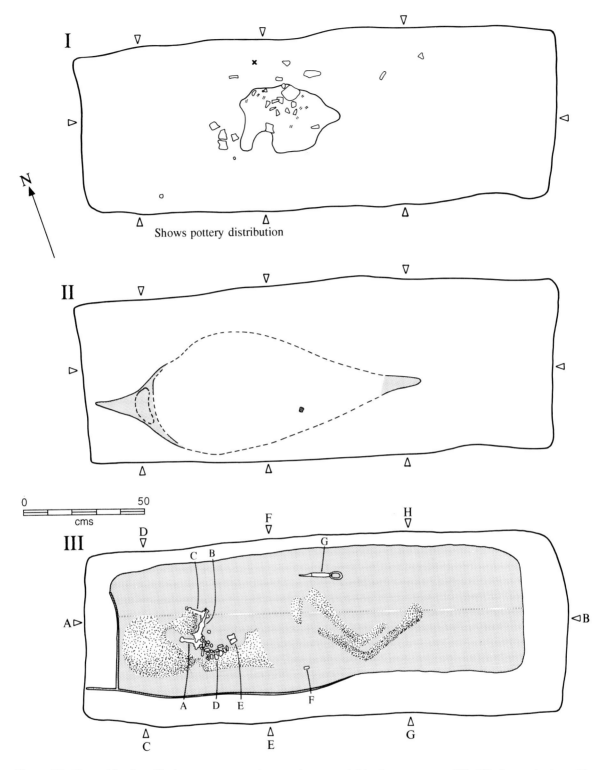

I

Shows pottery distribution

N

II

III

0   50

cms

D
F
H
G
C B

A
B

A   D   E   F

C   E   G

Figure 23 Grave 10, plan. (I) shows pottery and cremation material in the uppermost fill, (II) shows the boat-like stain midway down. Scale 1:15

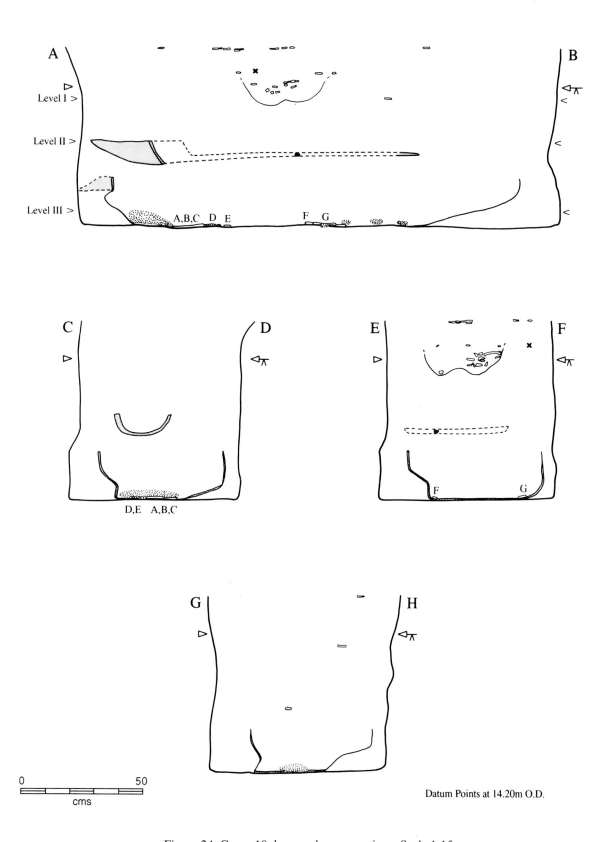

A

Level I >

Level II >

Level III >

B

C

D,E A,B,C

D

E

F

G

H

0   50
cms

Datum Points at 14.20m O.D.

Figure 24 Grave 10, long and cross-sections. Scale 1:15

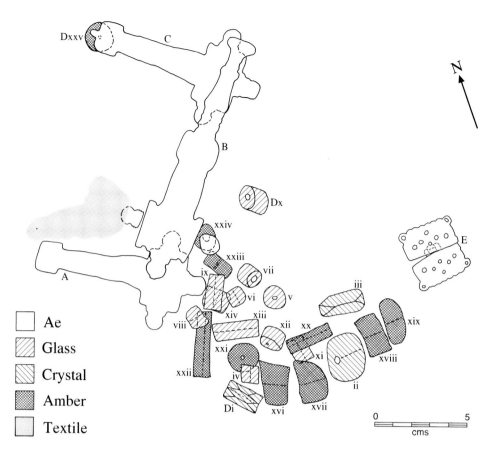

Ae

Glass

Crystal

Amber

Textile

Figure 25 Grave 10, detail of grave-goods. Scale 1:2

green and yellow with red blobs); cylinder with square section (ix; reticella with crossing ropes of green and yellow); cube (iv, xi; red with panels of confused green and yellow swirls). Crystal: irregular disc (ii); biconical, faceted (i, iii). [0788–0808, 0813–0815, 0819]

E: Decorated Ae **wrist clasp** suite, i and ii (Hines C5), with traces of a ?tin-lead solder on the three flattened areas of the inner bar, and paired, inturned beaked heads on the main panels. Length 30mm. Mineralisation has preserved bone and textile (*c.f. F*). Mineralised textile (c) is on the underside for 6 × 3.5mm. It shows Z, S-ply cords of decayed tablet-weave; coarse S-ply sewing threads survive in the holes. [0811]

F: Looped half only of Ae **wrist clasp** (Hines C5), with decoration matching *E*. Traces of solder on decorated face on inside panel as with clasp *E* and slight evidence of gilding on face. Length 30mm. An area of tablet weave (c) was preserved on the front. It lies next to the metal for 12 × 25mm, cords from 4-hole weave 16 on 10mm, spin Z, wefts Z, S-ply. The cords

lie 12–13 S, then 1Z, 1S, 1Z, ?9S. The remains of the pattern (Fig. 139.10), probably horsehair, are as on wrist clasp *D*, grave 5. The weave is of fine to medium wool. A detached, confused, fragment of twill weave is probably from (b). Mineralisation also preserved a specimen of the beetle *Grammostethus marginatus* (Er.) and a larva of the fly *Fannia* sp. (see below, p. 226–7). [0812]

G: Fe **knife** (i) and **ring** (ii). The knife, length 146mm, has a horn handle and traces of leather lying on both sides of the blade. It is wrapped over the back and extends down below the blade edge by 4mm and overlaps the handle junction by 3mm. The identification of a sheath is inconclusive but made by the manner of its arrangement. Two textiles are preserved in patches on both sides of the ring; (a) only 8 × 5mm, a mineralised coarse weave, Z-spun ?warp, S-spun ?weft; weave twill. (b) areas 31x13, 22 × 13mm, mineralised twill, both systems Z-spun. Thread count 10/11 on 10mm, no reverses visible. Ring diameter 62mm. [0810]

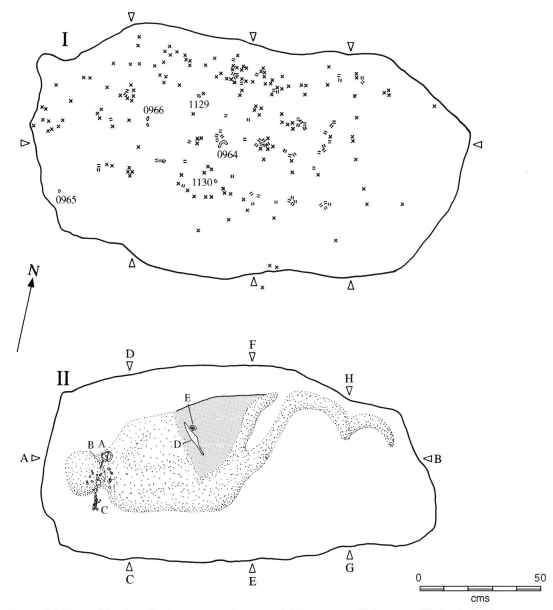

Figure 26 Grave 11, plan. (I) shows cremation material from grave 99 in upper fill. Scale 1:15

Grave 11 (inhumation) (Figs 26, 27, 28, 88 and 89)
Dimensions: 1.81 × 1.02m
Orientation: 258°
Container for body: None but body probably rested on an organic layer.
Sex/age: Female.
Body position: Supine flexed to left. Head to west, lying facing north.

Description: An irregular, sub-rectangular grave cut with edges undercutting on the south side. The grave was extremely difficult to identify at the surface level, which consisted of redeposited natural. The fill became an increasingly homogenous mid grey with some dark patches of black/grey sand in the upper levels and had several lumps of redeposited ironpan throughout.

The fill contained a dense layer of cremated bone at 14.28mOD, weighing 60.5g which included two pieces of burnt animal bone and a few burnt metal objects. These

are interpreted as a cremation burial and are catalogued as grave 99, although it is unlikely that they represent a disturbed cremation accidentally reincorporated, as suggested for the cremation (No. 80) in the fill of grave 5. Instead, the thick layer at a single level suggests a deliberate deposition, which is discussed further in Chapter 6 section II. Only a few cremated bone and metal objects were found lower down in the fill, stressing the concentration of material higher up. Several unidentifiable charcoal fragments were also found in the fill, which could relate to either the cremation or the inhumation.

The body stain was very poorly preserved but the corpse possibly rested on an organic layer, seen only as a smear, in which the upper legs could be distinguished. Several traces of bones survived, principally ribs, parts of the vertebrae and the clavicles, all in the area of the brooch and pins.

43

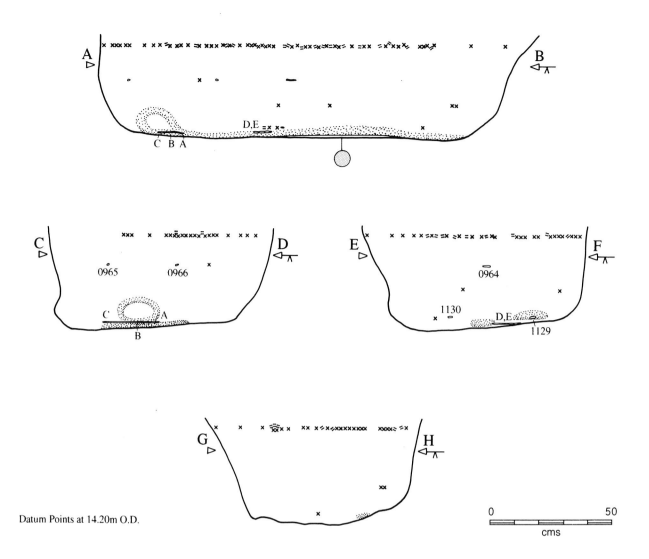

Datum Points at 14.20m O.D.

0   50
cms

Figure 27 Grave 11, long and cross-sections. Scale 1:15

Grave-goods:

A: Ae **annular brooch** (i), diameter 54mm, with Fe pin (ii). The brooch has a thin flange with a central line of ring-and-dot stamps. It was reconstructed in antiquity, in penannular form with ends overlapping by 14mm, held together by a simple Fe rivet. A second hole pierced both ends and was used to anchor the pin. Fe pin (ii), in a NW–SE orientation beneath the brooch, presumably represents its fixing pin. Mineralised textile adheres to both sides. (a), in several layers over 20 × 14mm, is dark brown, of undyed wool. The spin is Z/Z, loosely twisted, a 2/2 twill; thread count 12/9 on 10mm. No dye was detected. (b), the best area 11 × 7mm, has a Z/Z spin and hard threads with a tight twist. It is probably from a tabby weave, thread count *c*.8/6. There were a few fragments of animal fibre present. Coarse mineralised Z-spun threads wound round under the brooch may come from (b). No dye was detected. [1341, 2442]

B: Fe **pin** lying in a N–S orientation just south of brooch *A*. Length 51mm. [2406]

C: String of 38 **beads**, 20 of glass, 17 of amber and 1 of jet, together with an Ae **loop/collar** (xxxix) between beads (xvii) and (xxxi). There are degraded threads above and below the collar and the remains of cloth. Glass: disc-shaped (iii, xxi; grey opaque. vi, rust red with yellow dots and line); globular (iv; rust red with yellow crossing trails and dots. vii, grey with thin red crossing trails. xi, blue translucent. xii, dark brown with white crossing trails and dots. xiv, grey, opaque. xv, rust red with white crossing trails. xvii, xx; large, rust red with white crossing trails); barrel (i, red with yellow crossing trail and dots); biconical (ii, xix; large, white with red dots. x, small, blue translucent); dome (viii, ix; small, blue translucent). Jet: barrel (xiii). Amber: globular (xxii, xxiv); wedge (xxvi, xxviii, xxix, xxxvii); roughly shaped (xxiii, xxv, xxvii, xxx–xxxvi, xxxviii). [1291–1300, 1302–1331, 1333–1339]

D: Fe **knife**, length *c*.136mm, with horn on the tang. A thin and brittle layer of iron oxides curve over the blade back and extend a little below the cutting edge but could not be confirmed as leather. Sand particles separate it from the blade surface. Traces of textile (unidentifiable) overlie it. [1134]

E: Fe **buckle** with tongue uppermost, lying on top of *D*. Possibly degraded leather associated. Length of tongue 30mm. [2408]

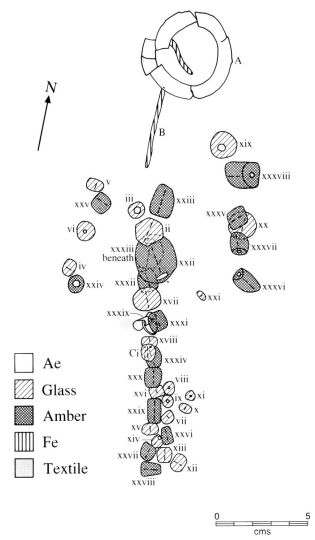

N

Ae
Glass
Amber
Fe
Textile

0   5
cms

Figure 28 Grave 11, detail of grave-goods. Scale 1:2

Grave 12 (inhumation) (Figs 29 and 89)
Dimensions: 1.76 × 0.86m
Orientation: 276°
Container for body: None.
Sex/age: ?Male; middle-aged or old.
Body position: Unknown as no body stain survived. Preserved bone and teeth indicate head at west end.

Description: An irregular rectangular cut with a fill of reddish brown sand at the surface, changing to a mix of grey and mid brown sand throughout the rest of the fill. The north-west corner contained a patch of redeposited natural. Several amorphous patches of black stain throughout the fill seem to be the remains of degraded wood/charcoal running especially down the centre of the grave; only the most definite piece (*2448*) is marked on the grave plan.

The west end was filled with 22.8g of cremated bone, with a mean fragment size of 10mm. The bone was concentrated in a darker circular area of fill, probably redeposited topsoil. This suggests that there may have been more such bone scattered in the topsoil throughout the cemetery; this bone cannot be related to the spreads of bone associated with grave 10 which are interpreted as the remains of a cremation pyre. Also within this patch of

darker fill was an Fe **stud** or **rivet**, *0619*, with a circular head and square distal end (Fig. 89).

Although no body stain survived, fragments of the skull and mandible (a) and proximal humerus (b) were preserved. The size of the mastoid process suggests that the individual was male although the (eroded) mandible is quite gracile. The few remaining tooth fragments show medium-heavy wear and suggest that the individual was middle-aged or old. Slight lipping around the tooth sockets on the mandible suggests a possible inflammation or infection of the gums.

Grave-goods:
A: Fe **object** of unknown type with mineralised bone attached. This piece is listed as a grave-good purely because it lies at the bottom of the grave (*not illus.*). [0921]

Grave 13 (inhumation) (Fig. 30)
Dimensions: 1.21 × 0.61m
Orientation: 238°
Container for body: Organic lining?
Sex/age: Unknown, infant.
Body position: No body stain survived.

Description: A squat rectangular grave cut with rounded ends, very shallow in depth, with a stone free fill of fine homogenous mid grey sand. An organic stain of dark grey rectangular shape appeared at 14.25mOD. A small fragment of charred wood (unidentified) was at the grave bottom (14.21mOD).

There was no trace of any body stain. The grave size suggests the occupant was a baby or infant.

Grave-goods: None.

Grave 14 (inhumation) (Figs 31, 32 and 90)
Dimensions: 1.78 × 0.71m
Orientation: 300°
Container for body: Coffin or ?textile lining.
Sex/age: Female, unknown.
Body position: Only skull survived. Head to west.

Description: A rectangular cut at the surface which became sub-rectangular in its lower levels. The fill was a pinkish-grey at the top, becoming a mix of mid brown and grey sand. The sand was fine but included several small stones redeposited from a band of ironpanning which the grave cut through. At 14.16mOD the fill became an homogenous dark grey, contrasting with the previous layers, with rectangular patches of pinkish-fawn sand possibly representing redeposited blocks of topsoil.

There was no clear evidence for a body container, although faint traces of an organic stain perhaps represented a textile lining. A length of charred wood of unidentified species, first seen at 14.16mOD at the grave east end, is probably analogous to the lengths seen in many other graves. The use of the brooches in this group is interesting, the annular and small-long brooches forming a pair with the more normally placed cruciform.

Only the skull survived as body stain. The lower jaw could be distinguished and there were remains of some teeth which were sampled. The head, and pot behind, appeared to rest on a slightly upstanding 'pillow' of ironpanned sand on the grave floor.

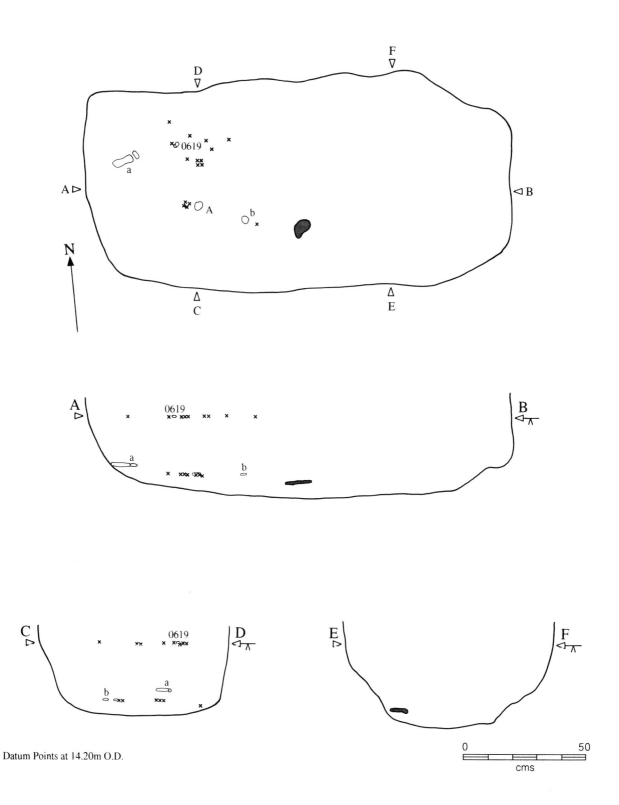

Datum Points at 14.20m O.D.

Figure 29 Grave 12, plan, long and cross-sections. Scale 1:15

46

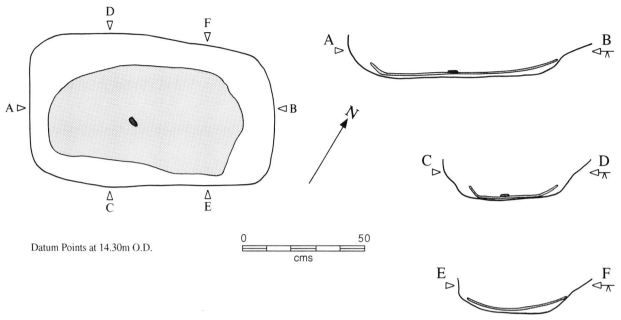

Datum Points at 14.30m O.D.

0   50
cms

Figure 30 Grave 13, plan, long and cross-sections. Scale 1:15

Grave-goods:

A: Small rounded **pottery bowl**, undecorated, with upright rim flattened above, placed immediately to the west of the skull. Complete, it collapsed on excavation as the fabric was too brittle. It has a brown sandy fabric with rounded grit and dark grey surfaces. Height 840mm. [0786]

B: Ae **small-long brooch**, Leeds trefoil-headed class, found face up in throat area of body. Square-headed plate with traces of lunate stamps on one side; flat knobs. Plain bow above catch-plate which is obscured by textile. Wide transverse moulding above triangular foot with further traces of lunate stamps. Fe spring and pin. Length 62mm. Three areas of textile were identified: (a), partially mineralised on the front plate over an area *c*.9x12mm, is of undyed wool, spin Z/Z, weave a 2/2 twill, thread count *c*.8/8 on 10mm but pulled diagonally. (b), detached from ?above the bow and head-plate, is 25 × 23mm; spin Z/S with coarse dark threads, it is a twill, thread count 8–10/8 on 10mm. Its fibre is unidentified and no dye was detected. (c), from below the bow, has five threads bound round, S, Z-ply or very coarse loose twisted Z. A 13 × 7mm fragment adhering may be from (a) folded, with light coloured ?fibres; no spin clear. [0783]

C: Ae **annular brooch** with Fe pin, found next to the chin. The brooch lay between the two brooches *B* and *D*, and beneath a layer of textile. Thick, plain dished flange with bevelled edges, diameter 34mm. Textile is attached to the front and back. On the back there is a mineralised lump on the ring 13 × 16mm in area, with fragments coming round to the front. The best area, 9 × 8mm, spin Z/Z, of 2/2 twill, has a thread count *c*.14/12 (7/6 on 5mm), with fine even threads. A fragment of finer Z, S-ply thread protrudes from beneath. A fragment (d) is detached. Of fine to medium undyed wool, it comes from a weave-edge preserved 12mm long. There are only three tablet cords, Z, S-ply on 2–3mm width, with protruding Z,

S-ply weft loops, 8 per cm, too fine to belong to (a). [0735]

D: Ae **cruciform brooch**, length 90mm, found face up to the north of the skull and forming a dissimilar pair with brooch *B*. Small head-plate edged with lunate stamps, barely defined from the narrow side wings. Both side knobs are missing. The terminal knob is three-quarters round but flattened behind, attached by a half-lapped projection (soldered) to the front of the head-plate. Plain swollen bow with end facets. Catch-plate small, faceted above a strong, double moulding and animal-head terminal with rounded eyes and undeveloped muzzle. On the reverse, the bow and the whole of the terminal area is hollowed. Remains of an Fe spring and pin, attached to the brooch by a single lug, the catch for the pin small. The brooch is clearly early in the cruciform series, with a close parallel from Holywell Row, Mildenhall, grave 48. It belongs with Reichstein's *Späte* brooches, with suggested dating of 475–525 by Hines (1984, 244–253; 1997, 244). A scrap of mineralised textile lying on top is preserved, Z/Z-spun with loose twisted threads, possibly from a twill. A small area of finer medium threads protrudes, one possibly S, curling under possibly indicating a selvedge. No dye was detected. [0784]

E: String of 19 **beads**, 13 of glass and 6 of amber (see detailed plan, Fig. 32). Glass: annular (iv, pale yellow, translucent); globular (i, bright apple green. ii, white with pale blue crossing trails, iii, v; yellow with green crossing trails. x, dark green. xi, white with blue trail. xii, yellow with rust-red crossing trails); drawn globular (viii, colourless with gold internally); cylindrical (iii, yellow with green crossing trails. vi, white with blue crossing trails. vii, yellow with rust-red crossing trails. ix, white with green crossing trails); drawn hexagonal cylindrical (xiii, light blue). Amber: wedge (xvi, xvii); biconical, long (xv, xviii); roughly shaped (xiv, xix). [0740–0750, 0755–0760, 0764, 1159]

47

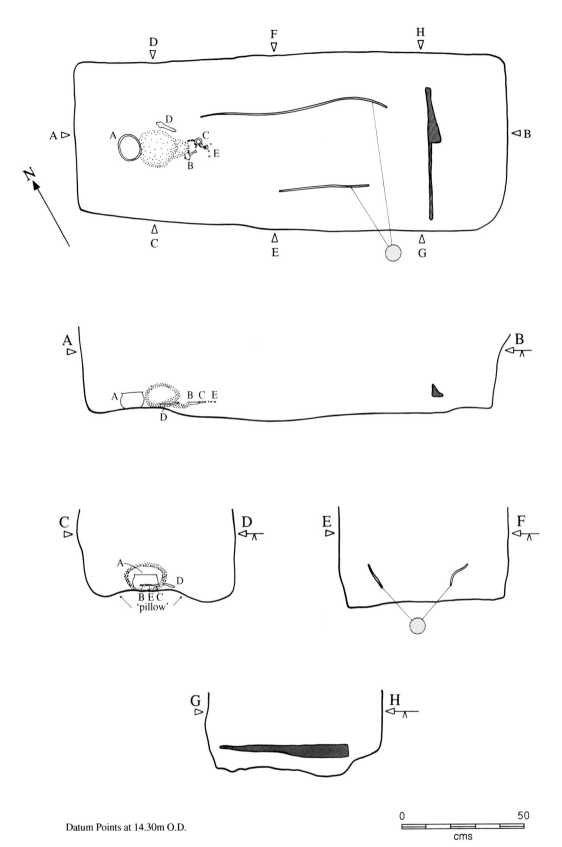

Datum Points at 14.30m O.D.

0   50
cms

Figure 31 Grave 14, plan, long and cross-sections. Scale 1:15

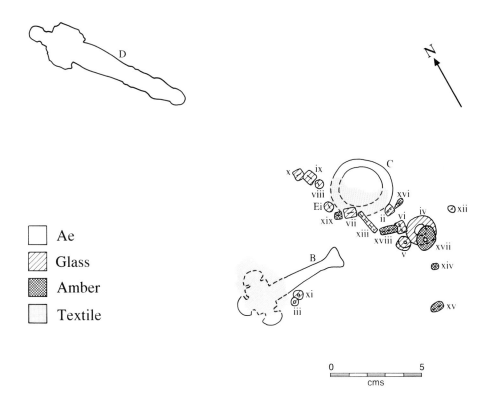

Figure 32 Grave 14, detail of grave-goods. Scale 1:2

Grave 15 (inhumation) (Fig. 33)
Dimensions: 1.77 × 0.73m
Orientation: 300°
Container for body: Coffin or organic lining.
Sex/age: Unknown, probably juvenile.
Body position: Very fragmentary traces of body stain suggest that the body was either flexed or, probably, supine extended with right leg crossed over left, head at east end lying on its right side.

Description: An irregular sub-rectangular cut at the surface evolving into a smoother sub-rectangular shape. The fill of light grey sand in the upper levels changed to an orange brown and mid grey. Frequent small stones from ironpanned gravel were redeposited within the grave. The ironpan formed a slight shelf along the south edge of the grave cut.

The first suggestions of a stain appeared at 14.14mOD along the grave south edge as a black organic line. This line was never very strong although quite thick when seen, and continued especially in the south-west corner to 13.98mOD, at which level stains appeared at both east and west ends. A short length of organic stain also appeared along the grave north edge at 13.81mOD. Although never very extensive, these together suggest some form of container for the body, probably an organic lining, perhaps of textile.

The body stain was almost non-existent except for the head with lower jaw in which were preserved several teeth.

Grave-goods: None.

Grave 16 (inhumation) (Figs 34, 35, 90, 91 and 92)
Dimensions: 1.93 × 0.77m
Orientation: 276°
Container for body: None.
Sex/age: Female, young adult.
Body position: Supine flexed, right leg possibly crossed over the left. The position of the wrist clasps suggest that the right arm was bent over the chest so the hand rests on or near the left upper arm. Wrist clasps suggest the left arm lay by the side of the body. Head to west.

Description: A rectangular cut with edges showing some undercutting. At the surface the ends were slightly rounded and became more elliptical further down. The fill was of a very light grey sand mixing with orange-brown redeposited natural. The grey sand was extremely light, appearing almost white when dry.

The backfill had a clear division with very light grey sand on the south side of the grave right down to the bottom. This seems to represent two spoil heaps being redeposited as the same time (see Chapter 6 section II).

Two small patches of charcoal were noted in the upper levels of the fill at 14.19m and 14.15mOD. One, *0953*, was of oak stem (*Quercus* sp.). A sherd of pottery, *0955*, was found at the grave east end at 14.19mOD (*not illus.*).

The body stain was poorly preserved and was very similar to the darker brown of the natural. It seems that the body may have been resting on a small organic layer although this could not be distinguished from the body stain; this may be a similar arrangement to that seen in grave 9. Fragmentary mineralised remains of the spine show fusing of the bone not yet complete, suggesting the individual to have been aged 18–25 years.

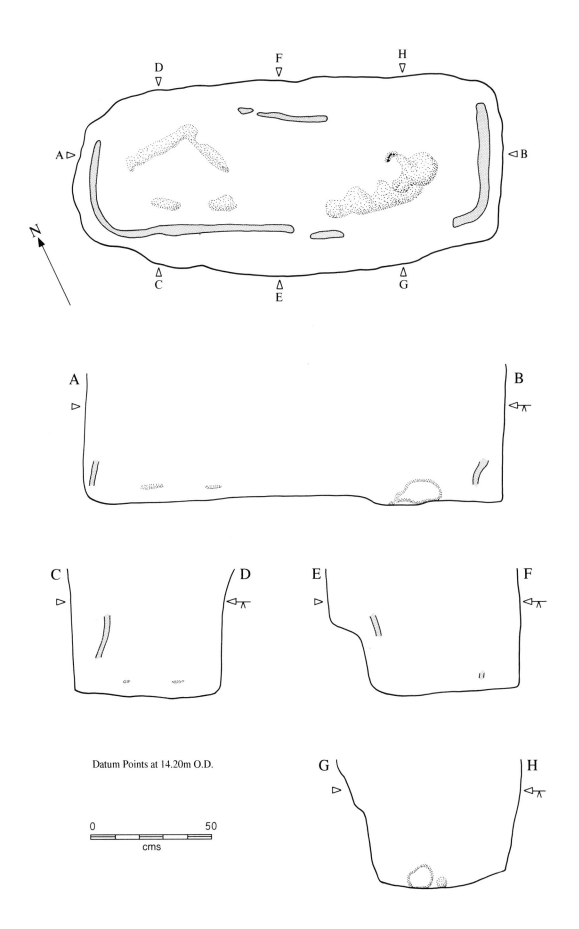

A

B

C D

E F

Datum Points at 14.20m O.D.

G H

0   50

cms

Figure 33 Grave 15, plan, long and cross-sections. Scale 1:15

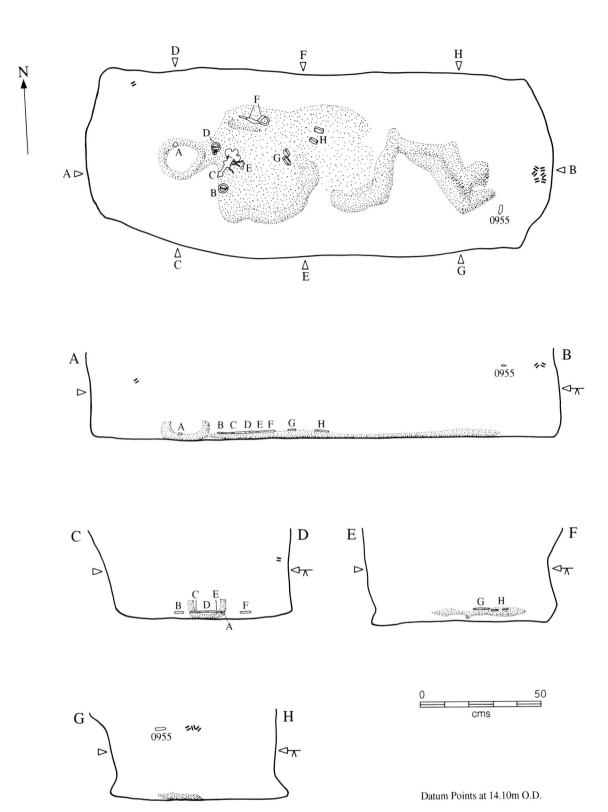

N

D   F   H

A ▷

B ◁

C   E   G

0955

A   B

0955

A   B C D E F   G   H

C   D

E   F

B   C E   F
    D
    A

G   H

0   50
cms

G   H

0955

Datum Points at 14.10m O.D.

Figure 34 Grave 16, plan, long and cross-sections. Scale 1:15

Grave-goods:

A: ?chain link of unknown material found isolated by the skull but at the same level as the other goods, not unlike grave 2, *C* and so perhaps a fastening for the bead string? Now missing (*not illus.*). [1286]

B: Cast Ae **annular brooch** with four faceted divisions and a double rebated seating for the Fe pin. Slightly oval in shape, 41 × 43mm, forming a pair to *D*. Overlying textile (b) associated. [1284]

C: Ae **florid cruciform** brooch, length 135mm. Plain rectangular head-plate, no demarcated side wings, side knobs detachable, held in place by a rectangular plate to the front of the head-plate and the Fe axial bar for the spring, which passes through two lugs on each side knob. The side knobs are exploded into full-face masks flanked by in-turned, beaked heads. The top knob is of the same design, but cast in one with the rest of the brooch. The bow is wide, with a flattened

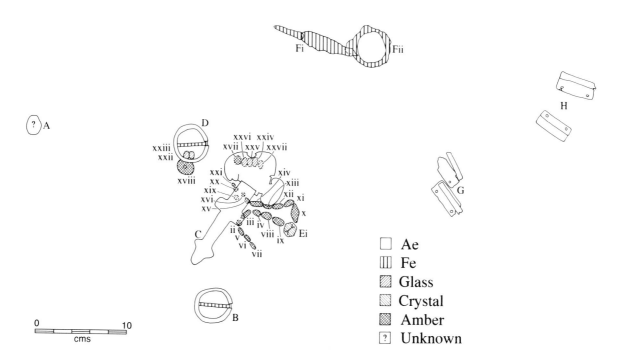

Ae
Fe
Glass
Crystal
Amber
Unknown

Figure 35 Grave 16, detail of grave-goods. Scale 1:4

profile, weak stops and a low central bar bearing a suggestion of a central, raised square. Plain catch-plate with up-turned beaked heads forming side lappets. Low double moulding above animal-head terminal. The head has round, protruding eyes and the muzzle expanded as a humanoid mask with heavy brows, protruding eyes and square nose above a horizontal 'S' scroll. On the reverse side there are traces of an Fe spring and a long but weak catch. The whole of the animal-head terminal is hollowed. The brooch belongs to the 'florid' class of cruciforms of Leeds and Pocock (1971), Class Vai, and very closely resembles the larger, damaged piece from Felixstowe (West 1998, fig. 15.2).

The decorative knobs on the east and west of the head had become detached; that to the west had traces of white solder on its surface. The brooch was extracted in a block for laboratory excavation, with brooches *B* and *D*, and in the mineralised textile associated, two weaves were distinguishable. Towards the head end of *C* over an area of *c*.45 × 30mm was (a), a fabric of animal fibre (?wool), with Z/Z spin, light twist, a twill weave, probably 2/2, with no reverses visible; thread count *c*.9/9 on 10mm. It appears to be a very open weave, but this is possibly due to deterioration. Under (a) lies (b), a slightly finer weave, best over an area *c*.90 × 90mm, in two clear layers at the foot of *C* and also present on *B* and *D*. It is of wool, the fibres finer than in (a); Z/Z spin, 2/2 twill, thread count 10–11/8–10 on 10mm, with fairly even spin and weave. The blue colorant indigotin was detected and almost certainly combined with a second brown or yellow mordant dye, indicating this weave to have been deep bluish black or possibly green. A tablet-woven weave border (c), 8mm wide, is preserved under the pin, six 4-hole cords lying in chevrons (Fig. 139.7); the warp and weft, Z-spun, must be a starting or closing border on weave (b).

Weave (a) may have been attached to the other side of this border but probably simply underlies it. [1282]

D: Ae **annular brooch** with four faceted divisions and a double rebated seating for the Fe pin. Of slightly oval shape, 41 × 43mm, forming a pair to *B*. Overlying textile (b) adheres and over the textile was a much degraded organic layer, probably leather, with at least one definite hole going through it. [1283]

E: String of 27 **beads**, 1 of crystal, 17 of amber and 9 of glass. Some beads preserve fragments of the stringing thread still *in situ*. Crystal: irregular four-sided cylinder. The central hole can be seen to have been drilled from both ends, with a smaller bore to join in the middle (i). Amber: roughly shaped long biconical (iii–vii, xi–xiii, xv, xvi); biconical (ix, x); biconical, square (viii); globular (xvii); disc (xviii). Glass: melon (xix, yellow); disc (xxii–xxiv; yellow); annular (xx, yellow); globular (xxi, xxv, xxvi, yellow). (*Beads xiv and xxvii not illus.*) [1295, 1360–82, 2446–7]

F: Fe **knife** (i), length 98mm, and **ring** (ii), diameter *c*.42mm. An amorphous deposit on one side of the knife blade could not be identified as a skin product. Fibrous organic remains overlying this and the other side of the knife blade derive from textile. [1291, 1292, 1294]

G: Ae **wrist clasps** (i–v) (Hines B13b), length 38mm. The clasps have attached tubes (ii and iv) and a single row of ring-and-dot ornament on the 'eye' plate. There is mineralised bone under, and mineralised wood overlying the clasps. The corrosion of the metal caused fragmentation on conservation. [1127]

H: Ae **wrist clasps** (i–iii) (Hines B13b), a matching pair to *G*. An organic material was attached but unidentifiable. Mineralised textile from (d) adheres; these detached tablet cords, loose and probably from the clasps, were polluted with an alkanet-like colorant. Probable wood traces overlie this, with grain running parallel to the length of the southern clasp. [1125]

52

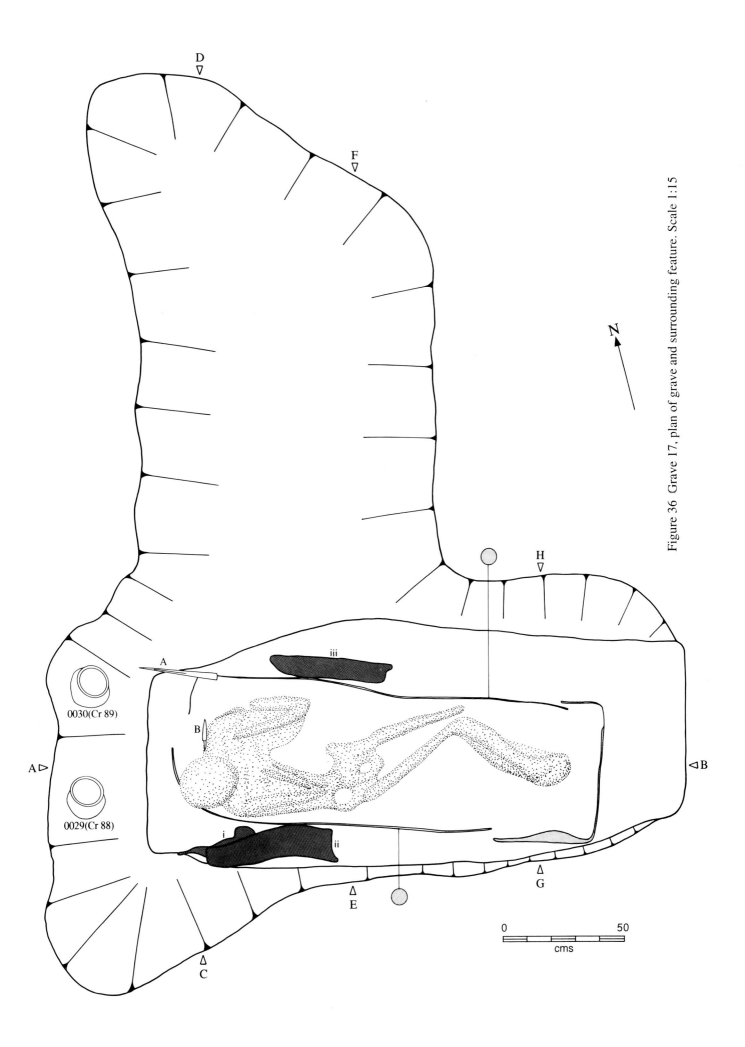

N

0030(Cr 89)

0029(Cr 88)

Figure 36 Grave 17, plan of grave and surrounding feature. Scale 1:15

0   50

cms

53

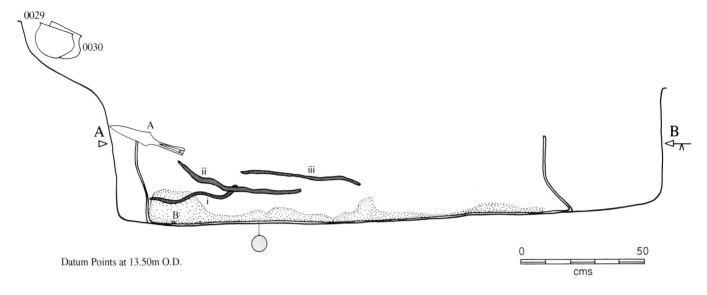

0029
0030

A
A
ii
iii
i
B

B

Datum Points at 13.50m O.D.

0   50
cms

Figure 37 Grave 17, long section. Scale 1:15

Grave 17 (inhumation) (Figs 36, 37, 38 and 92)
Dimensions: (Feature) 2.63 × 3.70m; (Grave) 2.22 × 0.99m
Orientation: 284°
Container for body: coffin.
Sex/age: Male.
Body position: Flexed to left, arms folded so hands meet on left shoulder. Head to west.

Description: A large rounded rectangular grave, cut through a larger amorphous feature of light grey sand. The fill was composed of light grey sand mixing with redeposited orange-brown natural to produce an amorphous fill whose cut was difficult to distinguish. A neat rectangular black coffin stain could be seen from 13.53mOD, set at an angle to the grave cut. The edges of the larger feature were also difficult to determine as they mixed into the natural sand. This feature may therefore be the remains of a natural hollow within the original heathland.

Two urns (*0029* and *0030*) were placed within the light grey sand at the west end of the grave on a 'shelf' in the natural. They contained the cremated remains of one or two juveniles (catalogued as graves 88 and 89 respectively) and are therefore treated as individual burials rather than grave-goods. However, the urns had no independent cut marks within the fill of the grave cut.

Although the amorphous nature of this type of sand makes the identification of such cuts difficult to recognise, it seems that the two cremations are contemporary with the inhumation.

The coffin stain was well-preserved and although sometimes fading completely away, was typically 10–15mm wide. The stain, approx. 1.76 × 0.58m in size, shows clearly the distortion caused by the pressure of the earth which caused it to collapse inwards. The dimensions are therefore based on its size as seen at or near its base. Three charred pieces of oak (*Quercus* sp.), (i)–(iii), flanked the coffin on the north and south sides. (i) was of stem, (ii) of softwood from a wide stem or branch and (iii) was of hardwood. There were no other wood traces nor any sign of a coffin lid. The position of the spearhead suggests that the spear was originally laid on top of the container.

Grave-goods:
A: **Spear**, with Fe head (Swanton H2), length 373mm. Mineralised wood in the socket is of mature ash (*Fraxinus* sp.). [0032]
B: Fe **knife**, length 139mm, with traces of mineralised horn handle and heavily mineralised leather. Unidentifiable mineral-replaced textile overlies it. [0177]

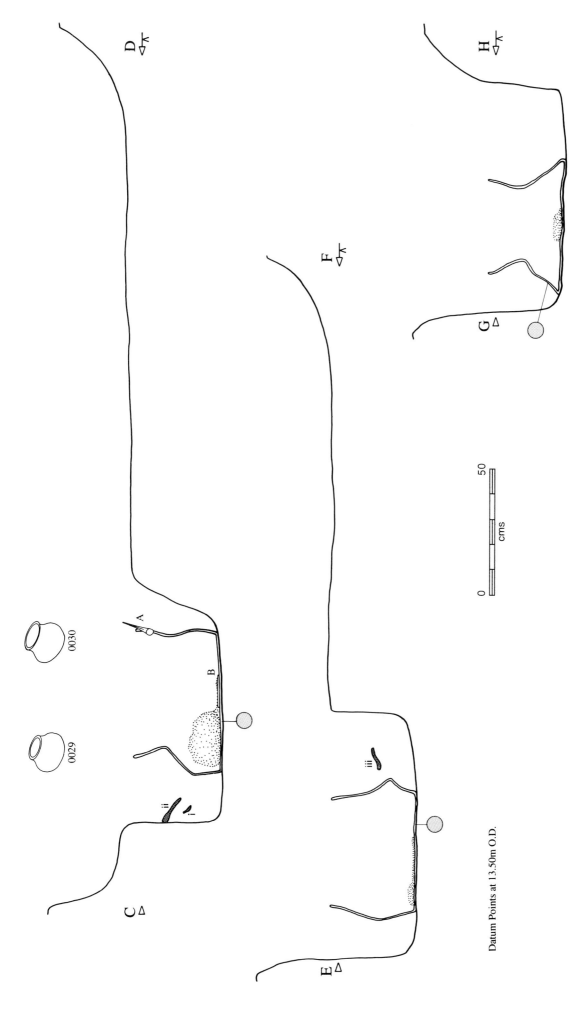

Figure 38 Grave 17, cross-sections across grave and surrounding feature. Scale 1:15

Datum Points at 13.50m O.D.

0030

0029

A

B

C

D

E

F

G

H

cms

0

50

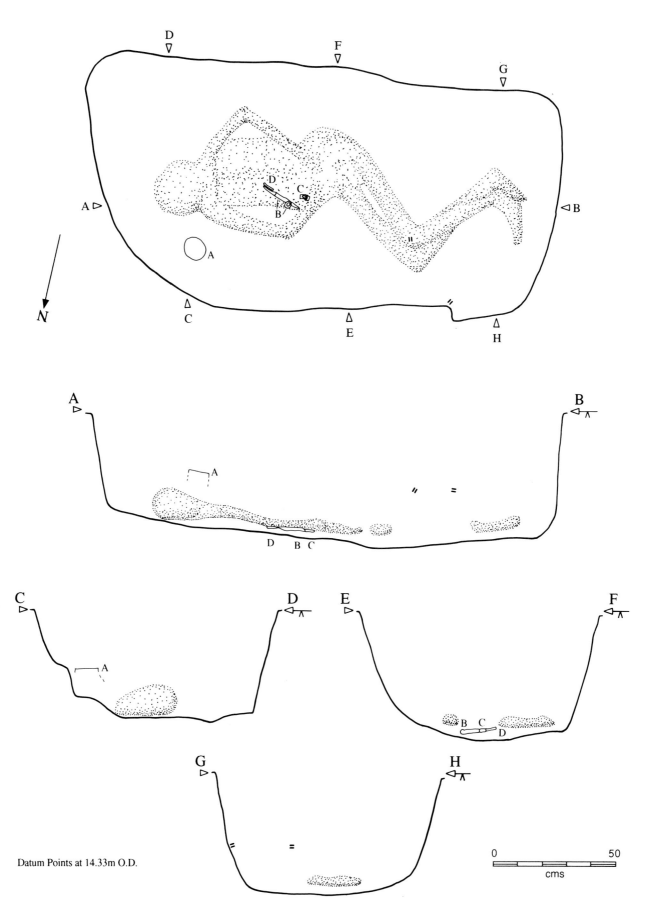

Datum Points at 14.33m O.D.

0   50
cms

Figure 39 Grave 18, plan, long and cross-sections. Scale 1:15

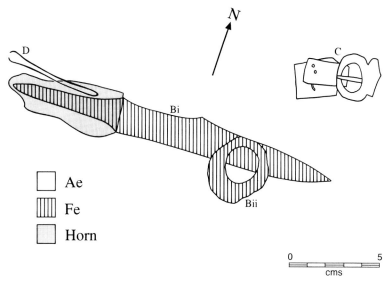

Figure 40 Grave 18, detail of grave-goods. Scale 1:2

Grave 18 (inhumation) (Figs 39, 40, 93 and 94)
Dimensions: 2.00 × 0.97m
Orientation: 251°
Container for body: None.
Sex/age: Possibly female.
Body position: Flexed, knees right, hands over pelvis. Head to east.

Description: An irregularly-shaped cut, initially rectangular with rounded corners, becoming increasingly apsidal-ended. At 14.01mOD the curious 'notch' shape appeared in the grave northern edge. The curved 'missing' north-eastern corner continued to the grave bottom. The fill was of a stone-free light grey and orange, and dark black sand, mottling together. The light grey sand was concentrated at the west end but mottled into the orange sand at the east end. These east/west concentrations continued down to the body stain. Several fragments of charcoal, *0615*, found in the fill were of oak stem (*Quercus* sp.).

The body showed as a reasonably clear stain, slightly disturbed by roots. There was no apparent organic stain accompanying the body. The knife and tweezers were presumably contained within a bag, mineralised remains being noted on the knife, tweezers and buckle. This bag may have been fastened by the possible iron ring adhering to the knife. Both bag and buckle were found below the body stain. A fragment of comb was seen mineralised, attached to the knife. The body is possibly that of a female if the identification of an Fe ring with the knife seen on the X-ray is correct; this can only be a very tentative identification though, because the whole object is so poorly preserved.

Grave-goods:
A: Horn **cup** or **drinking horn** with Ae rim mount with an approximate original diameter of 88mm. Horn survived only where in contact with metal, and there was no metal terminal fitting, hence the uncertainty about the original form of the vessel. The object seems to have been placed on a small ledge at the side of the head. It consists of a U-section moulding fitted over

an exterior collar of Ae sheeting approximately 17.5mm in height. Six plain strap clips with rounded ends pass over the moulding and are riveted in place through the collar and horn. The collar strip is not continuous but patched together, possibly made up of available cut-and-pieced scrap.

Two overlapping pieces of Ae sheeting extend below the collar and are both overlapped and were probably originally held in place by the collar at their top edges. The original shape of these pieces of Ae sheeting is difficult to determine as they are broken at the bottom, but the outer lateral edges, although damaged, suggest a concave sub-rectangular shape for the upper section. It is difficult to determine if these two pieces of sheet metal were originally separate or if a single mount was broken and overlapped due to compression of the body of the vessel.

Similar configurations of undecorated moulding, collar and clips have been found in grave 42 at Little Wilbraham, Cambs. and grave 15, Holywell Row, Suffolk (Kennett 1971, 10, 15–17; Lethbridge 1931, 12). The rim mounts at Little Wilbraham and Holywell Row have considerably greater vertical dimensions (60.4 and 26.9mm respectively) than the Snape rim mount, and their collars are continuous rather than pieced. These two mounts also come from richer graves. Little Wilbraham grave 42 also contained a cauldron, a sword with a gilt bronze mount, a spear and a shield boss. The rim mount here had a suspension loop; another band with suspension loop, thought to have been placed about halfway down the length of the horn, was also preserved. Holywell Row grave 15 had a spear with iron head and ferrule, a knife and a piece of bronze plating of uncertain function. [0528, 0543, 0592, 0632, 0633]

B: Fe **knife** (i) with horn handle, length *c*.176mm. X-rays show a possible Fe **ring** (ii) adhering. A dark brown layer less than 1mm thick on the blade surface appears to represent a leather sheath. The layer extends beyond the blade edge by 8mm where a wrinkled edge of double thickness and two or three possible stitch holes are visible. Both sheath and handle remains are overlain on one side by an area of mineralised textile 20 × 20mm, Z/Z spin, even, of medium to light twist; a 2/2 twill, thread count 7–8/8, even thread, medium to light twist. Also clear on the hilt, over *c*.7 × 7mm, Z/? spin, count 8/8 on the area preserved, weave not clear. [0629, 0776]

C: Fe **buckle** with double Fe plates, length *c*.42mm. Traces of mineralised textile adhere; Z/Z, twill scrap and all over the other side over 25 × 9mm, Z/Z, 2/2 twill, thread count 10–11/11, originally an even weave. All may be the same wrapping. [0776]

D: Ae **tweezers** with incised design on upper portion of each blade. Each blade is pierced below the decorated zone; one hole is open and seems to show a lining which projects fractionally on the inside. Length 49mm. Traces of mineralised Z-spun threads. [0630, 0776]

Grave 19 (inhumation) (Figs 41, 42, 94, 95 and 96)
Dimensions: 2.10 × 0.94m
Orientation: 295°
Container for body: None for upper; ?organic lining for lower.
Sex/age: Top body – Unknown.
Bottom body – Female.
Body position: Top body – bent over, head to east, left arm folded into waist, right arm lies along the body. Body is bent at waist so it follows the east and north edges of the grave. Left leg bent, knee over head of body below.
Bottom body – extended, head to east. Body slightly bent at waist and legs slightly flexed. Very fragmentary remains of upper body but faint traces of left arm lying alongside waist area.

Description: A large rectangular grave, 0.7m deep, with regular straight sides. The stone-free fill was of mid brown sand in the upper layers which made initial recognition difficult. Further down, the fill contained a mix of golden brown and light/mid grey sands. Small dark grey stains appeared throughout the lower levels, possibly representing the remains of organics deposited within the fill. They have not been marked on the plan as they were very amorphous.

There was no clear evidence for a container. However, a long black line running along the entire length of the grave south edge was seen first at 13.95mOD and continued to the bottom of the grave where it flattened out. No matching line was found along the north edge although some very slight traces were seen at various points down the fill at the east and west ends and in the grave south-east corner. None was very extensive. They possibly represent an organic lining for the lower body which has only survived well on one side. The base of the grave was of dark brown sand, very similar in colour to the body but, by its texture, not apparently an organic layer.

The large size of the grave was unusual and although the upper body has the appearance of having been thrown in, the size of the cut seems to have anticipated the two individuals contained within it. The nature of this burial is discussed more fully in Chapter 6 section II (pp. 248–9). Parts of the lower body's jawbone and teeth were preserved by metal salts from the brooches but gave no information about the body.

Grave-goods:
A: 'D' shaped Fe **buckle** with Fe tongue and mineralised remains of degraded textile, weave no longer discernible. It is perhaps associated with the upper body but this is unclear. Width 15mm. [0981]

B: String of 81 **beads**, 80 of amber, 1 of meerschaum. Meerschaum: large disc (ii). Amber: long biconical (ii–lxxxi). The meerschaum bead was apparently originally at the centre of the string. A ?mineralised thread protruding from some of the beads has the same structure as (e) on brooch D although there seem to be only three plyed ends. (*Bead lxxxi not illus.*) [1170–1204, 1224, 1225]

C: Fe **knife** (i), length 108mm, and **ring** (ii), diameter 36mm. Both the knife and ring have been repaired. The knife has traces of horn on the hilt and traces of mineralised wood on the blade. Patches of fine mineralised textile going round the edge suggest a garment fold or a wrapping; the surface is badly deteriorated but the very fine threads, probably Z-spun, and the weave, suggest a twill. [1223]

D: Ae **small-long brooch** (Leeds class D) with trefoil head and crescentic foot. The face is heavily obscured by textile but a band of transverse moulding is visible above the foot. The spring appears to be of Ae. Length 70mm.
Mineralised textile adheres, curled round. These suggest a twill weave with a fine tablet-weave border. (a), a fragment along the top, has coarse white fibres of hemp, spinning Z/Z with a loose twist. The weave is tabby, very even, with a thread count 11–12/14 (7 on 5mm). Screwed-up textile (b), semi-mineralised with fine Z-spun threads tucked round underneath, may come from the twill and a tablet-weave. Other fragments, from (d) at this end of the brooch, are of fine wool, dyed red-purple, probably lichen purple ('orchil' or 'cork'), spinning Z/S. The weave suggests a warp-faced tabby, perhaps a tape, but no edges are visible. (e), a white protruding fragment probably of hemp as in (a), is a fragment of guilloche plait, of four S-ply threads, only 5mm long. [1224]

E: Ae **small-long brooch** with trefoil head, Leeds class C, but with animal eyes on catch-plate close to the bow. On the reverse, a single lug for the attachment of the spring is visible through the textile and corrosion products. Heavy Fe staining suggests the spring and pin to be Fe. Length 62mm. An amber bead is embedded in this corrosion.
Mineralised textile adheres underneath. On the brooch pin is a strip 25 × 14mm of weave (c), a tablet-weave border or braid; the warps are very fine, Z-spun with a loose twist, the 4-hole cords lying S,Z,S,Z,S on 5mm and the wefts Z,S-ply 6–7 on 5mm. Another fragment, *c*.25mm long, has Z,S,Z cords with an edge, and a scrap of twill (b), here as far as can be seen, Z/Z spun. On the front of the brooch over 35 × 15mm, there are deteriorated fragments of the tablet cords. Another loose sample 20mm long, has an edge preserved and cords S,S,Z,S,Z,S,?Z,Z,S; The badly degraded fibres are probably wool and were dyed red. [1225]

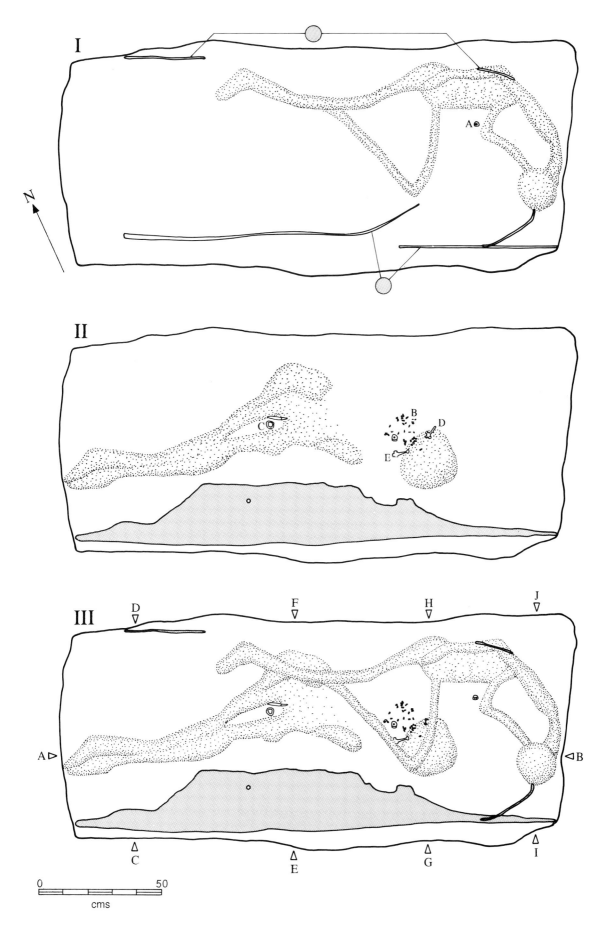

Figure 41 Grave 19, plan. Scale 1:15

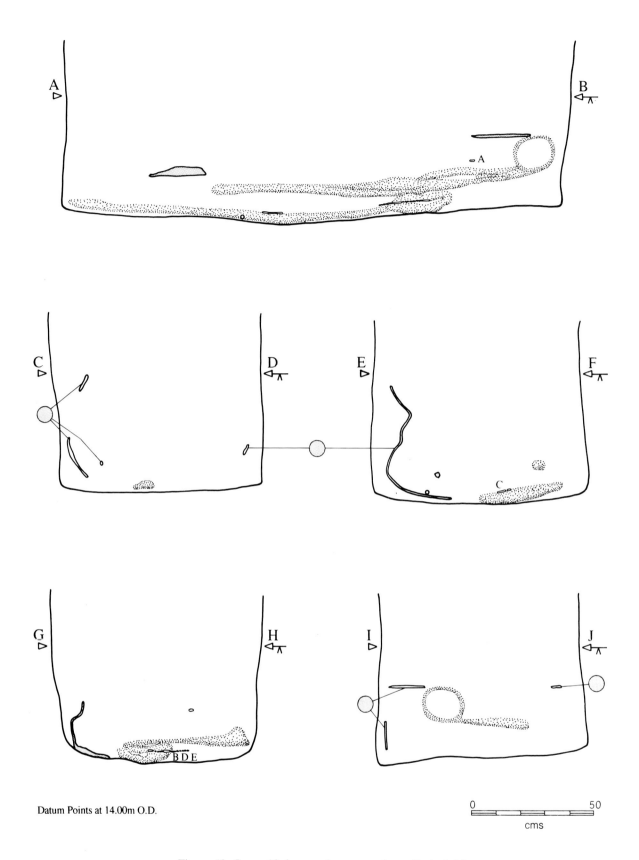

Datum Points at 14.00m O.D.

0   50

cms

Figure 42 Grave 19, long and cross-sections. Scale 1:15

Grave 20 (inhumation) (Figs 43, 44, 96 and 97)
Dimensions: 2.13 x 0.88m
Orientation: 276°
Container for body: Organic lining?
Sex/age: Male.
Body position: Supine extended, head turned to south. Right leg crossed over left, arms folded over the chest. Head to west.

Description: A sub-rectangular grave cut with a stone-free mid-orange brown sand with light grey patches mixing in throughout the fill. Two small charcoal patches (i and ii) of willow (*Salix* sp.) or poplar (*Populus* sp.) were found at 14.15m at the grave west end. Some dark grey/black patches, probably of degraded wood, appeared at 14.04mOD. The fill was of a slightly darker brown sand at the base of the grave, with a few patches of mid grey sand outside the organic lining.

The organic stain appeared at 13.86mOD as a dark brown/black stain 10–20mm thick, with a 'double edge' on the north side which quickly disappeared to produce a single edge sloping down to the grave bottom. An undercutting bulge in the grave north-west corner accommodated the spearhead, the spear apparently being too long for the grave as initially dug. This suggests that the original length of the spear was in excess of 2m long.

The form of the container used to accommodate the body is uncertain and is perhaps best interpreted as an organic layer, lining the base of the grave. It was rounded off at the corners and was thin and similar in colour and texture to the body stain. Contained within the layer was charred wood iii, of oak heartwood (*Quercus* sp.), immediately south of the body. Another wood-like stain in the sand, *0772*, was seen for a short stretch along the centre of the grave north edge and possibly represents remains of the spear shaft.

The body stain was poorly preserved, perhaps due to the strength of the organic stain. The head was reduced to a small lump and the chest area was especially thin. The legs, however, were reasonably easy to define.

The belt set was excavated *in situ* and contains a number of curious Ae objects presumably related to belt fittings/strap ends. Their fragile nature has meant that nearly all have disintegrated and they cannot be drawn except from X-rays.

In the grave upper fill, at 14.25mOD a fragment of a saddle quernstone, *0326*, was recovered (Fig. 97). The fragment, weight 120g, maximum thickness 38mm, retains a flat grinding surface and deliberately rounded underside. Although too small to give its original dimensions, the stone was probably fairly small. Such fragments are difficult to date, since they are often residual in later features and were in use from the Neolithic period to the Iron Age, and even occur in Roman contexts. A date within the late Bronze Age or Iron Age is preferred for the Snape quern and is supported by the careful shaping of the stone to an oval bun form with rounded underside, typical of 1st millennium stones.

Thin-sectioning of the quern showed the rock to be a microgranite composed almost entirely of feldspar and quartz. Three possible outcrop areas for this type of rock are the Scottish Highlands, Norway or Greenland, and although the quern could have been traded into the Snape area, a glacial deposit seems a more likely source than a quarried or natural outcrop. This has been the explanation for various other finds including those from Spong Hill, Norfolk (Buckley 1995), Goldington, Beds. (Williams 1992) and Spratton, Northants. (Ingle 1989). Full reports on the quernstone and its petrological identification are held in the site archive.

Ring-ditch *0302* (Fig. 128) which surrounded the grave had a fill of mid grey stone-free sand. It was 4.1–4.5m in external diameter, and looked as though straight stretches had been dug and joined to form the circle. Its width varied between 0.34–0.55m. It survived to only a shallow depth, being partly damaged by ploughmarks and for this reason it is unclear whether it was originally annular or penannular. The latter is a possibility, not least because the gap in the ditch east side is almost exactly on the axis of the grave cut.

No finds were made in the ditch fill although two scatters of pottery were located in the immediate area; within the ring-ditch area a scatter of 57 sherds, including 3 rim sherds was found in association with a few bone fragments and charcoal. The sherds all derive from vessel *1597*, interpreted as a smashed cremation urn (grave 90). A fourth rim was found to join another sherd deriving from vessel *0462*, found in the fill of grave 6 (Fig. 148). South-east of the ring-ditch, another scatter of sherds included 11 from vessel *1594* (scatters No. 18) which show it to have had incised lines and blurred stamps, although its original form is unknown.

Grave-goods:
A: **Spear** with Fe blade (Swanton H2), length 202mm, placed flat. Mineralised wood in the socket is probably of ash (*Fraxinus* sp.). [0582]
B: Fe **buckle** and Ae **belt plate** (i), length *c.*118mm, and matching **counterplate** (ii), length *c.* 101mm. Both are so heavily corroded they are illustrated from X-rays. Each appears to have an Fe body with Ae plates over the top at one end. Two textiles were preserved. On (i), textile (a) in a mineralised area 6 × 20mm is Z-spun in both systems with a thread diameter 0.5–0.6mm. It is a 2/2 twill, thread count 11/10 on 10mm. The diagonals appear to go different ways but this may be confused layers rather than reverses in the weave which is very friable. Weave (b) on top and beneath for 14 × 12mm, is a broken diamond twill with Z/S spinning and a thread count of *c.*20/18. Reverses are visible but no clear centre area is preserved. The textile on (ii) is in a detached fragment, 15 × 10mm, preserved against a solid mass of leather. (a) is of undyed wool, Z/Z, a 2/2 twill, with another probable area mineralised on the back-plate. [0692, 0695]
C: Tiny Ae **strip** with line-and-dot decoration. Heavy corrosion in the ground meant that the original size and shape of the object cannot be determined even from X-rays taken of the soil block it was lifted in. (*not illus.*) [0695]
D: A **patch of leather and textile**, destroyed in a latex mould when lifting on site was attempted. It lay directly above *E* and was possibly preserved by metal salts from this. Some mineralised textile of unpigmented coarse wool is preserved, over an area 50 × 13mm, on wood. It is a Z-spun twill, the threads 0.75mm in diameter. Thread count 8/8. [0675]

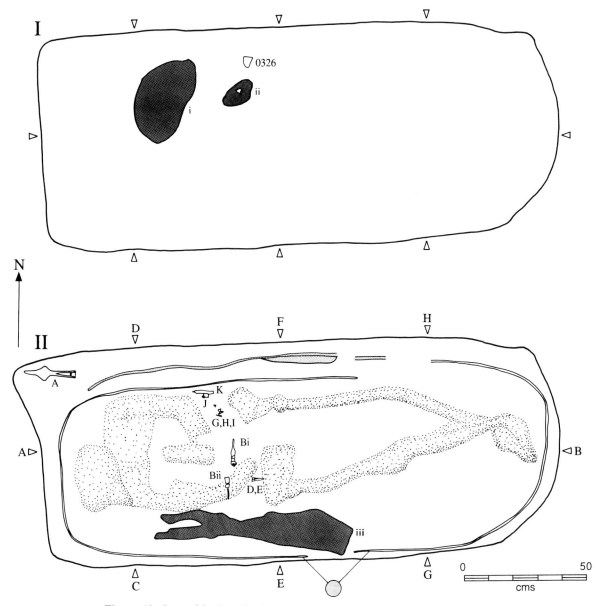

Figure 43 Grave 20, plan. (I) shows wood lumps in upper fill. Scale 1:15

E: Tapering Ae **strap end** of two plates, length 48mm, preserving organic material, decorated with two pairs of lines at the top, above the rivet hole. X-rays show three dots in an inverted arc between these lines. Midway down is another series of punched dots in a U-shape. This is possibly a strap end or counterplate from a thick leather belt. The leather would then be about 4mm thick, possibly indicating cattle skin. Charcoal flecks associated with this object are of oak (*Quercus* sp.). A detached area of textile, 15 × 10mm, is associated. It is Z/Z spun, a twill, with a very even spin and weave, of fine to medium wool. Illustrated from X-rays. [0694]

F: A layer or patch of **leather**, listed as a sample, also containing Ae object G (*not illus.*). [0676]

G: A highly corroded Ae lozenge **?belt mount**, length 35mm, with two rivets on one side, associated with *F* and *H*. It preserves small areas of textile (c); 7 × 7 and 12 × 13mm of degraded animal fibre, Z/Z, twill, mixed with leather. No dye was detected. The mount was so badly corroded in the ground that it could only be drawn from X-rays. [0690]

H: Ae **strip**, length 14mm, associated with *F* and *G*, possibly part of a belt mount. Highly corroded whilst in the ground, the strip could only be drawn from an X-ray taken whilst it was still in a soil block. One (broken) end, with three moulded ribs, is of D-section. The other end with an empty (?rivet) hole is flat. Small fragments of Ae seen scattered in the X-ray plate suggest the piece might originally have been symmetrical. [0691]

I: Small pointed piece of **wood** adjacent to *H*. Unclear if this is only a fragment of the original object or complete. (*not illus.*) [0515]

J: Ae **object** of unknown type or shape adjacent to knife *K*. This object is possibly a plate associated with the belt, and has tiny punched dot decoration forming a small circle. The severe corrosion meant that no shape can be determined even from X-rays of the soil block in which it was lifted. (*not illus.*) [0689]

K: Fe **knife** with horn handle, length 40mm. A powdery orange deposit on both sides of the blade has been identified as leather. [0688]

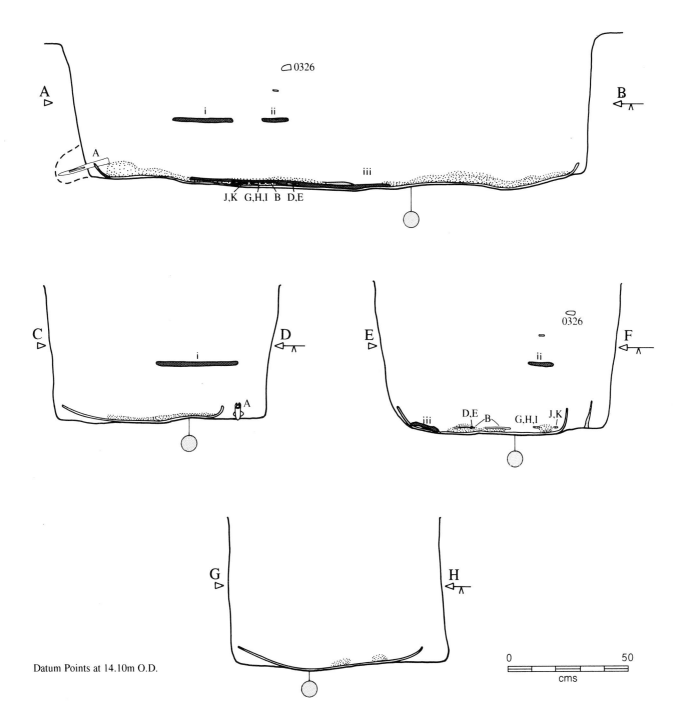

0326

i
ii
iii

J,K G,H,I B D,E

C
D

i

A

0326

E
F

ii

iii D,E B G,H,I J,K

G
H

Datum Points at 14.10m O.D.

0   50

cms

Figure 44 Grave 20, long and cross-sections. Scale 1:15

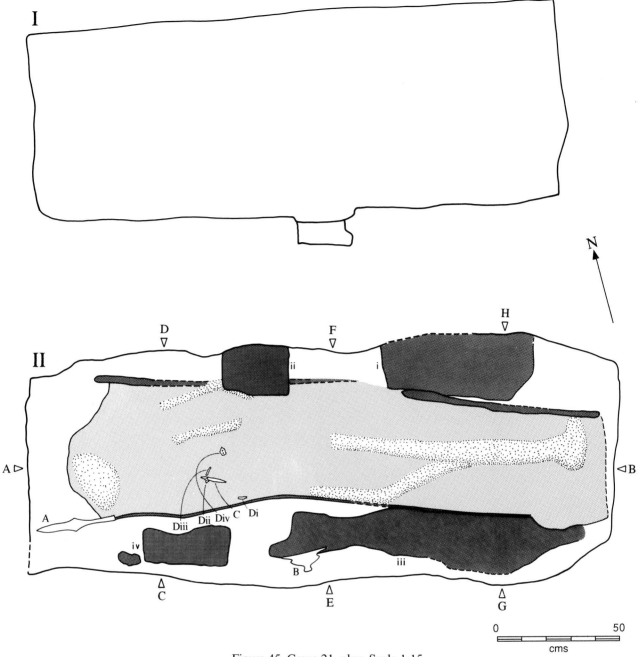

Figure 45 Grave 21, plan. Scale 1:15

Grave 21 (inhumation) (Figs 45, 46, 47, 97 and 98)
Dimensions: (Top) 2.18 × 0.8m; (Base) 2.4 × 0.95m
Orientation: 285°
Container for body: Shallow bier edged with plank or open-ended coffin.
Sex/age: Male.
Body position: Extended, legs crossed. Very fragmentary stains of upper body. Head to west.

Description: The grave was first seen as an extremely clear rectangular cut through the pinkish-brown relict Anglo-Saxon topsoil (Fig. 45 I and Pl. XIII). The grave undercut significantly, especially to the east, hence the surface and base grave plans. At surface level (14.37m OD), a rectangular feature was noticed slightly east of centre along the south edge. Measuring 220×150mm it would seem to represent a socket or post-hole associated

with the grave. The grey-brown grave fill extended 50mm into this feature before being sharply delineated by another fill of an homogenous grey-black sand, probably a wood stain. There was a slight extension of the feature to the east. There was no sign of any other similar features around the grave, although had they existed and their bases been at a slightly higher level, they would have been removed by agricultural activity. Charcoal, *0534*, found within the feature, was of oak (*Quercus* sp.) and hazel (*Corylus* sp.). Because the feature disappeared so quickly, no section was made and its profile was never seen.

The grave fill consisted of mottled grey-brown soil becoming increasingly brown in the lower levels. Throughout were patches of dark grey/black moisture-retaining sand, most probably the remains of wood contained within the fill. These patches first appeared at the east end and became pronounced at 14.04mOD with

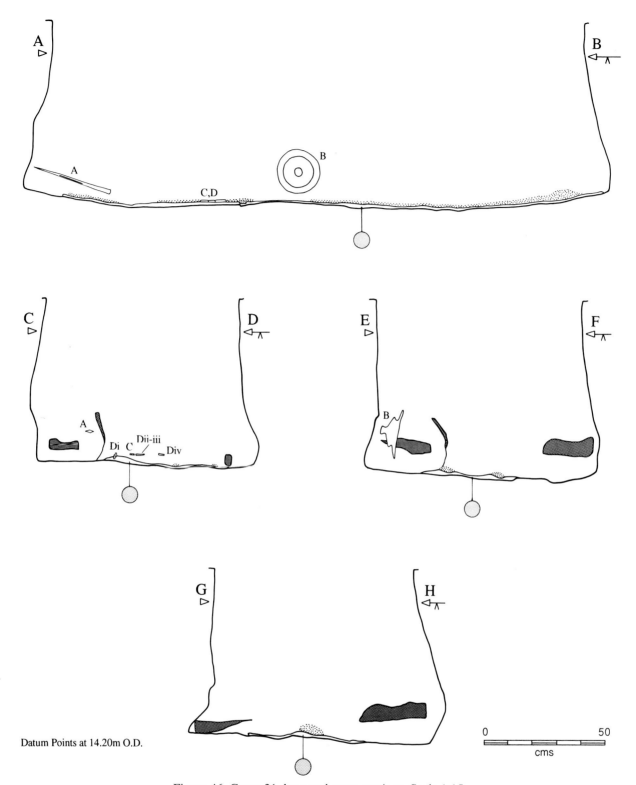

Datum Points at 14.20m O.D.

Figure 46 Grave 21, long and cross-sections. Scale 1:15

two spreads along the north side. More spreads, on the south side, appeared at 13.88mOD. These dark stains were all concentrated at the east end until the final levels of the grave were reached, when they became better defined and were seen to extend along the length of the cut. The wood illustrated represents only those most dense concentrations. Wood patches are omitted from the long section for clarity. Analysis of the charred remains gathered from these is of interest. Patch i, relatively homogenous in the ground includes oak stem (*Quercus*

sp.), willow (*Salix* sp.) or poplar (*Populus* sp.), and hazel (*Corylus* sp.). Patch ii contained charcoal of hazel and iii charcoal from hazel and willow/poplar. Neighbouring grave 20 also contained willow/poplar, distinguishing these graves from most others which had only oak.

The bottom layers of the grave were highly disturbed by roots from nearby trees which made distinguishing the body container difficult. The body appears to have lain on an organic layer whose form is unclear. The stain was very intense and might represent wood, in which case it might

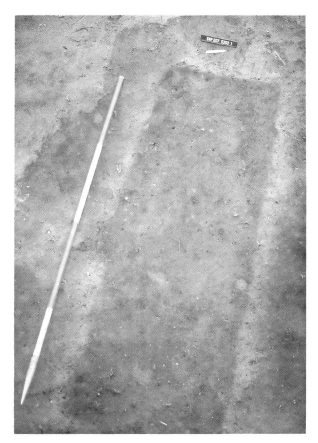

Plate XIII Grave 21 surface plan with ?socket on south (left) edge

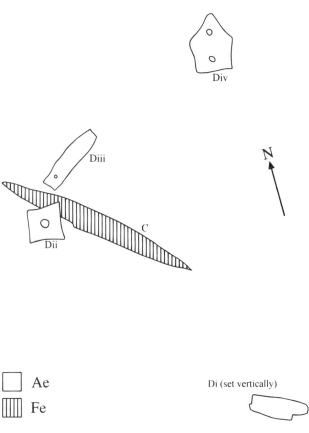

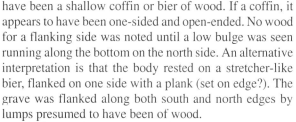

Figure 47 Grave 21, detail of grave-goods. Scale 1:2

have been a shallow coffin or bier of wood. If a coffin, it appears to have been one-sided and open-ended. No wood for a flanking side was noted until a low bulge was seen running along the bottom on the north side. An alternative interpretation is that the body rested on a stretcher-like bier, flanked on one side with a plank (set on edge?). The grave was flanked along both south and north edges by lumps presumed to have been of wood.

The body stain was very poorly preserved and only the legs could be seen clearly. The waist area was removed in a block for laboratory excavation of the belt set.

Grave-goods:

A: **Spear** with Fe head (Swanton H2), length 336mm. Mineralised wood in the socket is of ash (*Fraxinus* sp.) from mature timber. [0914]

B: **Shield** with buttoned Fe boss (i), diameter *c*.190mm, height 78mm, and Fe grip (ii), (Dickinson and Härke Group 3). The boss has a heavy button, low straight carinated dome and wide flange with five flat-headed rivets. The shield board is made of willow (*Salix* sp.) or poplar (*Populus* sp.) with an oblique tangential surface and was covered with leather at least at the rim of the boss. The five rivets securing the boss appear to be only folded over nails which give a shield board thickness of 8–10mm. The grip is a flat strip with one rivet, length *c*.120mm. A small fragment of wood on the central portion of the grip may lie on the grip's axis and perpendicular to the grain of the shield board, probably indicating the grip to have been of an inserted type. [0912, 0913]

C: Small **knife** with Fe blade and horn handle. Unidentified wood fragments are also associated but being of mainly pith-like material are probably root. Textile survives on the knife blade and belt fitting *Dii*. Of medium to fine fibred wool, it is in folds with Z spinning in both systems, of medium twist; weave 2/2 twill, noticeably even, thread count 14/14. There are no reverses but there is a clear fault, either from a broken thread or incorrect weaving. A partially mineralised area over the stud, again Z/Z, a 2/2 twill but pulled (count estimated *c*.10/10) could still be the same weave. Another sample with a similar thread has a count of *c*.14/12. No dye was detected. [1386]

D: **Ae belt suite** with traces of a silvered finish. (i), a shield-on-tongue 'D' shaped buckle. Cast bow, chamfered above with seating for pin, reducing to a bar for the attachment of the tongue and strap. Tongue with square shield. Width 27mm. Behind the bow the buckle plate is single-sided with the strap secured by one rivet. The plate is rebated to take the rear of the tongue and decorated with a roughly scored border line outlined with tri-lobed stamps and a row of double lunette stamps behind the tongue. The rivet projects 2mm, length 24mm. The buckle and plate are both heavy cast pieces.

(ii). Square stud with concave sides. Cast, with square sunken area behind the central rivet. The silvered front has a single line border with an irregular row of stamps of two kinds; tri-lobed stamps matching those on the buckle plate on three sides, with one side bearing what seems to be the centre and one lobe of imperfectly struck stamps of the same kind. 16×17mm.

(iii). Pointed strap end with single rivet and short backing plate. Two transverse lines, but much obscured by textile. Length 37mm.

(iv). Five-sided belt plate with thinner plate behind, secured by two rivets, sandwiching the remains of the leather strap between. Traces of a border-line and tri-lobed stamps can be seen beneath the corrosion products. Length 26mm.

Associated with this group were several traces of organic material, probably wood and leather, and some mineralised textile. The largest area, identified as of wool with medium to fine fibres, was 10 × 5mm, partly obscured but with Z/Z spinning, some threads dark brown, medium twist. The weave is a 2/2 twill, thread count estimated at *c*.8/8 on 5mm. No dye was detected. [1384, 1386]

Grave 22 (inhumation) (Fig. 6)
Dimensions: Unknown.
Orientation: Unclear.
Container: Unknown.
Sex/age: Unknown.
Body position: Unknown.

Description: A presumed inhumation grave, unexcavated, extending beneath the eastern baulk of Area A. No large-scale surface plan was drawn as too little was revealed for accurate measurement. The grave is possibly associated with a cremation (grave 91), which lay between this and grave 21.

Grave-goods: Unknown

Grave 23 (inhumation) (Fig. 6)
Dimensions: Unknown.
Orientation: Unclear (?276°).
Container: Unknown.
Sex/age: Unknown.
Body position: Unknown.

Description: A presumed inhumation grave, unexcavated, extending beneath the eastern baulk of Area A. Too little was revealed for accurate planning of the surface level or measurements.

Grave-goods: Unknown.

Grave 24 (inhumation) (Fig. 6)
Dimensions: 1.16+ × 0.47m
Orientation: 292°
Container for body: Unknown.
Sex/age: Unknown.
Body position: Unknown.

Description: An unexcavated inhumation grave extending beneath the eastern baulk of Area A. Only the surface was planned which showed a fill of dark grey sand with patches of black sand. The full length of the grave was not uncovered.

Grave-goods: Unknown

Plate XIV Grave 25 fully excavated within surrounding ring-ditch *0110*, from east looking west

Grave 25 (inhumation) (Figs 48, 49 and 98)
Dimensions: 2.45 × 0.80m
Orientation: 270°
Container for body: Coffin or, probably, an organic lining.
Sex/age: Male?
Body position: Supine extended, arms alongside body, head turned to south.

Description: A long sub-rectangular grave cut within annular ring-ditch *0110* (Fig. 129). The grave fill consisted of mid brown sand throughout, with some light grey and dark grey/black patches mottling the upper levels.

The stain of the organic container appeared at 14.06mOD as a dark grey line along the grave south edge. It did not appear at the ends of the grave until 13.76mOD, shortly before the body stain appeared. It had a curious 'double end' at the west (head) end. The thinness of the stain and its appearance at the grave ends only near the grave bottom suggest that this was perhaps a textile or animal hide, as does the fold in the stain seen on the south side. How the double end related to the stain bottom is unclear as it was only seen at one spit level. The long section drawn suggests one possibility. The body stain was poorly preserved in the chest area although the legs were well defined. The body could also be clearly seen to lie on the organic layer.

Contained within the fill of the grave were twenty sherds deriving from two vessels, *0405* and *0634* (Fig. 98). Vessel *0405*, represented by two sherds, has a soft sandy black fabric with light grey surfaces. It is of unknown form and shape, although one sherd displays an upright rim. Vessel *0634*, of a crumbly soft dark brown vesiculated fabric, was also of unknown form and decoration although a base sherd survives.

Annular ring-ditch *0110* had a fill of dark grey-brown sand showing against the light grey sand of the Anglo-Saxon topsoil, scarred by ploughmarks and post-holes from a modern fenceline. Its external diameter was approximately 5–5.2m, the width of the ditch varying from 0.6m up to 0.95m at a bulge on the west and up to 0.41m deep. It contained 22 sherds deriving from vessel *0407* (Fig. 98), a dark brown sandy fabric, vesiculated, with a simple upright rim. There is no decoration on any of the sherds. Slightly away from the concentration of sherds, an Fe nail, *0062*, was found at the top of the fill but is possibly modern (*not illus.*).

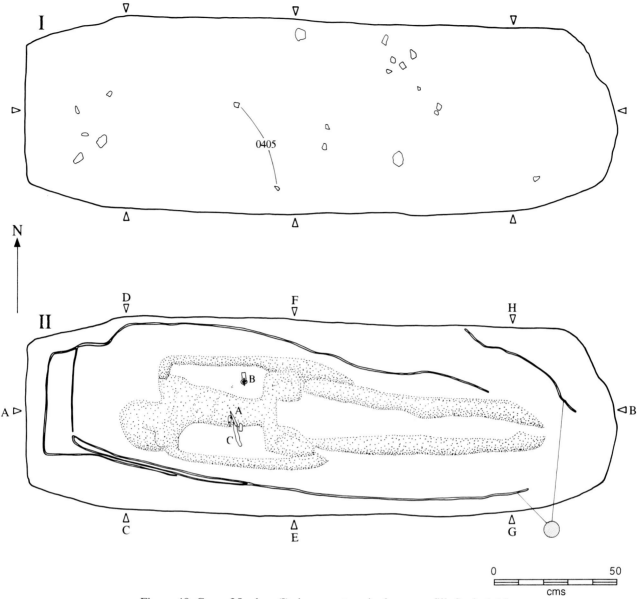

Figure 48 Grave 25, plan. (I) shows pottery in the upper fill. Scale 1:15

Grave-goods:
A: Ae **belt plates** (i–iii), matching buckle and plate *B*. Lengths, (ii), *c*.42mm, (iii) 65mm. The rivets appear to have circular washers. Remains of two textiles survive: (a), beneath and through the rivet hole, over an area 50 × 27mm of light brown wool with even Z-spun warp and weft, had threads of medium twist, diameter *c*.0.8mm. It was an even 2/2 twill weave without reverses, thread count 14/14–16 on 10mm. No dye was detected. (b), lying below (a) in an area 85 × 35mm is another wool Z-spun twill with finer threads of 0.6mm diameter. The spin and weave are both looser, the thread count 8/6–7 on 10mm. The complex was too poor and corroded to illustrate other than from X-rays. [0250]
B: Fe and Ae **belt buckle** with **plate**, length 50mm, matching *A*. Textile from either (a) or (b) is preserved lying in folds under ?leather on the buckle ring. Again it is a wool Z-spun twill; no thread count was possible and no dye was detected. The severe corrosion of the

buckle has destroyed the loop and tongue which are drawn from X-rays. [0251]
C: Fe **knife**, length 126mm, broken into three fragments in the ground. It has a horn handle and leather sheath with textile on both sides. [0518]

Grave 26 (inhumation) (Fig. 6)
Dimensions: c.1.45 × 0.7m
Orientation: 228°
Container for body: Unknown.
Sex/age: Unknown.
Body position: Unknown.

Description: A presumed inhumation grave, unexcavated, located during evaluation work in trench I. The full extent of the upper fill could not be clearly seen and so the grave apparently has a missing south-west corner, although this is probably an illusion caused by redeposited natural. The upper fill was of a mid brown and orange-brown sand.

Grave-goods: Unknown

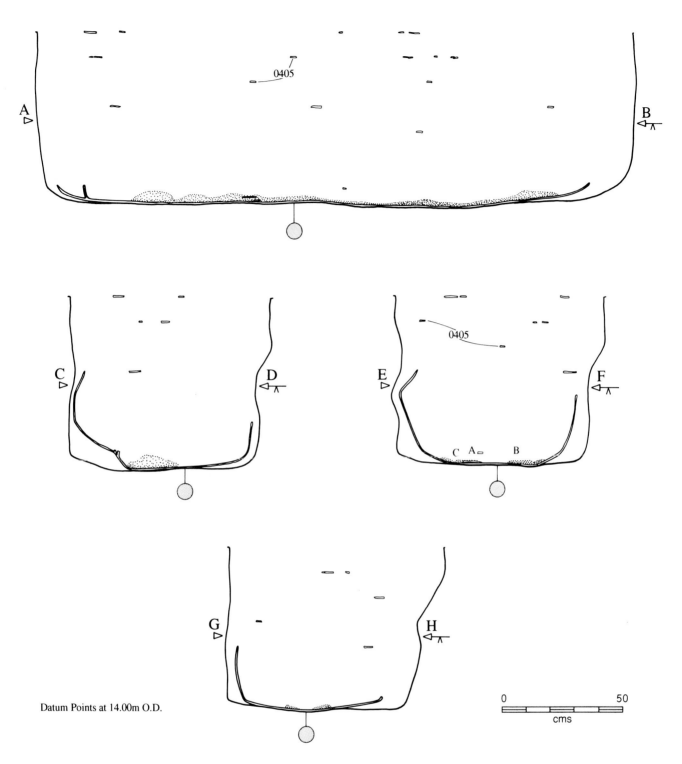

A

B

0405

C

D

E

F

0405

C A B

G

H

Datum Points at 14.00m O.D.

0   50
cms

Figure 49 Grave 25, long and cross-sections. Scale 1:15

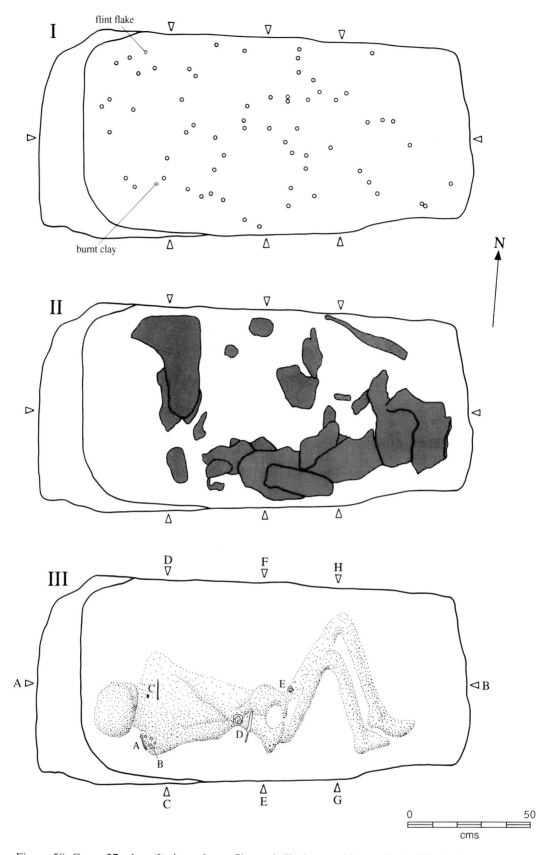

Figure 50 Grave 27, plan. (I) shows burnt flint and (II) the wood lumps in the fill. Scale 1:15

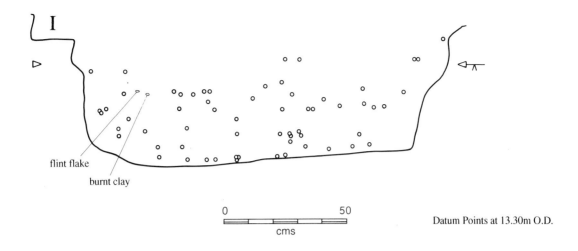

flint flake

burnt clay

0   50

cms

Datum Points at 13.30m O.D.

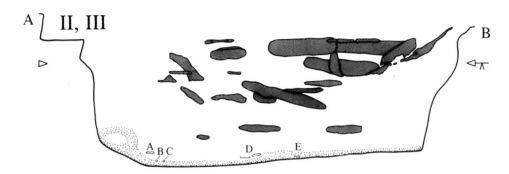

Figure 51 Grave 27, long section across the grave. (I) shows burnt flint in the fill

Grave 27 (inhumation) (Figs 50, 51, 52 and 99)
Dimensions: 1.79 × 0.83m
Orientation: 266°
Container for body: None.
Sex/age: Female.
Body position: Flexed supine with left arm possibly drawn across body so left hand meets right hand resting on pelvis. Right leg probably lies over left. Head to west.

Description: A squat rectangular grave cut with near vertical sides and some slight undercutting in places. The fill of a fine mid grey sand was cut through very mottled natural, with occasional small stones in the upper levels. The sand became more mottled with light yellow-brown redeposited natural at the lower levels, which made defining the grave cut difficult at times. The cut reduced in size at 14.40mOD to produce a shelf at the east end, as also seen in grave 9.

The fill of the grave was packed with twenty-four pieces of charred wood, nearly all badly degraded and which appeared as dense black stains rather than charcoal, so that no wood species could be identified. At times it was also difficult to distinguish between patches representing the same piece of wood and smaller independent lumps. The wood was distributed predominantly in the upper fill at the west end above the body's legs. The arrangement is very similar to that in grave 9 where eight pieces of charred wood were placed within the fill apparently arranged over the body.

Sixty-two burnt flint chippings with a total weight of 0.22kg were also recovered. The burnt flint was spread evenly throughout the lower two thirds of the fill, mostly beneath the wood fragments. It forms the most dense concentration of burnt flint found in any of the graves excavated, with the exception of grave 46 which cut burnt stone feature *1775*. A flint flake (*1461*) and small piece of burnt clay (*1462*) were also found in the fill.

The body stain was reasonably well preserved except in the chest area, making it difficult to define the position of the arms. However, the feet and legs were very well preserved. The body appears to have been laid directly onto the grave floor as no organic stains were seen.

Grave-goods:
A: Fe **dress pin** at right shoulder, length 79mm. The pin is slightly curved with a crosier-shape terminal and forms a pair with pin *C*. Almost entirely covered with poor condition mineralised textile, *c.*5 × 3mm, very fine ?twill, with coarser traces underneath. A three-ply thread is mineralised close to the point. [1539]
B: String of three amber **beads** with two Ae **pendant spacers** at the right shoulder, immediately adjacent to pin *A*. Beads: Amber; square cylinder (i, ii); globular (iii). Ae spacers: flat pierced tab, length 18mm (iv); flat with rolled-over loop, length 11mm (v). [1549–1553]
C: Fe **dress pin** at centre of upper chest, length 83mm. It forms a pair with pin *A* having a crosier-shape terminal but is straight rather than curved, the pin head being slightly flattened at the sides. The outer corrosion layers preserve coarse mineralised threads, Z-spun, loose twist, ?wound round below the eye. [1554]

71

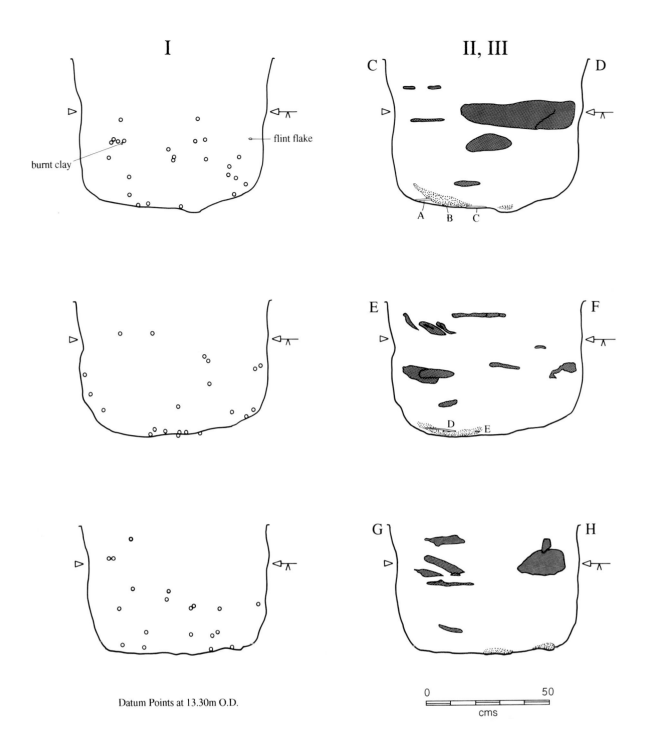

I

II, III

burnt clay

flint flake

C — D

E — F

G — H

A B C

D E

Datum Points at 13.30m O.D.

0   50
cms

Figure 52 Grave 27, cross-sections. (I) shows burnt flint in the fill, (II and III) the wood lumps and body stain/grave-goods. Scale 1:15

D: Fe **knife** (i), length 130mm, with Fe **ring** (ii), diameter c.40mm, from waist area just above the pelvis. The knife has traces of a horn handle. There are traces of mineralised textile along both faces of the blade and on part of the ring, over 12 × 10mm; Z/Z, medium/loose twist, 2/2 twill, with a thread count 9–10/8 on 10mm. The thread diameter is approx. 0.5mm. [1536, 1538]

E: Fe **buckle** and tongue, width c.24mm, lying on the left leg immediately beneath the pelvis. Very deteriorated mineralised textile remains on the tongue and all loop surfaces except the base, but there are no leather traces. The textile is of two qualities, (a), coarse, ?Z and (b) fine, Z/S. An unidentified organic material, probably bone, is preserved on the loop base. The position of the buckle in the grave makes it unclear if it was actually being worn on the body at burial. [1533]

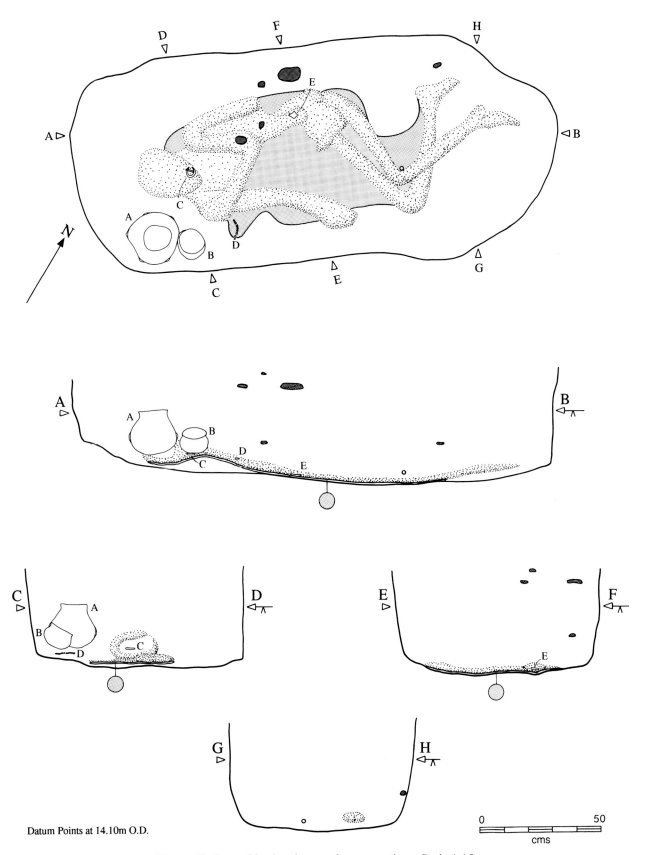

N

A

A
B
C
C
D

E

E
G

D
F
H

B

Datum Points at 14.10m O.D.

A

B

A
B
C
D
E

C
A
B
D
E

D

E

C

F

E

G

H

0   50

cms

Figure 53 Grave 28, plan, long and cross-sections. Scale 1:15

73

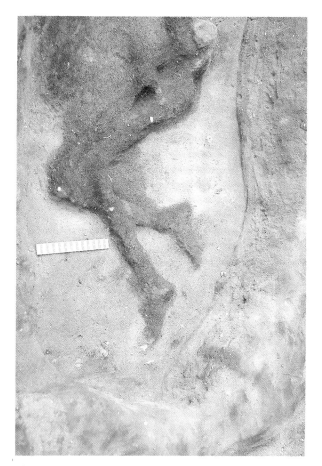

Plate XV Grave 28, detail of legs and feet. Scale bar 25cm

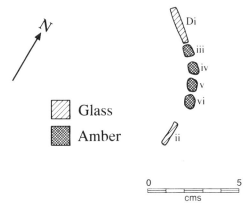

Figure 54 Grave 28, detail of beads. Scale 1:2

Grave 28 (inhumation) (Figs 53, 54, 99 and 100)
Dimensions: 2.00 × 0.91m
Orientation: 239°
Container for body: None but body rested on an organic layer.
Sex/age: Female.
Body position: Flexed, left leg over right, left hand on right shoulder, right arm extended. Head to west.

Description: A sub-rectangular grave cut with a rounded east end. The fill was a mix of coarse greyish brown sand at the west end and mixed grey brown sand at the east, turning to a reddish brown in the lower layers. Small patches of black 'greasy' sand were seen throughout the fill, probably from degraded wood or charcoal. Towards the bottom, the centre of the grave was marked by occasional flecks of charcoal. Two plain pottery body sherds, *1440* and *1446* were found in excavation, location unknown, but high in the fill (*not illus.*). A burnt flint fragment was found at the bottom. The annular brooch was used as a main brooch.

The body was laid on a thin organic layer of unknown type, which blended into the upper body stain, but the legs were well preserved (Pl. XV).

Grave-goods:
A: Complete tall biconical **pot**, height 180mm, with five hollow bosses; tooling marks visible on the inner surface. Fine sandy fabric with orange grog, inner surface grey, outer surface brown grey, both surfaces burnished. Placed to the south-west of the body's head. [1477]
B: Small undecorated globular **bowl**, height 90mm, with constricted neck and rounded rim. Fragments of the base and shoulder missing. Brown sandy fabric with red grog and grey burnished surfaces inside and out. Placed to the south of the body's head, east of pot A. [1490]
C: Ae **penannular brooch** with waisted terminals and single row of three-part 'arrowhead' stamps. Fe pin wrapped round. Slightly oval, max. diameter 45mm. Mineralisation preserved parts of the teeth and jawbone, and a lump of textile (a), at the junction of the pin, c.24 × 25mm, of very dark brown pigmented animal fibre, probably wool; spinning Z/Z, coarse twist, weave 2/2 twill, thread count 6/5 on 5mm. A 5mm length of tablet-woven border was preserved on the twill, the back damaged but cords probably Z,S,Z,S,Z. No dye could be determined. A mineralised fragment of (a) on the pin, 10×7mm, was possibly of the same twill, thread count 10/9. [1537]
D: String of 6 **beads**, 2 of glass and 4 of amber, from near to the left wrist, possibly originally a bracelet (see detail, Fig. 54). Glass: drawn cylinder (i, ii; dark blue, ii in fragments). Amber: biconical, four sided (iii); globular (iv); barrel (v); wedge (vi). [1542–1547]
E: Fe **belt fitting** of lozenge shape, central length c.25mm. Mineralised textile (b) with a damaged surface was all over one side, spin Z/S. [1548]

Grave 29 (inhumation) (Fig. 5)
Dimensions: ? × 0.66m
Orientation: 260°
Container: Unknown.
Sex/age: Unknown.
Body position: Unknown.

Description: A presumed inhumation grave, unexcavated, extending from the east baulk of trial trench VI, found during evaluation work in 1989. The feature had a fill of grey sand with patches of brown mixing in.

Grave-goods: Unknown

Grave 30 (inhumation) (Fig. 5)
Dimensions: 1.64+ × 0.62m
Orientation: 203°
Container: Unknown.
Sex/age: Unknown.
Body position: Unknown.

Description: A possible inhumation grave, unexcavated, located during site evaluation, extending from the eastern baulk of trial trench VI. Although the feature was on an extreme orientation in comparison with the other graves from the site, it had a good rectangular shape, one edge extending 1.64m out of the baulk, and its fill was of the common pale grey sand with mid brown patches.

Grave goods: Unknown

Grave 31 (inhumation) (Figs 55, 100 and 101)
Dimensions: 2.06 × 1.39m
Orientation: 262°
Container for body: Body rested on an organic layer.
Sex/age: Male.
Body position: Supine extended, both arms apparently folded over the waist. Head to west, slightly turned to the south.

Description: An ovoid cut with a fill of mid grey and orange-brown sand, mixing together to the base of the grave to become more grey with silver-grey lenses. The fill consisted of a medium fine sand with occasional small stones (deriving from ironpanned sand) and, to the south of the skull, a few tiny pieces of macroflora, *2216*, midway down.

Although various lenses of dark grey sand were seen near the edges of the fill, none appears to be identifiable with the organic layer visible at the bottom of the grave cut on which the body was laid. The excavator noted another possible organic stain at the shoulder area, of a more reddish colour, which perhaps suggests that the body was (at least partially) covered.

The body stain was reasonably well preserved, although quite thin in the chest area. The basic body position was extended supine. The position and orientation of the grave-goods suggests a belt set including buckle, knife and strike-a-light which was laid on top of, rather than worn by, the dead man.

Grave-goods:
A: **Spear** with Fe head (Swanton D1), length 172mm, blade lying flat to north of the left shoulder. Mineralised wood within the socket is probably willow (*Salix* sp.) or poplar (*Populus* sp.). [2204]
B: Tiny Ae **pin** or **tack**, length 6mm, with an oval cross-section tapering to a blunt point, found beneath the skull. [2365]
C: Large Fe **buckle**, maximum length 102mm, lying over the upper chest. The X-ray shows a narrow oval loop with wrapped-around tongue. A separate Fe plate is slotted to take the tongue and wrapped round the buckle-loop to take the strap. A large triangular buckle plate has four rivets. It is not clear how the slotted plate was attached to the strap or the buckle plate.
The whole appearance of the top surface suggests textile or leather fibres over an area c.60 × 90mm,

obscured by small stones. Three patches on the loop of the buckle, and fibrous traces, are probably leather. These have sharp cut edges with fine S and Z-spun threads showing beneath where broken, of ?twill. A patch on the loop, 15 × 15mm, with fine Z/Z spin may be (b). Z and S threads are mineralised on the pin tip. The buckle is so heavily corroded that the reverse side is illustrated, from X-rays. [2254, 2371]
D: A large straight-backed Fe **knife**, length 246mm, positioned on the left-hand side of the body over the arm, beneath strike-a-light *E*. The cutting edge undulates, possibly from wear. The tang, broken whilst in the ground, preserves traces of a horn handle; there is also a compact corrosion layer 1mm thick covering the blade. It is wrapped over the knife back and overlaps the handle junction by 20mm. This layer could not be confirmed as leather.
The knife and the strike-a-light preserve two textiles: (a), an area on top of the blade and over *E*, c.40 × 30mm, is largely covered by small stones but is clearly continuous, the spin of one system Z (loose), the other S-spun. The threads have a variable medium twist, dark brown in colour; the weave is 2/2 twill, thread count 9/8 on 10mm. (b), under a patch of (a), curls down over *E* for c.45mm, width 20mm. It is a weave with Z/Z spinning and finer threads. A small patch near the point of the blade, again with Z/Z spin (thread count c.17/12 (6 on 5mm)), shows probable reverses; the quality suggests a good broken diamond twill. Both (a) and (b) have degraded fibre but suggest the scale structure and irregular diameter of wool. [2253]
E: Fe **strike-a-light** with coiled terminals (i) and tapered rods (ii) and (iii), possibly **steels**, placed at the body left-hand side, overlying the knife *C*. Both rods have a round cross-section, tapering to a blunt point. (ii) has a loop head, (iii) has the 'head' turned over to form a thin end at right angles to the stem. Lengths; (i) 100mm; (ii) 90mm; (iii) c.86mm. [2373]
F: Ae **pin**, minimum length 28mm. Incomplete, it has a flattened ring-head and decorated stem. It was found in the same area as objects *D* and *E* and was perhaps part of the belt set. [2097]

Grave 32 (inhumation) (Figs 56, 101, 102 and 103)
Dimensions: 1.93 × 1.12m
Orientation: 274°
Container for body: Organic lining to base and grave sides.
Sex/age: Male.
Body position: Supine extended, head to west. Legs slightly flexed. Position of the arms unclear although left arm appears to be bent out to cradle the lyre.

Description: A large rectangular grave cut with sharp corners at the surface. The upper levels of the grave had been severely damaged by ploughing and a post-medieval road-side ditch which had passed directly overhead on the grave's east-west axis. The fill consisted of a stone-free fine silver-grey sand mixing with mid brown sand. At the lower levels, this silver-grey sand continued around the grave edges surrounding a large oval filling of mid brown sand, directly above an organic layer and the body. This probably represents a filling of topsoil sand which packed

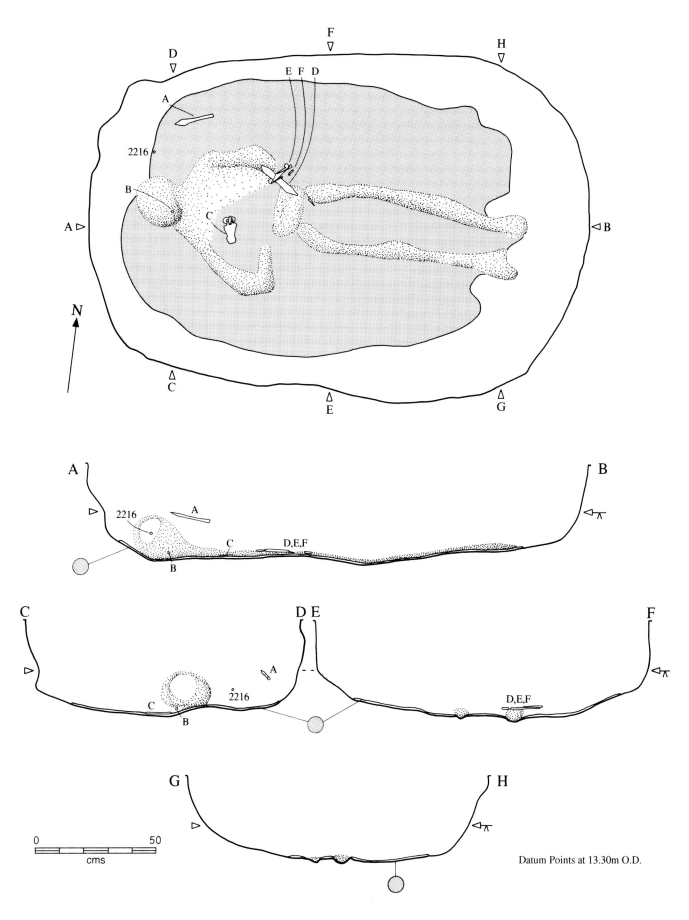

N

0 ——————— 50
cms

Datum Points at 13.30m O.D.

Figure 55 Grave 31, plan, long and cross-sections. Scale 1:15

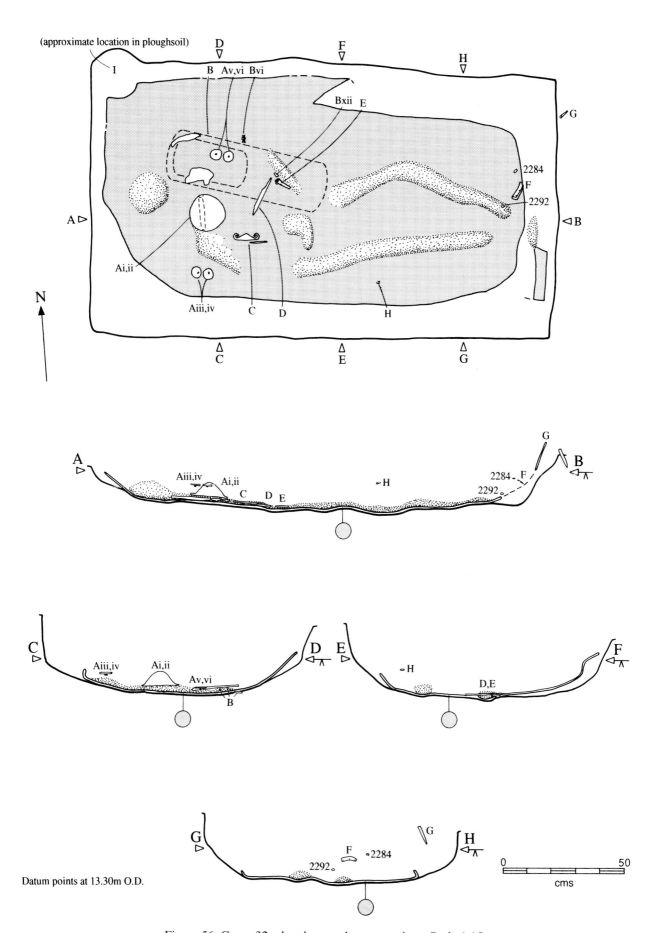

(approximate location in ploughsoil)

N

Datum points at 13.30m O.D.

Figure 56 Grave 32, plan, long and cross-sections. Scale 1:15

the edges of the grave when the organic lining was inserted. The subsequent backfill in the remaining central oval cavity was of mixed brown soil.

The organic layer on which the body stain rested was thin (about 5mm thick) and traces of it could be seen in the upper layers, as high as 13.42mOD and at one point there were two distinct lines running parallel. Although this edge was extremely fragmentary it would seem that the organic lining once enclosed the whole grave, quite probably to a level higher than the top of the grave as exposed. The edges of the cut as found were very straight; indeed the cut was one of the most regular seen on the site, but its corners quickly rounded off at the grave base.

The upper fill had numerous very small charcoal flecks (up to 5mm long). One fragment, *2284*, was possibly of gorse (*Ulex* sp.). In addition, the excavator noted that the organic stain line (*2274*) when it first appeared was 'flecked with charcoal'. A small fleck of cremated bone, *2292*, was found in the fill immediately above the left shin.

The damage caused to the grave by agricultural activity is demonstrated by the two spear fragments apparently from the grave but found *ex situ*. Also at a higher level, some 11m to the east, part of an Fe socket (scatters No. 39) was found. Whilst it has no obvious associations, it is possibly a spear ferrule and could conceivably represent a part of a second spear originally contained within this grave.

The excavator noted that the area of wood from the lyre was overlain by a much blacker wood. As this was the shield, it might be that the reason for this extra, darker, stain was an organic covering to the shield boards, for instance of leather.

Grave-goods:

A: **Shield** with Fe **boss** (i), diameter *c.*150mm, height *c.*84mm (Dickinson and Härke Group 6); **grip** (ii), length 110mm, and two pairs of decorative Fe **studs** (iii–vi) at the top and bottom edges, best preserved diameter 45mm. The shield had been laid over the body's upper chest. The boss has a tiny, pointed apex, narrow flange and low wall. The number of rivets is not clear. The cone can clearly be seen to have been made separately from the wall and flange.

The shield board appears to have been of slow-grown ash (*Fraxinus* sp.), *c.* 8 rings per 10mm, orientated with the grain running east-west in the grave. It appears to have been covered on the reverse with a thick layer of leather with possibly a thinner piece being used on the front or at least over part of the circumference; there is no obvious sign of leather between the wood and boss rim but it is present on the decorative studs. The flat Fe grip was offset from, and bent into, the centre of the boss. It had traces of its wooden handle on the inside, perpendicular to the grip axis with organic material, probably leather, on the other side, presumably from a binding. Rivets associated with the boss show the board and leather covering to have been 10mm thick and from decorative stud (vi), boards 9mm thick with a layer of leather approx. 4.5mm thick on the back. Most of the studs have fragments of random vegetation on the front. [2307, 2308, 2322, 2323]

B: Remains of a stringed musical instrument of **lyre** type, of multi-timber construction, with Ae and Fe fixtures and fittings (i–xvi: the lumps shown in Fig. 56 represent the blocks in Fig. 140). The surviving portions are of wood and metal, with textile, leather and other organic deposits adhering. Beneath these adhesions, timber surfaces survive in good condition, visible areas being smoothly finished. Timbers used include oak (*Quercus* sp.) and maple (*Acer* sp.). The joinery is of a well-developed form and particularly fine craftsmanship. Fe fittings include remains of two small looped strap-attachment terminals with studs, associated with a pair of Ae figure-of-eight hooks, probably from a wrist-strap (vi–vii). Structural pins were preserved *in situ* embedded in the timbers. Ae components include jointing pins also *in situ*, one of a pair of binding-strips with attachment pins (viii–xi) and two disc-headed studs (i, v); their original surfaces retain fine detail, but no visible decoration. Little or no actual metal remains beneath: the tin-richness of the residue may be due to selective leaching of the original copper content. The lyre is described and discussed in detail in Chapter 5 section V.

Textile (a) was associated with piece (v) at the edge of the wood in an area *c.*20 × 15mm, lying across from the underneath, perhaps from a garment, but the threads are very broken up, dark brown with red-brown patches (spinning Z/Z, threads with medium twist and an open weave; thread count estimated at *c.*8/8–10). Another fragment with a pin lies 30mm from the stud, probably an edge, with mixed dark and rusted threads. A broken-off fragment of leather, 16 × 12mm again has a pin or stud. The textile threads were of animal fibre and pigmented. Textile (b), a mineralised area 35×20mm associated with S-hook (vi), has a Z-spin medium thread twist coarse tabby weave. It is very open, with a thread count 11–12/7–8 on 10mm, but its openness may be due to deterioration. The textile was of wool with fine to medium fibres. Textile (c) was preserved on top of the stud in fragment (i), on the side of the wood and leather, over an area 25 × 15mm. It is very coarse and deteriorated, with Z/Z spin, probably a wool twill, with a knot at one edge. Parts adhering to the stud suggest a weave edge with loops on one side and broken ends the other, perhaps a starting-border, or braid edge curling for *c.*15mm. Other fragments show similar coarse Z threads, pushed aside by the studs. There is a scrap of twill on the edge of the pin. The textile is wool of fine to medium fibres; no dye was detected on any fibres. These textiles may represent, in part, a bag used to contain the lyre. (*fragments xii–xvi not illus.*) [2325– 2328, 2370]

C: Fe **strike-a-light** (i), length 108mm, and **steel** (ii) with a wooden handle (species unidentifiable), length 80mm. The strike-a-light was contained within a pouch whose grain pattern suggests deer leather (Pl. XXXVII). The steel was probably in the same pouch or at least in a leather wrapping of some kind. [2321]

D: Long Fe **knife**, length 170mm, with horn hafting extending onto the blade. An orange-brown layer 3mm thick with a rough granular surface encloses the blade. It is rounded over the blade back, tapers towards the blade edge and overlaps the handle junction by 20mm. Its arrangement suggests a leather sheath but this could not be confirmed. The blade had been covered or enclosed in textile 2–3mm thick, attacked in antiquity by insects. A mass of insect pupae and cuticles survive amongst a mass of chewed fibres (see *E* below). [2324]

E: Ae shield-on-tongue **buckle** with long, narrow triangular buckle plate, total length 73mm. The loop is a narrow oval; the shield on the tongue is broken at the rear. The buckle is attached to a leather strap by an Ae plate with two elongated strips which pass through the buckle loop. The triangular buckle plate is deeply recessed behind by 3mm; the recess filled by an unidentified material, possibly a metallic filler, making the surface flush. This has three longitudinal grooves on the surface which faced the leather strap. Leather is preserved beneath the Ae strips and around the rear rivet. The buckle plate bears three rivets which pass through domed heads mounted on circular Ae plates. Beaded collars of silver alloy survive on the two lateral rivets. The surface of the plate is without ornament, but there are slight traces of silvering. There are two slots in one edge of the buckle plate.

Mineralised textile (d) was preserved on this and knife *D* in a strip *c.*35 × 13mm, of light red-brown wool, Z/S spin, both thread systems variable, with a medium to loose twist. The Z thread is noticeably finer, the weave probably a regular 2/2 twill, thread count *c.*14 (Z)/9–10 (S), fragile with insect damage. A deteriorated lump of the same weave, *c.*25 × 25mm, preserved on wood or leather, has dark curling Z-spun threads curling loose on the surface, possibly from sewing. The textile is wool of fine to medium fibres with no dye detected.

About 250 **puparia** of the flies *Ophyra capensis* (Wied.) or *leucostoma* (Wied.) were preserved by mineralisation on the buckle and also on knife *D*. The posterior spiracles and respiratory horn show a close similarity to those of *O. capensis*, although it was not possible to compare the specimens with puparia of *O. leucostoma*. Also preserved were a pair of elytra and a pronotum of **beetle** *Trox scaber* (L.), four pinnae (leaflets) of *Pteridium aquilinum* (bracken) and a rodent-nibbled **plum stone** (*Prunus domestica* (L.). The insect remains are discussed further in Chapter 5 section VI. [2328]

F: Ae mount, length 64mm, for a lathe-turned **wooden bowl**, probably of walnut (*Juglans* sp.), attached with three rivets and crimped decoration along one edge. There is no sign of breakage in the mineral preserved wood and the strip is mounted just off the transverse section making it unlikely to be a repair. Where seen, the wood was 4mm thick. Tiny patches of charcoal flecking were noticed on its north side. Mineralisation had also preserved a weevil *Otiorhynchus ovatus* (L.), almost certainly an ancient specimen. [2280]

G: Fe **ferrule**, length 90mm, found point down, embedded in natural immediately outside the east end of the grave cut. It probably derives from a spear originally contained in the grave. Mineralised wood in the socket is from ash (*Fraxinus* sp.). [2273]

H: Two Fe **clamps**, one broken (ii). They originally lay with the plate side down, rivets sticking up, and were possibly used to join two flat pieces of wood although there is no sign of this in the wood grain. Mineralisation has preserved traces of wood, possibly maple or birch wood (*Acer* sp. or *Betula* sp.). The

Plate XVI ?Robber pit to grave 33, mound 6 during excavation, looking south. Scale rod 2m

board had a tangential longitudinal section and was only 3.5mm thick. The two clamps are of different widths, one 16.5mm the other over 19.5mm. [2309]

I: Fe **socket**, length 84mm, containing traces of a wood hafting of ash (*Fraxinus* sp.), found in initial cleaning above the north-west corner of the grave before the grave was identified. The socket is probably the lower part of a spearhead removed by agricultural activity from the upper fill of the grave, perhaps associated with ferrule *G*. [2179]

Grave 33 (robber or excavation trench; original burial method unknown) (Figs 57 and 104)
Dimensions: 1.33 × 0.80m
Orientation: 0° (due north)
Container for body: None.
Sex/age: Unknown.
Body position: Unknown.

Description: A regular rectangular cut filled with a mid grey sand. The cleanness of the cut and the uniform fill (Pl. XVI) make it likely that the feature is 'modern', and certainly post-medieval. The location of the feature, at the centre of where ploughed-out mound 5 is known to have stood, suggests that it is the bottom of a robber or excavation trench cut into the mound. This is perhaps complemented by the cut being oriented due north-south. The size of the original mound is unclear since no trace of it was found in excavation, but it was recorded in 1862 as being 25.5m in diameter and 2m high. These measurements probably represent a mound that had

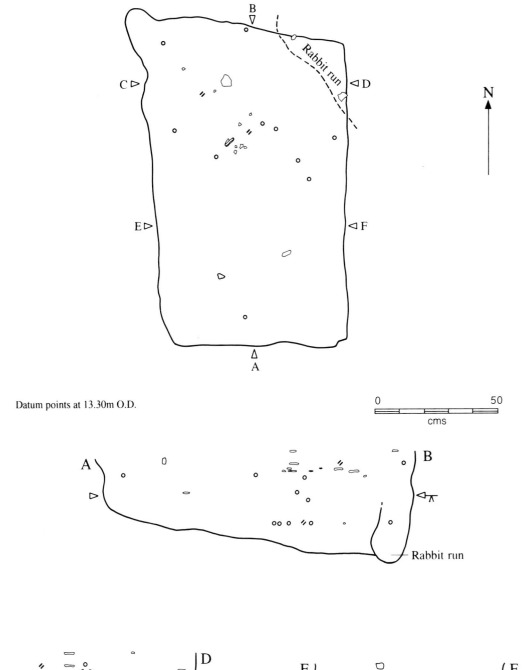

Datum points at 13.30m O.D.

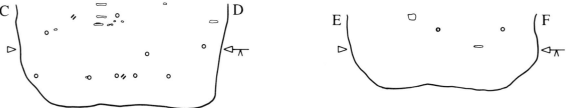

Figure 57 Grave 33, plan, long and cross-sections. Scale 1:15

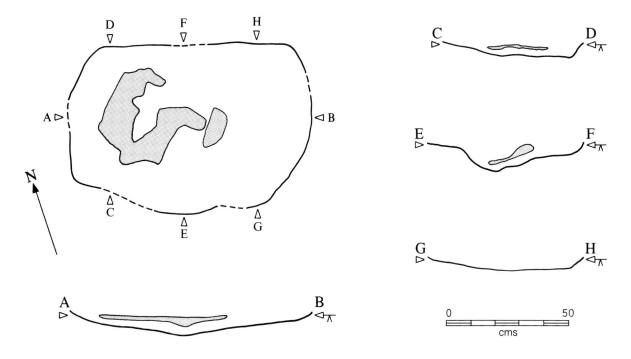

Datum Points at 13.50m O.D.
Figure 58 Grave 34, plan, long and cross-sections. Scale 1:15

slumped considerably from one originally more steeply banked, since at this size it would have swamped inhumations 31, 32 and 34, including ring-ditch *2062* (Fig. 5). Regardless, such a mound might naturally have attracted the attention of robbers or antiquarians, resulting in the proposed robber pit that was excavated. It could also explain the lack of any objects other than small sherds.

The fill of the feature contained fourteen sherds of Anglo-Saxon pottery, deriving from one vessel, *2177*. It has a soft dark grey-brown fabric internally, with slight burnishing. The exterior has a light orange-brown surface. Its core is coarse with frequent grass and vegetation inclusions. Three rim sherds show it to have been a straight-sided vessel.

Two charcoal fragments of gorse stem (*Ulex* sp.) and twelve small burnt flints (weighing 60g in total) were found in the upper levels of the fill. A tiny piece of orange fired clay of a sandy fabric was also recovered. This has the appearance of 18th or 19th-century brick, but the amount preserved is too small for a positive identification.

If the feature is the bottom of a robber trench it is impossible to gain any idea of the former contents of the mound from the fragments redeposited. The pottery could represent a container for offerings or be from primary or secondary cremations, although the total absence of any cremated bone makes this less likely.

Grave-goods: None

Grave 34 (inhumation) (Fig. 58)
Dimensions: 1.00 × 0.68m
Orientation: 284°
Container for body: ?Organic wrapping?
Sex/age: Infant.
Body position: Unknown.

Description: A short squat rectangular grave slightly off-centre within ring-ditch *2062* (Fig. 130). The grave was heavily truncated and disturbed by agricultural activity, and survived to a depth of 0.1m at best, and most typically 40–50mm. Remaining fill was of a light grey sand, homogenous throughout its depth. Showing at the surface on cleaning was a dark grey-black stain in a vaguely rectangular shape. This was also badly damaged but would appear to be the remains of an organic wrapping. There was no body stain discernible but the size of the grave suggests an infant burial in which a body stain would not be expected to survive well.

The ring-ditch was also severely damaged (Pl. XXXI). It had a maximum external diameter of 4.6–4.8m and was narrow with a width of between 0.15–0.42m. This is possibly a result of its upper levels having been truncated, since the U-profile ditch was only between 0.04 and 0.15m deep. It is possible that the ditch was originally penannular; the two ends were reasonably clear of plough activity and occurred at the east end, almost in line with, and on the same orientation as, the grave. Against this, the ditch was shallowest at this point, with no certain evidence of predetermined terminals.

A small piece of burnt flint, *2191*, was found to the north-west of the grave cut within the area of the ring-ditch. Two burnt flint fragments, *2239*, were found within the ditch fill as was a small fragment of charcoal, *2240*, of *Prunus* spp. (which includes wild cherry, blackthorn and bird cherry).

Grave-goods: None

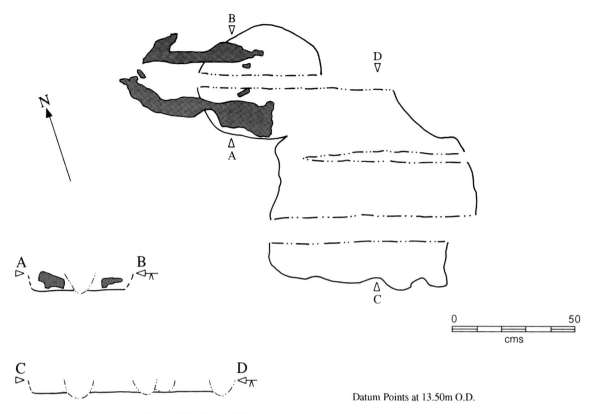

N

A   B

C   D

Datum Points at 13.50m O.D.

0 _____ 50
cms

Figure 59 Grave 35, plan, long and cross-sections. Scale 1:15

Grave 35 (inhumation) (Fig. 59)
Dimensions: 1.14 × 1.03m
Orientation: ?290°
Container for body: None.
Sex/age: Unknown.
Body position: Unknown.

Description: An extremely heavily plough-scarred area in which traces of charred wood, possibly retaining its original structure, were seen. The area was planned and lowered in the usual way to reveal a very shallow layer of mid grey sand. The area is tentatively identified as the ploughed-out base of a grave containing charred wood planks or branches similar to those seen elsewhere on the site. There were no other features nearby from which this charred wood could have been dragged by the plough. The charcoal (*2181*) was all of oak (*Quercus* sp.), including stem (some fast grown) and heartwood (some slow grown).

It is interesting to note that the remains are on a similar orientation to the two nearby graves, 34 and 36, perhaps adding weight to the interpretation of this being a severely truncated inhumation. The shallow nature of the feature and lack of a body stain suggest that if this is indeed a grave, it is that of an infant or young child.

Grave-goods: None

Grave 36 (inhumation) (Figs 60, 61 and 104)
Dimensions: (Feature) 3.22 × 2.01m; (Grave) 2.22 × 1.19m.
Orientation: 299°
Container for body: Body rested on an organic layer, probably of textile.
Sex/age: Male.

Body position: Supine flexed, arms alongside or folded over the body. Head to west.

Description: A large ovoid feature with a fill of fine light grey sand mixing into coarse dark brown natural, containing an irregular sub-rectangular grave cut. The grave appears to have been deliberately cut into a feature best interpreted as an existing hollow within the heathland, since its fill mottles almost imperceptibly into the surrounding natural. The edges of the grave cut were extremely difficult to identify since the fill of light grey sand and light brown sand mixed into that of the feature. The secondary cut of the grave was first seen clearly at 13.22mOD to the east, as a rounded end and showed best when the sand had completely dried out. The cut edge was never visible at the very west end where its presence could only be determined by a more homogenous light grey sand fill, hence the somewhat irregular west end shown on plan. In the upper levels of the fill at the west end and along the northern edge many small flint pebbles were removed. These continued further down, albeit slightly fewer in number, and seem to derive from a band of coarse ironpanned gravel in the surrounding natural.

The body lay on an organic layer which rested on the grave bottom of ironpanned gravel natural. The identification of this organic layer is uncertain. An isolated patch, *2288*, *c*.70 × 70mm, with a solid thickness *c*.2–3mm deep was possibly of leather and was stained with an alkanet-like colorant (no dye was detected). No threads were distinguished and it is unclear whether the patch was originally of textile or leather, or perhaps both. A larger area, 180×23mm, was examined on site, preserved best in the area of *B* and *D*. The textile (a), a rather open 2/2 twill, spinning Z/S with a very loose thread twist, had an even

82

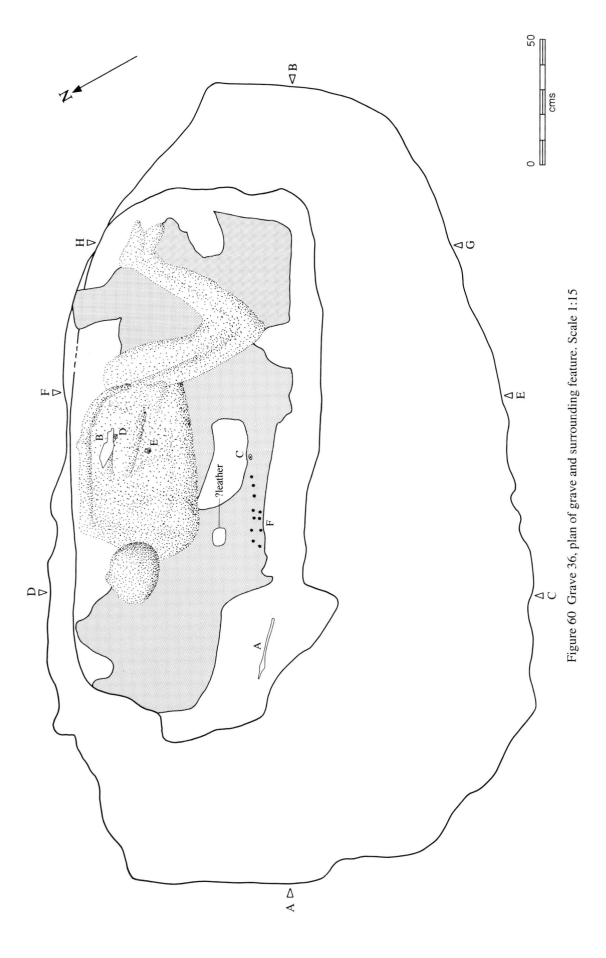

Figure 60 Grave 36, plan of grave and surrounding feature. Scale 1:15

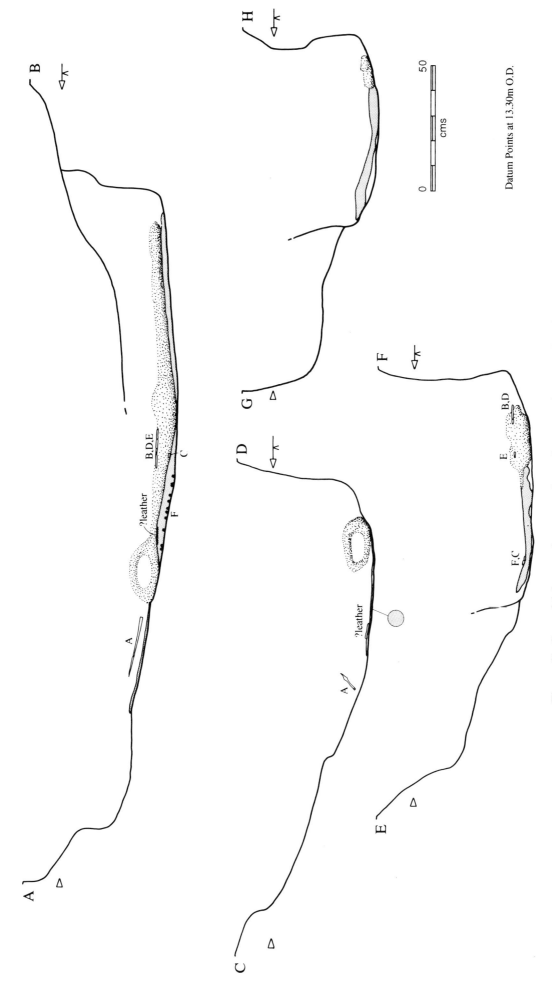

Figure 61 Grave 36, long and cross-sections of grave and surrounding feature. Scale 1:15

weave and thread count 6–9/8 on 10mm. The piece showed one clear reverse of the twill diagonals in the middle, that is, the weave had either a herringbone pattern or a very widely spaced broken diamond. The fibre was of wool; no dye was detected. One other small fragment (b) with light-coloured threads, the spin and weave unclear, was probably a tabby weave.

With the exception of the skull, the body stain was very poorly preserved above the waist. It seems to have been laid supine flexed with the arms by the sides of the body, the right arm possibly folded back up over the chest.

Grave-goods:
A: **Spear** with Fe blade (Swanton D2), length 496mm, lying flat to right of body. Mineralised wood in the socket was of beech (*Fagus* sp.). [2279]
B: Fe **knife**, length 168mm, with traces of the horn handle, which extended beyond the tang. The leather sheath survives as a compact layer patchily surviving over the blade surface and folded over the blade back. It has impressed decoration on one side in the form of four parallel ridge lines spaced 2mm apart running lengthways. Textile remains enveloped the sheath and knife handle but were too intermittent for identification. [2286]
C: 'D' shaped Fe **buckle** loop, width *c*.15mm, in leather binding immediately east of the line of wood *F*, on grave south side. Textile (c) of Z-ply threads were wound round the buckle loop. [2291]
D: **Buckle** with silver-alloy loop and tongue, width 10mm, Ae plate and three dome-headed rivets (no longer *in situ*), placed next to knife *B*, lying upside down on lower chest left side. Textile associated: ?(a), preserved underneath the buckle in an area *c*.15 × 15mm, spin Z/S, of coarse threads with a loose twist. The weave was 2/2 twill, thread count 7–8/8 on 5mm. Coarse 20mm threads (d) lying across (a) were possibly roots. (e), fragments of fine textile of ?wool, Z-spun, were from a 4-hole tablet-weave with cords lying alternately Z and S (estimate *c*.12 on 5mm, wefts *c*.5 on 3–4mm), probably from a fine belt or strap. One separated scrap shows a cut end with the threads curled over, *i.e.* where turned under and sewn to the buckle. No dye was detected. [2343]
E: Ae **buckle** and **plate**, length 21mm. The riveted plate was already broken in the ground and the buckle had become decuprified and disintegrated; it is drawn from an X-ray taken while the buckle was still in a soil block. A 20 × 15mm textile patch associated had dark brown fibres; spin Z/S, weave 2/2 twill, thread count 10/12 on 10mm. The textile was possibly (a), as a reverse in the weave suggests that it was a herringbone or broken diamond weave. The threads were probably animal, but were too degraded for identification. An alkanet-like colorant was detected. Mineralised traces of (e) ?tablet cords also found. [2287, 2344]
F: **Wooden object** along grave south edge to east of spearhead. Traces of wood with the grain running east-west were seen in several patches. The wood identification of one patch of oak (*Quercus* sp.) or beech (*Fagus* sp.), mineralised by association with an Fe corrosion bubble means the object could possibly be part of the spear. (*not illus.*). [2350, 2352, 2353, 2355, 2357–2363]

Grave 37 (inhumation) (Figs 62, 63, 104 and 105)
Dimensions: 1.86 × 0.91m
Orientation: 296°
Container for body: Textile lining to grave.
Sex/age: Male, juvenile?
Body position: Unknown as no body stain survived.

Description: A sub-rectangular grave, cut into ironpanned sand becoming neat and elliptically ended at its lower levels. The fill was predominantly of a mid grey sand with occasional small stones and, in the upper levels, amorphous patches of black humic sand probably representing degraded wood. Two of the more clearly defined patches of unidentified wood are shown on the plan. A tiny piece of iron, *2210*, about 5mm in diameter was recovered at 13.26mOD but fell apart on excavation and could not be identified. In the upper fill a difference was distinguishable between an outer and inner fill, also of elliptical shape, which seemed to reflect the presence of the subsequent textile lining; it disappeared at 13.27mOD when the lining appeared (Pl. LVI).

This grave's excellent surviving textile lining was the best encountered in the excavations, and was examined *in situ* by Elisabeth Crowfoot and extensively photographed. The view of three of these photographs (Pls XVII–XIX) is marked on Fig. 62 I. The textile first appeared as a thin dark brown organic line. The fragmentary nature of the stain means that its top level is incomplete on plan. Lower levels are not included except at the south-east corner. The stain sloped inwards and formed a curious pointed crescent at 13.24mOD at the east end. This shape soon disappeared and perhaps reflects a fold in the textile to bring it around the grave edge. The grave quickly bottomed out and in places the excavator noted that the stain seemed to be in a double layer. It was also noted as being difficult to distinguish between body stain and textile stain. A loose fragment of charcoal from the textile layer was of hazel stem (*Corylus* sp.).

Three weaves were distinguished lining the grave. (a), nearest the probable body position, was of fine blackish wool threads. The largest clear area was exposed to the left of the ?head in an area 380 × *c*.240mm. The spinning was Z/S with one system noticeably finer, the weave a damaged 2/2 twill. (b), in two areas, one 300 × 180mm to the right of the ?head position, and another *c*.110 × 100 lying over the ?head, were from another textile of wool. The spin was Z/Z, both coarse threads very loosely twisted, from a striped weave based on a 3/1 twill with reversing ribs (*Rippenköper*; Fig. 139.3). Over another area, for *c*.200mm length, S-spun threads could be seen; floats, 10mm long, possibly an added stripe to (b), or remains from another weave were followed by a damaged area for *c*.450mm, with another clear area of weave (b) for 65mm. Another fragment of this, *c*.100 × 20mm near a broken edge, could be seen lying over (a). Small preserved samples may indicate other textiles present, possibly of garment remains. The best piece encountered, 5 × 3.5mm, from (b) has all threads Z/Z, loosely twisted. The ?warp is dark brown-black, the weft reddish. Both yarns are of the same quality, of wool, with a thread count 7/7 on 10mm. A few other samples were taken of small scraps, details of which are held in the site archive. No dye was detected, but all the weaves had an alkanet-like colorant. A third possible textile (c) on the back of (b) occurs as 3 × 2mm scraps of Z/Z twill, black, with thread count *c*.9 × 9 on 10mm.

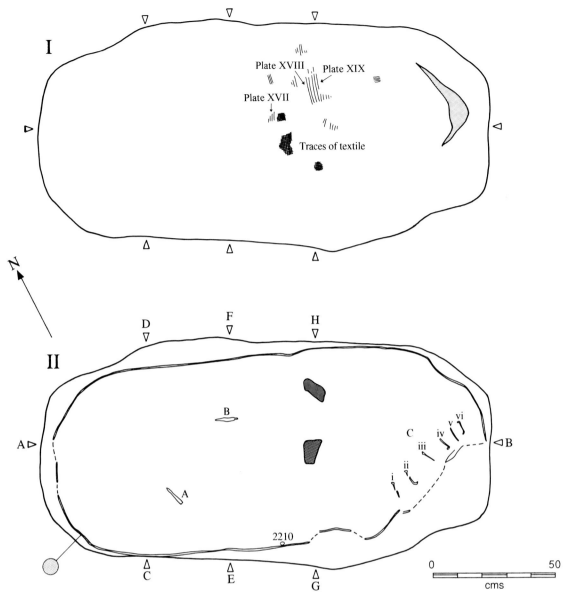

Figure 62 Grave 37, plan. (I) shows specific areas of textile at bottom of grave. Scale 1:15

Plate XVII *Rippenköper* twill weave *in situ*, grave 37
lining (shot located in Fig. 62)

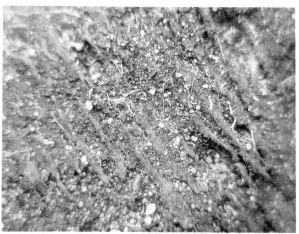

Plate XVIII *Rippenköper* twill weave *in situ*, grave 37
lining (shot located in Fig. 62)

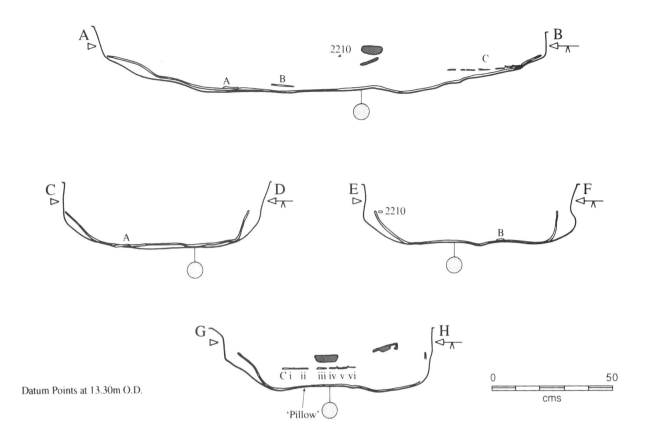

Datum Points at 13.30m O.D.

'Pillow'

Figure 63 Grave 37, long and cross-sections. Scale 1:15

Plate XIX *Rippenköper* twill weave *in situ*, grave 37 lining (shot located in Fig. 62)

87

The plan shows no body stain as the difficulty in isolating it also meant that no parts could be certainly identified. This and the small spear tends to suggest that the body was of a juvenile or child. The position of knife B suggests that the head was at the west end, although the uneven grave bottom formed a possible 'pillow' at the east end like those in graves 7 and 14.

Grave-goods:
A: Small **spear** with Fe head (Swanton ?F1), length 90mm, lying at an angle to the grave south side at the grave base. Mineral-preserved wood in the socket (which was probably butt-joined) was of beech (*Fagus* sp.) or holly (*Ilex* sp.). It had pith present so it is likely to have come from a branch or very young stem. Unidentified degraded textile remains are preserved on the exterior surface. [2277]
B: **Knife** with horn handle, length 92mm. The mineralised leather sheath had hairs protruding from the outer surface (Pls XXXVIII and XXXIX), possibly of calf. Part of a seam survives along the blade edge where a thong fragment is still attached. Two weaves of textile were found beneath the knife. (d) was of S-spun threads *c.*20mm long, Z loose open ply, with traces of Z threads passing through, *i.e.* probably tablet cords from a braid or border; weft count 5–6 on 10mm. Analysis by S. Hardman suggests the fibres are wool. (e), of very deteriorated scraps with medium coarse threads, Z-spun in both systems, is probably the remains of a medium coarse twill, with a thread count of 5–6/6–7 on 10mm. No dye was detected in either but there was pollution from an alkanet-like colorant. [2278]
C: Row of six Fe **staples** (i–vi), some broken, of squared C-shape lying in an east-west orientation at the grave east end. The staples appear to derive from a single object of unknown type and an organic stain line could be seen associated with them in the ground. The object must have been at least 0.4m long but could have been up to 0.6m. Mineralised wood survives with the grain following the line of the clamps. It cannot be identified further but has predominantly uniseriate rays. The thickness of the object as reflected in the clamps varies from 12–23mm and is thicker in the centre. As the wood cross-section becomes oblique towards both ends this suggests the tapering was done by trimming the outer edge after putting the object together but before the addition of the clamps. The clamps were presumably used to join together two boards but there is no obvious sign of this. Lengths: i, 78mm; ii, 70mm; iii, 64mm; iv, 32mm; v, 78mm; vi, 56mm. [2232, 2242–2247]

Grave 38 (inhumation) (Figs 64 and 105)
Dimensions: 1.87 × 1.08m
Orientation: 267°
Container for body: Organic layer at base of grave.
Sex/age: Uncertain.
Body position: Unclear but probably flexed. Head to west.

Description: A shallow sub-rectangular grave cut with a stone-free fill of fine silver-grey sand and some pale brown-grey patches. The uppermost fill also produced several smears of unidentifiable soft charcoal.

Several patches of dark grey staining were seen in the upper levels of the fill and these seem to represent parts of the organic stain seen most clearly at the base of the grave. Whether this organic stain formed a lining to the grave or just a layer beneath the body is unclear; only a few stains, including one reasonably-sized length along the north edge, east end, were seen higher up in the grave fill.

The body stain was difficult to distinguish as it was poorly preserved with the exception of the skull and two longbone lengths, probably representing the thighs. The most likely body position is therefore flexed, facing south, the body possibly lying prone.

Grave-goods:
A: Fe strip, length 70mm, possibly the tip of a **knife blade**. Mineralised macroflora adhere. [2211]
B: Fe **knife**, length 127mm, with traces of the horn handle. The blade is enclosed in a compact layer 1mm thick, which is wrapped over the back and extends over the handle junction by 3mm, but its identification as a sheath is inconclusive. The handle extends just beyond the blade/tang junction. Three areas of a textile nature were associated: (a), an area rusted and deteriorated but with fibres preserved in an area 25 × 30mm, of dark brown threads, ?wool; spin Z/Z, weave twill, probably 2/2, but one system is damaged. The thread count is estimated at *c.*8/9 on 10mm. The weave is loose and in one dark area some of the threads appear to be finer. (b), a very coarse-fibred wool fragment is preserved lying in a curved fold. The threads are spun, some S, some Z, but not regularly in the different systems. Occasional threads suggest this is a twill weave, possibly with stripes or checks, indicated by the change of spin direction. (c), in an area *c.*10 × 15mm, of S-spun threads again lies in a curve, side by side, *c.*7 on 5mm; these were possibly tied round the top of the knife sheath. No dye was detected, but an alkanet-like colorant was. [2212]
C: Fe **nail**, length *c.*20mm, the head bent over at 90°, close to chest area of body. [2213]
D: Fe **strip**, length 48mm, overlying the suggested pelvic area of the body. Mineralised macroflora adhere. [2214]

Grave 39 (inhumation) (Fig. 65)
Dimensions: 1.6 × 0.4m
Orientation: 262°
Container for body: None.
Sex/age: Uncertain.
Body position: Very unclear but possibly tightly flexed in a 'foetal' position. Head to west.

Description: A very fragmentary and badly damaged grave. The northern side was accidentally truncated when seen on the very edge of trial box 11 during trenching in 1985. The grave was only positively identified during further evaluation work in 1990. The upper levels were destroyed by plough damage and the skull of the body had been burrowed through by an animal.

That fill remaining was of light grey sand with darker brown patches mixing in, especially to the east. Soil disturbance made identification of the grave edge very unclear even at the bottom levels. Directly above the head was charcoal smear (i) containing twelve fragments of oak (*Quercus* sp.) stem and heartwood, and nine fragments of

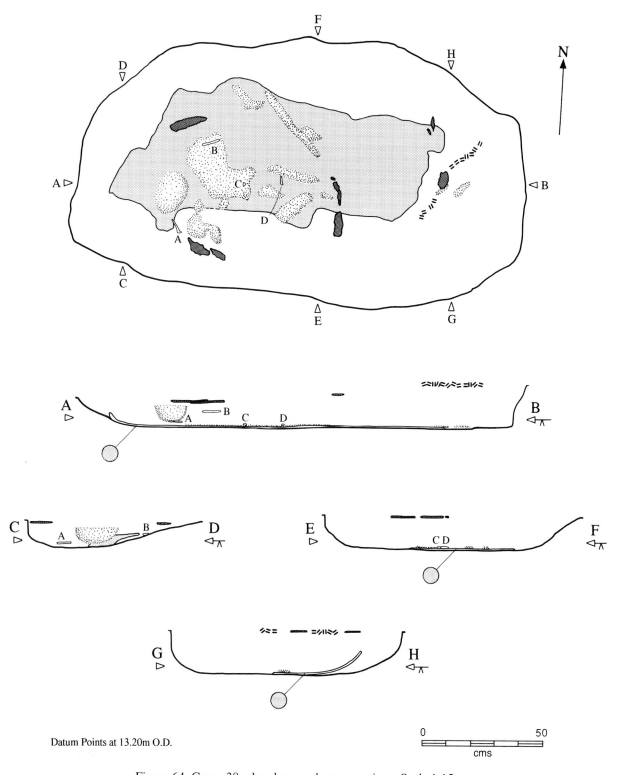

Datum Points at 13.20m O.D.

0   50

cms

Figure 64 Grave 38, plan, long and cross-sections. Scale 1:15

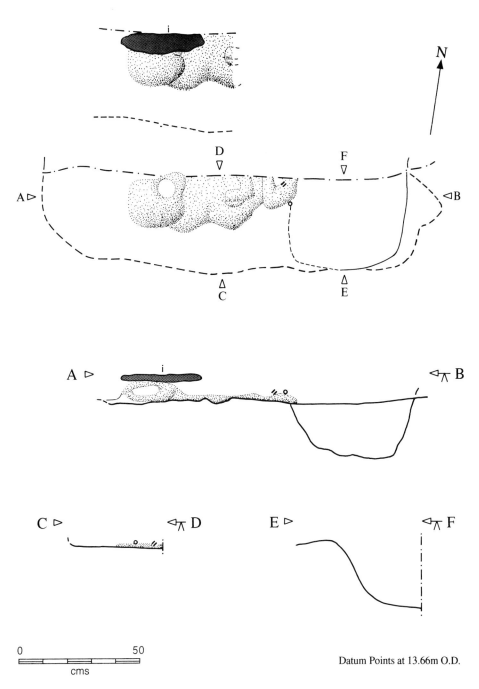

N

0 _____ 50
cms

Datum Points at 13.66m O.D.

Figure 65 Grave 39, plan, long and cross-sections. Scale 1:15

gorse (*Ulex* sp.). The fill yielded a small fragment of burnt flint, *1733*, and a small fragment of charcoal, *1734*. Burnt flint collected from the feature when first excavated weighed 10g. The one piece from the re-excavation was under 5g.

Although very unclear, the body was possibly resting on organic material. The east end of the grave had a curious small pit with a very fine white, almost ash-like sand fill; the body appears to have been laid over this pit.

Grave-goods: None

Grave 40 (inhumation) (Figs 66 and 105)
Dimensions: 1.87 x 0.65m
Orientation: 284°
Container for body: None but rested on an organic layer.
Sex/age: Female?
Body position: Supine extended, right arm crossed over chest, the left crossed so that the hand was by the throat. Head to west.

Description: A highly damaged inhumation. The sub-rectangular cut was difficult to distinguish clearly as ploughing had affected its definition in the upper levels. In addition, ploughing had sheared off the top of the body stain head. A rabbit run swept through the middle of the grave and a probable ferreter's hole had destroyed most of

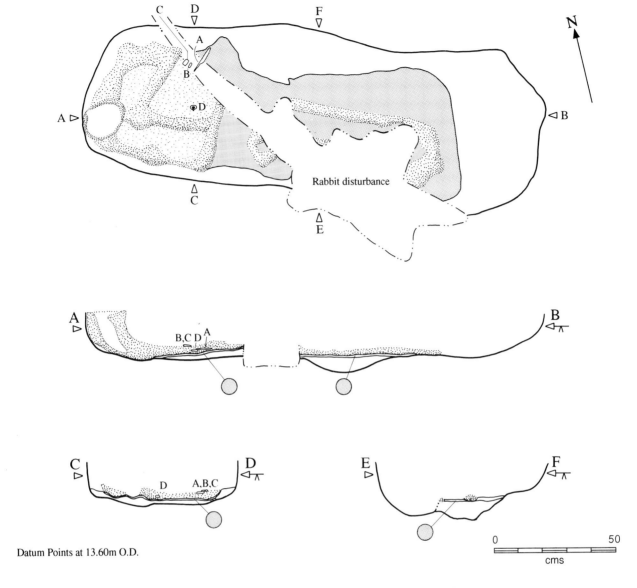

Figure 66 Grave 40, plan, long and cross-sections. Scale 1:15

Datum Points at 13.60m O.D.

0   50
cms

the legs. That fill which survived was light grey and pinkish grey at the surface, and a mix of light and mid brown sand, with some grey mixing lower down. The soil was relatively stone-free except fairly high up at the west end.

The body stain was reasonably well preserved and rested on an organic layer of unknown type which, in the chest area, mixed into the body stain. Although shown as in the rabbit run on plan, the grave-goods were in fact just beneath its bottom and apparently undisturbed by this activity. Elsewhere around the edge of the grave was light yellow sand, possibly trample.

Grave-goods:

A: Fe **knife**, length 126mm, badly corroded with traces of a horn handle. Only textile survives on the blade, probably from two weaves; (a) near the handle, a clear patch 9 × 11mm, spin Z/Z, threads medium twist, hard fibres with worsted appearance. It is an even tabby weave, thread count 9/13. A deteriorated area lies across the blade and round the side, suggesting a tape or wrapping, but no edges are preserved. (b), a fragment 13 × 7mm on the point of the handle, shows a thread count of 9/9 on another scrap, probably tabby, spin not clear, with a very smoothed surface. A small area beneath is more like (a). [1747]

B: Fired clay **bead** with large hole, incomplete, found next to knife *A*. The orange colour may derive from its proximity to Fe knife *A*. An associated mineralised fine **textile**, spin ?Z, is possibly a tabby weave but is too deteriorated for identification. [1748]

C: Small **sherd** of pottery found near *A* and *B* (*not illus.*). [1749]

D: Fe **buckle** of small size, width 25mm, completely covered in badly degraded mineralised textile (c), spin Z/S, apparently fine twill. (d), above the tongue, was seen in a small area, 4 × 7mm. It was coarser and again probably a twill. [1761]

91

Grave 41 (inhumation) (Figs 67 and 106)
Dimensions: 1.10 × 0.67m
Orientation: 270°
Container for body: None.
Sex/age: Unknown, probably juvenile.
Body position: Unknown as no body stain survived.

Description: A shallow irregular rectangular grave cut. The fill was an amorphous mix of coarse silver-grey and pale brown sand throughout, with frequent root disturbance. The fill had several inclusions of peagrit gravel. The upper fill contained several small unidentified charcoal patches; no other stains were noted. Some burnt flint was collected in the uppermost levels but was not otherwise recorded. The size of the grave cut and the complete absence of any body stain suggests that the grave was that of a child.

Grave-goods:
A: Mineralised **textile lump** preserved in an area *c.*30 × 17mm. Z/S spin, thread twist medium to loose. The weave is a slightly open 2/2 twill with thread count *c.*11/12–13, and no reverses. It was originally an even weave but the surface is poorly preserved (*not illus.*). [1921]
B: Fe **knife**, length 116mm, with horn handle and traces of a leather sheath. No grain pattern survives but fine hairs protruding from the outer surface layer of corrosion products were identified as calf. Bulky deposits of mineralised textile on both sides could not be identified. [1922]

Grave 42 (inhumation) (Fig. 68)
Dimensions: 1.10 × 0.34m
Orientation: 294°
Container for body: None.
Sex/Age: Infant/child.
Body Position: ?Extended. Head to east.

Description: A rounded rectangular cut filled throughout with an homogenous coarse-grained dark grey sand. Within the upper levels were two black organic stains, possibly of degraded wood. A ring of dark brown/black body stain with coarse fawn sand inside, probably representing the skull remains, was seen at 12.98mOD and an organic stain was noted following the cut line down at the grave east end. No other traces of body stain were noted.

Grave-goods: None

Grave 43 (inhumation) (Figs 69, 70 and 106)
Dimensions: 2.87 × 1.18m
Orientation: 280°
Container for body: Coffin or ?textile lining.
Sex/age: Uncertain, juvenile?
Body position: Unclear but probably extended supine with head to west.

Description: A long sub-rectangular grave cut with a fill of mid grey and grey-brown sand with occasional small stones. These probably derive from a band of ironpanned gravelly sand through which the grave cuts. The fill had lenses of a darker brown sand in parts which highlighted a long central oval shape of a light grey stone-free sand.

This oval lens faded out midway down the fill but does not seem to represent a later cut into the grave. The extent of this oval is shown on the sections but not on the grave plan.

Within the oval lens, a series of charcoal and black degraded wood stains were found. They lay in the upper levels at the west end above where the body's head is suggested to have been. This apparent placing of material over the head seems to be paralleled in other graves (see Chapter 6 section II, pp. 243–4). The charcoal was of oak (*Quercus* sp.), mostly stem although some was sapwood (not from a narrow stem) and heartwood.

The organic lining in the grave was first noticed at 13.28mOD, patchily at first but eventually extending to an oval shape at the grave base (Pl. XX), about 10mm thick at most. A number of patches of textile were seen within this organic stain at the grave base and they suggest that the whole stain represents a single textile lining to the grave, as is suggested in several other graves. The layer was seen higher up within the fill along the north and south edges but only appeared at the east and west ends very low down, suggesting that it was principally lining the long sides of the grave cut. Two samples were examined. *2002* included Z and S threads some very coarse and lightly spun, probably from a twill weave. The deteriorated fibres were of fine to medium wool with an alkanet-like colorant present. *2003* had similar threads, some finer and redder, again of wool with an alkanet-like colorant.

The body stain was very poorly preserved, typically a smear within the bottom organic stain, of slightly different colour and texture. The body seems to have been laid supine extended, with the head at the west end. If this interpretation is correct then the knife may not have been worn but laid on or by the side of the body as it was upside down relative to the head.

Grave-goods:
A: Wooden **box** or **casket** represented by a small group of fittings including the drop handle (i), length 60mm, a fragment of the split-spike loop (ii) and possible corner brackets (iii and iv). The drop handle has only the remains of textile and roots but the loop that attached it to the box pierces a cross-section which means that it was probably mounted on the edge of one of the sides. Textile is also preserved in a position which suggests that it was possibly present between the handle and the box. The possible corner brackets, with rectangular section pins, appear to be mounted on the cross-section. Their length may indicate the board thickness as being a minimum of 15mm. The box appears to have been made from maple (*Acer* sp.), but could be lime (*Tilia* sp.) or cherry (*Prunus* sp.). Corrosion has meant that the objects are drawn from X-rays taken whilst in a block of sand, with details of sections added. [1942]
B: Fe **knife** with horn handle, total length 180mm. A layer of corrosion product encrusts part of the knife block and overlaps the handle by 7mm; it may be the remains of a sheath but the identification is inconclusive. The blade is covered on both sides by extensive textile remains of five weaves, also extending onto buckle *C.* (a), over the upper knife blade, an area *c.*30 × 30mm showed decayed textile with Z/Z spin and loosely twisted threads in a very loose weave, probably twill but distorted; count originally *c.*8–10 range in both systems. The wool fibres are now very

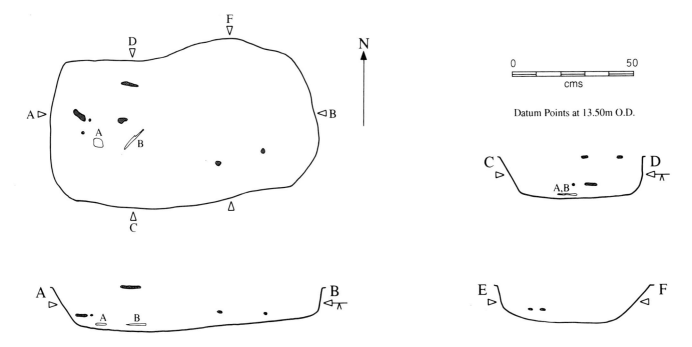

Figure 67 Grave 4, plan, long and cross-sections. Scale 1:15

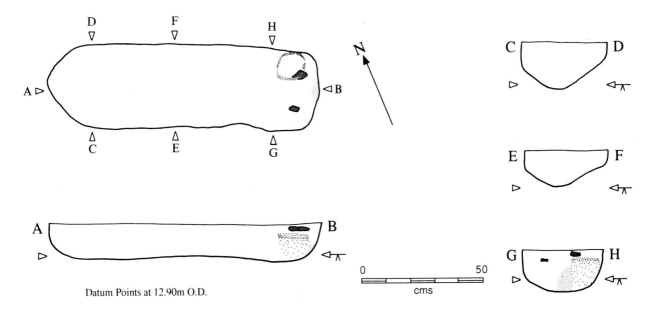

Figure 68 Grave 42, plan, long and cross-sections. Scale 1:15

Plate XX Organic lining in grave 43, during excavation

Plate XXI Grave 44 within larger oval feature 0738.
Mound 4 in background

black and friable with some scale pattern. (b), lying along the blade edge for *c*.70 × 15mm are the remains of a fine textile, again very black, spinning Z/S; here it is certainly a 2/2 twill with thread count *c*.16–18/*c*.20 on 10mm. Over an area 30 × 25mm lies one clear patch of textile, (c), spin Z/S, both threads medium to loose twist. The Z?warp is much broken, the S?weft very coarse. This must also have been a twill with a thread count *c*.5/3–4 on 10mm. This fabric may be responsible for coarse overlying threads on other pieces. Present on all pieces of (c) with some clear patches (the best 15 × 20mm) lies (d), a fine Z/S-spun 2/2 twill; thread count at least 16–18/14, the colour here is slightly reddish. The fabric is very like (b). (e), in large areas, the best 40 × 40mm; at least two layers of a very dark brown wool survive with spinning Z/S. The threads are pulled and deteriorated, the weave twill but not clear; thread count *c*.8–9/8 on 10mm. (All the wool samples were similar, with the addition of an occasional coarser fibre with a medulla.). There is a slightly clearer scale structure on some fibres; all are of wool and all are stained with an alkanet-like colorant. During conservation it was noted that the textiles had a rough inner surface caused by the weave and a smooth outer surface. [1943]

C: Ae **buckle** with rectangular **plate**, length 17mm. The plate is broken at the end and the tongue and half of the loop were already broken in the ground. Detached from the buckle was an area *c*.45 × 35mm of crushed layers of two weaves similar to those on *B*, one resembling weave (e), but at one end a clear patch 15 × 15mm of (d), reddish, with a count *c*.20/18 (9 on 5mm). The quality of both is that of good broken diamond twills, but there are no signs of clear reverses. [2087]

Grave 44 (inhumation) (Figs 71 and 72)
Dimensions: (Feature) 3.51 × 1.88m; (Grave) 1.74 × 0.58m
Orientation: 270°
Container for body: None.
Sex/age: Unknown, adult.
Body position: Prone, head resting against grave west end. Right arm resting alongside body beneath pelvis, left arm folded across the waist beneath the body.

Description: A neat rectangular grave, cut through a large oval area (*0738*) of fine light grey/white stone-free sand (Pl. XXI). It is unclear how this feature was formed. Although its proximity to mound 4 raises the possibility of it being a quarry pit, the fill suggests that it could be a natural hollow in the heathland. The fill of the grave cut showed from the top of this area and was a slightly darker mid grey colour. Some small pieces of ironpan were found in the upper layers of excavation as was a small quantity of burnt flint but it is unrecorded whether this came from the grave cut or from the wider feature.

The body was buried without any grave-goods (at least any that survived). It was a well-preserved stain showing the body to have been pushed up against the grave west end as though thrown in from the east. Although the fill was stone-free, a large flint was found immediately east of the head overlying the shoulders. This apparently deliberate inclusion, and its implications for the body buried, are discussed more fully in Chapter 6 section II, pp. 249.

Grave-Goods: None

94

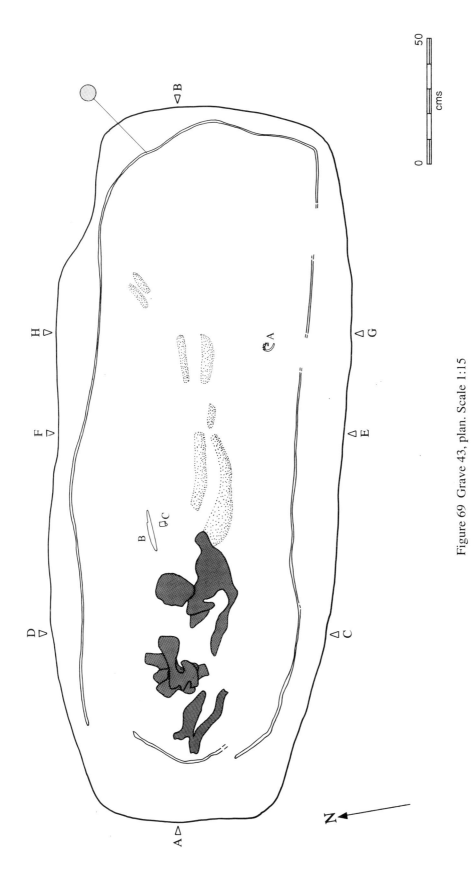

Figure 69 Grave 43, plan. Scale 1:15

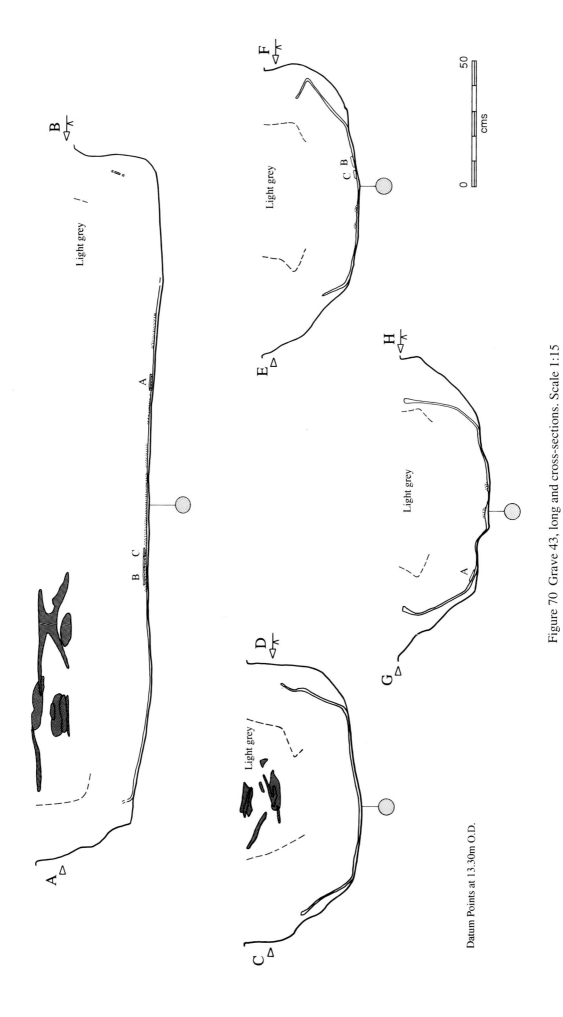

Figure 70 Grave 43, long and cross-sections. Scale 1:15

Datum Points at 13.30m O.D.

96

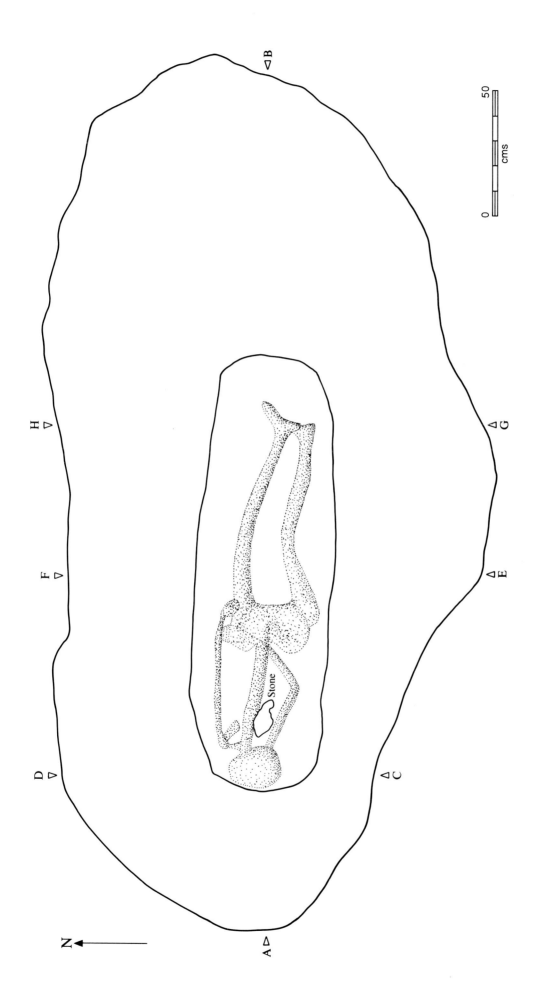

Figure 71 Grave 44, plan of grave and surrounding feature. Scale 1:15

97

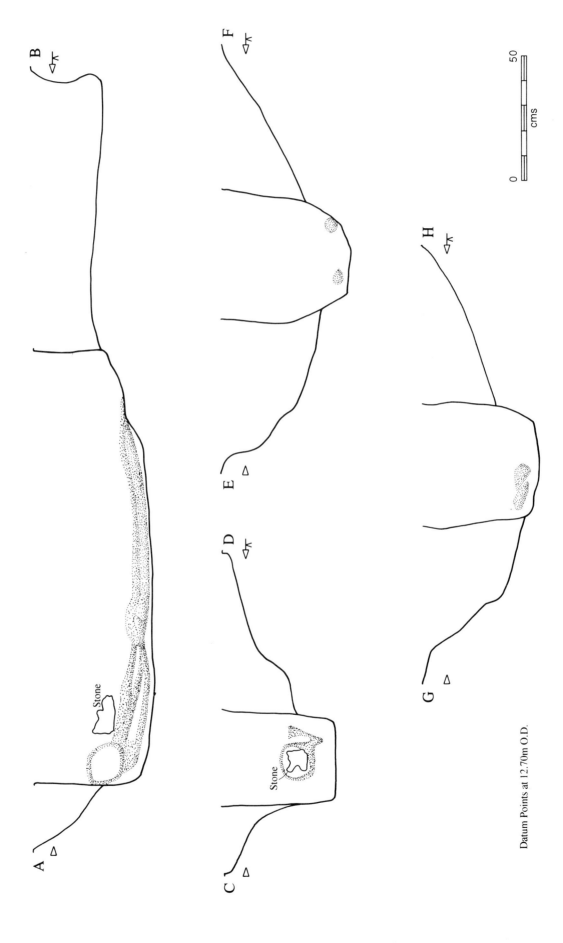

Figure 72 Grave 44, long and cross-sections across grave and surrounding feature. Scale 1:15

Datum Points at 12.70m O.D.

Stone

Stone

cms

0

50

98

Grave 45 (inhumation) (Figs 73 and 106)
Dimensions: 1.95 × 0.65m
Orientation: 309°
Container for body: Coffin or organic lining, probably of textile.
Sex/age: Male.
Body position: Supine extended, legs straight and arms laid alongside body. Head to west.

Description: A regular sub-rectangular cut with steeply sloping sides, severely damaged in its upper levels by the plough. The cut contained a mixed fill of stone-free coarse brown and fine grey sand with some ironpan inclusions, mixing in as amorphous patches. Tip lines could be seen in places throughout the fill, the inner lenses of dark brown gravelly soil resting on orange-brown sand. A few patches of soil containing burnt flint were noted at the very top and bottom of the fill but are not marked on the plans.

The organic lining was first seen running along the grave south edge at 13.13mOD, soon extending all around the grave although always very fragmentary at the east end. The stain divided into a double line at the upper levels of the west end. This was originally thought to represent the dipping away of a bowed container lid and the top edge of the container wall. Subsequently the lines rejoined making this unlikely. The effect might have been created by a flexible organic that had been folded — the top edge could then divide into two lines which subsequently rejoined.

The organic material was probably textile, as three samples of the stain, taken when it first appeared along the south edge all proved to contain threads. Unfortunately, these did not survive in a weave. An organic stain obscuring, and apparently over, the body stain perhaps represents a covering of textile. Three fragments of charcoal from this organic stain were of *Prunus* sp., probably blackthorn (*P. spinosa*).

The body stain was generally poorly preserved, especially in the area of the chest and skull, merging into the associated organic stains. Although thin, enough survived to demonstrate the extended supine position with arms lying at a slightly higher level to the rest of the body. The legs were well preserved with a central core of very dense body stain.

Grave-goods:
A: **Spear** with Fe head (Swanton C2), length 275mm, blade lying (edge vertical) along southern side of grave, west end. Mineralised wood in the socket is of hazel (*Corylus* sp.). [1856]
B: Fe **knife** with a horn handle, length 148mm, leather sheath and unidentifiable mineralised textile remains. The sheath, 1.5mm thick, is folded over the blade back and overlaps the handle junction by 2mm. Fine hairs protrude from the outer surface of the layer, confirming the identification of leather. [1923]
C: A patch of very deteriorated **textile** initially thought by the staining to represent a belt buckle. The textile fragments survive over an area 11 × 8mm, spin Z/Z of loose to medium twist with occasional finer threads in one system; ?2/2 twill, thread count *c*.10/8 (4 on 5mm). Some coarser loose-spun Z threads are stained by Fe. No dye detected (*not illus.*). [1917]

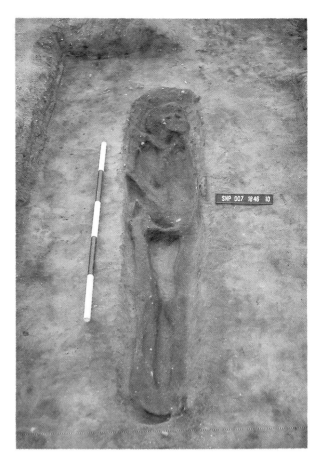

Plate XXII Grave 46 fully excavated, showing body stain. Scale rod 1m

Grave 46 (inhumation) (Fig. 74)
Dimensions: 1.94 × 0.52m
Orientation: 248°
Container for body: None.
Sex/age: Unknown, adult.
Body position: Supine extended, right arm bent over waist. Body squeezed into the grave.

Description: The grave cut burnt stone feature *1775*. It was first excavated as a quadrant in the south-west corner until recognised as a grave and was then lowered in spits in the normal way. The fill consisted of an homogenous light grey-brown sand with numerous inclusions of charcoal (0.71kg) and burnt flint (4.18kg) redeposited from the burnt stone feature. The concentration of these thinned out to the east. The abundant charcoal and burnt flint in the quadrant first excavated was unrecorded. The charcoal derives from a large mass of gorse (*Ulex* sp.) roundwood/stems but also includes three fragments of *Prunus* spp. which includes wild cherry (*P. Avium*), bird cherry (*P. padus*) and blackthorn (*P. spinosa*).

The body stain was perfect and the best preserved on the site (Pl. XXII). Some bone was preserved within the core of parts of the body stain, notably the skull, but all were too badly degraded to say anything other than the body was that of an adult. The grave cut was barely large enough to take the body which had been squeezed in, the bottom of the cut being slightly sloped down to the north.

Grave-goods: None

99

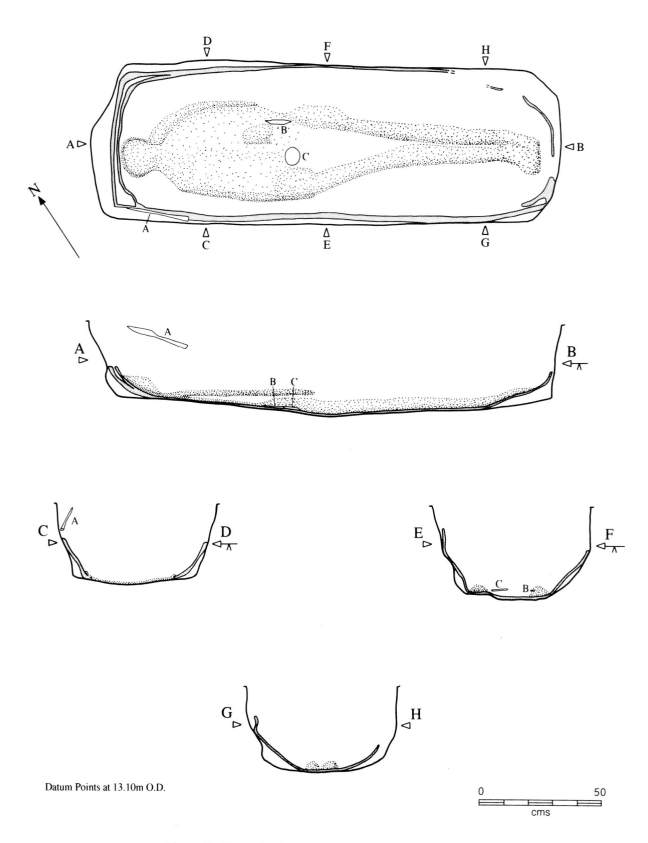

Datum Points at 13.10m O.D.

0   50
cms

Figure 73 Grave 45, plan, long and cross-sections. Scale 1:15

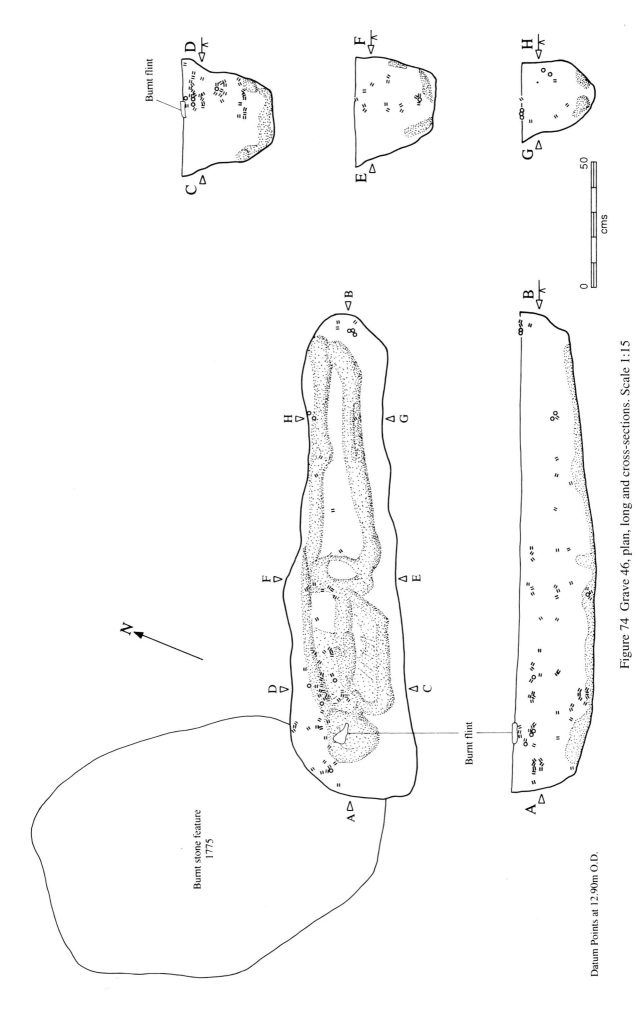

Figure 74 Grave 46, plan, long and cross-sections. Scale 1:15

Burnt flint

Burnt stone feature 1775

N

Burnt flint

Datum Points at 12.90m O.D.

50

0

cms

Grave 47 (inhumation) (Figs 75, 76, 77, 107, 108, 109 and 110)
Dimensions: 3.53 × 1.37m
Orientation: 289°
Container for body: Small dugout logboat.
Sex/age: Male, possibly adolescent.
Body position: Unknown, possibly supine extended. Head to west.

Description: A large sub-rectangular grave cut filled with a mix of mid grey and yellow sand. The upper levels were of a dark/mid grey sand which soon developed into a tripartite division running the length of the grave, with a southern band of yellow sand, northern band of yellowish grey and central band of mid grey sand (Pl. XXVI). These bands subsequently developed into the approximate edges of the logboat contained within the grave. The north edge of the grave at the lower levels had a fill of redeposited yellow natural which made locating the cut line very difficult. The upper levels of the grave had been very severely damaged by ploughing and animal activity, narrowly missing bucket *F*, damaging horse head *S* and destroying pot *2026*. This vessel is represented by six sherds found at the surface level of the grave and in a rabbit run descending from the area of the scatter. It is possibly once a cremation urn judging by the three small cremated bone fragments recovered from the scatter. It is of a mid brown fabric with small sandy inclusions and is decorated with an applied linear boss. The fabric is of a uniform colour throughout, except the boss, which has a lighter brown core and is orange-brown immediately beneath the surface. The exterior has burnishing, the interior has wipe marks. Because of the fragmentary remains it cannot be said whether this was an urn buried in the upper fill of grave 47 or immediately adjacent to it.

The grave cut maintained a regular shape throughout, gradually narrowing to form more of a trench in which the boat was deposited (Pls XXVII and XXVIII). The edges sloped steeply in and formed a step along the north edge of the cut at about 12.70mOD, especially at the centre, evening out to the west end. The fill was relatively stone-free, including only very small stones (up to 10mm in diameter) and the grave was cut into almost pure yellow sand ironpanned in parts.

At its upper levels the cut had an almost oval outline with two bulges at the west end, on the north and south sides. Two more clearly defined D-shaped bulges were seen at the very uppermost levels at the east end, north and south sides. Together they form a regular arrangement, almost certainly representing four post-holes of a structure originally above the grave cut. The features all disappeared quickly, suggesting that only their very bases were seen, the upper levels having been destroyed in the ploughsoil. These features are omitted from the long section for clarity. Three pieces of burnt flint with a weight of over 10g and two flint flakes, *1829* and *1909* (*not illus.*) were found in the grave fill.

The grave had several traces of organic materials, the most significant being patches *1826* and *1827* which first emerged at 13.09mOD. It is not certain whether the two joined, although this is likely. *1826* was of textile, the best area 13 × 7mm in two layers of reddish staining. It was of Z/Z spinning with loose thread twists, very variable with some threads very coarse. The weave is uncertain with an estimated count of *c*.6 on 5mm in one system. No dye was detected but like all textiles from the grave tested for dye,

it had an alkanet-like colorant (see pp. 214). Both patches seem to have been laid over the eastern bow and into the boat, lapping over the gunwale although they were not seen immediately adjacent to the boat stain. The arrangement suggests that the boat was interred and slightly backfilled before being covered or lined in textile and having grave-goods placed within and upon it. The stain was very thin (1–2mm thick) but quite distinct. In addition to the textile, a pillow seems to have been deposited, judging by the mineralised feathers associated with the spearhead bundle *D*. Esther Cameron comments that they parallel those thought to be goosedown found in the mound one ship burial at Sutton Hoo, that had filled a woven linen pillow-case (Bruce-Mitford 1983, 889). Other discoveries of feather pillows in Merovingian graves are cited by Bruce-Mitford.

Other small and amorphous organic patches were seen, which possibly represent patches of turf incorporated into the backfill. Organic stain *1881* included charcoal of *Prunus* spp. which includes wild cherry (*P. avium*), bird cherry (*P. padus*) and blackthorn (*P. spinosa*) perhaps suggesting that it was a piece of wood. A small fragment of charred roundwood, *1938*, from alder (*Alnus* sp.), hazel (*Corylus* sp.) or dogwood (*Cornus* sp.) lay at the bottom of the boat. A concentration of thin spreads along the line of the cut at the west end, characterised by retaining moisture, may possibly represent some form of organic lining or revetment to the grave. However, they may also be associated with the animal activity following the edge of the cut in this area.

The horse head could be directly linked to the grave through the identical form of its tack *U* with fragments *B* and *R* found within the boat. These show that the head was buried resting on its chin, wearing its harness, which was perhaps draped down into the main burial deposit. The difficulty with this interpretation is the lack of clear stratigraphic evidence to link the head with the upper edge of the boat grave. The head had been buried at a shallow depth and the cranium heavily plough-damaged, leaving only the lower part of the skull and jawbone undamaged. Although looked for, no cut for the head was recognised, perhaps as a result of the plough damage but also possibly because of its presence in the upper 'intermediate' soil layer in which cuts were often not visible (as noted with cremations elsewhere on the site). To the north of the boat grave, the line of another feature was seen extending a few centimetres out from the baulk but this disappeared before it could be planned accurately. It is unknown whether this represents another inhumation or another type of feature. The possibility that it was a cut containing the rest of the horse must be stated, but given the position of the head (on its chin, not its side), its location (to the north-west of the grave cut) and the lack of other bone elements in the surrounding topsoil, notably vertebrae, this seems unlikely. The head should therefore be considered a single deposit.

The boat left one of the best stains recovered in any of the graves at Snape, and its clarity enabled planning accurate enough for a computer-reconstruction and hydrostatic assessment to be made. This and further aspects of the boat's design and construction are discussed elsewhere (Chapter 5 section II). The stain was first seen at 12.93mOD at the west end bow, which rapidly assumed a regular pointed shape. Both bows showed before the rest of the stain gradually emerged, linking the two ends. They

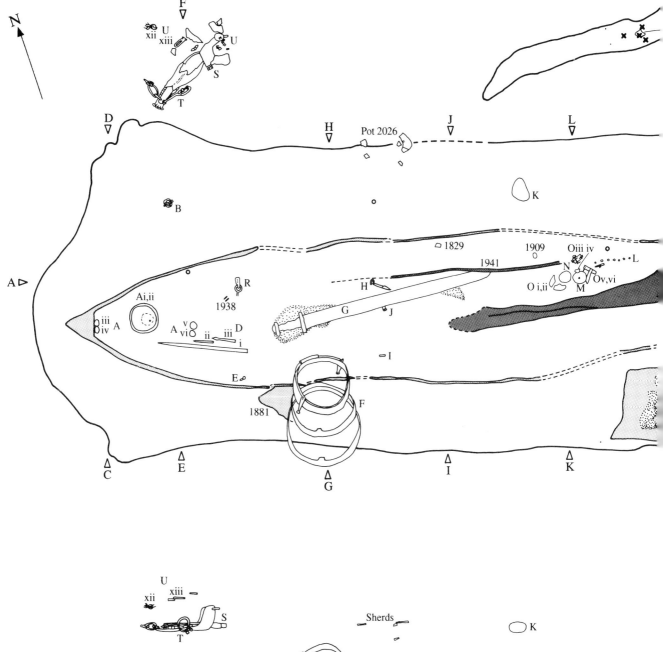

Figure 75 Grave 47, plan and long section. Scale 1:15

N

Pot 2026

P

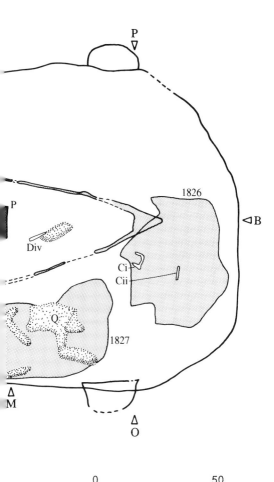

1826

◁ B

Div

Ci
Cii

Q

1827

Δ
M

Δ
O

0 _____ 50
cms

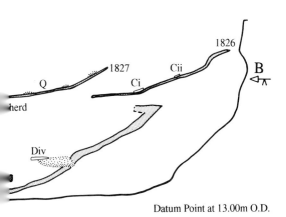

1826

1827

Cii

B
◁

Q

Ci

herd

Div

Datum Point at 13.00m O.D.

show the boat to have been approximately 3.09m from bow tip to bow tip, with a beam of about 0.62m. The grave plan uses dotted lines to show the highest original extent of the stain.

Both bows remained as regular V-shapes, forming a solid triangular stain. There was no evidence for the type of thick internal thwart or bulkhead fitting seen in the boat from grave 4. There was also no evidence for any patching, although Fe nail *E* was recovered from the centre of the stain. Sections showed a well-rounded base to the boat (Pl. XXIX). A small area of the boat's north side had been charred at the west end. The thinness of this charring (about 5mm) makes it likely to have been only on one surface of the boat, probably the interior. This charring and other small fragments mineralised by association with various metal objects show the boat to have been made of oak (*Quercus* sp.).

The base of the boat proved to be a complex of stains, mixing with many grave-goods, notably the complex *L–O*. Those areas identified as body stain were very small and it was impossible to use them to suggest the body position. However, the suggested pillow implies that the head was at the west end. In addition, the space restrictions at the bottom of the boat, not least because of the many grave-goods, make it most likely that the body was laid supine extended, with the sword placed on the chest.

Grave-goods:

A: **Shield** with Fe **boss** (i) (Dickinson and Härke Group 6), diameter 130mm, height 80mm; straight Fe **grip** (ii), length 132mm; and two pairs of decorative Fe **studs** (iii–vi), diameter *c.*32mm set some 0.15m from the shield boss along top and bottom edges. The shield had apparently been laid over the gunwale of the boat's western bow (Pl. XXIII) and subsequently slumped in. The boss is a low curved cone with rod apex and five rivets, one of which has an internal Ae washer. The board studs have slightly domed heads; two of the rivets have washers visible, marking the inside of the board. The rivets are the same length as those on the boss, of *c.*9mm. The boss preserved mineralised traces of two *pinnae* (leaflets) of bracken (*Pteridium aquilinum* (L.) Kuhn) on the surface. The shield board was of willow (*Salix* sp.) or poplar (*Populus* sp.), the grain running vertically to the axis of the grip, with a radial surface. The same orientation on the grip probably indicates a cut-out type. Leather is present between the wood and iron on both the boss rim and grip suggesting that the shield board was covered on both sides by this material. The eastern pair of studs (v) and (vi) preserve mineralised shield board with an oblique surface and leather between the shield board and head of the stud. The thickness of the shield board at this point, 9.4–11.8mm, suggests that it tapered towards the edge. [1908, 1886, 1890, 1916]

B: Fragment of **tack** associated with horse tack fragments *T, U* and horse head *S*, consisting of an Fe ring with two Fe distribution loops each terminating in a pair of flat plates with three Ae rivets for securing the straps. [1831]

C: Pair of Fe **clamps** resting on textile layer *1826*, immediately south-east of the boat east end. On (i), width 44mm, mineralisation has preserved on the outer side, layers of coarse textile overlain with random organic material including stems and leaves.

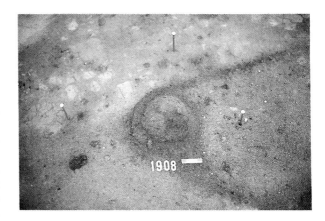

Plate XXIII Grave 47, shield boss *Ai* laid over boat west bow

The clamp was attached to wood of alder (*Alnus* sp.) or hazel (*Corylus* sp.) with the grain at an oblique angle on both points. Associated with the clamp is a nail (*not illus.*) with mineral-preserved alder wood (*Alnus* sp.). The nail pierces a cross section of the timber and the grain is diagonal on the shank which may mean that the nail was used to secure the wood, or as a repair (in a mitre joint?). Coarse textile is also preserved on the nail head. Clamp (ii), width 62mm, is slightly larger, with alder (*Alnus* sp.) all over the inside and over the points but with no indication of a joint. The points pierce a tangential surface board, with grain perpendicular to the length of the clamp. Coarse textile is preserved on both sides of the clamp. The evidence therefore suggests that both (i) and (ii) clamped the same object, that was of alder. [1830, 1876]

D: Bundle of three **spears** with Fe heads. Spear (i), length 384mm (Swanton C3), has an Fe **ferrule** (iv), length 78mm, giving an approximate spear length (tip-to-tip) of 2.3m. Mineralised wood in the socket of the head is of ash (*Fraxinus* sp.) from mature timber, and mineralised traces in the ferrule socket suggest a possible surface coating on the wood, perhaps of paint or a varnish.

Mineralisation has preserved the remains of feathers (Pl. XXIV) on the underside of the head, suggesting the former existence of a **pillow**. The feather shafts, 15–25mm long, are slightly curved but are too poorly preserved to enable the genus to be identified. Prof. C Perrins (Dept. Zoology, University of Oxford) considered them to be consistent in size and shape with those from the body parts of birds comparable in size to a chicken or duck.

Some fine mineralised threads lie across the spear shaft end. On the upper side, for 90mm along the metal, mineralised textile (d) is preserved, the widest patch 20mm with spin Z/Z, thread twist medium to loose, weave probably twill; thread count in one system ?10, the other deteriorated, ?7–8. Its general appearance suggests (a) on sword *G*, but it is probably another finer twill wrapping the spears.

Spear (ii), length 90mm (Swanton F1), preserves mineralised wood, possibly hazel (*Corylus* sp.) in the socket and the remains of an adjacent spear shaft on the outside of the head. Textile survives in a mineralised area 60 × 15mm, spin Z/Z, threads

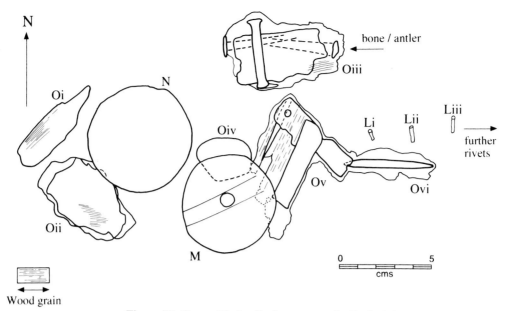

N

Oi

N

Oiv

bone / antler

Oiii

Li   Lii   Liii

Ov   Ovi

further rivets

Oii

M

0   5
cms

Wood grain

Figure 77 Grave 47, detail of grave-goods. Scale 1:2

medium to loose twist, ?(d) twill very similar to that on spear (i) but one thread system badly decayed; a small fine fragment is possibly only the fibre side of leather.

Spear (iii), length *c*.107mm, a pair with (ii) (Swanton F1), preserves mineralised hazel wood (*Corylus* sp.) in the socket and areas of possible textile. Textile remains in the soil from round the spearheads and shafts. Twisted threads from a damaged weave, ?(d), are scattered over an area *c*.20 × 30mm; coarse threads, medium twist, occasionally lying in pairs suggesting a twill weave. No count is possible. (e), a small area, 9 × 17mm, is clear among scattered scraps on wood from the shafts, showing ten threads, S-spun, medium twist, lying closely side by side. There are possible traces of a cross-system, also S-spun, spaced *c*.5mm apart, in one place passing over two of the ?warps, suggesting that this may be the remains of a tape or braid going round the shaft. Another scrap, detached, is shaped as if to curl round an edge. A loose sample from the grave, *c*.15 × 13mm, again shows seven S-spun threads. [1914]

E: Fe **nail**, head diameter 16mm, found within the boat stain preserving mineralised traces of oak (*Quercus* sp.). The nail pierces a tangential surface and seems to have been positioned in the side of the boat. The nail head preserves mineralised stems or roots. [1907]

F: Wooden **stave bucket** of flat sawn yew planks (*Taxus* sp.) bound by three Fe hoops with a twisted Fe handle. Mineralisation had preserved *pinnae* of bracken (*P. aquilinum*) on all three hoops, especially on the upper two. The bucket appeared to have been forced into the natural, most probably at burial, because the bottom hoop straddled the edge of the grave cut. Post-depositional forces are unlikely to have pushed the bucket so far laterally into natural so the bucket was probably rammed snugly into the grave edge, which might also account for the bucket hoops later slumping into the grave cut. Original height *c*.0.46m, diameter 0.53m. [1822–1824]

G: Fe **sword** with two-edged pattern-welded blade and horn grip, within a mineral-preserved scabbard, total length *c*.0.924m. The scabbard had a leather covering, over willow (*Salix* sp.) or poplar (*Populus* sp.) stiffening sheets with a longitudinal radial surface orientation. Its length is unknown as it is incomplete; width 62mm, total thickness of extant remains 17mm. Two wooden plates, hollowed to a thickness of 2.5mm at the central axis, 1.5mm at the edges, enclose the blade. They are lenticulate in cross-section. The wooden scabbard edges survive in two lengths, 60mm on one, 27mm on the other, marked 1.5mm in from one edge with a scriber or similar tool. The consistent thinness of the wood and the neatness of its edges attest a level of precision in Anglo-Saxon scabbard manufacture which has only recently been recognised (*c.f.* Schiek 1992, tafel 35). Similar signs of carpentry practice are a feature of wooden debris from the scabbard of an unpublished 6th/7th-century sword from grave 91, Mill Hill, Deal, Kent. A hairy animal skin, cut to the dimensions of the sword blade, lined each scabbard side, hair innermost against the sword blade. This technique was designed to accommodate the pelt in a confined space and was a common practice in scabbard construction of the Early Medieval period. The hair fibres, short and densely grown, were too encrusted for identification. The scabbard was originally covered with leather but only a few small fragments survive, insufficiently preserved to identify the genus. A 10 square mm area shows a wrinkled effect, the cause of which is not at present understood. Unusually, the scabbard mouth is reinforced with an incomplete wooden binding, the grain direction transverse; metal fittings, binding tapes or cords occur more frequently. Another wooden example, in Maidstone Museum (cat. KAS 827), belongs to a scabbard known to come from the cemeteries of Sarre or Bifrons in Kent. A thin willow wood belt from Buckland, Dover (grave 20) provides further evidence for the use of flexible wooden strips in the 6th and 7th centuries AD. The sword had broken into three pieces by corrosion whilst still in the ground. The uniquely well-preserved sword grip is presumed to be of cattle horn and was moulded with individual finger recesses (Cameron and Filmer-Sankey 1993).

Along the blade for 210mm, an area shows patches of two mineralised textiles: (a) in crumpled folds, the widest area c.45mm, of a very coarse weave, spin probably all Z/Z with thread twist loose to medium; weave 2/2 twill, variable, thread count 7/6 on 10mm. (b) is in patches further up the blade, the best c.18 × 22mm. This may be more of (a) but seems noticeably coarser. It is again Z/Z spin, weave 2/2 twill, with thread count 5/5 on 10mm. One lump has a visible coarse knot which includes one S-spun thread. (c); other fragments mineralised round the tip of the blade, and in a double layer or fold may include part of the scabbard; these show finer layers underneath, coming up round the sword hilt. Other mineralised areas again suggest fine scraps, the best lengths c.80 and 50mm, lying in folds, apparently a fine tabby weave but not clear under microscope examination. The textile is not related to the scabbard's construction but may have been burial wrappings for the weapon. There is no indication of the means by which the scabbard was suspended although buckle J was found midway along the blade's length. [1939]

H: Fe **knife** with horn handle, length 102mm, tucked into or attached to belt J. The blade is enclosed in a leather sheath 1.5mm thick, folded over the blade back. It is joined along the cutting edge and overlaps the handle junction by 8mm. Part of the seamed edge survives as a 13mm sinuous line running from the blade tip; further along the blade edge, a 5mm thick length of thong is embedded in the seam. A mineralised lump of **textile** (g) was preserved immediately adjacent along one side; above, an edge curls up from a woven ?tape, width 8mm, simple selvedges, spinning Z/Z, very even. Thread twist medium to loose, a fine tabby weave, thread count c.32/22–24 on 10mm. Underneath this is another tabby fragment, possibly the same but it looks coarser. The appearance of both suggests flax. Underneath both are traces of a coarser weave, Z/Z-spun threads with loose twist, probably 2/2 twill, ?(d). [1954, 1955/2076]

I: Fragment of loop-headed Fe **pin**, length 20mm, probably of round cross-section, possibly a buckle tongue. Attached is mineralised macroflora mostly of feathers (strays from the pillow associated with *Bi*?). [1956]

J: Ae **buckle loop** and **plate** shattered by decuprification whilst in the ground. No pin survives and the fragility of the piece has meant that only the loop, width 10mm, could be illustrated. [2078]

K: A large stone of quartzite with slight bruising on the edges, possibly representing a **maul**. This identification is perhaps strengthened by the general lack of large stones occurring naturally on the site (*not illus.*). [1819]

L: Large **comb** associated with object complex M, N, O, represented by seven surviving Fe rivets, each 6 to 8mm long, which preserve three sections (c.3mm thick) of mineralised antler, presumably the comb's component plates. A radiograph of the block from which the rivets were extracted seems to show a curved back suggesting that the comb was single-sided and approximately 130mm long. Rivet (ii) has a piece of mineral-preserved horn from an adjacent object on the head; (iii) has a thin platelet of a tabby weave across its base. Rivets (vi) and (vii) have fibres lying across their tops, not twisted into a yarn. They were identified by Anna Cselik as of sheep/goat or horse body hair, and may belong to an object that the comb was lying on, or under. Rivet (vii) also has a sliver of wood associated, possibly ash (*Fraxinus* sp.) that could have been from a possible **container** for the comb and objects M, N and O. Poorly-preserved oak wood (*Quercus* sp.) with a tangential surface associated with the line of rivets probably represents the floor of the boat although there might also have been a box in the area. [1950]

M: Pottery **spindle-whorl**, diameter 51mm, made from the wall of a pot, of an even, well fired grey-brown fabric with a few sand grains. The interior and exterior surfaces are a dark grey-brown, with crazed surfaces. There is no sign of burnishing. The edges are uneven and irregular but well smoothed. The fabric appears to be Anglo-Saxon. Associated with L, N, O. [1952]

N: The footring and very base of a **Roman greyware pot**, diameter 57mm, of a well fired even light grey sandy fabric, wheel-thrown with smoothed under-surface to the footring. The upper edges that form the base of the bowl are well clipped down to form a rough circular shape. It was found footring down. Associated with objects L, M, O. [1953]

O: A **complex** of objects (i–vi) (see 1: 2 detail, Fig. 77) contained within several layers of dark organic staining. Many pieces are mineralised but are difficult to differentiate by material even after conservation. (i) and (ii) are confirmed by SEM as of leather, consisting possibly of three layers. (i) contains an iron fragment, (i) and (ii) wood and possibly textile. (iii) is also an agglomeration of iron and organic material, mainly wood, including beech (*Fagus* sp.) and fleece. A patch of mineralised textile (f) is associated, c.25 × 30mm, with fine threads, Z/Z-spun, loose twist, even tabby weave, thread count 15/16 threads on 10mm. A radiograph shows three iron components. First is a fragment of a plate or band, width 22mm, embedded in wood. A rivet, 35mm long and 5mm wide with two flattened terminals passes through the complex N–S and finally an iron nail, barely traceable, extends E–W. A small peg, possibly of bone/antler, 9mm in diameter at the head and 38mm long, was also revealed. (iv) is a sliver of horn preserved as a black substance, beneath spindle whorl M, in a layer 1–2mm thick.

Piece (v) is another agglomeration that contains wood and iron fittings. The longer of two iron strips lay beneath the spindle whorl M at one end. There were possible textile fibres at one end of the wood nearest the iron, and animal fibres lay on a small platelet of iron corrosion (perhaps similar to those seen on one of the rivets to comb L?). The block included two iron tools, an awl with a hazel (*Corylus* sp.) handle and a tool with a handle probably of beech (*Fagus* sp.). (vi), length 50mm, is a small iron awl with a mineral-preserved handle, probably of willow (*Salix* sp.) or poplar (*Populus* sp.), made from a branch (as the pith is present), mounted centrally on the tang. The

Plate XXIV Grave 47, mineralised feather on spearhead *Di*

Plate XXV Grave 47, possible animal offering *Q* on organic layer *1827*

Plate XXVI Grave 47 upper grave fill with logboat bow stain emerging to west (right) with organic layers *1826* and *1827* to east (left). Note division of the soil fill colours

Plate XXVII Grave 47 at excavation level 14. The spear bundle is emerging to the west (right) as is horse tack fragment *R* to its north (below)

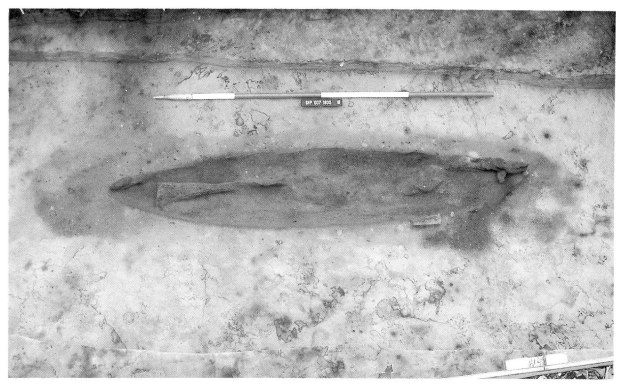

Plate XXVIII Grave 47 fully excavated. Sword *G* at centre, spear bundle *D* to west (right) and object *P* to the east (left)

Plate XXIX Section through Grave 47, looking west, midway between section K and M shown in Figure 76. In centre of boat is ?wood object *P*, to the right comb *L* rivets are being isolated for extraction as a block

outer surface is flattened and has traces of spun yarn, mineralised antler (from the comb) and horn.

The group is most curious and difficult to make much sense of as a whole. Some pieces are possibly fittings to some form of a container, perhaps a rectangular wooden box that also contained items *L*, *M* and *N*. (*i and iv not illus.*) [1951]

P: Wooden **object** at grave base, with some charred wood, one deriving from ash (*Fraxinus* sp.) and two of maple (*Acer* sp.). This was initially interpreted as a paddle but the charcoal could make it another example of an inclusion of charred wood. (*not illus.*) [1936]

Q: Body stain interpreted as an **animal offering**, resting on organic layer *1827* (Pl. XXV). It is likely that the organic layer was of textile like the other spread, *1826*, immediately to the east. The body stain was seen in two spits, best at the second level. The overall plan suggests a complete animal rather than a joint of meat. (*not illus.*) [1825]

R: **Strap connector**, length *c.*60mm, forming part of the horse tack *T* and *U* associated with the horse skull. The piece consists of two interconnected Fe rings, the ends beaten into flattened plates, each pair clasping mineralised leather from straps, secured by three Ae rivets. [1915]

S: **Horse's head** (*Equus caballus*) recovered at the surface level of the grave north-west corner. The bone had been damaged by ploughing and parts had begun to form a body stain. Ploughing had scattered bone and the tack *U* around the immediate area. The head is associated with the boat grave through the tack fragments *U* found at the surface and *B* and *R* found within the grave fill. The upper skull had been mostly destroyed, leaving only the roof of the mouth, maxillary teeth and mandible, still clenched around bit *T*. From the cheek teeth, the horse was probably an old individual at death, at some 20–30 years and was rather small in stature, probably a pony; its canine teeth show it to have been a stallion. A full discussion is contained in Chapter 5 section IX. Bone from the skull was radiocarbon dated to cal AD 430–670 at 2σ (GU–5233; 1460±70BP). [1773, 1774, 1778, 1787, 1789]

T: Fe two-link **snaffle bit** found *in situ* between the jaws of horse head *S*. It is now broken in two (i and ii). Fragment (ii) has a second ring corroded together with the cheek ring, not apparently fixed by any metal hook or riveted plate. This may possibly have been attached originally by means of only organic loops to the cheek ring. Diameter of cheek rings *c.*62mm. [1783, 1784]

U: Scattered Ae and Fe fragments of **horse harness tack** (i–xiii). The fragments are all small, typically broken, and apparently removed from their original position by ploughing. The fragments are characterised by being parts of thin Fe strips or plates, sandwiching leather strap elements, secured by two or three simple Ae rivets (i–x). One fragment (xi) has a 10mm diameter circular mark, apparently the void of a larger-sized rivet head with a 3.5mm diameter shaft, which might have acted as an anchor for additional support or was perhaps a repair.

Two other fitting types, again found scattered loose around the horse skull, were (xii), an Fe figure-of-eight hook with two Fe D-loops for fixing straps, and (xiii), an Ae plate, broken so that just over half survives of what was apparently a symmetrically arranged piece (surviving length 40mm). As it remains, the plate has a rounded end, and an end that steps in, then out, ending with two prongs. This may originally have been the edge of rectangular slot, mirroring that which survives. A rivet at each end of the piece suggests that it was probably originally placed or used lengthways. XRF shows it to be copper alloy with tin and lead, the latter two enhanced on the coated surface at the front. The reverse is clearly scoured by file marks. Other fragments of the harness, *B* and *R*, were found within the boat itself, to the south. All fragments except (xiii) are drawn from X-rays. [1773, 1776, 1778, 1786, 1788, 1790]

	1	2	3	4	5	6	7	8	9	10	11	12	13	14	15	16	17	18	19	20	21	22	23	24
Annular brooch		×			×			×			×			×		×								
Penannular brooch																								
Small-long brooch														×					×					
Cruciform brooch										×				×		×								
Pins											×													
Beads: glass		×						×		×	×			×		×								
amber		×			×			×		×	×			×		×			×					
crystal										×						×								
other											×								×					
Pendant spacer																								
Loop/collar/bead fastening		×									×					×								
Wrist clasps					×					×						×								
Spindle whorl																								
Tweezers																		×						
Knife		×	×	×	×	×		×	×	×	×					×	×	×	×	×	×			
Knife ring		×						×		×						×		×	×					
Buckle			×	×	×		×				×							×	×		×			
Belt-plate/belt fittings				×																×	×			
Strap-end																				×				
Drinking vessel				×														×						
Ae bound vessel									×															
Fe bound bucket																								
Pottery vessel		×			×	×	×							×										
Sword																								
Shield boss			×			×															×			
Shield studs			×																					
Shield grip			×																		×			
Spearhead	×		×			×											×			×	×			
Spear ferrule			×																					
Lyre																								
Awl																								
Animal offering																								
Staples/nails																								
Glass claw beaker	×																							
Finger ring	×																							
Strike-a-light and steels																								
Box/casket																								
Miscellaneous metal																				×				
Comb																								
Sherds				×	×	×										×				×				
Textile/leather	×																			×				
Miscellaneous glass	×																							
Unidentified object	×	×										×								×				
Horse tack																								

Table 1 Grave-goods from inhumations

25	26	27	28	29	30	31	32	33	34	35	36	37	38	39	40	41	42	43	44	45	46	47	
																							Annular brooch
			×																				Penannular brooch
																							Small-long brooch
																							Cruciform brooch
		×				×																×	Pins
			×																				Beads: glass
		×	×																				amber
																							crystal
															×								other
		×																					Pendant spacer
																							Loop/collar/bead fastening
																							Wrist clasps
																						×	Spindle whorl
																							Tweezers
×		×				×	×				×	×	×		×	×		×		×		×	Knife
		×																					Knife ring
×		×				×	×				×				×			×				×	Buckle
×			×								×												Belt-plate/belt fittings
																							Strap-end
																							Drinking vessel
							×																Ae bound vessel
																						×	Fe bound bucket
			×																				Pottery vessel
																						×	Sword
							×															×	Shield boss
							×															×	Shield studs
							×															×	Shield grip
						×	×				×	×							×			×	Spearhead
							×															×	Spear ferrule
							×																Lyre
																						×	Awl
																						×	Animal offering
												×	×									×	Staples/nails
																							Glass claw beaker
																							Finger ring
						×	×																Strike-a-light and steels
																		×				×	Box/casket
							×						×									×	Miscellaneous metal
																						×	Comb
×			×					×							×							×	Sherds
												×				×				×			Textile/leather
																							Miscellaneous glass
											×											×	Unidentified object
																						×	Horse tack
25	26	27	28	29	30	31	32	33	34	35	36	37	38	39	40	41	42	43	44	45	46	47	

Grave	Sex	OP	Object	Position on object	Measurement	Fibre	Dye	Spin	Weave	Thread Count	Comments
2	F	0940	Ae link?	round metal	-	min.	-	Z or Z-ply	threads	fine	-
		1254–9	Teeth	traces and fragments jammed round	10×8	unident.	n.d.d.	Z/S	not clear	-	-
		1261	B, detached	loose (a)	13×9	wool	?pigment n.d.d.	Z/S	2/2 twill	10/10	loose spin
		1262	C, chain, ?beads	patches	-	min.	-	Z	not clear	-	fine
		1267	D, annular brooch	underneath (b)	10×10	det.	n.d.d.	Z/Z	2/2 twill	est. 13/10	with skin (?)
		1268	E, annular brooch	above (a)	traces	-	-	Z/S	2/2 twill	est. 6/5 5mm	dark brown loose twist
				other side (b)	18×10, 9×8	det., min.	n.d.d.	Z/Z	2/2 twill	c.10/12 and 6/7 on 5mm	even spin, fine thread and strip 14×9
		1272,	F, knife and Cu	under half, area (a)	width 25mm	?wool	n.d.d.	Z/S	2/2 twill	15/12	2 layers, reddish and dark brown
		1274	alloy ring	nearer ring (b)	c.15×10 exposed	?wool	n.d.d.	Z/Z	2/2 twill	7/9 on 5mm	loose spin, finer
				under ring (c)	-	?wool	n.d.d. no pigment	-	-	-	fine fibres, not hair
		1280	F, knife	from (a) over ring	width 5.5	leather	-	Z,S-ply	-	-	?strap of bag
				other side of ring	L.20mm	min.	-	one Z/S	thread	-	loose
				patches	-	min.	-	-	-	-	traces wood, leather, threads
				sheath fragment (d)	13×12	min.	-	Z/Z	2/2 twill	c.15/13	appearance flax
3	M	0777	A, spearhead	patch, ferrule	20×9	min.	-	Z/Z	2/2 twill	c.7/6–7	damaged, thread missing; thread diam c.1mm
		0954	C, Cu alloy buckle	underneath (a)	30×38	?wool	n.d.d.	Z/Z	2/2 twill	c.8 on 5mm	fine, loose spin
				pin, next to metal (b)	32×22	?wool	n.d.d.	Z/Z	2/2 twill	12–14/12–14	even spin, weave
				G, K, N scraps ?(a)	-	-	-	-	-	-	-
4	J	0960	B, Fe buckle	all over inside ring	9×9	min.	-	Z/S	2/2 twill	-	very fine, damaged
		1001	C, Fe stud, wood ?box	top and edge	-	min.	-	Z/-	-	-	damaged textile underneath, leather
5	F	0696	A, annular brooch	top of brooch (a)	13×10, 30×13	wool	indigotin	Z/Z	2/2 twill	10/10, 10/8–9	3 folds round
			L, shoulder	under (a), ?(b)	27×12	wool	n.d.d.	Z/Z	2/2 twill	10/8	?surface raised
									tubular selvedge	11–12 warps	damaged
		0753	B, annular brooch	under (a)	55×35	wool	n.d.d.	Z/Z	2/2 twill	10/10	folds over pin
			R, shoulder	under (b)	15×10	wool	?tannins	Z/Z	2/2 twill	12/6–8	folds under pin
		0737	C, wrist clasp	detached (c)	35×8	wool	n.d.d.	Z/Z-ply	tablet 4-hole	10–12/12	cords S; edge
				fragments edge	13×30	hair	pigmented	-	pattern, wrapped	-	guilloche plait
		0699	D, wrist clasp	sewn, S-ply (c)	14×45	wool	pigmented	Z/Z/Z-ply	tablet braid	cords 6 5mm	sewn, underside to sleeve
				(a) or (b)		hair	pigmented	-	pattern, wrapped	-	
		0751	E, buckle: waist	area above ?(a)	38×35	wool	n.d.d.	Z/Z	2/2 twill	8–9/8	fragmentary
						wool	-		2/2 twill		with ?leather
				adhering (d)	3×3	hair or silk		unspun	?tabby	3/c.24 in 3mm	?warp bundles
		0845	G, knife	detached (a) or (b)	13×5	min.	-	Z/Z	twill	-	threads

Grave	Sex	OP	Object	Position on object	Measurement	Fibre	Dye	Spin	Weave	Thread Count	Comments
6	M	0779	D, knife	end blade, near hilt	10×13, 5×5	min.	-	-	?twill	fine	underside, leather
7	?	0990	B, textile	lump	16×15	min.	-	Z/Z	2/2 twill	9/10 on 7mm	loose spine, even weave
8	F	0848	A, annular brooch	front, over bone (a)	18×10	wool	-	Z/Z	2/2 twill	10/8	loose weave
				and under pin	10×6						
				under, protruding (b)	L. 9mm	semi-min.	-	Z, S-ply	4-whip cord	-	fastened to (a) by thread
				through beads (c)	L. 19mm	-	-	Z, S-ply	threads	(3)	-
		0849	D, knife	along ring; detached ?(a)	30×15, 12×11	-	-	Z/Z	?twill	-	degraded
		0851	C, annular brooch	above, and under pin (a)	26×24, 45×13	wool	n.d.d.	Z/Z	2/2 twill	10/8	loose twist; ?all same weave
				under (a), (d)	5×6	min.	-	Z/Z	tabby	7/8–9 on 5mm	?2 double lines, stripe?
9	?	0661	A, wood bowl	on Cu rim	-	min.	n.d.d.	Z	?string	-	traces
		0847	scraps from 0661	loose	20×18	wool	-	Z/Z	2/2 twill	-	
				on metal and wood	c.23×20		pigmented and unpigmented	Z/Z	2/2 twill	c.6/6	loose twist, striped light and dark threads
				lump from rim	40×40					-	
10	F	0810	G, knife and ring	on both sides (a)	8×5	min.	-	Z/S	2/2 twill	10/11	loose spin and weave
				(b)	31×13, 22×10	min.	-	Z/Z	2/2 twill	c.10/11	no reverses
		0811	E, wrist clasp	underside (c)	6×3.5	min.	-	ZZZ, S-ply	tablet weave	-	decayed. Sewing, hole, S-ply thread
		0812	F, wrist clasp	front (c)	12×25	wool	n.d.d.	ZZZ, S-ply	tablet weave 4-hole	16/16	Cords, 12–13S, 1Z, 1S; pattern as on 0699, grave 5
						hair			wrapped pattern	(8 on 5mm)	
				detached ?(b)	-	?wool	-	Z/Z	twill	-	medium, confused
		0816	B, cruciform brooch (large)	under front (d)	25×23	min.	-	Z/Z	tabby	16/14–16 (8/7–8 5mm)	tight folds, tucked under catch
				under (d) ?(b)	35×18	min.	-	Z/Z	2/2 twill	-	fine
				on detached knob (d)	20×18	min.	-	Z/Z	tabby	16/17	even
		0817	A, cruciform brooch (small)	on bone, back of head (b)	34×30	wool	-	Z/Z	2/2 twill	9–10/12	very even spin, weave, no reverses
				front, head and behind ?(b)	52×35	min.	-	Z/Z	2/2 twill	12/12	layers, deteriorated, no reverses
		0818	C, cruciform brooch (small)	front ?(b) area against cross	40×40	min. animal	-	Z/Z ?S or S-ply/Z	2/2 twill ?border	12–14/12	all down back patches
		0820	B, detached	?from brooches (d)		min. ?flax	-	Z/Z	tabby	17–18/16	folds; even spin, weave; thread diam 0.3mm
11	F	1341	A, annular brooch (frags)	under ring, pin (a)	20×14	unid.	n.d.d.	Z/Z	2/2twill	12/9	coarse fibres, loose spin
				D (with bones)		animal ?wool					
				G detached (b) ?wrapped around	11×7	animal ?wool	n.d.d.	Z/Z	?tabby	c.8/6	hard thread, tight twist
14	F	0735	C, annular brooch (small)	on back (a)	13×16	min.	-	Z/Z	-	-	-
				and to front (a)	9×8	wool	n.d.d.	Z/Z	2/2 twill	c.14/12	fine, even spin
				protruding (c)	-	-	-	Z, S-ply	thread	-	?from beads
				detached (d)	25×2–3	wool	n.d.d.	Z/S-ply	tablet 4-hole	est. 10 cords/16 wefts	8 weft loops visible

115

Grave	Sex	OP	Object	Position on object	Measurement	Fibre	Dye	Spin	Weave	Thread Count	Comments
14 (cont'd)	F	0783	B, small-long brooch	front plate (a)	9×12	semi-min.	-	Z/Z	2/2 twill	c.8/8	loose, pulled diagonally
				below bridge (c)	-	semi-min.	-	Z or S, Z-ply	threads	-	coarse, bound round
				detached (b)	25×23	det.	n.d.d.	Z/S	2/2 twill	8–10/8	-
				?from above ?(a)	13×7	-	light brown	no spin	-	-	folded fibres
						?wool			threads		
								Z,S ply	?twill	-	
16	F	1282	C, cruciform brooch	head end (a)	45×30	wool	n.d.d.	Z/Z	?2/2 twill	c.9/9	open weave, distorted
				under (a) 2 layers (b)	90×90	wool	indigotin & yellow (alkanet)	Z/Z	2/2 twill	c.10–11/8–10	finer threads
				border (b) (c)	width 8mm			Z/Z	tablet, 4-hole	6 cords/8–9	S,Z,S,Z,S
		1283	D, [pair annular	layers on top and pins (b)	35×13	wool	as above	Z/Z	2/2 twill	10/10	thread medium twist; layers
		1284	B, [brooches	detached (c)		wool	as above	Z/S-ply	tablet cords, 4-hole	-	loose in block
		1125	H, [pair wrist	area under plate (b)	40×22	wool	n.d.d.	Z/Z	2/2 twill	12/11	medium spin, folded double
		1127	G, [clasps					Z/Z	tabby	-	
				behind broken clasp (d)	13×14	wool	n.d.d.	Z, S-ply/Z	tablet braid 4-hole	10 cords on 9mm	fine reddish (sewing threads seen by KW)
18	M	0776	B, knife	on blade	20×20	min.	-	Z/Z	2/2 twill	7–8/8	even, tight spin
				other side, hilt	7×7	min.	-	Z/?	-	8/8 on 7mm	weave not clear
			C, buckle with knife	alloy strip	25×9	min.	-	Z/Z	2/2 twill	10/10–11	originally even weave (all frags prob. same)
19	F	1223	C, knife, ring	both sides blade	-	det.	-	?Z	?twill	-	with wood, badly damaged
		1224	D, small-long brooch	top of brooch (a) and sample E	L.40mm 10×6	hemp	undyed	Z/Z	tabby	11–12/14	loose twist even spin and weave
				screwed up (b)		semi-min.		Z	twill and tablet tabby	-	fine threads
				end of brooch (d) (sample R)	25×8–9	wool	?red dye	Z/S	tabby	20 (10 on 5mm) /5	?tape, brown, no edges preserved
		1225	E, small-long brooch and bead	protruding (e)	L.5mm	?hemp	undyed	Z, S-ply	guilloche plait	4 threads	as on grave 5 wrist clasp 0737
				underneath (c)	25×14	min.	see A below	Z/Z, S-ply	tablet weave 4-hole	5 cords/6–7 wefts on 5mm	loose twist, cords S,Z,Z,S
				adhering to (c) (b)				Z/S, Z/Z	twill	-	underneath
				detached ?(c)	L. c.25mm			Z/Z, S-ply	tablet weave	-	edge, cords Z,S on twill Z/Z
			sample A	detached (c)	L.20mm	wool	red/purple ?orchil	Z/Z, S-ply	tablet weave	4 hole, 7 cords	edge, S,S,Z,S,Z,Z
			beads sample M	protruding (e)	-	-	-	?Z, S-ply	guilloche plait	4 ends	
20	?M	0692	B, buckle	top, strap end (a)	60×20	min.	-	Z/Z	2/2 twill	11/10	folds; thread diam 0.5–0.6mm
				on loop (b)	14×12	.min.	-	Z/S	2/2 twill	-	
				detached (b) ?under (a)	9×8	min.	-	Z/S	2/2 broken diamond twill	c.20/18	reverses clear; even spin

Grave	Sex	OP	Object	Position on object	Measurement	Fibre	Dye	Spin	Weave	Thread Count	Comments
20 (cont'd)	?M	0694	E, strap end	detached on ?(a) ?leather	15×10	wool	-	ZZZ	2/2 twill	-	even spin, weave
		0695	B, ?buckle plate	on pieces ?(a)	17×15	det.	-	ZZZ	2/2 twill	c.12/10	damaged
		0675	D, on wood	detached (c)	30×13	wool	unpigmented	ZZZ	2/2 twill	c.8/8	thread c.0.75 diam
		0690	G, with rivets	small areas ?(a)	7×7, 12×13	wool	pigmented n.d.d	ZZZ	2/2 twill	-	with leather
21	M	1384	D, buckle (frags)	plate and loop	10×5	wool	n.d.d.	ZZZ	2/2 twill	c.9/8 on 5mm	medium twist, reddish staining
		1386	C, knife and stud	under stud, folds	-	wool	n.d.d.	ZZZ	2/2 twill	c.10/10, 14/14	medium, pulled blackish stain ?all same weave
25	M	0250	A, belt plate	through rivet hole (a)	50×27	wool	n.d.d.	ZZZ	2/2 twill	14/14–16	thread diam 0.8 medium twist
		0518	C, knife	below (a) and blade (b)	85×35	wool	-	ZZZ	?twill	8/6–7	thread diam 0.6
		0251	B, buckle, plate	on loop, leather; under (a) or (b)	15×15	wool	n.d.d.	ZZZ	twill	-	folds on loop
27	F	1533	E, Fe buckle	with bone, adhering	-	min.	-	-	-	-	damaged
		1536	D, knife	both sides blade, and end	12×10	min.	-	ZZZ	2/2 twill	9–10/8	one clear patch; yarn medium–loose
		1539	A, Fe pin	along	5×3	min.	-	?Z	?twill	-	layer, very fine under coarser threads
		1554	C, Fe pin	wound round below eye	-	min.	-	Z	threads	-	coarse, loose twist
28	F	1537	C, penannular brooch	junction of pin on back (a)	24×25	?wool	pigment	ZZZ	2/2 twill	6/5 on 5mm	dark brown lump
					L. 5mm	wool	n.d.d.	ZZZ	tablet border	5 cords, 5mm	?Z,S,Z,S,Z
				loose (a)	10×7	-	-	ZZZ	2/2 twill	10/9 (on 7mm)	-
		1548	E, Fe plate	over one side (b)	-	min.	-	Z/S	?twill	-	damaged
31	M	2253	D, knife	top of blade of 2253 and top of 2273 (a)	c.40×30	?wool	-	Z/S	2/2 twill	9/8	dark brown, Z; yarn loose, S
				patches under (a) lying along 2273	L.45/26	?wool	-	ZZZ	2/2 twill	17/12	variable fine threads
				near point blade 2253 small patch (b)	-	?wool	-	ZZZ	2/2 twill ?broken diamond	c.17/12, (6 on 5mm)	hard thread, good quality
		2254	C, Fe buckle	top surface and patches	c.60×90, 1×20	?leather	-	-	-	-	and threads
				loop (?a)	10×10	min.	-	Z/S	twill	-	-
				under loop (b)	15×15	min.	-	Z/S	twill	-	-
32	M	2325	B, fragments of lyre: wood, studs, nail nail and pin	edge of wood (a)	c.20×15	animal	n.d.d.	ZZZ	2/2 twill	est. 8/8–10	dark brown, Fe patches, open weave
				broken off	16×12	leather	-	-	-	-	-
		2326	Ae links	against (b)	c.38×20	min.	-	ZZZ	tabby	11–12/7–8	very open, damaged
		2327	wood and studs	top of stud (c) or (a)	25×15 L. c.15mm	wool	n.d.d.	ZZZ Z	2/2 twill ?starting border	-	knot edge; loose coarse loops, curling along edge
		2328	E, knife and buckle	on strip (d)	c.35×13	wool	n.d.d.	Z/S	?2/2 twill	c.14/9–10	Z finer, no reverse
				lump (d) on wood, leather	c.25×25	wool	n.d.d.	Z/S	2/2 twill	-	loose dark thread. ?sewing, insect pupae
36	M	-	(on site) over burial	centre area	c.70×70, 2–3 deep	?leather	-	-	-	-	black, decayed leather and/or textile
				overall area (a) above Ae plates	180×23	wool	n.d.d.	Z/S	2/2 twill ?broken diamond	6–8/9	remains, even weave
			B, Fe knife	under knife (b)	-	-	light, undyed	ZZZ	tabby	-	tiny scraps, traces
		2291	C, Fe buckle loop	on ring (c)	20×15	min.	-	Z-ply	threads	-	wound round

Grave	Sex	OP	Object	Position on object	Measurement	Fibre	Dye	Spin	Weave	Thread Count	Comments
36 (cont'd)	M	2343	D, Ae buckle and ring	under buckle (a)	15×15	wool	n.d.d.	Z/S	2/2 twill	7–8/8 on 5mm	variable, loose twist
				across (a) (d)	L.20	-	-	-	threads	-	coarse, roots
				fragments (e)	best 5×3–4	wool	n.d.d.	Z/Z	tablet, 4-hole	12 cords 5mm	cords Z, S, belt or edge; cut end curled under
		2344	E, buckle	traces (e)	-	min.	-	-	tablet cords	-	-
		2287	textile	detached ?(a)	20×15	animal	(alkanet)	Z/S	2/2 twill, broken diamond	10/12	diamonds widely spaced
37	M	-	on site, all over burial	area nearest body (a) L. of head	380×240	wool	n.d.d. (alkanet)	Z/S, Z	2/2 twill	?8–9/-	damaged; Z fine
				samples 7, 8	4×3, 3×2	wool	n.d.d.	Z/S, Z	2/2 twill	6–9/10	
				R. of head (b)	300×180	wool	(alkanet)	Z/Z, S	3/1 striped twill, reversing (rippenköper)	c.7/7	loose twist, S coarse, ?wp dark ?weft reddish
				samples 6, 9–10 ?(a) or (c)	3.5×2, 2.5×3.5	-	-	Z/Z	?twill	c.9/9	
				samples 4, 13 (c)	3×2, 3×2	-	-	Z/Z	?twill	c.9/9	blackened
		2278	B, knife	below knife (d)	L. c.20mm	wool	n.d.d. (alkanet)	S, Z-ply/?Z	tablet braid or border on (e)	-/5–6	scraps, ?cords
				scraps, ?(c) or (e)	-	-	-	Z/Z	?twill	5–6/6–7	coarse
38	U	2212	B, Fe knife	area blade (a)	25×30	?wool	(alkanet)	Z/Z	?2/2 twill	est. 8/9	dark brown; fine threads, loose weave
				curved fold (b)	-	-	-	S, Z	?twill	-	S and Z irregular
				?top of sheath (c)	10×15	-	-	S	threads	7 on 5mm	coarse fibres, tied round
40	?, adult	1747	A, Fe knife	near handle round one side (lying across blade) (a)	9×11	min.	-	Z/Z	tabby	9/13	?worsted thread, even wear, ?tape (no edges preserved
				point, other side	-	min.	-	-	-	-	patches ?leather
		1748, 1762	B, clay beads	pommel handle (b)	13×7	min.	-	-	tabby	?9/9	?tape, possibly (a) but coarser
				lying against	-	replaced	-	Z/?	?tabby	-	deteriorated
		1761	D, Fe buckle	covered both sides (c)	-	min.	-	Z/?	?twill	-	fine, surface damaged
				above pin (d)	4×7	min.	-	-	?twill	-	coarser
41	U	1921	A, textile	fragment, damaged	30×17	min.	-	Z/S	2/2 twill	c.11/12–13	slightly open weave, yarn medium twist, no reverses
43	U	2002	sample H ?lining	edge of grave (a)	-	wool	(alkanet)	Z, S	?twill	-	very coarse, loose spin; mixed roots
		2003	sample I	?higher in grave	-	wool	(alkanet)	similar	-	-	
		2087,	B, knife and buckle	overlying (a)	c.30×30	wool	(alkanet)	Z/Z	?twill	c.8–10/8–10	black, distorted
		2088		blade edge (b)	70×15	wool	(alkanet)	Z/S	2/2 twill	c.16–18/20	very black
				(c)	30×25	wool	(alkanet)	Z/S	twill	c.5/3–4	?weft very coarse
				detached (d) ?(b)	15×20	wool	(alkanet)	Z/S	2/2 twill	16–18/14	red-brown
				detached (e)	40×40, 40×40	wool	(alkanet)	Z/S	2/2 twill	c.8–9/8	very dark brown crushed layer
				detached (layer) ?(d) and (e)	45×35	wool	-	Z/S	2/2 twill	20/18	reddish
45	M	1917	C, Fe traces, textile	(best scrap)	11×8	unid.	n.d.d.	Z/Z	2/2 twill	c.10/8	loose spin. Fe stain

118

Table 2 (rotated). Catalogue of textiles — Grave 47.

Grave	Sex	OP	Object	Position on object	Measurement	Fibre	Dye	Spin	Weave	Thread Count	Comments
47	M	1826	patches, textile	in two layers	best 13×7	-	(alkanet)	Z/Z	?	c.6 on 5mm/?	loose threads, some coarse; variable
		1939	G, sword	patches along blade, crumpled folds (a)	areas 210mm L. c.45mm wide	min.	-	Z/Z	2/2 twill	c.7/6	threads coarse, loose
				further up blade (b)	c.18×22	min.	-	Z/Z	2/2 twill	c.5/5	?(a) but coarser, knot of S thread
				top of blade (c)	c.L. 80mm	min.	-	Z/	?tabby	-	fine; in folds
				fold on scabbard and hilt	c.L. 50mm	min.	-	Z/Z	-	-	feathers and fine
		1914	D [spearhead i /shaft	under socket and upper blade (d)	c.90mm L. 20mm widest	min.	-	Z/Z	?twill	10/?7–8	like (a) on 1939 but ?wrapping
			D [spearhead ii	as above (d)	area 60×15	min.	-	Z/Z	2/2 twill	decayed	?with fragment leather
			D [spearhead iii	areas textile, none clear	-	min.	-	-	-	-	sand grains
			D [soil lump from	damaged ?(d)	area 20×30	min.	-	Z/Z	?twill	-	coarse threads
			spearheads	clear areas, wood from shafts (e)	9×17, 15×13	min.	-	S	threads, 7	-	possible tape or braid round shaft
		1951	O, unidentified complex, Fe	patch ?(f)	25×30	min.	-	Z/Z	tabby	15/16	fine threads, loose twist
		1954	H, Fe knife, min.	one side (g)	width 8mm	min.	-	Z/Z	tabby	c.32/22–4	tape, full width, simple selvedge
			lump textile	under (g) (f)	-	min.	-	Z/Z	tabby	-	protruding, coarse, prob. (f) appearance flax
				under (f), (g) ?(d)	traces	min.	-	Z/Z	2/2 twill	-	loose spin ?(d)

Notes:
1) Measurements in millimetres, thread counts per 10mm unless otherwise stated
2) (a), (b), etc indicate different fabrics present in a grave
3) min. or semi-min. indicates fibres mineralised ('replaced') by metal oxides from grave goods
4) Dye identification by Penelope Walton Rogers (n.d.d. = no dye detected)
5) Fibre identification by Harry Appleyard

Table 2   Catalogue of textiles

Grave 1

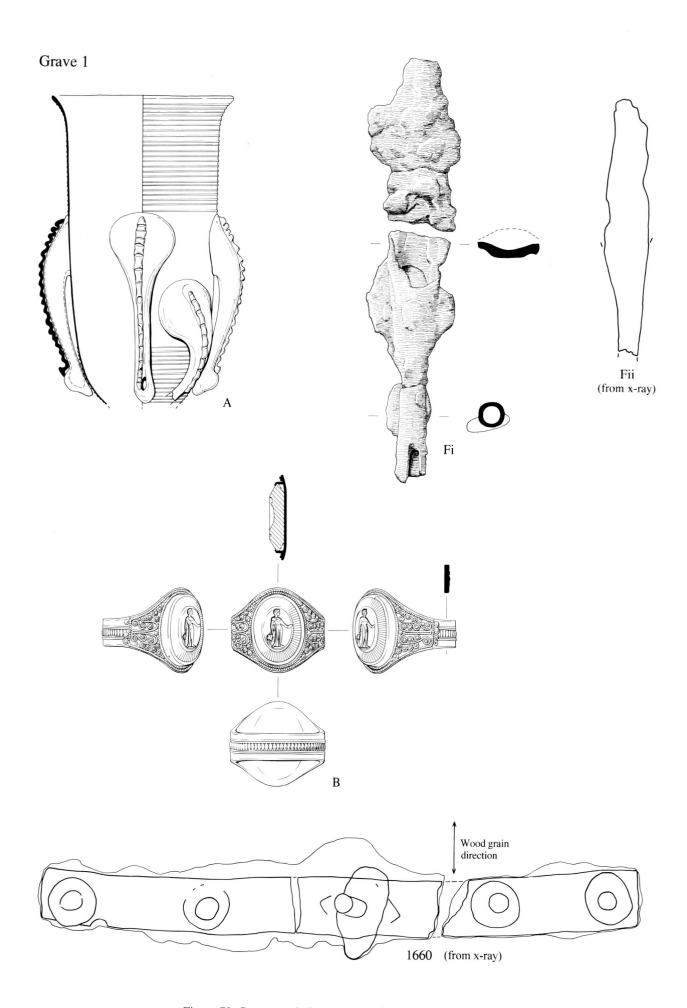

A

Fi

Fii
(from x-ray)

B

Wood grain
direction

1660   (from x-ray)

Figure 78 Grave-goods from grave 1. Scales: *B*; 1:1. Others 1:2

Grave 2

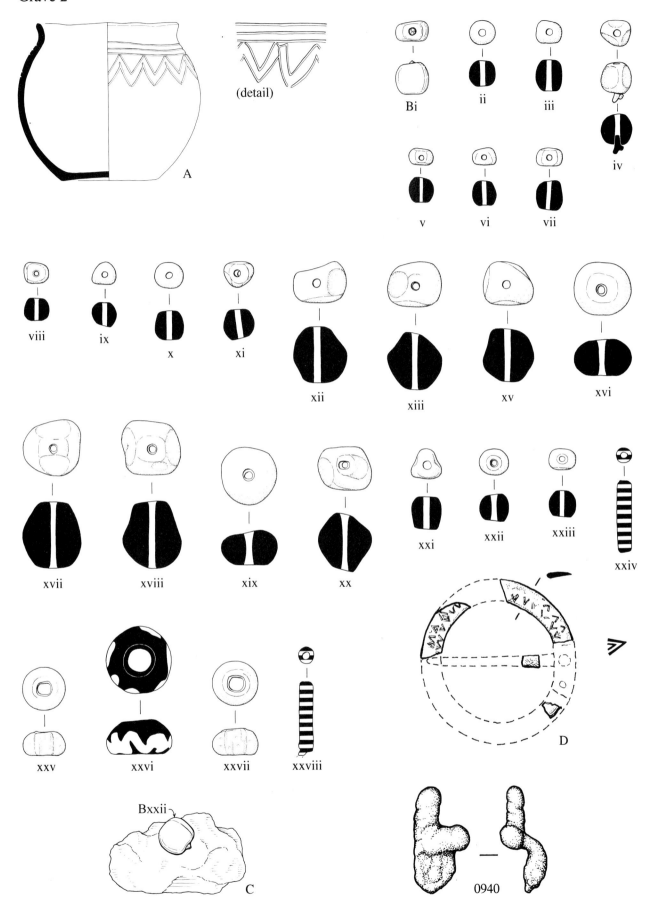

Figure 79 Grave-goods from grave 2. Scales: *A*; 1:3, detail 1:2. Others 1:1. Punch stamp at 2:1

121

Grave 2(cont.)

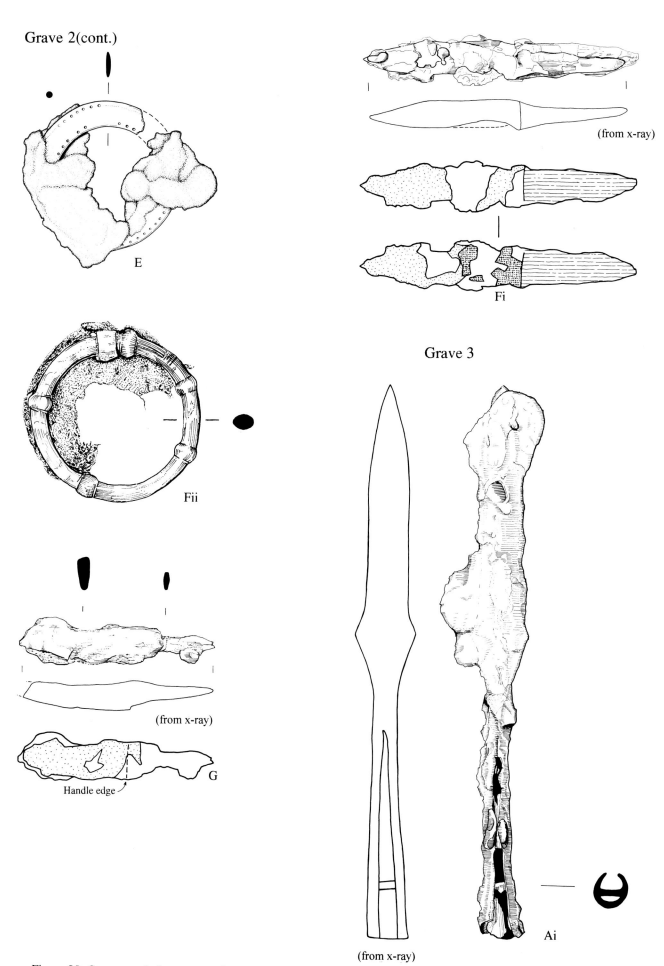

Grave 3

E

Fi

(from x-ray)

Fii

(from x-ray)

Handle edge

G

(from x-ray)

Ai

Figure 80 Grave-goods from graves 2 (cont'd) and 3. Grave 2. Scales: *E* and *Fii*; 1:1, *Fi* and *G*; 1:2. Punch stamp at 2:1. Grave 3. Scale: *Ai*; 1:2

Grave 3(cont.)

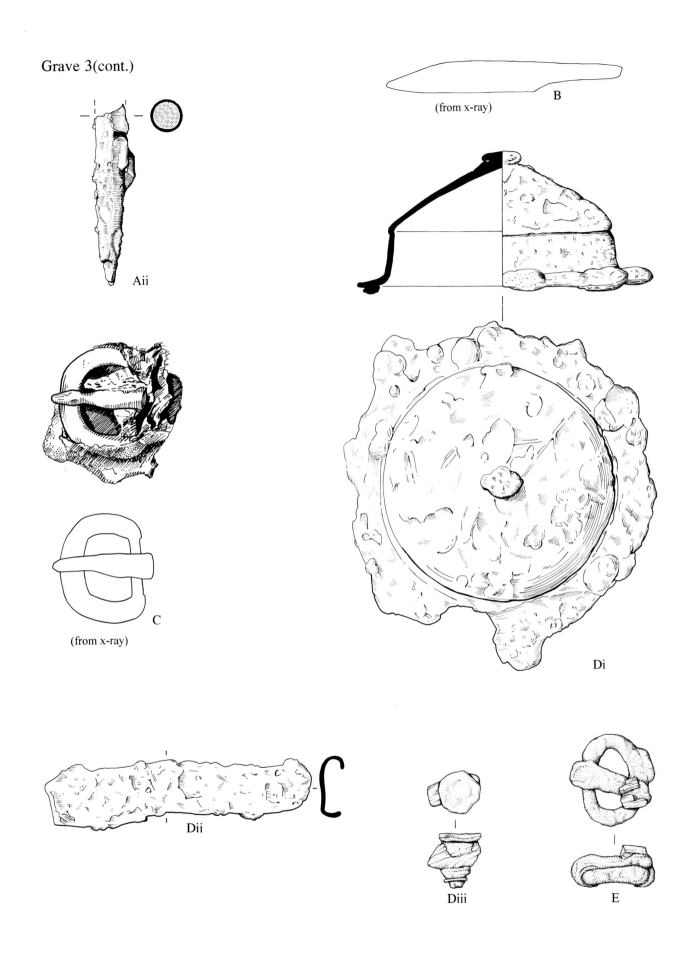

Figure 81 Grave-goods from grave 3 (cont'd). Scales: *C, Diii* and *E*; 1:1. Others; 1:2

123

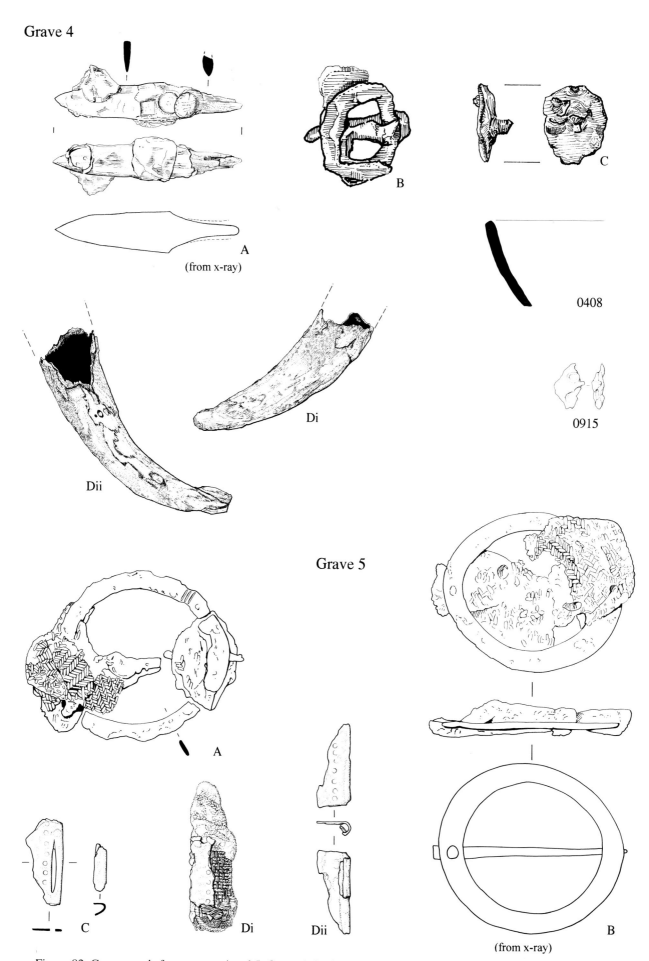

Grave 4

A

(from x-ray)

B

C

0408

0915

Di

Dii

Grave 5

A

B

(from x-ray)

C

Di

Dii

Figure 82 Grave-goods from graves 4 and 5. Grave 4. Scales: *B*, *C* and *0915*; 1:1. *0408*; 1:3. Others; 1:2. Grave 5. Scale: All 1:1

Grave 5(cont.)

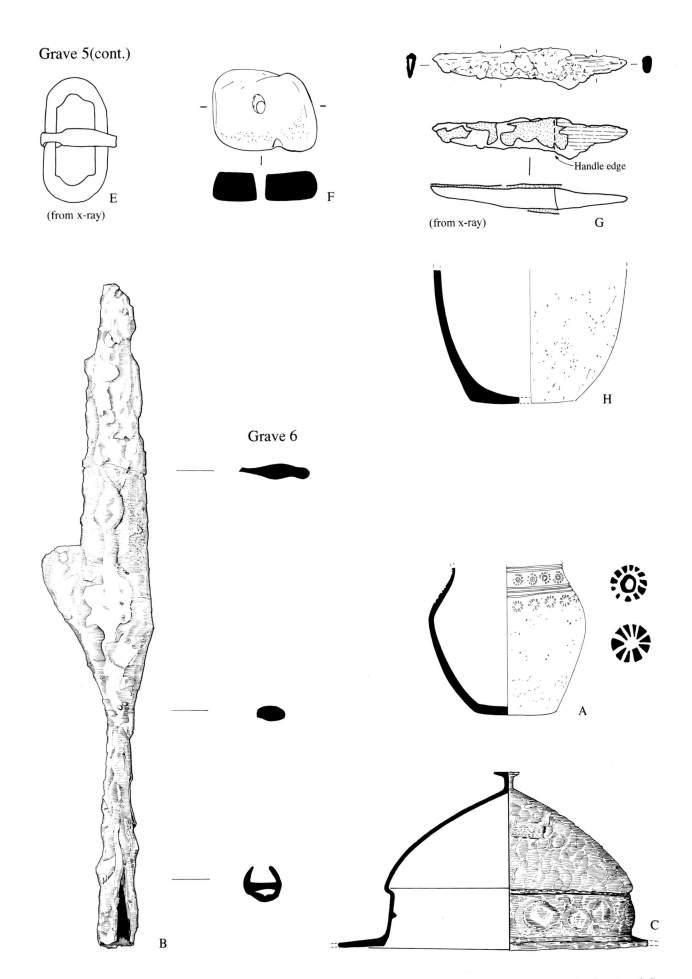

(from x-ray)   E

(from x-ray)

F

Handle edge

(from x-ray)   G

H

Grave 6

A

B

C

Figure 83 Grave-goods from 5 (cont'd) and 6. Grave 5. Scales: *E* and *F*; 1:1. *G*; 1:2. *H*; 1:3. Grave 6. Scales: *B* and *C*; 1:2. *A*; 1:3, pot stamps at 1:1

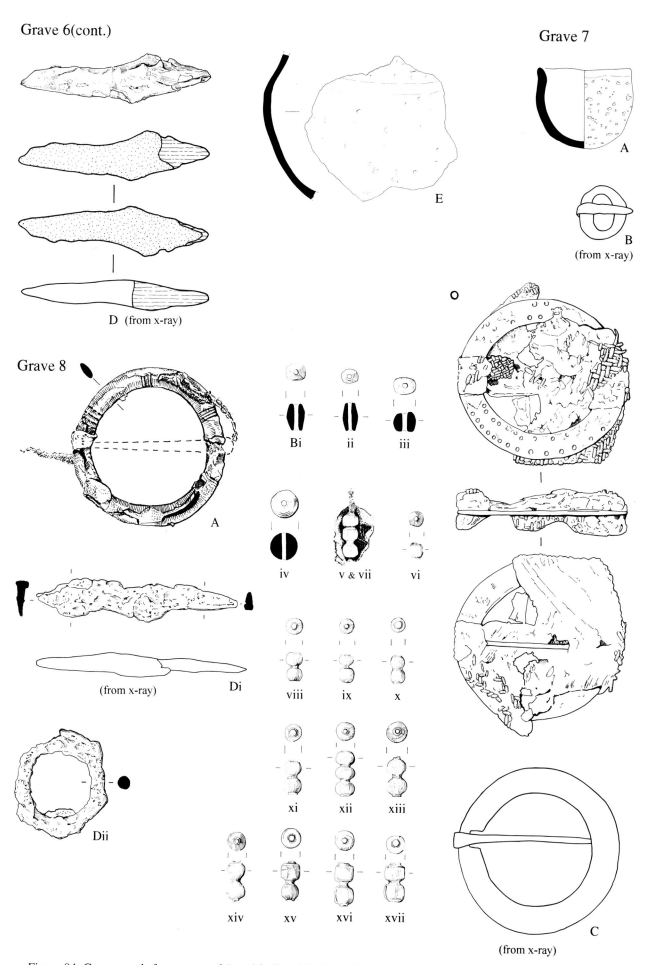

Figure 84 Grave-goods from graves 6 (cont'd), 7 and 8. Grave 6. Scales: *D*; 1:2. *E*; 1:3. Grave 7. Scales: *A*; 1:3. *B*; 1:1. Grave 8. Scales: *Di* and *ii*; 1:2. Others; 1:1. Punch stamp at 2:1

Grave 9

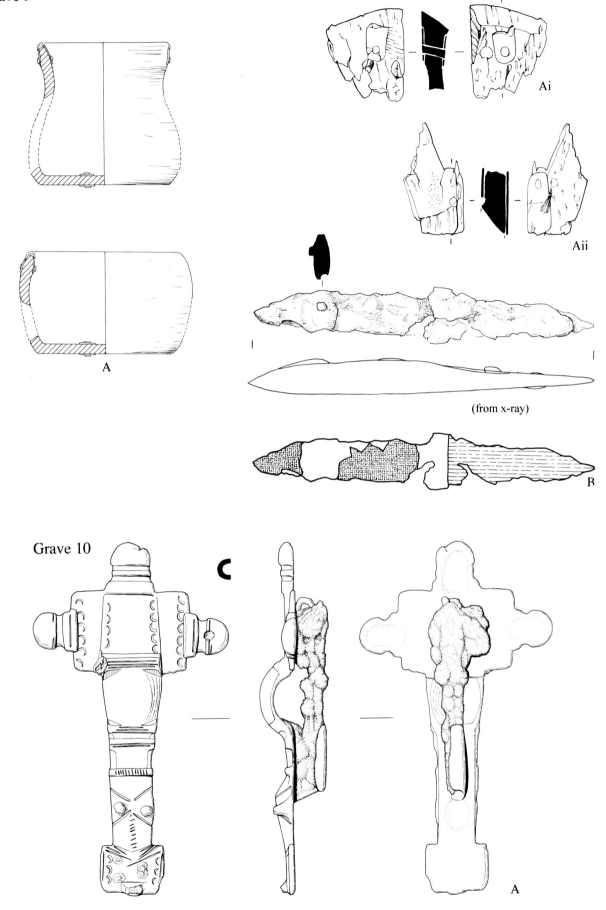

Grave 10

Figure 85 Grave-goods from grave 9 and 10. Grave 9. Scales: *Ai* and *ii*; 1:1. Reconstructions of *A*, and *B*; 1:2. Grave 10. Scale: *A*; 1:1. Punch stamp at 2:1

Grave 10(cont.)

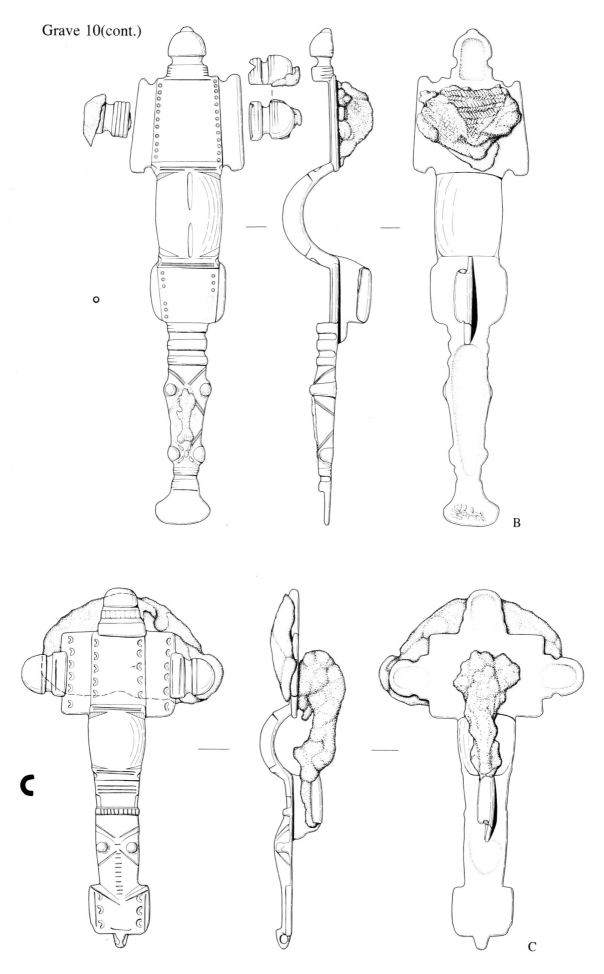

Figure 86 Grave-goods from grave 10 (cont'd). Scale: 1:1. Punch stamp at 2:1

128

Grave 10
(cont.)

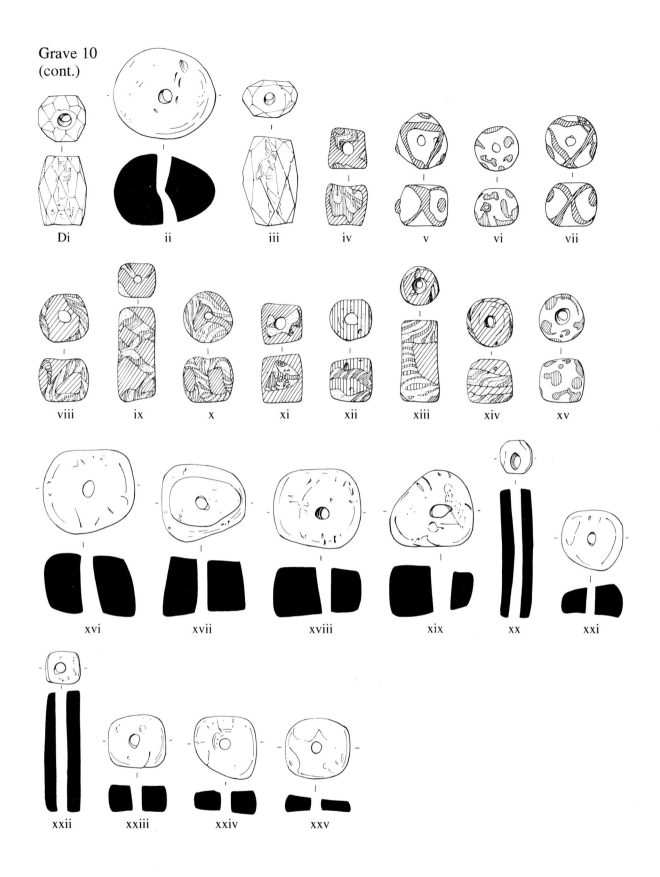

Figure 87 Grave-goods from grave 10 (cont'd). Scale: 1:1

Grave 10(cont.)

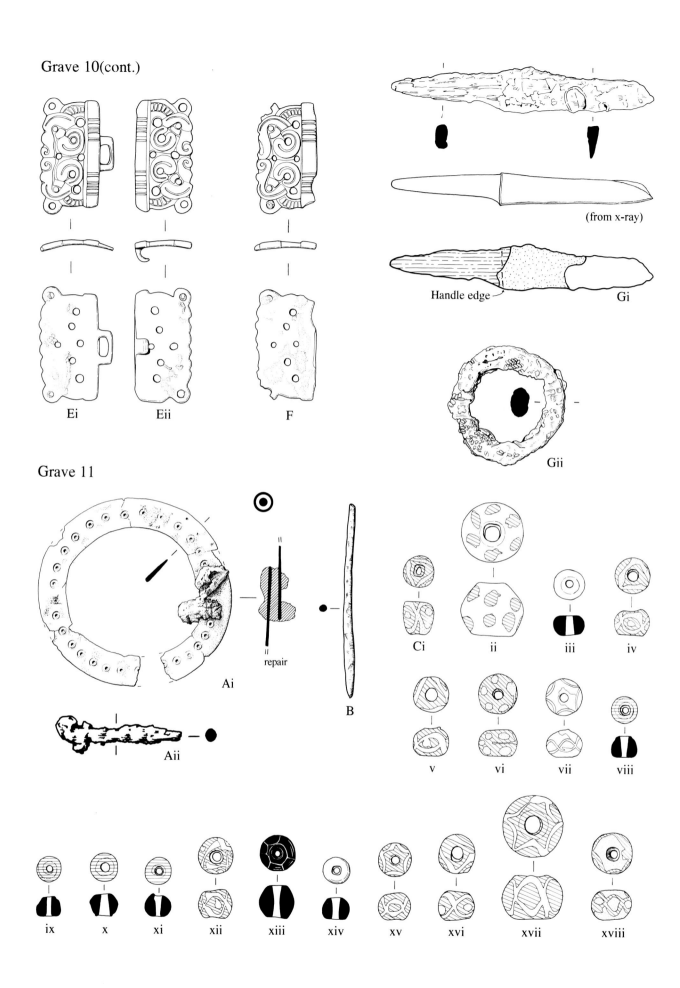

Ei   Eii   F

(from x-ray)

Handle edge   Gi

Gii

Grave 11

repair

Ai

Aii

B

Ci   ii   iii   iv

v   vi   vii   viii

ix   x   xi   xii   xiii   xiv   xv   xvi   xvii   xviii

Figure 88 Grave-goods from graves 10 (cont'd.) and 11. Grave 10. Scales: *E*, *F*; 1:1. *Gi* and *ii*; 1:2. Grave 11. Scale: 1:1. Punch stamp at 2:1

Grave 11(cont.)

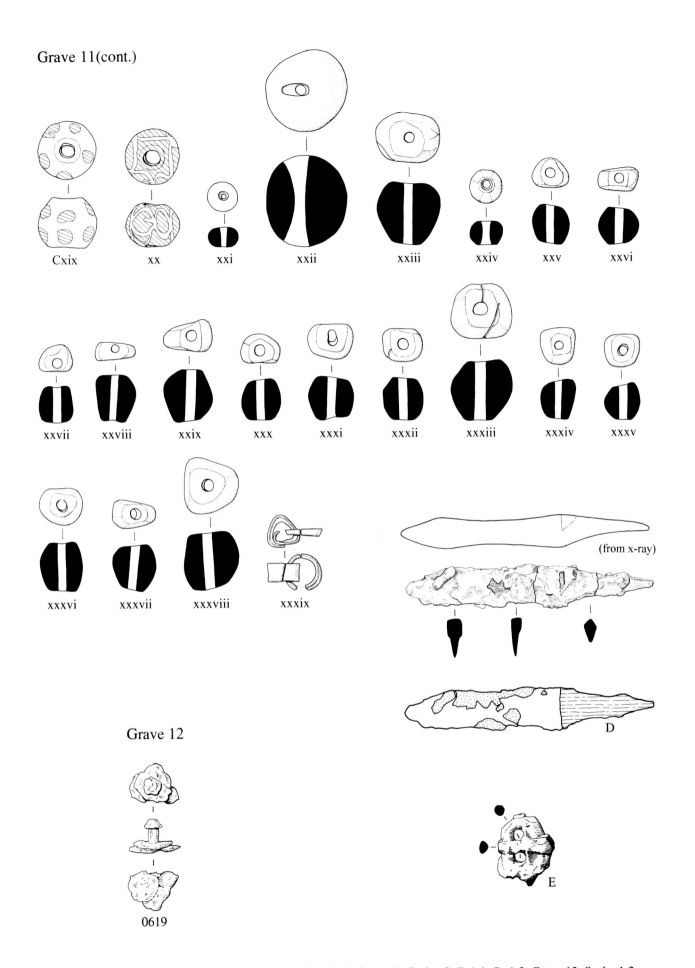

Cxix xx xxi xxii xxiii xxiv xxv xxvi

xxvii xxviii xxix xxx xxxi xxxii xxxiii xxxiv xxxv

xxxvi xxxvii xxxviii xxxix

(from x-ray)

D

Grave 12

0619

E

Figure 89 Grave-goods from graves 11 (cont'd) and 12. Grave 11. Scale: *C, E*; 1:1. *D*; 1:2. Grave 12. Scale: 1:2

Grave 14

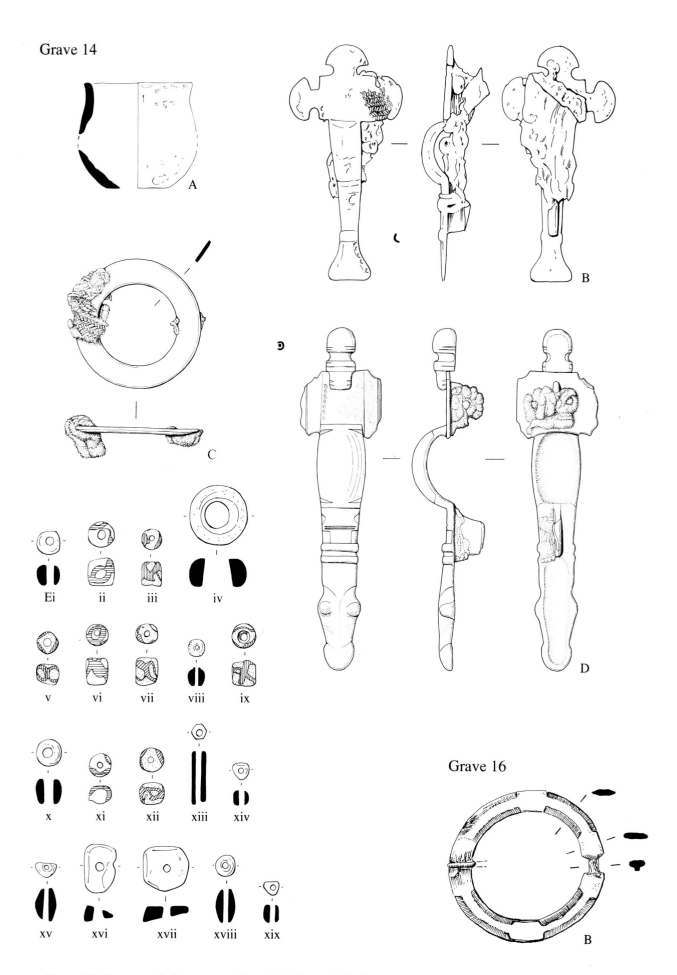

Grave 16

Figure 90 Grave-goods from graves 14 and 16. Grave 14. Scale: *A*; 1:3. Others; 1:1. Punch stamp at 2:1. Grave 16. Scale: 1:1

132

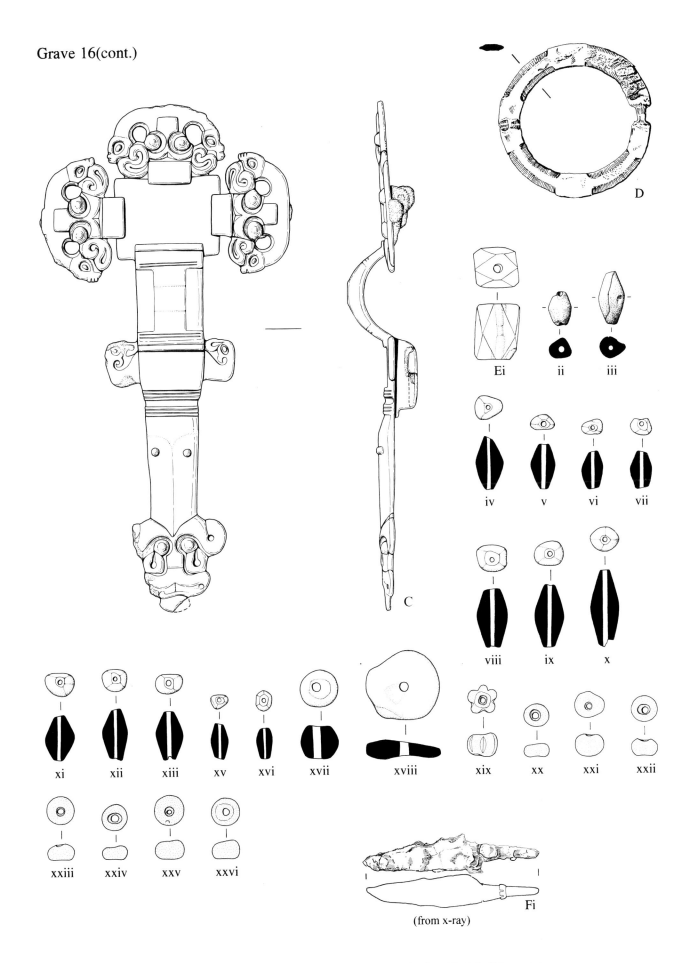

Figure 91 Grave-goods from grave 16 (cont'd). Scales: *Fi*; 1:2. Others; 1:1

Grave 16(cont.)

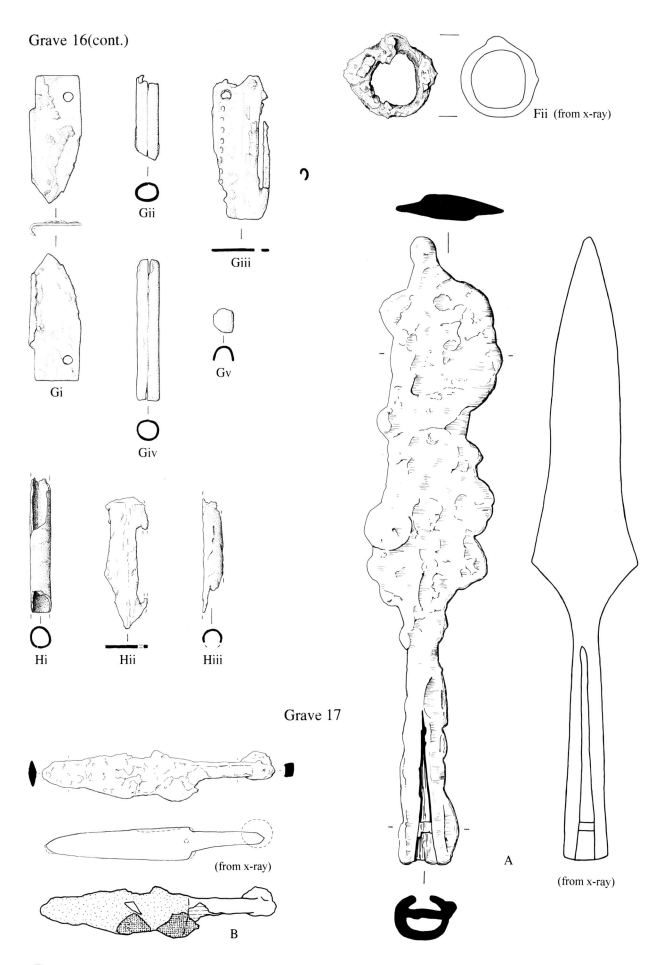

Gii

Giii

Gi

Giv

Gv

Fii (from x-ray)

Hi

Hii

Hiii

Grave 17

(from x-ray)

B

A

(from x-ray)

Figure 92 Grave-goods from graves 16 (cont'd) and 17. Grave 16. Scales: *G* and *H*; 1:1. *Fii*; 1:2. Punch stamp at 2:1. Grave 17. Scale 1:2

134

Grave 18

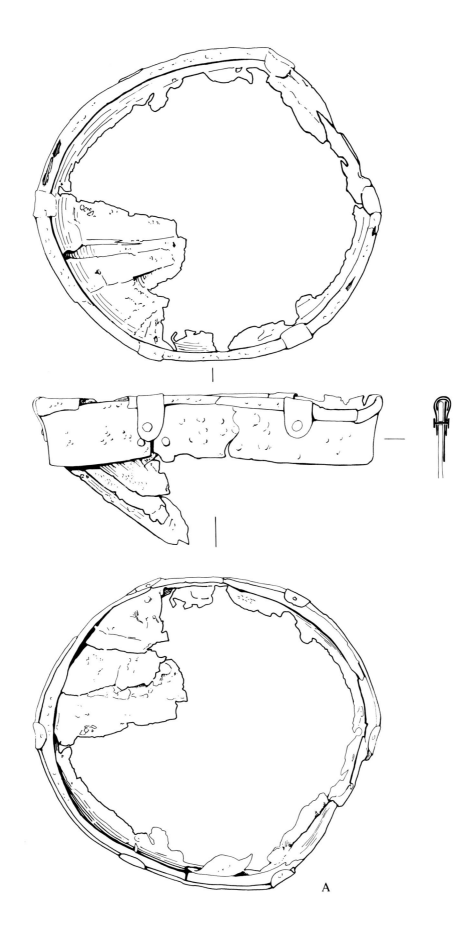

A

Figure 93 Grave-goods from grave 18. Scale: 1:1

Grave 18(cont.)

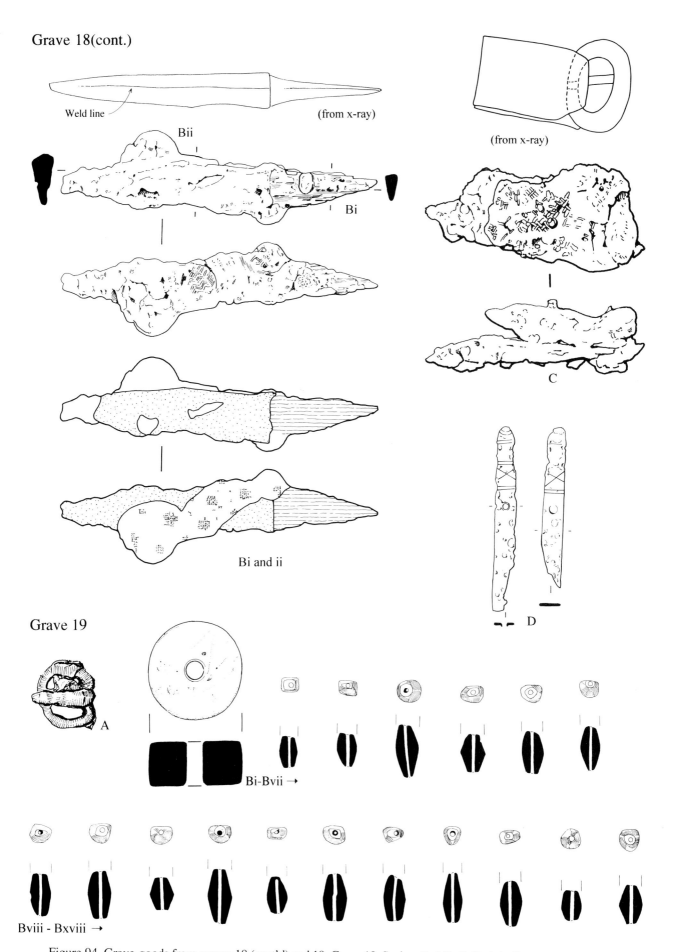

Weld line   (from x-ray)

Bii

Bi

(from x-ray)

C

Bi and ii

D

Grave 19

A

Bi-Bvii →

Bviii - Bxviii →

Figure 94 Grave-goods from graves 18 (cont'd) and 19. Grave 18. Scales: *B*; 1:2. *C, D*; 1:1. Grave 19. Scale: 1:1

Grave 19(cont.)

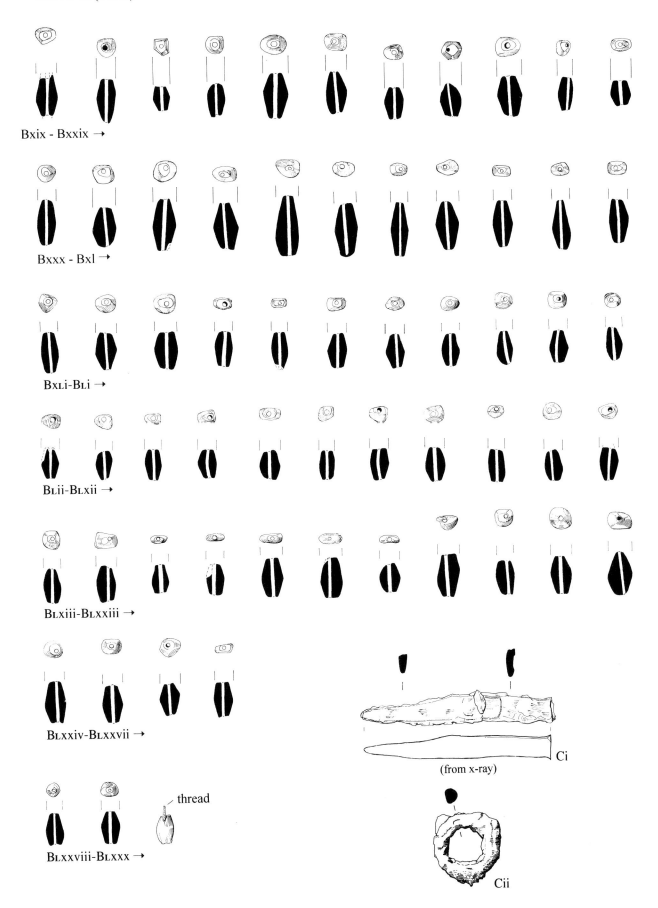

Bxix - Bxxix →

Bxxx - Bxl →

BxLi-BLi →

BLii-BLxii →

BLxiii-BLxxiii →

BLxxiv-BLxxvii →

thread

BLxxviii-BLxxx →

Ci

(from x-ray)

Cii

Figure 95 Grave-goods from grave 19 (cont'd). Scales: *B*; 1:1. *C*; 1:2

137

Grave 19(cont.)

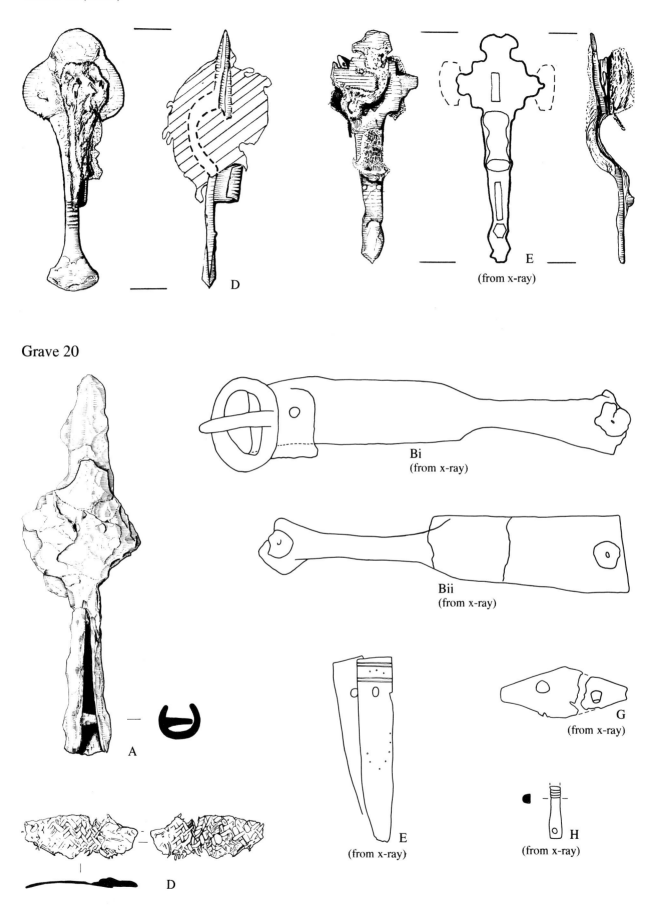

D

E
(from x-ray)

Grave 20

Bi
(from x-ray)

Bii
(from x-ray)

A

D

E
(from x-ray)

G
(from x-ray)

H
(from x-ray)

Figure 96 Grave-goods from grave 19 (cont'd) and 20. Grave 19. Scale: 1:1. Grave 20. Scales: *A*; 1:2. Others; 1:1

Grave 20(cont.)

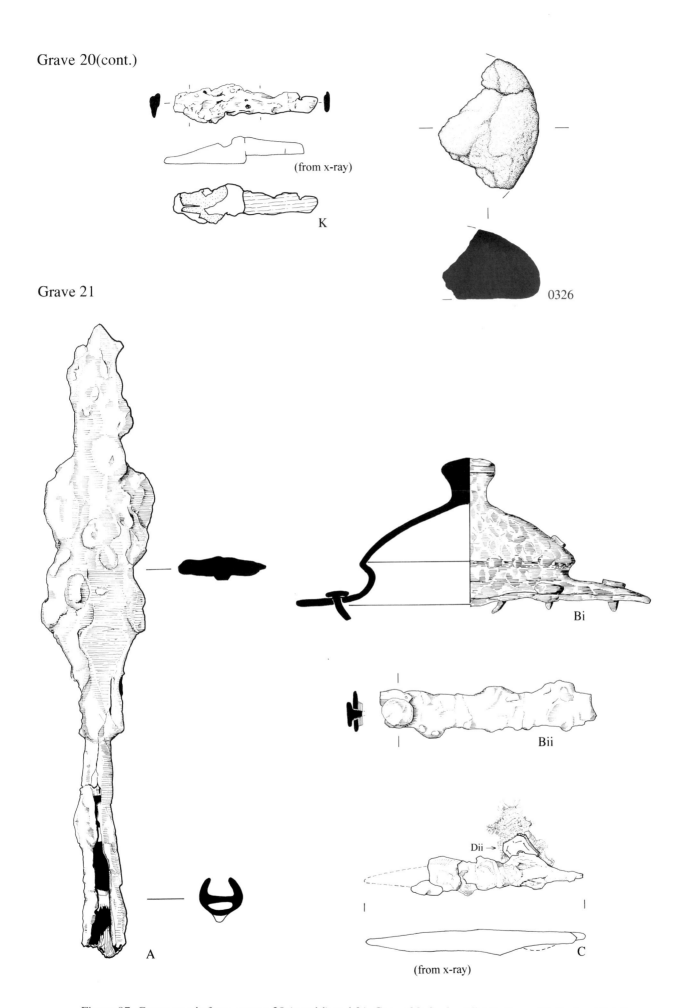

Grave 21

(from x-ray)

K

0326

Bi

Bii

Dii →

A

C

(from x-ray)

Figure 97 Grave-goods from graves 20 (cont'd) and 21. Grave 20. Scale: All 1:2. Grave 21. Scale: All 1:2

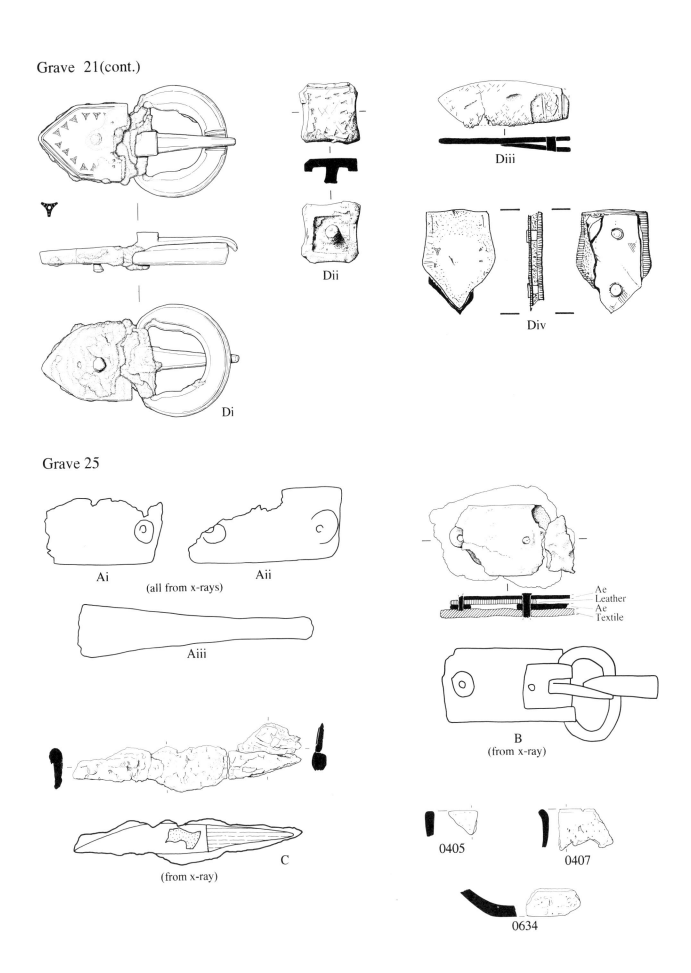

Grave 21(cont.)

Di

Dii

Diii

Div

Grave 25

Ai

Aii

(all from x-rays)

Aiii

Ae
Leather
Ae
Textile

B
(from x-ray)

C
(from x-ray)

0405

0407

0634

Figure 98 Grave-goods from graves 21 (cont'd) and 25. Grave 21. Scale: All 1:1. Punch stamp at 2:1. Grave 25.
Scales: *A, B*; 1:1. *C*; 1:2. *0405, 0407* and *0634* 1:3

Grave 27

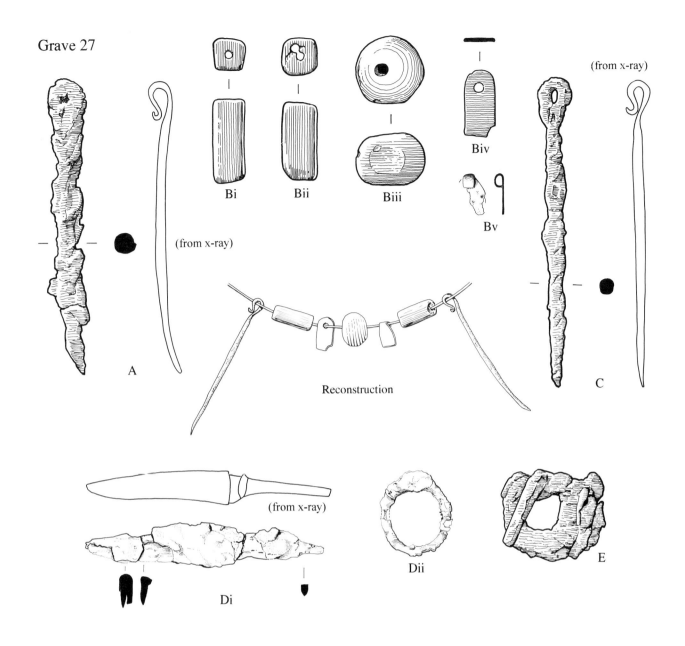

A

(from x-ray)

Bi Bii Biii Biv

Bv

(from x-ray)

C

Reconstruction

(from x-ray)

Di Dii E

Grave 28

A B

Figure 99 Grave-goods from graves 27 and 28. Grave 27. Scales: *Di* and *ii*; 1:2. Others; 1:1. Grave 28. Scale: Both 1:3

141

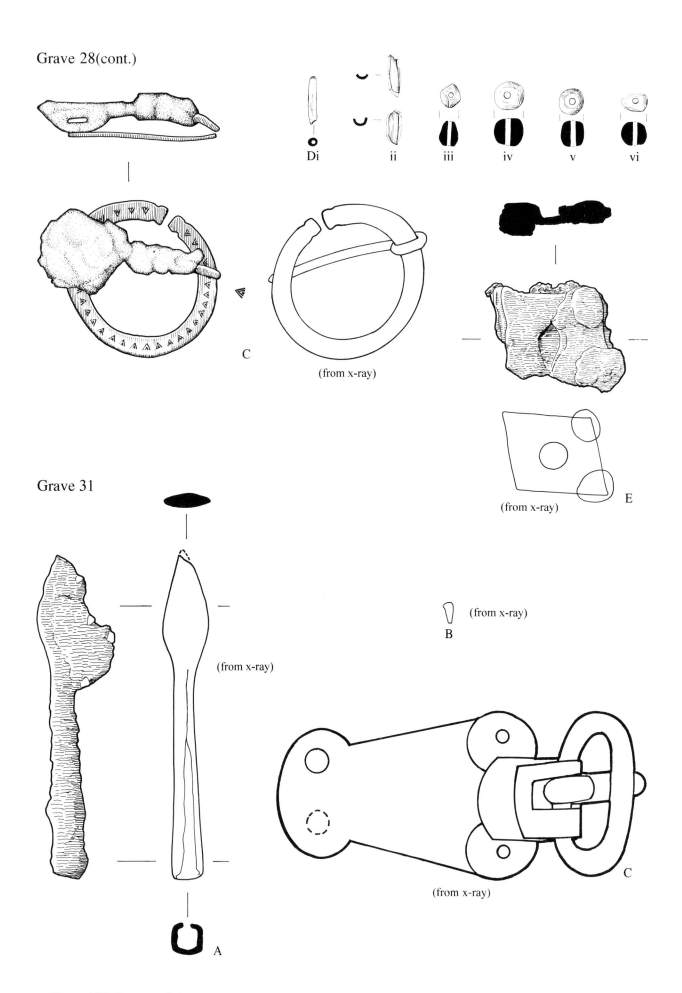

Grave 28(cont.)

Di   ii   iii   iv   v   vi

C

(from x-ray)

E

(from x-ray)

Grave 31

B (from x-ray)

(from x-ray)

C

(from x-ray)

A

Figure 100 Grave-goods from graves 28 (cont'd) and 31. Grave 28. Scale: All 1:1. Punch stamp at 2:1. Grave 31. Scales: *A*; 1:2. *B*, *C*; 1:1

Grave 31(cont.)

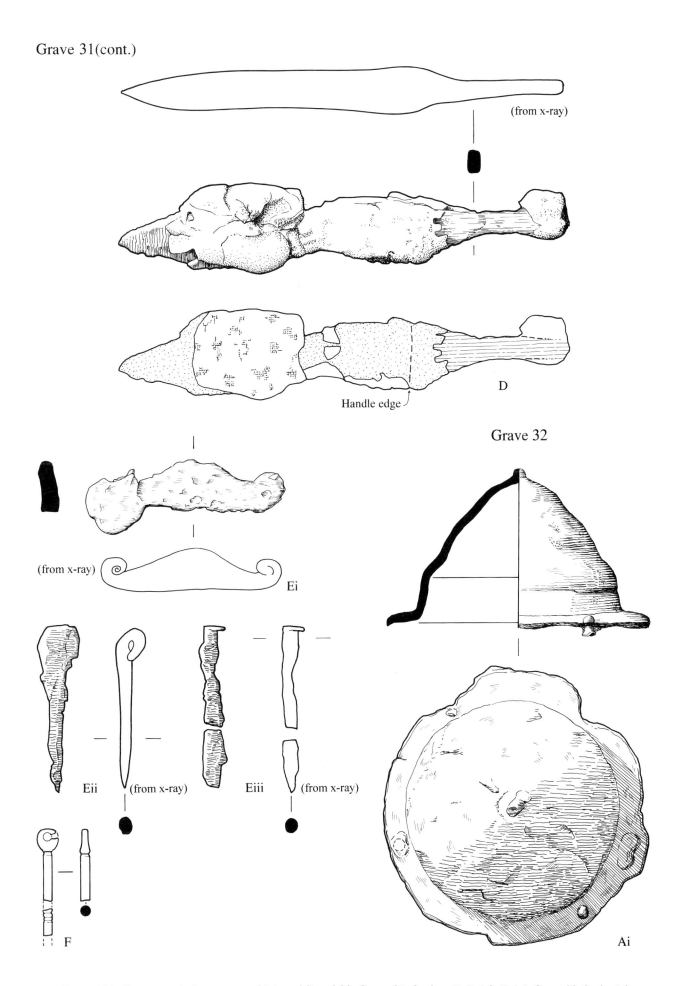

(from x-ray)

D

Handle edge

Grave 32

(from x-ray)

Ei

Eii

(from x-ray)

Eiii

(from x-ray)

F

Ai

Figure 101 Grave-goods from graves 31 (cont'd) and 32. Grave 31. Scales: *D*, *E*; 1:2. *F*; 1:1. Grave 32. Scale: 1:2

Grave 32(cont.)

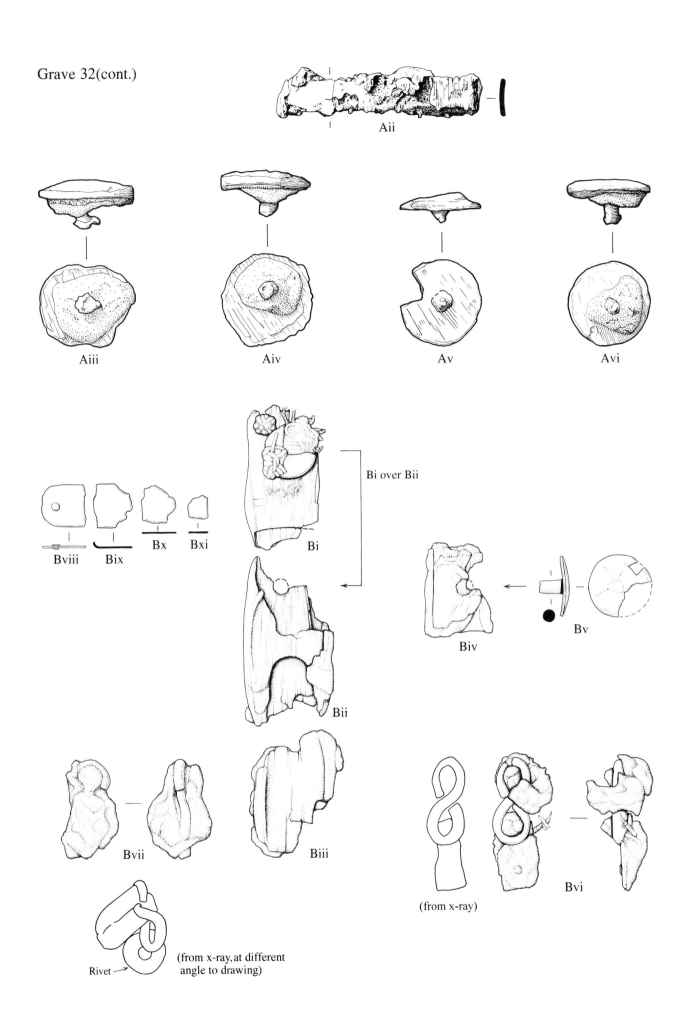

Aii

Aiii

Aiv

Av

Avi

Bi over Bii

Bviii Bix Bx Bxi

Bi

Biv

Bv

Bii

Bvii

Biii

Bvi

(from x-ray)

Rivet →

(from x-ray, at different
angle to drawing)

Figure 102 Grave-goods from grave 32 (cont'd). Scales: *A*; 1:2. *B*; 1:1

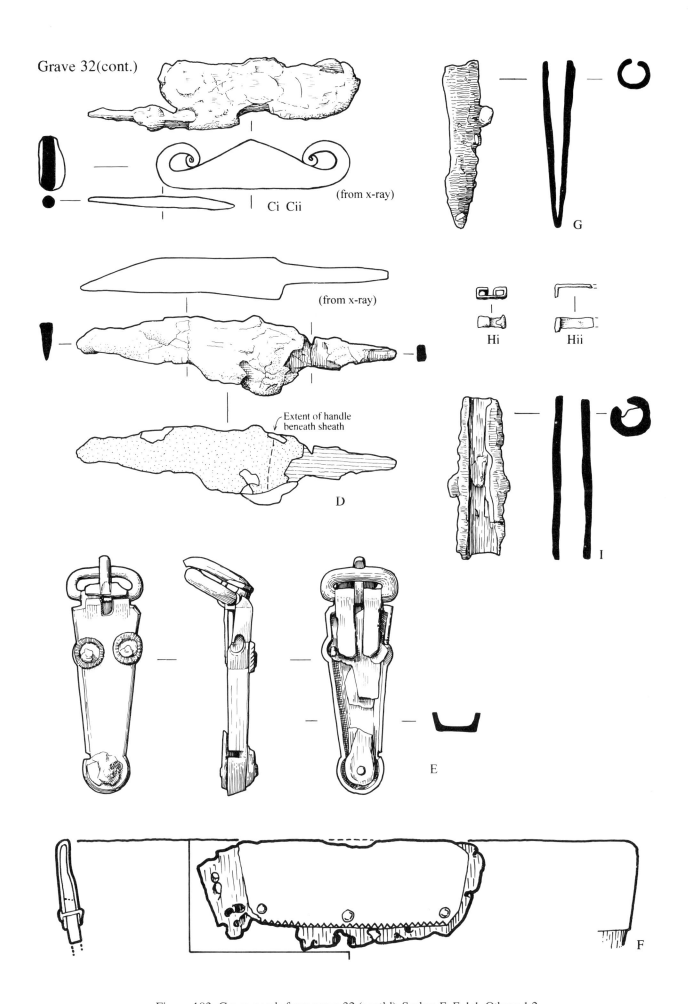

Grave 32(cont.)

(from x-ray)

Ci Cii

(from x-ray)

Extent of handle
beneath sheath

D

G

Hi   Hii

I

E

F

Figure 103 Grave-goods from grave 32 (cont'd). Scales: *E, F*; 1:1. Others; 1:2

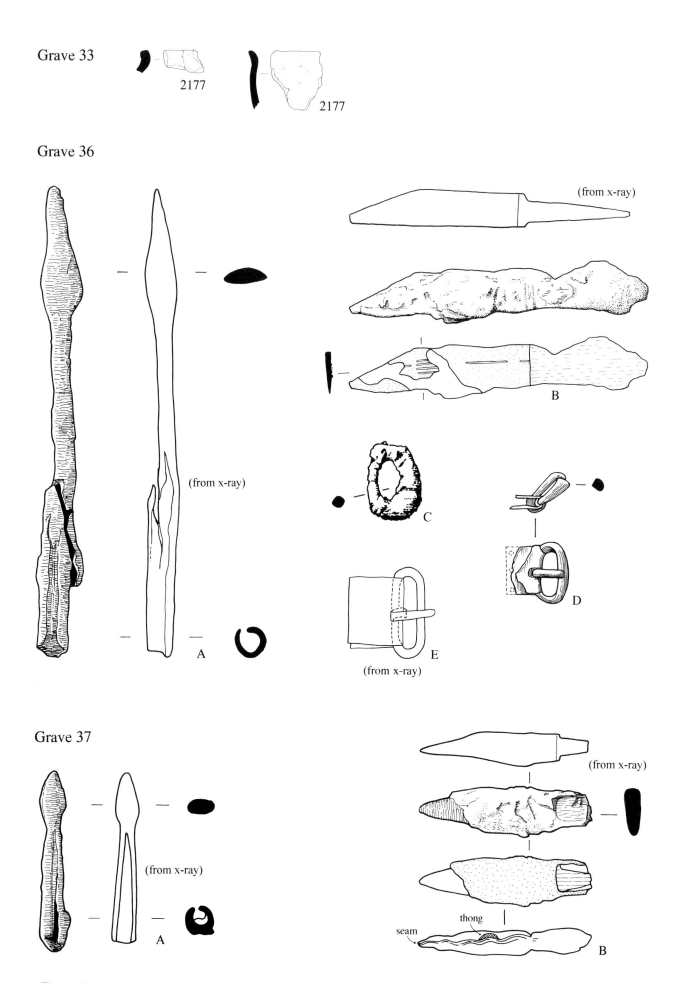

Figure 104 Grave-goods from graves 33, 36 and 37. Grave 33. Scale: 1:3 Grave 36. Scales: *A, B*; 1:2. *C, D, E*; 1:1.
Grave 37. Scale: 1:2

Grave 37(cont.)

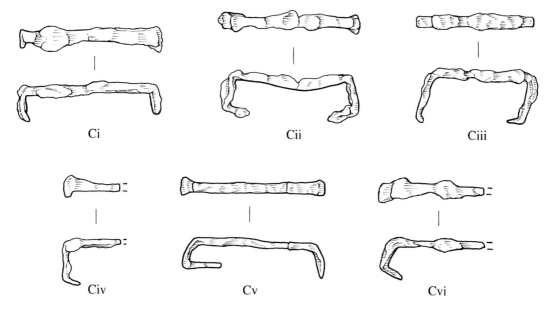

Ci   Cii   Ciii

Civ   Cv   Cvi

Grave 38

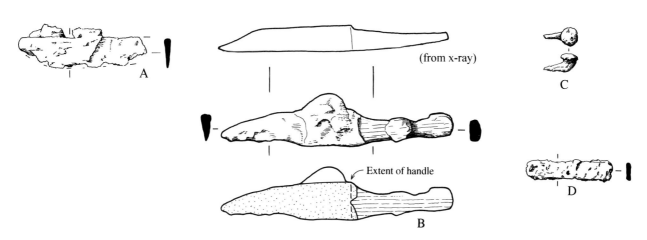

A

(from x-ray)

C

Extent of handle

B

D

Grave 40

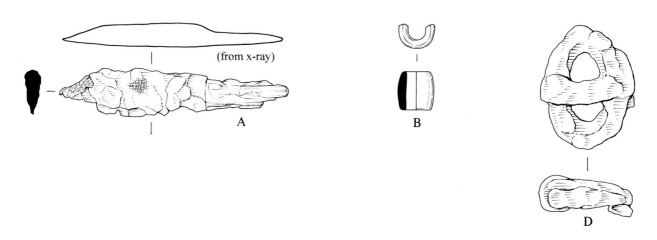

(from x-ray)

A

B

D

Figure 105 Grave-goods from graves 37 (cont'd), 38 and 40. Grave 37. Scale: 1:2. Grave 38. Scale: All 1:2. Grave 40. Scales: *A*; 1:2. *B*, *D*; 1:1

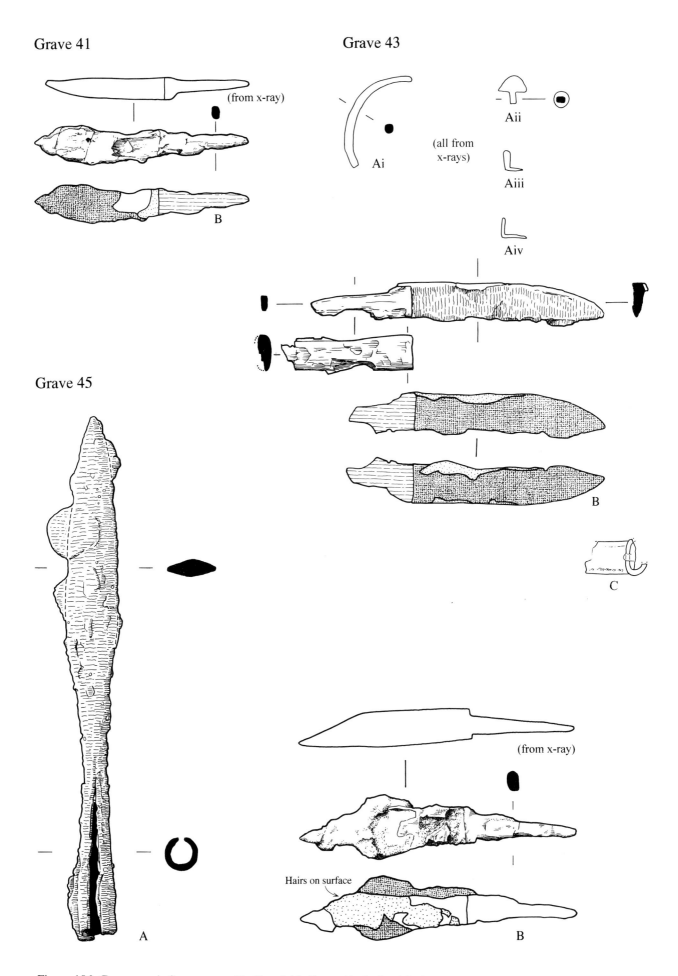

Figure 106 Grave-goods from graves 41, 43 and 45. Grave 41. Scale: 1:2. Grave 43. Scales: *A*, *B*; 1:2. *C*; 1:1. Grave 45. Scale: 1:2

148

Grave 47

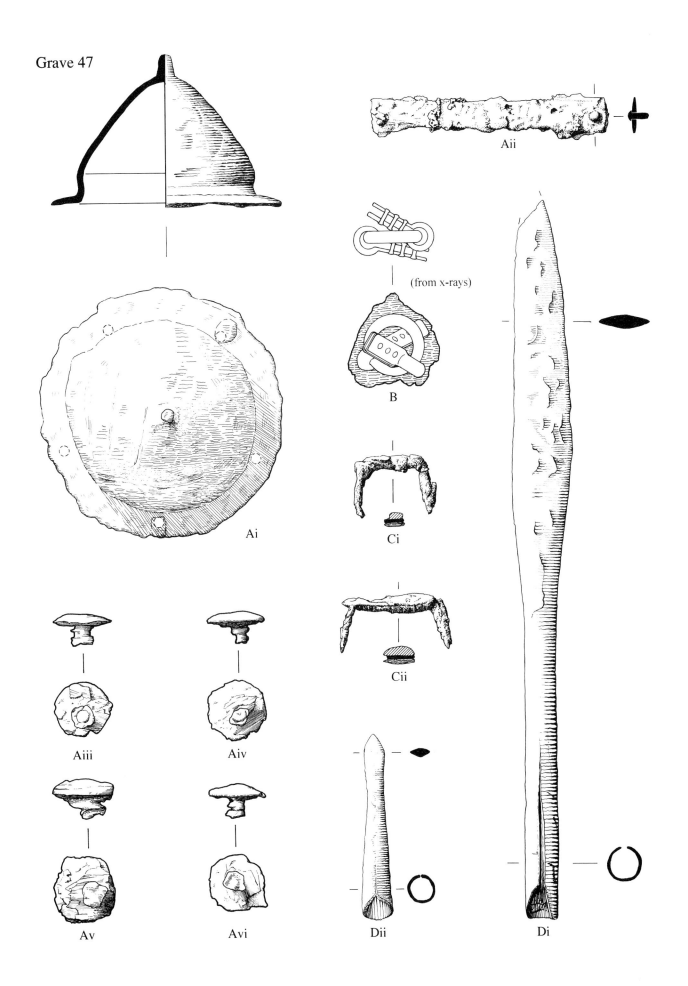

Ai

Aii

(from x-rays)

B

Ci

Cii

Aiii

Aiv

Av

Avi

Dii

Di

Figure 107 Grave-goods from grave 47. Scale: all 1:2

149

Grave 47(cont.)

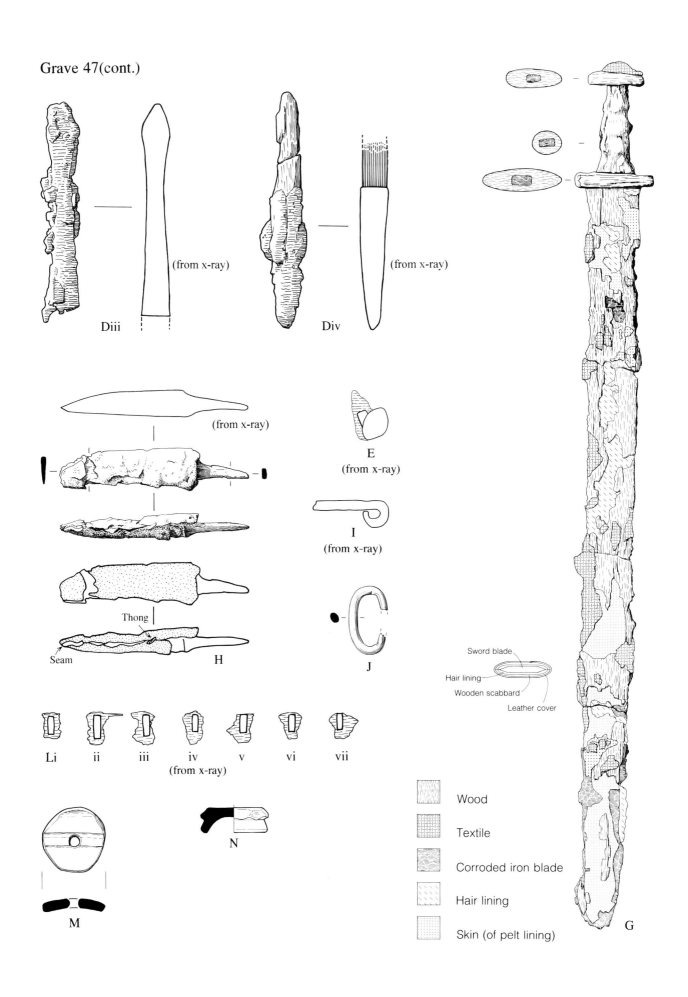

Figure 108 Grave-goods from grave 47 (cont'd). Scales: *G*; 1:4. *D, E, H, L*; 1:2. *I, J*; 1:1. *M, N*; 1:3

150

Grave 47(cont.)

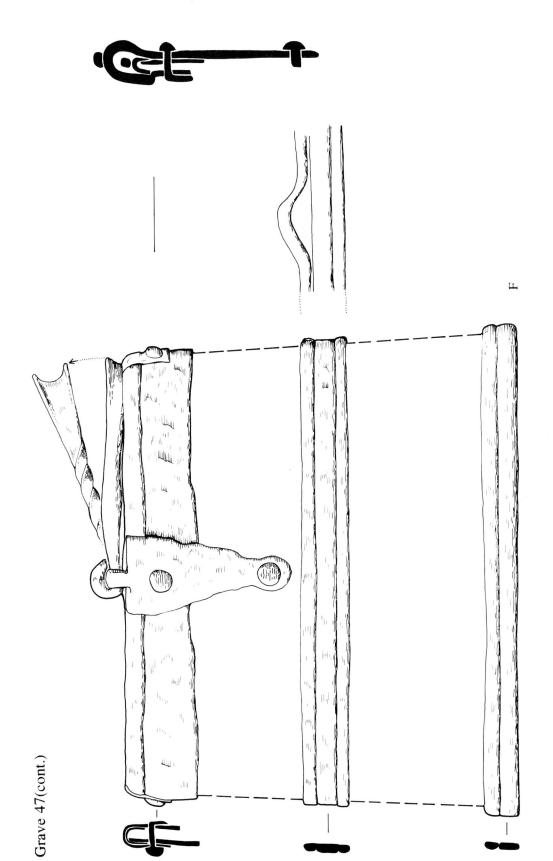

Figure 109 Grave-goods from grave 47 (cont'd). Scale: 1:4

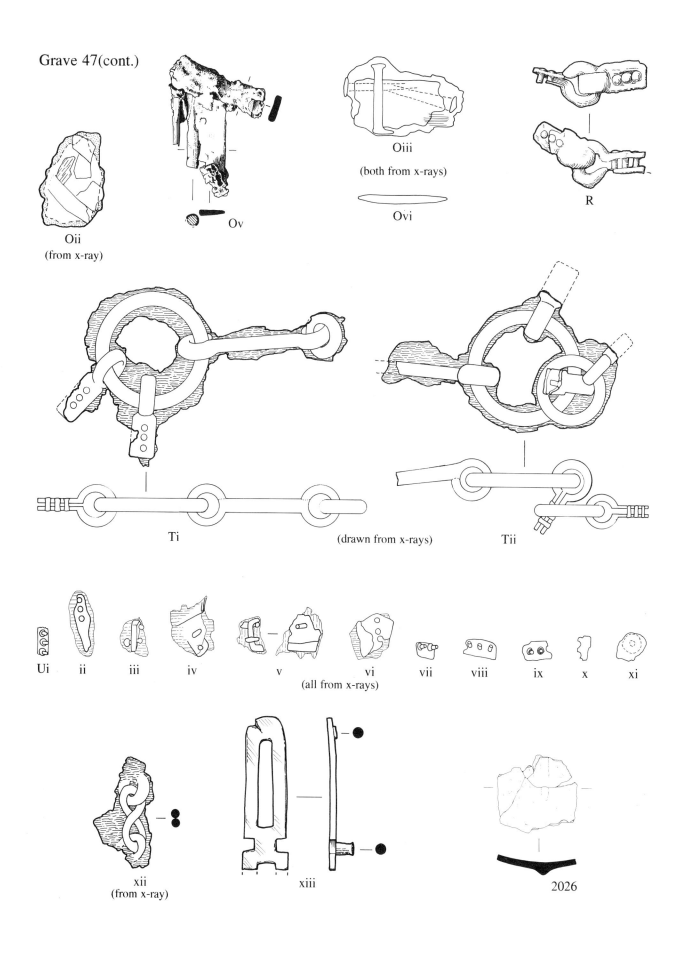

Grave 47(cont.)

Oii
(from x-ray)

Ov

Oiii

(both from x-rays)

Ovi

R

Ti

(drawn from x-rays)

Tii

Ui   ii   iii   iv   v   vi   vii   viii   ix   x   xi

(all from x-rays)

xii
(from x-ray)

xiii

2026

Figure 110 Grave-goods from grave 47 (cont'd). Scales: *Uxiii*; 1:1. *2026*; 1:3. Others; 1:2

III. Catalogue of Cremations

by Tim Pestell and Shirley Carnegie, incorporating material by Teresa Briscoe (pot stamps), Elisabeth Crowfoot (textiles), Rowena Gale (charcoal), Simon Mays (cremated bone), Peter Murphy (seeds) and James Steele (cremated bone).

Grave 48 (cremation) (Fig. 111)
Cut dimensions: Unknown
Container for bone: Urn
Condition: Only urn survives
Sex/age: Unknown

Description: A Bronze Age collared urn, *0558*, height 366mm, virtually complete. The collar is decorated with alternating zones of vertical or slightly diagonal, and horizontal, lines of cord impressions, numbering between four and nine in each zone. The grit-tempered fabric is mid-brown with a surface which is now crazed and which has probably been varnished since excavation.

The urn was found upside down in mound one in 1862, making it likely that the ship burial mound re-used an earlier prehistoric barrow. Hele recorded that the urn 'contained human bone, the femur or thighbone and part of the pelvis being perfect' (1870, 25–6) but Davidson commented that it was empty (1863, 179) and Francis 'almost empty' (1863a, 61). [Ald A122]

Grave-goods: None

Grave 49 (cremation) (Fig. 111)
Cut dimensions: Unknown
Container for bone: Urn
Condition: Only urn survives
Sex/age: Unknown

Description: A damaged biconical urn, *0559*, lacking all of the rim and much of its hollow neck. Decoration consists of four incised lines just below the outward curve of the neck. Beneath are two bands of circular stamps of plain centre with radiating lines (Briscoe A5di), divided by three bands of incised lines. Beneath are two more bands of incised lines, above a band of segmented horseshoe stamps (Briscoe G2bii). The decoration finishes just above the carination which has a slight flange. The fabric has a dark grey core and inner surface with a pink-brown layer immediately beneath the outer surface. The outer surface is pale brown with a large dark grey patch. The fabric is generally rough and gritty though smoothed in some areas. Surviving height 201mm.

The urn's date of discovery is unknown but it was placed in the Ashmolean Museum in 1885 from the University of Oxford Natural Science Museum. Nothing is known of its arrival in Oxford, although George Rolleston, Professor of Anatomy, acquired a great deal of archaeological material in the 1860s and 1870s. The urn is not mentioned in his correspondence but its accompanying label states 'Found at Snape, Suffolk. From the collection of Antiquities formed by the late J. M. Spalding, Esq., of Westleton' (David Brown, Asst. Keeper, Dept. of Antiquities, pers. comm. 5/7/82). The urn is therefore assumed to derive from the 1862–3 excavations. The urn was drawn by Pat Jacobs. [Ash 605–1885. Myres 1977, No. 2040]

Grave-goods: None

Grave 50 (cremation) (Fig. 111)
Cut dimensions: Unknown
Container for bone: Urn
Condition: Urn now missing
Sex/age: Unknown

Description: A small biconical vessel, *0640*, with wide mouth, hollow neck, slightly elevated rim and a low footring base. It is known only from Myres' Corpus (1977, 40, fig. 209, No. 2421) and its location, if it still exists, is unknown. Its decoration consists of three horizontal grooves above short diagonal slashes on the carination around the urn's circumference. Its fabric is a dark brown coarse ware. Height 126mm. The urn is assumed to have been found during the 1862–3 excavations.

Grave-goods: None

Grave 51 (cremation) (Fig. 112)
Cut dimensions: Unknown
Container for bone: Urn
Condition: Only urn survives
Sex/age: Unknown

Description: A shouldered urn, *0641*, with tall neck and everted rim. It is decorated with a grooved corrugation low on the neck, interspersed with wider grooves. The three panels contain a diagonal grooved cross and vertical and diagonal grooved swastikas (Briscoe J1aii) of the same size. The drawing has been rearranged to show both swastikas, the vertically-set one being in the place where the diagonal cross should be. The soft pale brown core fabric has a grey surface, burnished black above the shoulder. The tempering has burnt out leaving *c*.1mm diameter holes. Height 155mm.

The urn was about half full of mixed loose earth and cremated bone with some cremated bone concreted to the side wall near the base. The material was possibly undisturbed but was not examined.

The urn was mentioned by Davidson (1863, 178 and fig. 1), Francis (1863a, 61 and fig. 2) and Hele (1870, 25–6 and figure), having been found in 1862 during the excavation of the ship burial (mound one). [Ald A126. Myres 1977, No. 2423]

Grave-goods: None

Grave 52 (cremation) (Fig. 112)
Cut dimensions: Unknown
Container for bone: Urn
Condition: Only urn survives
Sex/age: Unknown

Description: A shouldered urn, *0642*, with wide mouth and a short upright rim. There is a possible hole in the lower part of the urn but this was blocked when the urn was restored by Ipswich Museum and cannot now be examined properly. The decoration consists of three horizontal incised lines forming two bands with a zone of pendant triangles beneath. The upper band contains a row of bow-edged triangular stamps (Briscoe E1di), the lower band, a row of plain circular stamps (Briscoe A1bi). The pendant triangles, probably originally five in number, are irregularly spaced and contain stamped rosettes (Briscoe A5ai). The fabric is of a smooth grey-brown ware with a red oxidised band immediately beneath the outer surface. It has occasional inclusions of small stones. Height 159mm.

The urn is assumed to have been found in the 1862–3 excavations. [Ald A130, Myres 1977, No. 2424]

Grave-goods: None

Grave 53 (cremation) (Fig. 112)
Cut dimension: Unknown
Container for bone: Urn
Condition: Only urn survives
Sex/age: Unknown

Description: A bossed globular urn, *0643*, with only the lower half surviving. It has four, originally five, small hollow bosses at the shoulder evenly spaced. Each is enclosed on its sides and base by three straight incised lines. Between each boss is the lower portion of a triangle formed by three incised lines; the bases are roughly level with the base lines beneath the bosses. There were originally five triangles, each apparently filled with stamps following the edges and bisecting them vertically. Two stamps are used; in three triangles there is a key-hole design (Briscoe E5ai) and in the other surviving triangle a small cross-in-square (A4aiii). At one point there is a horizontal incised line between a boss and a triangle near the (surviving) top of the pot. This is possibly the base of another decorative feature. The dark grey fabric is grog-tempered and has a pinky-brown layer just beneath the outer surface. The outer surface is burnished very dark grey from the base of the decoration up. The interior surface is dark grey with the surface largely flaked away. Surviving height *c.*171mm.

The urn was found in 1862 in mound 2 according to Francis (1863a, 61 and fig. 1). [Ips, no accession number; Myres 1977, No. 2425]

Grave-goods: None

Grave 54 (cremation) (Fig. 112)
Cut dimensions: Unknown
Container for bone: Urn
Condition: Only urn survives
Sex/age: Unknown

Description: A shouldered urn, *0644*, with slightly everted rim. Just below the rim is a line of 'tree'-shaped stamps with a grid pattern, set vertically (Briscoe M6ai). At each quadrant a pair of vertical lines, each made up of five stamps, reaches down to the shoulder. The dark grey sand-tempered ware has a pink layer immediately beneath the outer surface. The outer surface is rough and gritty with smoothing, especially above the shoulders. Surviving height 165mm.

The urn is labelled simply 'Snape, Aldeburgh 1863' and is assumed to come from the 1862–3 excavations. There is no other information and the urn does not appear in the British Museum accession book. [BM. OA 4300. Myres 1977, No. 3626]

Grave-goods: None

Grave 55 (cremation) (Fig. 112)
Cut dimensions: Unknown
Container for bone: Urn
Condition: Only urn survives
Sex/age: Unknown

Description: A shoulder-bossed urn, *0645*, with its rim missing. Its only decoration is of five regularly spaced hollow bosses. The fabric is dark grey with grog tempering and a thin pale brown oxidised layer immediately below the outer surface. The dark grey surface is burnished on its upper half. The lower third of the urn shows possible traces of horizontal knife trimming. Surviving height 165mm.

The urn is assumed to have been found in the 1862–3 excavations. [Ald A128. Myres 1977, No. 3862]

Grave-goods: None

Grave 56 (cremation) (Fig. 112)
Cut dimensions: Unknown
Container for bone: Urn
Condition: Only urn survives
Sex/age: Unknown

Description: A plain sub-globular urn, *0648*, with wide mouth and inverted rim. Its fabric is a smooth black ware, originally burnished. Height 175mm. It is assumed to have been found during the 1862–3 excavations. [Ald A127. Myres 1977, No. 3865]

Grave-goods: None

Grave 57 (cremation) (Fig. 113)
Cut dimensions: Unknown
Container for bone: Urn
Condition: Only urn survives
Sex/age: Unknown

Description: A tall, plain, sub-biconical urn, *0649*, with everted rim. Its mid grey core fabric is grit-tempered. The surface is a hard brown-grey, patchily burnished especially above the shoulder. The fabric is a pale grey immediately beneath the outer surface. Height 220mm. The urn is assumed to have been found in the 1862–3 excavations. [Ald A129. Myres 1977, No. 3866]

Grave-goods: None

Grave 58 (cremation) (Fig. 113)
Cut dimensions: Unknown
Container for bone: Urn
Condition: Only urn survives
Sex/age: Unknown

Description: A biconical urn, *0651*, with its rim missing. The neck and shoulder has three horizontal lines above a line of 'Union Jack' stamps (Briscoe C4ai). Beneath this zone are two more incised horizontal lines. The lower is interrupted by long hollow bosses demarcated by variously one or two incised vertical lines. At the shoulder between the bosses are lines of three circular cross stamps (Briscoe A4ai). Incised lines lower down on one part of the pot (not shown) are classified by Briscoe under 'doodles' (M7bi). Surviving height 99mm.

The urn was donated to the Verulamium Museum, St Albans by Sir John Evans, having been in his possession for a number of years. He was at Aldeburgh frequently around 1866 and he probably acquired this single pot at about this time (B. Adams pers. comm. 3/2/89). The urn is therefore assumed to have been found in the 1862–3 excavations. [Ver 80.548]

Grave-goods: None

Grave 59 (cremation) (Fig. 113)
Cut dimensions: Unknown
Container for bone: Urn
Condition: Only urn survives
Sex/age: Unknown

Description: Fragments of the conical neck of an urn, *0652*, with a slightly thickened vertical rounded rim. The decoration still surviving consists of two wide horizontal grooves beneath an irregular line of impressions formed by a stamp (Briscoe G1aiii) used six times, to create a rectangular shape. The sand-tempered dark grey fabric has a smooth mid grey inner surface. The outer surface is a smooth dark grey with a thin pink layer immediately beneath. Surviving height 92mm. This urn is assumed to have been found in the 1862–3 excavations. [Ips, no accession number — wrongly entered under 1972.120]

Grave-goods: None

Grave 60 (cremation) (Fig. 113)
Cut dimensions: Unknown
Container for bone: Urn
Condition: Only urn survives
Sex/age: Unknown

Description: A decorated sub-biconical urn, *0653*, mostly complete in its lower half. The sandy dark grey fabric has dark brown inner and outer surfaces and evidence of its coil manufacture at the shoulder. The outer surface is burnished and the inner has scrape marks. Decoration consists of elongated hollow bosses, both on their own and contained within slightly diagonal incised lines. One sherd suggests some incised lines may have formed a pendant triangle. A band of irregularly-spaced oval cross stamps (Briscoe D4ai) is contained beneath two, and above three, incised horizontal lines at the shoulder. Height 198mm. No associated contents are known. It is assumed to be from the 1862–3 excavations. [Ips, no accession number]

Grave-goods: None

Grave 61 (cremation) (Figs 114 and 119)
Cut dimensions: Unknown
Container for bone: Urn
Condition: Only urn survives
Sex/age: Unknown

Description: A complete urn, *0560*, of sub-biconical form with an upright rim. It has a variety of decorative stamps used within a field of triangles set beneath a single incised band below the neck. Those triangles with their bases uppermost have a line of stamps following each side. Those with their apexes uppermost are not always stamped along their bases and one has no stamps outlining any of its sides. Each triangle is bisected vertically by a line of stamps except for one which is filled with stamps. There is a group of three solitary stamps above the upper line (shown in the 'unrolled' illustration, Fig. 114). The stamps used are two concentric circles (Briscoe A2ai), concentric triangles (E1ei), a cross stamp (A4aii) and a lattice square (C2di). Each triangle normally contains two stamp types, used eight times, but on occasions only one stamp type is used. The fabric consists of a dark grey core with a pale brown layer just beneath the surface. The upper half is pale pinky-brown and oxidised, the lower dark grey and reduced. The surface lacks tempering and is flaking away from the body. Height 270mm.

The urn was found to contain quite a large amount of cremated bone which was not examined; it is presumed to be a mix of material as two sherd fragments (from other urns), matchsticks and paper scraps were also contained. Sherd (i) possibly derives from urn *0643* (grave 53). A large fragment of charcoal from the bone, up to 19mm in diameter, was identified as of gorse or broom (*Ulex* sp. or *Cytisus* sp.), of ring porous structure. The urn is assumed to come from the 1862–3 excavations. [Ald A123. Myres 1977, No. 2419]

Grave-goods: None

Grave 62 (cremation) (Fig. 114)
Cut dimensions: Unknown
Container for bone: Urn
Condition: Only urn survives
Sex/age: Unknown

Description: A large shouldered urn, *0639*, with conical neck and slightly everted rim. It is decorated at the shoulder with four incised horizontal lines forming three bands, each decorated with incised diagonal lines forming chevrons. The narrow upper and lower bands contain single line chevrons and frame a wider band of three-line chevrons. The fabric is pale grey, chaff-tempered, with a roughly burnished surface of oxidised pale brown, with pink and grey patches. There are numerous chaff impressions. Height 273mm.

The urn has a smear of the original cremation concreted to the base but this was not examined. The urn is assumed to derive from the 1862–3 excavations. [Ald A125. Myres 1977, No. 2420]

Grave-goods: None

Grave 63 (cremation) (Fig. 115)
Cut dimensions: Unknown
Container for bone: Urn
Condition: Only urn survives
Sex/age: Unknown

Description: A plain shoulder-bossed urn, *0646*, with missing rim. Its nine applied bosses are evenly spaced. The pale grey grog-tempered fabric has a hard, dark grey surface, with an oxidised patch of pale pinky brown. The surface is burnished above the shoulder. Surviving height 180mm.

The urn contained a mix of loose soil and cremated bone; the bottom 40mm appears to be intact with the bone and sand concreted together. This bone was not examined.

The urn is assumed to have been discovered in 1862–3. [Ald A124. Myres 1977, No. 3863]

Grave-goods: None

Grave 64 (cremation) (Figs 115 and 119)
Cut dimensions: Unknown
Container for bone: Urn
Condition: Incomplete
Sex/age: Unknown

Description: A plain shouldered urn, *0647*, with wide mouth, hollow neck and a smaller, slightly squared-off, rim. The fabric is a rough dark grey ware with a thin red oxidised layer immediately beneath the outer surface. Height 155mm.

The bottom 50mm of the urn contained the unexcavated remains of cremated bone concreted within a dark grey sand. The bone was mainly in small fragments and has not been examined. The urn is assumed to have been found during the 1862–3 excavations. [Ald A131. Myres 1977, No. 3864]

Grave-goods:
A: Opaque fused **glass lump**, length 25mm, of dark blue colour with a small green patch, possibly from beads. [1165]
B: Opaque fused **glass lump** of dark blue colour, from beads? [0654]
C: Three small melted **Ae fragments** from unknown objects. [0655]

Grave 65 (cremation) (Fig. 115)
Cut dimensions: Unknown
Container for bone: Urn
Condition: Only urn survives
Sex/age: Unknown

Description: A plain sub-biconical urn, *0650*, with a hollow neck and everted rim. The pale grey fabric is grog-tempered with chaff and occasional angular flint fragment inclusions. It has a smooth grey and brown surface burnished above the shoulder. Height 210mm.

The bottom 45mm of the urn contains a mix of grey sand and cremated bone, concreted together so hard that the material could not be extracted. The urn is assumed to derive from the 1862–3 excavations. [Ald A132. Myres 1977, No. 3867]

Grave-goods: None

Grave 66 (cremation) (Fig. 119)
Cut dimensions: Unknown
Container for bone: Urn (*not illus.*)
Condition: Incomplete
Sex/age: Possibly female, adult

Description: A cremation with no details other than that it derives from Snape, making it likely to be from the 1862–3 excavations. The fragments of urn *0769*, surviving only as a base, were held together by the bottom 120mm of the concreted cremated bone it originally contained. The urn remains have a dark grey core and inner surface, with an outer surface of smooth mid grey-brown. The fabric is chaff-tempered. No decoration is visible. The form is

uncertain as the weight of earth had caved in the base which was also root damaged, making reconstruction or drawing impossible.

Over four thousand fragments (1146.8g) of well fired cremated bone survived, deriving from a middle-aged adult, possibly female. The bone was excavated in two equal spits for the present study. Forty-four fragments (98.9g) of animal bone from a horse/donkey were identified, including an equid second carpal and a (possibly horse) mandible, and occipital fragments. As nearly 10% of the total bone by weight was of animal bone, it may represent the deliberate burning of part or all of the animal with the corpse (see Chapter 6 section IV for further discussion). [Ips, no accession number — wrongly entered under 1972.90]

Grave-goods:
A: Four Fe **rivets**, length *c.*12mm. (i–iii) were found within 60mm of each other during retrieval of the bone. (iv) was found in sieving the top spit of bone from the urn. The first three rivets all have wood impressions and their position in a line within the bone suggests that all four originally came from the same wooden object, presumably placed in the urn unburnt. [1387, 2437–2439]

Grave 67 (cremation) (Fig. 115)
Cut dimensions: Unknown
Container for bone: Urn
Condition: Probably truncated
Sex/age: Possibly female, adult

Description: An urned cremation located by Major-General Scott-Elliott by dowsing, at approximately TM 4010 5937, that is, north-west of Area A (roughly located in Fig. 5). The urn, *0658*, of chaff-tempered fabric, has only the lower two thirds surviving, with detached fragments of the rim and decoration. These show it to have been probably biconical with a rounded, everted rim. Its interior is dark grey, with a mid grey core and a pale pink layer beneath the exterior surface. This exterior is dark grey-brown and pockmarked, with slight burnishing on the upper half. The decoration consists of chevrons, each formed by four incised lines, beneath a single incised horizontal line. A single quatrefoil stamp (Briscoe A4aiii) survives above this line. Reconstructed height 219mm.

The cremated bone, *1166*, surviving as over 2000 fragments (407.1g), is of a middle- to old-aged adult, possibly female. The bone was well fired. A fragment of ossified cartilage, *2415*, probably from an animal, was also identified.

Amongst the bone were two small pieces of unworked burnt flint (*1167*) and some tiny pieces of charcoal (*2425*). One fragment was probably of heather (*Ericaceae*) and one probably of gorse (*Ulex* sp.) or broom (*Cytisus* sp.); the sample was too small to specify which. A third fragment was vitrified with distortion of the structure.

Published by Owles (1970, 103). [Ips 1970.90]

Grave-goods:
A: Bone **spindle-whorl** fragment, now missing (*not illus.*). [1168]

156

Grave 68 (cremation) (Figs 115 and 119)
Cut dimensions: 0.55m diameter
Container for bone: Ae bowl
Condition: Complete
Sex/age: Probably female, adult or possibly adolescent

Description: A cremation buried in a flat-bottomed pit, its base at approximately 13.70mOD. The bone was contained in an open Ae bowl, *0770*, spun rather than beaten (Dr S.J. Plunkett pers. comm.), diameter 327mm. The rim has a thickened triangular section, the sides curving down to a flat base. The bowl had been wrapped in an uneven Z-spun plain tabby weave cloth. One corner of this had fallen inside, leaving its impression on the rim and inner side. The cloth fibres have the appearance and structure of flax *Linum usitatissimum*. L., and all the preserved remains derive from the same fabric. The warp is generally coarser than the weft, thread counts per cm varying from 25–6/18, 23/17 and 19/16. Identification of the weft was through the preservation in three places of a return thread only halfway across the fragment, used to straighten up an uneven shed. The parallels of early Scandinavian textiles and the Z-spinning suggest a local/European origin is more likely than one further east. The position of the fragments and the lack of any string under the bowl rim suggest that it was completely wrapped in cloth rather than tied on; both methods have been found used in bronze bowls from Anglo-Saxon graves.

The cremated bone consisted of a few hundred minute fragments and a few larger identifiable pieces. These suggest a female, probably adult but possibly adolescent. The bone had been well fired but the collection of the remains was poor. Four fragments (5.4g) of unidentifiable animal bone were included (*contra* Calvin Wells in West and Owles 1973, 55).

When *in situ* the bowl had pieces of wood (*2427*) adhering to its west side, suggested at the time of excavation to have been probably tree roots. The wood was mineralised and has been re-examined, showing it to be of oak (*Quercus* sp.) with a ring-porous structure indicating that it derived from aerial parts of the tree, *i.e.* branch or trunk, and therefore possibly deliberately included. A small amount of burnt flint (*2426*) was also found.

The cremation was exposed in the sewer trench excavated in 1972 where it was called 'burial 1' (West and Owles 1973). [Ips 1972.120]

Grave-goods:
A: Fe **rivet**. [1385]

Grave 69 (cremation) (Fig. 116)
Cut dimensions: None observed
Container for bone: Urn
Condition: Incomplete
Sex/age: Male, young adult

Description: A cremation contained within urn *0882*, a large biconical vessel with its rim missing, surviving height 226mm. The urn is of light grey fabric with a reduced surface and was originally well burnished. The upper body is decorated with a band of triangles whose sides are each formed of four incised lines. The triangles are enclosed at the top by two, and bottom by four, bands of horizontal lines; each triangle contains a group of seven

open rosette stamps (Briscoe A7ci). All are sharp, clear, deep and clearly made with the same die. A further sherd from the urn, also decorated with lines and stamps, came to light in 1991 from a private collection; it has now been reunited with the pot.

The bone, a few hundred small fragments, are from a young adult male and include small fragments of cranial vault, some with unfused sutures. Firing of the bone was efficient although collection was poor. No animal bones were present.

A small flint flake (*2422, not illus.*) was also found mixed in with the bone, as was a charred wheat grain (*2421*) of *Triticum* sp., probably emmer.

The cremation was excavated in the 1972 sewer trench and called 'burial 2' (West and Owles 1973). [Ips 1972.120]

Grave-goods: None

Grave 70 (cremation) (Figs 116 and 119)
Cut dimensions: None observed
Container for bone: Urn
Condition: Incomplete
Sex/age: Unknown, infant

Description: A cremation contained within *0883*, a plain, squat, dark brown biconical urn of soft fabric with some chaff backing, burnished all over. Height 192mm. Decoration consists of five small hollow bosses around the girth of the pot.

The several hundred minute bone fragments were from an unsexable infant, probably 9–10 months old and included two crowns of deciduous teeth (a molar and an incisor). Two cranial vault fragments had porotic lesions — pitting on the surface of the bone — which are often classified as porotic hyperostosis. This condition is most frequent in infants in the 6 months–2 years age range (Stuart-Macadam 1989), and seems to be the result of iron-deficiency anaemia. This condition can be caused by poor diet, but it is perhaps most commonly caused by intestinal parasites (Stuart-Macadam 1991). It particularly affects individuals during phases of rapid growth and immunological vulnerability (*e.g.* weanlings) and was a common disease in antiquity.

The firing of the bones was good. A small fragment of an adult (?tibia) bone was present. There was no animal bone. Two small fragments (0.1g) of 'cremation slag' were found (*2411*).

Some tiny pieces of charcoal (*2420*) were identified as being of oak (*Quercus* sp.), probably alder (*Alnus* sp.) and probably cherry or blackthorn (*Prunus* spp.). A small piece of burnt flint (*2419*) was also present.

Excavated in the 1972 sewer trench and published as 'burial 3' in West and Owles (1973). [Ips 1972.120]

Grave-goods:
A: Bone **object**, length 10.5mm, possibly a pin terminal. An alternative interpretation would be as a bone cosmetic pick but these normally have a hole at the flattened end for suspension. The flat end has four notches, rounded and therefore possibly made by friction from an abrasive thread rather than a saw (R. D. Carr pers. comm.). [2412]

Grave 71 (cremation) (Fig. 116)
Cut dimensions: None observed
Container for bone: Urn
Condition: Incomplete
Sex/age: Unknown, infant

Description: A cremation contained within urn *0884*. This shouldered vessel has a rounded profile, short upright rim and a soft fine pale buff fabric with grey-brown reduced surfaces, apparently unburnished. The shoulder is decorated with five hollow bosses. Reconstructed height 190mm.

The small amount of bone contained was from an unsexable infant probably 3–6 months old, including the partly formed crown of an unerupted molar. The firing of the bones was good and their collection moderately so. No animal bones were present.

Excavated in 1972 and published as 'burial 4' in West and Owles (1973). [Ips 1972.120]

Grave-goods: None

Grave 72 (cremation) (Fig. 116)
Cut dimensions: None observed
Container for bone: Urn
Condition: Incomplete
Sex/age: Unknown, adult

Description: A cremation contained within urn *0885*. The urn survives only as fragments of a globular vessel with a high shoulder, its rim and base missing, surviving height 140mm. The fabric is a dark red-brown with smoothed surfaces.

The few small fragments of bone show an unsexable adult with few identifiable pieces. Firing was efficient but collection bad. There were two fragments (10.9g) of animal bone (*contra* Calvin Wells in West and Owles 1973, 55), one fragment petrous, from a ?pig, cow or horse.

The cremation was from the 1972 sewer trench and published by West and Owles (1973) as 'burial 5'. [Ips 1972.120]

Grave-goods: None

Grave 73 (cremation) (Figs 116 and 119)
Cut dimensions: None observed
Container for bone: Urn
Condition: Incomplete
Sex/age: Unknown, adult

Description: A cremation contained within an open biconical urn, *0886*, height 168mm. The fabric is grey with red-brown oxidised surfaces. Most of the upper half was lost but enough survives, including a rim fragment, to show that it had been decorated with a single row of cross-hatched stamps in a band below three horizontal incised lines under the rim and above three more horizontal incised lines. The shoulder had a zone of pendant triangles beneath the lower lines, each of their edges formed by three incised lines, containing six stamps made with the same cross-hatched die (Briscoe A3aii).

The cremated bone consists of several hundred very small fragments from an adult. Three fragments of leg bone, one probably of the tibia, show evidence of chronic periostitis. There is longitudinal striation of the kind which

is commonly found in early, especially Anglo-Saxon, leg bones. The striae, about 2mm apart, have in between, occasional fine pits, 0.25mm or less in diameter, which indicate a reaction to a low grade inflammation of the legbone membrane or vascular congestion.

There is a slight underfiring of several fragments of the bone and collection of the remains was poor. A fragment (0.9g) of unidentified mammalian animal bone (*2414*) was present.

The cremation was excavated in 1972 and published as 'burial 6' by West and Owles (1973). [Ips 1972.120]

Grave-goods:
A: Bone **spindle-whorl**, max. diameter 30mm, laminated during firing. [0887]
B: Fragment of double-sided bone **comb**, length 13mm, shrunken during firing. Now missing. [0888]
C: A **girdle ring**, diameter *c.*46mm, made from the burr of a red deer antler, shrunken during firing. [0889, 2414]

Grave 74 (cremation) (Fig. 119)
Cut dimensions: None observed
Container for bone: None
Condition: Incomplete
Sex/age: Male, youngish adult

Description: An unurned cremation recovered immediately east of ring-ditch *2449*, beneath the present road.

The bone was of a male, possibly youngish adult, represented by several hundred fragments. Some pieces of the cranial vault showed unfused sutures or barely starting fusion. A short length of mandible showed three incisors had been present at death although not now surviving. The bones had all been well fired but not well collected. They include a tiny fragment of the superior orbital margin of a young child. No animal bones were present.

Excavated in the 1972 sewer trench and called 'burial 7' by West and Owles (1973). [Ips 1972.120]

Grave-goods:
A: Four fragments of a double-sided bone **comb**, the tooth-plates originally clamped between a central band on either side. A rivet hole is visible on fragment (iii). [2409]

Grave 75 (cremation) (Fig. 116)
Cut dimensions: None observed
Container for bone: Urn
Condition: Incomplete
Sex/age: Unknown, infant

Description: A cremation contained within biconical urn, *0890*. It has a hard fabric of fine-grained buff with oxidised patches of dark red-brown, decorated with six small applied bosses. Height 63mm.

The bone, consisting of a few hundred tiny fragments mostly of the cranial vault, show the body to have been from an infant ?8–12 weeks old. The bone was well fired and reasonably well collected. Two small fragments of adult radius or ulna bones were also present. There was no animal bone.

Excavated in the 1972 sewer trench and published by West and Owles (1973) as 'burial 8'. [Ips 1972.120]

Grave-goods: None

Grave 76 (Figs 117 and 119)
Cut dimensions: None observed
Container for bone: Urn
Condition: Incomplete
Sex/age: Probably female, (?young) adult

Description: A collection of cremated bone found in a restricted area of the spoil heap from the 1972 sewer trench, well away from any other cremations. In the same area were found fragments of pottery and the spindle-whorl, hence the group is interpreted as deriving from a single urned burial. The pottery consists of rim and shoulder sherds from a biconical urn (*0891*), surviving height 105mm, of hard grey fabric with overall burnishing and red-brown oxidised surfaces. One fragment has an applied boss.

The cremated bone is limited to a few tiny scraps, including fragments of thin cranial vault, some with unfused sutures. The bones were well fired but no new assessment of the bone collection has been made. There was no animal bone.

Published by West and Owles (1973) as 'burial 9'. [Ips 1972.120]

Grave-goods:
A: Clay **spindle-whorl**, found in the same area of spoil as the bones and urn sherds. [0892]

Graves 77–99 were discovered in 1985–1992 excavations.

Grave 77 (cremation) (Fig. 119)
Cut dimensions: None observed
Container for bone: Urn (*not illus.*)
Condition: Truncated
Sex/age: Unknown, middle/old-aged adult

Description: A damaged cremation contained within urn *0013* found in trial box 3 in 1985, about 3.5m from grave 67. The urn survives only in fragments and is in too poor condition to be reconstructed or drawn. Its form is unknown and no decoration exists on any of the surviving sherds. The underfired fabric is dark brown with occasional grit and in crumbly condition. The outer surface is smoothed, the inner surface decayed.

The bone was well fired, and consists of about 750 fragments (181.2g). It represents a middle/old-aged adult of unknown sex. No animal bone was identified.

Grave-goods:
A: A **droplet** of melted Ae adhering to a fragment of cremated bone. [0021]

Grave 78 (cremation) (Figs 117 and 119)
Cut dimensions: 0.34 × 0.59m
Container for bone: Urn
Condition: Truncated
Sex/age: Unknown

Description: A plough-damaged cremation contained in urn *0073*. The 109 sherds that survive all derive from the lower half showing it to have been of a squat globular form; the highest surviving fragment appears to be inturning. Surviving height 96mm. Its red-brown sandy fabric has occasional large flint grit inclusions and dark brown inner and outer surfaces with chaff impressions on the base. The inner surface has tooling marks and the outer surface is burnished.

This problematic deposit is listed as a cremation although no cremated bone was found within the pot. Two joining rim sherds (*0074*) were found in the base of the urn and derive from vessel *1152*, an open bowl, fragments of which were also found in the fill of grave 4 and loose in topsoil layer *0273* (Scatters No. 20). This whole 'cremation' is therefore most curious.

Grave-goods: None

Grave 79 (cremation) (Fig. 117)
Cut dimensions: 0.3 × 0.24m
Container for bone: Urn
Condition: Intact
Sex/age: Probably male, middle/old-aged adult

Description: An intact cremation placed in a regular round cut, contained within urn *0268*, height 245mm, that had collapsed in on itself (Pl. VI). The 148 sherds show the urn was globular with a rounded upright rim. It has a dark brown fabric with grit/sand tempera and some angular flint grit inclusions. Both surfaces are dark brown and smoothed with internal tooling on the shoulder. Decoration consists of three horizontal lines enclosing two rows of simple cross stamps (Briscoe A4ai). Beneath the bottom horizontal line are spaced six single-line pendant triangles enclosing rows of the same cross-shaped stamps.

The 6,600 bone fragments (576.8g) were of a middle/old-aged adult, possibly male. The bone was white and well fired, with some internal blackening. One vertebral fragment had a Schmorl's node. There was no animal bone.

Grave-goods: None

Grave 80 (cremation) (Figs 16, 117 and 120)
Cut dimensions: None — scattered within fill of grave 5 (an inhumation)
Container for bone: Urn originally
Condition: Scattered
Sex/age: Unknown, adult

Description: A scatter of cremated bone fragments and sherds found principally at the uppermost levels, but also lower down the fill of grave 5. Together, they are interpreted as deriving from a cremation disturbed by the digging of the inhumation and scattered throughout the grave on backfilling. Sherds from another pot (*0677*) were found directly associated with the body and are considered to relate to the inhumation. No sherds or bone fragments from grave 80 were found in the bottom layers of grave 5 or associated with the body.

The 118 sherds from the suggested cremation urn, *0318*, show the vessel to have been large, with a simple upright rim, reconstructed height 145mm. It was decorated with a zone of four horizontal lines on the shoulder above a line of stamps with a central club shape between two dots with barely discernible transverse grooves (Briscoe M3ci), apparently made using the foot of a brooch (Chapter 5 section VIII, pp. 228–31). Beneath are three horizontal lines and although incomplete, the shoulder appears to have had eight three-line pendant triangles, every other triangle containing one of four hollow bosses.

159

Its fabric is of fine brown clay, the inner surface showing extensive tooling, the outer surface grey-brown and burnished.

The 80 bone fragments (19g) scattered throughout the fill of the grave are from an adult of unknown sex. The bone is white, well fired and contains no animal bone. The fill of grave 5 contained 29 charcoal fragments (*0465*, *0486*) but it is unclear whether they relate to the inhumation or the cremation. Some were of a reasonable size suggesting that they are more likely to relate to the inhumation, although all were high up in the fill where the cremation material was most dense; they are described in the catalogue entry for grave 5.

Grave-goods:
A: Ae **buckle**, burnt and twisted, found within the fill of grave 5 and interpreted as belonging to the cremation. [0165]
B: Fe **nailhead** or **tack**, also found within the grave fill and interpreted as belonging to the cremation. [0185]

Grave 81 (cremation) (Figs 117 and 120)
Cut dimensions: None observed
Container for bone: Urn
Condition: Truncated
Sex/age: Possibly female, young adult

Description: A damaged cremation contained within urn *0042*. The urn survives only as fragments with no rim sherds, to 75mm high. They show a convex base and body sherds with two horizontal grooves on the shoulder above a zone of diagonal lines, apparently in groups. The fabric is sandy with occasional large grit inclusions. It has an oxidised dark grey outer skin with burnished inner and outer surfaces of dark grey.

The cremated bone was well fired and survives as over 460 fragments (156g). They derive from a young adult, possibly female. Three fragments (1g) of unidentified animal bone were identified, similar in appearance to the animal bone fragment from grave 73.

Grave-goods:
A: Circular clay ?**counter** with one face flat, the other convex. Diameter 17mm. [0044]

Grave 82 (cremation)
Cut dimensions: 0.6 × 0.57m
Container for bone: None
Condition: Truncated
Sex/age: Unknown

Description: A deposit of bone contained within an irregular round cut. The 300 fragments (53.7g) of bone were white and well fired but could not be used to determine either the age or sex of the individual. Two fragments (3.1g) of unidentified animal bone were recognised.

Grave-goods: None

Grave 83 (cremation) (Fig. 120)
Cut dimensions: 0.38 × 0.36m
Container for bone: None
Condition: Truncated
Sex/age: Unknown

Description: A tightly restricted scatter of cremated bone associated with pottery fragments from pot *A*, contained within or just outside a shallow round cut. The deposit was contained within a shallow scoop south of grave 7. Whilst the deposit was obviously truncated, the bone within the scoop was concentrated and clearly not originally contained within the pot, which had no base fragments; the pot is therefore listed here as a grave-good. There were in addition two sherds deriving from at least one other (unidentifiable) vessel.

The 360 fragments of bone (119.3g) represent an individual of unknown age or sex. The bone was well fired, white and includes some yellow trabecular material. Eight fragments (28.1g) of animal bone were mixed in, including mandible fragments from a large animal, ?horse/cow tibia shaft fragments and rib fragments from a smaller animal.

Several fragments of burnt flint and charcoal were also mixed in with the bone and sherds.

Grave-goods:
A: Fragments from a **pot**. The sherds (total weight 0.22kg) derive from the rim, neck and body. The pot was undecorated, of a soft grey fabric with external surfaces of red/brown colour. [0635]

Cremation 84 (cremation) (Figs 117 and 120)
Cut dimensions: None observed
Container for bone: Urn
Condition: Truncated
Sex/age: Unknown, adult

Description: A plough-damaged cremation contained within urn *0048*. As excavated, it appeared as a scatter of bone, pottery and the grave-goods. This was cleaned to reveal the base of the urn *in situ*, containing bone with spindle-whorl *A* sitting at the centre of the urn base. The vessel sherds can be reconstructed to show a well-made biconical urn, *c.*147mm tall, with upright rounded rim with a slight external bead. The vessel is of a fine light grey sandy fabric with slightly oxidised outer layers. Both surfaces are dark grey and burnished. Decoration consists of a band of circular cross and rosette stamps (Briscoe A5ai and A4ai), used alternately above two horizontal incised lines on the shoulder. Spaced pairs of shallow vertical lines extend from the lower horizontal line onto the urn's lower half. The decoration is, perhaps surprisingly, badly executed for such a well-made pot.

The bone collected was well fired, the 480 fragments weighing 126.7g. They represent an adult of unknown sex, although possibly female based on the presence of the spindle-whorl and the possible melted beads. Three pieces of burnt flint (*0196*) were recovered from the scatter. No animal bone was identified.

Grave-goods:
A: Two burnt and fused **fragments**, (i) of glass, possibly deriving from beads, (ii) of Ae. [0050]
B: Antler **spindle-whorl**, maximum diameter 33mm, nearly complete and burnt. A chip from the top of one edge (ii) has several circular incised lines apparently the result of the object being turned. [0192, 2418]
C: Large melted glass **fragment**, possibly deriving from beads. [0193]

D: Eight melted and fused glass **fragments** (i–viii), possibly deriving from beads, and a separate lump of melted Ae (*none illus.*). [0194]

E: Fe **object**, possibly a part of a nail or rivet shaft. The broken section shows a square core within the corrosion. [0195]

F: Twenty-one fragments of a double-sided **comb**. The comb originally had central tooth-plates of bone or very compact antler clamped by iron rivets between two decorated antler side-plates. Four joining fragments show a curved end (*selectively illus.*). [0049, 2417]

Grave 85 (cremation) (Fig. 121)
Cut dimensions: 0.39 × 0.48m
Container for bone: None
Condition: Truncated
Sex/age: Unknown, adult

Description: A discrete area of cremated bone containing several burnt fragments of grave-goods suggesting an unurned cremation. The bone was immediately beneath plough level and enclosed within a patch of dark greyish-brown sand which perhaps formed the base of the cut.

The bone, in a truncated deposit, consisted of about 113 fragments (11.7g) from an adult of unknown sex. The bone was well fired, mainly white with some yellowish trabecular material. No animal bone was identified.

The deposit also included a mass of charcoal fragments (*0255*), all of oak (*Quercus* sp.) including stem and heartwood, some slow grown.

Grave-goods:
A: Ten fragments of Ae **sheet**. All are warped, possibly after softening by fire but not actually melted. None is decorated. Nine are of thin sheet and one is of thicker gauge with a straight edge and a rounded profile. They suggest that, if all are from the same object, it was either a binding or more likely a thin-walled vessel such as a bowl. Only the three best pieces are illustrated. [0047, 0247, 0248, 0256]

B: Two fused glass **lumps**; (i) translucent blue, (ii) a droplet of opaque red and translucent blue. [0254, 0256]

Grave 86 (cremation) (Figs 117 and 119)
Cut dimensions: 0.24m diameter
Container for bone: Urn
Condition: Truncated
Sex/age: Unknown, adult

Description: A badly damaged cremation with associated material scattered over a wide area. The cremation was originally contained within urn *1157*. Although the pottery found in the scatter could be matched with that left in the base of the cremation cut, the identification of the remainder of the material as having constituted grave 86 is interpretative. The material is not considered a part of the cremation pyre spreads, and it seems to have been independent from that contained in grave 12.

The cremated bone from the scatter (11.1g) is from an adult of unknown age or sex, although the associated grave-goods suggest a female. Amongst the material was a fragment (1.3g) of animal bone of unknown type. Two samples of charcoal from the scatter (*0136, 0168*) were both of oak stem (*Quercus* sp.), that from *0136* fast grown.

Three fragments of burnt flint, *0054*, were found mixed in with the scatter.

Grave-goods:
A: Distorted fragment of Ae **cruciform brooch**, possibly the bow, with decoration of three ring-and-dot stamps. [0053]

B: Two **fragments** of Fe from an unknown object of flat rectangular shape. One possibly has a hole through one end — ?part of a **belt fitting**. [0069]

C: Melted **lump** of Ae, original object unrecognisable. [0125]

D: Five joining fragments of Fe from an object, possibly a **stud head** badly blistered by corrosion. [0126]

E: Fe **buckle** with tongue, width 23mm. [0234]

F: Fe **plate** with large rivet, possibly from a buckle. [0235]

Grave 87 (cremation) (Figs 118 and 121)
Cut dimensions: 0.28 × 0.27m
Container for bone: Urn
Condition: Slightly truncated
Sex/age: Possibly female, middle/old-aged adult

Description: A cremation within urn *0138*, placed within an irregular cut, only the base of which survived. The urn is tall and straight-sided with a wide mouth and rounded upright rim, reconstructed height 195mm. Its fabric is a dense dark brown with grit, chaff and some red grog inclusions. Its outer skin is oxidised to a darker brown and both inner and outer surfaces are rough. It is decorated with a faint horizontal line on the neck, crossed with spaced vertical lines. The fragments from the neck and rim show there to have been at least one row of coarse, open, four-leafed rosette stamps (Briscoe A4aiii) on the shoulder above another row of spaced, coarse, vertical lines.

The 4500 bone fragments (487.3g) were mainly white with some blackening internally and some yellowish trabecular material. They were possibly of a middle-aged female (35+). A fragment (2.2g) of possible animal bone was included in the cremated material.

Grave-goods:
A: **Object** with a porous structure, probably of clinker or slag. [0115]

B: Fragments of a double-sided bone **comb** (i–iv). Fragment (ii) from the connecting plate has ring-and-dot decoration and (iii) has a rivet still *in situ*. [0130, 2433]

Grave 88 (cremation) (Figs 36, 37, 38 and 118)
Cut dimensions: None — contained in upper fill of grave 17 (an inhumation)
Container for bone: Urn
Condition: Intact
Sex/age: Unknown, child

Description: An intact urned cremation within the upper fill of an inhumation (grave 17) adjacent to grave 89. The undecorated urn, *0030*, 95% complete, is hollow-necked with an upright rim, flattened above. The fabric has a dark grey core with grit tempera. Both surfaces are smoothed, the inner dark brown, the outer reddish brown. Height 129mm.

The 2700 bone fragments (172.2g) are unsexable, but come from a child, about 7 years old. The bones are white and well fired. Two longbone fragments apparently from this cremation are included in grave 89 (see below) and suggest that the two were buried at the same time. No animal bone was present.

Grave-goods: None

Grave 89 (cremation) (Figs 36, 37, 38, 118 and 121)
Cut dimensions: None — contained in upper fill of grave 17 (an inhumation)
Container for bone: Urn
Condition: Intact
Sex/age: Unknown, child

Description: An intact cremation contained within urn *0029*, deposited at the east end of an inhumation (grave 17), adjacent to grave 88. The globular undecorated urn, height 126mm, is 75% complete with a rounded upright rim, most of which is missing. Its fabric is gritty, of a dark brown colour. It has a brown interior and exterior, with a red-brown layer beneath the skin of the outer layer. The exterior is smoothed and the interior has tooling marks on the inside.

The 1100 bone fragments (172.2g) are of a child, unsexable, aged between 2–7 years. The bone includes a 'woven' bone, probably indicative of an infection, and a sutural ossicle ('wormian bone') like those from the pyre spread and grave 91. Wormian bones are supernumerary bones growing in the sutures of the cranial vault. Although sutural ossicles are to some extent hereditary (Sjøvold 1984), they have been found to be so common in Anglo-Saxon skeletons that their occurrence cannot be used at Snape to infer a familial relationship.

The bone was white and well fired. In addition, there were two longbone fragments, more robust than the rest of the assemblage, which would be consistent with the age of the older juvenile in the adjacent cremation, grave 88. Whilst intrusive, the fragments were evidently placed within the urn when originally deposited and suggest that cremations 88 and 89 were buried contemporaneously. They were apparently buried at the same time as the inhumation in grave 17, as no secondary cuts for the cremations were found in the grave fill. No animal bone was present.

Grave-goods:
A: Square-shaped bone **object** with a hole drilled through the centre, maximum width 14mm. [0270]

Grave 90 (cremation) (Fig. 118)
Cut dimensions: None — found in a scatter
Container for bone: Urn
Condition: Truncated
Sex/age: Unknown, infant/juvenile

Description: A scatter of pottery and cremated bone contained within ring-ditch *0302*, immediately south of the enclosed inhumation (grave 20). The scatter comprises 60 fragmentary sherds from an urn (*1597*) of unknown form other than having a simple upright rounded rim. The sandy fabric has a black inner surface and a smooth outer one of dark brown, showing signs of scraping. The only decoration visible is of faint horizontal lines on the neck sherds. One other sherd from this scatter (*0623*), from a rim, joins urn *A* in grave 6 (see discussion in Chapter 6 section II, pp. 244–6).

The six bone fragments (1.4g), all white, are from an infant or juvenile (0–12 years old) of unknown sex. Three unidentified fragments of charcoal, *0622*, were found in the scatter. No animal bone was identified. The tight distribution of the scatter fragments suggest that they are from a single truncated cremation perhaps associated in some way with the occupant of ring-ditch grave 20, and through sherd *0623*, maybe also with that of grave 6.

Grave-goods: None

Grave 91 (cremation) (Fig. 118)
Cut dimensions: 0.46 × 0.37m
Container for bone: Urn
Condition: Truncated
Sex/age: Possibly male, young adult

Description: A disturbed cremation originally contained within urn *0507*, placed in an oval cut. The cremation was between graves 21 and 22 (unexcavated) and was possibly associated with one or other. The urn has been reconstructed, height 169mm, showing it to be of globular form with a rounded, everted rim. It had no decoration, but a small hole 5mm in diameter had been drilled off-centre through its base. Its fabric has a dark brown core, the inner surface black, the outer, a lighter red-brown.

The cremated bone associated with the pottery fragments was spread over a restricted area. The 1300 fragments (572.3g) are from a young adult, 18–35 years old, possibly male. The bone was white, with occasional blackening internally and included a sutural ossicle or 'wormian bone' (*c.f.* those from the pyre spread and grave 89). There was no animal bone present.

Mixed in with the bone were a few charcoal fragments of oak (*Quercus* sp.) and gorse (*Ulex* sp.); there were also a few fragments of cokey-looking material.

Grave-goods: None

Grave 92 (cremation) (Fig. 118)
Cut dimension: None observed
Container for bone: Urn
Condition: Intact
Sex/age: Possibly male, adult

Description: A cremation contained within urn *0025*. Only the lower three-quarters of the tall straight-sided urn, height 180mm, survives. Its dense dark brown fabric has burnt-out chaff impressions on the outer red-brown to grey surface, which also shows wipe marks. The inner surface is dark brown to grey.

The bone was well fired with some subsidiary blackening internally. The bone survives as over 1500 fragments (369.8g), from an adult, possibly male. No animal bones were identified. A small fragment of burnt flint (*0033*) was collected from amongst the bone.

Grave-goods: None

Grave 93 (cremation) (Figs 118 and 121)
Cut dimensions: None observed
Container for bone: Urn
Condition: Truncated
Sex/age: Unknown, adult

Description: A plough-damaged cremation contained within urn *1423*, surviving height 60mm. Only the bottom can be reconstructed of what was probably originally a large vessel. There is no decoration on the remaining sherds. The dark grey, sandy fabric has an oxidised outer buff layer. The inner surface of the pot is dark grey, the outer dark brown; both are smoothed.

The 1100 cremated bone fragments (136.2g) are from a young/middle-aged adult (18–50 yrs) of unknown sex. The bones are white and well fired. No animal bone was present but there were two fragments of burnt flint, *1428*, weight under 5g.

Grave-goods:
A: Small Ae **fragment**, distorted by heat (*not illus.*). [1426]
B: Fe ?**nail** shaft, height 24mm, drawable only from X-ray. Found close to the main scatter of cremated bone, its association is only interpretive. [1421]

Grave 94 (cremation)
Cut dimensions: None observed
Container for bone: Urn
Condition: Truncated
Sex/age: Unknown, child

Description: A plough-damaged cremation placed close to cremations 95 and 96, in which only the bottom 80mm of urn *1495* survived (*not illus.*). Its form is not known, nor whether it was decorated. The surviving sherds show a fabric with a fine, pale grey core with red/brown surfaces, and smoothed on the exterior. One sherd shows evidence of a coil.

The surviving 500 bone remains (64.7g) are from an unsexable child about 2 years old. The bone is all white and well fired. No animal bone was present.

Grave-goods: None

Grave 95 (cremation)
Cut dimensions: None observed
Container for bone: Urn
Condition: Truncated
Sex/age: Unknown, adult

Description: A badly plough-damaged cremation (Pl. V) buried close to cremations 94 and 96. It was contained within urn *1494* (*not illus.*) which had completely lost its structure. Only remains of the base survived and its form, and whether it had any decoration, is unknown. The dark brown, soft, sandy fabric has a powdered red grog filler. One sherd is burnished.

The bone is made up of 1000 fragments (197.8g), all white and well fired, from an adult of unknown sex. No animal bone was present.

Grave-goods: None

Grave 96 (cremation)
Cut dimensions: None observed
Container for bone: None
Condition: Truncated
Sex/age: Unknown, adult

Description: A plough-damaged cremation found in close proximity to cremations 94 and 95. The 150 bone fragments (19.7g) are from an adult of unknown sex. The bone is white, well fired and includes no animal remains.

Grave-goods: None

Grave 97 (cremation)
Cut dimensions: 0.16 × 0.19m
Container for bone: None
Condition: Truncated
Sex/age: Unknown

Description: An unurned cremation located in evaluation work in trial trench VI and left unexcavated, hence no further information, except that it was adjacent to possible post-hole *1562* (Fig. 133).

Grave-goods: Unknown

Grave 98 (cremation)
Cut dimensions: None observed
Container for bone: Urn
Condition: Truncated
Sex/age: Unknown

Description: A heavily plough-damaged urned cremation located in evaluation work in trial trench VII and left unexcavated, hence no further information.

Grave-goods: Unknown

Grave 99 (cremation) (Figs 26, 27, 28 and 121)
Cut dimensions: None — scattered within fill of grave 11 (an inhumation)
Container for bone: None originally?
Condition: Probably incomplete
Sex/age: Unknown

Description: A scatter of cremated bone fragments with burnt metal objects from the fill of grave 11 (an inhumation), the majority from a thin, single, layer. Like grave 80, the material is considered to derive from an individual cremation. It appears to have been a deliberate rather than accidental inclusion, only a few bone sherds being found other than in the main layer (for an interpretation of this see Chapter 6 section II, pp. 246). The association of the burnt metal objects with the cremation rather than the inhumation is, naturally, interpretive.

The bone weighs 60.5g in total but the age, sex or number of individuals represented by it is unknown. Amongst the bone are two burnt animal bone fragments, weighing 2.1g. One is ?zygomatic, the other possibly of calcaneum. Both were from a large animal, possibly a horse or cow. The fill of grave 11 also contained a few charcoal fragments, although these might relate to the inhumation rather than the cremation.

Grave-goods:
A: Ae fragment possibly from a **brooch**. [0964]
B: Ae **droplet** or ball (*not illus.*). [0965]
C: **Strip** of rolled Ae. [0966]
D: Ag **droplet** attached to a fragment of burnt bone. [1129]
E: Two conjoined **balls** of Ag. [1130]

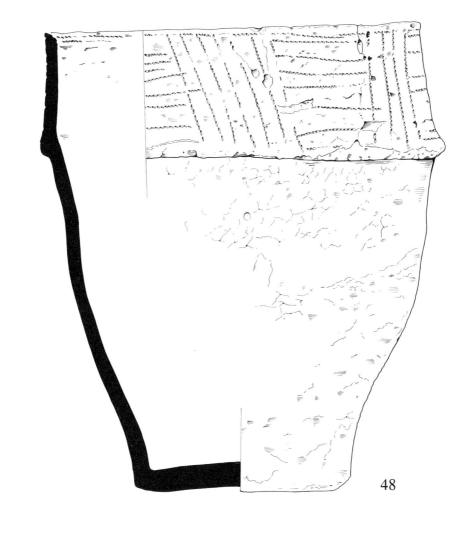

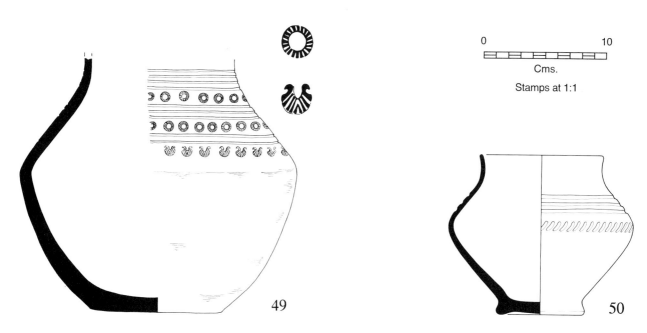

Figure 111 Cremation urns, graves 48, 49 and 50. Scale 1:3, pot stamps at 1:1

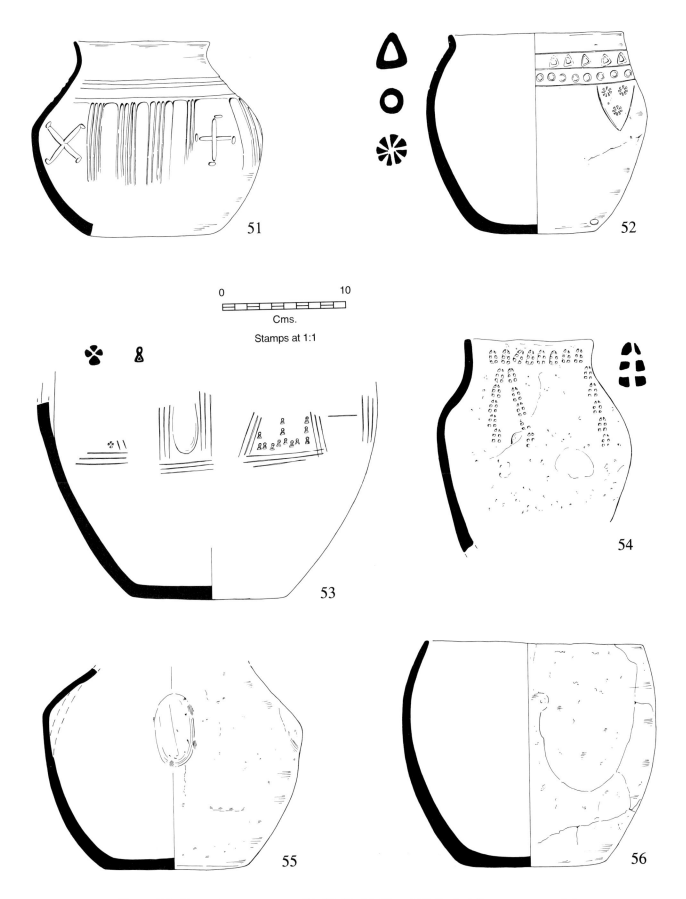

Figure 112 Cremation urns, graves 51, 52, 53, 54, 55 and 56. Scale 1:3, pot stamps at 1:1

165

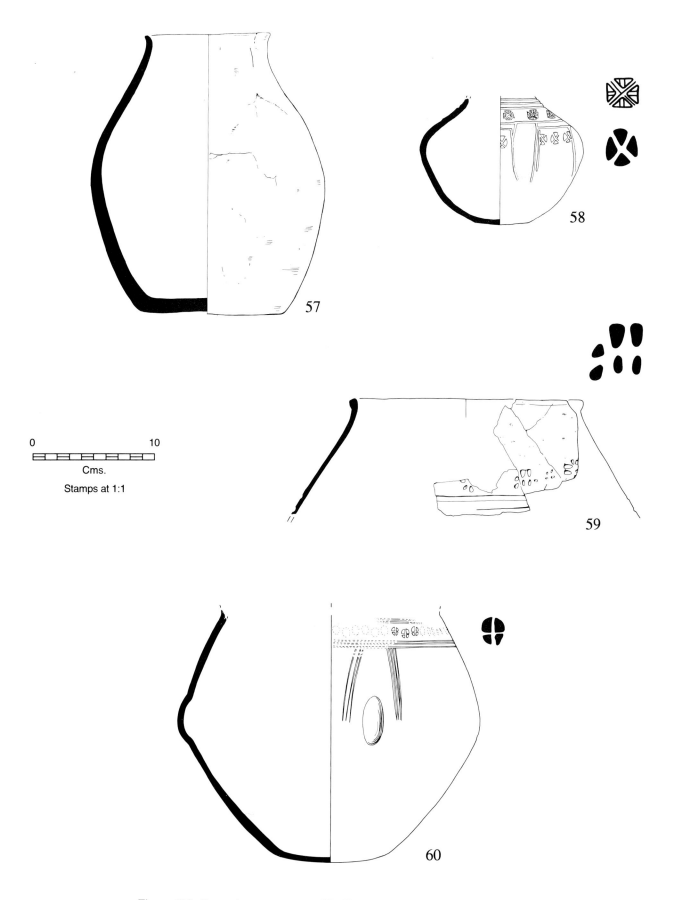

0
10
Cms.
Stamps at 1:1

57

58

59

60

Figure 113 Cremation urns, graves 57, 58, 59 and 60. Scale 1:3, pot stamps 1:1

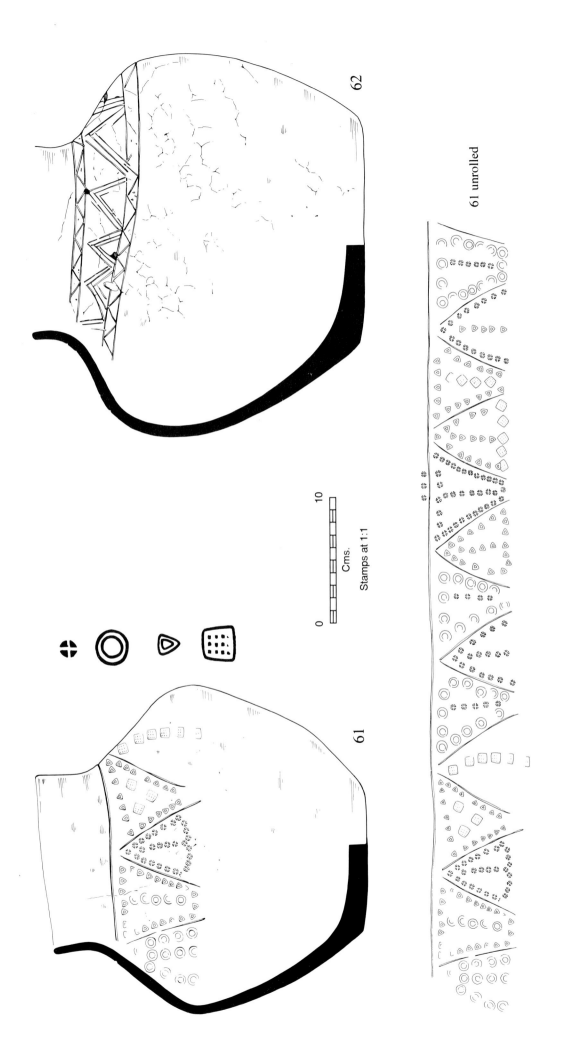

61 unrolled

Cms.

Stamps at 1:1

62

61

Figure 114 Cremation urns, graves 61 and 62, decoration on pot from 61 unrolled. Scale 1:3, pot stamps at 1:1

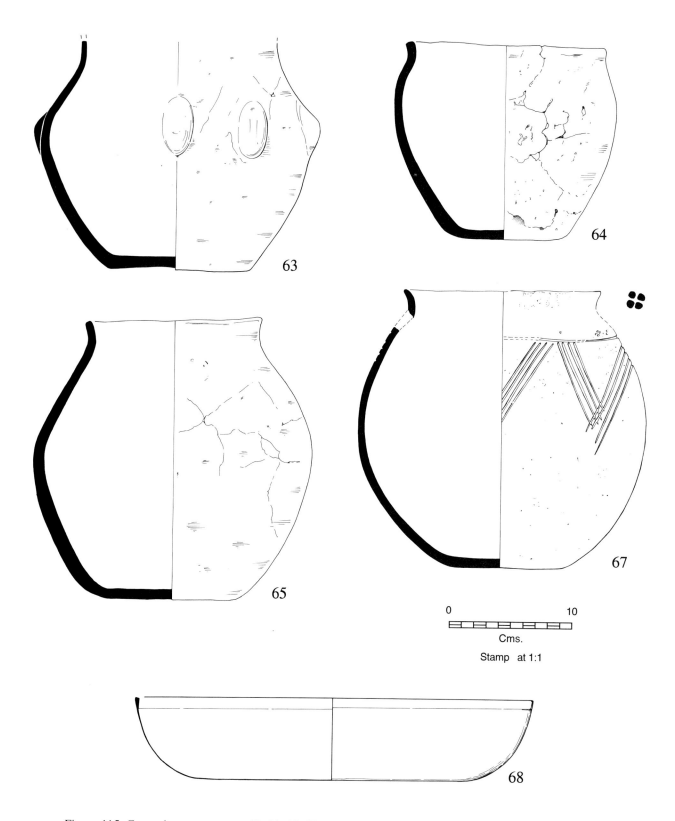

63

64

65

67

0   10
Cms.

Stamp at 1:1

68

Figure 115 Cremation urns, graves 63, 64, 65, 67, and bronze bowl from grave 68. Scale 1:3, pot stamp at 1:1

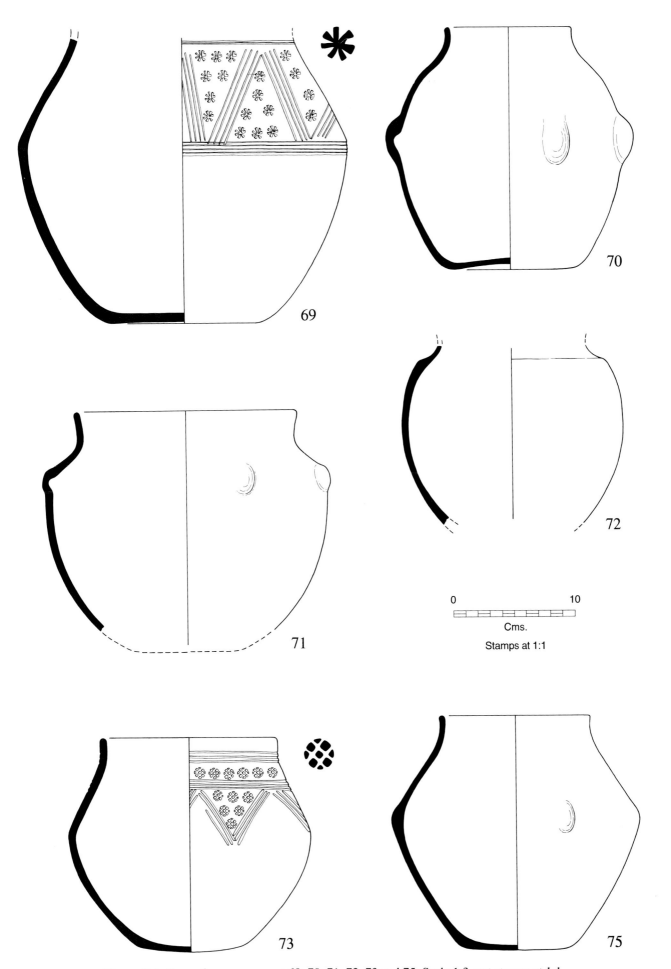

Figure 116 Cremation urns, graves 69, 70, 71, 72, 73 and 75. Scale 1:3, pot stamps at 1:1

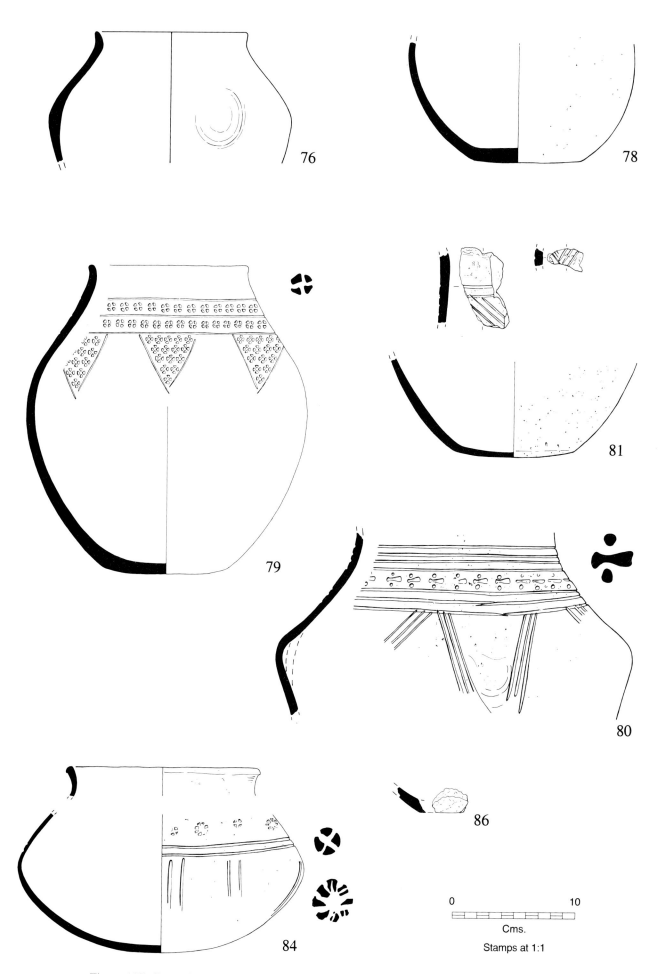

Figure 117 Cremation urns, graves 76, 78, 79, 80, 81, 84 and 86. Scale 1:3, pot stamps at 1:1

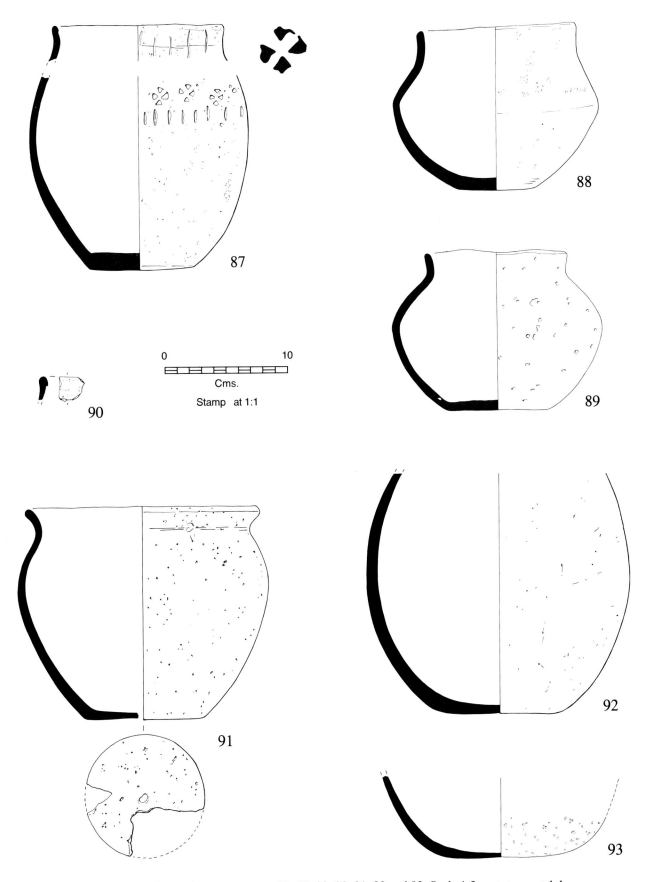

Figure 118 Cremation urns, graves 87, 88, 89, 90, 91, 92 and 93. Scale 1:3, pot stamp at 1:1

171

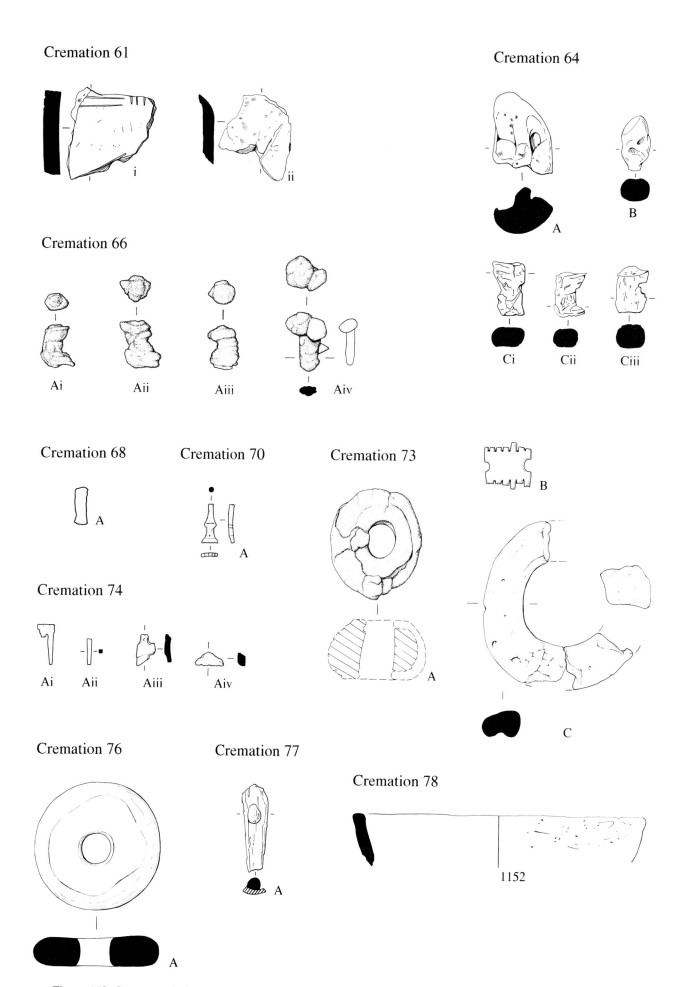

Figure 119 Grave-goods from graves 61, 64, 66, 68, 70, 73, 74, 76, 77 and 78. Scale 1:1 except 61 and 78 at 1:3

172

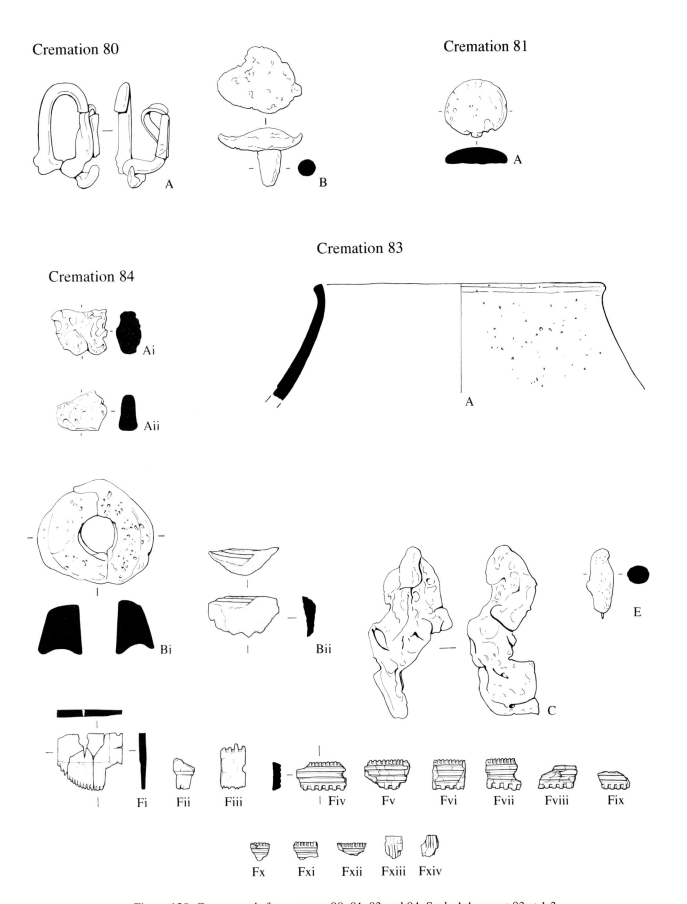

Cremation 80

A

B

Cremation 81

A

Cremation 83

A

Cremation 84

Ai

Aii

Bi

Bii

C

E

Fi Fii Fiii Fiv Fv Fvi Fvii Fviii Fix

Fx Fxi Fxii Fxiii Fxiv

Figure 120 Grave-goods from graves 80, 81, 83 and 84. Scale 1:1 except 83 at 1:3

Cremation 85

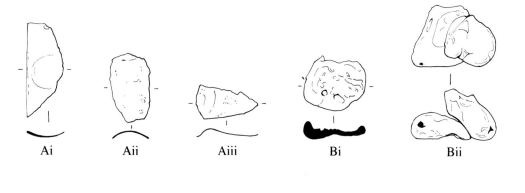

Ai   Aii   Aiii   Bi   Bii

Cremation 86

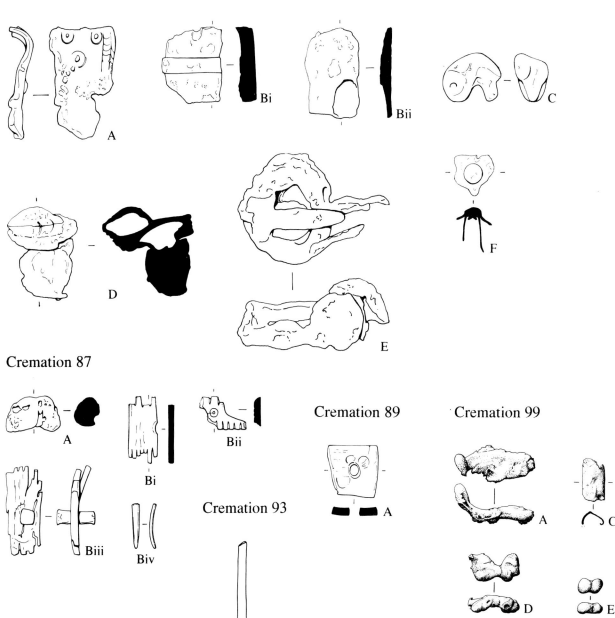

Cremation 87

Cremation 89

Cremation 99

Cremation 93

B (from x-ray)

Figure 121 Grave-goods from graves 85, 86, 87, 93 and 99. Scale 1:1

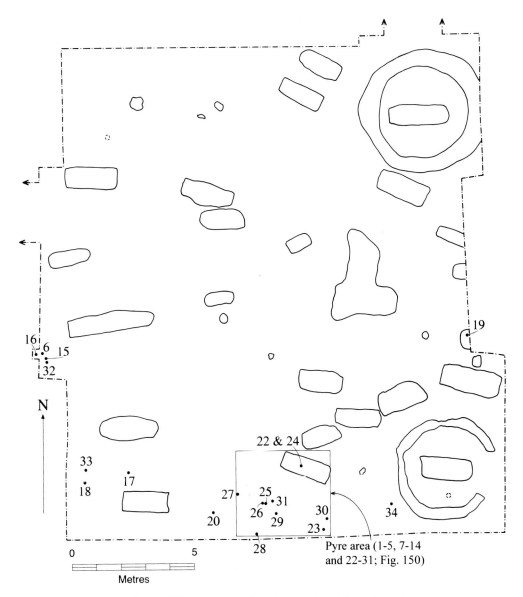

Figure 122 Location of scatters material from Area A

IV. Scatters and Unstratified Material

by Tim Pestell, incorporating material by Shirley Carnegie (pottery), Rowena Gale (charcoal), Vanessa Fell (metalwork), Simon Mays and James Steele (cremated bone)

Within soil layer *0273*, interpreted as being the remains of the Anglo-Saxon topsoil (above, pp. 15), were a number of fragments of pottery, cremated bone, burnt and unburnt metal, charcoal and burnt flint. This material was principally found in Area A because of the survival of the topsoil there.

The scatters were first seen during initial cleaning, following ploughsoil stripping. Thought to be the remains of smashed cremations, they were all numbered (mostly as individual finds, occasionally in small groups), planned and levelled. When the spreads became clearer they were planned at 1: 20. As soon as material could be related to the fill of a grave it was planned (and has been catalogued) as part of that grave. Scattered material obviously deriving from plough-damaged cremations is catalogued elsewhere as part of the relevant cremation.

Material is presented by type and includes original site numbers. Much of the material found in an extensive scatter in Area A is interpreted elsewhere as being the remnants of a cremation pyre (Chapter 6 section III, pp. 252–5). The remaining material from the site, including unstratified finds, is catalogued here, with the exception of a few individual sherds of pottery and cremated bone that cannot be assigned to component vessels or features. These are listed in the site archive, under the topsoil layer *0273*. All categories of artefacts considered to have been a part of the pyre area are distinguished by an asterisk accompanying their catalogue number. All items catalogued within this section are located in Figures 122 and 150 except No. 21 (on Fig. 5) and Nos 38 and 39 (on Fig. 7).

Cremated bone

Cremated bone was collected in several separate contexts, with individual fragments being planned in many cases. Those that cannot be related to the main spread of 'pyre' material, or to individual cremations, were all very small in extent and are listed in the site archive under the component number for the Anglo-Saxon topsoil, *0273*.

These fragments, being often individual pieces, were considered too small to yield any useful information and were not examined. Those spreads that can be associated with the pyre weighed 211.6g in total and represent the remains of a minimum of one individual, possibly male. The full cremated bone report in the excavation archive lists those individual contexts examined as part of the pyre spread. [components 0083, 0216, 0245, 0273, 0327]

Animal bone
The scatters included four small fragments of burnt animal bone, total weight 11.9g, none of which could be identified. All were from the pyre area. [0141, 0416, 0531]

Charcoal
Charcoal was recovered from various locations within the pyre area. That associated with the cremated material in the upper fill of grave 10 included six fragments of hazel (*Corylus* sp.). A scatter west of grave 10 produced the remaining charcoal, containing hazel and oak (*Quercus* sp.) possibly of stem. Uniquely it also contained several fragments of pine (*Pinus* sp.) of the *sylvestris* group which includes Scots pine, discussed on p. 226. Only one piece of charcoal is recorded from the surface scatters outside of the pyre area (No. 6).

Catalogue
(Figs 122 and 150)
1* 6 fragments of hazel (*Corylus* sp.). [0422]
2* 5 fragments of pine (*Pinus* sp.), *sylvestris* group which includes Scots pine. [0443]
3* 1 fragment of oak ?stem (*Quercus* sp.) and 1 fragment of hazel (*Corylus* sp.). [0458]
4* 6 fragments of pine (*Pinus* sp.), *sylvestris* group. [0479]
5* 4 fragments of pine (*Pinus* sp.), *sylvestris* group and 1 fragment of hazel (*Corylus* sp.). [0482]
6 3 fragments of oak stem (*Quercus* sp.), partially vitrified. Possibly associated with scatters vessel No. 16. [1393]

Pottery
The sherds from the scatters were all examined individually by Shirley Carnegie. In many cases their distinctive fabrics enabled isolation and grouping as components of identifiable vessels. The possibility that sherds listed as deriving from a vessel could be part of another pot was considered. Whilst the pottery of this period is notably crude and badly fired, close study was made of the fabric colour, fabric type, inclusions, style, method of manufacture, part of the vessel and finish (*e.g.* burnishing). Attribution to a particular vessel has been made on these criteria and it has proved possible to identify at least fifteen separate pots. This is in fact a conservative estimate of the total, as a number of odd sherds remain, apparently unassociated with these or any of the other vessels from the site, but which cannot be described easily for cataloguing; they are therefore omitted. The location of the sherds/vessels is shown in Figures 122 and 150.

Nearly all the fragments are plain bodysherds but where evidence for form or decoration exists, this is noted. In the absence of any evidence for their use, the term 'urn' has been avoided; instead 'vessel' or 'pot' is used. A sherd found in a service trench dug in 1976 (No. 21) is also published.

Catalogue
(Figs 122, 123 and 150)
7* *0406.* Form and decoration unknown. Vertical rim and body sherds survive. The fabric is a hard, dark grey sandy clay with sparse grit and external burnishing. Fracturing of the sherds clearly shows the coils used in its manufacture. [0057, 0109, 0219, 0307, 0319, 0323, 0352–3, 0356, 0412–3].
8* *0616.* Form unclear although probably from a biconical urn with everted rim. The only surviving decoration is of two horizontal incised lines around the vessel neck. The fabric is a hard dark grey sandy clay with sparse grit. The outer dark grey-brown surface was originally burnished. [0109, 0411, 0481, 0544].
9* *0617.* Appears from fragments to be a tall, straight-sided vessel, with two horizontal incised lines at the bottom of the neck and a slightly everted rim. It has a hard, light grey fabric with coarse angular grit, and a brown outer surface. Both interior and exterior surfaces are tooled smooth. Decoration consists of a horizontal row of coarse ring-and-dot stamps (Briscoe A2ai) between two lines both above and below. Another sherd has part of a larger zone of deeply impressed oval stamps with an internal 'V' shape (Briscoe D5ci). It is impossible to tell whether the oval stamps were originally arranged above or below the ring-and-dot stamps, although the latter seems most likely. [0109, 0220, 0285–6, 0354, 0437, 0480, 1220].
10* *0636.* A straight-sided open bowl of fairly hard dark grey sandy fabric with a dark brown smoothed external surface and angular rim. It is unknown if it was originally decorated. [0210, 0213].
11* *0899.* A vessel of unknown form and decoration as only body sherds survive. The fabric is a hard dark grey and sandy with an orange-brown outer surface, burnished in parts. The interior sherds have some wipe marks (*not illus.*). [0214, 0218, 0290, 0294, 0309]
12* *0930.* A vessel represented by a number of sherds but not reconstructable. The body sherds are all fairly straight-sided and preserve evidence of the coils used in the pot's manufacture, just over 60mm wide. The hard orange-brown fabric has small grit/sand and red grog inclusions. The dark brown inner surface is well burnished and shows scraping and wiping marks. The exterior is also dark brown but less well burnished and some sherds have a pronounced orange layer just beneath the outer surface. It seems to have been decorated in part with hollow bosses. [0275, 0277, 0283–4, 0287, 0297–8, 0404, 0410, 0446, 0454, 0456–61, 0478, 0487, 0489–90, 0505–6, 0525–6, 0545]
13* *1153.* With its form and decoration unknown, this vessel is represented by small body sherds of a hard dark grey-brown fabric with small sand inclusions. There is evidence for an orange-brown interior surface (*not illus.*). [0412, 0441, 0444]
14* *1588.* A vessel of unknown form and decoration but probably small in size as the pot walling is thin. The dark grey sandy fabric has an orange-brown outer core with a mid/dark brown outer surface slightly burnished in parts; the inner core is grey-brown with a dark brown inner surface, partially burnished. Some traces of burnishing remain on the outer surface. One small sherd has an evertion, probably indicating the neck. There is no surviving decoration (*not illus.*). [0227, 0245, 0306, 0308, 0320–22, 0325, 0414–5]
15 *0902.* A vessel, probably globular, with a simple rounded rim of a dark brown gritty fabric. Its inner and outer surfaces are brown and oxidised beneath the outer surface, with external burnishing. Decoration consisted of at least four horizontal incised lines on the neck with a row of square stamps beneath, probably arranged horizontally, featuring a central dot and radiating lines (Briscoe C4ai). A shoulder sherd has three lines from a ?chevron with the same stamps and two vertical lines, possibly the edge of a boss. Found west of grave 4 like No. 16. Only sherd with stamps illustrated. [0901, 0902, 0904, 0906]
16 *0903.* Form and decoration unknown. A soft powdery brown fabric with minute, rounded, quartz grains. Found west of grave 4 like No. 15 (*not illus.*). [0903]
17 *0184.* A vessel of unknown form with soft brown fabric and burnished dark grey surfaces. Decoration is of a slight solid boss bordered with two lines. A second sherd bears two broad grooves. Found between graves 2 and 3. [0184]
18 *1594.* A vessel of unknown form but decorated with three indistinct stamps and two horizontal incised lines. Two stamps, probably Briscoe A3aii and A4aiii are above or below these lines. The third stamp seen on another sherd is, like the first two, applied very indistinctly; it is probably Briscoe A5giv. The vessel fabric is of a hard sandy type with a dark brown burnished inner surface. The outer surface has an orange layer immediately below the partially burnished brown top skin. There are some internal scraping lines. The thickening of sherd *0206* indicates either the former presence

176

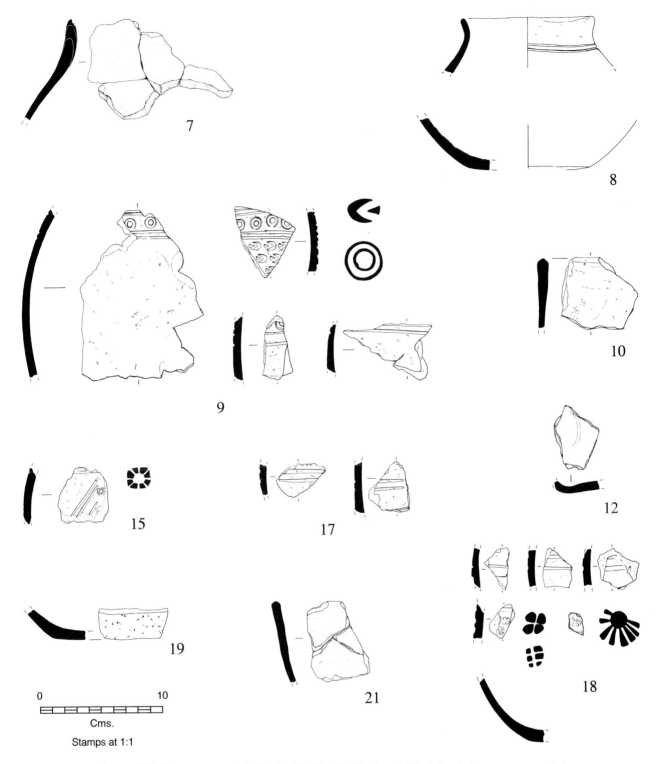

Figure 123 Scatters material, Nos 7–10, 12, 15, 17–19 and 21. All at 1:3, pot stamps at 1:1

of an applied boss or the curvature of the sherd to the pot base (as shown). [0206, 0347–8]

19 *0579*. The incomplete base and body of a vessel of unknown form or decoration. The black fabric has rounded quartz grit and some red grog inclusions. The inner surface is black and the outer reddish-brown to black. Found in the baulk section above grave 22. [0578]

20 *1152*. A vessel represented by sherds in layer *0273*, and also from within the fill of grave 4 and within the urn of grave 78 (a cremation). It has a soft dark brown fabric with angular grit and pitted surfaces. Two joining rim sherds found in grave 78 show it to have been a shallow open bowl. (*illus. under grave 78*). [0278, 0280]

21 *0637*. A vessel represented by three joining sherds, found in a Post Office service trench in the road north of mound 4 in 1976 (located on Fig. 5). The sherds are of a dark brown sandy fabric. Both surfaces are dark brown, the exterior having slight burnishing; both surfaces have wipe marks. The inner fabric is light brown. The sherds are from the rim and body of an open bowl or possibly the upper part of a biconical pot. [0637]

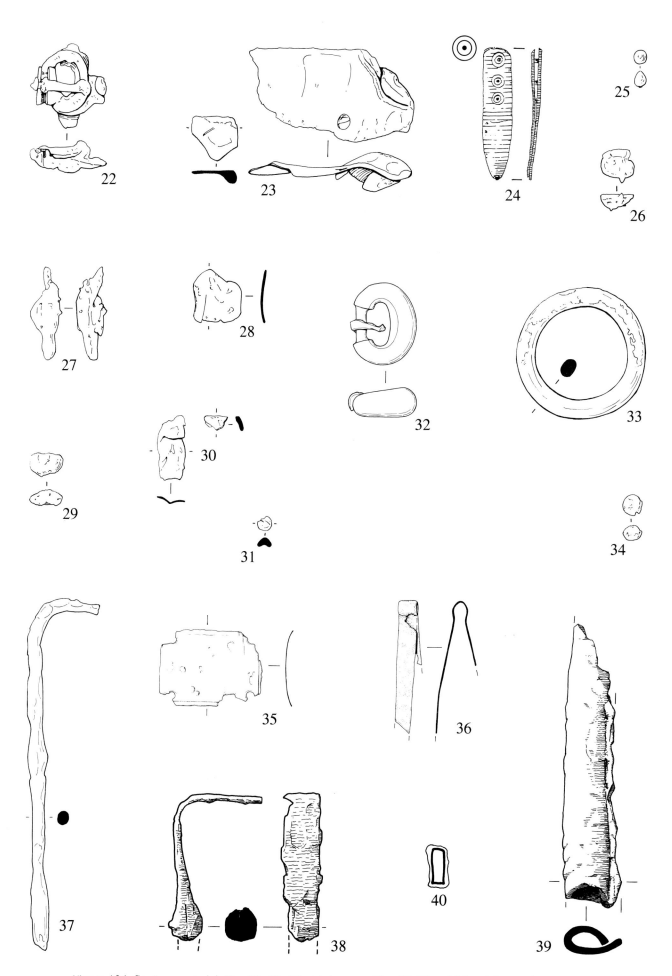

Figure 124 Scatters material, Nos 22–40. All at 1:1 except Nos 37, 38 and 39 at 1:2, punch stamp at 2:1

Metalwork

A number of metal objects were found but present problems in interpretation. Unless otherwise stated, all are burnt and most have been distorted beyond recognition into droplets of metal making identifications difficult and tenuous. Three unstratified finds from the 1972 sewer trench (Nos 35, 36 and 40), previously unpublished, are also included but cannot be located any more accurately.

Catalogue
(Figs 7, 122, 124 and 150)

22* **Fe buckle**, width 15mm, contained within the fill of grave 10 (an inhumation) in association with sherds relating to the 'pyre' spreads and thus catalogued here rather than with the grave. [0351]

23* Two fragments of Ae **sheet**, length 45mm, possibly the remains of an open bowl or repair/binding strips to a wooden object. The larger piece has a small hole punched through it. [0493]

24* Two Ae fragments from a **strap end**, length 35mm, with three stamps of a ring-and-dot design, on one side only, at the end nearest the rivets. The fragments do not appear to have been burned but were contained in the fill of grave 10 (an inhumation) with other material from the 'pyre' spreads, hence their being catalogued here. [0410]

25* Ae **droplet**. [0446]

26* Ae fragment, possibly from a **brooch**. [0458]

27* Ae fragment, possibly from a **brooch**, width 25mm. [0281]

28* Ae fragment, possibly from a **wrist clasp** or **small-long brooch**, width 13mm. [0488]

29* Ae **fragment**, unidentifiable, length 10mm. [0491]

30* Two Ae **fragments**, longest length 17mm, unidentifiable. [0494]

31* Ae **fragment**, unidentifiable. [0461]

32   Ae **buckle** and tongue, width 17mm, possibly associated with scatters vessels Nos 15 or 16. Not apparently burnt. [0905]

33   Small Ae **ring**, possibly part of a belt/knife fitting, diameter 37mm. Apparently unburnt. Possibly associated with scatters vessels Nos 17 or 18. [0124]

34   Burnt Ae **droplet** found just west of ring-ditch *0302*. [0282]

35   Unburnt Ae **sheet**, length 29mm, found amongst the 1972 sewer trench material in Ipswich Museum. Its provenance from Snape seems assured as it is labelled with the site code. It is slightly curved and has a circular rivet hole at each corner with faint traces of an internal line running around the edge. Probably a binding or repair patch. [2440]

36   Unburnt Ae **tweezers**, now broken, found amongst the 1972 sewer trench material in Ipswich Museum, also labelled with the site code. Only one arm survives to any length (35mm). [2441]

37   Unburnt Fe **?pin**, length 21mm, found unstratified in layer *0273*. It is a length of thin square-section Fe bent into a right angle at one end. It is apparently broken at each end. [0066]

38   Unburnt Fe **strip**, length 12mm, found in plough-disturbed topsoil in the extension opened up on the south side of mound 4, Area B (located in Fig. 7). [1840]

39   Unburnt Fe **object** found within the fill of modern ditch *2176* running along the north side of Area B (located in Fig. 7). The object has the appearance of a spear ferrule, being a rolled iron sheet forming a point, length 150mm. If Anglo-Saxon, it is unclear whence the object derives, although components of a spear were found in the topsoil apparently ploughed out of grave 32. [2184]

40   Fe **rivet**, length 9mm, found amongst cremated bone recovered from the 1972 sewer trench, in a bag marked only 'manhole bone' (drawn from X-ray). [2430]

Burnt Flint

In common with many graves and a few cremations, several burnt flints were found in the spreads of material. Their presence was originally thought to be indicative of natural heathland fires and they were not systematically recorded. Their subsequent occurrence in large numbers elsewhere on the site and the discovery of the burnt stone features meant that this view had to be revised. Six pieces are recorded in the pyre area but no further instances are considered worth listing here as the recovery was too erratic. A full list, for those interested, is held in the site archive. [0289, 0357, 0441, 0447, 0460, 0479].

V. Burnt Stone Features

by Tim Pestell, incorporating material by Rowena Gale
(Fig. 7)

Stone feature 1771 (not illus.)
Dimensions: 1.55 (to baulk) × 1.30 × 0.16m
Samples recovered: Charcoal 0.23kg Burnt flint 31.2kg

Description: A shallow ovoid feature filled with burnt
flint and charcoal, heavily plough-damaged. It was found
at the edge of Area B when first cleaned and was initially
considered a tree-clearance pit. A section cut across it
showed that the feature had no real structure, hence it is
not illustrated. The charcoal included a large mass of
roundwood with fragments of gorse stem (*Ulex* sp.),
Rosaceae, subfamily Pomoideae (which includes
hawthorn (*Crateagus* sp.), apple (*Malus* sp.), pear (*Pyrus*
sp.) and rowan, whitebeam and wild service tree (*Sorbus*
spp.). Fragments of oak (*Quercus* sp.) were also present.

Stone feature 1775 (Fig. 125)
Dimensions: 1.5 × 0.99 × 0.35m
Samples recovered: Charcoal 1kg Burnt flint 61.98kg

Description: A sub-rectangular feature, initially quite
irregularly shaped. Cleaning revealed the well defined
profile of a flat base and steep sides with a rounded break
of slope. The feature had been truncated in its upper levels
by agricultural activity which had mixed the contents of
charcoal and burnt flints with the surrounding natural
sand. In its lower levels a deposit of charcoal was overlain
by medium to large size burnt flints with several larger
fragments of charcoal included. The pit had been cut by
grave 46 at its south-east corner. Flint from the first
quadrant of the grave excavated was not recorded but the
respective weights of the charcoal and burnt flint include
the material subsequently recovered from the grave. The
charcoal from the feature included a large mass of roundwood,
principally gorse stem (*Ulex* sp.), oak stem (*Quercus* sp.),
Prunus sp. and Rosaceae subfamily Pomoideae.

Stone feature 1779 (not illus.)
Dimensions: 0.56 × 0.54 × 0.16m
Samples recovered: Charcoal 0.08kg Burnt flint 92.1kg

Dimensions: A near circular shallow scoop found when
first cleaning off the site. Also initially considered a
modern feature, no large-scale plan was made although a
detailed section was drawn. This showed that it
maintained some of its structure with a bottom layer of
charcoal resting on natural sand turned a pinkish colour by
burning. Above the charcoal was a more mixed layer of
small to medium size flints with some charcoal mixed in.
The feature was shallow and truncated by agricultural
activity although that part beneath plough depth was
substantially undamaged. The charcoal preserved consisted
of oak stem (*Quercus* sp.) and gorse stem (*Ulex* sp.).

Stone feature 1794 (Fig. 126)
Dimensions: 0.9 × 0.69 × 0.17m
Samples recovered: Charcoal 0.59kg Burnt flint 151.6kg

Description: A sub-rectangular pit of shallow depth
disturbed in its upper levels by agricultural activity
(gyrotiller and plough). This had distorted the original

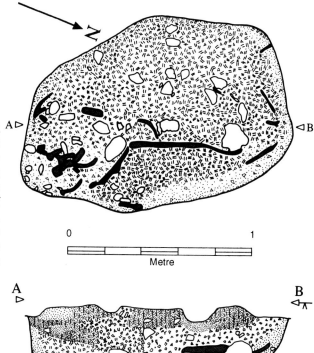

Figure 125 Burnt stone feature *1775*. Scale 1:20

shape of the feature, probably rounding off its ends,
notably that to the east. It contained a mixture of small to
medium size burnt flints, many of which had been broken
up from larger pieces. The pit had a flat bottom with edges
rounded at the bottom break of slope. The sides above had
been destroyed. The natural sand of the edges had been
turned to a pink-red colour by the heat and were covered
with a layer of charcoal. The charcoal examined from the
sample taken was of gorse stem (*Ulex* sp.), hazel (*Corylus*
sp.) and oak (*Quercus* sp.).

A sample of charcoal from the feature was radiocarbon
dated to cal AD 380–600 at 2σ (GU–5234; 1580±50BP).

Stone feature 1815 (not illus.)
Dimensions: approx. 1.36 × 1.17 × 0.2m
Samples recovered: Charcoal 0.27kg Burnt flint 51.5kg

Description: An irregularly shaped feature, probably
originally sub-rectangular, much damaged by agricultural
activity. This activity, principally ploughing, has
destroyed nearly all evidence for any structure within the
feature, except in a few parts between plough furrows.
Here, the characteristic layering of charcoal beneath a
mixture of medium-sized shattered burnt flint was present.
The edges were too severely truncated to give any idea of
their original shape. The charcoal derived from stems of
gorse (*Ulex* sp.), oak (*Quercus* sp.) and a fragment of
Prunus sp.

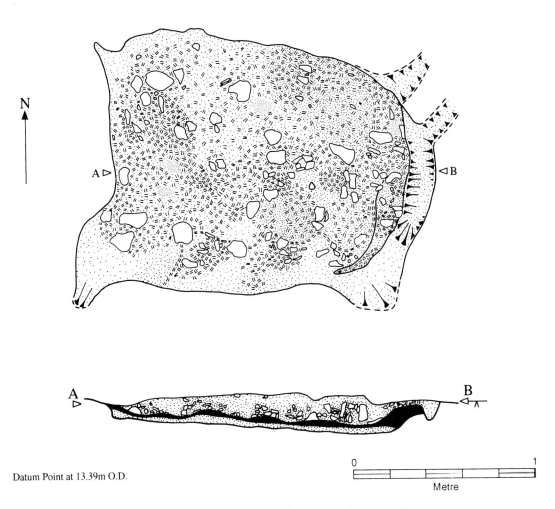

N

A▷ ◁B

A▷ B◁

Datum Point at 13.39m O.D.

0   1

Metre

Figure 126 Burnt stone feature *1794*. Scale 1:20

Stone feature *1849* (Fig. 127, Pl. XXX)
Dimensions: 1.92 × 1.26 × 0.26m
Samples recovered: Charcoal 3.27kg Burnt flint 176.53kg

Description: The best preserved of all the burnt stone features, despite much disruption and damage in its upper levels by agricultural activity. The initial spread of material in this area, some 3.14 × 2.12m, was cleaned to reveal a well-defined pit about half this size. The feature was rectangular with rounded corners and had gently sloping sides with rounded bottom edges. The feature had the natural sand along the bottom and sides burnt pink. The bottom layer of the fill was of charcoal, many pieces of which preserved their structure showing that the pit appears to have been lined with branches. Above this was the usual thick infilling of burnt flint of small and medium stones including many shattered fragments. The amount of charcoal mixed in with this suggests a possible second layer of wood above or between the stones. There appears to have been a small layer of gravel near the top of the fill although this may simply reflect later disturbances by agricultural machinery.

A sample of charcoal from the feature was dated by radiocarbon to cal AD 240–440 at 2σ (GU–5235; 1680±50BP). This feature also contained fragments of burnt clay of uncertain origin (*not illus.*). These had a lighter, softer feel than brick but an apparent lack of inclusions or impressions compared with daub. They

Plate XXX Burnt stone feature *1849* during excavation showing its well-defined rectangular shape

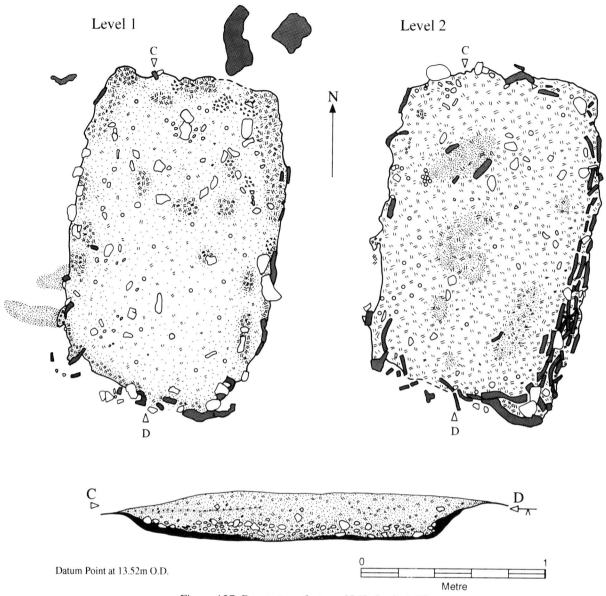

Level 1   Level 2

N

C → D

Datum Point at 13.52m O.D.

0   1
Metre

Figure 127 Burnt stone feature *1849*. Scale 1:20

appear to lie somewhere between examples of both brick and daub recovered from the Middle Anglo-Saxon site at Staunch Meadow, Brandon (A. Tester pers. comm.) and resemble pieces of furnace or oven (E. Martin pers. comm.). Their inclusion in the feature would appear to be accidental, perhaps arriving with a load of flint. Despite the large quantity of charcoal present, the samples examined contained only stems of gorse (*Ulex* sp.) and oak (*Quercus* sp.).

Stone feature *2251* (*not illus.*)
Dimensions: 1.34 × 0.9 × 0.13m
Samples recovered: Charcoal 0.98kg Burnt flint 23.86kg

Description: A medium-sized feature that had been almost totally destroyed by ploughing, only retaining its shape between furrows. Its original shape appears to have been rectangular with a flat base, rounded bottom edges and steeply sloping sides. The profile of the sides is uncertain, as ploughing had removed most edges. The fill was mixed but had a bottom layer of 90% charcoal and small heat-shattered flint. The upper layer consisted mainly of burnt flints, some large, mixing with structureless fragments of charcoal. This consisted of a large mass of roundwood, principally oak stem (*Quercus* sp.), some fast grown, and gorse stem (*Ulex* sp.). Some oak stem fragments had annual rings of up to 14 years. Present in smaller quantities were *Prunus* spp. and rose or bramble (*Rosa* sp. or *Rubus* sp.). The base of the feature had natural sand burnt pink to a depth of up to 50mm.

VI. Ring-ditches and Other Features

by Tim Pestell

The site produced a few features in addition to those already catalogued, the most important of which were the ring-ditches. Those surrounding inhumations are described in their relevant grave catalogue entries, but are illustrated here (Pl. XXXI, Figs 128–130) for ease of comparison with the other ring-ditches. The majority of other features were natural or modern, and often related to agricultural activity; only features of possible relevance to the cemetery are considered here. All measurements given are *maxima*.

Ring-ditch *1735* (Fig. 132, Pl.XXXII)
Diameter: 6.6m (approx.)
Width: 0.95m
Depth: 0.2m (approx.)

Description: Area B. This ring-ditch, first located during trial trenching in 1990, was very fragmentary, having been scarred by ploughing, subsoiling, rabbit holes and tree roots from the adjacent road hedgeline. Additionally, the northern part had been removed by a modern roadside ditch. The ring-ditch's original diameter can only be estimated, but there is some evidence that it was penannular, since a section through the south-western end showed a steep slope, suggestive of a terminal. The depth of the ditch on the west side contrasts with the extremely shallow traces to the east. The ditch fill contained 0.17kg of burnt flint; a single flint flake, *2248*, was found immediately adjacent to the ditch. The stratigraphic relationship between this ring-ditch and ring-ditch *2265*, which would overlap if fully reconstructed (Fig. 7) could not be determined from the sparse remains of both that were left. If penannular, it is possible that *1735* was added to *2265*, since its gap occurs on the western side, in the region of where *2265* would have extended.

The ring-ditch contained three features, *2174*, *2311* and *2346*, none centrally positioned, and none of which could be interpreted clearly. Feature *2174* to the south was apparently a sub-rectangular cut with a mixed grey sand fill, but was only 50mm deep at best, being completely disturbed by surrounding animal activity. No section could be drawn and nothing diagnostic was contained in the fill. Feature *2346* in the northern end was cut by feature *2311*. Again, it was apparently originally a sub-rectangular feature, showing a clear layering of soil in its fill. Finally, feature *2311*, a large sub-rectangular cut, oriented north–south, contained a fill of mixed grey sand with coarser brown sand at the bottom. Although fully excavated and sieved, no finds were made within the pit and its date and function are unknown.

Ring–ditch *1780* (Fig. 131)
Diameter: 7.3m (approx.)
Width: 0.65–0.95m
Depth: 0.48–0.5m

Description: A ring-ditch located at the far east end of Area B. The ditch showed that an apparent hummock within the scheduled area to the north was in fact the remains of a small barrow (mound 6). Only about one-third of the ditch was uncovered and so its edge-to-edge diameter can only be estimated; nor could

the ditch be proven to have been penannular or annular. As exposed, it seems to show straighter lengths joined together to form an arc. It had a very steep section to the outer edge, sloping slightly more in the internal edge, and, in parts, a flat bottom, 0.2m wide. The narrow width of the ditch and its steep profile may suggest that it once contained a retaining fence although there were no other indications of any former palisade in the ditch, nor any obvious post-hole bases at the bottom of the ditch cut. The ditch fill was a mixed grey and brown sand, coarser brown at the bottom, but mixed by much root disturbance. Only this small stretch was excavated because the ditch extended into the scheduled area.

Ring-ditch *2066* (Fig. 131, Pl.XXXII)
Diameter: 4.6m (approx.)
Width: 0.32–0.58m
Depth: 0.21m

Description: A ring-ditch to the west of ditches *1735* and *2265*, located against the northern edge of Area B. Over half of the ditch was exposed, although it was unclear whether the ditch was fully annular or not. The ditch had been damaged by a modern field ditch running across the southern part of its arc, and the whole area was heavily disturbed by root action, being adjacent to the hedgeline. The ditch was open in section, with a rounded bottom, becoming almost V-shaped in one part. The fill was of a coarse grey-pink sand, with a slightly more coarse, browny sand silting the bottom. The ditch was 100% sampled and yielded 0.27kg of burnt flint.

At the projected original centre of the ring-ditch, possible feature *2185* was located, but this was uncertain as the whole area was disturbed by animal burrowing. The feature could not be seen in the baulk for the same reason, and proved to be only a few centimetres deep. If it did represent a central deposit within the ring-ditch, this was only its base, and no objects or stains were found within the feature.

Ring-ditch *2265* (Fig. 133, Pl.XXXII)
Diameter: Estimated at 4.2m
Width: 0.38m
Depth: 0.07m

Description: Area B. A curved linear feature interpreted as the fragmentary remain of a ring-ditch, 1.1m away from ditch *2066* and possibly once overlapping (or overlapped by) ditch *1735*. The short curved stretch was both very shallow (at no point deeper than 70mm) and much disturbed by animal and agricultural activity. 100% sampling failed to recover any finds. The fill was of light to mid grey sand with some grey-brown sand mixing in. No trace of silting could be seen. No feature possibly once central to this ditch was seen, if indeed one once existed. It is possible that if penannular, this ditch could have formed an 'add-on' to the west of ring-ditch *1735* or, if annular, had been added to by a penannular *1735*.

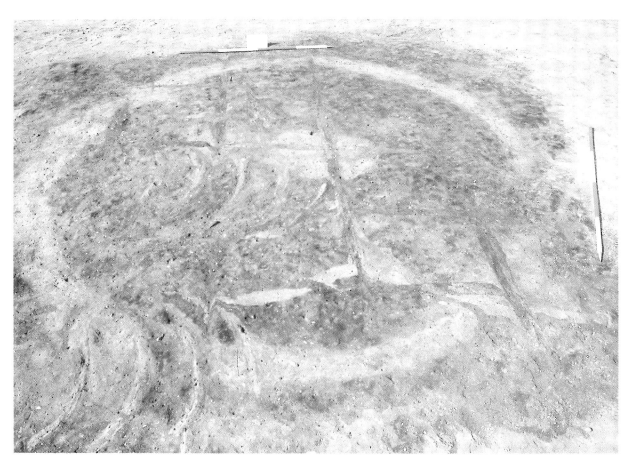

Plate XXXI Ring-ditch *2062* surrounding inhumation grave 34; view from south looking north

Plate XXXII Ring-ditches *1735, 2066* and *2265*, Area B, from the south looking north

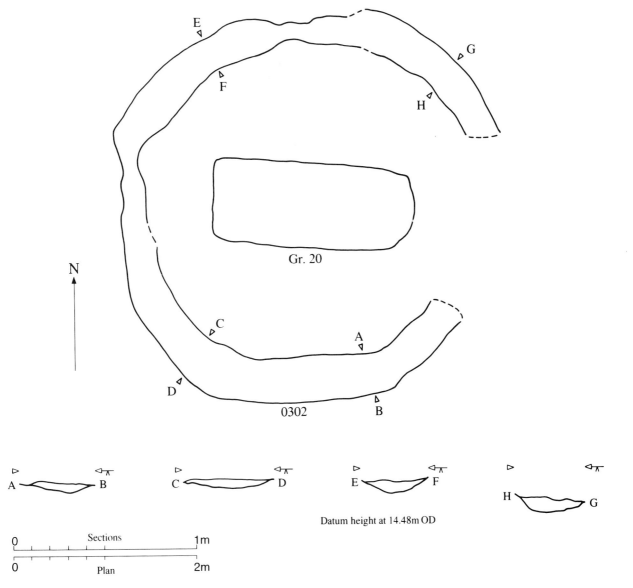

E

F

G

H

N

C

A

D

B

Gr. 20

0302

A ◁T B   C ◁T D   E ◁T F

Datum height at 14.48m OD

H G

0   Sections   1m

0   Plan   2m

Figure 128 Ring-ditch *0302*. Scale 1:40, sections 1:20

Ring-ditch *2449* (Fig. 5)
Diameter: Estimated at 5.5–6.2m
Width: 0.55–0.85m
Depth: 0.8–1.1m

Description: A ring-ditch seen in section only, in the two walls of the sewer trench dug along the A1094 road in 1972. The estimated diameter is based on its description by West and Owles (1973, 47) as 'reaching a depth of 1.8m from the present ground surface ... [*i.e.* about 12.80m OD] The inner lips of the ditches on the north side of the trench were 3.4m apart and they were just over 1m wide; those on the south face were almost touching and, since the section was more oblique, appeared 1.6m wide'. Reconstruction of the diameter measurement assumes the trench to have been approximately 2' (0.7m) wide, which seems reasonable based upon photographs taken at the time, now held in Ipswich Museum. This suggests an approximate external diameter of 5.5–6.2m, rather than the 8m that West and Owles proposed (1973, 48).

The ring-ditch yielded six plain Anglo-Saxon body sherds, although these cannot now be isolated from the other 1972 material held in Ipswich Museum. Since the centre of the ring-ditch has not been seen, it is impossible to date the feature.

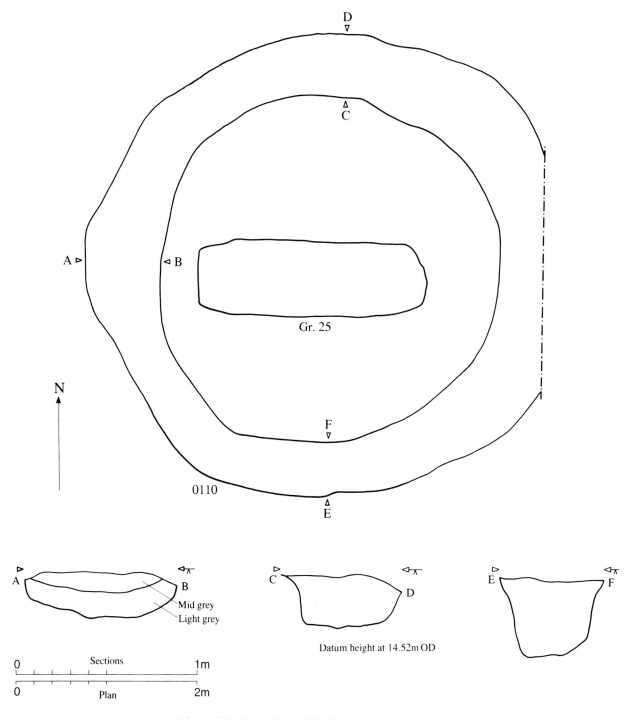

D

C

A ▷   ◁ B

Gr. 25

N

F

0110

E

A   B
Mid grey
Light grey

C   D

E   F

Datum height at 14.52m OD

0   Sections   1m

0   Plan   2m

Figure 129 Ring-ditch *0110*. Scale 1:40, sections 1:20

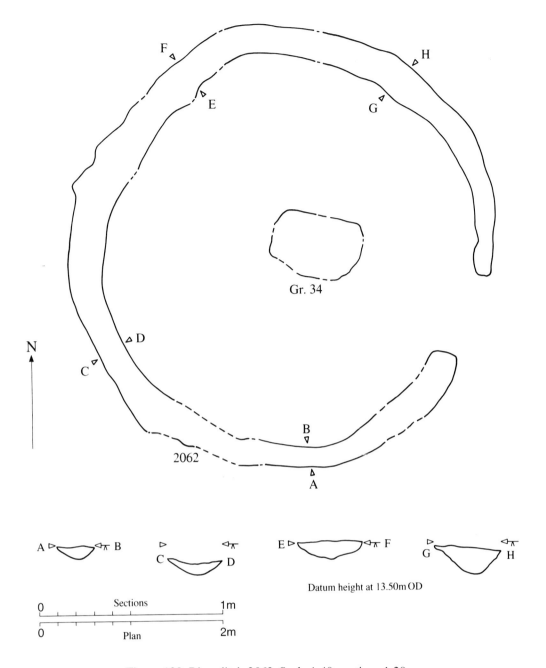

N

Gr. 34

F

E

H

G

D

C

B

2062

A

A ▷⌣◁⊼ B

C ⌣ D

▷ ◁⊼

E ▷⌣◁⊼ F

G ⌣ H
▷ ◁⊼

Datum height at 13.50m OD

0   Sections   1m

0   Plan   2m

Figure 130 Ring-ditch *2062*. Scale 1:40, sections 1:20

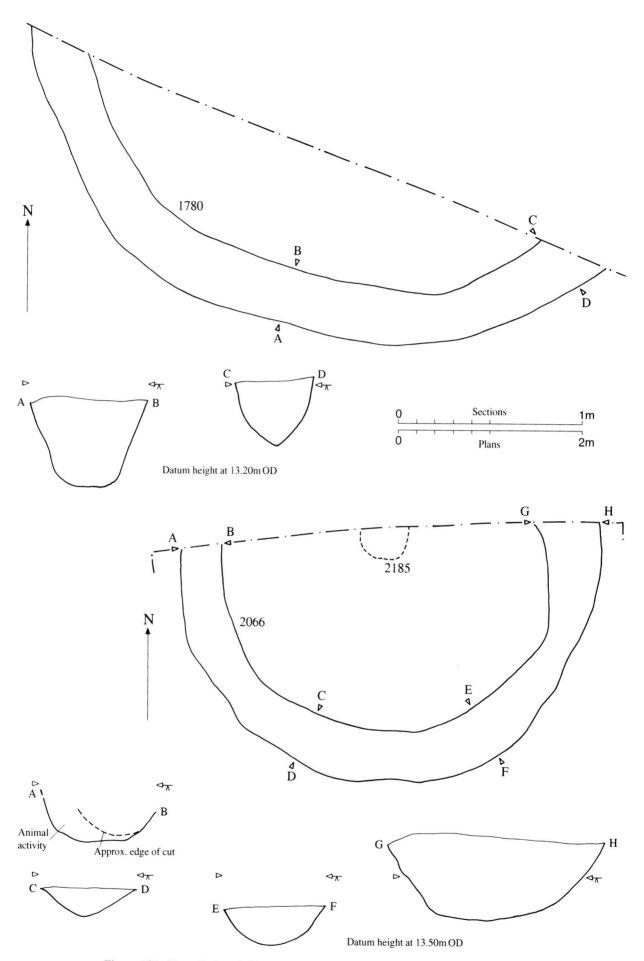

N

1780

C

B

D

A

C D

A B

Datum height at 13.20m OD

Sections
0 1m

Plans
0 2m

G H

A B

2185

N

2066

C E

D F

A

Animal
activity

Approx. edge of cut

B

C D

E F

G H

Datum height at 13.50m OD

Figure 131 Ring-ditches *1780* and *2066*, and feature *2185*. Scale 1:40, sections 1:20

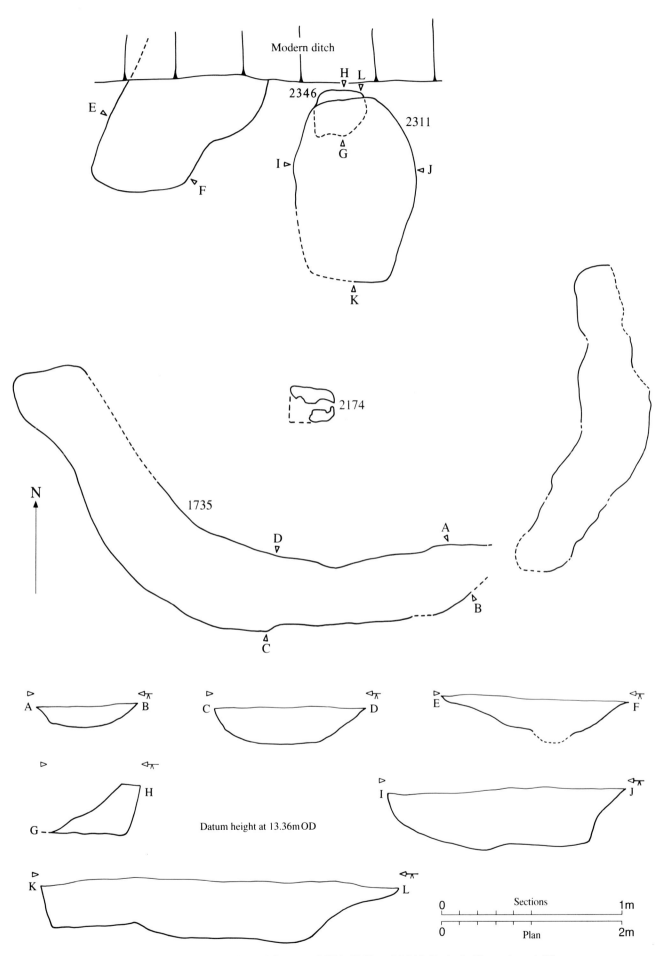

Modern ditch

2346

2311

2174

1735

N

Datum height at 13.36m OD

0   Sections   1m

0   Plan   2m

Figure 132 Ring-ditch *1735* and features *2174, 2311* and *2346*. Scale 1:40, sections 1:20

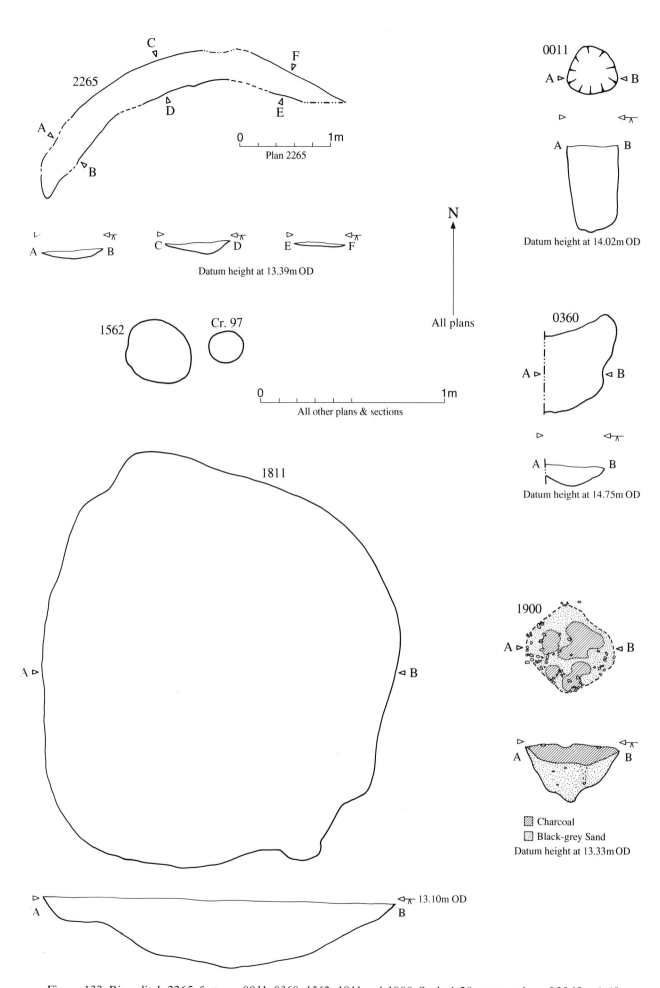

Figure 133 Ring-ditch *2265*, features *0011, 0360, 1562, 1811* and *1900*. Scale 1:20, except plan of *2265* at 1:40

Post-holes/pits (Figs 133 and 134)

A few post-holes, other than those directly associated with graves, were located during excavation, but none (other than the charcoal in feature *1900*) contained any material that could be dated. A possible post-hole, *0011*, was found in 1985 trial box 2 but was unassociated with any other feature in the box. It was steep-sided with a rounded base and contained a fill of mid grey sand. *1562*, in trial trench VI, was a small circular feature with a fill of pale grey sand adjacent, and possibly related to, grave 97 (a cremation); because they were found during evaluation work, both were left unexcavated. Of more interest was post-hole *1900* in Area B, south of burnt stone feature *1794*. This was filled with a mass of charcoal in its upper levels, of oak stem roundwood (*Quercus* sp.). The feature was 0.31m deep with a fill of light grey sand in its lower edges that could not be clearly defined. Finally, features *2340* and *2341* in Area B were possible post-holes, with fills of light grey sand. Although perhaps paired, they were isolated from any other feature.

The proximity of post-holes *1562* and *1900* to Anglo-Saxon features encourages belief in their antiquity, although their purpose is unclear. It is conceivable that they represent post-holes associated with former pyre structures as discussed by Genrich (1981a, 60); any pyre material could then have been lost with the destroyed topsoil layer. This interpretation might seem especially tempting for *1900* given the charcoal content, but its composition of stem wood fragments demonstrates that the fragments did not derive from an *in situ* post.

Finally, in Area A, a patch of clay with chalk flecks, *0360*, was noted during initial site cleaning. At the time it was assumed to have been a modern deposit, possibly associated with marling, since it was at the interface of the ploughsoil and the archaeological horizon. Subsequent analysis has shown how two similar patches, *0358* and *0359*, lay almost directly over the corners of grave 2 and possibly represented post pads. Thus, *0360* may also be the remains of a clay post pad, perhaps for an inhumation immediately outside the excavated area.

Other features (Figs 133, 134 and 135)

There were several other categories of features encountered during excavation. A single feature to the south-west of mound 4, *1811* (Fig. 133), has been interpreted as a quarry pit, created in the construction of that tumulus. The feature was near circular at the surface and had been damaged by agricultural activity in its upper layers. Its fill of light and mid grey sand was stone-free and consistent in colour, mixing down into the natural brown sand at the base. Its interpretation as a quarry pit rests on its proximity to mound 4, and its size and shape bears comparison with the known scoops surrounding the mound to the north and west, that were revealed by contour survey (Fig. 7). The level of its bottom (12.73mOD) was also consistent with the bases of these scoops in the scheduled area (*c.* 12.65mOD).

Only three other clear features could be defined, all from the west end of Area B. *2175* (*not illus.*), a sub-rectangular feature, was aligned east-west, the stone-free fill of mixed mid grey and brown sand being removed to reveal a smooth base. There were no finds. Feature *2348* (*not illus.*), near grave 32, was also aligned east-west but was not investigated since it extended beneath the north baulk adjacent to the road. Feature *2263*

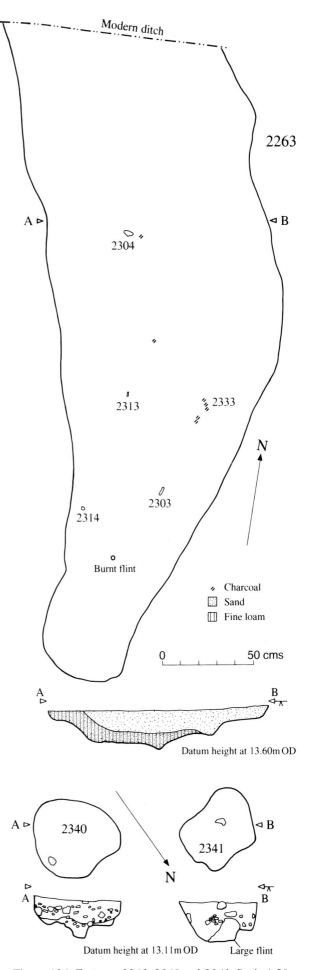

Figure 134 Features *2263*, *2340* and *2341*. Scale 1:20

(Fig. 134) was of an irregular shape, on a north-south alignment. Like *2175*, it was much disturbed by animal and agricultural activity in its upper layers. Its sides sloped down gently to a slightly uneven bottom, the silver-grey fill mixing into the natural brown sand at the base. Contained within the fill was a small fragment of burnt flint, several fragments of charred oak stem (*Quercus* sp.), and four pieces of iron. One of these was shapeless, but the remaining three finds (Fig. 135) consisted of a **staple/clamp** with a rivet *in situ* (*2313*); a round-headed **nail** with a square-section stem, *2314*; and an iron **clamp** with two rivets, *2303*. The amorphous nature and light colour of the fill graded into the natural sand making the definition of an edge difficult.

Several more amorphous features were found across the site, for instance *1404* and *1407* from trial trench V and *2271* in Area B (*not illus.*); they cannot be dated and have no apparent relevance to the cemetery. These and other amorphous features are excluded from the catalogue since they are probably natural and are not shown on the site plans, although full details of them are contained in the site archive. These features all seem to represent hollows in the natural heathland surface, larger examples

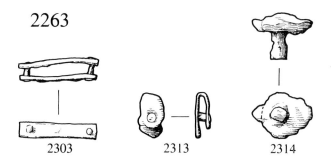

2263

Figure 135 Small finds *2303, 2213* and *2314* from feature *2263*. Scale 1:2

of which seem to have been exploited by the excavators of graves 17, 36 and 44. Their presence is a reminder of how the original ground surface apparently undulated when the cemetery was in use, and how radically the now flat fields have been changed by intensive agriculture in the last forty years.

Chapter 5. Detailed Results

I. Grave 1 (the 1862 Ship Burial): Analysis and Interpretation
by William Filmer-Sankey

Introduction
The excavation in 1862 of a mound containing a ship burial was described in Chapter 2 (above, pp. 6–7). This grave (grave 1) and its contents are of very great importance and deserve detailed examination, individually and collectively. At the same time, as the sources of information on the grave — the surviving finds and the contemporary accounts — are less than complete and leave a number of important issues unresolved, it is vital that any interpretation is soundly based. The following discussion therefore looks carefully at the evidence to see how far it can be used to address the unresolved issues of the mound's location, its relationship with the cremation burials, and the orientation of the ship within the mound. It then assesses the significance of the boat and the other finds as objects in their own right, before suggesting how they can be used to draw conclusions about the sex and status of the person buried, and about the date of the burial. The wider question of the relationship of the grave to the rest of the cemetery is discussed in Chapter 6.

The location of the mound
Perhaps the most important of the issues left unresolved by the contemporary accounts is the location of the mound containing the ship burial. As already discussed (above, pp.5–6), we know that it was the westernmost (and largest) of the three mounds north of the road; we know also that it was close to the road, since a considerable part of it had been sliced off by passing traffic. Unfortunately, all traces of the three mounds have been completely obliterated in the subsequent years. The only possible evidence is an area of rough ground, containing what might be the remains of spoil heaps, which lies in the south-west corner of the present garden of St Margaret's. There was no trace of any mound in the 1986–8 excavated area immediately to the west of this (Area A: Fig. 6), so that, if these mounds are spoil heaps, they must come from the ship burial mound. For want of any better evidence, the ship burial has been tentatively marked in this location on Fig. 5. This would then allow the remaining two mounds excavated in 1862 to be placed in the garden to the east, between the house and the road.

The relationship between the mound and the cremation burials
There is further uncertainty over the important question of the stratigraphic relationship between the mound and the cremation urns, and thus to the question of whether the ship burial pre-dates, is contemporary with, or post-dates the urns found within it (above, p.16). The excavators, unaware of the significance of this question, leave only unsatisfactory and inconclusive evidence in the accounts. Thus Francis Francis, the only one to make a general statement, writes 'we found them [urns], or portions of them, at all depths (from one to three feet deep), as well as in all parts of the mound' (Francis 1863a, 62). Dr Hele, recounting specifically the discovery of the urn with swastika decoration (grave 51) and of the Bronze Age urn (grave 48), writes: 'The pot [with swastika decoration] was about three or four inches below the surface of the ground [...] We afterwards came across a second example [the Bronze Age urn], just beneath the surface as in the former case' (Hele 1870, 25). All that can sensibly be concluded from these accounts is that some intact urns were apparently near the surface, while others, or fragments of others, were found at greater depth. It is impossible to draw any valid stratigraphic conclusions from this. It might have been tempting to conclude that the shallowly buried whole urns were later insertions into the mound, were it not for the fact that one is Bronze Age and the other, a distinctive Anglian type with swastika decoration, is of a relatively early form, which Myres dates to the late 4th or first half of the 5th century (Myres 1977, I, 37–41, type II.6; for comments on Myres's chronology, see below p. 235)! Francis Francis' mention of portions of urns at depths of up to three feet might be interpreted as evidence for the later insertion of a mound into a pre-existing urnfield, with the consequent disturbance of cremations, but given the methods of excavation and the fragility of the pottery, cannot be absolutely trusted. In short, there is no definite stratigraphic evidence to establish the relationship between ship mound and urnfield. Before leaving the subject, it is worth noting that Rupert Bruce-Mitford argued that the ship mound was later, 'possibly appreciably later' than the urnfield. The reason for this was not so much the evidence of the original accounts, but rather his own dating of the ship burial to c.600–625. If there were later cremation burials on the site, it would 'be proof of a wholly unexpected persistence of cremation in this corner of Suffolk right up to the Christian period' (Bruce-Mitford 1974, 136). In order to avoid this unwanted conclusion, it was necessary to assign the cremations to an earlier period.

The orientation of the ship within the mound
The final area of uncertainty, about which the excavators make no clear statement, relates to the orientation of the ship within the mound. It is possible, however, to deduce that the boat lay E–W, for several reasons. In the first place, the watercolour plan from the Society of Antiquaries' library (Pl. I), shows a section along the length of the ship with an undisturbed profile through the mound, with no trace of truncation by the road. Secondly, the excavators would surely not have aligned their trench through the mound so as to start or finish on the road. It would make much better sense to dig it (as they had done with the first mound) parallel to the road. In fact it was a very fortunate coincidence that the east-west road made an east-west trench the most convenient way to proceed, since this meant that the excavators came directly down onto the full length of the boat, rather than cutting obliquely across it.

Had this happened, it would have been far harder for them to recognise what they had stumbled across.

The ship

The ship thus recognised and excavated by Septimus Davidson in 1862 is of considerable importance. In archaeological terms, it was the first ship burial to be recognised in England, and it was the first in Europe to have its plan published (Müller-Wille 1970, 9). It is also reasonably securely dated, with the mid to second half of the 6th century date of the burial providing a *terminus ante quem* for the construction of the boat (see below, pp.195–6). In nautical terms, it remains (after the Sutton Hoo mound 1 ship) the only example of a complete pagan Anglo-Saxon clinker-built boat, a testimony to the constructional skills of 6th-century boat builders, and a clue to the types of vessel in which the Anglo-Saxon immigrants arrived in East Anglia. It is important therefore to extract the maximum possible amount of detail about its construction. There are three sources of evidence. The first is Septimus Davidson's 1863 account, which is worth quoting in full:

It was therefore decided to increase the depth of the excavation, and a highly interesting result ensued. A few pieces of metal or wood, of dubious structure and use, were discovered. They scarcely held together, and the scraping the earth from them broke them. They appeared to have been originally of the thickness and length of a finger or a little more, with a head the size of a florin, sometimes set diamond-wise, sometimes not, and knobbed rather than flat, and sometimes with a short projecting point. An examination of the broken ones seemed to show that they were composed of laminae of metal and wood, with a bolt or handle through them.

The number of these articles increasing, it was determined to avoid disturbing any more, but to trace them out in the earth, removing the superincumbent soil. This plan of operations laid bare what seemed to be a floor of considerable size, with rows of these knobs protruding at regular intervals of a few inches, and led to the impression that perhaps this was the substitute for a cist or coffin. Carefully scraping or sweeping with the hand only between the rows, it became apparent that the interval was of wood, but so disintegrated and crumbling as to be almost of the colour of the soil. The same plan of operations being pursued disclosed a continuance of these rows at an obtuse angle from the floor upwards; and the excavation being yet further extended, both on each side and at each end, gave to view the shape of a boat, and it appeared that the knobbed pieces of metal and wood above alluded to, were the rivets that fastened together the planks laid clinkerwise, and that the boat was probably flat-bottomed. This boat, or at least boat-like structure, was 48 feet in length, 9 feet 9 in. in width, and 4 feet deep. In each row of rivets seven were included within a distance of 3 feet. The rows were six in number on either side, and four or five in number in the bottom of the boat. At the sides the rivets lay horizontally, at the bottom they rested vertically on the sand. All the rows terminated in two rivets lying parallel with each other — the one at the stem, the other at the stern.

The second source of evidence is the plan, of which there are two versions. The first, the watercolour in the Library of the Society of Antiquaries (Pl. I), is unsigned and undated but must have been done either during or shortly after the excavation. In addition to a plan, a section through the mound and along the length of the boat, and a cross-section of the boat, there are pencil annotations of the different soil layers, and a drawing of a sand-encrusted rivet. The second version of the plan was published in the *Proceedings of the Society of Antiquaries* in 1863, to accompany Septimus Davidson's communication, and is also reproduced by Hele (Davidson 1863, 180; Hele 1870, 26; here Fig. 4). It is an engraving based on the watercolour, but altered in several ways. The plan and sections have been trimmed to omit the full section through the mound, while the pattern of rivets, shown only partially on the watercolour, has been extended to fill the entire area of the boat. The resulting number of lines of rivets, seventeen, and the spacing of the individual rivets, broadly reflect Septimus Davidson's account, but it is clear that the pattern is schematic and not intended to represent what was observed. Septimus Davidson in a footnote says that 'The plan not having been made by a professional surveyor may not be minutely accurate, especially as to the exact position of the rivets at the smaller end' (Davidson 1863, 181). On the cross-section, the profile of the boat has been made less rounded while the number of rivets shown in the cross-section has been reduced from the eighteen shown on the watercolour to seventeen, presumably so as to match up with the plan. Of the two versions, there can be no doubt that the watercolour is both the more reliable and the more informative.

The final source of evidence for the Snape ship is the collection of ironwork — principally rivets — which survives in Aldeburgh Museum. As Septimus Davidson noted, the iron is almost totally mineralised and surrounded by thick layers of corrosion and of mineralised wood which recent examination showed to be slowgrown oak heartwood (Rowena Gale, report in site archive). It is a credit to the 1862 excavators that they recognised the rivets for what they were.

The metalwork from the ship can be divided into three categories:

a) **rivets**; these are of the usual type with round, domed heads, and diamond roves. Bruce-Mitford distinguished two different lengths, with head and rove 30mm (1.2in) and 44mm (1.75in) apart;

b) **rib-bolts**; Bruce-Mitford identified only one piece, 64mm (2.5in) in length;

c) portions of an **iron strip**, at least 328mm in length, with regularly spaced rivets, which appears from the mineralised wood impressions to have been fastened vertically to the outside of the hull (Fig. 78, *1660*). The significance of this object is discussed below.

From this evidence it is possible to say that the Snape ship was of clinker built and riveted construction, identical to that used in the Sutton Hoo mound 1 ship. The rivets were spaced at 140mm intervals and were of at least two lengths. For comparison, the rivets on the mound 1 ship were spaced at *c.*170mm intervals and were *c.*50mm in length (Bruce-Mitford 1975, figs 279 and 309). The number of strakes in the Snape ship cannot be known exactly but was either sixteen or eighteen (eight or nine per side). The latter is the more probable, since it would match the Sutton Hoo mound 1 ship, and it is the number shown in the cross-section of the watercolour plan.

A striking feature of the plan is the ship's squared end or 'transom stern'. That the Snape ship was in fact 'double ended' (or 'pointed at both ends' as a non-sailor would say) is proved by Septimus Davidson's account, which records that 'all the rows terminated in two rivets lying parallel with each other — the one at the stem, the other at the stern'. It is also indicated on the watercolour where the outer two lines of rivets do not continue around the 'stern'.

The effect of the transom stern was probably produced by the boat having been more truncated by the erosion of the mound at one end than at the other. Looking at the full section through the boat and mound (Pl. I), it is clear that (as at Sutton Hoo) the bow and stern of the boat must have been left sticking out above the surface of the mound. If one end protruded further than the other, and if the boat was broader in the beam at the same end, then the removal of the end would result in a more rounded profile beneath the surface. It is interesting that the stern of the Sutton Hoo ship appeared 'slightly rounded' to the excavators (Bruce-Mitford 1975, 360).

The flat bottom of the boat, mentioned by Septimus Davidson and particularly emphasised in the engraved version of the plan, must also be the result of post-deposition factors, in this case the settling of the boat, as the wood decayed and was pressed down into its trench (Bruce-Mitford 1975, 347).

Although Septimus Davidson gives the length of the boat as 48 feet, it must originally have been somewhat longer. Allowing for the lost bow and stern, the total length must have been in the region of 54 feet. There is no reason to question Septimus Davidson's figures for its beam and depth, so the overall dimensions were thus 16.45m in length, 2.97m in the beam and 1.22m in depth. This compares with 27 × 4.25 × 1.37m of the Sutton Hoo mound 1 ship and 8.5 × 1.6 × 0.8m of the ship from mound 7 at Valsgärde (Arwidsson 1977, 95–8).

In default of any direct evidence, we must assume that, like the Sutton Hoo ship, the principal method of propulsion for the Snape ship was oars. This does not of course rule out the use of sail and it is possible to interpret the iron strip attached vertically to the outside of the hull as the remains of a 'chain plate' to attach stays to support a mast. Against this interpretation is the fact that the use of iron chain plates is unparalleled at this period (McGrail 1987, 229); stays seem to have been attached directly to the hull. It is also worth remembering that diamond-roved rivets were not just used for boats. In Valsgärde 7, a wooden sea chest or wagon body using identical rivets to those used in the ship had been placed within the grave (Arwidsson 1977, 99–103). It is possible that the strip from Snape derives from some other object altogether.

The other finds

In addition to the ship itself, the 1862 excavators found a number of objects as they dug down into the mound and cleared the ship. Virtually all the conclusions about the sex and status of the person buried, and about the date of the burial, have to be based on these objects which were:

> fragments of two iron **spearheads**
> a single fragment of **blue glass**
> fragments of **'jasper'**
> a **bundle of 'red hair'** wrapped in cloth
> fragments of a glass **claw beaker**
> a gold **ring**, set with a Roman intaglio

Of these finds, the single fragment of blue glass has disappeared, making any interpretation of its significance impossible. Francis Francis felt that it was Roman, which is by no means impossible; a surface scatter of Roman material has been located 250m to the west of the site (SNP 024). The jasper fragments have also gone and remain wholly enigmatic. The 'red hair' and its associated cloth were at Aldeburgh Museum before the last War, whence it was transferred to Ipswich for safety (Stanley West, pers. comm.). It was seen in Ipswich Museum, but seems to have been lost in the subsequent return of the Snape material to Aldeburgh. Despite its loss, the accounts are sufficiently precise for it to be identified by Rupert Bruce-Mitford as the remains of a 'shaggy cloak, in which the long matted tufts of animal hair or fur were inserted into a cloth base' (Bruce-Mitford 1974, 117). Similar finds were made in the Sutton Hoo ship burial and in the Broomfield barrow, Essex.

The glass claw beaker (Pl. IV and Fig. 78), almost every fragment of which was collected by the excavators, survives in Aldeburgh Museum, and is of Evison's Type 3c, which she dates broadly to the mid-6th century (Evison 1982). The magnificent gold ring is now in the British Museum (Pls II and III, Fig. 78). It was illustrated by Septimus Davidson, and passed by inheritance to his granddaughter Mrs Christie, who generously gave it to the British Museum in 1950, just as Rupert Bruce-Mitford had given up hope of finding it (Bruce-Mitford 1974, 122–3). It is a signet ring, with a Roman onyx gemstone, depicting the standing figure of *Bonus Eventus* (Happy Outcome), mounted in a Germanic gold setting. Bruce-Mitford, the first after the original excavators to discuss the ring in any detail, argued that it was an Anglo-Saxon piece (Bruce-Mitford 1952). He was unable to find any Anglo-Saxon rings of similar form to support his thesis, but instead drew parallels with details of the decoration, such as the 'hook and eye' motif which appears on the ring's shoulders, which he linked with that on the Sutton Hoo sword clips. He also felt that the use of granulation on the shoulders was most closely paralleled by objects dating to as late as the second half of the 7th century. Based on these parallels, and writing at a time when the Sutton Hoo ship burial was still put at *c*.650, he 'found it difficult to assign the manufacture of the Snape ring ... to a date earlier than 625AD' (Bruce-Mitford 1952, 19).

Bruce-Mitford's conclusions, both on provenance and date, were strongly challenged in 1966 by Joachim Werner (Werner 1971). He had the advantage of the discovery in 1962 of a ring very similar to that from Snape in grave 1782 at Krefeld-Gellep, in the Rhineland (Fig. 136a), a grave securely dated to *c*.525 (Pirling 1974, 61–8; 1986, 139–64). Based on this find, Werner suggested that the ring was of early 6th-century Germanic manufacture.

There is no doubt that the parallels between the Snape and Krefeld-Gellep rings are very close. Both are Germanic settings for a re-used Roman intaglio and have a similarity of form and feel that Bruce-Mitford was unable to find among the Anglo-Saxon material; both furthermore have 'hook and eye' and granulation, arranged in a very similar way to give a characteristically Germanic zoomorphic effect (Müller-Wille 1970, 45).

It is, however, not just the parallels between these two rings which prove a continental origin for the Snape ring.[1] There are similarly close parallels of detail with other continental rings, such as that from Lorsch (Roth and Wamers 1984, 137). More significant, however, is the fact that, as Bruce-Mitford had found, there is no ring of comparable form to that from Snape among early Anglo-Saxon rings, numerous as these are (Fisher 1979). Although some five other intaglio rings have been found in reliable Anglo-Saxon contexts, these are all actual Roman rings. They are not Anglo-Saxon resettings of Roman intaglios. On the continent, the situation is the reverse. Of the thirty or so intaglio rings from reliable contexts, only two retain their original Roman settings. The rest are all Germanic resettings of Roman intaglios. The Snape ring is so clearly at home in this continental setting that it would be foolish to argue otherwise.

Werner's suggestion of an early 6th-century date for the ring is also clearly correct. Once again, it is not only the close parallel with the securely dated Krefeld-Gellep grave 1782 ring that proves this, but the wider context of continental rings. The form of the Snape ring, with its wide and heavily decorated shoulders is current on the continent only in the first half of the 6th century, after which it is superseded by a less sumptuous form. This date is further confirmed by the high gold content (86% pure; Bruce-Mitford 1978, 625).

The sex of the burial

The burial seems to have been that of a man. Although none of the grave-goods found within the ship (*i.e.* ring, claw beaker, cloak) give any clue as to sex, the finding of the two spearheads higher up appears conclusive. As Bruce-Mitford suggested, it is probable that they were disturbed by the 'Gentlemen from London' in 1827 (above, p. 5). The diameter of the ring neither supports nor contradicts this (*pace* Bruce-Mitford, who describes it as 'unusually large. It must have been worn by a man, either on the thumb or forefinger' (Bruce-Mitford 1974, 124)). The 22mm diameter is well within the range of both male and female rings (Filmer-Sankey 1990b, 36 and table 4). Bruce-Mitford's statement nearly landed the author in serious trouble when he attempted to remove the Aldeburgh Museum's replica ring from his thumb!

The date of the burial

The ring is of crucial importance in establishing a *terminus post quem* for the ship burial. As discussed above, Bruce-Mitford in 1952 saw the ring as an Anglo-Saxon piece which, on account of the parallels with the Sutton Hoo material, he could not 'assign to a date much earlier than AD 625'. The redating of the Sutton Hoo ship burial from 650 to 625 shifted the date of the Snape ring earlier, to *c.*A.D. 600 (Bruce-Mitford 1974, 129). In deciding the gap between the ring's manufacture and its burial, Bruce-Mitford noted 'signs of wear upon the shoulders which show that it must have been worn for some little while'. By 'some little while', Bruce-Mitford appears to have meant fifteen years, since he dated the ship burial to *c.*615.

In support of this relatively late date, Bruce-Mitford also quoted the solitary fragment of blue glass, mentioned only by Francis Francis and now lost. He interpreted it as the remains of a Cuddesdon-Broomfield type bowl, of known 7th-century date.

This interpretation cannot be accepted. Francis Francis' description of the fragment as 'being more an opaque blue, and being thicker glass of better manufacture, more in fact like a fragment of Roman glass' does not sound like a Cuddesdon-Broomfield bowl. Since only one fragment of the vessel was found (in contrast to virtually all of the claw beaker) it may well have been a stray object, or even a fused glass bead from a disturbed cremation.

The dating of the ship burial was given a radically different slant by Werner's dating of the ring to the early 6th century, based on its parallels with the Krefeld-Gellep grave 1782 ring. As already discussed, Werner is definitely right both in assigning a continental provenance and in his date. In consequence, the ring now gives a *terminus post quem* for the burial of *c.*525. At the same time, however, the continental provenance adds a further level of uncertainty, since it is now necessary to allow time for the ring to make the journey from the Rhineland to Suffolk.

The only other finds which can contribute anything to the dating are the spearheads and the claw beaker. The former are not helpful. Only one is sufficiently preserved to allot a Swanton type, H2, 'the vast majority of which belong to the latest 5th and the 6th century' (Swanton 1973, 107–111). The claw beaker is better and has been discussed by Evison as part of her overall study of claw beakers. She allots it to her type 3c, which she dates broadly to the mid 6th century (Evison 1982, 48).

In short, the surviving datable objects give a reasonably good *terminus post quem* of *c.*525 for the ring and a very vague *c.*550 for the claw beaker. Taken together (and combined with the evidence from the 1985–92 excavations, which are discussed in detail below) it seems reasonable to date the Snape ship burial to the mid to second half of the 6th century. It is thus, of course, definitely earlier than the mound 1 ship burial, and probably earlier than any of the other excavated mounds, at Sutton Hoo (Carver 1993, 17–19).

The status of the burial

Turning finally to the question of the status of the burial, the use of a ship of at least 14m as a coffin is in itself indicative of high status, albeit in a rather vague and ill-defined way. A rather more precise picture can be gained by a study of the Snape ring, both in a continental setting, and in an Anglo-Saxon setting.

As already discussed, the Snape ring is undoubtedly of continental manufacture. It should thus be seen first as one of a group of thirty intaglio rings from continental contexts, where they are one of the few types to be found in male as well as female graves. As already remarked, all but two of these rings are Germanic resettings of Roman gemstones; they are not re-used Roman rings. At the same time, however, the inspiration for the forms of the Germanic settings derives from late Roman and contemporary Byzantine, rather than from native Germanic styles. As with the Snape ring, so on the continent, the bulk of these Germanic settings are of gold (twenty out of thirty), thus qualifying for *Qualitätsgruppe* D, the highest rank, in Christlein's widely adopted system for ranking graves (Christlein 1973, Abb. 11). Analysis of the subjects chosen for resetting suggests that Germanic jewellers were selecting, wherever possible, intaglios with standing or seated figures, and it seems reasonable to

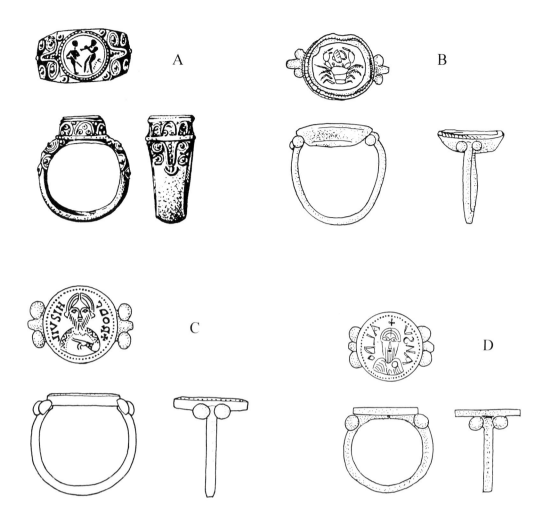

Figure 136 The finger-rings from (a) Krefeld-Gellep (after Pirling 1974) and (b–d) Trezzo sul'Adda
(after Roffia 1986: (b) tav. 5; (c) tav. 13; (d) tav. 31). Scale 1:1

conclude that this reflects a symbolic role for the rings, most likely as an indicator of rank or status (Filmer-Sankey 1990b, 104–5). Once again the figure of *'Bonus Eventus'* on the Snape ring fits this pattern.

Although direct evidence in the form of surviving impressions is lacking, it is further likely that these Continental intaglio rings were used for sealing. In the first place, they were used as seals in both the preceding Roman and the succeeding Carolingian period, where the earliest surviving impressions include some probably from re-used Roman intaglios (Posse 1909, Taf. 1, A–C; Christlein 1974, 582, n. 22).

Strong, if still indirect, evidence for the use of intaglio rings as seals comes also from the small and aristocratic north Italian cemetery of Trezzo sul'Adda (Roffia 1986). The excavated area contained five graves: three adult males and two juvenile males, all dating to the 7th century. The two later adult graves, no. 4 (*c.*600–650) and no. 2 (*c.*650), both contained purpose-made gold seal rings, complete with a bust and surrounding inscription giving the name and, in the case of grave 2, the abbreviated title (*Vir Illuster*) of the owner (Fig. 136, c–d).

The earliest adult grave (no. 1, with a *terminus post quem* of 607–8) contained not a seal ring, but an intaglio ring, in which a gemstone showing a crab has been incorporated into a typical Germanic setting (Fig. 136b). The juxtaposition of these three graves, with their one intaglio and two seal rings, indicates very strongly that the intaglio ring fulfilled the same function as the purpose-made seal rings and that they belonged to succeeding generations of the same family of office holders.

In short there is good evidence to conclude that intaglios reset in Germanic ring settings were not just a symbol of rank or status, but that they also had a practical function, and were used to seal documents in exactly the same way as the genuine seal rings, such as those from graves 2 and 4 at Trezzo sul'Adda, and (more famously) that from the grave of the Frankish king Childeric (Chiflet 1655). This group, twenty-one examples of which are known from continental Germanic contexts, is clearly to be linked with the highest ranks of Germanic society, not least because several of them belonged to known kings or queens. In addition, the fact that they incorporate reversed inscriptions (to make the resultant seal legible) means that they must have been made by coin-die cutters. Since in the Germanic kingdoms it was, in theory at least, the king who controlled the coinage, it must also have been the kings who commissioned the seal rings, either for their own use, or for the use of their highest officials.

In using this information to define more precisely the continental status of intaglio rings, several avenues can be used. In the first place, the fact that not only the form of the intaglio rings, but also the use of rings as signets, derives from late Roman and contemporary Byzantine practice links the group clearly with the desire to follow Byzantine fashions, which was such a hallmark of aristocratic Germanic society in the 5th–7th centuries (see for example Schulze 1976).

Furthermore, though accurate quantification is impossible, the number of documents requiring seals in the 6th century (to take the date of manufacture of the Snape and Krefeld-Gellep rings) would clearly have been very small. A person thus equipped with a signet would therefore be of the very highest status in the Germanic world, as clearly was the man buried in grave 1782 at Krefeld-Gellep.

If the Snape ring had been found on the continent, there is no doubt that the grave would have been attributed the highest status, with its occupant as one of a very restricted group who had reason to seal documents, and who was concerned to follow Byzantine fashion.

Turning to see the ring in its Anglo-Saxon context is equally revealing. The ring, as a continental piece, belongs to a very small and select group of nine Anglo-Saxon ring finds which are of continental origin. Associated with this group are a further seven rings which are clearly based on continental Germanic types[2]. This group represents a tiny proportion (some 5%) of the corpus of Anglo-Saxon rings as catalogued by Fisher (Fisher 1979), but it stands clearly apart from the majority in several ways.

In the first place, their forms differ totally from 'native' rings. The majority of Anglo-Saxon ring types, such as the well known 'wire rings with twisted bezels', are based on native Germanic forms. Like the native Germanic rings of the Roman Iron Age, furthermore, they are made of a wide range of materials, with gold and silver forming only a small percentage of the whole. The Merovingian and Merovingian-inspired rings, by contrast, owe little to northern European forms, but rather take their inspiration from late Roman or contemporary Byzantine styles. They are predominantly of precious metal (eleven out of the sixteen are of gold or silver).

A further factor distinguishing these sixteen Merovingian and Merovingian-inspired rings from the bulk of Anglo-Saxon rings is that they virtually all have a potentially practical, as opposed to purely decorative, function. There is one purpose-made seal ring, for example, even if it is a particularly crude example (an unstratified find from Richborough). Six of the sixteen rings are intaglio rings, which could be used as seals. There are three rings which use a coin as a bezel. Native Anglo-Saxon types, by contrast, have no features like intaglios or coins which could give them such a function, and they must be assumed to have had a purely decorative function. The fact that three of this Merovingian group (the rings from Snape, Mucking cemetery II, gr. 933 and Milton-next-Sittingbourne) were found in male graves further distinguishes it from the native Anglo-Saxon tradition, where rings are only found in female graves.

In short, it seems that the Anglo-Saxons were aware of the practical and symbolic use of certain types of continental Germanic rings, and were emulating that use. In the case of the Snape ring, they were able to get hold of an actual continental intaglio ring. In other cases where a seal ring was needed, no continental ring was available, so that a Roman ring had to be found for re-use. This pattern of reusing a Roman object in place of an unavailable continental example has been noticed elsewhere in Anglo-Saxon England (White 1988, 163). In the case of five re-used Roman intaglio rings, moreover, it is very notable that every effort was made to find a gold or silver example, itself an indication of the status that was attached to the possession of a seal ring.

On the continent, as argued above, intaglio rings like that from Snape were used as seals. Clearly in England in the 6th century there would have been no documents to seal. This fact, however, can only increase the status represented by the ring's presence in the Snape ship burial. The more restricted the potential use, the higher the status accorded to the possessor. A modern analogy would be the spread of mobile telephones: they were at their height as a status symbol when they were so technologically restricted as to be virtually useless. The fact that the Snape ring may never have been used thus increases the status that must be accorded to the grave. On this basis it is reasonable to suggest that the grave may have been that of an early East Anglian king. The only difference between the Snape ship burial and Sutton Hoo mound 1 is that, while the former was plundered, the latter survived intact for its royal nature to proved.

The presence of the ring can be seen as more than just a sign of the highest (royal?) status. It is also a sign of a conscious desire to emulate Frankish and, more distantly, Roman and Byzantine customs. This is in itself a sign of the highest status, and here too there are parallels with mound 1 at Sutton Hoo, where the Frankish coins and Byzantine silver emphasise that man's Roman and Frankish aspirations, and the royal nature of the burial (Filmer-Sankey 1996).

Endnotes:

1. For more detailed discussion of the Continental parallels for the Snape ring and of the function of rings in the Early Medieval Germanic world, see Filmer-Sankey 1990b.

2. Continental rings in Anglo-Saxon graves:

Site	Metal	Sex	Date
Aldeburgh, stray find	gold	-	-
Finglesham, grave 58	gilded bronze	male	600–700
Harnham Hill, grave 40	silver	female	500–550
Harnham Hill, grave 54	bronze	female	500–600
Mucking II, grave 933	silver	male	-
Richborough, unstrat.	gilded silver	-	-
Richborough, unstrat.	silver	-	-
Sibertswold, grave 163	gold	male	-
Snape	gold	male	-
Alfriston, grave 28	gilded bronze	female	525–550
Chatham Hill	gold	-	-
Highdown Hill, stray	bronze	-	-
Howletts, grave 4	gold	female?	500–550?
London, Euston Square	gold	-	-
Milton-next-Sittingbourne	gold	male	-
York, stray find	gold	-	-

(After Filmer-Sankey 1990b, table 27)

II. The Logboats from Graves 4 and 47
by Tim Pestell

Background

Two of the most important discoveries in the recent campaign of excavations were the stains from graves 4 and 47, of logboats re-used as burial containers. Their identification as such is discussed in Filmer-Sankey (1990a). Briefly, both stains share the same shape, well-documented in expanded dugout logboats. They also have fittings normally associated with such boats, they derive from a site known for the use of a boat burial rite, and they are strikingly well paralleled by the expanded dugout boats excavated in the cemetery at Slusegård on the Baltic island of Bornholm (Klindt-Jensen 1978; Crumlin-Pedersen 1991). As this report was in press I was made aware of the two fundamentally similar dugout boats preserved by waterlogging and excavated in 1994 at the German cemetery of Fallward, Wremen, Kr. Cuxhaven (Schön 1999). It has therefore not been possible to take these new discoveries into account in the present discussion, although the boats, of 5th to 6th-century date, are slightly larger at 4.4m and 5m long, like the Slusegård vessels. I am grateful to Dr Chris Loveluck for drawing my attention to this site. Another inhumation, grave 3, produced a charcoal-edged stain that possibly represents a third logboat cut up for use as a burial container. Its identification can only be made by comparison with the two complete boats and gives no additional information on dugout boat design.

Both complete boats were excavated in plan according to the techniques used for the other inhumations (p. 16), except that excavation was undertaken in smaller spits, 25mm at a time, with more frequent planning levels, often every 50mm. Sections were cut through the boat bases at more regular intervals — every 50mm in grave 4, every 100mm in grave 47.

The stains of both boats preserved evidence of constructional details, that in grave 47 generating records from which a three-dimensional computer reconstruction has been made by Peter Marsden (below). By applying the naval architect computer program *Boatcad*, its theoretical nautical performance has been assessed. The full report of this study, with supporting data and calculations, is held in the site archive but is extensively summarised below. The close similarity in size and design between the boats from graves 4 and 47 suggests that the theoretical performance figures can be applied to both safely.

Size and design

As excavated, the boat in grave 4 had a length of 2.96m, beam of 0.7m and depth of 0.4m. That in grave 47 was 3.09m long, 0.62m in beam and 0.35m deep. In fact, these are all probably minimal measurements, this is especially true of the boat in grave 4, which survived at its western end from only a relatively low height. The original thickness of the boats was also unclear. The stain in grave 4 was always patchy except at the eastern bow and in several places it did not exist. It survived up to 20mm thick at the eastern bow and even more in some parts where the 'fin' of the bow point survived. The boat in grave 47 survived far better with a stain some 10–20mm thick throughout. Again, it was thicker at both bows and on the bottom, where it measured up to 30mm. A patch of charcoal within the boat stain was about 5–10mm thick

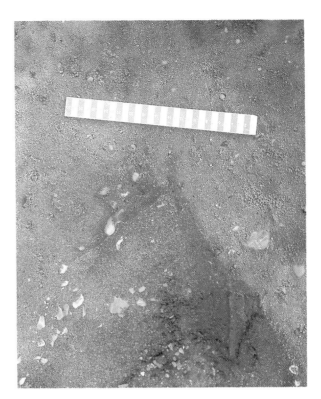

Plate XXXIII Grave 4, fin end to east bow of logboat with possible repair patch *1019*

and would seem to reflect a charring of one side of the boat, probably the inside.

The original thickness of the boat from grave 47 (and by implication of that from grave 4) seems slight in comparison with other British logboats recorded by McGrail (1978, ii), which show bottoms ranging from 30–130mm in thickness and sides of 20–80mm. Originally, all were probably slightly thicker as they were recorded dry and shrunken. The stain of both Snape boats may suggest unusually thin-walled craft although Edwin Gifford (pers. comm.) suggests that, like expanded dugouts, the Snape boats could indeed originally have been some 10–30mm thick. Understanding the construction of both relies on more ephemeral clues.

Although clinker-built construction with strakes fastened by wooden pegs is possible, the lack of evidence for any planking, and absence of any keel in the cross-sections, suggests that the boats were a dugout form of logboat. This identification is strengthened by their tapering plan, their rounded bottoms and the lack of any characteristic metal fittings. Whilst there is little positive evidence in support, it suggests that both the Snape logboats were expanded like those from Slusegård, a thin-walled cut-out being stretched under heat into a more open form. The shape was then maintained by the insertion of cross-pieces or breasthooks at the bows (seen at Slusegård in boats 1129, 1131, 1139 and 1391; Crumlin-Pedersen 1991, 253). Certainly, the boat from grave 4 preserved stains of substantial curved wooden fittings inside the bow fins at both ends (Pl. XXXIV). The small size of the boat makes it unlikely that they were thwarts, as the user probably sat at the centre of the boat on the floor (see below). An alternative possibility is therefore that they were breasthooks strengthening the boat. The boat

199

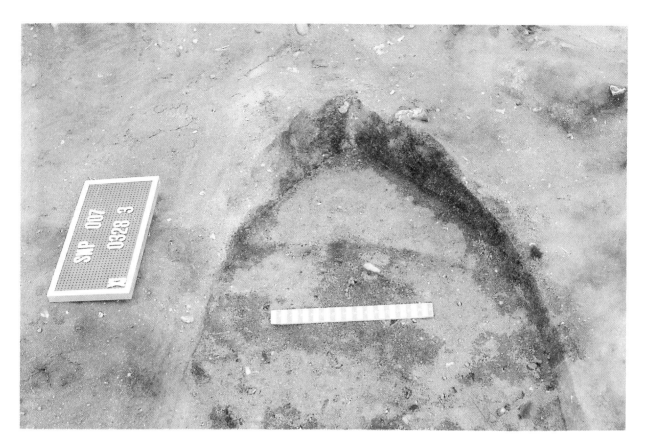

Plate XXXIV Possible thwart inside eastern bow of logboat from grave 4

from grave 4 finds at least one close parallel from Slusegård in boat 1131, which was 2.8m long and 0.7m in beam (Klindt-Jensen 1978, 110). The parent timber from which the boat in grave 4 was made is unknown but is presumed to have been of oak (*Quercus* sp.). Tiny fragments of charcoal found in its western bow stain were of oak but being possibly of softwood, it is unclear whether these derived from the actual boat. The boat in grave 47 was confirmed as oak by a large charred patch within the stain and several mineralised wooden fragments associated with small-finds in the burial deposit.

The shape of both Snape boats, pointed at each end, is uncontroversial in dugout logboats. Indeed, the distinctive 'fin' shape of the boat from grave 4 (Pl. XXXIII) is well-known in many of the Slusegård boats, for instance those from graves 1072, 1129, 1131 and 1139 (Klindt-Jensen 1978, ii; 177, 179–180, 182). However, neither of the Snape boats appeared to exhibit the lower extension to this fin, the 'skeg' (Crumlin-Pedersen 1991, 105). The uneven shape in section along the lengthwise axis of the boat from grave 47 is also unusual. This might be the result of the boat base slumping into the burial pit but the many sections show a smoothness and consistency which suggests that this need not be the case. The boat stain from grave 4, whilst far more fragmentary, also seems to have an uneven bottom and these may reflect both dugouts' original design. A possible implication is that the boats, whilst pointed at each end, could originally have been perceived or designed as having a bow and stern. Both deeper ends were to the east when buried, suggesting that if a 'front' and 'back' were recognised, this might have influenced the orientation of the boat in the grave. The evidence is slight and if intentional, it remains unclear which end was seen as the bow.

Both Snape boats provide other smaller hints for being expanded. The process of expansion often led to internal cracking which required caulking. Two patches of greasy grey organic material, suggested to be caulking, were found in the boat from grave 4 (Pl. XXXIII), a presence matched by numerous examples of resin caulking from Slusegård (Crumlin-Pedersen 1991; 104, 254). Finally, more slender evidence supporting the expansion of the boats perhaps comes from that in grave 47; this retained the U-shape section necessary for expansion and the area of charring at its west end could, like several examples from Slusegård, relate to the boat's heating over an open fire (Crumlin-Pedersen 1991, 254).

Fittings or accessories to the boats were limited. A charred stain at the bottom of the boat in grave 47 was suggestively paddle shaped but analysis of the charcoal showed that it derived from two wood types and this is probably yet another instance of charred wood accompanying a body for burial. If it does represent a paddle Slusegård again provides a possible parallel, with two or three oars placed outside the boat in grave 1224 (Crumlin-Pedersen 1991, 150–1). The boat in grave 47 also had Fe nail *E* in the boat interior but it is unclear what function this might have had.

The reconstruction and hydrostatic assessment of the boat from grave 47
by Peter Marsden

The shape of the boat
In order to conduct an assessment of the boat's seaworthiness and performance it was first necessary to create a computer reconstruction of the vessel. There are five objectives in reconstructing any boat: its type of construction, its shape, the distribution of its weight, its methods of propulsion, and its steering. Construction determines strength, and shape and weight distribution determine stability.

It was first necessary to establish what was the boat's original centre-line, since for the purpose of stability its shape and weight would have been the same on either side. The centre-line clearly ran between the sharp ends of the vessel. As the boat's stain was far better preserved on the south side it was decided to use this entire half of the boat as the basis for reconstruction, using the shape of the north side as a check.

The naval architect's computer program *Boatcad* was used, initially drawing the vertical sections reconstructed every 100mm through the boat's length into the computer using a digitizing tablet. These were related to the centre-line of the vessel and site datum. The result was that *Boatcad* could represent the excavated shape of the southern half of the boat in three dimensions. This could then be copied to form the northern half of the vessel giving an image of the whole, which could be turned to any angle. The shape was also represented by 'waterlines' (horizontal sections through the boat at vertical intervals) and buttock lines (vertical longitudinal sections parallel to the central axis of the vessel) (Fig. 137a).

The minimum reconstruction
The next objective was to 'fair' the lines of the vessel with minimum alteration. This was achieved by rotating the image of the boat and by eye averaging out the hull shape between the irregularities. The basic form of the vessel was not altered. The surviving top of the south side was uneven but in places reached a horizontal line drawn between the tops of stem and stern, as if originally the top of the vessel's sides were straight. The resultant reconstruction is very close to the shape of the boat as found, showing a vessel 3.08m long with a maximum beam of 0.62m and a height of the sides of 0.35m (Fig. 137b). It was slightly sharper at the west end than at the east and its rounded bottom was a little deeper in the western half of the vessel. This was the minimum reconstruction of the boat's original shape.

The maximum reconstruction
Uncertainty over the uneven bottom to the boat, unusual although not unique amongst dugout finds, led to the creation of a 'maximum' reconstruction. This modified the bottom to make it parallel with the gunwale throughout the vessel except at its ends, on the assumption that the bottom of the western part of the boat was the true shape (Fig. 137c). This slightly altered the beam of the boat (length 3.08m; beam 0.52m; depth 0.35m).

Weight
The distribution of the weight of the vessel is one of the most important factors determining its stability and therefore whether or not the object was a boat. The total hull area was computed by *Boatcad*, taking into account the presence of any structural weight in the boat other than the sides. If the vessel was bottom-heavy it would be more stable than one that was top-heavy, for the latter would tend to capsize. Determining weight relies upon establishing the volume of wood that comprised an average square metre of the hull. This can be converted into weight by multiplying the volume by the weight of a cubic metre of timber, a density of about 800kg per cubic metre for oak. Estimating the original hull thickness is difficult but the bottom is likely to have been at least 30mm thick and the sides at least 20mm thick. The stem and stern hull stains were much thicker and would have added weight compensating for the thinner sides. For assessing weight distribution, the boat probably had an average minimum hull thickness overall of 30mm giving the following hull weights; as found 0.059 tonnes; minimum and maximum reconstructions 0.058 tonnes. These figures confirm how the reconstructions very closely follow the excavated shape.

Hydrostatic study
The measure of any boat's stability is its ability to right itself when heeled. This righting lever is proportional to the transverse Metacentric height (GMt), which is the distance between the Centre of Gravity (CoG) above the keel, and the transverse Metacentre above the keel (KMt). For a boat to be stable the righting moment must be positive; that is, that Mt must always be above the CoG (Fig. 138). The vessel was examined in both minimum and maximum reconstructions for unladen and laden states.

Unladen: The minimum reconstruction in its unladen state, as if the empty boat was placed in the water, was found to have a displacement of 0.058 tonnes and a draught of 0.127m. Its Centre of Gravity was at 0.17m above the bottom, and its Centre of Buoyancy lay 1.39m from the east end and at a height of 0.08m above the bottom. This is important as it is about the mid point of the vessel, and therefore the best position for a seat for the user of the vessel. *Boatcad's* calculations showed that when the boat was launched empty it would remain upright. In the maximum reconstruction *Boatcad* calculated a displacement of 0.058 tonnes and a draught of 0.114m, with the Centre of Gravity 0.15m above the bottom. This vessel would also have been stable when launched.

Laden: Once laden the hydrostatics change as the vessel lies deeper in the water with a combined Centre of Gravity of the boat and person which can make it top-heavy. On the basis of certain standard parameters as advanced by McGrail (1978, 131) calculations presume a representative person to be 1.65m high with a weight of 60kg, *i.e.* short, lean and wiry. The Centre of Gravity of a standing person should be at 1.1m above the feet, of a kneeling person it would be at 0.45m, and it would be at 0.4m above the backside when seated. Only by establishing the combined CoG relative to the metacentre of the vessel in a static state can the theoretical stability of the boat, and therefore its uses, be made. The maximum heeled righting moments are calculated to occur at a displacement of about 0.118 tonnes, from which the weight of the boat (0.058 tonnes) is deducted, giving an extra load of 0.060 tonnes (*i.e.* about the weight of a person). On the basis of a standard two-fifths freeboard of

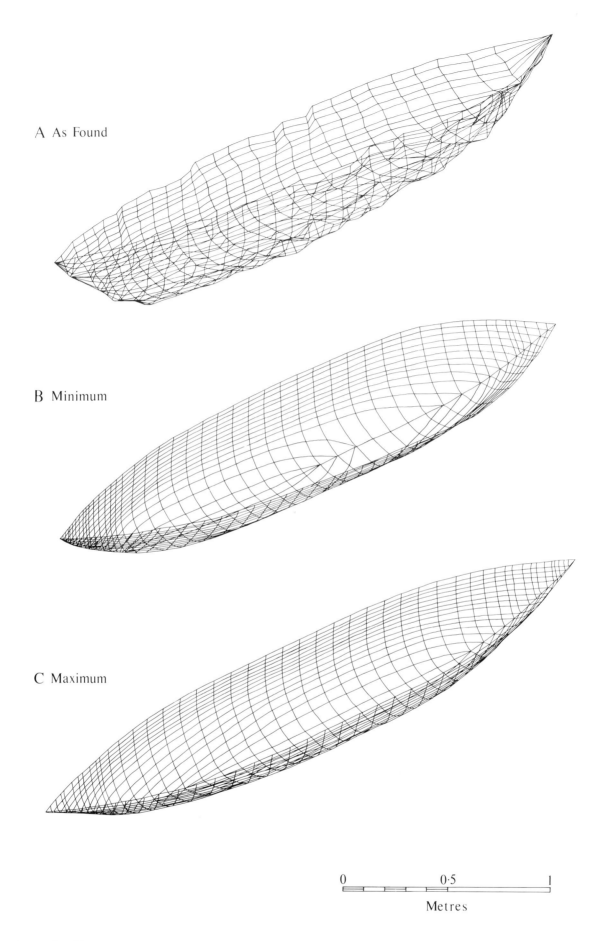

A As Found

B Minimum

C Maximum

0   0·5   1

Metres

Figure 137 Three-dimensional computer-generated plots of the logboat from grave 47 as found (a), and as minimum (b) and maximum (c) reconstruction

FORCES   RIGHTING   HEELING

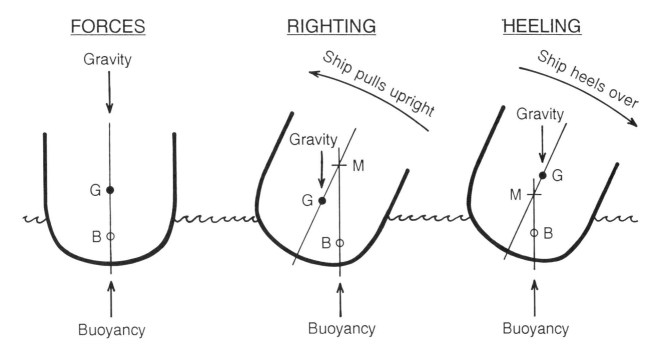

G = Centre of Gravity B = Centre of Buoyancy M = Metacentre

Figure 138 The forces of buoyancy

the depth of the hull amidships (the 'ideal' load as indicated in a medieval Icelandic Law: McGrail 1987, 13) the Snape boat would have a draught of 0.21m giving a displacement of 0.135 tonnes. The boat could carry a load of 0.077 tonnes in this state. In the maximum reconstruction the maximum righting moments occur at a draught of 0.193m, at a displacement of 0.118 tonnes, and would accommodate a load of 0.060 tonnes. A two-fifths freeboard would give a draught of 0.21m and a displacement of 0.148 tonnes. This would give a load of about 0.090 tonnes, about the weight of a large man. If the weight of a 60kg person is deducted, this gives a baggage load of 17kg in the minimum and 30kg in the maximum reconstructions. If the hull was only 10mm thicker *Boatcad* calculates that its weight would be 77kg, an increase of 19kg leaving little or no room for a baggage load. By comparison, the boat from grave 1131 at Slusegård is estimated to have been able carry 123kg at two-fifths freeboard (Crumlin-Pedersen 1991, 182). However, this calculation is based upon the beam originally having been some 0.9m after expansion, rather than the 0.7m as excavated.

Speed
The theoretical maximum speed is calculated by *Boatcad* to be 4 knots. This is the 'one wave' speed, based upon the fact that at slow speed the vessel is supported on its bow and stern waves. If that speed is increased beyond 4 knots the stern will sink into the trough behind the bow wave and consequently much power will be expended in trying to climb the slope of the bow wave rather than on going faster.

Conclusions
Although the calculations are very precise, the results can only be considered approximate as it is not clear what the exact shape and weight of the Snape boat was. Moreover, two alternative reconstructions were necessary, although their similarities suggest that they are close to the shape of the original vessel. The slightly negative transverse Metacentric height in all loaded situations indicates that the boat was probably a little unstable, though if the bottom was thicker and baggage was carried on the boat floor to lower the Centre of Gravity, the vessel would be less inclined to capsize. However, this tendency might not be significant as the boat seems to have had the characteristics of a modern canoe that is kept upright by using the paddle, and the user constantly moving to change their Centre of Gravity. The similarity to a modern canoe does not end there, since the boat was light enough (58kg) to be dragged, and its sharp ends show that it was designed for speed. As the Centres of Buoyancy and Gravity lay amidships in both reconstructions this was evidently where the user sat and either end could have been used as a bow.

Although there are many uncertainties, this study confirms that this vessel was indeed a working boat which had subsequently been re-used as a coffin. It could only have been used by one ordinary 60–70kg person, possibly with a little baggage, as fast and light personal transport on local rivers. In this respect, both the boats from Snape would have been ideally suited to the broad local Alde, Deben and Stour/Orwell estuaries of Suffolk.

III. The Remarkable Survival of Organic Materials

by Esther Cameron and Vanessa Fell

Introduction

It was clear while the excavation was still in progress that the survival of organic remains at Snape differed markedly from the norm. On the one hand, virtually no skeletal material survived from inhumations at Snape where shapes of bodies were preserved as darkly-stained cohesive lumps of sand, similar to those at the nearby site of Sutton Hoo (Bethell and Carver 1987; Bethell and Smith 1989). On the other hand, objects which would normally have perished, or survived only in mineralised form, such as horn, leather, textile and wood, were recovered apparently intact. Since this curious variety of survival had not been noted before, a small study was undertaken to investigate its possible causes.

Methodology

Organic materials endure burial only under conditions which prevent biological activity. This normally occurs through waterlogging, charring, mineralisation and by contact with biocidal agents such as metals, in particular copper (Biek 1963, 125).

At Snape, preservation of organic materials in the vicinity of metal artefacts is common, but there are several occurrences where they have survived without apparent contact with biocidal agents, or through any of the other conditions mentioned above. Most notable are two horns from grave 4 (Pl. XXXV) and a spread of textile from grave 37 (Pls XVII–XIX). Further textile examples are from graves 2, 11, 16, 20 and 36, as well as the bundle of red hair and textile (now lost) found during the excavation of the ship burial in 1862 (Grave 1, above p. 7 and 195; see also Bruce-Mitford 1974, 117).

In order to look for evidence which might help to explain why these materials had survived and to investigate aspects of their physical and chemical change during burial, samples were analysed in three ways:

1   The physical condition of four samples each of bone, horn, leather, animal fibre, and wood was examined by scanning electron microscopy (SEM);
2   Chemical composition in respect of stable isotope and carbon/nitrogen (C/N) ratios of sample duplicates was determined on four specimens each of horn, leather, animal fibre, and wood in order to assess the degree of organic survival (Report by the Research Laboratory for Archaeology and History of Art, University of Oxford in the site archive);
3   Fibre analysis of samples from fifteen textiles were investigated by Fourier transform infrared (FTIR) microscopy for identification of fibres and for degree of deterioration. A full report of the analyses, by Susan Hardman, is in the site archive.

Summary of results

Bone and antler

The exceptional survival of the horse skull (grave 47, S) is difficult to explain. Bone and antler did not normally survive except for fragments that had been partially burnt or were associated with metal artefacts. The morphology of the compact bone and cancellous bone appears undegraded. Although the bone weights from individual cremations are low, reasons other than soil dissolution are proposed for this, such as plough damage and incomplete retrieval from the pyre (Section VII below, p.227).

Horn

Two horn tips from within the prow of the logboat in grave 4, apparently not associated with metal artefacts, are so well preserved that they resemble relatively fresh specimens. A slightly porous appearance and the presence of hyphae strands indicate a degree of fungal activity. This might even be of recent occurrence, perhaps caused by the alteration of soil pH (Filmer-Sankey, n.d.). By contrast, an object of horn from the other boat burial (grave 47, O) did not survive and left only a crumbly black trace, 20 × 30mm, while another drinking horn or cup from grave 18 (A) is only preserved in proximity to its copper alloy rim. All horn handles from knives appear to be mineralised and C/N ratios of two of them did not indicate any significant degree of organic survival.

Leather

Leather survives only where it has been in contact with metal artefacts (Pl. XXXVI). Grain patterns are sometimes preserved on leather sheaths and pouches surrounding iron artefacts (Pl. XXXVII). Occasional details of construction survive such as a seam edge of a knife sheath. Finer details, such as collagen bundles characteristic of the internal structure of leather, are almost entirely absent. The C/N ratios of leather preserved near to iron confirm substantial mineralisation whereas one sample associated with a copper alloy buckle (grave 25, B) was appreciably organic.

Animal hairs

Fine hairs protruding from mineralised leathers are flexible and scale patterns on their outer surfaces are intact (Pls XXXVIII and XXXIX).

Spreads of woollen textile which appeared matted and soft on site became brittle on drying, but weave pattern and lengths of spun yarn are still preserved (Pl. XL). Examination of their fibre surfaces shows that erosion of the cuticle cells has exposed the hair cortex (Pl. XLI). Despite this condition, FTIR analysis confirms a high state of organic preservation (see report by Susan Hardman, site archive).

Wood

Wood survives in the charred condition and in immediate or close proximity to metalwork. The appearance of wood found near to copper alloy suggests a degree of organic survival, for example the remains of the lyre (Pls LIII and LIV) and of vessel F from grave 32. Wood found in association with iron is more friable and degraded, and is preserved through partial mineral replacement (Pls XLII and XLIII). C/N ratios suggest some survival of the organic content in samples associated with either of the metal types. Evidence for ancient fungal activity within samples of wood microstructure (Pl. XLIII) is minimal yet each wood sample shows depletion of hemicellulose (Dr B. Juniper, pers. comm.), possibly by the acid environment.

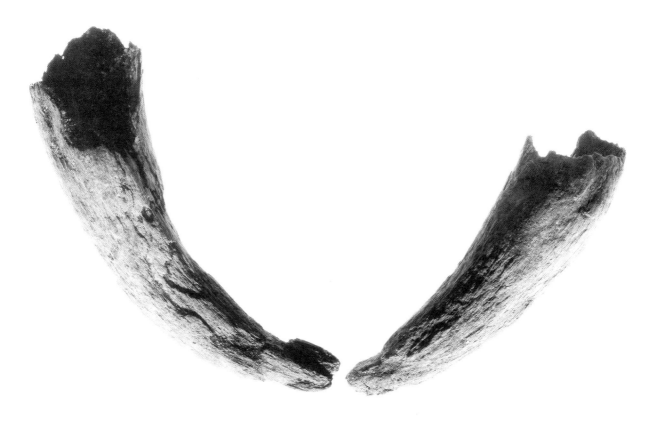

Plate XXXV The two horn tips from the prow of logboat grave 4

Plate XXXVI Mineralised leather loop on knife ring
Fii, grave 2

Plate XXXVII Grain pattern on a mineralised deer skin
pouch, grave 32 *C*

Plate XXXVIII Hair protruding from a mineralised bovid skin sheath of knife *B*, grave 37

Plate XXXIX Scale pattern on a hair shaft from a mineralised bovid skin sheath, knife *B*, grave 37

Plate XL Woollen textile from the base of grave 37

Plate XLI Individual fibres from the woollen textile from grave 37, showing loss of outer cuticle layer

Plate XLII Partly mineralised wood from a spearhaft, grave 47. Longitudinal radial section

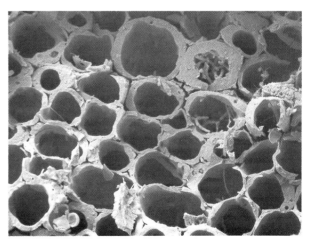

Plate XLIII Partly mineralised wood from a spearhaft, grave 47. Transverse section. Fungal hyphae occupy vessel cavities top right

Discussion

The well-drained glacial deposits of sand at Snape have a pH of 4.5 which until the recent past supported heathland. It should not be assumed that this was always so; soil conditions at Snape hold several features in common with Sutton Hoo where the acid brown earth in which the ship was buried is thought to have been under cereal cultivation in the Early Anglo-Saxon period (Bruce-Mitford 1975, 48–77). A thin iron pan which had developed at Snape is now disturbed by the burrowing of rabbits and by the recent work of the plough and subsoiler.

With the exclusion of charring — as well as the notable horse head remains mentioned earlier, and some bone fragments from grave 12 — bone, antler, leather and wood have not survived except where they have been in contact with, or in close proximity to, copper or iron artefacts. Physical appearance as well as C/N ratios suggest that the biocidal effects of copper have been more effective in preservation, though less extensive than mineralisation by iron salts. On the evidence of soil stains and incomplete objects, the disappearance of organic materials from elsewhere on site might suggest a broad variety in the microbial population. Wood-destroying fungi are known to prefer a low pH whereas bacteria utilising collagen in leather, bone and antler favour a more neutral range.

The notable class of materials to survive is the keratinous group which includes horn, woollen textiles and animal hairs. These do not normally survive burial. Acid has little effect on the protein keratin, but some fungi and bacteria living in a neutral pH range can hydrolyse it. The survival of this particular group of materials would at first suggest that the pH of the soil remained consistently low during most of the period of burial. This explanation would seem adequate if materials made wholly or largely from keratin had survived equally, but this is clearly not the case. The horn tips from grave 4 were buried as complete drinking horns, two other objects of horn (already described) have survived as traces only, while the knife handles and sword hilt of horn were not in their original state, but mineralised by iron compounds. From Sutton Hoo, Mound 1, two auroch horn tips were also well preserved (Bruce-Mitford 1983, figs 234 and 251), although this might have been due to their encasement by the decorative metal terminals of the drinking horns. More comparisons are needed (*e.g.* Taplow and Broomfield) but the remarkable survival of horn tips in particular suggest to us that structural differences between the sheath part and the tip of a horn may render the latter more resistant to biodeterioration and dissolution.

Animal hair has survived well, including isolated hairs on the surfaces of leather knife sheaths, and occurring in quantity as spreads of woollen textile. The interesting contrast between the two — survival of cuticle cells on the former and their loss from the latter — are further evidence of biological differentiation. Reasons for this might be due either to a localised pattern of colonisation among soil microbes away from accumulations of iron corrosion products in leather knife sheaths or to a focusing upon textiles as a source of nutrition. The two sorts of hair (animal pelt and woven yarn) might have been prepared in different ways which rendered the textiles more prone to biodeterioration. Similar survival of hair cuticles on finds from the Sutton Hoo ship burial include otter and beaver pelt-hair, identified partly from scale patterns on the fibre surfaces (Bruce-Mitford 1983, 723 and fig. 652).

However, a scientific description of the condition of woollen textiles from the ship is still to be published.

Feathers, thought to have filled a pillow in the Sutton Hoo ship burial, were so well preserved that they were described as a 'white flock-like material' (Bruce-Mitford 1983, 888). Traces only of mineralised feathers in grave 47 at Snape, as well as the absence of hair from the horse skull, and of human hair from any of the graves, add weight to the argument that, despite the extreme acidity of the soil, keratinous materials were subject to bio-deterioration and that the survival of the horn tips and woollen textiles cannot at this stage be adequately explained.

It is evident that more comparative material and a great deal more scientific analysis will be needed if further study of burial conditions at Snape and similar sites is to progress. Moreover, if we wish to heighten the sensitivity with which we reconstruct and interpret finds, then our understanding of soil processes and agents of decay needs to be more highly developed.

IV. The Textiles
by Elisabeth Crowfoot

Introduction

The places chosen for Anglo-Saxon burial grounds are usually higher positions, with light dry soil. But though the acidity at Snape has resulted in the deterioration of bone, and human skeletons are in most cases only represented by soil shadows, preservation of other organic remains in the inhumation burials was exceptionally good by English standards, and this applies particularly to wood and textile. As in all pre-Christian Anglo-Saxon cemeteries the Germanic funeral customs have continued; the dead were obviously interred fully clothed, and textile evidence is preserved by corrosion on metal grave-goods with which these less durable possessions came into contact; scraps from clothing or wrappings on brooches, buckles, wrist clasps, knives and weapons. Much of this material is mineralised, surviving as 'replacements' in which the characteristics of spin and weave can still be clearly identified. At Snape this evidence also includes a high proportion of samples in which some of the fibres have escaped mineralisation. The fragments preserved, however, are small; though well-to-do, none of the burials was immensely rich, and there was no pile-up of large metal objects under which layers of valued fabrics could survive, as at Sutton Hoo under the silver dishes (Crowfoot 1983, 412).

Apart from the remains of the important boat burials, an unusual quantity of wood has also survived, or been noted as soil shadows *in situ*. These wood fittings — coffins, biers and even planks — throw an interesting new light on burial practices, and they are also sometimes associated with textile. In grave 43 the excavators described an 'intensely organic stain' with a clearly defined edge which they interpret as a chamber, lined with textile. Samples taken from this area included rather coarse woollen threads. These, and lumps of crushed textile, some similar, some with noticeably finer threads from areas overlying the buckle and knife, suggested that the chamber had perhaps been lined with a coarse woollen twill and the clothed body covered with a layer of similar fabric (grave 43, a and b); or that the body had lain on a blanket or cloak, large enough to lap over the entire contents of the grave.

The excavators were fully aware of the interest in evidence obtainable from textile remains; they were able to consolidate an important area of the contents of grave 16 in a block, so that study of the brooches and surrounding organic matter might be undertaken later under laboratory conditions; similarly, textile layers in graves 36 and 37 were examined during excavation on site. The suggestion of fibres in a noticeably blackened area in the centre of grave 36 perhaps indicated that some garment or object placed on top of the body was of leather, while on and around the upper surface of the grave-goods there was again enough evidence of a coarse woollen twill fabric to indicate an all-over covering. This practice was even clearer in grave 37 where remains of at least two different heavy wool weaves, one decorated with stripes, could be identified (Pl. XLIV, Fig. 139.3). There was no suggestion in the placing of these fabrics that they could have been more intimately connected with any wooden furniture, unlike the results found during recent study of bed burials from Swallowcliffe and Barrington, Cambs. (Malim and Hines 1998, 261–8). Evidence of textile overlying Anglo-Saxon burials has been noted elsewhere; at Little Eriswell, Suffolk (Hutchinson 1966) one grave was described as being 'covered with a blanket' (pers. comm. from Capt. Le Bard, USAAF to the late Lady Briscoe) but in view of this urgent wartime excavation, before the erection of buildings, nothing from this layer was preserved.

Fibres

(See also below, p. 214). With one exception (grave 19) all fibres identified in the textiles were of animal origin, mostly sheep's wool with medium or fine fibres; in some cases these were well enough preserved to show whether pigment was present (graves 5, *A*; 20, *G* and 28, *C*); in one twill weave (grave 9, *A*) yarns with pigmented and unpigmented fibres were used to form a striped pattern (Fig. 139.2). Animal fibres used for pattern work on tablet-woven braids were probably horsehair, again naturally pigmented, two colours (chestnut and black) being still visible on the wrist clasp in grave 5, *D* (Pl. XLV, Fig. 139.9). The one vegetable fibre preserved, as fine shiny white threads in a tabby weave (grave 19 *D*), was identified as well-preserved undyed hemp. A tiny fragment of plait from the same grave, possibly a bead string, appears to be of similar origin.

Dyes

(See also below, pp. 212–214). Evidence for dyes was perhaps disappointing, particularly as rather larger samples were available for testing than can usually be detached, and colour sometimes seemed to be visible, notably in the striped covering in grave 37, where to the eye the ground weave was blackish and the stripes distinctly redder (but see Undyed cloth p. 214). There was little sign of the range of reds, blues and purples occasionally found from other Anglo-Saxon sites and identified in Viking material at York. There were a few traces in tablet braids from graves 16 and 19 and one blue twill (grave 5). As mentioned above, natural pigmentation was preserved in some wool, and still clearly visible in one striped twill (grave 9), but it seems probable that some garments and coverings were indeed white, or the light tan

of natural fleeces. It is also possible that the pollution of an area of the graveyard with a purple colorant (discussed below pp. 214) may have been responsible for masking the presence of some weak or fugitive dyes. The sample of hemp, as in that recently found at Harford Farm, Norfolk (Walton Rogers in Penn 2000, 90), was strikingly white and shiny.

Spinning and weaves

Most of the textile types are those general in 6th-century Anglo-Saxon weaving, but two show clear connections with earlier continental practices. As usual with people recently come from northern areas, twill weaves, whose structure gives a warm double layer of threads, are noticeably predominant. There are remains from over forty examples, compared with only fourteen tabby (plain) weaves, and eight tablet-weaves including two weave-borders, and six bands, *i.e.* ornamental pieces made separately, to be sewn to decorate garments. As in Scandinavian fabrics of the earlier Migration Period, the high number of those with Z-spun yarn in warp and weft is noticeable — at least twenty-eight of the twills, all the tabby weaves and the tablet-bands, with one possible exception (from grave 37).

Twill weaves

A high proportion of the twills are medium to coarse grade but this is perhaps due to the survival here of outer coverings, which in most cemeteries may have disappeared long before excavation. Of the simple 2/2 (four-shed) constructions, only one, the coarsest preserved, originally used to wrap a wooden bowl in grave 9, has any decoration, the narrow stripes of unpigmented single ?warps on a naturally pigmented dark brown wool fabric (Fig. 139.2). This is a type of weave familiar from other sites, with fragments from two graves at Mucking, Essex (graves 767 and 878; Hirst and Clark forthcoming), Sewerby, E. Yorks. (Crowfoot and Appleyard 1985, 52, 55) and a very well-preserved example from Broomfield Barrow, Essex (Crowfoot 1983, 468–471). Fourteen of these twills have the 'mixed spinning' (Z-spun yarns in one weave system, S-spun in the other) often associated in other cemeteries with fabrics of superior quality. Two of the finer twills here have evidence of broken diamond or herringbone structures, though the whole pattern cannot be recovered, but none have the heavy warp-thread count preponderance, or the shiny appearance which suggests that they were made of high-grade worsted wool, so noticeable in the fine broken diamond twills from the rather later very rich barrow burials at Sutton Hoo and Broomfield (Crowfoot 1983, 418–24, 468).

Ribbed twill

(Fig. 139.3, Pl. XLIV)

The coarse striped wool cloak or blanket lining the male burial in grave 37 connects the Snape settlers with travels further afield. This is an example of the *Rippenköper*, a twill weave with reversed ribs, of which many examples were published by the late Professor H-J. Hundt from Alamannic graves in Germany (Hundt 1984, 141–3 and fig. 6). This is the first example of the structure so far recorded from an English burial. Hundt's examples were all based on a 2/1 twill but the weave here, based on a 3/1 construction, works on the same principle and seems likely to have a similar origin. Dr J. P. Wild (pers. comm.)

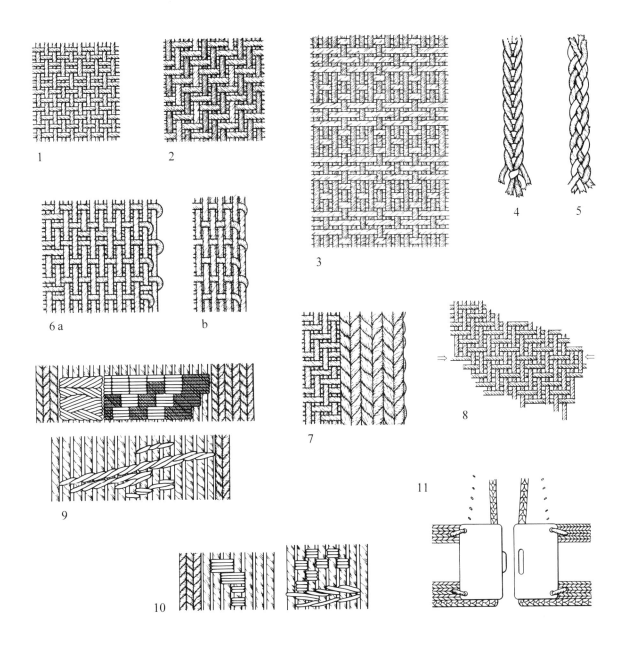

Figure 139 Textiles. 1) Tabby weave with paired threads, ?stripe, grave 8 *C*. 2) 2/2 twill, stripes in ?warp, pigmented wool, grave 9 *A*. 3) Textile layer, 3/1 twill with stripes, *Rippenköper*, grave 37. 4) Guilloche plait from edge of sleeves, grave 5 *C* and *D*. 5) 4-thread cord, ?from beads, grave 8 *A*. 6) Tubular selvedge on twill; (a) passage of wefts (b) wefts pulled in to cord, grave 5 *A*. 7) Tablet-woven border on 2/2 twill, grave 16 *C*. 8) Fine 2/2 twill with mistake arrowed, grave 21 *C*. 9) Tablet-woven bands from wrist clasp edge cords, centre pattern in horsehair on stationary cords, *D*, 'soumak' wrapping, *C*, wraps tapestry blocks, chestnut and black hair, grave 5 (reconstruction). 10) Patterns on tablet-woven band, wrist clasp *F*, grave 10. 11) Reconstruction of wrist clasps on sleeve of garment from grave 5, with tablet-woven cuff band, seam opening and guilloche plait edging

has pointed out that the 2/1 *Rippenköper* appears first in a Roman context at Mons Claudianus and its presence at Snape perhaps suggests service in the military Roman world.

Tabby weaves
The tabby weaves are all tiny fragments, two perhaps from tapes; one of these, from grave 19, of wool, showed the fine Z-spun warp and coarse S-spun weft yarns characteristic of narrow bands, though no selvedges are preserved. All the others are Z-spun yarn throughout. The appearance of the fibre of a possible tabby scrap from grave 5 suggested fine hair, but was too deteriorated to be sampled. Fragments preserved in grave 10 under two brooches, one in close folds with tight spin and thread count 16/14–16, the other from grave 8, a finer scrap with

Plate XLIV 3/1 twill with stripes (*Rippenköper*), grave 37 (both sides shown)

Plate XLV tablet-woven band from wrist clasp *D* grave 5, horsehair pattern, tapestry blocks. Scale in mm

Plate XLVI tablet-woven band from wrist clasp *D* grave 5, horsehair pattern, wrapped, 'soumak'. Scale in mm

Plate XLVII Tablet-woven border on twill, grave 16 *C*

two paired throws suggesting a stripe (Fig. 139.1), could have come from women's veils. They were probably of flax, though these must have been soft even weaves, of very different quality from the unevenly spun and woven flax of the remains of the cloth wrapping the bronze bowl in grave 68. The hemp tabby curling round a brooch in grave 19 again suggests a headveil, tucked under the pin to keep it in place; the good preservation here allowed a positive identification.

Tablet-weaves
Tablet-woven borders on twill cloaks or blankets, like that on the twill covering a woman's burial in grave 16 (Pl. XLVII; Fig. 139.7) made simultaneously with the fabric, are a feature from the Roman Iron Age onwards (Nockert 1991, 82–3; Hald 1950, 63ff.). This border is narrow, only six cords, and perhaps comes from the side edge of a weave. Tablet-woven bands of which fragments survive as here in the metal wrist clasps from women's burials were made separately and sewn as cuffs on the long sleeves of their garments. Other well-preserved Anglo-Saxon examples, from Mildenhall and Mitchell's Hill, Icklingham, Suffolk (Crowfoot, G. 1951, 26–28 and 1952, 189–191) were solid undecorated bands, but the fragments from graves 5 and 10 from Snape have sufficient remains of fine horsehair pattern to indicate that they were woven in an elaborate technique that has been described by Margareta Nockert as 'a complete innovation of the Migration Period' (Nockert 1991, 83).

In her study of the magnificent textiles of that period from Högom in Sweden Dr Nockert suggests that the origin of these braids should perhaps be looked for in the Near East or Mediterranean region (1991, 88–89). Bands like those from Snape come under her classification of 'warp-twined bands with patterns in different kinds of weft-wrapping and a tapestry-like technique' (1991, 83). As far as can be seen, the Snape bands from the grave 5 wrist clasps had edge borders with tablets threaded alternately in pairs at both sides; the stationary tablet warps of the centre pattern section are clear where they have lost much of their horsehair decoration, but remains of two of the different kinds of pattern wefts described by Dr Nockert can still be identified:

> A pattern section always begins and ends with one or more lines of weft wrapping, which run from edge to edge. The pattern weft can, for example, pass over all threads from two tablets, back under the threads from one tablet, under one and so on. This kind of weft wrapping is synonymous with *soumak*. (1991, 83–84).

Remains of this soumak wrapping can be seen on the band fragment from wrist clasp 5 *C* (Fig. 139.9b, Pl. XLVI).

> The contours of the pattern are done in weft-wrapping. The weft passes several times round all threads from one or two tablets. In this way vertical slits can be formed in the weave between the differently coloured fields, just as in tapestry weave or *kelim*. (1991, 85).

This pattern was clear when grave 5 *D* was first examined and drawn, with slanting lines of wraps in alternate wrapping in black and chestnut horsehair, though some of the delicate hairs disintegrated before photography (see Pl. XLV). The tiny scraps from grave 10 (Fig. 139.10) show remains of both types of pattern wefts. An even smaller fragment recently excavated, in a wrist

clasp at Barrington, Cambs., shows traces similar to the soumak wrapping (Crowfoot 1998, 246). Dr Nockert has pointed out that the pattern wefts cover the entire warp and there is no active main weft in the pattern sections, so that the patterns are not, as sometimes previously described, brocaded (Nockert 1991, 83).

Many of the pieces from Scandinavian sites, particularly those from the Högom warrior's grave published by Dr Nockert, are in magnificent condition (Pls XLVIII and XLIX), wide bands with colour preserved showing animals and human praying figures. The slightly later date of the Snape fragments, compared with these examples of the Migration Period perhaps suggests that they should be regarded as old pieces, treasured and re-used, as so often happens with beautiful fragments in medieval ecclesiastical material.

One interesting feature of the grave 5 bands is a very neatly made 'guilloche' plait, surviving on the fragments from both clasps. On *C* it is preserved for 16mm, fastened to the edge of the tablet cuff; on *D* a fragment hangs loose from the corner, suggesting that it continued down to decorate the sleeve opening, like the ornamental stitching on a sleeve from Högom (Nockert 1991, 76–8). A similar plait was used to decorate the edges of bands of the 10th century among the relics of St Cuthbert at Durham; it can be simply made with two 2-hole tablets (Crowfoot, G. 1956, 447, fig. 13.6).

Much of the published work on Anglo-Saxon textiles comes from the Anglian region; of southern and western cemeteries, though studied and catalogued, many remain unpublished. The available comparative northern material has been recently very much expanded by the work of Penelope Walton Rogers at Textile Research, York, on cemeteries at Norton-on-Tees, Teesside; Castledyke, North Lincs; and on the very large collection from West Heslerton, N. Yorks. (Walton Rogers, forthcoming). Two of these sites have produced fragments of tablet-woven bands with remains of similar patterning to the Snape bands — at West Heslerton again in horsehair, and at Norton-on-Tees possibly in silk.

Costume
As usual in Anglo-Saxon cemeteries, the costume evidence at Snape depends on the arrangement of the grave-goods and the interpretation of the fragments of textile that they may have preserved. The best provided of the women's graves (5, 10 and 16) follow the usual Anglian pattern (Owen-Crocker 1986, 28ff.) — an undergarment with long sleeves, their cuffs decorated with tablet-woven bands and fastened with wrist clasps, worn with an overgown either tubular or of the 'peplos' pattern, fastened on the shoulders with a pair of brooches; a necklace of beads; a belt with a buckle. None have the array of 'girdle hangers' worn by later colonists, only the essential knife. Seven women had pairs of shoulder brooches, the others pins or a brooch and pin to fasten their overgowns. Only three had wrist clasps and two had a third central brooch which may have held up the loose front of the gown as there was no sign of cloak material on it.

The fabric of these garments at Snape is always twill for both under and overgown; there is very little variation in quality. As far as can be seen from the small fragments surviving in the brooches and wrist clasps, both garments were of very similar weights and where best preserved, of well-spun even weaves. The only lightweight fabrics, the tabby fragments probably of flax and hemp, are always found associated with brooches and their position suggests that they come from the headveil rather than any undergarment such as a shirt. Evidence from later sites suggests that the overgown could be of linen tabby (as at West Heslerton; Walton Rogers forthcoming a), a lighter garment falling into the soft folds shown in manuscript paintings and sculptures (Owen-Crocker 1986, figs 25–31); at Snape there is no available evidence of anything but solid woollen garments, of fabrics like coarse tweeds.

The evidence on men's clothing is always more difficult to find, since they wore no jewellery and textile remains come only from belt buckles and fittings and their knives. Weapons may sometimes have lain in contact with their clothing but in most cases fabric traces suggest that they were wrapped when buried with their owners; the sword and spears in boat grave 47 show folds of coarse twill and threads, some possibly from ties, including one fine tabby tape. It can be assumed that like the Scandinavians of the Migration Period graves, they wore tunics and trousers and were covered by their cloaks. The fragments left on buckles often show two twill weaves of slightly different quality. There is no way of knowing if their garments were carefully cut and sewn, with shaped sleeves and skirt gores (Nockert 1991, 125–130), or loom-shaped like the earlier Germanic bog-finds, woven in four pieces, rectangular front and back, with tablet-woven borders at neck and hem and the sleeve pieces tapering to the wrists (Owen-Crocker 1986, 70–71). The large areas of textile in graves 36 and 37 suggest cloaks or blankets — the originally handsome ribbed twill in grave 37 probably the former — but unfortunately no borders survived, nor any brooches or pins for fastening.

The fragments of wood and metal in grave 32, identified as parts of a lyre, show patches of coarse woollen textile, probably twill. Some even coarser threads curling round the stud pins at first suggested a selvedge or starting border but their position indicates that this could have been a fragment of the wrist-strap fastened by the pins (see below, p. 217). No fabric was found in this position at Bergh Apton (Lawson 1978, 92–95) or with the very small wood remains at Morning Thorpe, but perhaps the other traces of textile indicate that here at Snape the lyre was buried in a bag, as suggested for that found at Sutton Hoo, although there the evidence indicated one probably of beaver-skin (Bruce-Mitford 1975, 451–2).

Tests for dye in textile samples
by Penelope Walton Rogers

Introduction
Altogether sixty samples of textile were provided for dye analysis by Elisabeth Crowfoot. The samples came from twenty-three different graves and included twills, tabbies and tablet weaves. Most of the textiles sampled were wool (above, p. 208), as it seemed unnecessary to test the obviously white plant-fibre textiles. Preservation ranged from poor to excellent.

Each sample was exposed to our standard examination procedure for natural dyes, namely extraction into solvents, followed by absorption spectrophotometry (Walton 1988). Where tannin dyes were suspected, thin-layer chromatography was also used (Walton and Taylor 1991).

Few authentic dyes were detected and it is beginning to appear likely that many Early Anglo-Saxon textiles were used undyed (see below). An unusual purple colorant was, however, detected in a number of graves and this has posed some intriguing questions concerning the source of the colorant and its relation to Anglo-Saxon burial practice.

Woad-dyed cloth and braid
The blue colorant indigotin was detected in a twill from grave 5 brooch A and a tablet braid from grave 16 brooch C. Indigotin may be derived from woad, indigo or related species but in an Anglo-Saxon context the dye is most likely to be woad. The woad plant, *Isatis tinctoria* L., was grown in Britain long before imported indigo became available — probably as early as the Iron Age — and was used for shades from sky-blue to deep blue. The behaviour of the dye in the braid from grave 16 suggested the presence of an additional yellow or brown dye, which would have changed the blue to green or black.

Lichen purple on a tablet braid
A trace of purple dye was detected in the tablet braid from grave 19 brooch D. Although weak, the dye appeared in two separate extractions, one in alkaline conditions, the other acidic. The spectra obtained in both cases indicated the presence of the lichen dye, variously known as orchil, cork or lacmus (Taylor and Walton 1983). Lichens which yield this dye, such as *Ochrolechia* spp., *Umbilicaria* spp. and *Evernia prunastri*, are to be found on rocks in northern and western Britain, although they do not appear to be available in East Anglia or southern England. The Anglo-Saxons seem to have made limited use of the purple dye (Walton 1988), apparently eking it out on small items such as embroidery yarns, as at Kempston, Beds. (Taylor 1990, 41–2; Crowfoot 1990, 51–2) and tablet braids, as at Snape.

A red tape
The narrow tape from grave 19 brooch E also showed a trace of dye, in this instance a red, comparable with a very dilute dyeing with madder or bedstraw. Madder from Dyers' Madder, *Rubia tinctorum* L., was commonly used in the Late Anglo-Saxon period (Walton 1988) but wild madder or bedstraw may have been used instead in the 5th and 6th centuries (Walton and Taylor 1991, 7). The Snape dye was unfortunately too weak to allow the exact dye-plant source to be identified. Madder-type dyes have previously been identified in an Early Anglo-Saxon braid at Mucking, Essex (Crowfoot 1998); in the head-dress of a richly dressed woman at West Heslerton, N. Yorks. (Grave 2BA604; Walton Rogers forthcoming a); in two patterned soumak weaves, one from the boat burial at Sutton Hoo (Whiting 1983), the other from Taplow Barrow, Bucks. (Taylor 1990, 42); and in fine diamond twills from Broomfield Barrow, Essex (Whiting 1983). In the pagan period therefore, the use of this dye is only attested in fine cloth and patterned weaves, especially those worn by the wealthy and aristocratic, and in small items such as braids.

Plate XLVIII Tablet-woven band with horsehair pattern from Högom

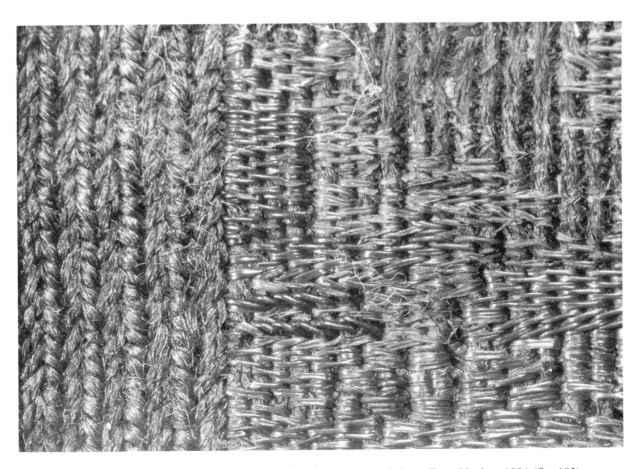

Plate XLIX Enlarged detail of Plate XLVIII, showing pattern technique. From Nockert 1991 (fig. 103)

Tannin dyes

Two samples of a textile on brooch *B* in grave 5, on extraction showed strong absorption at short wavelengths. This suggested the presence of a yellow or brown organic substance, although not necessarily a dye. The extracts were further examined by thin-layer chromatography, using systems designed for yellow and brown colorants (Walton and Taylor 1991). The chromatograms showed no indication of yellow dye (from comparison with the behaviour of known dyestuffs) but both samples showed two spots comparable with the tannins of, for example, oak galls. Tannins occur in many natural substances, such as autumn leaves, tree-barks and nuts. We cannot therefore be sure whether the textile from grave 5 was dyed with tannins or heavily stained by some contaminant in the grave. Since, however, there was none or very little of the same substance in other textiles from this grave and since it appeared in both samples of the same textile, a tannin-bearing dye is possible. This would mean that the textile was originally brown, grey or black.

Undyed cloth

The remaining fifty-four samples from textiles showed no evidence for having been dyed. In previous work on Early Anglo-Saxon cemetery textiles this typically small number of positive results has been attributed to the poor preservation of the samples. More recently, work on the remains from Hochdorf in Germany, has shown that dye may still survive in considerable strength on mineralised textiles (Walton Rogers 1999). Furthermore, some of the Snape samples were in excellent condition. The decay of dyes during burial is poorly understood, but if dye had ever been present in a textile such as the well-preserved twill from brooch *C* in grave 28, surely some residue would have survived in detectable form?

It has already been shown that, as far as the Early Anglo-Saxon period is concerned, dyes, especially reds and purples, tend to be more frequently detected in textiles from high-status burials and in small items such as braids and embroideries. Only woad blues and relatively dull tannin colours have been found in ordinary full-size cloths, at Snape as elsewhere; natural fleece colours also provided some variation from white (see above p. 208). The evidence, therefore, is beginning to suggest that bright colours were used only in a limited way in the 5th to 7th centuries and that most clothing was blue, brown, grey or natural white — perhaps with more lively colours in the braids at cuff and neckline.

Alkanet-like purple colorant

In fourteen of the textile samples taken from six graves (16, 36, 37, 38, 43, 47), another purple organic material was detected. Its absorption pattern was very close to that of the dyestuff alkanet, although there is a strong yellow component in the Snape colorant which is only faintly recorded in acidic extracts from alkanet.

The dye alkanet derives from the roots of the plant Dyers' Alkanet, *Alkanna tinctoria* Tausch (formerly *Anchusa tinctoria* L.) which was reportedly used by early civilisations of the Mediterranean (Brunello 1973, 329). However, it has rarely been detected on early textiles and there are no records of it in any other samples from archaeological sites in Britain. The number of examples in the Snape cemetery — sometimes including all of the textiles in one grave — was suspicious and samples of a

soil block from grave 37 were therefore tested. The soil samples proved to contain the same alkanet-like material. This suggests that the colorant is a contaminant permeating the burial, rather than a deliberately applied dyestuff. The following theories for the presence of the purple may be considered:

a) The colorant is from some modern agricultural spray. Although possible, modern synthetic colorants tend to have simpler absorption spectra than those noted.

b) It has formed as a result of the decay process of the body. Yeasts and metabolic products can stain bones but not, in the author's experience, the surrounding soil.

c) It is the result of contamination from plants growing on the site. Originally open heathland, the site has most recently been farmed for oil-seed rape. Dyers' Alkanet, *A. tinctoria*, is a native of southern Europe (Cardon and du Chatenet 1990, 29 and 160–1) and it is unlikely to have been growing in the area at any stage, but other members of the Boraginaceae, the family to which alkanet belongs, contain the same colouring principle, alkannin (Thomson 1957, 111). It is possible that there is some native species which yields alkannin plus the yellow substance recorded in the Snape spectra. On the other hand, there is no recorded evidence that the colorants from dye plants can wash out and stain the surrounding environment while the plant is still growing. Plant roots that had invaded grave 37 were tested for dye content but these did not show any greater concentration of dyestuff than in the textiles or soil-sample.

d) The colorant derives from some material placed in the grave at burial. The presence of grasses, bracken or flower stems strewn over the body has been noted in several Early Medieval graves (see p. 240). It is therefore possible that an alkannin-containing plant has been placed on some of the bodies as part of the burial ritual. A root of dyers' alkanet *A. tinctoria* has been found in the shrine of 3rd-century St Maurua in Bohemia, for example (Samhylová 1993).

On the present evidence the third and fourth theories seem the most likely candidates, and the fourth the most tempting given the evidence for a wide range of organic inclusions in graves at Snape.

Fibre identifications of textile samples
by Harry Appleyard

The identification of animal fibres is determined by the following criteria: general appearance of the fibres, *i.e.* regularity of fibre diameter along the length of the fibre and the amount by which cuticular cells protrude from the fibre, scale pattern, cross-sectional shape, thickness of cuticle, presence and type of medulla and pigment distribution.

Some of the fibres were so badly damaged by bacterial action that much of the detail had been destroyed and then it could only be said that they were of animal origin. Some fibres were very friable, and useful cross-sections could not be cut.

V. The Lyre Remains from Grave 32

by Graeme Lawson

Introduction

Remains of lyres, an ancient class of stringed musical instrument of ultimately prehistoric origin, form an established category of grave-goods amongst pagan Anglo-Saxon and contemporary Germanic inhumation cemeteries. Whilst earlier, ancestral types included instruments with simple and in many cases naturally hollow resonating bodies (such as gourds and tortoise-shells) the Early Medieval lyre, we now know, was typically of dug-out construction, carved from a solid block of wood. Moreover, its superstructural framework, comprising two arms and a connecting cross-bar (to which the strings were attached), was by this time so firmly integrated into its design that arms and body were carved in a single continuous unit, from one piece of timber. Only the cross-bar remained structurally discrete, and in most cases steps were taken to disguise even this separateness, resulting in an elegant structure of smooth, uninterrupted outline. It is, however, the essentially tripartite form of this superstructure which distinguishes the lyre from the two other important groups of stringed instrument, the harp and the lute, both as yet unrepresented in the Early Anglo-Saxon archaeological record, and which gives the lyre much of its unique musical character.

Amongst Early Medieval examples the two well-known, richly ornamented instruments from the royal barrows at Sutton Hoo, Suffolk and Taplow, Bucks., support historical and iconographical evidence for the importance of lyre-playing as one of the various accomplishments expected of the aristocratic male in traditional Germanic societies. However, occasional discoveries of similar instruments in simpler inhumations, as at Saxton Road, Abingdon, Oxfordshire and at Bergh Apton, Norfolk, confirm that they were owned and played at other, less elevated levels too (Bruce-Mitford R.L.S. and M, 1970; Lawson 1978). In their fine, specialist manufacture and complex structure these apparently lower-status instruments are indistinguishable from their royal counterparts; only their decorative metalwork seems notably less sophisticated. The simpler, diagnostically less sensitive forms of these metal attachments and the ephemeral nature of the fragile wooden structures which they support combine to make their remains notoriously difficult to identify. Recent recovery of extremely fragmentary evidence from sites such as Morning Thorpe, Norfolk (Lawson 1987), suggests that such instruments may be less rare than their survival rates have seemed to indicate hitherto. Finds of stray components from later, largely urban contexts confirm the long-term vitality and ubiquity of the lyre-playing tradition throughout the North Sea and Western Baltic areas: such instruments clearly continued in circulation, in much the same form, until at least the 11th century, as at York (Hall 1984), Hedeby, Schleswig-Holstein (Lawson 1984) and Birka (Björkö), Sweden (Arbman 1939, 129; Reimers 1980).

The discovery and ongoing research

The recovery of the lyre remains from grave 32 was a piece of great good fortune, not only because of the rarity of such finds in general but because grave 32 was the last major feature of the site to be investigated, completed on the final day of the excavations. Fortunately, while the finds and associated organics were still *in situ*, it was already suspected that the fragmentary wooden remains beneath the shield and in the region of the body's left shoulder might represent a single complex structure of some unusual significance. It was therefore decided to remove these soil blocks intact for micro-excavation in the laboratory. Once there, suspicions that the remains might belong to a musical instrument comparable with the Sutton Hoo and Bergh Apton finds hardened when Jacqui Watson, while conducting timber identifications, recognised similarities to the shapes of parts of the instrument from Taplow Barrow, Buckinghamshire, now in the British Museum. In October 1993 the present writer was able formally to confirm its musical identity, as a lyre, on the basis of the remains of components *Bi–iii*, the form of which is entirely consistent with the upper part of one arm of a lyre's superstructure. It was also possible to suggest that two small copper alloy figure-of-eight loops with associated iron and organic remains (*Bvi* and *vii*) might represent parts of one of that instrument's most important performance-related features, its wrist-strap.

The recovery, identification and ongoing conservation and analysis programmes may provide a useful case study for future excavation and post-excavation treatment, both of potentially music-related remains and of fragile composite wooden structures in general. Instruments of this type must have been familiar objects in Anglo-Saxon times, but it is extremely rarely that we are able to identify their remains in the ground today: indeed musicians' graves may well have been present amongst many of the pagan Anglo-Saxon cemetery sites so far excavated, but the odds are inevitably stacked against the survival of a lyre's fragile, mainly organic, diagnostic elements. Perhaps as a result, only a handful have so far been recognised, the most recent properly excavated example being that of the musician's burial, grave 97, at Morning Thorpe, Norfolk. Even that find was so insubstantial that several years were to elapse before its musical character was first suspected, during routine finds-survey work by the present writer (Lawson 1987), and indeed this was to remain largely tentative until corroboration was finally provided by details of the present find. This is in fact an important distinguishing feature of the Snape discovery, which has affected the course of its study almost from the outset: it was in a very real sense a discovery waiting to be made. Consequently it was possible to institute quickly a specially tailored, fully integrated scheme of conservation, analysis and documentation. This work is ongoing and is to be the subject of further publications as results emerge.

The instrument

All the pieces and traces associated with, or thought to be associated with, the lyre were located within an area of the grave both well-defined and broadly consistent with the placements observed in all but one of the other simple musical inhumations of the Early Medieval period: set against and slightly to one side (in this case the left) of the upper torso and cradled in the crook of the left arm, almost as though in preparation for performance (Lawson 1987, fig. 462). Within this area there were four concentrations of lyre-related material (Fig. 140), all more or less sheltered beneath the shield: one over the left shoulder (*Biv–v*), a second (the most substantial) over the right

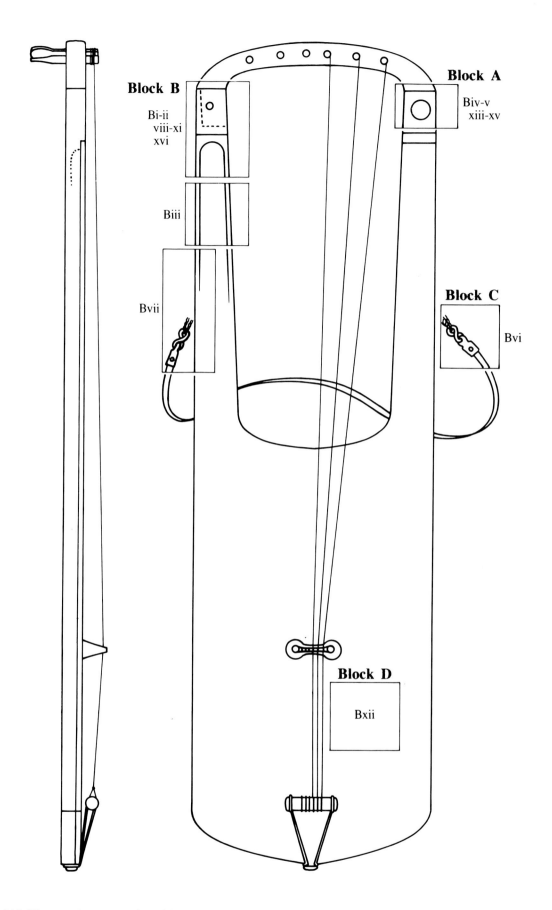

Figure 140 The constituent remains of the lyre (framed) showing their probable original juxtaposition and context; the suggested form of the missing structure is derived from other Early Medieval instruments. Scale approx. 1:3

collar-bone (*Bi–iii*), and two single items (*Bvi* and *xii*) next to the left elbow and wrist respectively.

(a) The first complex, located over the left shoulder, beneath the shield, was lifted and excavated off-site. It yielded a small composite wooden structure representing the mortice-and-tenon joint at the upper end of the instrument's right[1] arm (*Biv*). Remains of a copper alloy disc-headed rivet (*Bv*) were still in place, penetrating both mortice and tenon and apparently positioned in order to secure the joint. Remains of a further piece of wood, comprising wooden sheet perhaps from a carrying case, lay flat against the head of the disc and its parent structure, sandwiching between them a layer of textile in which an impression of the disc can still be seen (*Bxiii*). Other associated organics included, next to the joint itself, a quantity of fibrous material (*Bxv*) and, nearby, one detached small wooden fragment bearing a copper alloy pin *in situ*, probably one of the fixtures around the rim of the wooden sound-board (*Bxiv*).

(b) This soil block, located over the right collar-bone, beneath the shield, was also lifted and excavated off-site. It was found to contain the best-preserved portion of the instrument, representing much of its left arm (*Bi–iii*) (Pls L, LI, LIII and LIV). At the upper end it includes a mortice-and-tenon joint which is a mirror image of that of *Biv*, again pierced by the copper alloy shaft of another disc-headed rivet. A thin sliver of wood is inserted alongside the shaft and may have acted as a tightening wedge to secure it firmly in place. Metal salts from the rivet are most likely the agent responsible for preserving the whole structure. The tenon shows the wood selected for the now otherwise missing arch of the instrument to have been maple (*Acer* sp.). At its lower extremity the arm, which is also of maple, has been neatly and extensively hollowed out from the front (Pl. LIII). Remains of a cover of thin wooden sheeting pinned across the cavity, representing the sound-board, probably of oak (*Quercus* sp.), survive *in situ*. Also preserved are its means of fixture: one of a number of copper alloy attachment pins (compare *Bxiv* above) and a number of fragments from a binding-strip which held down and concealed its upper end. The two pins and the rounded ends of this strip, which they pierced, are still located *in situ* (*Bi* and *iii*) (Pl. LIV). Closely comparable strips have been identified at Bergh Apton and Morning Thorpe where they perform exactly the same function (Lawson 1987, fig. 461), but this example is now easily the best-preserved. Other associated finds include, amongst miscellaneous organics, one small fragment of wood with an iron nail *in situ* (*Bi*) and two more substantial pieces, one representing more of the hollowed arm (*Biii*) and another which, with textile adhesions resembling *Bxii* above, may also be part of a carrying case (*Bxvi*). A small figure-of-eight loop of copper alloy with textile adhesions and an iron concretion appear to represent one of a pair of attachments for a thin leather strap, probably a wrist-strap (*Bvii*) (Pl. LII). Such straps have been identified in two later Anglo-Saxon manuscript illustrations and among the lyre fittings at Bergh Apton (Lawson 1978, 92–5) and Taplow (Bruce-Mitford R.L.S. and M. 1983, 713–5).

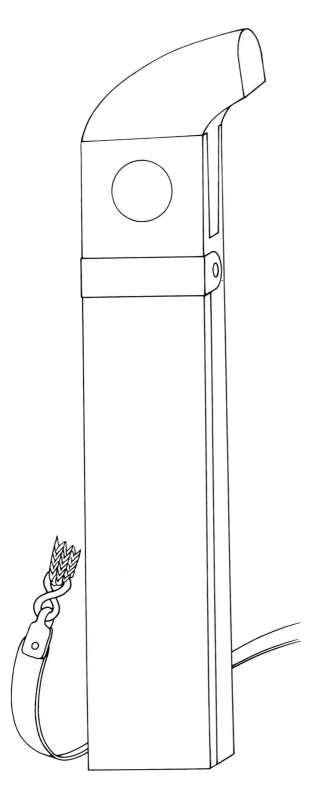

Figure 141 Oblique view of the lyre left arm top, showing its probable original external appearance. It features the mortice-and-tenon joint, disc-headed rivet, resonator cover of thin wooden sheet held in place at the upper end by an Ae strip, and the ?wrist strap (attachment point uncertain). Scale approx. 1:1

(c) A second, matching copper alloy figure-of-eight loop lay in the vicinity of the left elbow (*Bvi*): attached to it, once again, are textile adhesions and remains of a looped and riveted iron strap-terminal (compare *Bxiv* above). The strap residue preserved between the iron plates shows it to have been of leather. Identification as the other end of a wrist-strap may be further supported by its placement in the grave, some distance down the opposite arm of the instrument.

(d) One further small piece of wood, found next to and preserved by the corrosion of belt buckle *E*, may also belong to the instrument. Its location in the region of the left wrist is consistent with its identification as a fragment of the main part of the body or resonator of the instrument, which is otherwise lost (*Bxii*).

The instrument thus has several unusual and interesting features. First, the presence of the pair of figure-of-eight strap-loops lends strong support to the previously tentative identification of such straps at Bergh Apton and Taplow. The musical importance of such an accessory can hardly be overstated: by suspending the instrument from the wrist it offers the player's left hand complete freedom of access to the rear of the strings, enabling the development of sophisticated two-handed playing techniques. Without it the left hand would be reduced merely to a supporting role.

Second, the presence of the copper alloy binding strip, and its clearly defined relationship with the attachment of the thin wooden sound-board (Fig. 141), ties in closely with comparable features at Bergh Apton and Morning Thorpe. Omitted both at Sutton Hoo and in the lyres from Cologne and Oberflacht, its intended purpose is still unclear; in the absence of any obvious structural explanation, it is tempting to suggest a cosmetic role. Similar structural redundancy has been noted elsewhere in respect of the rivets and plates supporting the main mortice-and-tenon joints at Sutton Hoo, Taplow and Bergh Apton (Lawson 1980, 121) where they appear if anything to weaken rather than strengthen their structures. Indeed, this might equally apply to the disc-headed rivets surmounting the joints at Snape too.

Third, identification of the use of more than one (and at least two) wood species in a single instrument represents another important breakthrough in our evaluation of the sophistication in instrument manufacture at this time. Materials were clearly being chosen in order to suit the particular and contrasting requirements of each individual component: oak, easily split into thin sheets, for the sound-board; maple, favourite of cup and bowl manufacturers, for the dug-out body and curved arch. Such considerations, incidentally, confirm the need to keep under close review the significance of the subject of that problematical Old English riddle, *Exeter Book* No. 53, for which multiplicity of timbers has previously been used, curiously, to argue *against* the reading 'lyre' (Lawson 1980, 77; *c.f.* Williamson 1977, 301).

Finally, and perhaps most strikingly, the instrument is remarkable for the fineness of its construction. Even within the context of fine Anglo-Saxon instrument-building it has unusually refined features. The extension of the body cavity into the arms, for example, is in no other lyre so far advanced as it is in *Bii* and *iii*, where barely 10mm of solid wood separate it from the lowest point of the joint-mortice (Fig. 142). With its thin walls the result must have been an extremely lightweight structure, considerably lighter than at Sutton Hoo. Curiously, the other delicate lyre so far excavated, that of grave P100 at St Severinskirche, Cologne, also shares with the Snape instrument the unusual curvature at the upper extremity of its arm cavity (*c.f.* Lawson 1987, 168; fig. 461 i & ii). Whether this represents simply independent evolutionary convergence or whether it suggests a closer technological relationship, it is not yet possible to say.

Discussion of the man

Although the lyre is the most obviously unusual item in grave 32 it is by no means the only feature of importance to music archaeologists. If lyres are still poorly represented in the archaeological record, their cultural context, and in particular the nature of their ownership, is even less well understood; consequently such finds may yield crucial contextual evidence, not only through study of associated objects and deposits but also through consideration of the location of the burial, both within the cemetery and in the broader human landscape.

In common with many of the other, non-musical graves at Snape, grave 32 is notable for its exceptional preservation of textiles and other organics, including grave-lining materials, clothing and even insect remains deriving from post-depositional decay. These afford a detailed insight into funerary practices and the physical circumstances of burial unique among Early Medieval musicians' graves excavated since 1945. Beyond the general placement of grave-goods, adornments and clothing accessories, which were quite modest and undistinguished, little remained at Bergh Apton or Morning Thorpe to suggest just how those graves were prepared, furnished and covered. Textile remains were limited to small mineralised fragments and impressions, presumably of clothing, adhering to copper alloy and iron objects (Crowfoot 1987, 176). At Snape, in addition to a normal range of male Anglo-Saxon grave-goods, including a spear and shield, an organic liner probably once of textile and traces of a covering of vegetal matter were preserved (pp. 75–9). These represent the most comprehensive record yet found of any Anglo-Saxon musician's equipment. Only grave P100 at St Severinskirche, Cologne, provides a more complete assemblage. There, unusual conditions in a stone-lined cist, preserved not only the instrument but the player's clothing, right down to his woollen outer garments, leather gloves, leather footwear, linen underclothes and stockings. Also remaining, strewn around the body, were traces of vegetal matter identified as flower stalks (Fremersdorf 1943, 133–9). Now paralleled at Snape, these serve as a poignant reminder that such burials, whilst clearly of musicians, nevertheless represent the work, and the loss, of others as well.

Of actual grave-goods, other than items of personal equipment, a wooden bowl is the only piece represented, attested by the presence of a small copper alloy rim reinforcement found at the foot of the grave. Although this is paralleled at Morning Thorpe by a small pottery vessel, positioned to the right of the head, and at Cologne by a wooden flask set beside the right foot, such vessels are a common enough feature of pagan Germanic provision for the dead and do not constitute special, music-related furnishing.

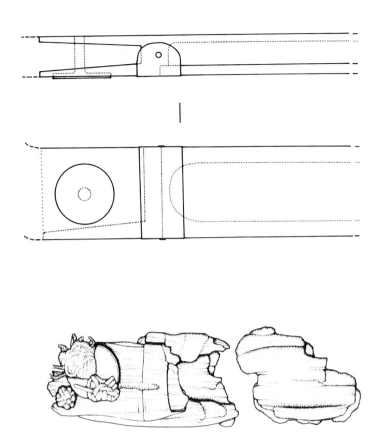

Figure 142 Montage of components of the lyre left arm top, interpreted without allowance for shrinkage (*c.f.* Lawson 1987, fig. 460). Scale approx. 1:1

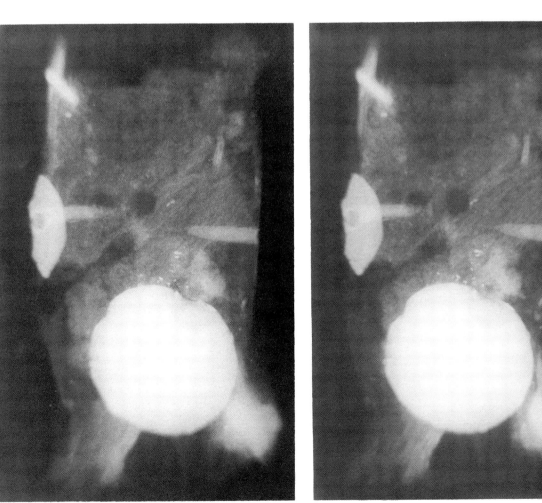

Plate L Stereo-radiograph of top left arm of lyre (*Bi–ii*): frontal view showing disc-headed rivet, Ae strip-end and pins, and other metal tacks and pins still *in situ*

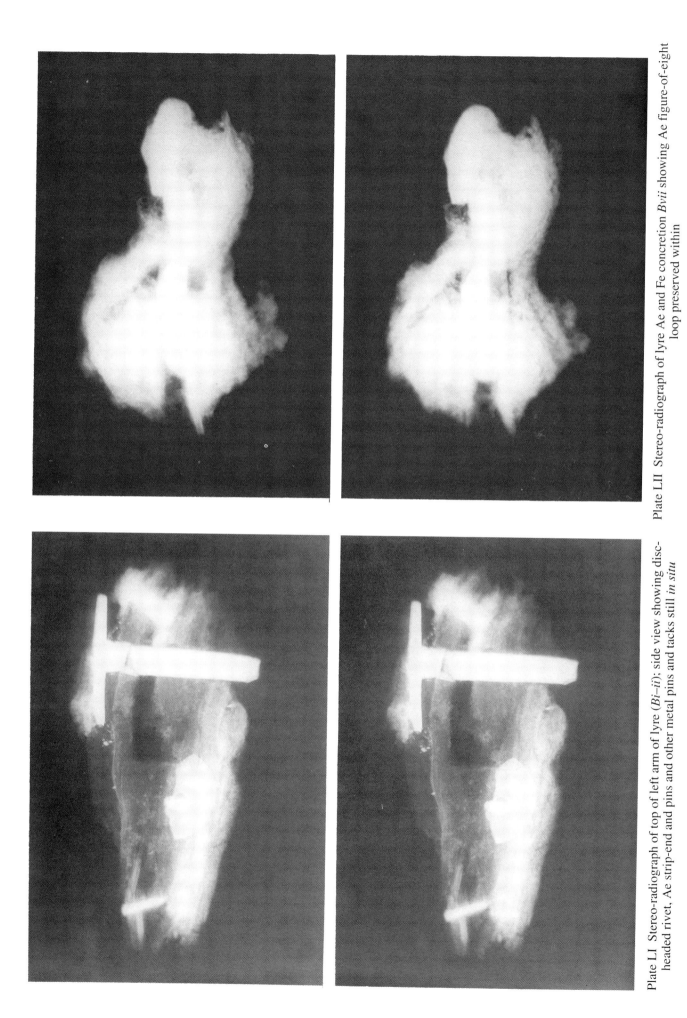

Plate LII Stereo-radiograph of lyre Ae and Fe concretion *Bvii* showing Ae figure-of-eight loop preserved within

Plate LI Stereo-radiograph of top of left arm of lyre (*Bi–ii*): side view showing disc-headed rivet, Ae strip-end and pins and other metal pins and tacks still *in situ*

220

Plate LIII Stereograph of top of left arm of lyre (*Bi–ii*); frontal view with detached frontal portion (below) set aside to show (upper right) joint mortice and (upper centre-left) round top of arm cavity visible in longitudinal section in fracture surface

Plate LIV Stereograph of top of left arm of lyre (*Bi–ii*); side view showing Ae strip-end *in situ*. Front surface of instrument is uppermost, top is to right

The smaller items of personal equipment found in the grave seem equally unspecific: the knife lying at waist level and the strike-a-light and steel found nearby. However, larger items of equipment contribute significantly to establishing the identity and status of the person with whom they were buried. Most obviously, the presence of weaponry confirms that the body is male, as in all the lyre graves so far excavated; indeed the only female association yet noted, at Morning Thorpe, is residual. Moreover, the presence of such a fine musical instrument implies that the burial was not merely that of a musician but that of a specialist musician, someone for whom music was more than just one of a number of casual interests or activities. This conclusion has already been argued elsewhere in respect of the lyre graves of Bergh Apton and Morning Thorpe, and seems equally appropriate to Continental finds such as Cologne (Lawson 1978 and 1987; see also Fremersdorf 1943). There must have been some compelling reason for such an elaborate and costly item to be disposed of in this fashion: although now fragmentary, there is no evidence that it was in anything other than good working condition at the time of burial, nor is there anything amongst the accompanying grave-goods to suggest that either the individual or those responsible for his burial were especially wealthy. Moreover, the precise location of the instrument within the grave, cradled in the arms of the body, is particularly prominent, evidently symbolic of a significant, indeed intimate relationship with the dead. In both these respects

it follows closely the pattern observed at Bergh Apton, Morning Thorpe and their Continental parallels, and contrasts with the instruments in the royal barrows at Sutton Hoo and Taplow, which were evidently of less central importance, included and positioned peripherally amongst the other grave-goods and the furnishings of the chambers.

Whether such specialist musicians represent professional entertainers or musically trained amateurs is difficult to assess. Such a distinction may itself be of doubtful validity in 6th- and 7th-century England. Nevertheless from these three East Anglian individuals a pattern does now seem to be emerging: that of a modestly furnished inhumation, with simple but functional weaponry, in which the lyre is prominently situated, resting in the arms of the dead man. Seen in this context the only other Anglo-Saxon inhumation for which records exist, adolescent male grave B42 at Saxton Road, Abingdon, Oxfordshire, takes on an increasingly irregular appearance: there, prominence was given to the sword while the instrument was laid instead at his feet, more after the manner of the royal graves (Leeds and Harden 1936). For the time being unique, its exact significance and relation to the East Anglian finds remain unclear. Nevertheless, it seems increasingly likely that somewhere amongst these graves we may now have the first archaeological evidence for the Anglo-Saxon *scop* or poet-musician, that pivotal yet, today, still shadowy figure of our earliest English literature.

221

York

Morning
Thorpe ● ● Bergh
Apton

▲
Scole

Snape ●

Sutton ◆
Hoo

● Abingdon

◆
Taplow

◆ Aristocratic grave
● Cemetery find
■ Urban find
▲ Metal detector find

0   50   100
Kms

Figure 143 Distribution of Early Medieval lyres. The Snape find set within the current distribution of finds of
established identity (unconfirmed examples not included)

What do we know about the *scop* of pagan Anglo-Saxon England? Surviving poetic records, both Old English and Latin, yield tantalisingly few clues, yet enough remains to confirm his role as poet-musician with stringed instrument, typically (though not necessarily exclusively) in the context of court and mead-hall. In *Beowulf* we hear of Hrothgar's *scop* performing the story of the Creation, no doubt sitting by the king's feet after the manner of the musician in the poem *The Fates of Men*. In the lament *Deor* the eponymous poet describes his sadness and loss at having yielded his place as *scop* to the court of the Heodeningas, a loss that was evidently financial as well as artistic in its impact. The poem *Widsith*, originally composed by such an individual some time during the closing years of the pagan period, is often taken to be a fuller autobiographical statement of the *scop's* way of life. It includes amongst his roles that of praise-singer and, although exaggerated and complicated by later interpolation, a clear reference to travel as a significant element in his life.

What do grave 32 and the East Anglian group as a whole add to this historical picture? First, he is equipped as a fighting man with shield and spear, a warrior-musician in fact, an aspect which curiously figures nowhere in the Old English literature, although it is plainly repeated at Morning Thorpe. Indeed, it is interesting to note that if this really is the grave of a *scop*, apart from the instrument itself, there is nothing either in the form or the contents of the grave to distinguish it from other non-musical graves nearby. This is repeated in all such lyre-graves so far identified. There are, as far as can be seen, neither ornaments nor tools, nor any other gadgets, exclusive to a musician's craft or way of life. There is no sign of anything which might represent a plectrum or a tuning-key, and no specialist instrument-making tools. Moreover, except remotely at Sutton Hoo[2], no lyre has yet been found in association with any other musical instrument, despite the fact that instruments of several other, contrasting types are known, or are believed, to have existed at this time: from simple folk whistles to elaborate, composite pipes of reed, wood, bone and horn. Even the remarkable use of horsehair in reinforcing, perhaps darning, the edges of the musician's garments, which might otherwise have suggested a possible link with the use of hair in stringing (as preserved in Later Medieval traditions), is not unique to grave 32.

Perhaps most intriguing of all, however, is the addition which this new musician makes to what was already becoming a noticeable cluster of such finds within the east of the East Anglian region. Despite continuing music-archaeological survey work throughout England, no fewer than five of the seven graves now firmly identified from the pagan Anglo-Saxon period lie in north-east Suffolk and south-east Norfolk, within a circle of less than eighteen miles radius (Fig. 143). Cemetery excavations further afield merely reinforce this singularity, which is becoming increasingly difficult to dismiss as a mere artefact of taphonomy or technique. Some degree of local specialization may well be indicated, perhaps deriving from the presence nearby of an important cultural centre. The emerging emporium of Ipswich, the royal presences in both the Sutton Hoo and Snape cemeteries, and the royal estates at Rendlesham (Bede, *HE* iii. 22) provide no shortage of possible associations.

The existence of such foci of artistic activity and patronage should in a general sense come as no surprise, but hard evidence associating them with particular sites or regions must be of considerable interest, not only to the prehistory of music and musicians but also to the study of the cultural background to *Beowulf* and our oldest English poetic relics. Even without more concrete proofs, graves like Snape 32 already provide us individually with direct archaeological links, and if not with the very creators of *Beowulf* itself, then at least with those directly responsible for the preservation and communication of the body of ancient traditions within which it was composed. It is to be hoped that future finds will continue to provide much-needed clarification.

Endnotes
1. In the convention used here, the right arm of the instrument is the arm set towards the right, seen from the audience's (and illustrator's) viewpoint: this of course lies to the player's left during performance.
2. A small copper alloy bell 28mm in height was found during post-excavation examination of an iron concretion from Area IV.2 at the west end of the Sutton Hoo ship-burial chamber, probably between the gilt shield-rim and the sceptre (Bruce-Mitford 1983, 890–899). Although not in intimate association with the lyre, this is nevertheless the only such juxtaposition to have yet emerged.

VI. Other Organic Remains

The Charcoal
by Rowena Gale

Charcoal was associated with inhumations, cremations, ring-ditches and burnt stone features as well as a few other features and surface scatters. Nearly all charcoal was sampled and analysed for species identification, including pieces discovered amongst the material from the 1862–3 and 1972 excavations. All identifications are listed individually in the relevant catalogue entries and together in Table 3.

Methods
Samples containing large amounts of charcoal, for example those from the burnt stone features, were sub-sampled to produce realistic quantities for identification. These samples mainly contained relatively large, firm-textured fragments (>10mm in the longest axis). Samples from contexts including logboat grave 4, some coffin stains and from the cremation pyre area, contained few fragments of charcoal and these tended to be small (measuring <2mm in the longest axis) and friable. Because of the paucity of material from these contexts, identification was attempted and usually produced some results. Some fragments, notably from graves 8, 9 and the pyre area, were partially vitrified: when wood or charcoal is burnt at temperatures above C800°, modifications (including plasticity of the cell walls) may occur in the cellular structure (Prior pers. comm.).

Charcoal fragments from each sample were sorted into groups based on the anatomical features present on the transverse surface when viewed using a ×20 hand lens. Representative samples from all groups were selected for detailed examination at higher magnification.

Grave	OP	Object	Description
Inhumation burials			
2	0939	Fill	Several fragments *Quercus* sp., oak, stem,
3	0568	Coffin stain	11 fragments *Quercus* sp., oak, heartwood
	0732	Shield grip	*Quercus* sp., oak, heartwood
4	0931	Boat grave	Few narrow fragments (<2mm), too small for positive identification, transverse surfaces *cf.* Rosaceae/Ericaceae, ?root
	0945	Boat bow stain	Mass of very small fragments, *Quercus* sp., oak, ?sapwood (no tyloses visible) but not narrow stem
	1003	Above boat floor	4 fragments *Quercus* sp., oak, sapwood
	1004	Above boat floor	5 fragments *Quercus* sp., oak
	0121	-	2 fragments *Quercus* sp., oak, stem
5	0465	-	3 fragments *Quercus* sp., oak, heartwood
		-	9 fragments *Quercus* sp., oak, ?stem
6	0780	-	2 fragments *Quercus* sp., oak, very small fragments
8	0809	-	Large quantity *Quercus* sp., oak, probably sapwood but not from narrow stem
	1002	-	Large quantity *Quercus* sp., oak, sapwood and heartwood
	0823	-	20 fragments *Quercus* sp., oak, stem burnt at high temperature (partially vitrified)
	0625	Plank/branch	46 fragments *Quercus* sp., oak, stem
	0135	-	1 fragment *Quercus* sp., oak, ?sapwood, slow grown
9	0483	Plank/branch	Large quantity *Quercus* sp., oak, stem and sapwood
	0521	Plank/branch	Large quantity *Quercus* sp., oak, stem
	0603	Plank	*Quercus* sp., oak, sapwood and heartwood
	0604	Plank	*Quercus* sp., oak, sapwood, probably from wide stem/narrow pole, fast grown
	0626	Plank/branch	Large quantity *Quercus* sp., oak, stem, almost vitrified
	0697	-	*Quercus* sp., oak, heartwood
	0736	Plank/branch	Large quantity *Quercus* sp., oak, stem
	0771	-	Large quantity *Quercus* sp., oak, stem
16	0953	-	7 fragments *Quercus* sp., oak, stem
17	0142	Plank	*Quercus* sp., oak, heartwood
	0190	Plank	Large quantity fragments *Quercus* sp., oak sapwood from wide stem or branch
	0197	-	45 fragments *Quercus* sp., oak, stem
18	0615	Grave fill	32 fragments *Quercus* sp., oak, stem
20	0450	Ring-ditch	1 fragment *Salix* sp., willow/*Populus* sp., poplar
	0775	Ring-ditch	Large quantity *Quercus* sp., oak, heartwood
21	0934	-	13 fragments *Quercus* sp., oak, stem
		-	9 fragments *Salix* sp., willow/*Populus* sp., poplar
		-	4 fragments *Corylus* sp., hazel
	0935	-	1 fragment *Corylus* sp., hazel
	0950	-	2 fragments *Corylus* sp., hazel
		-	1 fragment *Salix* sp., willow/*Populus* sp., poplar
	0534	-	4 fragments *Corylus* sp., hazel
		-	2 fragments *Quercus* sp., oak
27	1447	-	14 fragments *Quercus* sp., oak, sapwood and ?heartwood
		-	3 fragments *Quercus* sp., oak, probably root
32	2284	-	1 fragment, poor condition, ?*Ulex* sp., gorse
33	2259	Upper level of pit	1 fragment *Ulex* sp., gorse, stem
	2269	Upper level of pit	1 fragment *Ulex* sp., gorse, stem
35	2181	Sample 1	26 fragments *Quercus* sp., oak, stem
		-	11 fragments *Quercus* sp., oak, heartwood
		Sample 2	15 fragments *Quercus* sp., oak, stem, fast grown
		-	6 fragments *Quercus* sp., oak, heartwood
		Sample 3	7 fragments *Quercus* sp., oak, stem
		-	5 fragments *Quercus* sp., oak, heartwood slow grown
37	2283	-	1 fragment *Corylus* sp., hazel, stem
39	1729	-	12 fragments *Quercus* sp., oak, stem and heartwood
		-	9 fragments *Ulex* sp., gorse
43	2021	-	1 fragment, friable, ? *Quercus* sp., oak
	2022	-	8 fragments *Quercus* sp., oak, stem
	1893	-	5 fragments *Quercus* sp., oak, sapwood (not narrow stem) and heartwood
	1895	-	1 fragment *Quercus* sp., oak, stem
	1896	-	13 fragments *Quercus* sp., oak, stem
	2020	-	3 fragments *Quercus* sp., oak, stem
45	1993	Coffin stain	3 fragments *Prunus* sp., probably *P.spinosa*, blackthorn
46	2018	Quadrant 1841	Large mass of roundwood – *Ulex* sp., gorse, stem
	2019	-	Large quantity roundwood – 55 fragments *Ulex* sp., gorse, stem
	-	-	3 fragments *Prunus* spp., which includes *P.avium*, wild cherry, *P.padus*, bird cherry, *P.spinosa*, blackthorn
47	1881	Logboat grave	3 fragments *Prunus* spp., which includes *P.avium*, wild cherry, *P.padus*, bird cherry, *P.spinosa*, blackthorn

224

Grave	OP	Object	Description
Cremation burials			
85	0255	-	Mass of fragments *Quercus* sp., oak, stem and heartwood, some slow grown
Cremation pyre			
	0422	-	6 fragments *Corylus* sp., hazel
	0443	-	5 fragments *Pinus* sp., pine, *sylvestris* group, which includes Scots pine
	0458	-	1 fragment *Quercus* sp., oak, ?stem
		-	1 fragment *Corylus* sp., hazel
	0479	-	6 fragments *Pinus* sp., pine, *sylvestris* group, which includes Scots pine
		-	1 fragment *Corylus* sp., hazel
Ring-ditches			
2062	2240	-	3 small fragments, very friable, *Prunus* spp., which includes *P.avium*, wild cherry, *P.padus*, bird cherry, *P.spinosa*, blackthorn
Burnt flint features			
1771	1781	-	Large mass of roundwood:
		-	18 fragments *Ulex* sp., gorse, stem
		-	8 fragments Rosaceae, subfamily Pomoideae which includes *Crateagus* sp., hawthorn, *Malus* sp., apple, *Pyrus* sp., pear, *Sorbus* spp., rowan, whitebeam and wild service tree
		-	6 fragments *Quercus* sp., oak
1775	1791	-	Large mass of roundwood:
		-	35 fragments *Ulex* sp., gorse, stem
		-	10 fragments *Prunus* spp.
		-	8 fragments *Quercus* sp., oak, stem
		-	1 fragment Rosaceae, subfamily Pomoideae
1779	1795	-	Large mass of roundwood:
		-	15 fragments *Quercus* sp., oak, stem
		-	11 fragments *Ulex*, sp., gorse, stem
1794	1828	-	5 fragments *Ulex* sp., gorse, stem
	1859	-	42 fragments *Ulex* sp., gorse, stem
		-	Large quantity of roundwood: 56 fragments *Ulex* sp., gorse, stem
1815	1817	-	3 fragments *Ulex* sp., gorse, stem
		-	2 fragments *Quercus* sp., oak, stem
			1 fragment *Prunus* spp.
1849	1861	-	Large mass of roundwood:
		-	35 fragments *Ulex* sp., gorse, stem
		-	14 fragments *Quercus* sp., oak, stem
2251	2317	-	Large mass of roundwood:
		-	68 fragments *Quercus* sp., oak, stem, fast grown
		-	40 fragments *Ulex* sp., gorse, stem
		-	1 fragment *Prunus* spp.
	2260	-	12 fragments *Quercus* sp., oak, stem
		-	8 fragments *Ulex* sp., gorse
		-	5 fragments *Prunus* spp.
	2230	-	Large mass of roundwood:
		-	32 fragments *Ulex* sp., gorse, stem
		-	6 fragments *Quercus* sp., oak, stem
2251	2318	-	Large mass of roundwood:
		-	15 fragments *Quercus* sp., oak, stem, some with 14 annual rings
		-	8 fragments *Ulex* sp., gorse, stem
		-	1 fragment *Rosa* sp., rose/*Rubus* sp., bramble
Other features			
1900	1901	Post-hole	Large mass of roundwood: 54 fragments *Quercus* sp., oak, stem
2263	2333	-	6 fragments *Quercus* sp., oak, stem
2306	2305	-	6 fragments *Quercus* sp., oak, sapwood (not narrow stem) and heartwood
1392		Urn in area 0907	3 fragments *Quercus* sp., oak, stem, partially vitrified
Miscellaneous			
	0168	-	2 fragments *Quercus* sp., oak, stem
	0136	-	1 fragment *Quercus* sp., oak, stem, fast grown
	0495	-	1 fragment *Quercus* sp., oak
		-	1 fragment *Ulex* sp., gorse, plus some cokey looking material
1782	1785	Charcoal scatter	6 fragments *Ulex* sp., gorse, stem

Table 3 Charcoal identifications

Each fragment was fractured to expose clean flat surfaces in the transverse, tangential longitudinal and radial longitudinal planes and mounted in washed sand. These were examined at magnifications up to ×400 and anatomical features were matched to authenticated reference material.

The origin of the fragments (*i.e.* roundwood, sapwood and heartwood) was noted. Samples arising from stems or branches measuring up to 25mm in diameter were classed as roundwood, whereas samples arising from wider stems or branches but not apparently from heartwood (*i.e.* with some curvature of the annual growth rings; tyloses absent) was noted as sapwood. Samples with little or no curvature of the annual growth rings and with tyloses present were classed as heartwood.

The genera identified, or tentatively identified, are classified according to *Flora Europaea* (Tutin *et al.* 1964–80).

Results
(Table 3)
The majority of the graves in which charcoal was found included oak (*Quercus*) and in many cases this was the only woody species identified. Few charred wooden grave-goods, morphologically recognisable as such, accompanied the bodies. A few graves included oak heartwood, for instance the burial container in grave 3 which strengthens its interpretation as a logboat fragment. In the majority of graves though, there was a mixture of roundwood, sapwood and heartwood or only roundwood, which would appear to support the observations made elsewhere of planks or branches being incorporated into the fill of the grave. However, in some instances, the origin of the charcoal was less evident and the inclusion of roundwood in so many graves may indicate perhaps the use of some structure (such as a hurdle), which incorporated stems and poles. The possible implications of these various wood remains is discussed further in the section on burial rite (below pp. 243–4).

Use of wood resources
The charcoal derived from several distinct groups of features and indicated well defined preferences in use. For example, oak was strongly associated with both inhumation and cremation burials. Oak is strong, tough and durable, and suited to many forms of construction and carpentry, particularly for outdoor use. It may therefore have been deliberately selected for funerary artefacts such as coffins or hurdles for carrying cadavers (as in grave 21), especially as oak also had many mystical and religious connotations (Cooper 1978).

The presence of oak in the cremation graves again appears to show this deliberate selection. The complete absence of other wood fuels, such as gorse (*Ulex*), seen so abundantly in the burnt stone features, suggests the preferential selection of oak for funerary use; it also argues against the burnt stone features having been used as cremation pyres.

The presence of pine (*Pinus*) charcoal in the cremation pyre area was unique on the site. The status of *Pinus* in southern England by the Anglo-Saxon period is uncertain. It is known to have been common in the Mesolithic (Rackham 1990) but pine communities declined significantly during the following millennia. Its gradual retreat from southern England to more northerly latitudes allowed (perhaps isolated) stands to survive in some areas

as, for example, at the Wytch Farm Oilfield, Dorset (Cox and Hearne 1991), where pollen and charcoal were identified from Mid Iron Age deposits (3rd and 2nd century BC).

It is therefore conceivable that in some regions small pockets of pine were still present in the early centuries of the next millennium. By the 12th century locally grown pine timber was apparently unavailable in East Anglia and consignments were imported from the Baltic (Rackham 1986). The pine fragments from Snape were small and gave no clue to their likely origin, whether locally grown or imported as an artefact.

Woodland management
A great quantity of roundwood was present in many of the contexts but most notably in the burnt stone features. Potential evidence of morphological features characteristic of coppice rods had been lost through fragmentation of the charcoal. The dimensions of wood cells are greatly reduced on charring, depending on the temperatures and period of burning. Therefore, the comparative assessment of the fragments from Snape from unmonitored pyrolysis as to their likely origin from fast grown stems was difficult. A few oak fragments appeared to have wide annual growth rings typical of fast grown stems but, in general, it was impossible to assess the bulk of the material with any accuracy. The predominance of stem material tended to suggest that coppice woodlands were present in the area.

Gorse has many economic uses (Lucas 1960) and has been cultivated and coppiced in regions where other wood was sparse (*e.g.* parts of Ireland). However, at Snape where other species were evidently available, gorse was perhaps more likely to have been cut at random from plants growing in scrub.

Conclusions
The identification of the charcoal has indicated preferential use of the woody resources available. Oak (*Quercus*) was evidently important in economic terms and probably in ritual practices in both inhumation and cremation burials. Woods used for fuel included oak and gorse (*Ulex*) roundwood. While this may have been gathered from coppiced woodlands, the evidence is inconclusive.

Insect remains preserved by metal corrosion products
by Mark Robinson
During conservation of the metal small-finds, it was noticed that invertebrate remains had been preserved by corrosion products in the vicinity of several copper alloy objects (Table 4). Material was identified at the English Heritage Environmental Archaeology Laboratory at the University Museum, Oxford.

Discussion
The flies *O. capensis* and *O. leucostoma* have both been reared from a variety of foul organic materials, including carrion (Smith 1989, 136). *O. leucostoma* and perhaps *O. capensis* are strongly attracted to corpses once they have reached a stage of ammoniacal fermentation. *O. capensis* larvae comprise the second stage of faunal succession on buried human corpses, probably appearing several months after burial, especially when the corpse has not been exposed to the open air for long before burial, which would

Grave	Object	Taxon	Quantity
10	F	Beetle — *Grammostethus marginatus* (Er.)	1
10	F	Fly — *Fannia* sp. Larva	1
32	E	Fly — *Ophyra capensis* (Wied.) or *Ophyra leucostoma* (Wied.) larvae	c.250
32	E	Beetle — *Trox scaber* (L.)	pair of elytra and 1 pronotum
32	F	Weevil — *Otiorhynchus ovatus* (L.)	1

Table 4 Mineralised invertebrate remains identified from small finds

result in colonisation by other species of Muscidae and Calliphoridae (blow-flies) (Smith 1973; Smith 1986, 126). The larvae of the fly *Fannia* sp. have also been recorded from corpses (Smith 1986, 122).

The beetle *Grammostethus marginatus* is usually found in moles' nests (Halstead 1963, 10), but as a beetle which feeds on Diptera larvae underground, it would probably have found a suitable habitat around a buried corpse. *Trox scaber* is associated with dry carcasses and carrion in very advanced stages of decay amongst other foods (Smith 1986, 149). It was perhaps able to gain access to the corpse in grave 32 at a late stage down a rodent burrow as evinced by the nibbled plum stone. The weevil *Otiorhynchus ovatus* feeds on various plants and does not provide any useful information on the burial.

VII. The Cremated Bone
by James Steele and Simon Mays

All cremated bone known from the site was submitted for analysis including the material recovered between 1985–92, the contents of an 1862 urn, one found in 1970 and the cremations from the 1972 sewer trench first examined by Wells (1973). All material was sieved through 2mm and 4mm meshes with any non-bone removed. In total, data has been compiled on thirty-two individuals from the site (see Table 5 for a breakdown by age and sex). Additionally, several spreads of bone suggested as being from a cremation pyre and a few tiny scatters of bone insufficiently large to yield information were examined. The identified animal bone is discussed further elsewhere (Chapter 6 section IV). The nine cremations from 1972 were excluded from the calculation of summary statistics as some bone appears to have become mixed since Wells' examination (notably graves 73 and 74) and some material may have been lost. These made Wells' identifications, reached by different methods, uncheckable and they are distinguished in the table below.

Demographic aspects
Estimation of sex was made from sexually dimorphic aspects of the skull, or failing this, from overall skeletal size/robusticity. Juveniles could not be sexed; their age at death was estimated using dental development, epiphysial fusion or bone size. Cranial suture closure (Perizonius 1984) was used as a very approximate guide for ageing adults. Sexing of the remains is often uncertain, ranging from probable identifications for most, to possible for a few.

	Male	Female	Unknown	Total
Sex/age unknown			4	4
Infant/juvenile			4	4
Juvenile			(3)	3
Adolescent/young adult		(1)		1
Young adult	1 (2)	1 (1)		5
Young/middle adult	1			1
Middle adult		1		1
Middle/old adult	1	2	1	4
Old adult				
'Adult'	1	(1)	6 (1)	9
Total cremations				32

Table 5 Breakdown of cremations by age and sex. Identifications by Wells (1973) in brackets

Quantification
Quantification of the bone weights, fragment numbers and sizes for the non-sewer trench material is shown in Table 6. Modern studies suggest that a burnt adult corpse will yield about 2–2.5kg of bone (Wahl 1982) although the Snape cremations yielded only about 10–15% of that figure. This is probably partly due to the serious truncation to sixteen of the twenty-three caused by ploughing. Comparisons show that the intact adult cremations contain (on average) over four times as much material as the truncated assemblages although these are still considerably less (about only 25%) than the total bone weights that might be expected. Notwithstanding the difficult conditions for the rescue of the 1972 sewer trench material, Wells' reaction was that this bone had also been collected initially 'with gross inefficiency' (Wells 1973, 57).

The intact adult cremations contained a greater representation of the lighter, smaller-sized fragments of bone, and truncation *per se* appears to correlate with a loss of these smaller fragments. Skull and postcranial/ unidentified fragment weights from the 4mm sievings suggested that there was no noticeable collection bias in favour of either skull or postcranial fragments for burial. This accords with Wells' findings with the 1972 cremations ('fragments seem to have been preserved randomly from most parts of the body'; West and Owles 1973, 57).

Bone colour and pyre temperature
Experiments by Shipman *et al* (1984) have shown that the temperature reached by burnt bone can be estimated from bone colour. Most of the bone in the Snape cremations is of a white or greyish-white appearance, indicating a sustained pyre temperature probably in excess of approximately 940°C. This is similar to the evidence from other cremations of this period (*e.g.* Illington, Norfolk: Wells 1960; Mucking, Essex: Mays 1992), and is similar to temperatures achieved in modern crematoria (Wahl 1982).

In the Snape assemblages, fragments of cortical bone sometimes occur which appear dark grey or blackened on broken surfaces (as seen in section), suggesting that the

Weights of bone (grams)

	All cremations				Adult cremations only			
	No	Mean	S.D.	Range	No	Mean	S.D.	Range
Intact	7	476.0	331.9	172.2–1146.8	5	597.6	317.2	369.8–1146.8
Truncated	16	111.9	138.4	1.4–572.3	10	142.9	168.1	11.1–572.3
Total	23	222.7	269.1	1.4–1146.8	15	294.5	309.9	11.1–1146.8

Estimated number of fragments

	All cremations				Adult cremations only			
	No	Mean	S.D.	Range	No	Mean	S.D.	Range
Intact	7	3303.0	1973.6	1120–6628	5	3859.0	2043.5	1558–6628
Truncated	16	467.4	401.8	6–1306	10	585.7	459.1	61–1306
Total	23	1330.4	1718.2	6–6628	15	1676.8	1969.7	61–6628

Estimated mean fragment size (mm)

	All cremations				Adult cremations only			
	No	Mean	S.D.	Range	No	Mean	S.D.	Range
Intact	7	7.6	1.8	5–10	5	6.8	1.5	5–9
Truncated	16	10.0	2.7	6–14	10	10.4	3.3	6–14
Total	23	9.3	2.8	5–14	15	9.2	3.0	5–14

Table 6 Summary statistics for bone from the cremations excluding the 1972 sewer trench material

broken surfaces were less burnt. This indicates that the bone has shattered during incineration, and fragments have fallen to cooler parts of the pyre. Additionally, fragments of yellowish white trabecular bone were occasionally noted in some assemblages. It is probable that these fragments were not fully burned due to their shifting to cooler parts of the pyre as the bones disintegrated during the cremation process.

Pathologies and skeletal variants
The bone examined had few pathologies. Each is described in detail within its own catalogue entry. Pathologies noted included:

Porotic hyperostosis (pitting in orbital roofs likely indicative of anaemia); grave 70.
Sutural ossicles (supernumerary bones in cranial vault sutures); graves 89 and 91, and from the pyre cremated bone.
Tibial periostitis; grave 73.

Conclusions
Of the twenty-three cremations from the 1985–92 excavations, fifteen were adults (four male, four female, the rest unsexable) and four children; the age of the remaining four could not be determined. Many of the burials were truncated by later disturbance, but even those not affected contained relatively little bone — on average about 25% of the weight expected from a complete individual. This, in part at least, appears to reflect incomplete recovery of bone from the pyre in antiquity. This same inference was made by Wells when he studied the sewer trench material. Firing temperature in excess of about 940°C appears to have been attained, similar to other Anglo-Saxon cremations.

VIII. The Pottery Stamps
by Teresa Briscoe

The Anglo-Saxon cemetery at Snape has produced a total of thirty-five pot stamps, many of interest (Fig. 144; *n.b.*, three are doodles and not illustrated). The Archive actually lists some forty stamps but four of these cannot be traced amongst the Ipswich Museum's Snape material and it cannot be certain that they derive from Snape. The other stamp is a double numbering. The following discussion is based on the corpus of 20,000 stamps contained in the Archive of Anglo-Saxon Pottery Stamps. One consideration that needs taking into account from the outset is the considerable number of stamp types from Spong Hill, Norfolk and Loveden Hill, Lincs., (2,282 and 1,909 respectively). One must therefore expect uncommon stamps to turn up in both these places, especially as some appear to have stamp links with each other.

As with all cemeteries, the very common stamps are largely undiagnostic; by these I mean the circular cross stamps (A4ai/ii), which are the most common motif in the archive, the rectangular grid stamps (C2ai–vii) and the rosette type (A5ai). The only useful information which may be helpful at the present time is if a site produces a preference for one stamp type against the other ones. At Snape we have four A4ai/ii stamps against three of the rosette type, and in addition there are four examples of the A4aiii, which have the bowed cross edges. Unlike the ubiquitous A4ai stamps, the D4ai stamp from pot *0653* (grave 60) is comparatively rare. In the area in which we are concerned, examples come from Spong Hill, Brooke, Morning Thorpe and Illington in Norfolk and from Lakenheath and Boss Hall (Ipswich) in Suffolk. In the Thames area, examples come from Northfleet and Canterbury as well as Eynsham, Oxon., and Barton

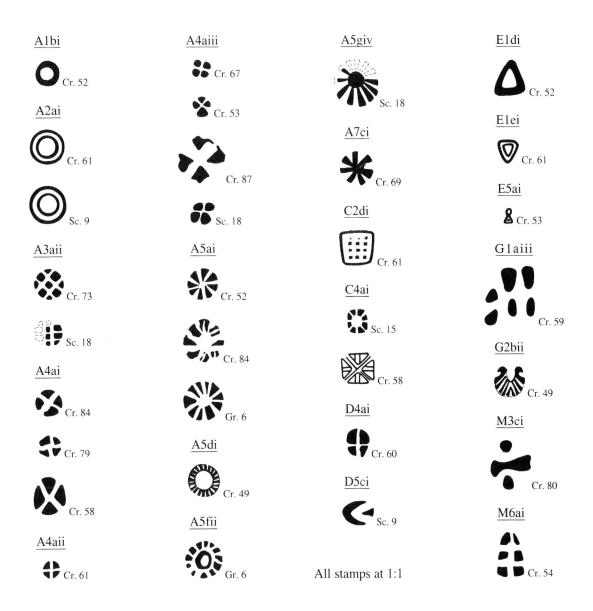

Figure 144 All pot stamps known from Snape, arranged by type. Scale 1:1

(Cirencester) in the Upper Thames complex. There are no C2a types, but two examples of the less common circular version (A3a). Two of the very common stamps found in East Anglia and eastern England generally are the double concentric circle (A2ai) and the dot-in-circle (A1bi). Of these, Snape has only two examples of the A2ai type and one of the A1bi. There are two examples of the rectangular 'Union Jack' (C4ai) stamp from Snape. They are of different sizes and appear on pots *0651* (grave 58) and *0902* (scatters, No. 15). This type is fairly common and the distribution is widespread, as is the C2di stamp on pot *0560* (grave 61).

Of the less common stamps, the A7ci on pot *0882* (grave 69) has parallels at Spong Hill, and Longthorpe, Cambs. The plain outlined triangular stamp E1di on pot *0642* (grave 52) is a very simple stamp but there are only eight other examples in the archive. These come from Loveden Hill (4), West Keal, Lincs. (2), Lackford and Sudbourne, Suffolk (Fig. 145a). The last is, in my opinion, a visually identical stamp with the Snape example, being of the same size. Moreover, both stamps are associated

with the simple single-ring stamp (A1bi), both of which are of the same size. The proximity of the two places makes the supposition that they are the work of the same potter extremely likely. The E1ei stamp on pot *0560* (grave 61) belongs to a small variant group of ten examples within what is, in itself, a not very common type. It is marked by having a shield shape rather than a true triangle. The distribution is interesting, examples coming from Loveden Hill (3), Cleatham (5) and one each from Ixworth and West Stow, Suffolk (Fig. 145b).

The G2bii stamp on pot *0559* (grave 49) is a unique stamp. It resembles examples from Mucking and from the continent, but the two wings at the tips of the crescent do not appear anywhere else. Similarly, the 'keyhole' stamp (E5ai) on pot *0643* (grave 53) is a rare stamp, of which the Snape example belongs to the smallest type. There are other examples of about this size from Loveden Hill, and Field Dalling and Gt. Ellingham, both Norfolk (Fig. 145a). These very small examples suggest that they might relate to similar stamps applied to some great square-headed brooches.

229

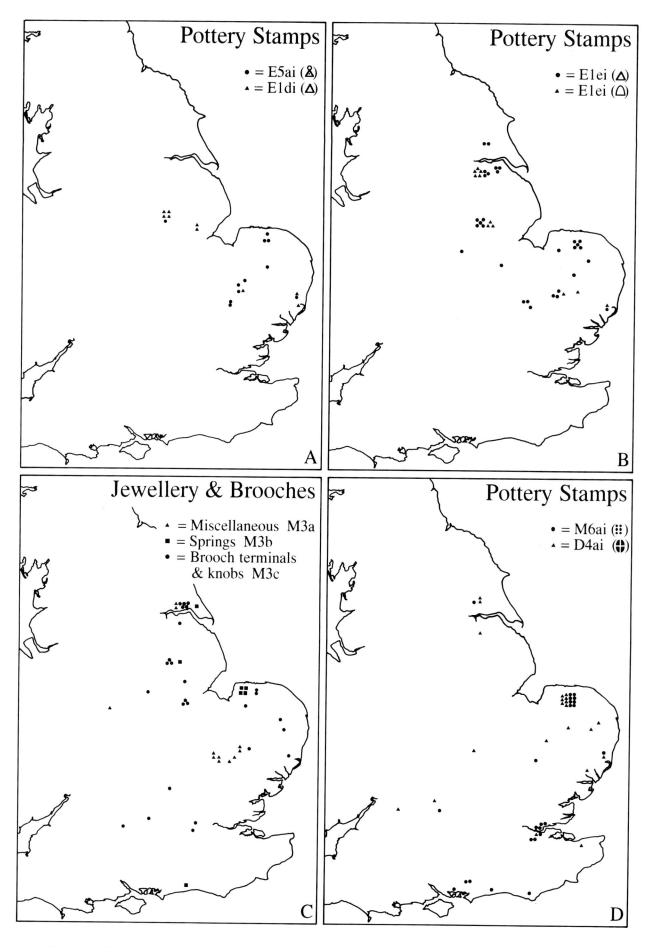

Figure 145 Pot stamp distributions. a) E5ai, E1di. b) E1ei, E1ei subgroup. c) M3a, M3b, M3c. d) M6ai, D4ai

The M3ci 'brooch' stamp on pot *0318* (grave 80) is of great interest. When brooches are used to decorate Anglo-Saxon pots, it is usually the lower finial of cruciform brooches that are used, or the side-knobs. In the case of the Snape pot, the lower middle part has been used, presumably from a broken brooch, but from a cruciform of unusual type. An example of a similar whole brooch comes from the cemetery at Brough-on-Humber. The way that the decoration has been applied, in a line round the neck of the pot, is paralleled by the use of brooch terminals on pots from Spong Hill and Castle Acre (Fig. 145c), but these are all made with the same type of brooch terminal, and are associated with other stamps and/or decoration. The Snape example has the brooch stamp on its own with no other decoration.

The 'tree' stamp (M6ai) on pot *0644* (grave 54) is another rare stamp which is found mostly in the Thames estuary and the south coast cemeteries (Fig. 145d). There are however, ten examples from Spong Hill and one each from Sancton, N. Humbs. and Lt. Wilbraham, Cambs. The most westerly examples come from Abingdon, Oxon. and Southampton.

The A5fii stamp on pot *0462* (grave 6) is a fairly uncommon version of this type but it has a widespread distribution. A similar rosette stamp comes from No. 18 of the scatter material. Although a poor impression, the segments appear to 'swirl', suggestive of the 'wheel-of-fire' type, A5giv. The distribution is widespread but there is a group of examples from the Cam/Lark area, and another from the East Norfolk sites of Markshall, Spong Hill and Witton with yet another from Eye, Suffolk.

The two versions of the right-facing swastika (type J1aii) on pot *0641* (grave 51, Fig. 112) are probably hand drawn rather than stamped. They are larger than many and the 'club' ends have one parallel from Loveden Hill.

Discussion

Overall, the Snape stamps seem to relate rather more to the sites in Essex and the Thames estuary than to the more inland East Anglian sites, especially those of the Lark Valley. The presence of brooch terminals at the more easterly Norfolk sites and of course at Spong Hill are consistent with this and would suggest a common cultural origin. The complete absence of the use of brooch knobs at Snape would seem to reinforce this as they are missing from all the Norfolk sites except Spong Hill. The assemblage generally seems to suggest a people somewhat isolated and one might have expected more links with the sites north of the Waveney. Martin Carver's suggestion of a kingdom or tribal area of the Sandlings (Carver 1989, 152) is perhaps borne out by this distribution. A similar pattern can be discerned for Norfolk north of the Yare and the area stretching from Illington to Cambridge. There are two examples of the dot-in-circle stamp which are found at Caistor St Edmund and these are common in the cemeteries and sites of the Lark Valley, around Cambridge and in central Suffolk.

The use of the lower central part of a cruciform brooch is, as stated above, unique to Snape. The brooch used would have been one similar to that from Brough-on-Humber. The brooches shown by Reichstein (1975) do not include any of this type. The use of protruding 'eyes' each side of a raised line, above the actual terminal, appears to be Scandinavian and he

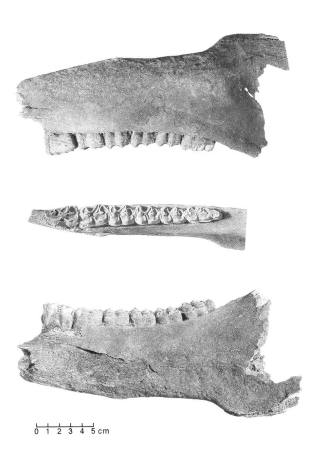

Plate LV External, occlusal and internal views of the left mandible of horse head *S* grave 47

illustrates a number from Norway. They do not, however, have the central 'dumb-bell' of the Snape and Brough brooches. The only British brooches of this type that I have been able to find are two from West Stow.

The distribution of the M6ai stamps appear to bear out the ties which Snape seems to have with the south-eastern part of the country. With ten examples from Spong Hill but none from Loveden Hill, this would appear to confirm this idea.

IX. The Horse Head from Grave 47
by Simon Davis

During excavation of Area B in 1991 an equid skull was found associated with grave 47. The skull had an iron snaffle-bit in its mouth and the remains of tack were scattered in the surrounding ploughsoil. The top of the skull and upper jaws had been ploughed away, but the mandibular tooth rows and adjacent rami, especially of the left side, are well preserved. The rest of the skeleton has not been found and the burial, it is suggested, was an intentional horse head burial (Chapter 6 section IV). It is interesting because finds of equid skulls with a bit are rare, and the Snape find is well dated.

The Snape equid is without doubt a horse, *Equus caballus* since the molars and premolars have 'U' shaped internal folds, and in the molars the external fold partially penetrates between the metaflexid and entoflexid (Fig.

Tooth	ACH	L_1	L_2	L_3	W_a	W_b	W_c	W_d
P_2	15	-	12.6	13.8	10.4	13.4	13.6	6.9
P_3	18	25.7	16.5	9.0	14.6	15.7	14.4	4.2
P_4	24	23.7	14.9	8.0	14.6	14.3	12.1	3.5
M_1	17	22.3	13.6	4.9	14.2	13.3	11.6	2.5
M_2	17	23.2	13.2	6.4	12.7	12.1	10.4	2.3
M_3	20	29.8	12.3	8.1	11.7	11.0	10.1	2.2

Table 7 Measurements of the left mandibular cheek teeth of the Snape horse, in mm. ACH is the approximate crown height measured from root 'saddle' to occlusal surface, as shown in Levine (1982)

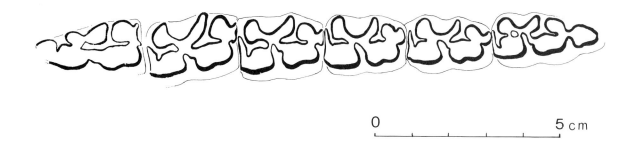

0 _____ 5 cm

Figure 146 The cheek teeth of the left mandible, horse head from grave 47, in occlusal view to show the enamel folds. Scale 1:1

146 and Pl. LV). The third molar has an anomalous circle of enamel between the metaflexid and external valley.

Age at death

The cheek teeth are all well worn, with crown heights ranging between 15 and 24mm. Comparison of these heights with data from New Forest ponies (Levine 1982) suggests an age at death greater than 17 years. The Snape horse was certainly an old individual and I would suggest that it may have been 20–30 years old. Only one, unidentifiable, isolated and broken incisor is preserved with part of its occlusal surface. It still possesses a near circular infundibulum, which suggests a somewhat younger age than that indicated by the cheek teeth. Given the poor state of the incisors, the cheek teeth would seem to provide a better guide for an age estimate.

Size and sex

Comparison of the Snape tooth measurements (Table 7) with those from an Iron Age pony from Hampshire (Davis 1987) indicates that the Snape horse was rather small, probably a pony. The presence of a canine tooth suggests that the Snape horse was more probably a stallion.

Bit wear

The mammalian tooth comprises three hard tissues, cementum and dentine which are bone-like substances and a much harder crystalline enamel which, in equids, is arranged as a series of complicated folds. This structure, and the high crown, has evolved as an adaptation to grazing tough grass and the inevitable soil and sand particles which enter the mouth. Their abrasiveness cause

the tooth gradually to wear down. Since enamel is harder than dentine and cementum, the enamel folds stand proud and give the occlusal surfaces of the cheek teeth a rough surface rather like a carpenter's file.

A horse bit lies within the space (diastema) between incisors and first premolar (P_2) and rests on the sensitive gum of the mandible. Application of pressure via the reins and bit onto the gum of the diastema gives the rider control of the horse's head, and hence the ability to control the animal. However, a resting horse is sometimes able to 'take the bit between its teeth' by lifting it with its tongue onto the front half of P_2. The bit cannot usually be pushed any further back than the anterior half of the first lower premolar since it is effectively stopped by the fleshy corners of the mouth. Continual biting on an object as hard as an iron bit, unlike the grass and soil particles, produces equal wear on both enamel and dentine/cementum. In addition the enamel in this region suffers 'spalling' damage (*i.e.* cracking/crazing; Anthony and Brown 1991).

Despite the presence of an iron bit in the Snape horse skull, no signs of the kinds of damage and wear described by Anthony and Brown can be observed. The Snape P_2s show normal wear surfaces with the enamel folds standing proud of the intervening dentine and the P_2 enamel lacks spalling damage. There are several possible explanations for the lack of 'bit-wear' on the Snape P_2s. For example the Snape horse may not have been wearing a bit during its last few weeks of life, but was merely buried with it in its mouth. An alternative possibility is that the Snape horse did indeed wear a bit during its last few weeks of life, but it did not behave in the manner described by Anthony and Brown.

Chapter 6. Overall Results

I. The Cemetery
by William Filmer-Sankey

Introduction

Having presented the evidence derived from both the 1985–92 excavations and from the earlier work in the Catalogue (Chapter 4), and having looked at the detailed interpretations of selected aspects (Chapter 5), the time has come to see what broader conclusions can be drawn about the Snape Anglo-Saxon cemetery. This chapter therefore covers the interpretation both of the cemetery as a whole, and of different burial types and other features.

In discussing the character of the cemetery, it is vital to remember that we can do no more than interpret the existing, partial evidence in order to draw wider conclusions. The dangers of this approach were made clear early on in the project. The fact that (with the exception of the 1862 ship burial) only cremation burials had been found was interpreted as meaning that the cemetery was similar in character to Spong Hill, where densely packed cremations are in the overwhelming majority. This, with hindsight wholly incorrect, interpretation was then used as the basis for a sampling strategy to determine the size of the cemetery (described above, pp. 11–12). If it had not been for the chance discovery of an inhumation grave, the true nature of the site would have remained totally unknown. At the same time, however, the factual basis for making deductions about the nature of the entire cemetery has improved vastly as a result of the 1985–92 excavations. These examined a total of 2300m², forty-six inhumation graves, twenty-three cremation graves and various other features (Table 8).[1] Assuming that the limits of the cemetery derived from the 1989–90 2m wide trenches are correct, the total area of the cemetery would have been in the region of 11,200m². The 1985–92 excavated area is thus equivalent to a 20% sample, large enough to draw statistically valid conclusions. It should always be borne in mind, nevertheless, that a 'statistically valid' conclusion is not necessarily the same as the truth!

Location

The Anglo-Saxon choice of that particular site for their cemetery must have been influenced by the presence of at least one Bronze Age barrow. The collared urn (grave 48) found upside down and containing cremated bone, just below the surface of the ship burial mound excavated by Septimus Davidson, can surely only derive from an existing tumulus which had been built over to make the ship burial mound. In addition to this, it is at least possible that some of the other mounds noted by the 1862 excavators may have been prehistoric, while a number of the ring-ditches in Area B may well also pre-date the Anglo-Saxon use of the site (below, pp. 236–8). No other features of pre-Anglo-Saxon date were found during the excavation.

The siting of important Anglo-Saxon cemeteries and settlements in the area of existing prehistoric earthworks has been noted at Sutton Hoo and elsewhere, and cannot be coincidental. Richard Bradley has interpreted the practice as demonstrating the way in which newly arrived elites laid claim to new areas by establishing links with their 'predecessors' (Bradley 1987). In this context, it is of particular interest that the buriers of the 1862 ship apparently chose deliberately to swamp an existing barrow, thus demonstrating not so much a continuity with the past, but a desire to be seen to overwhelm it. The significance of this, when taken together with the dating evidence, is considered further below (p. 266).

There must, however, have been more to the choice of site than simply the presence of an existing burial mound (or mounds). There are at least two other tumuli of presumed prehistoric date known to lie within 1000m of the cemetery (Fig. 2), so the question of 'why there?' still

Date of excavation	1862—3	1970—2	1985—92	Totals
Cremations (total 52; 1 empty)				
urned	19	8	17	44
unurned	-	1	6	7
bronze bowl	-	1	-	1
male	-	2	3	5
female	1	3	2	6
uncertain/empty	18	5	18*	41
infant	-	3	4	7
adult	1	7	13	21
uncertain	18	-	6	24
Inhumations (total 47 graves; 48 bodies)				
ship/boat	1	-	3	4
lining	-	-	11	11
layer	-	-	12	12
coffin	-	-	1	1
bier	-	-	1	1
none/uncert/unexc	-	-	18	18
male	1	-	13	14
female	-	-	11	11
uncertain	-	-	23	23
infant/juvenile/adol	-	-	10	10
adult	1	-	2	3
uncertain	-	-	35	35
Ring-ditches (without central burial)				
	-	1	4	5
Cremation pyre	-	-	1	1
Burnt stone features	-	-	7	7

* includes cremation 78 which had no bone and therefore total cremations = 52

Table 8 Summary of excavated features

needs answering. The key may lie in the fact that, as argued above (p. 1 and Fig. 3) the site was visible both from the sea and the river Alde. Indeed, when viewed from out to sea, the ship burial mound (assuming that it had a not unreasonable original height of 5m or more) would actually have appeared as a silhouette against the sky. Anyone familiar with the problems of navigating along the Suffolk coast line will know that landmarks along the shore line are very hard to pick up against the uniform and relatively featureless background of the land behind. The most easily visible landmarks are those which, although perhaps some distance inland, appear as a silhouette against the skyline. It has long been known that Suffolk church towers were used as navigational marks for precisely this reason, with even the distinctive spire of Wickham Market church (12.5km inland) being used as a sea mark (Arnott 1955, 25).

If church towers were used as navigational marks in the medieval period, why should tumuli not have had a similar function in the Early Medieval period? We know in fact that they were: the dying Beowulf asks that his mound be positioned on Hronessness, so that it will be visible to sailors. If, as Sam Newton has argued, *Beowulf* is a product of the East Anglian kingdom, the poet was in all likelihood reflecting his own experience (Newton 1993).

In short, the location of the Snape Anglo-Saxon cemetery (or at least of the ship burial and any other Anglo-Saxon mounds with it) is likely to have been decided not only by the presence of existing mounds, but also by the fact that it could serve a navigational purpose, identifying the mouth of the river Alde. There is of course no reason why the Bronze Age tumuli should not have been placed for the same purpose.

Size and layout

The Anglo-Saxon cemetery is best described as 'pear-shaped', with its long axis on a WNW–ESE alignment. Its dimensions are 200m × 70m, which compare with c.90m × 70m at Spong Hill and c.140m × 70m at Mucking Cemetery II. The tumuli are clustered around the southern and eastern sides of the cemetery, with the cremation and inhumation burials intermixed with the mounds in those areas, but extending further to the north and west.

The only area of excavation which undoubtedly included the edge of the cemetery (Area B), showed that the graves thinned off at the edges, rather than coming to an abrupt halt, as is so clearly the case (for example) at Morning Thorpe and Yeavering. If the cemetery was surrounded by some form of boundary, as must have been the case at Morning Thorpe (Green *et al* 1987, fig. 5) and Yeavering (Hope-Taylor 1977, fig. 26), the density of graves never became great enough for it to act as a constraint. Indeed, the overall density of graves in Area A is unusually low, with (on average) one inhumation per 16.3m^2, and one cremation per 21.45m^2 (Fig. 6).[2] Although there are some areas of relatively dense concentrations (notably graves 10–12 and 16–18 in Area A; Fig. 6), the overall impression is of a sprawling cemetery, in which space was not a constraint.

It was argued above (p. 15) that the finding of fragments of cremated bone in the fills of two inhumation graves and in a rabbit burrow adjacent to boat grave 47, combined with the particularly severe soil erosion,

indicated that cremation burials had once existed in Area B, but had been totally destroyed by ploughing. Certainly, the evidence from Area A and those trenches north of the road which produced graves, indicates that the inhumation and cremation burials are intermixed throughout the cemetery, and that there are approximately equal numbers of each type. There is in short no evidence for 'zoning' of burial rites as has been noticed at Spong Hill.

Assuming that the grave density does remain reasonably constant throughout the cemetery, and that the roughly equal proportion of inhumation to cremation burial is also constant, the Snape Anglo-Saxon cemetery would have contained a total of 1000 burials, divided equally between inhumation and cremation.

Date

Although there is no evidence for spatial 'zoning' of the different burial methods, with the two rites appearing totally intermixed, this should not be taken to imply that they are also chronologically indistinguishable. Accurate dating of the individual graves and other structures is hampered by the usual problems of Anglo-Saxon cemeteries. The site has produced only three 'absolute' dates, from C14 samples taken from two 'burnt stone features' and from the horse's head associated with grave 47. There are no cases of multiple overlapping or intercutting graves, so that the construction of a 'horizontal stratigraphy' (so useful on continental sites) is impossible.

At the same time, there are a few individual relationships between cremation and inhumation graves, a burnt stone feature and a funeral pyre. Thus the pottery, burnt bone, burnt copper alloy and iron fragments found in the upper fill of an inhumation (grave 5) are interpreted as the remains of a pre-existing cremation burial disturbed by the digging of grave 5. The two urned cremations (graves 88 and 89) found at the head of an inhumation (grave 17) appear to have been placed in the inhumation grave cut during backfilling and are thus exactly contemporary with it. The substantial scatter of cremated bone (grave 99, with no pottery and only five fragments of metal) in the upper fill of an inhumation (grave 11) is, in itself, hard to interpret, but is most likely to be contemporary with or later than the inhumation. Finally, the very badly truncated remains of an urn and cremated bone (grave 90) were found within the area of the ring-ditch surrounding an inhumation (grave 20). Other cremations in the immediate area were much better preserved (*e.g.* graves 87 and 92) and the poor state of grave 90 could be explained by its having been inserted into the top of an existing tumulus covering grave 20. It would thus have been particularly vulnerable to plough damage as the mound was flattened.

In summary, there are possible examples of individual cremation burials pre-dating, being contemporary with and post-dating individual inhumation burials.

A burnt stone feature (*1775*) was cut by an inhumation (grave 46), with a considerable amount of burnt stone from the former being found in the fill of the latter. Finally, it seems most likely (though certainty is impossible) that the suggested cremation pyre (below, p. 252) underlay an inhumation (grave 10).

These relationships provide some elements of a relative chronology. For an absolute chronology, however, we remain largely dependent on dates derived from object typologies. Although many of these have been reworked and immensely improved during the past few years, they remain a less than perfect tool, not least because of the impossibility of knowing the relationship between the date of the grave-goods and the date of the grave. In any case, Snape has produced relatively few of the most clearly diagnostic types.

Despite these caveats, a picture of the chronological development of the cemetery can be built up. To begin at the most basic level, all features (with the exception of the Bronze Age collared urn in grave 48, and the possible exception of some of the ring-ditches (see below)) are what is conventionally labelled pagan Anglo-Saxon (*i.e.* broadly 5th to 7th century). It will be noted that the C14 date for one of the burnt stone features (*1849*) gave a rather early date range of cal AD 260–416 at 1σ (GU–5235; 1680±50BP). The other however, from burnt stone feature *1794*, fell clearly within the period cal AD 415–544 at 1σ (GU–5234; 1580±50BP), and the early date may be accounted for by the incorporation of a long-living species (oak) into the sample.

For more detailed dating, and particularly for deciding the chronological relationship between the cremation and inhumation burials, we must rely on typology-based dates. The following objects can be used in this way: urns (following Myres 1977 in default of a more up-to-date system), spearheads (following Swanton 1973), shield bosses (following Dickinson and Härke 1992), cruciform brooches (following Mortimer 1990) and wrist clasps (following Hines 1993).

To begin with the urns, it is particularly unfortunate that the promised analysis of the Spong Hill urns is not yet available. It has been clear for a long time that Myres' dating is suspect, but nothing has yet replaced it. None of the Snape urns belong to any of Myres' more distinctive types, though some (such as that from grave 51) would appear to be early (5th century? or earlier 6th century) and some (such as that from grave 54) to be late (7th century?) (Myres 1977, I, 37–41 for the urn from grave 51 and I, 56 for the urn from grave 54). The bulk is undistinguished and could date from any time within the pagan period (Stanley West pers. comm.).

Ten inhumation graves from the 1985–92 excavations contained a total of twelve spearheads. In addition to this are the fragments of two spearheads found associated with, and believed to derive from, the 1862 ship burial (above, p. 7). All the blades are very corroded, making confidence about their exact form difficult (impossible in the case of one of the two ship burial blades). Seven different Swanton types can be identified, however, most represented by a single example. The spearheads in graves 1, 3, 6, 17 and 21, are of Swanton's types H2, the 'vast majority of which belong to the latest 5th and the 6th century', though there are rare indications of a later survival (Swanton 1973, 107–111). The blade in grave 45 is of type C2, which spans the entire pagan period (Swanton 1973, 51). The larger C3 version of the same leaf-shaped form was found in grave 47, the boat grave, as one of a bundle of three. It is a 6th-century type, but has a strong survival into the 7th century (Swanton 1973, 55–9). Types D1 and D2 are also represented by single examples, from graves 31 and 36 respectively. Type D1 spans the entire pagan period, while D2 (an example of which occurs in mound 1 at Sutton Hoo) is a 6th-century development.

There is a possible example in grave 20 of Type H1, for which Swanton suggests a relatively early date, describing the type as 'characteristic of the latest 5th and earliest 6th centuries, with a strong likelihood that the whole was entirely superseded by the second half of the 6th century' (Swanton 1973, 103–7).

Finally there are three spearheads (the final two in the bundle in boat grave 47 and one from grave 37) which may fall into Swanton's type F1. The uncertainty derives not so much from their corroded state as from the fact that they do not match Type F1 (or any other type) very closely, being very small (*c.*110mm) and having virtually no blade. It was initially thought that they might be arrow heads, but the finding of two in a bundle with the Type C3 spearhead in grave 47 indicates that they are spears. Given that we have suggested that both graves 37 and 47 may have contained juveniles, it is possible that this is a young man's spear type. If they are of Type F1, they have a 6th-century date range (Swanton 1973, 91–2).

Five inhumation graves (3, 6, 21, 32 and 47) contained shield bosses. Those from graves 3, 6 and 21 belong to Dickinson and Härke's Group 3, which they date broadly to the 6th century, while noting a bias towards the mid to later part of the century (Dickinson and Härke 1992, 15). The shields from graves 32 and 47 seem to have been identical, both having not only Group 6 bosses but also two pairs of *c.*30–50mm diameter studs placed vertically on the board. Group 6 is dated to the later 6th–early 7th century (Dickinson and Härke 1992, 20–1), which ties in well with the radiocarbon date of cal AD 543–652 at 1σ (GU–5233; 1460±70BP) from the horse's head burial adjacent to grave 47.

Three inhumation graves produced a total of five cruciform brooches. In grave 10 were three brooches, while graves 14 and 16 produced one each. Although the particularly florid brooch from grave 16 is of a distinctive type (paralleled by that from Sporle, Norfolk, for example (Leeds and Pocock 1971, fig. 4a)), a date for four of them more precise than '6th century' is impossible (Dr C. Mortimer, pers. comm.). The exception is brooch *D*, one of the trio from grave 10, which may be as early as the 5th century.

Dates for the three pairs of wrist clasps are similarly vague. Those from grave 10 (the most decorated) belong to Hines' type C5, for which 'a 6th-century date may be presumed' (Hines 1993, 72).[3] The pairs from graves 5 and 16 fall into Hines Type B7, the majority of members of which are 6th-century (Hines 1993, 41), and Type B13b, which has a similarly 6th-century focus.

In summary, the grave-goods from Snape (with the slight exception of the shield bosses, some of the spearheads and one of the brooches) are generally not of types that allow for a very precise dating. Any hope, therefore, of phasing the individual graves is forlorn. At the same time, a tentative conclusion about the chronological relationship between the inhumation and cremation burials can be reached by combining all the slender threads of dating evidence.

It seems that, while the cremation burials span the entire 'pagan' Anglo-Saxon period from the late 5th/early 6th to the 7th centuries, the inhumation burials may be more restricted, perhaps to the latter half of the 6th and early 7th centuries. Only two of the datable grave-goods — the brooch from grave 10 and the spearhead from grave 20 — fall outside this range, which would fit in well with the 1862 ship burial for which a date of around the mid 6th century was suggested (above p. 196). It seems probable therefore that the cemetery originated (like Spong Hill) as a cremation cemetery. The 'burnt stone features', with their relatively early C14 dates, were an element of this cemetery. In around the mid 6th century, the rite of inhumation was introduced alongside cremation, which continued in use. It is tempting to see the 1862 ship burial as a 'founder grave', initiating the rite of inhumation in an already existing cemetery. Both rites then continued in tandem until the early 7th century, when the site was abandoned.

Endnotes
1. The actual area of the excavation was *c.*3450m^2, but a proportion of this was, of course, outside the limits of the cemetery.
2. These figures on grave density have been derived from Area A only. Area A was the only part of the excavation where we can be reasonably confident that most, if not all, the graves survived to be excavated.
3. Hines' Type C5 has only two examples. He writes 'There is as yet no dating evidence for this form; a 6th-century date may be presumed but further discussion must wait upon a comprehensive publication of the cemetery at Snape'. Sorry!

II. Inhumation Graves
by Tim Pestell

Ring-ditches
Excavation at Snape revealed eight ring-ditches, of which one was definitely annular (around grave 25) and two were possibly penannular (around graves 20 and 34). Ring-ditch 2066 (extending beneath a baulk) was probably annular. Traces of four more ring-ditches, 1735, 1780, 2265 and 2449, (seen in the 1972 sewer trench) were either too fragmentary to categorise, or only partially excavated.

Ring-ditches have usually been taken to indicate the former existence of barrows, ditch upcast being used to form an earthen mound. However, it is equally clear that not all barrows had ditches (for example Snape mound 5), nor is it certain that all ring-ditches necessarily contained mounds.

The principal difficulty in interpreting the ring-ditches is their lack of dating evidence. Only those around graves 25 and 20 were definitely Anglo-Saxon, although that around grave 34 almost certainly was too. A prehistoric use of the site is attested by the Bronze Age collared urn found in mound 1 in 1862 (grave 48), suggesting that a tumulus had been re-used by the Anglo-Saxons, in common with many other examples at this time (Van de Noort 1993, 70). The possibility therefore exists that several or all of the other ring-ditches may be of a Bronze Age date. Since Bronze Age ring-ditches are morphologically identical to their Anglo-Saxon counterparts, when surviving as only faint plough-damaged examples it is impossible to distinguish between the two. This difficulty is heightened by the fact that no dating evidence was found in any of the five remaining ring-ditches excavated or partially excavated (1735, 1780, 2066, 2265, and 2449), despite 100% sampling where possible. Prehistoric material from the site is scant, restricted to the collared urn from the 1862 ship burial; a possible Bronze Age sherd probably from Snape, amongst

the loose pottery fragments from the 1972 sewer trench;[1] and a small collection of struck flint, excavated 1985–92, which has 'nothing really diagnostic ... so one cannot even attach a prehistoric date with much confidence' (E. Martin, flint report in site archive). This paucity of evidence, coupled with the lack of datable material in the features associated with ring-ditches 1735, 2066 and 2265, makes it difficult to present a positive case for their prehistoric date. However, an absence of datable finds from such sites is not uncommon and this may have been exacerbated at Snape by finds loss through plough damage. The features within ring-ditches 1735 and 2185, apparently empty, are also known from other prehistoric barrow excavations. Similar examples were found in recent excavations at Bixley, Norfolk, where several have been interpreted as Bronze Age graves, where soil conditions have destroyed all traces of the burials (Ashwin and Bates 2000). In particular, the lack of central features to many prehistoric ring-ditches make it possible that, for instance, ring-ditch 1735 may derive from an earlier use of the site. The arc of ring-ditch 1780, apparently a curve made from straighter sections, is also paralleled in a number of prehistoric examples, for instance Sweet Briar Road, Norwich (Lawson *et al* 1986, 61). A difficulty with the Snape ring-ditches is that only 1780, with a diameter of 7.3m, approaches the usually larger size of Bronze Age examples. However, the clustering of small ring-ditches around larger barrows is known elsewhere in Suffolk in this period (*e.g.* Nayland with Wissington; Lawson *et al* 1981, 23), so it is possible that a relict Bronze Age barrow cemetery may also be represented at Snape. Certainly, such a concentration of tumuli would be consistent with their known distribution in Bronze Age Suffolk, which has four main concentrations, including the East Suffolk Sandlings (Lawson *et al* 1981, 75).

Equally, the possibility of an Anglo-Saxon date for many or all of the ring-ditches must be considered. Although three ring-ditches were apparently buried with nothing at their centre, most obviously ring-ditch 2066 which had three-quarters of its arc revealed, there are several possible explanations. Grave 34 demonstrated that plough damage could cause the removal of nearly all of an inhumation, the ditch here being deeper than the actual burial, in contrast to those around graves 20 and 25. Several graves may therefore have been completely destroyed, their former presence now signalled only by the fragmentary survival of their surrounding ditches, for instance 1735 and 2265. Moreover, such graves need not have contained inhumations; the small feature at the centre of ring-ditch 1735 had more in common with the base of a cut for a cremation than with either an inhumation or robber-pit. Alternatively, there may have been no central burial, empty ring-ditches of Anglo-Saxon date also occurring at Portway, Andover, Hants. and Brightlingsea, Essex (Cook and Dacre 1985, 58–9; Clarke 1991, 272). Finally, the size of the ring-ditches is more consistent with those found in many Anglo-Saxon cemetery excavations (Hills 1977, 171).

What is certain is that two, definitely, and three, almost certainly, of the ring-ditches excavated were of Anglo-Saxon date. In being a visible marker of a grave, they have often been seen as indicating high status because of the increased effort expended in their construction (Welch 1992, 72). Some caution is necessary. The potential for other markers such as canopies or structures around graves

| | | BODY | | | GRAVE CUT | | FILL INCLUSIONS | | | | | | |
No	Sex	Age	Body position	Head	Orientation	Container	Grave goods	Sherds	Wood 'planks'	Wood lumps	Burnt flint	Cremated bone	Object
1	M				E–W	ship	y						
2	F		EC	W	269	lining with posts	y			SL			
3	M		EC	W	270	?logboat	y			SL			
4		?juv	F	W	263	logboat	y	y		SL	y		
5	F		E	W	259		y	y		F			?smashed cremation
6	M		F	W	269	lining	y	y		F		y	
7		juv		W	271		y			SL			
8	F		E	E	269	layer	y		y				
9			EC	W	289	layer	y		y				
10	F		F	W	290	lining	y	y		F	y	y	boat bow cremation
11	F		F	W	258	layer	y			BS			cremation
12	?M	mid-old		W	276		y			SL	y		
13		infant			238	layer				F			
14	F	juv		W	300	lining			y				
15		?juv	?F	E	300	lining							
16	F	y. adult	F	W	276	layer	y	y		F			
17	M		F	W	284	?coffin	y		y				2 cremations
18			F	E	251		y			F			
19	F+?		F & O	E&E	295	lining	y			SL			
20	M		EC	W	276		y		y	SL			quern stone fragment
21	M		EC	W	285	?bier	y		y	F			
22					?	?	?						
23					276	?	?						
24					292	?	?						
25	?M		E	W	270	liner	y	y					
26					228	?	?						
27	F		F	W	266		y		y	SL	y		
28	F		F	W	239	layer	y	y		F&SL	y		
29					260	?	?						
30					203	?	?						
31	M		E	W	262	layer	y			F			
32	M		EC	W	274	lining	y			F		y	
33					0	?	?			F			
34		infant			284	layer							
35					290					SL			
36	M		F	W	299	layer	y			F			
37	M	juv			296	lining	y			SL&F			
38	.		?F	W	267	layer	y			SL			
39				W	262	?layer			y		y		
40	?F		E	W	284	layer	y						
41		?juv			270		y			F	y		
42		inf/juv			294					Smear			
43			E		280	lining	y						
44			O	W	270								large stone on back
45	M		E	W	309	lining	y			F	y		
46											cuts BSF		
47	M	adoles	?E	W	289	logboat	y	y	y	SL	y	y	included flint flakes

Abbreviations
Body position: E extended; EC extended, feet crossed; F flexed; O other
Wood lumps: BS black sand; F flecks; SL small lump

Table 9 Summary of inhumation grave attributes

should make us wary of automatically attributing status to burials having small barrows or ring-ditches. This is perhaps reinforced by the general lack of discernibly richer or 'higher status' grave-goods found within those graves surrounded by ring-ditches. Ditchless small barrows formerly over inhumations, implied by their isolation from surrounding graves (for example Morning Thorpe, Norfolk, grave 246; Green et al 1987, 102), might also have once been far more common than excavated remains need necessarily show. Nevertheless, there does seem to be a clustering of graves around the ring-ditch to grave 20 which might indicate a more important burial surrounded by satellite graves in much the same manner as the founder graves seen in Merovingian cemeteries

(James 1979, 81) or Hope-Taylor's model of 'polycentric' cemetery development (1977, 262). A wider view of the site makes it clear that the ring-ditches themselves form satellites to larger barrow burials, for instance that of grave 34 to mound 5, and grave 20 to the presumed site of the mound 1 ship barrow. These relationships may be further strengthened if ditch *1780*/mound 6 and ditch *2449* are Anglo-Saxon, being satellites to mounds 4 and 1 respectively.

Similarly, if Anglo-Saxon, the empty ring-ditches *1735*, *2066* and *2265* are reminiscent of the curious features 14 and 20 from Sewerby, E. Yorks. Hirst discussed the possibility that these might have formed slots to hold wattle fences or perhaps even the foundation slot for a circular building 'perhaps a mortuary house or shrine' (1985, 25–7). Such an interpretation might also be applicable to Snape although Blair (1995) has suggested there was a development of square-shaped shrines. The possibility of there having been a structural element to ring-ditches may be suggested in the case of ring-ditch *1780* around mound 6. This was narrow and had a steep profile more reminiscent of a palisade trench for retaining a fence than an open ditch. A later parallel is the tumulus over the Danish ship burial at Ladby which was surrounded by posts (Thrane 1987, 45–6). Anglo-Saxon instances of 'annular palisade ditches' include examples from St Peter's, Broadstairs, Kent, where the (penannular) ditches surrounding graves 277, 280 and 339 revealed 'evidence of numerous stake holes' (Hogarth 1973, 113). None of the latter were seen at Snape but the proportions of the ditch relative to its diameter (Fig. 131) make it reasonable to suggest that this could also have contained some form of structure. More importantly, it stresses another variation in which Anglo-Saxon graves, and indeed tumuli, might be marked.

Barrows

Of the tumuli, only mounds 4 and 5 (both scheduled monuments) remained to be investigated. Mound 4 still stands as a well-defined round barrow *c.*15m in diameter, standing up to 0.8m above the surrounding ground surface. Mound 5 had been eroded from a shape recorded in 1862 as 25.5m in diameter and 2m high, to an irregular 10m diameter blob, some 50mm (*sic*) above the ploughsoil by 1990 when a contour survey was made as part of the site evaluation.

Both barrows have been robbed, mound 4 displaying a clear dishing in its top, whilst at the centre of where mound 5 stood was a square feature, 'grave 33', apparently the base of a robber pit. The mounds seem to have differed in their construction. The clearing of undergrowth around mound 4 revealed it to have an intermittent series of hollows on the north and east sides. Limited excavation to the south revealed feature *1811*, a large but shallow scoop. Together, these suggest that the mound had no ditch as such, but had been surrounded by a series of shallow quarry pits. In contrast, mound 5 produced no evidence for either a surrounding ditch or quarry pits. If Anglo-Saxon, they exhibit parallels to the barrows at Sutton Hoo. Here too, a variety in their construction can be seen, mound 1 having no apparent ditches whilst mound 5, like Snape mound 4, was surrounded by a series of smaller quarry pits (Carver 1992, 357).

The date of both Snape barrows is unclear, although the pottery from robber pit/'grave 33' in mound 5 is Anglo-Saxon. Similarly, no stratigraphic relationships could be observed between the mounds and surrounding flat cemetery. However, if mound 5 was indeed once 25m in diameter, and grave 33 represents its original centre, then it would have covered graves 31, 32 and 34. This would suggest a late, probably 7th-century, building of this barrow. A more likely alternative is that the mound was originally far more steeply banked and had slumped to this size, covering other graves in the process. The positioning of the burnt stone features, graves 44, 45 and 47 (especially), and mound 6, all indicate that they are later than mound 4, which they surround. If the barrow is Anglo-Saxon in construction, it seems to contradict Shephard (1979, 49) who has suggested that barrow burial began in flat-grave cemeteries in the middle and later 6th century AD with a scattering of ring-ditches, gradually supplanted by the more general employment of tumuli. A preferable alternative is that mound 4 is a surviving, possibly re-used, Bronze Age barrow. The question of the relationship between the barrows and surrounding cemetery will inevitably remain a thorny one as long as the dating evidence is so restricted.

Structural features

In common with a number of other Anglo-Saxon cemeteries, Snape produced evidence of structural features associated with graves. They can be divided into those found above and below ground. The most often quoted article in connection with such structures is Hogarth's short 1973 paper on the features discovered at St Peter's, Broadstairs (Kent). Since then, there have been several more cemeteries excavated containing a variety of features similar to the types discovered by Hogarth.

At Snape three inhumations produced evidence for post-holes associated with some form of surface structure. The clearest example was boat grave 47, which had a post-hole on both the north and south sides at the east end. Both were very shallow, only that to the south surviving beneath the surface planning level. The west end of the grave had no actual post-holes but the bulging grave sides to north and south suggest a matching arrangement, and that the grave originally had some four-posted structure above it. Indeed, this structure may have been more complex if these had represented only the main load-bearing posts. A similar arrangement appears to have been used over grave 148 at Morning Thorpe, Norfolk (Green *et al* 1987, 76–77).

Another structure, possibly four-posted, is suggested to have once existed over grave 2. In this case, the grave itself had a complex internal structure (see catalogue and below p. 241) but above ground, two thin clay deposits, *0358* and *0359* were preserved at the east end. These were planned and removed as part of surface cleaning of the site but their position directly adjacent to the south-east and north-east corners of this grave suggests that they once formed pads in the soil to support a structure.

The final example of a feature indicative of an above ground post was found centrally along the south side of grave 21 (Pl. XIII and p. 64). The feature was very clear and straight-edged, strongly suggesting that it contained a plank or post of some form. The lack of a larger hole suggests such a post was driven into the ground. Its disappearance before the next planning level reflects its shallow and vestigial nature; there was no sign of any similar arrangement to the north of the grave, but bearing in mind the fragmentary nature of this example, any matching arrangement may well have already been destroyed in the ploughsoil.

In themselves these three instances are unremarkable, but they demonstrate the presence of such features in yet another Anglo-Saxon cemetery, and the often fugitive nature of such remains. They force the recognition that many similar structures may have formerly existed both at Snape and in other cemeteries. If the wider use of such above-ground structures is appreciated, it also helps to explain the general lack of intercutting graves found in many Anglo-Saxon cemeteries.

The structure of the graves below the ground also proved varied. Structural features defined by the shape of the grave cut were seen in three instances. In graves 9 and 27 a step or shelf was found within the sand. In grave 9 this was at the east end, in the top of a band of ironpanned natural. In grave 27 the length of the grave was again reduced, at the west end, high up in the grave cut, to produce a narrow shelf. In grave 47 the effect was more of a sloping ledge on the grave north side, as though the grave pit had been dug deeper to the south to produce a trench into which to rest the logboat. A fourth example, running along the southern edge of grave 15 and most marked in the centre may have been caused accidentally by a partial collapse of the grave edge when being dug. However, given that several other cemeteries, notably St Peter's, Broadstairs, Kent, have also produced such ledges and shelves dug into chalk (Hogarth 1973, 111), these features may also have been deliberately constructed.

Three graves, 7, 14 and 37, had apparent 'pillows' of ironpanned sand, upon which the bodies' heads rested. A similar 'pillow' was reported in the chalk natural of a grave at Saffron Walden, Essex (Smith 1884, 314). Finally, grave 39 seemed to overlie a small feature with a fill of very fine light grey/white sand at the east end, noted at the time as almost ash-like. The feature does not seem to have been natural and its relative date is unclear. As the inhumation is directly above, its position is probably not coincidental. It could conceivably represent a deposit, perhaps of ash given the apparent emphasis on burnt matter in so many other graves.

The incorporation of graves in other features
In several cases it seems that there was a practice of digging graves within areas that were visible at the time as semi-silted hollows in the heathland surface. This was first seen in 1985 with the discovery of grave 17, apparently cut through an amorphous patch of light grey sand. Subsequently, two more amorphous patches were found to contain graves 36 and 44. The reasons for believing these patches to represent hollows are their very light silvery-grey fills and very fine sand, reminiscent of the Anglo-Saxon topsoil, although less pink in colour. Their imperceptible grading into the natural subsoil reflects their natural rather than artificial deposition. Similar, smaller, pockets of such sand — down to about 0.2m diameter — were found and removed in many places across the site when cleaning of the subsoil ensured that all graves had been identified. Grave 7 appears to have been cut through a low part of this subsoil but not a true hollow as in the cases of graves 44 and 36.

The use of a hollow in which to dig a grave is untypical but recalls the use of ditches being re-used for inhumations, for instance in Norfolk, graves 43, 44 and 47 in the ring-ditch to grave 40 at Spong Hill (Hills *et al* 1984, 12) and graves 38–40, 43 and 44 in ring-ditch *1021* at Harford Farm (Penn 2000), and with graves 1, 2, 4, 5 and 68 in a ?boundary ditch at Portway, Andover, Hants. (Cook and Dacre 1985, 13–16). The re-use of ring-ditches for burial may have been through association with whoever was buried in the central grave but in the case of hollows, there are no obvious relationships. Alternatively, using hollows may have involved less effort, a shallow grave cut being buried deeper by levelling off the surrounding area into the dip.

Grave depths
In the past there has been some discussion of grave depth as a possible indication of the occupant's status. The evidence from Snape would broadly suggest that the deeper the richer, but contradictory results have been found at different sites, for instance shallower graves being richer at Melbourn, Cambs. (Wilson 1956, 29). A more fundamental problem is that at Snape a formerly uneven ground surface has been levelled by modern agricultural activity. The depth of a grave as excavated need not, therefore, reflect its depth when originally dug, and so further discussion has little merit.

Burial containers
The most remarkable feature of the Snape inhumations is the number and variety of funerary structures or containers associated with the body. The principal difficulty in their interpretation is that they existed only as soil stains, the clarity of which was essential to understand their character. In the case of some, for instance the logboats, this is relatively straightforward. For the majority of others this is not the case. There are three fundamental difficulties in interpretation.

First, the nature of the staining was affected by soil conditions which could show great variety between even small areas of the site. Those graves dug into heavily ironpanned sand were generally the most difficult in which to see stains clearly. The logboat from grave 4 was an example of this, the ironpanned natural (both *in situ* and redeposited) making the isolation and recording of the stain difficult. Soil was also difficult to excavate at the east end of Area A due to the presence of tree roots from the adjacent garden which had disturbed and rapidly dried the sand.

Secondly, the original material from which the container was made was often difficult to determine, remaining only as a different soil colour. It was also clear that charcoal flecks within these stains need not be an indicator that the container was of wood, as several examples from Area B, for instance from graves 37 and 45, had such flecks but when the stain dried out proved to be large areas of textile weave. Consequently, the identification of the material represented by an organic is often extremely difficult to determine. On occasions, identifications may be proposed on interpretative bases, usually the excavators' acquired knowledge of the 'feel' of a stain. These impressions are difficult to relate in words; whilst the identification of organic stains by their colour and feel seems subjective, in many cases their accuracy has been proven. Less clear is whether the material was of, for instance, wood, textile or hide, and as will be seen this can have a fundamental affect on the interpretation of a burial container.

Thirdly, it was possible that in many graves the container had been distorted in the soil by post-depositional forces. This is reflected in the sections of many grave containers which show a wobbling line which would probably have been straight or curved originally, for example those in graves 3, 17 and even parts of the good boat stain from grave 47. However, these wobbling lines can (and in some cases certainly were) caused partially by even only minimal misalignment of sequential grave plans. Additionally, the stone-free sand is an excellent, mobile, packing material, quickly moulding itself around objects, not only allowing the degrading material to form a stain, but to represent its shape with reasonable accuracy and stability in the ground.

As a result, it has been possible to suggest the use of several forms of container. Of the forty inhumations excavated between 1985–91, twenty-eight (70%) had containers or structures of some form (not including those above the ground) leaving only eleven (30%) without. They can be divided into several types.

Coffins

Coffins have been the most widely recognised form of mortuary container in pagan Anglo-Saxon cemeteries. However, as such stains have normally been very fragmentary, and usually concentrated only on the grave floor, this identification is probably at least partially misplaced. The identification as coffins is natural. They are known as a container used for the disposal of the dead, with both a wide geographical distribution and a currency throughout the Anglo-Saxon period and up to the modern day. Stains interpreted as those of coffins have been seen in several Anglo-Saxon cemeteries, for instance at Spong Hill, Norfolk (Hills et al 1984), in graves 32, 46 and 57. Their recognition compared to other container types may well have been biased in reports, being archaeologically more recoverable due to the better survival of wooden planks as stains, especially given the enforcedly speedy excavation of many cemeteries in the past. However, the use of wooden elements such as planks (as used to construct the chamber in grave 31 at Spong Hill; Hills 1977, Hills et al 1984) should not lead to an automatic interpretation of a coffin having been used. In only a few cases can it be proven conclusively that the stains observed are those of a coffin, and recent excavations in the churchyard of St Lawrence Jewry, Guildhall, London, have shown that even in the 11th century coffins as we might think of them were not being used, but that planks (here surviving through waterlogging), could consist of loosely-pegged trays, boards under or over the body, or even two planks resting against one another like a pitched 'roof' (Bateman 1997, 116–117). Although these examples are from a Christian context, it serves as a warning that burial containers in the pagan Anglo-Saxon period may also have taken a number of forms. At Snape, evidence for a coffin was particularly strong in only one instance, grave 17. Here, a regular rectangular shape with straight sides was formed of a dark organic stain. There was no evidence that there had ever been a lid, and in common with the suggestion often made for other Anglo-Saxon coffins, a lack of metal fittings suggests that it was held together by wooden pegs. A number of other organic containers were found which might be identified as coffins, in graves 6, 10, 14, 15, 25, 43 and 45. All had reasonably straight edges but the rounded corners of most, very clear in a number of cases, suggest that they may have more in common with other forms of organic container such as those of textile (see below).

Boats

The use of boats for burial was previously known only from the ship graves at Sutton Hoo and Snape, although the practice was more widespread abroad (Müller-Wille 1970; Schönbäck 1983). The discovery of two organic stains consistent in shape and size with dugout-type logboats, used as burial containers in graves 4 and 47, was therefore important in showing the variety of objects used as funerary structures. This was reinforced when analysis of the container used in grave 3 suggested that a part, perhaps half, of a boat may have been used. The container was of heavily charred oak heartwood (as used for the boat from grave 47), with a 'double skin' visible in several stretches, suggesting burning on both sides of the object. During excavation it was thought to be a coffin, possibly made from a hollowed-out tree trunk. Reconstruction from the grave plans and sections showed the sloping west end and the open east end, the curved sides, and especially the rounded bottom of the object, not unlike those seen in the boats from graves 4 and 47 (Figs 15 and 76). There is evidence for the incorporation of bits of boats in graves in later Anglo-Saxon England (Rodwell 1993; Carver 1990b, 117–9) and, at an earlier period, abroad at Slusegård (Crumlin-Pedersen 1991, 249). The major objection to interpreting the grave 3 container as part of a boat would seem to be the essentially parallel-sided shape of the stain and the blunt western end. If the bow tip had been removed (a possibility given the stain suggested to be a piece of bow seen in grave 10; see below, pp. 242–3), this might have caused a loss of rigidity to the structure, allowing the east end to open out and attain the flat, blunt, more rectangular shape seen. Alternatively, if it were a boat made from a hollowed-out log, there is no reason for it not to have had a blunt end, like a punt. It would be dangerous to link this container with the suggested bow tip found in grave 10, but it is of interest that these two graves and boat grave 4 should be clustered so closely together, possibly implying some form of grouping. The implications and use of boat burial are discussed in more detail in Chapter 7.

Biers

The use of biers on which to carry bodies is well known, but the distinction between a bier and other forms of funerary structure is more difficult to determine from organic soil stains alone. The identification of a bier at Snape has therefore been made tentatively in only one instance, grave 21, where a rectangular-shaped organic layer beneath the body was found, perhaps associated with a single vertical edge. The use of the term is here understood to mean some form of rigid structure upon which the body was lain. Rowena Gale points out that the mixture of charred roundwood of hazel, willow/poplar and oak may support this suggestion, perhaps deriving from a burnt wicker hurdle. The charcoal is also atypical, as the first three *genera* are almost totally absent from other graves. The only other possible bier might have been from grave 8 where the body lay on a layer of dark staining and charred oak which had no vertical edges.

Textile linings and layers

In four cases, the organic staining seen in many graves was proven to consist of textile, when hot weather dried out the stain and lengths of woven thread appeared. This was seen most clearly in grave 37 where large areas of textile were exposed (p. 208). That the whole of these stains were of textile, rather than just the base in the area of the body stain, is suggested by the threads seen in the upper stain in grave 45, and that used draped, perhaps over the gunwhale, into the logboat in grave 47. The presence of entire linings of textile (Pls XVII–XIX and LVI) might also help to explain why the stains encountered in many graves were so thin and could disappear and reappear, as in grave 32, or could be shown to have such a well-rounded bottom, as in grave 2. Nevertheless, it is clear that making positive identifications of the nature of an organic from only a brown soil stain is difficult and another possibility for the material underlying the stains is animal hide. In two cases (graves 20 and 38) the stains were described by the excavators as having the body stain-like greasy 'feel' and look of degraded leather. Their use might be supported by the use of animal hides in cemeteries elsewhere, for instance in graves 1 and 9 at Great Chesterford, Essex. Here it was suggested that hide may still have been attached to horn cores that were found in the graves (Serjeantson 1994, 66–67).[2] Similarly, bear claws in some of the Spong Hill cremations suggest the incorporation of bearskins in the pyre assemblage (Bond 1994, 134).

The use of textile (or hide) rather than wood is helpful in explaining the form of many container stains in those graves with oval shapes, curves, folds and double lines. Thus, the stain at first thought to represent a slumped coffin lid in grave 45 was revealed by surviving threads to have been textile. Similarly, the odd line at the west end of grave 10 could have been one end of a textile length stretched around the grave; the pointed shape of the stain in the upper levels of grave 37 might have been a fold and the curved base associated with post-holes in grave 2 suggests some form of structure holding a lining together. The way in which the textiles may have been incorporated as a container is still not clear, as some rigidity would have been necessary for backfill not to have collapsed a lining. It is possible that other organic incorporations, for instance withies, may have acted as stiffeners, or perhaps more likely, textiles were leaned up against a packing of backfill as was demonstrated in graves 32 and 47 (see below). Since many stains were relatively shallow in depth, it need not have been difficult to create a textile lining. This may also account for many sections which show the organic stain sloping down into the grave (for instance graves 6 and 10; Figs 17 and 24). If post-depositional forces were to act in any way, it is more likely that a rigid structure like a coffin would (especially if lidded) collapse inwards, or if unlidded retain straight edges through backfill packing it on either side. Exactly such an inward collapse trajectory was seen in the staining of the proposed coffin in grave 17 (Fig. 38).

The use of textile linings seems directly related to the use of organic underlayers to several bodies. In a number of cases, for instance grave 19, it is unclear whether the organic should be seen as a 'liner' or 'layer' having a

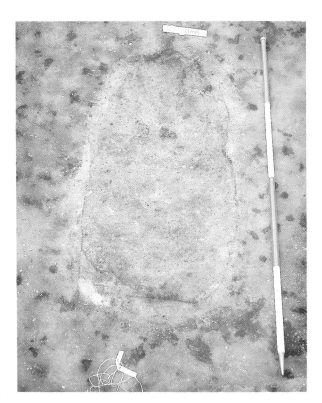

Plate LVI Grave 37, textile lining seen as organic stain lines in the upper fill

vertical edge on one side of the grave only. Organic stains beneath bodies were seen in ten graves (9, 11, 13, 16, 28, 31, 34, 36, 38 and 40) or 25% of the total number of inhumations excavated. The fact that the upper parts of an organic stain might easily be lost is perhaps best seen in grave 32 where only two stretches of stain were seen in the upper spits. Had these not survived, the organic seen would have been interpreted as only an underlayer to the body.

The widespread use of these additions to the internal grave structure does not seem to relate to sex, age or phases of the site's use. Indeed, whilst only graves generally 'poor' in terms of grave-goods do not have organic body containers/layers, there are exceptions. For instance, grave 13 was unaccompanied yet had an underlayer, whilst grave 5 was furnished with a respectable assemblage of grave-goods but had no organic stain.

Discussion

On the evidence from Snape it might be that the general interpretation, that dark stains in Anglo-Saxon inhumation graves are the remains of coffins, has been overstated. Instead, linings and underlayers of textile or hide may once have been far more common than the published material suggests. The soil conditions of Snape have been principally responsible for their survival and other East Anglian sites with similarly sandy conditions have also recently begun to produce such stains, for instance Harford Farm, Norfolk (Penn 2000) and the Boss Hall and Buttermarket sites, Ipswich (Scull forthcoming). An older excavation at Little Eriswell, Suffolk also seems to have had such remains, grave 33 being noted as having 'heavy fabrics over the entire body' (Hutchinson 1966, 12).

Grave fill and inclusions

Backfill

As the graves from Snape were excavated in shallow spits and regularly planned, it was possible to note aspects of the fill in detail. Often, the backfill was a patchy mix of grey topsoil and bright orange natural sand, but in several graves it was distinctly separated when redeposited, showing that the topsoil and natural had been piled up independently, probably one heap on either side of the cut. To have remained unmixed when redeposited suggests the involvement of at least two people backfilling the grave at the same time. This process was observed in graves 2, 6 and 16, whilst boat grave 4 perhaps had three people backfilling, as the grave centre was filled with grey topsoil throughout, and each end was of orange natural. In grave 11, the topsoil was clearly backfilled first and the orange natural last, again suggesting two distinct heaps for the gravedigger's spoil. In other graves, for instance grave 45, distinct tip lines were observed, mixing within the fill. Graves 37 and 43 had at their surface distinct ovals of grey sand within redeposited natural, directly above the body position. Neither were recuts and they seem to reflect a subsequent slumping of grey topsoil further into the grave fill (Fig. 70).

Finally, two graves produced evidence of spoil being used in the arrangement of structures within the grave. Grave 47 had a tripartite division of fill extending into the boat stain with grey topsoil fill at the centre and yellow-brown redeposited natural on either side. This is best explained as redeposited natural sand being used in the lower levels to pack the boat into its cut. This packing may have been maintained above the gunwhale level where one or possibly two pieces of textile (stains *1826* and *1827*) appear to have been draped over the sand and into the boat at the south-east corner (Figs 75 and 76). Grey topsoil may then have been backfilled straight into the gap at the centre when the grave was filled in. A second case of sand packing a cut was in grave 32. Here grey topsoil (deeper and cleaner than simple trampled earth) appears to have been used at the base for the organic layer's edges to be laid on. As excavated topsoil would have been at the bottom of a single spoil heap, two separate heaps may again be indicated.

Trampled sand was only noted at the bases of graves 9 and 40. Three graves, 4, 7 and 47, produced rectilinear patches of dark sand which suggested that turves were incorporated into the backfill.

Organics

The grave fills produced many instances of organic inclusions, stressing the possible involvement of a far wider range of ritual attributes to inhumation burial than simply the deposition of a body and grave-goods. In many cases all that could be distinguished as 'organic' were patches of sand with a 'sticky' texture, usually retaining moisture longer. Some were possibly originally of wood and there were numerous instances of graves with odd small charcoal flecks. There may well have been other types of inclusions but the acidic sand of the site meant that any animal/meat joint offerings, wood or textile would all have degraded into a very similar-looking sand. Indeed, a few graves had small lumps akin to body stain suggesting meat buried with the body but only in grave 47

was the shape of such a patch clear enough to warrant such an identification (Pl. XXV). One other instance of a possible food offering came from grave 32 where a rodent-nibbled plum stone was preserved by mineral salts. A parallel to this is found in the provision of hazel nuts from a grave at Burwell, Cambs. (Lethbridge 1926, 73).

Three graves produced more certain evidence for the incorporation of vegetation. In grave 47 a random mass of stems and leaves were seen covering iron clamp *Ci*. Additionally, all three hoops of bucket *F* and the boss of shield *A* were encrusted with pinnae (leaflets) of bracken (*Pteridium aquilinum* (L.). The large quantities of the latter especially, suggest their deliberate inclusion as some form of covering. Similarly, shield *D* in grave 3 and shield *D* and belt buckle *E* in grave 32 produced·evidence for similar coverings of vegetation. A twig on brooch *C* in grave 8 may represent the same practice.

Coverings of vegetation have been seen in other Anglo-Saxon cemeteries, for instance grave 19 Sewerby, E. Yorks. (Hirst 1985, 31); at Mucking, Essex (Jones and Jones 1975, 175); probably from a grave at Warren Hill, Mildenhall, Suffolk (Prigg 1888, 59); at the Buttermarket, Ipswich (K. Wade pers. comm.); and in grave 18 Swaffham Paddocks, Norfolk, where the impression of a bracken leaf was preserved on the shield boss (Hills and Wade-Martins 1976, 9 and pl. VIII). The practice therefore seems to have had a wide distribution. Interpretations of its significance should perhaps be restricted due to the lack of detailed knowledge of the plant species often involved. Given the use of wood in many graves from Snape, a ritualistic interpretation is possible and the observations of Penelope Walton Rogers regarding the alkanet-like colourant in six graves (p. 214) are of interest here. She notes the possibility that alkannin-containing plants had been deliberately placed on the bodies in some graves, and comments that the Romanesque shrine of 3rd-century Saint Maurus, in Bohemia, contained silks, resins and plant remains including laurel leaves (a Christian symbol of everlasting life) and a root of dyers' alkanet *A. tinctoria* (Samhylová 1993). Whilst the reason for placing the root in the shrine is not known, its deliberate inclusion suggests that alkanet may have had a symbolic importance in the medieval world. Moreover, it emphasises the likely symbolic and certainly deliberate nature of the other organic inclusions noted.

Objects

A few inhumations contained objects within their fill which were not amongst the usual run of Anglo-Saxon grave-goods. Whether their inclusion was deliberate in all cases is unclear.

Grave 20 contained a fragment of a granite saddle quern, whilst grave 47 contained a large quartzite stone with some bruising, possibly a maul. Their presence may well be accidental; they were both found in the upper fill of the graves, the most likely position for objects redeposited from the topsoil layer, and they had no other apparent association with these graves.

A more certain case of a deliberate inclusion was found in grave 10. Here, a soil stain directly comparable to those of the body containers in other graves, appeared halfway down the fill (Pl. XII and Fig. 23 II). A small fragment of charred wood was found within the outline of the stain but could not be identified. The stain had a well-defined beak shape at its western end, widening out with a loss of definition to a pointed 'tail' at the east. It was clearly once an object of some sort and continued to the next planning level. Its positioning seems to have been deliberate, the 'beak' being placed directly over the head of the body with the rest of the stain covering the area of the torso and part of the legs.

The object is difficult to interpret. Its pointed, beak-like shape is most obviously paralleled in the bow shape of the Snape and especially Slusegård boats (see Chapter 5 section II, pp. 199–200). Whilst this example was fragmentary, its shape was so clear and distinctive that such an identification is very attractive. The burial of bits of boats is known from Slusegård and has already been suggested as being represented at Snape by the container in grave 3. Given the practice of cutting up boats to use in graves, it seems most likely that the piece in grave 10 was from a genuine one. However, as its incorporation in the grave was not for containing the body it might, arguably, not have mattered whether the object was real, or merely symbolic. Logically, such an interpretation lends weight to there having been a wider meaning for the two definite and one suggested logboat burials other than simply their re-use as coffins (see further Chapter 7 section II, pp. 262–4). Finally, the arrangement of the piece above the body and more specifically, the bow being above the head, corresponds closely to the placing of charred wood branches above bodies in other graves and implies that this too is related to a burial rite.

Charred wood
Incorporating material by Rowena Gale
A striking feature of the Snape inhumations is the inclusion of charred wood, both in terms of size (grave 9, piece i; 1.2m long) and quantity (grave 27, with twenty-four lumps). Examination demonstrated that the pieces were indeed of charcoal rather than the ferrimanganiferous replacement of wood (Fryer and Murphy 1992). Species identified include oak (*Quercus*), gorse (*Ulex*), willow/poplar (*Salix/Populus*), hazel (*Corylus*) and blackthorn/cherry (*Prunus*). The frequent incorporation of charcoal was such that an amorphous area with charred fragments seen in Area B has been tentatively interpreted as a grave (35). Being inert, charcoal is unaffected by different soil conditions and its inclusion in pieces is well known from many other Anglo-Saxon cemeteries. However, Snape seems to differ from most other cemeteries through the quantity of material found in many graves.

In all, thirty-three (82.5%) of the forty inhumation graves excavated 1985–92 contained charred wood of some description, ranging from small flecks to large burnt timbers. A few pieces were preserved as no more than dense black soil stains although they obviously derived from burnt wood, often incorporating small charcoal flecks. In the majority of cases there were remains with a clear structure. Together, the pieces can be broadly categorised as flecks (in twelve cases: 30% of all graves), lumps and smears of various sizes (fifteen graves; 37.5%), and larger pieces with structure (six graves; 15%). Only seven graves had no burnt wood inclusions.

The inclusion of larger pieces in graves was clearly deliberate and ranged from single pieces to the extremes seen in graves 9 and 27. In several instances the wood

Plate LVII Knot in charred wood from grave 9

structure remained in such excellent condition that the grain and knots could be seen (Pl. LVII). These examples, and occasionally the charcoal identifications including softwood, suggest that most lumps were branches rather than planks or shaped wood. At first sight it would seem that the presence of charred wood inclusions was simply accidental, perhaps the result of vegetation clearance on the cemetery site. However, closer observation demonstrated that the larger pieces especially, were carefully positioned, for instance forming a covering layer above the body in grave 9. Likewise, in graves 8 and 39 although the pieces were small, like the 'bow' stain in grave 10, they were placed directly over the head. In grave 17 the three pieces flanked the coffin, level with the torso, as did the piece in grave 20. Similarly, in grave 21 the body was flanked all along its length by mixed charcoal pieces. The incorporation of smaller smears and lumps tended to be in the upper levels of grave fills and with fewer indications of deliberate positioning. The charcoal flecks seen in many varied even more greatly between both the upper and lower levels of the grave fill; in several cases, for instance graves 32, 36 and 45, they were caught up with the textile containers. As there are examples of both larger and smaller lumps, it is difficult to be clear where deliberate deposition ends and chance inclusion begins. The presence of charcoal in so many graves suggests that such incorporations were made throughout the life of the cemetery, reducing the chance of these having been accidental incorporations residing in the topsoil as a result of, for instance, slash and burn clearance of the cemetery site.

Perhaps the most obvious relationship with the burnt wood is to the 'burnt stone features' which contained largely gorse and oak charcoal and which, like the graves, included many oak stems. Whatever the use of these burnt stone features, their Anglo-Saxon date means they could have been the easiest source for such large pieces of charred wood, or that they were used to burn branches for inclusion. If there is a relationship, the absence of gorse fragments in the graves compared to those in the burnt stone features would seem to be a consequence of larger wood pieces being selected for burial.

Clearly, the incorporation of wood was considered necessary or significant in many burials and the overwhelming presence of so many pieces suggests that their being charred was an important element. The presence of burnt material in Anglo-Saxon inhumations elsewhere has been remarked upon by several scholars who have interpreted its presence in various ways. Meaney suggested an association with cremation ritual which served 'to release the spirit of the dead' (1964, 17) whilst Salin put forward several explanations including charcoal being brought from the family fire to indicate an association between the living and the dead (1952, 206–7). For Wilson, the use of charcoal 'might represent the symbolic purification of the grave' (1992, 126). Two observations may be made. First, the larger pieces were clearly carefully positioned, over or around the body. The apparent derivation of the wood from branches rather than artefacts implies a ritual use and seems to emphasise the pieces as coming from the wild tree rather than, for instance, being spare planks. Secondly, most accounts of other cemeteries speak only of charcoal and do not specify the actual wood species involved. This is, potentially, a crucial omission since the use of charred wood perhaps finds a parallel in the spreading of vegetation in graves which, as has been seen, may have had specific symbolic connotations according to the species. The identification of most of the charred pieces as oak, especially the larger pieces, may therefore be significant.

Oak has had many mystical and religious connotations (Cooper 1978) and it may be that it was considered particularly apt for use in funerary rituals. Oak is known to have had ritual associations with Donar, the Germanic predecessor to Thor, who had strong associations with forest groves and especially oak woods (Todd 1987, 164–5). Indeed, if we are to believe Adam of Bremen, a 'guardian' tree, once familiar in Germanic and Scandinavian areas, was next to the great heathen temple at Uppsala. Such trees echoed Yggdrasill, the World Tree described by the late 12th-century author Snorri Sturluson, which formed a universal link between mankind, the dead and the gods (Davidson 1964, 191). The difficulty of using such later material should warn us against making too direct a link between these recorded beliefs and the material from Snape. Nevertheless, it is an analogy requiring careful thought; the long-lived maintenance of such associations can be seen in the pagan Prussians still celebrating their thunder god Perkuno — linked with Latin *quercus* (oak) — with a fire and images of gods placed in a holy oak, as late as the 16th century (Davidson 1964, 87). Similarly, the use is known of partially charred wood coffins in the later Anglo-Saxon period, apparently having symbolic associations with eternity (Rodwell 1981, 150). A direct parallel for these associations could be the charred ?boat in grave 3. Just as the use of boat burial might imply adherence to a particular deity (pp. 262–3), such an interpretation could be possible for those graves using branches of charred oak, especially when the pieces had been carefully arranged in the ground as seen in grave 9. The deliberate covering of the body with charred wood might, therefore, be a direct analogy for the deceased's protection by a particular deity symbolised by the wood. In connection with this, it may be no coincidence that the only burial container to be found charred, the ?boat in grave 3, was made of oak.

Burnt flints

Within the fill of several graves (and also ring-ditches and other features) were inclusions of burnt flint.

Unfortunately, their presence and frequency was not fully recorded until the later years of the excavation as they were initially considered to be residual within the topsoil, deriving probably from heathland fires. Following the discovery of the burnt stone features, their presence is perhaps better explained, like the charred wood inclusions, as deriving from such features. Alternatively, they may represent material burnt on the topsoil, for instance the sites of cremation pyres.

Their presence was recorded in only seven graves, of which one, grave 46, cut burnt stone feature *1775*, so it was impossible to distinguish between flint that might have been deliberately rather than accidentally included. There were many more graves which contained small fragments that were simply not recorded.

The inclusion of the pieces can be seen as either deliberate or accidental; the latter is most likely but the mass of material (sixty-two pieces, or 0.22kg) from grave 27 also makes it possible that these could have been consciously deposited. The flints are probably best seen as an adjunct to charred wood since, where recorded, they always occurred in graves containing elements of burnt wood.

Pottery scatters

Eight graves contained sherds. In the case of grave 47, sherds found in the uppermost fill probably represent a plough-damaged cremation, perhaps buried at the same time as the inhumation, as in grave 17, or inserted later into the top of, or beside, the grave. If these inclusions were made accidentally, it implies a scattering of many vessels or their fragments across the Anglo-Saxon topsoil, some of which became incorporated into graves. For instance, the pottery and bone fragments which made up grave 80 seem to have been smashed and subsequently backfilled within grave 5. Likewise, a loose scattering of fragments was seen in mixed backfill in grave 25. Other examples of pottery deriving from individual vessels but scattered across the topsoil seem to be either the remains of plough-damaged cremations, or to relate to the cremation pyre discussed below (section III, pp. 252–5). However, it is also clear that more structured deposits of pottery were made.

Analysis by Shirley Carnegie of all the sherds from Snape revealed several instances of matching or joining fragments, deriving from different features (Fig. 147). In grave 4, pottery sealed in the fill derived from vessel *1152*, sherds of which were found in a scatter to the south of Area A and sealed within the remains of urn *0073* in grave 78. Similarly, grave 6 produced pot A (*0462*), complete except for a chip out of the rim. The missing fragment was found some 20m away at the opposite corner of the area, mixed with sherds from the shattered urn *1597* of grave 90. Pot *1154* was made up of sherds that derived from the lens of topsoil sealed within grave 10, in the 'cremation pyre' scatter on the southern edge of Area A and from directly above grave 22. Finally, in the scatters of pottery from the topsoil, sherd *0206* from the south-west corner of Area A came from the same vessel, *1594*, as sherds *0347* and *0348* some 17m away, in the south-east corner of the area.

If all these sherds were accidental inclusions, their final resting places provide impressive evidence of the mobility of sherds across the original Anglo-Saxon ground surface during the cemetery's use. The alternative is that some represent deliberate depositions of pottery, of

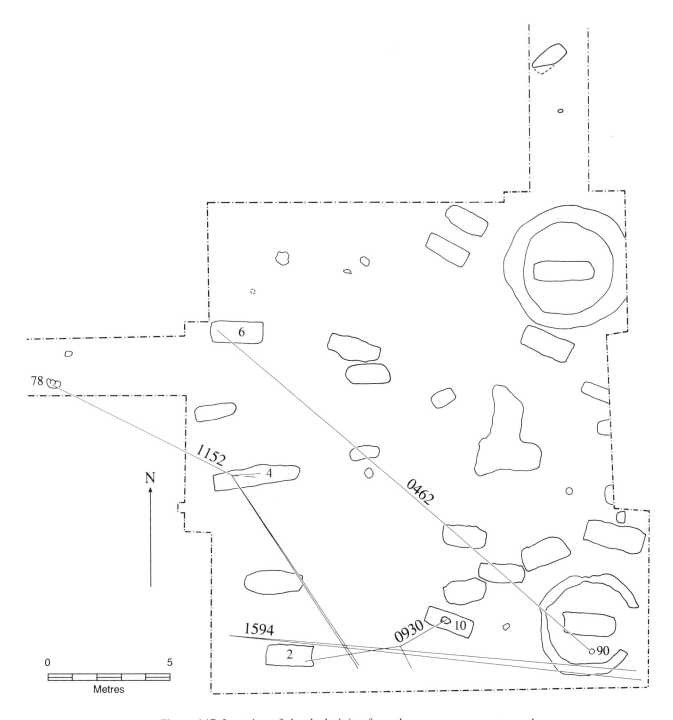

Figure 147 Location of sherds deriving from the same component vessel

which the missing piece from pot *A* in grave 6 seems a good example.

More compelling evidence for the deliberate deposition of sherds comes from other graves. For instance, in grave 5 the remains of vessel *0677* were all found in the lower levels of the grave in a dense cluster directly over the pelvic area, apparently deliberately placed. Similarly in grave 6 the large sherd, *E*, lay directly above the chest of the body, just east of the shield boss. Finally, in boat grave 47, separate from the probable cremation urn already described, two sherds were found in the feet area at the bottom of the boat, associated with a mass of other grave-goods, possibly once contained in a box. One had been converted from the wall of a pot into a ?spindle whorl and the other was the base and footring of a Roman wheel-turned pot subsequently broken and deliberately shaped. It is tempting to see the latter

especially as a 'high-class' sherd inclusion, concomitant with the status of the grave.

The presence of these sherd depositions raises two questions. First, what is the reason for the inclusion of sherds linked with pottery found elsewhere on the site? Second, and more generally, why was pottery deposited in graves?

The demonstrable cross-linking of sherds invites explanation beyond pottery always being incorporated in grave fills accidentally. Inclusions of pottery have been noticed in other Anglo-Saxon cemeteries, most notably at Wakerley, Northants., where the deliberate deposition of sherds was seen in forty-one of eighty-five inhumations. Here, in two cases, sherds from the same vessel were found in different graves (Pearson 1988–89, 160). At Sewerby, E. Yorks., five graves contained Anglo-Saxon sherds and burnt flints. Hirst cites Johnson's (1912) discussion in which he saw these as representing fire (flints) and water (the vessel) enabling the deceased the means of perpetuating life. In considering the fifty-seven inhumations at Spong Hill, Hills *et al* (1984, 7) have suggested that some sherds could have been deliberately included, perhaps being deliberately broken as a 'ritual killing' of pots. The Snape material does not contradict either of these views and could be similarly interpreted. More impressive though, is the similarity with the pottery at Wakerley, which suggests that individual sherds could take on a proactive meaning. As at Wakerley, the appearance of cross-linked pottery, sometimes over large distances, suggests a relationship between the individuals in these graves, perhaps coming from the same family (Pearson 1988–89, 160). The conclusion must be that loose sherds need not be simply accidental inclusions in graves, although only in certain cases can deliberate deposition be demonstrated.

Cremated bone
Cremated bone was found within the fill of seven inhumations. Its incorporation appears to be the result of three possibilities; accidental inclusion, the redeposition of a disturbed cremation, and deliberate inclusion. Although distinguishing which is represented is difficult, it is suggested that all three can be seen at Snape.

Accidental inclusion is the easiest option for interpretation. Since bone collection from pyres is known to have been poor at times (McKinley 1994, 85), the topsoil may have had much loose bone that could be incorporated into the backfill of graves by chance. This might explain the odd bone fragments in graves 6 and 32, the amorphous spread in grave 12, and the loose scatter of bone concentrated in a distinct lens of redeposited topsoil in grave 12 (intriguingly, once again found over the position of the head in the grave).

Slightly more difficult is when to call the material a redeposited cremation, because the bone weights can be quite small. This seems the most likely explanation for the material found in grave 5, an inhumation. Although only 19g of bone was recovered, this seems to have belonged to pot *0318* (recovered as 118 sherds) along with two burnt objects (grave 80). Had they been seen on the surface, they would have been interpreted as a truncated cremation and there seems no reason to alter this view simply because they were contained in the fill of a grave. The association with pot *0318* and the burnt objects cannot be proven but seems reasonable, not least given the shattered nature of the vessel.

Altogether more difficult to prove is the presence of a deliberate inclusion, yet it is suggested that this is represented by the material from grave 11. Here, a mass of bone (60.5g) and a few burnt objects (grave 99, a cremation) were sealed in the fill across the whole area of the grave but at only a single level. The amount of bone is still far short of the average to be expected from an intact cremation (p. 227) which suggests that this is not the bone of an entire cremated individual. However, it is difficult to see the bone as an accidental inclusion. It was found in one horizon, spread over the whole area of the grave, yet the fragments were at a single, even, level, with a height difference of no more than 50mm. Had the bone been the result of accidental incorporation, or the redeposition of a smashed cremation (which must have been unurned as no

pottery was found in the grave fill), a more widely-spaced distribution within the grave backfill might be expected as was found with the cremation (grave 80) in grave 5 and the pottery in grave 25. The flat level of the bone instead suggests both an even backfilling of the grave and a deliberate scattering of bone at what would probably have been originally mid-depth, if the height of the topsoil is added. This interpretation has two points commending it. First, the incorporation of cremated individuals, albeit urned, has been seen in other inhumations like grave 17, hinting that at least a part of a cremated individual's bones might be saved for burial later, perhaps with the inhumation of a loved one. Second, this scattering is perhaps analogous to the coverings of wood or objects seen in other graves.

Orientation
There has been much discussion over the years about the possible implications of grave orientation for understanding burial ritual and cemetery analysis. It is felt here that the difficulties associated with using grave orientation makes it of only limited application, and all the more so at Snape where the sample of graves is relatively small. A brief survey and orientation chart (Fig. 148) is given in the interests of consistency with other Anglo-Saxon cemetery reports. At the outset it is perhaps best to distinguish between orientation, that is, positions of the solar arc, and alignments which can relate to more general associations in the direction of graves.

Orientation has been argued by some as relating to the ethnic origins of the person buried (Faull 1977) and, by relating it to the solar arc, even to the time of year that the grave was dug (Hawkes 1976). Various objections have been found to such approaches and one might add that if the exact orientations suggested as necessary were important, the position of the body itself rather than the grave might be the crucial factor. In practice, the body, its container (if any) and the grave cut frequently all differ in orientation. A more fundamental objection is that, in general, grave cuts from Anglo-Saxon cemeteries are irregular, making a measurement of their exact orientation impossible.

Nevertheless, it is evident that orientation had some importance, as most Anglo-Saxon cemeteries have bodies buried either east-west or north-south rather than at all angles of the compass. Such considerations would seem to be present in most East Anglian cemeteries where east-west graves are almost universal. Snape has only east-west graves with the exception of possible grave 30, unexcavated, seen in trial trench VI. Similarly all east-west are the far larger samples of graves from Westgarth Gardens, Suffolk (West 1988), and Bergh Apton, Spong Hill, Morning Thorpe and Harford Farm, all Norfolk (Green and Rogerson 1978; Hills *et al* 1984; Green *et al* 1987; Penn 2000). It would seem to be of little relevance to try comparing the detail of such bearings (West 1988, 7–8) as the general range is consistent.

Of the forty graves with sufficient remains to determine, twenty-seven (67.5%) had their heads at the west end and five (12.5%) to the east; a further eight burials (20%) left no trace. Such a preponderance of west-east burials is consistent with the East Anglian examples cited above and suggests the perception of a 'usual' direction in which to lay out the dead.

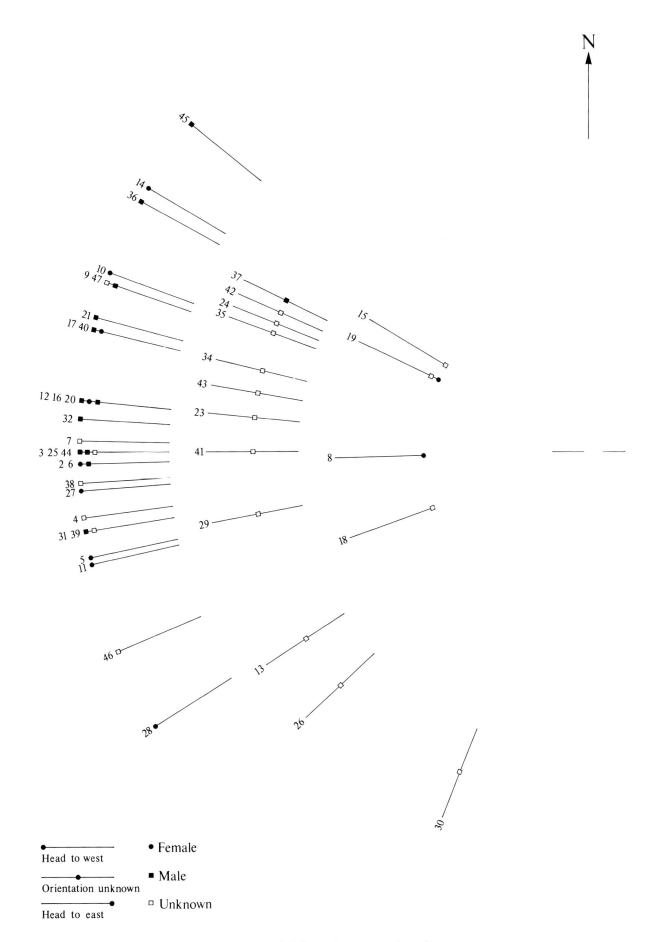

Figure 148 Inhumation grave orientations

Alignments

The role of alignments in influencing the orientation of grave cuts is far clearer. Both Rahtz (1978) and Rodwell (1981, 132) have pointed out the influence that topographical features often had in determining the alignment of a grave and at times 'deflecting' them from the desired direction. Instances of this from Snape are arguably graves 18 and 21 affected by the ring-ditch around grave 20 and perhaps graves 45 and 47 relative to mound 4. The suggestion made for Norton, Cleveland, that a possibly Bronze Age mound influenced the orientation of surrounding inhumations on lines radiating from a central point (Sherlock and Welch 1992, 15) cannot unfortunately be made for Snape. There are no apparently sequential topographical foci to influence possible groups of graves sharing alignments and the dating of the grave-goods is not considered accurate enough to confirm any possible phasing. The influence of the presumed prehistoric barrows in both attracting Anglo-Saxon burials and influencing clustering has, though, already been noted (above, pp. 236–8). The orientation of graves can, arguably, be seen most profitably as relating to the topography of the site than in any detailed discussion of their relationship to the solar arc.

Body positions

The nature of the acid sand meant that bone from all inhumations had been destroyed, except small fragments mineralised by contact with grave-goods and, exceptionally, a few tiny pieces in grave 12. This has made the detailed appraisal of body positions difficult. In eleven cases either only the head or no body stain at all survived; in the remaining twenty-nine inhumation graves excavated, the thirty bodies gave some indication of the way in which they had been laid out.

There are three main types of position represented: supine extended (eight cases); supine extended with feet crossed (six cases), and flexed (thirteen cases). Other variations were present, notably the sprawled upper body from the double burial in grave 19 and the prone burial in grave 44. A tightly flexed, possibly crouched, burial was seen in grave 39. As Table 10 makes clear, there are no real preferential trends for body positions; flexed burial is nominally more popular, especially in female burials, being selected in thirteen cases, but if supine extended, with and without legs crossed are counted together, they occur in fourteen cases, balancing up the numbers. The positions are all quite consistent with Anglo-Saxon inhumations in general, for instance Faull's study of 5,300 examples (1977, 5) and correspond to the available evidence for other East Anglian cemeteries. Of more interest are the exceptions to these rules, from graves 19, 39, and 44.

	Male	Female	Unknown	Total
Flexed	3	6	4	13
Extended	3	3	2	8
Extended, feet crossed	4	1	1	6
Other	-	-	3	3
Blank/head only	2	1	8	11
Total	12	11	18	41

Table 10 Body positions by sex

Grave 39

The body in grave 39 is the most difficult to discuss because it was so unclear and badly preserved when excavated (see catalogue). The body was only tentatively identified, its stain merging with the organic layer it rested on or was wrapped in. If interpreted correctly, then the body seems to have been in a crouched position most similar to prehistoric and Roman burials. The absence of grave-goods and the lack of any obvious association with other graves or features makes this inhumation undatable, although the charred wood stain above the head perhaps indicates that it was Anglo-Saxon. This grave is something of a curiosity, perhaps reflecting insular burial practices although also finding parallels in the tightly positioned post-Roman burial from grave 1188 Poundbury, Dorset and graves 26 and 32 Little Eriswell, Suffolk (Farwell and Molleson 1993, 83; Hutchinson 1966).

Grave 19

In grave 19, a body with no grave-goods except possibly a small iron buckle, was left in a sprawled position directly above a normally-furnished female inhumation burial (Pl. LVIII). The above-average size of the cut indicates that two burials were envisaged when the grave was first dug, but the manner of the deposit is in stark contrast to the double burials known in other East Anglian cemeteries, especially in the Cambridgeshire area, for instance Edix Hill, Barrington (Malim and Hines 1998). Here, grave cuts are made wide enough for both bodies to be laid out side by side on the grave floor, in the manner of single inhumation burials. The upper body from the Snape grave, by contrast, rested in an uncentral position, lying against the north-eastern corner of the grave. This, and the lack of grave-goods, raises the possibility that the body may be categorised a 'deviant' burial (Geake 1992), although the absence of skeletal remains for information on the age, sex and especially cause of death is unfortunate. An obvious parallel for this double burial is that of the burials in graves 41/49 at Sewerby, E. Yorks. Here, a middle-aged woman was found buried face down in a contorted position and was suggested to have been buried alive, above the body of a young female in a well-furnished grave. Other parallels to this type of burial exist, for instance grave H3 at Finglesham, Kent (Chadwick 1958, 25), and Cheesecake Hill, Driffield, Yorks. (Meaney 1964, 285). Further examples are enumerated by Hirst (1985, 41) but most are of less certain application in deriving from antiquarian or poorly recorded excavations, often with stratigraphic uncertainties about the relationship between upper and lower bodies. The burials in grave 19 at Snape are clearly contemporary, as seems also to have been the case at Sewerby (Hirst 1985, 39). Double burials of this type are self-evidently unusual, and the placement of the upper body with less apparent care and often few or no grave-goods seems characteristic. Their interpretation has always been more problematic but the apparent lack of respect shown to the upper body at Snape raises the possibility of its having been a ritual killing, subsequently incorporated into the main grave. If it is so interpreted, it could have been a slave buried with the mistress, and therefore included perhaps as a form of grave-good.

The nature of sacrificial or ritual killing in Anglo-Saxon England is poorly understood. Reynolds (1996) has pointed out that there is a general absence of clear examples of such killings, even though Davidson

(1992) has argued that the Anglo-Saxons may have carried out human sacrifice. Whilst the upper body from grave 19 may, therefore, add to the archaeological evidence for such practices, the absence of palaeopathological data makes it remain an equivocal case.

Grave 44

Grave 44 raised the possibility of its occupant having been killed, as it was buried face down. It is true that prone burials are known from several Anglo-Saxon cemeteries and have been seen by Faull (1977) as perhaps indicating continuing Romano-British burial customs, especially in the north of England. Indeed, this was considered one of the possible explanations for the relatively high number of seven examples found at Norton, Cleveland (Sherlock and Welch 1992, 26–27). There are, though, fewer examples in East Anglia and their appearance in Anglo-Saxon cemeteries across England lacks any otherwise distinctively 'British' element. Recent research has suggested that prone burials are a phenomenon originating in Anglo-Saxon cemeteries in the 6th and 7th centuries, in which the individuals were probably judicial killings and viewed 'very differently from other members of the community' (Reynolds 1997, 34). Prone burial was not only an exception, but a calculated opposition of the normal supine or flexed ways of laying out the body, and with it, implications of a normal body being able to 'rise up' at some future point are reversed, so that the body continues down (Hirst 1985, 36–7).

In the case of the Snape burial, a number of features indicate that the treatment of the body was disrespectful. First, the body was not placed exactly in the grave, which was dug to the correct length for the individual. Instead, the head was pushed back sharply, the face being pressed against the grave west end, leaving a gap to the east of the feet. The clear impression was that the body had been thrown into the grave from the east. Secondly, no grave-goods were found buried with the body, unlike nearly all the other Snape burials. Finally, a large flint cobble was found resting on the back of the body, between the shoulder blades. Given the paucity of flint from the site, and its total absence in nodules of this size, this must have been imported and be a deliberate inclusion within the grave. The use of a stone also finds a striking parallel in those found on the shoulders and pelvis of the body, once again, in grave 41 at Sewerby. Here, Hirst suggested that they might have been used to prevent the woman moving, or were used to weigh her down (1985, 39). Whilst Grainger argued that the stone on the Sewerby body would not in itself have prevented the person from moving if still alive (1986, 161) this presumes the individual not to have been unconscious or disabled in some way, perhaps by beating or drugging (Hirst 1993, 43). A similar interpretation is possible for the Snape body, that it was alive when buried, although the awkward body position would suggest that the individual may not have actually been conscious. The stone may, therefore, have been either thrown in to apply a *coup de grâce*, or have been the result of a final insulting 'parting shot' at the body.

Whether the individual in grave 44 was a sacrificial or judicial killing is less obvious. Reynolds has pointed out that Anglo-Saxon execution sites, originating in the 7th century with the institution of kingship, can often be seen to stand on the boundaries of territories, and are often to

Plate LVIII Upper body in grave 19 emerging from the fill, apparently thrown on its side against the northern edge of the cut

be found associated with extant barrows (1997, 34–37). An example is the recently-excavated site at South Acre, Norfolk, where at least 119 'deviant' burials were found placed around the mound, producing radiocarbon dates suggesting interment from pagan to Late Anglo-Saxon times (Wymer 1996, 88–89). The proximity of grave 44 to mound 4 at Snape would fit this pattern and perhaps also provides an explanation for the body in grave 46, which was curious. Although the body here was buried supine extended, it had no accompanying grave-goods, no organics related to grave structures, and had been squeezed into a very narrow grave cut, more akin to a slit trench. Like grave 44, this burial is undated although is stratigraphically later than burnt stone feature *1775*, which it cut. These burnt stone features surround mound 4 and radiocarbon determinations show them to date from the cemetery's use. How much later grave 46 might be is a moot question. If it, and grave 44, are Middle or Late Anglo-Saxon in date, interpreting them as judicial killings is clearly preferable, despite there only being a pair of them. A similar situation appears to have been found at Galley Hills, Surrey, where only five execution victims were found around one of several mounds (Barfoot and Price-Williams 1976) and 'there is no good reason why execution burials should necessarily focus on one particular mound if several are available' (A. Reynolds, pers. comm.). If belonging to the pagan period, both graves might be of either a sacrificial or judicial nature. Given their presence on a site including aristocratic, presumably royal, involvement through ship burial, either could be acceptable.

Endnotes:

1. The sherd from the 1972 material held in the Ipswich Museum cannot be provenanced to Snape with certainty, due to some mixing of material in the storage boxes. It is, however, quite likely. One might also add to the list of possible prehistoric finds the granite saddle quern found in the upper fill of grave 20, for which 'a date within the late Bronze Age or Iron Age is preferred' (David Buckley, report on saddle quern in site archive).

2. The horn in grave 1 was found under the left shoulder of the skeleton (Serjeantson 1994, 66), which would support its use as a layer for the body to rest on. That in grave 9 was also at the bottom of the grave 'by the right foot' (Evison 1994, 92).

3. Like that above grave 4 from urn *1152*, its retrieval from the surface meant that it could not be seen whether it was contained within the fill of the grave cut and therefore sealed.

III. Cremations

by Tim Pestell

Burial types

Only twenty-one cremations from Snape have been excavated under controlled conditions and the damaged nature of most of these means that there can be only limited discussion. Like the inhumations, the cremations were found buried in a variety of ways. Only the copper-alloy bowl had evidence of having been covered for burial, although many of the urns may have originally been sealed by organic covers which have left no trace. This may be reflected in covered urns having been more likely to collapse due to the pressure of earth upon them, than those left uncovered and packed inside and out by backfill.

In urns

This was the most common form of cremation burial, represented in the vast majority of cases (forty-three of fifty-one burials, or 84.3%). The urns all fall within the standard range of pagan Anglo-Saxon forms. The damage caused to the most recently excavated urns and the lack of bone in the complete ones from earlier excavations means that no attempts at correlation between the containers and contained can be made as Richards (1987) has attempted elsewhere. One urn, *0507* (grave 91) had a hole deliberately made in its base. Pot *H*, apparently associated with the body in grave 5, had a sherd missing from the centre of its base. This may have been a deliberate break but since the urn was reconstructed from fragments found at the bottom of the inhumation fill, this cannot be proven.

Grave 78, as outlined in the catalogue, is problematic. The urn was plough-damaged, only the bottom half surviving within its cut, but no cremated bone was found associated. Notwithstanding this rather important omission, the urn was like the other cremations, hence its listing as such. It has no readily apparent explanation as it is unlikely to have been deliberately emptied at some point after deposition only to be re-buried; a 'cenotaph' cremation burial seems equally unlikely.

Unurned

Seven cremations (13.7%) from the site were buried without any apparent container, one from the 1972 sewer trench (grave 74) and six from the recent excavations (graves 82, 83, 85, 96, 97 and 99). It is unclear whether any unurned cremations were found during the 1862–3 excavations. Unurned burial is a rarer form of the cremation rite but still widely known from many Anglo-Saxon cemeteries. It is unclear whether the bone was wrapped in cloth or placed in organic containers which have rotted and left no trace although this seems likely. No evidence for any such containers was found at Snape. One of the unurned burials, grave 83, contained the upper parts of a pot but none of its base. Although plough-damaged, because the deposit was mostly contained in a shallow scoop, the pot is considered a grave-good.

Copper-alloy bowl

The use of an open metal bowl as a container for a cremation is unusual, the Snape example (in grave 68) being one of only nineteen (possibly twenty) examples according to a recently published list (Dickinson and Speake 1992, 128–9). The majority of these are from 'high status' burials frequently of late 6th/early 7th-century date. Whilst seven of these nineteen were found beneath barrows, the Snape example seems to have been more modestly interred, although the nature of its recovery from a narrow service trench makes it difficult to be certain.

Instead, the Snape cremation appears to take as its closest parallel 'urn' 204 from Illington, Norfolk (Davison *et al* 1993, 36 and 48), also apparently interred as a flat burial in the cemetery, with nothing other than the bowl itself to mark it out as unusual. Like many other instances of cremations in bronze bowls, that from Snape had been wrapped in a cloth, apparently of north-west European manufacture (Crowfoot 1973). The Snape cremation differs from several of its more exalted parallels by having a solitary grave-good, an iron rivet. The small quantity of animal bone included is also quite consistent with many Anglo-Saxon cremations (see p. 258 and Richards 1987).

Nevertheless, the use of a bronze bowl for burial appears to indicate some status, since their use as containers for cremations is so limited. Bronze bowls are generally considered an item associated with wealthy (if not always 'rich') burial assemblages. When used to contain cremations they are most common in East Anglia, appearing within a small area in south-east Suffolk, in the barrow at Brightwell Heath and most notably from Sutton Hoo in mounds 4, 5, 6, 7 and 18 (Carver 1992, 368–69). However, they are not a purely East Anglian phenomenon, as examples have been found at Coombe, Kent, Loveden Hill, Lincs. (two burials), possibly at Asthall (Oxon.), and at Baginton, Warwicks. (five burials) (Fig. 149).

The Snape bowl or its burial cannot be dated accurately but it conforms to a known type of cremation assemblage in this area of Suffolk. Similarly, the incomplete information about the cremation's exact context is unfortunate but its proximity to the presumed site of the ship burial mound may not be coincidence, perhaps representing a clustering of graves of the local leading family.

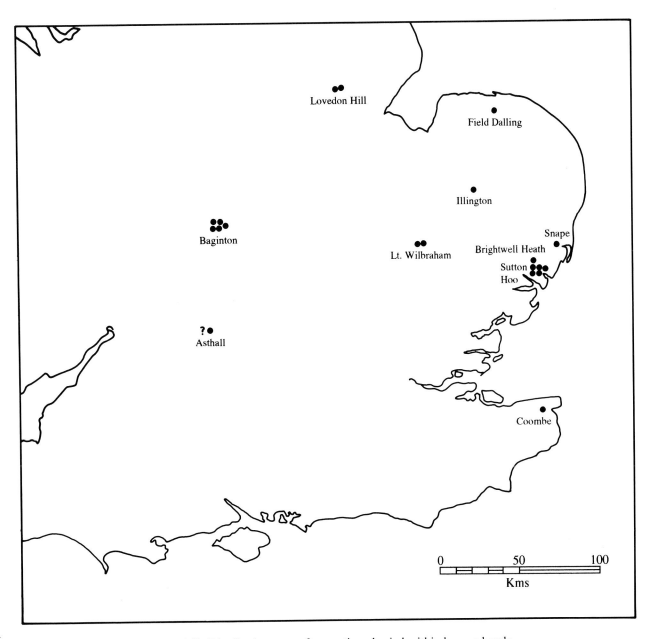

Figure 149 Distribution map of cremations buried within bronze bowls

Inclusions

Just as the inhumation graves were found to contain a wide variety of extraneous material, often deliberately placed in the grave, so did several cremations, albeit on a lesser scale. The small number excavated, especially in the latest campaign, means that there can be no statistical validity attached to the results. Nevertheless, the inclusions are of interest. In common with many other Anglo-Saxon cremation assemblages a number of burnt animal bones were detected. These are discussed below in section IV.

Charcoal
incorporating material by Rowena Gale

The inclusion of charcoal fragments might be expected given the involvement of pyres with cremations, but as with the inhumations, the inclusion of wood may also have had some ritual connotations. Six cremations included charred wood, including a bone collection from the 1862–3 urns. Species represented were oak (*Quercus*), gorse (*Ulex*), gorse/broom (*Ulex/Cytisus*), heather (*Ericaceae*), alder (*Alnus*) and cherry/blackthorn (*Prunus*).

The charred wheat grain found in grave 69 is an unusual occurrence although Peter Murphy remarks (pers. comm.) that if cremations were routinely floatated their presence might be seen more often. Small amounts of crop remains were also found in some cremations at the Springfield Lyons cemetery in Essex and in nine urns (from over 2000) from Spong Hill, Norfolk (McKinley 1994, 91). There is some evidence that spelt, a characteristic Roman grain crop continued in use into the Early Anglo-Saxon period. It is unclear whether the inclusion was deliberate or not, although Whitelock (1954, 25) refers to a pagan Anglo-Saxon practice of burning grain after death 'for the health of the living and the house'.

Although not strictly contained in a cremation, some charcoal from the pyre area (see below) proved to be fragments of pine (*Pinus*) of the *sylvestris* group which includes Scots pine. As Rowena Gale points out (p. 226), its presence is unusual, which suggests particular selection — perhaps with some assumed importance reflecting its rarity value. Alternatively, it may have been of artefactual derivation either imported as wood or as a ready made item. Its presence in the cemetery was also of interest since pine trees have sometimes been associated with immortality and the wood has been used to make coffins in the belief that it protected the body from corruption (Cooper 1978).

Wood

Only grave 68 (the bronze bowl) preserved actual wood fragments through mineralisation. The wood had been assumed to be from modern tree roots (West and Owles 1973, 50) but examination by Rowena Gale showed them to be of oak (*Quercus*) with a ring porous structure, indicating their origin from an aerial part of the tree such as a branch or trunk. The wood could, therefore, derive from an object placed in the cut (although not now morphologically recognisable as such) or perhaps be from a piece used originally for some internal structure. The possibility of a totemic inclusion must also be considered, and the wood might have been part of a scatter of vegetation as seen in some of the inhumations.

Sherds

Several cremations included sherds deposited in the cut unrelated to the burial urn. The clearest instances of this were seen in graves 78 and 83. In grave 78, a sherd from vessel *1152* appears to have been a deliberate deposition, being found in the bottom of urn *0073*; sherds from this vessel were also found in topsoil layer *0273* and in the fill of grave 4 (an inhumation; Fig. 147). In grave 83, the upper fragments of a smashed pot were collected from a scoop containing bone. Other examples of inclusions (as the cremations were themselves scattered) were the lip sherd from grave 6 pot *A* found in the shattered remains of urn *1597* (grave 90), and, less certainly, two sherds from at least one other vessel mixed in with the remains of grave 83.

The damaged nature of many cremations means that other examples may simply have been destroyed. The inclusions of cross-linked pottery are often too far apart to be the result of simply accidental incorporation and in common with the sherds in inhumations (above, pp. 244–6), their presence seems more likely to have been for symbolic or ritual reasons.

Other

In one case (grave 69) a flint flake of uncertain origin was included. More common were small amounts of burnt flint which were seen in eight different assemblages, always of small size and in small quantities. Their origin is probably accidental, being scraped up with the bone collected from the pyre site.

In two cases residues from the pyre were noted, a 'cokey' looking material being seen in the bone from grave 91, and a small piece of 'cremation slag' coming from grave 70. This slag seems to be principally silica fused at high temperatures in the cremation pyre and, according to Henderson *et al* (1987), occurs most often in cremations in areas of sandy soil — like Snape.

The cremation pyre

by William Filmer-Sankey, Shirley Carnegie and Tim Pestell

Introduction

Within Area A a number of scatters of pottery sherds, cremated bone, charcoal, metal fragments and burnt flints were found preserved in the Anglo-Saxon topsoil layer (*0273*). These were excavated in detail and the finds have all been individually catalogued (above, Chapter 4 section IV). A similar range of material — notably pottery — from the upper fills of several graves suggest that further scatters within the topsoil through which the graves were dug may have been destroyed by ploughing. The main scatter was spread over 2 square metres on the southern edge of the excavation area, in and adjacent to an inhumation (grave 10; Figs 6, 23 I and 150).[1] Rather than being simply the remains of cremations badly truncated by ploughing, these surface scatters seem best interpreted as the remains of a cremation pyre. This suggestion was first presented by Carnegie and Filmer-Sankey (1993) and has been refined as a result of further post-excavation analysis.

Dating

The nature of the material itself, catalogued pp. 175–9, makes it virtually impossible to date the 'pyre' scatter beyond being contemporary with the cemetery. Pottery from vessels found in the scatter was contained within a patch of grey topsoil sealed in the fill of the inhumation and so the grave appears to be stratigraphically later. The body from this was furnished with wrist clasps of 6th-century date so a broadly mid 6th-century date for the scatter is suggested.

Interpretation

Difficulties in the interpretation of this area were first raised by analysis of the pottery. This demonstrated that the sherds, in the largest density found anywhere in the cemetery, derived from at least eight separate pots. Moreover, the most natural interpretation, that they represented a group of plough-damaged cremations, seemed highly unlikely as the scatter included only a very small amount of cremated bone (total weight 211.6g). Given that even the truncated cremations at Snape have a mean weight of 119.9g (and adults of 142.9g), this was clearly insufficient for eight cremations.[2] Doubts were increased by the presence in the scatter of numerous pieces of charcoal and burnt flint. Neither was normally seen in cremation assemblages, except as only very small and occasional inclusions.

A far more likely explanation for this scatter is offered by the Roman Iron Age and Early Medieval Saxon cemetery of Liebenau, Kr. Nienburg, Germany. The site is notable for the remains of several funeral pyres (*Scheiterhaufenplätze*). Aspects of their interpretation are still problematic but their overall identification and characteristics have been established in the various reports of the site (Cosack 1982, 10–14; Häßler 1983, 15–21; 1990, 14–20). These pyres are characterised by spreads of material up to 4m in diameter and between 0.01–0.3m in depth. Typically, they contain burnt bone (usually in smaller quantities than in cremation urns), charcoal (which has often stained the surrounding clean sand), burnt metal fragments, glass objects and the sherds of a

URN No.	Container	Decorated	BODY Sex	Age	CONTENTS Grave goods	Animal bone	Charcoal	Burnt flint	Comments	From
48	Urn	Y								1862/3
49	Urn	Y								1862/3
50	Urn	Y								1862/3
51	Urn	Y								1862/3
52	Urn	Y								1862/3
53	Urn	Y								1862/3
54	Urn	Y								1862/3
55	Urn	Y (bosses)								1862/3
56	Urn									1862/3
57	Urn									1862/3
58	Urn	Y								1862/3
59	Urn	Y								1862/3
60	Urn	Y								1862/3
61	Urn	Y								1862/3
62	Urn	Y								1862/3
63	Urn	Y (bosses)								1862/3
64	Urn				Y					1862/3
65	Urn									1862/3
66	Urn		?F	middle aged adult	Y	Y				1862/3
67	Urn	Y	?F	middle/old adult	Y	Y	Y	Y		1862/3
68	Bronze bowl	Y	?F	?old adult	Y				mineralised wood	1970
69	Urn	Y (bosses)	M	young adult			Y	Y	included flint flake	1972
70	Urn	Y (bosses)	?	infant	Y		Y		cremation slag	1972
71	Urn		?	infant			Y	Y		1972
72	Urn		?	adult	Y	Y				1972
73	Urn	Y	M	adult	Y	Y				1972
74			?	young adult						1972
75	Urn	Y (bosses)	?	infant	Y					1972
76	Urn	Y (bosses)	?F	?young adult	Y					1972
77	Urn		?	middle/old adult	Y					1972
78				contained no bone						1985/9
79	Urn	Y	?M	middle/old adult					contained sherd from grave 4	1985/9
80	Urn	Y	?	adult	Y		?			1985/9
81	Urn	Y	?F	young adult	Y	Y			scatter in fill grave 5	1985/9
82					Y	Y				1985/9
83					Y	Y	Y	Y	contained sherds from another vessel	1985/9
84	Urn	Y	?	adult	Y					1985/9
85			?	adult	Y					1985/9
86	Urn		?	adult						1985/9
87	Urn	Y	?F	middle/old adult	Y					1985/9
88			?	child						1985/9
89			?	child	Y					1985/9
90		Y	?	infant/juvenile						1985/9
91			?M	young adult						1985/9
92			?M	adult						1985/9
93			?	young/mid adult	Y			Y		1985/9
94	Urn		?	infant						1985/9
95	Urn		?	adult						1985/9
96	Urn		?	adult						1985/9
97									unexcavated	1985/9

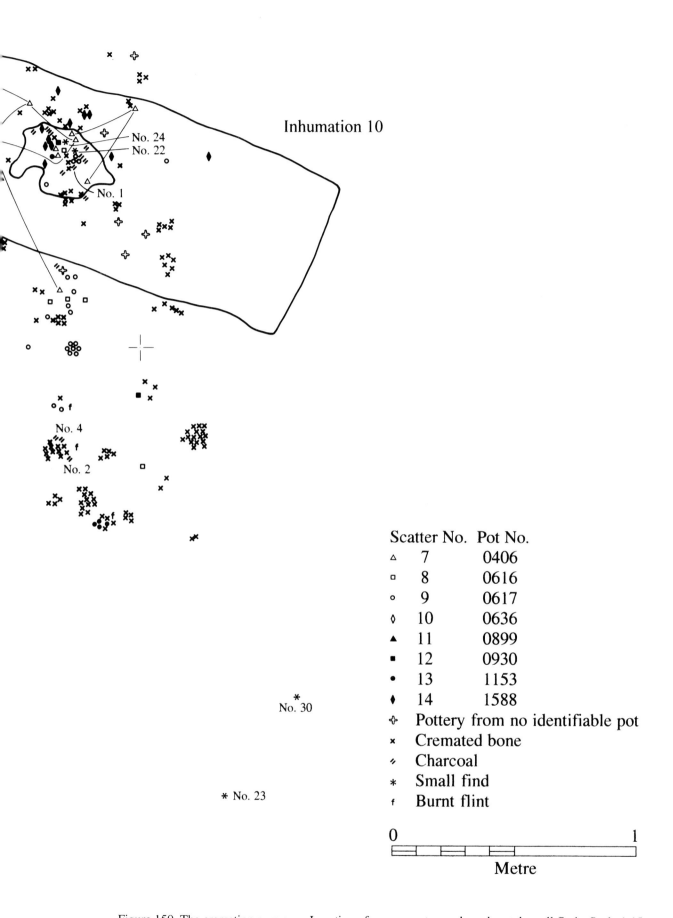

Inhumation 10

No. 24
No. 22
No. 1

No. 4
No. 2

*
No. 30

* No. 23

Scatter No.	Pot No.	
△	7	0406
▢	8	0616
○	9	0617
◊	10	0636
▲	11	0899
▪	12	0930
●	13	1153
♦	14	1588
✧	Pottery from no identifiable pot	
×	Cremated bone	
✓	Charcoal	
*	Small find	
f	Burnt flint	

0   1
Metre

Figure 150 The cremation pyre area. Location of component vessels and metal small finds. Scale 1:15

N

* No. 27

No. 3

* No. 25

*
No. 31

*
No. 26

No. 29

No. 28
*f

	Urn					
98		Y	Y		unexcavated	1985/9
99				?	scattered in fill grave 11	1985/9

Table 11 Summary of cremation burial attributes

number of pots, some of which have secondary burning. Occasionally, pyres contained post-holes arranged variously in circles, triangles or 'as the ground plan of miniature houses' (Genrich 1981a, 60). These have been interpreted as belonging to a pyre superstructure which, when an orientation survives, is often north-south, corresponding to the orientation of the inhumation graves in the cemetery. Cremation urns, containing only burnt bone and grave-goods, are sometimes found buried with the spread or close to it; in some cases they have been linked to the pyres by joining fragments of burnt bone or grave-goods (Cosack 1982, 10–14).

The body to be cremated appears to have been placed on the pyre accompanied by grave-goods and surrounded by food offerings placed in pots. After burning, most of the bone and grave-goods were collected for burial in an urn within or close to the pyre site. In a few cases the bone and grave-goods were left uncollected and the pyre itself formed the grave, being covered by a low mound. The frequent association of a pyre with an urn implies that most were used only once although some with both male and female bones may represent repeated use or a single multiple cremation.

The size, nature and components of the spread of cremated material from Snape have obvious and close similarities with the Liebenau pyres, although there are some differences. The principal distinction is the lack of staining in the sand caused by burning. The burnt stone features from Snape exhibited the red staining seen at Liebenau, albeit in only a very thin layer but no such patches were seen in the spread area. However, this reddened sand was only ever seen at Snape in the yellow natural sand, whereas the suggested pyre spreads were found in the light grey topsoil.

Other differences between Snape and Liebenau are trivial and can be disregarded. The absence of any post-holes in the Snape spread is not applicable as not all examples at Liebenau had these. The lack of secondary burning of the sherds is similarly not universal at Liebenau. In contrast, the Snape spread shares other more essential features with the Liebenau pyres. At both sites the pyre spreads follow the same orientation as their inhumations, east-west at Snape, north-south at Liebenau.

It can be seen that the Snape pottery forms coherent groups, around a central area in which only bone occurs, immediately to the south of the inhumation (Fig. 150). This presumably reflects the arrangement of pots around the body in the centre. The bone was collected as several constituent components and could derive from more than one individual, although only one gathering of material (*0083*) indicated a sex, probably male. Most of the components contained adult bone, and one included a sutural ossicle ('wormian bone', *c.f.* graves 89 and 91). Four unidentifiable fragments (11.2g) of animal bone were also included. The fragments of metal small-finds found in the scatter may also be interpreted as grave-goods accompanying the dead on a pyre and tend to suggest a female. They include fragments of brooches and of a wrist clasp (Fig. 150; scatters, Nos 26–28). These pieces were also found reasonably close together within the spreads, brooch bits 26 and 27, 1.17m apart, and brooch and wrist clasp fragments 26 and 28, 1.26m apart. More elements of a personal dress assemblage are represented by the strap-end and buckle (Fig 150; scatters Nos 22 and 24) found in the fill of grave 10.

Implications

If the Snape material is accepted as representing the remains of a cremation pyre, it is important in being the first identified and recorded in detail from Anglo-Saxon England. Other suggested instances have mostly been observations with the actual material left unrecorded, as for instance at Coombe, Kent (Davidson and Webster 1967). The example from the large cremation cemetery of Sancton in the Yorkshire Wolds is similarly based on rather tenuous evidence; accounts of the site describe it as being 'an area of burnt clay, charcoal and bone measuring two feet by one foot' (Myres and Southern 1973). The absence of any detailed plans or photographs of the area make it possible that this could be no more than an urned cremation that had been smeared across the subsoil.[3]

According to Genrich (1981b, 18), pyres of the Liebenau type have a distribution restricted to the Weser area where examples date back to the Iron Age, demonstrating their long tradition in the area. They are strikingly absent from the large Anglian cemeteries such as Bordesholm and Suderbrarup (Saggau 1985, 26; Bantelman 1988, 73) which have only simple urn burial; one might see such large cemeteries as Spong Hill also conforming to this same pattern. The example of Sancton, if seen as a cremation area, does not conform to the Liebenau type.

The identification of this particular type of pyre has other implications. Burial customs have been argued to be a reliable way of distinguishing the ethnic origins of Anglo-Saxon settlers in England. Arguably, the burial rite employed and the way that it was structured, are just as, if not more, diagnostic than the objects contained within a grave in terms of the ethnic affiliation of the settlers. In this case, the funeral pyre from Snape could be interpreted as that of a genuine Saxon or Saxons, demonstrating the survival and translation of this tradition of burial rite into mid 6th-century England from the Continent.

Endnotes:

1. The scatter of cremated bone in grave 11 may possibly be associated but other interpretations exist for this (p. 246); as it cannot be proven to have any relationship to the 'pyre' spreads, it is catalogued independently (as grave 99).
2. The Bronze Age cremation is excluded from these statistics which relate only to the Anglo-Saxon burials.
3. We are grateful to Mr B. Sitch, Assistant Keeper of Archaeology, Hull Museum, for his help in supplying details of this area from the site archive held there.

IV. Animal Burials
by Tim Pestell

Animal inhumations

Snape produced evidence for two animal inhumations, both associated with grave 47. Only one of these, the horse head, could be positively identified (see below). The second animal was seen on the south side of the grave (Pl. XXV), resting on an organic layer and its identification is interpretive. Whilst the sand cast was of the distinctive 'body stain', exactly what was represented was difficult to determine. The inclusion could possibly have been only a joint of meat rather than a whole animal, and as recovered, the stain was not clear enough to resolve this point.

However, since the stains represent the skeletal elements of a body, they appear to be convincing enough to have belonged to a whole, articulated, animal.

If the animal is taken to have been complete, its species is impossible to determine. A dog might seem to be the obvious candidate, having good parallels in a number of other Germanic and Anglo-Saxon graves, usually associated with male burials (Prummel 1992). The diminutive size of the Snape animal might make this seem less likely, although a lap-dog is known from a female grave at Minster Lovell, Oxfordshire (Meaney 1964, 211) and there was a small dog buried in a high-status male grave at Mitcham, Surrey (Bidder 1906, 58–9). An alternative is that the body was of a very young animal. Various other species of animal have been found incorporated in Anglo-Saxon graves, but these are almost always characterised by being odd or selected bones, suggestive of either accidental or amuletic incorporations, or meat offerings. Thus, if the Snape animal is indeed complete, it is impossible to make any closer suggestions as to its identity.

Horse head

The horse's head associated with grave 47 was an unusual find with relatively few Anglo-Saxon parallels. It can be securely dated as Anglo-Saxon both by a radiocarbon date of cal AD 430–670 at 2σ (GU–5233; 1460±70BP), and by its matching elements of harness tack found within the inhumation grave, a deposit of *c.* 600AD.

Horse burials have been seen by some as a substantially east European/central Asiatic rite. Popular amongst Eurasian nomadic peoples, the horse's socio-economic importance led to the development of rituals connected with it (Genito 1992, 47). Müller-Wille's work (1970–71) has made it clear that horse burials are also widely known in Germanic western Europe, amongst which some of the most famous are those from the Swedish ship burials at Valsgärde and Vendel.

The now rather dated starting point for examining horse burials in England is Vierck's catalogue (in Müller-Wille 1970/71), which listed twenty-nine sites, although twenty-one of these were from antiquarian excavations for which detailed information is lacking and one (Kemp Town) is in fact erroneous (Welch 1983, 431–2). Three sites mentioned in his list have since been published; Wanlip/Birstall, Leics. (Liddle 1979), Willoughby-on-the-Wolds, Notts. (Dean and Kinsley 1993) and Great Chesterford, Essex (Evison 1994). To these sites may be added the further examples of horse burials from Snape, Icklingham, Sutton Hoo and Lakenheath, all Suffolk (Prigg 1888, 70; Carver 1992, 362; K. Wade pers. comm.); West Heslerton, N. Yorks. (Powlesland *et al* 1987) and Springfield Lyons, Essex (D. Buckley pers. comm.) (Fig. 151). It is important to recognise the variety in the types of horse burial, as several of Vierck's sites have no more than the burial of bits of horses such as odd teeth and, at Milton, near Sittingbourne, Kent, the leg of a horse found interspersed amongst graves (Payne 1893, 103). Vierck also included examples of cremated horse remains. This latter category of horse burial, also now more widely recognised, will be considered later. Omitting these other types leaves fifteen sites with entire horse burials, four with head burials and four of unknown type. Of the entire horse burials, one from

Reading can be omitted from the present discussion as it appears to have been of 10th-century date. It may be that the more fragmentary nature of head-only burials has led to fewer being identified. Of the four uncertain types listed by Vierck, the original sources cited usually imply that the burials were of whole or nearly whole horses.

Inhumed horses are normally considered an element of high status burial (Piggot 1992, 116), typically associated with males. A few female associations exist, such as those from Selzen and Gammertingen on the Continent (Brown 1915, 420), but there is only one clear English example, from Willoughby-on-the-Wolds (Dean and Kinsley 1993, 60). The apparently status-based treatment of horse burials as grave accoutrements accords with Bede's description of a good horse being seen as a status symbol (Bede, *HE* iii, 14), and Richards has seen the horse as having had a powerful symbolism in defining status, wealth and mobility in a society becoming increasingly settled (1992, 139). This is perhaps also reflected in the 'rider and fallen warrior' panels on the Sutton Hoo helmet (Bruce-Mitford 1978, 190). The tack buried with most horses shows that they were for riding, and maintaining these animals for warfare was an expensive and therefore high-status activity in contemporary societies (Piggot 1992, 116).

It would seem that the burial of a head rather than the whole body of a horse has little bearing on the status of the grave it accompanies; both, after all, necessitated the slaughter of the whole animal. Additionally, both types have been found with tack; only one of the four English horse head burials has been unaccompanied (Barham, Kent, Meaney 1964, 111). The Snape horse head conforms in other respects to many complete horse burials. From a canine tooth, it appears to have been male (above, p. 232), like the majority of Germanic horse burials (O'Connor 1994, 32). More important, the head had been placed in an apparently formulaic pattern, to the north of the grave with which it was associated, and to the left-hand side of its owner. This pattern is found regularly in those burials for which sufficient information exists (horse burial 3 at Willoughby is a possible exception but it is unclear whether it is in fact associated with the nearest grave). Like the inhumations they accompany, horse burials tended to be placed with their heads to the west; the Snape head, although lacking a body, was similarly placed at the north-west corner of grave 47.

The distribution of horse burial types is difficult to plot with any degree of accuracy as the information for the majority of them is old and unclear. One can, however, reject Evison's assertion that 'complete skeleton horse burials are confined to the Anglian areas surrounding the Wash' (1994, 29) as there are a number of examples in the Midlands and several at Fairford, Gloucs. Moreover, if elements of horses are also considered, the distribution extends to virtually all areas of the pagan Anglo-Saxon settlement. Horse head burials, though, are apparently restricted to the south-east, and are all close to the coast. Horse bones identified in cremation assemblages at present have a biased distribution as the sites with such detailed bone studies are still relatively rare. Their distribution cannot therefore be taken as significant, although at present it appears to be essentially Anglian.

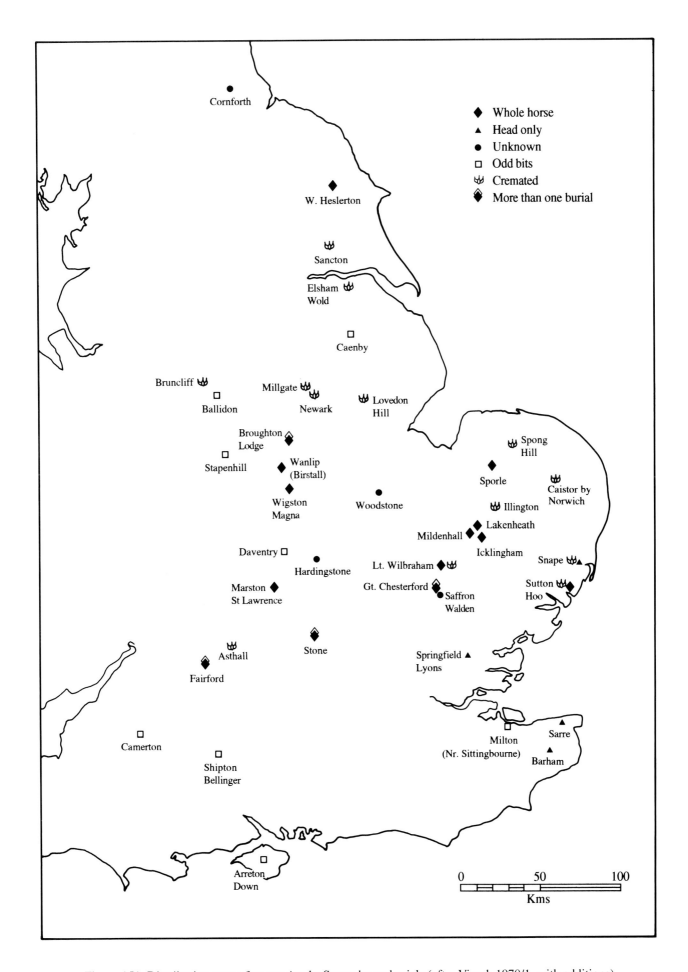

Figure 151 Distribution map of pagan Anglo-Saxon horse burials (after Vierck 1970/1, with additions)

Cremated animal burials

Snape produced burnt animal bone in eleven of the thirty-two cremations examined (34.4%), a frequency within the range of other Anglo-Saxon cremation assemblages, for example Loveden Hill 15% (Richards 1987, 125) and Spong Hill 46.4% (Bond 1994). The Snape examples could only be identified in four of the eleven instances. Two of these were of horse/cow (graves 83 and 99), one of horse/donkey (grave 66) and one of ?pig/horse/cow (grave 72). Fragmentation of the bone precluded any more precise discussion, such as the possible bias in the skeletal elements represented, to parallel or to contrast with other sites. In all cases the animal bone was fired to the same degree as the human remains, suggesting their deliberate rather than accidental inclusion on the pyre. It also made it impossible to tell where the animal or part of animal had been positioned on the pyre during cremation.

Whilst the proportion of cremations with animal remains is far higher than that for the inhumations, only one instance, grave 66, had a large amount of bone. This burial, a cremation recovered in the 1862–3 excavation, contained nearly 10% animal bone by weight, of horse/donkey. This might represent the deliberate burning of part or all of the animal on the pyre with the body. Such a practice is known elsewhere in the Germanic world for instance at Vallentuna, Sweden (Sjosvard et al 1983) and is a practice mentioned by Tacitus (Germania 27). More usually, bone appears as a few odd fragments.

Discussion

Two points are of interest. First, the proportion of animal bones, both at Snape and in general, is far higher in cremations than inhumations. Second, of the cremated animal bone, the proportion identifiable as from horses is very high, especially when compared to the overall number of horses inhumed with their owners. Explaining the reason behind this apparent patterning is more difficult.

Whilst the number of animal bones in inhumations may have been underestimated,[1] especially as contamination by residual animal bone is difficult to distinguish from deliberate depositions, their number remains very small. Consequently, it may be asked whether animal bone was more likely to be included within a cremation as a result of the ritual surrounding that form of burial, compared with inhumation.

The evidence is difficult to interpret because of the fragmentary nature of the cremated bone. In an interim discussion of the Spong Hill material, McKinley suggested that many bone elements found were those normally encountered in the detritus of butchered animals. This suggested that the missing parts might perhaps have been used in a ritual funerary feast (1989b, 244). This would accord with the non meat-bearing elements seen in many other burials across the Germanic world (Müller-Wille 1970/71, 181). It would also help to explain the presence of the mandible, tibia shaft and carpal in two Snape cremations (graves 66 and 83), and potentially to explain the fate of the rest of the horse originally belonging to the head buried with grave 47.

However, in the final report, Bond commented that the general evidence suggested whole animals were burnt, the presence of apparent 'head and hoof' burials argued to be largely the result of taphonomic processes, with these denser bone elements surviving cremation better. This not only detracts from a 'funeral feast' theory, but is supported by the general absence of butchery marks amongst the cremated remains (compared, for instance, with those few bones from the Spong Hill settlement; Bond 1994, 123). Complementary results from Sancton (Bond 1993) seem to confirm the high number of horses included in cremation burials. It would appear that horse burial was far more common in cremations, contrasting with the number of instances associated with inhumations.

It seems advisable to retreat a step in examining the inclusion of horses, to their ritual involvement in burial. The symbolic importance of horses in the material culture of the Germanic world has been variously noted, appearing for instance as stamps on pots and on metalwork such as cruciform brooches (Richards 1992, 139). This may well have been because of the position of the horse in popular religion on the Continent, a role that seems to have grown from the late Roman Iron Age onwards with Tacitus, writing in AD 98, mentioning white horses being kept in sacred groves to be used for divination (Germania 10). Similarly, Todd has commented of the remains from the Skedemoss votive deposits, that as both horse trappings and horse bones 'were very much to the fore...it has been suggested that a horse-god held sway' (1987, 174). By the Viking Age, a horse cult, possibly with earlier origins, was associated with the Vanir and especially Freyr, chief god of fertility in Norway and Sweden (Davidson 1964, 97). For the Anglo-Saxons, the horse seems to have had associations with the war-god Tîw (Davidson 1964, 60) which might have made it especially suitable for burial with warriors.

The association of several horses with high-status graves, especially those accompanied by tack showing their capacity for being ridden, has tended to reinforce the view of inhumed horses as being accoutrements to rich burials. The wealthy grave 47 at Snape, the recent double grave beneath mound 17 at Sutton Hoo and the formulaic positioning of many associated burials would tend not to contradict this. The question remains though, why decapitate the horse and bury only its head? If the funeral feast explanation is rejected, a deeper, meaningful reason must be sought. The Snape head may in fact represent the interface between concepts of high-status burial and the ritual incorporations represented in cremations.

Several examples of ritual horse inhumations exist, with the animals actually being buried alone, for instance that at Wanlip; horse 2 at Great Chesterford; horse 4 at Willoughby, and the horse head at Springfield Lyons (although, intriguingly, possibly associated with a nearby group of cremations; D. Buckley pers. comm.). Perhaps most interesting is horse 1B103 from West Heslerton, which was buried on its own, with tack, but with the head cut off and placed in the centre of the grave (Powlesland et al 1987, 163). The role of the head is perhaps also to be recognised in many of the horse burials in Vierck's original list, where those horse elements mentioned included teeth (for instance Arreton Down, Shipton Bellinger, Camerton, Daventry and Ballidon). The West Heslerton horse emphasises the importance of the head in ritual and provides a clearer context for the selection of only this element for burial at Snape. Its inclusion was clearly considered not only appropriate, but must have carried with it further associations or implications that made deposition of the rest of the body superfluous. A possible explanation is that the head was understood to be powerful in itself, carrying protective qualities for the burial of the dead as Rowell noted was later the case in medieval Lithuania (1994, 122–123).

In this way, the Snape horse head could be understood to have had an importance in burial as, arguably, those animals found in cremation burials had. It might be that the elements of tack best emphasize the aspirations of the buried individual to be identified with the warrior class. At the same time, the horse, as with the head at Snape, arguably fulfilled deeper ritual associations that caution us against making the assumption that horse burials simply indicate 'high status'.

Endnotes:

1. Some account must also be taken of the bias in the cemeteries excavated; many have been dug in advance of gravel extraction operations where the soil conditions result in poor bone survival. By contrast, cremated bone survives reasonably well in acidic soil as it contains a reduced organic component (McKinley 1989b, 241).

V. Burnt Stone Features
by Tim Pestell

The seven 'burnt stone features' excavated in the south-east of the site were initially thought to represent bonfires from modern tree-clearance. Subsequent investigation showed that they were all features of antiquity, and all were examined in detail throughout.

Size and structure
All examples shared a very similar structure and dimensions. Deep ploughing and the 'gyrotiller' (above, pp. 8–9) had affected all features' upper levels and mixed up some others lower down, for example *1771* and *2251*. All except *1771* and *1779* preserved a basic rectangular shape with slightly rounded corners and a flat base. There does not appear to have been any attempt to orientate the features. They ranged in size from 1.34 × 0.9m to 1.92 × 1.26m and from 0.13 to 0.35m deep. The sand around the edges and bases of them all had been burnt pink. In the best preserved pits, notably *1849* (Fig. 127 and Pl. XXX), the bottom and edges were lined with charcoal, typically firm-textured fragments of roundwood (branches and stems) up to 25mm in diameter. Within this lining were packed fire-crazed flints of nearly uniform small to medium size (50–100mm diameter) with, occasionally, larger nodules. Mixed throughout were more charcoal fragments and smaller burnt flint chippings. It was often difficult to determine what structure, if any, there had been at higher levels due to the agricultural activity; this damage had probably caused further fracturing of flints in the upper layers.

Those features that were relatively undisturbed showed a level layering of the flints over the wood, with some additional wood mixed in (for example *1849*). The careful arrangement of these layers is an aspect noted by O'Kelly (1954) as advantageous for heating stones. The presence of the flints is especially noteworthy; the soil at Snape is almost purely stone-free glacial sand with occasional bands of peagrit. The flints could not have been collected from the site or its immediate area but had been carefully selected, gathered and imported from further

afield. The amount of stone recovered from these features — or at least those parts surviving — demonstrates the effort involved in their construction. The average content was some 83.51kg with a range of 23.86kg (*2251*) to 176.53kg (*1849*). There was also a reasonable quantity of charcoal, with a mean weight of 0.82kg and a range of 0.08kg (*1779*) to 3.27kg (in *1849*, despite not being substantially larger than the others). Including the charcoal and burnt flint redeposited in grave 46 from feature *1775* gives the same range, but raises the means to 84.11kg (burnt flint) and 0.92kg (charcoal).

Wood species
by Rowena Gale
The species represented, usually as roundwood, consisted mainly of gorse (*Ulex*) and oak (*Quercus*) with small representations of *Prunus*, members of Pomoideae (which include hawthorn, apple, pear and rowan) and rose/bramble (*Rosa/Rubus*). The inclusion of oak and gorse in large quantities is unsurprising as traditionally both have been exploited for their high calorific values when used as charcoal or wood fuels. They have proved particularly important for use in kilns, ovens and other industrial purposes (Lucas 1960; Keepax 1974; Lambrick 1985).

It was impossible to tell whether the fuel was used as charcoal or wood but it may be concluded that these species would have heated the flints more rapidly than many others. Gorse in particular could have been used for an initial 'quick burn' whilst the wood/charcoal lining the feature, denied enough oxygen for fast combustion, may have prolonged the period of burning, maximising heat efficiency.

The inclusion of a wide variety of wood types, many being found in only very small quantities, could suggest their deliberate selection, perhaps related to symbolic associations or ritual importance. The possible ritual associations with oak have already been discussed (pp. 243–4) and the use of rowan may also have had such connotations. Wróblewski has argued that rowan was widely known in Scandinavia as having apotropaic powers (1992, 185–6) and possible associations with Thor, being described in the *Skáldskaparmál* (Poetic Diction) of Sturluson's *Edda* as 'Thor's salvation' (Faulkes 1987, 82). Certainly, given the energy used in the importation of the flint cobbles there may have been similar care exercised in the selection of wood types.

Date
The interpretation of features filled with burnt stone has normally revolved around the general discussion of 'pot-boiler' mounds, usually from prehistoric contexts. An Anglo-Saxon date was not originally suspected since an underlying prehistoric site was anticipated (see p. 236) and this type of feature did not seem to have been identified in any other cemetery. Additionally, the only stratigraphic relationship was where unfurnished grave 46 (presumed to be Anglo-Saxon) cut pit *1775*. Subsequently, it was recognised that similar features of uncertain date had been encountered at West Stow (West 1990, 27–30) and radiocarbon determinations were sought.

Pit *1794* yielded a date range of cal AD 415–544 at 1σ (GU–5234; 1580±50BP) and pit *1849* of cal AD 260–416 at 1σ (GU–5235; 1680±50BP). Whilst the latter is potentially of late Roman date, the range brings it into the

5th century, and the determination from *1794* shows that the features should be associated with the Anglo-Saxon use of the site. The date range of feature *1849* may additionally have been affected if oak heartwood amongst the charcoal sample submitted had been dated although Rowena Gale notes that many of the charcoal fragments were from stems. Difficulties in dating were also encountered at West Stow where 'fire pit' *383* contained Anglo-Saxon sherds but pit *46* was cut by a suggested Phase III Iron Age feature (West 1990, 29).

Uses and parallels

Burnt stone features have usually been interpreted as pits for cooking although Barfield and Hodder (1987) raise the possibility of certain examples having been used for bathing. Finally, in the context of an Anglo-Saxon cemetery, the identification of these features as cremation pyres is naturally seductive.

The possibility that the features at Snape are the remains of sauna baths is the easiest to dismiss since they differ in several fundamental respects: they are not close to water, have no very large accumulations of material, and lack the crucial trough-type lining of clay, stone or wood used for boiling water. Thus, although there is wide ethnographic evidence for saunas having been used for ritual purification, their presence in a cemetery set in free-draining sandy soil is extremely unlikely.

The two other alternatives appear more credible. Whilst interpreting the pits as cremation pyres is superficially attractive, there are several difficulties in sustaining such a view. The features are generally smaller than an average body size and do not show any apparent concern for orientation as do pyres elsewhere (see above, section III). It might also be expected that more examples would have been encountered in other Anglo-Saxon cemeteries. Finally, analysis of cremations from many sites has demonstrated that the collection of bone after burning was often inefficient (McKinley 1989a, 69); Snape is no exception in this respect (see p. 227). Notwithstanding the plough-damage seen, it might be expected that some pieces of bone would have been left mixed in the fill of such pits, perhaps along with droplets of melted grave-goods as encountered in many cremations. The fills of all the Snape burnt stone features were 100% sieved and no finds were recovered. Although such items might have been difficult to identify if sooted by charcoal, they were carefully sought and their absence seems damning. The existence of near-identical parallels from the Anglo-Saxon settlement at West Stow encourages identification with the third option, of cooking pits.

Outdoor cooking pits are known chiefly from prehistoric contexts but continued in use into the Early Medieval period in north-west Europe, for instance known as *fulacht fiadh* in Ireland (O'Kelly 1954). Similarly, Ólsen (1909) noted the Norse word *seyðir*, used for instance in *Landnámabók* ('H') in reference to a cooking pit. Olsen (1966, 284) mentioned 'the oval pit... [with] sooty stones in it' from Hofstaðir, Mývatnssveit (Iceland) being possibly a feature 'which could be the trace of a ritual baking pit... well-suited for the ritual preparation of sacrificial animals for a convivial meal'.[1] In common with many (prehistoric) examples, the lack of food elements need not detract from the Snape examples being thus interpreted; indeed the high natural acidity of the

surrounding heathland soil could easily have destroyed unburnt animal bones left from cooked joints of meat. If such features are associated with a form of ritual feasting or cooking at the time of burial, it perhaps provides a link with the food or animal offerings known to have been placed in Anglo-Saxon graves (Wilson 1992, 98–99).

Other various uses, for instance industrial, have been assigned to burnt mounds and alternative interpretations exist, although it should be noted that the Snape examples yielded no waste products such as slags. An intriguing possibility is a connection between the pits and the charred wood encountered in the fill of many of the Snape inhumations not least given the burnt flint recovered from several grave fills, most notably that of grave 27. Finally, it is interesting to note the distribution of the features. They all occur in the south-east corner of the site and with the exception of *2251*, are loosely arranged around the standing mound 4. They might, therefore, reflect ritual activity around the barrow.

Despite the unusual nature of the burnt stone features, there are a few other parallels to Snape beyond those at West Stow. An example is pit *248* from Norton, Cleveland, which contained several fills of burnt material with the stones at the bottom (Sherlock and Welch 1992, 13–14). A single example, close to Anglo-Saxon inhumations, was excavated in August 1998 at Flixton, Suffolk (S. Boulter pers. comm.). More certain Anglo-Saxon parallels are pits *22* and *43* from Nettleton Top, Lincolnshire (Field and Leahy 1993) which had similar dimensions to those from Snape. Charcoal samples from these features suggested that they had contained wood, some probably dead, from hedge trimming or scrub clearance which was used as tinder. These pits had no evidence of industrial use and, intriguingly, seem to have been sited on a Bronze Age barrow. Most important, from the evidence of three *grubenhäuser* in close proximity, the site appears to have been a settlement rather than a cemetery. This again seems to weaken the case for these types of features having been used for cremation. There are several other more enigmatic possibilities, typically from old excavations where detailed information is lacking. For instance, Humphreys *et al* (1923, 97) mentioned a large hearth from the cemetery at Bidford-on-Avon, Warwicks., consisting of 'about a wheelbarrow-full of large pebbles, charred and split by the action of fire' but not apparently related to the nearest body buried about three feet away. Similarly, Lethbridge (1931) noted 'the site of a large fire' which 'had been about 4' in diameter' in the cemetery at Little Wilbraham (Cambs.). Clearly, it will be of interest to see whether future excavations of Anglo-Saxon cemeteries bring to light further examples. It may well be that such features can be shown to have been far more common in Anglo-Saxon cemeteries and to have played a regular part in the ritual associated with burial.

Reconstructed burnt stone feature: performance and observations

At the end of the final excavation season (1992) it was decided to attempt to build a reconstruction burnt stone pit to gain some idea of its performance and characteristics. As the decision was made very much on the spur of the moment, the more rigorous approaches to experimental archaeology as advocated by, for example, Coles (1979) could not be applied. Nevertheless, the experience is considered worth relating.

A combination of materials was used, limited to those growing in the immediate area. A shallow rectangular pit was first excavated and filled with a mixture of long grass, branches and stems, of varying species including gorse. This mixture was used to line the pit before a layer of flints was added on top. Many of these were complete stones that had been excavated from the original features; where possible 'new' stones were also incorporated but the nature of the site meant that nearly all were of small size. Indeed the difficulty of finding enough stones on the site meant that this layer was relatively thin. Above was placed a covering layer of more long grass and branches before ignition (with the aid of a 20th-century match).

The initial result was a bonfire which gave off much smoke and a good flame. The stone layer underwent a rapid heating, fracturing and spitting small chippings out up to 5m away. Possibly because the stone layer was so thin the fuel layer threatened to burn out. The flames were lightly doused with water at which point the feature continued to burn steadily much like a barbeque. Although continued observation became less rigorous during the ensuing site party, the feature maintained a high temperature for in excess of seven hours, sufficient to melt at least one wine bottle. The evidence from our reconstruction, although crude, demonstrates that cooking or any other activity requiring a steady and high heat, could have been conducted for several hours.

Endnote:

1. I am grateful to Professor Ray Page for this reference.

Chapter 7. Discussion

I. Introduction
by William Filmer-Sankey

Although a relatively small number of graves has been excavated at Snape, the site has the potential to make a far greater contribution to the understanding of Anglo-Saxon archaeology than many more extensively excavated sites.

The reason for this lies in the unusual organic survival which has resulted in the preservation of the remains of burial containers, textiles, and other objects placed in the graves. This adds an entirely new dimension to the study of Anglo-Saxon burial rite which has traditionally been dominated by grave-goods and, to a lesser extent, by grave structure, and has concentrated largely on calculating the status of individual corpses[1]. The fact that the excavation could be carried out without any undue pressure of time meant that every effort could be made to record these features in detail.

II. Pagan Anglo-Saxon Burial Rite, Religious Belief and Ethnic Origin
by William Filmer-Sankey

The most remarkable aspect of the new information which the site has provided relates to the variety and complexity of pagan Anglo-Saxon burial rite. The evidence for this has been discussed in detail above, but is worth summarising here. Those arranging a funeral had an enormous number of choices to make. They must first decide whether the body should be inhumed or cremated. If the former, then they must decide whether the body should be placed in a container, such as a coffin or boat, and whether the grave should be lined with textile or other organic material. In digging the grave, they had to decide whether to keep the topsoil and subsoil separate, for distinct backfilling. In which of a restricted number of ways should the body be laid in the grave? Once the body had been placed in the grave, was it appropriate for charred wood to be placed in the backfill and, if so, how much? Should a layer of bracken be placed in the grave? Finally, once the grave had been backfilled, they had to decide whether there should be a structure over it and, if so, what form it should take (mound or post-built structure). If they chose a mound, should it be constructed from a ring-ditch, or from quarry pits or from somewhere else altogether? The choice of grave-goods, traditionally seen as the main element of decision, pales into insignificance compared with the multitude of other choices which had to be made.

If the body was to be cremated rather than inhumed, it is clear from the Snape evidence that a wholly different set of questions had to be asked. How should the body be burned? Should animals be included among the objects placed upon the pyre? If so, what animals? Should the burnt remains be placed directly in the ground or in an urn or other container, such as a bronze bowl. If in a container, should the remains be covered by a lid or not. Although there is no direct evidence for surface structures (whether of earth or wood) over cremations at Snape, we know from Sutton Hoo mounds 3–7 and Appledown (Welch 1992, 66) that they did exist and could be as varied as those over inhumation burials.

Cremation burial has often been assumed to be no more than a simple version of inhumation burial (Welch 1992, 87). The evidence from Snape shows that this was not the case. Rather, as Richards (1987) has argued, it was a completely separate ritual, just as complicated but abiding by a different set of rules.

In short, burying a pagan Anglo-Saxon required a huge number of choices. It is worth noting that the evidence for this variety relates only to those parts of the burial ritual which leave an archaelogically recognisable trace. There is no reason to doubt that there were many other choices (as in the initial laying out of the body, the funeral procession and feast) which have left no direct archaeological trace. There is nevertheless indirect evidence that they were of importance. The insect *puparia* found on the body of the ?musician in grave 32 indicates that his corpse was not buried immediately and it is tempting to speculate that it may have been laid out prior to burial. We know from the wailing woman and the sons of twelve noble warriors who galloped around Beowulf's barrow that considerable ceremonial accompanied the burial. Such displays, though archaeologically invisible, were of course a much more powerful medium for display than the actual placing of the body and accompanying objects in the ground.

The evidence from Snape shows further that the process was not random, but was carefully thought out and controlled. This is seen most clearly in the choice of containers in the inhumation graves. The boats used in grave 1 (the 1862 ship burial) and in graves 4 and 47 were clearly not just convenient boxes which happened to be lying around. The use of a boat of whatever size can only reflect a decision carefully taken, in full light of the not inconsiderable practical implications. A boat was needed in certain cases because of the message that it gave to the mourners. If one accepts that the choice of a boat for three graves was not random, then one must logically accept that the choice of a coffin, or a textile lined chamber or indeed of no container at all, was also a conscious one, and that the use of a particular type of container was a significant message. If one accepts this, it must surely follow that all the choices which had to be made were dictated not by whim, but by regulation. Every aspect of pagan Anglo-Saxon burial rite was chosen for the message that it gave.

The question is, of course, what message was being given? More accurately, what messages were being given, since it is likely that the complexity of the burial rite reflects a similarly complex symbolic language. Is it possible to isolate a dominant message? We suggest that it is possible, and that dominant message has nothing whatsoever to do with status as has traditionally been assumed (Welch 1992, 71–87; see endnote 1). That status is not the prime concern of the buriers is proved by the fact that there is no pattern to link graves with 'richer' contents to any of the other elements of variety, such as the provision of a grave marker or of charred wood. The signals of status, where they occur, are obscured. The case of boat grave 4 makes the point very well. On most sites, without the benefit of Snape's unusual preservation, the grave would have been found to contain no more than a simple iron knife, an iron stud and a buckle. It would thus have been a candidate for a low score in any of the more popular status scales (Arnold 1980, Shephard 1979). The additional evidence provided by Snape, however, gives a quite different slant. In the first place, the use of a boat, however small, raises the status level simply because of the effort required to bring it the 2.5 km from the river. Then there is the evidence provided by the pair of ?drinking horns remarkably preserved at the east end of the boat. Their significance lies in the fact that they are a pair, implying that the dead person was intending to provide drink for another and was thus a feast giver, a person of high standing in the Early Medieval Germanic world (Werner 1986 and 1992). Pairs of drinking horns are, of course, rare finds in Anglo-Saxon archaeology, occurring in only the grandest graves such as Sutton Hoo mound 1 and Taplow (East in Bruce-Mitford 1983, 385–95).

In short, the evidence from Snape indicates that, where status was signalled by grave contents, it is in a highly symbolic way, with relatively humble objects (such as the undecorated cows' horns in grave 4) used to convey a complex message. In the case of the 1862 ship burial (grave 1), it is not the fact that the ring is of gold that implies the high status, but the fact of its potential function as a seal (above p. 198). It follows that, lacking the detailed knowledge required to interpret these symbols, it will in most cases be impossible for us today to understand what such objects may have meant to the 6th-century onlooker. Any attempt to interpret the social hierarchy of Anglo-Saxon society from its graves can only fail. Härke has already made the same suggestion in his discussion of the symbolic function of weapons in graves (Härke 1989).

The best way to begin to understand the complexity of the symbolism of Anglo-Saxon burial rite is to see it at its most basic level, which is as an expression of religious belief. The prime reason why it was thought necessary to mark out the sex of the dead person by dressing the corpse rather than just wrapping it in a shroud (to take the most obvious example) was because pagan Anglo-Saxon religion demanded it. The same is true of all the other attributes signalled by the burial rite. If status was shown in a burial, it was because 6th-century religious belief felt it important, or (at the very least) tolerated it. The burial rite of pagan Anglo-Saxon England is thus first and foremost a statement of religious belief.

Seen in this light, the extraordinary variety of burial rite visible at Snape becomes much easier to understand. Relatively little is known about pagan Anglo-Saxon religion, but that which is points to great diversity, with many different deities having different attributes and being worshipped in different ways (Wilson 1992). There is furthermore no evidence to suggest, as the bland label of 'paganism' is often taken to imply, that it was a morally and spiritually bankrupt force, with the late 6th-century Anglo-Saxons simply waiting for a decent religion to come along! As Mayr-Harting has pointed out, the conversion to Christianity was no push-over, with virtually every single kingdom reverting to paganism after initial conversion (Mayr-Harting 1972, 29–30). East Anglia, of course, was no exception to this rule with Rædwald's famously ambivalent attitude to the new religion followed by the murder of his converted son Earpwald by the heathen Ricbert (Bede; HE ii, 15).

The evidence of the complexity of burial rite at Snape is best interpreted as an archaeological reflection of the richness and variety of pagan Anglo-Saxon religious belief, which persisted until the eve of conversion to Christianity. It is tempting, but probably fruitless, to try to identify particular methods of burial with particular strands of belief or even deities though a link between oak charcoal and the god Donar was noted above (p. 244). In this context, furthermore, it is also of interest that Crumlin-Pedersen has argued for the identification of boat burial with the cult of Frey, whose magic ship *Skiðblaðnir* is an important feature in Norse mythology (Crumlin-Pedersen 1991, 216–22). It is tempting to do the same at Snape: the worship of Frey is suggested from place-name evidence at Friday Street in Rendlesham, 8km to the south-west.

The archaeological evidence thus fits very well with the scanty written evidence to suggest a wide variety of religious beliefs still thriving on the eve of conversion to Christianity. The archaeological evidence can be taken one step further, to explain why there was such a diversity.

It has long been recognised that ethnic origin (actual or perceived) is an important message of Anglo-Saxon burial rite (but see Lucy 1995). Thus certain dress accessories (particularly brooches and wrist clasps) have clear links with the areas whence the settlers came. Snape both widens and reinforces this link, by suggesting that it was the ethnic origin of the settlers that determined their religion and thus dominated their burial rite. The use of boat burial is accepted to be evidence of Scandinavian origin. The funeral pyre identified at Snape (above, pp. 252–5) has its only parallels with the Saxon cemetery at Liebenau. None of the great Anglian cemeteries, even though extensively excavated, have produced anything remotely resembling the Saxon examples, indicating that this particular method of cremation was a marker of Saxon origin. It seems unlikely, given the identification of only one pyre, that all the cremations were burnt in this way. Some at least of the urns show parallels with the Anglian types (*e.g.* that from grave 51; Myres 1977 I, 37–41, type II.6), and it is tempting to suggest that their occupants were cremated elsewhere in a traditionally Anglian way which has left thusfar no archaeologically identifiable trace either in England or in the Anglian homelands. The wearing of wrist clasps by the women buried in graves 5, 10, and 16 should be seen in the same light: demonstrating their ethnic link with Scandinavia, where the fashion of fastening cuffs with metal clasps originated (Hines 1984, 1993). The inclusion of wrist clasps in the grave must not be seen in isolation, since they were presumably stitched onto an equally 'national costume', which must have served to demonstrate the ethnic origin of the person being buried. Although it is usually assumed that the dress fittings and clothing remains found in burials were part of everyday dress, it could equally be that there was a special costume that was used only for burials, certainly for corpses and perhaps for mourners too. It is of particular interest that Swedish-style horse-hair embroidery was found attached to a wrist clasp in grave 5, giving a rare hint of the sort of costume that might have been involved.

Elisabeth Crowfoot (above, p. 211) suggests that the piece of textile may have been old (even perhaps pre-migration) when used in the burial costume, further reinforcing the case for seeing these garments as purpose-made to indicate the ethnic origin of the dead women, and as a vital part of the burial ritual. Her study of the textile remains showed what may well be part of a different 'national costume' in grave 37, the fragments of textile which are paralleled only in Alamannic graves (above, p. 208–9).

The use of boats, of a particular type of funeral pyre and of a particular type of burial costume, distinctively woven and/or needing wrist clasps are the most obvious indications that the affirmation of ethnic origin was a vital part of the symbolism of burial and thus, probably, the determinant of religious belief. There are other, less certain, indicators, such as the crouched burial in grave 39. Such burial, elsewhere, has been interpreted as a Romano-British style and its presence in Anglo-Saxon cemeteries thus evidence for the continued existence of an 'indigenous' population (Hills *et al* 1984, 41). Even if no further links between a type of burial rite and an area of origin can be proved in the fugitive archaeological record, it is surely probable that they existed. If the choice of a boat as burial container demonstrated ethnic origin, why should a textile-lined chamber not give a similar message? If one type of burial costume proclaimed Scandinavian or Alamannic descent, why not all of them?

If one accepts that the assertion of ethnic origin (as the chief determinant of religious belief) was an important (if not the important) message of burial rite at Snape, two further conclusions can be drawn. The first is that the population of 6th-century Snape contained elements drawn from a wide area of northern and middle Europe. Caution is needed, as it is impossible archaeologically to distinguish between those who actually came from those areas, and those who adopted its uniform for political, social or economic reasons. However, there were Scandinavians from the wrist clasp and boat-burying traditions, Alamanni with distinctively woven textiles, there were Saxons using on-site cremation pyres, and Angles using other cremating methods. There were survivors of the indigenous population. Finally, since the name of the adjoining village is Friston, it is possible that there were Frisians too (Ekwall 1960, 188; but see Scarfe 1972, 84).

The second conclusion is that, at Snape at least, the memory of where your ancestors had come from remained of importance long after the migration had taken place. To some extent this is what we should expect. Bede, as is well known, displays a reasonably detailed (and accurate) knowledge of the origins of the Anglo-Saxon settlement (most notably in *HE* i, 15 and v, 9) which must have survived in the oral tradition into the 8th century for him to record. At the same time, however, there was clearly a general tendency to assimilate these smaller, diverse elements into the simpler ethnic blocks (basically Angles and Saxons) of the emerging kingdoms. This process was indirectly helped by the introduction of Christianity which deprived the Anglo-Saxons of the chance to display ethnic identity in burial rite.

More research is needed before we can know whether this concern to remember ethnic origin, perhaps for more than a century after the initial migration, is a phenomenon which occurs in all Anglo-Saxon cemeteries, or whether it is more restricted. It will be argued below that the

Sandlings lay between two of the emerging simpler ethnic blocks of the East Saxons and the East Angles, and this may have encouraged the maintenance of a separate (and diverse) identity longer than in other areas. Martin Carver, in his discussion of Sutton Hoo, has drawn attention to the way that burial rite may be used for political ends, so that the maintenance of diversity in burial rite at Snape (and Sutton Hoo — see below) could be seen as a way of demonstrating independence from the emerging might of the 'Saxons' to the south and the 'Angles' to the north and west.

III. Snape, Sutton Hoo and the Emergence of the Kingdom of East Anglia
by William Filmer-Sankey

The past ten years have seen an enormous increase in the amount of archaeological evidence to help us to understand the process of the Anglo-Saxon settlement of the Sandlings and the consequent emergence of the kingdom of East Anglia. In addition to the parallel projects at Snape and Sutton Hoo were the wider field survey carried out by the Suffolk Archaeological Unit (Newman 1992), the excavation of the Boss Hall and Buttermarket cemeteries in Ipswich (Newman 1993; Scull forthcoming), and the reassessment of the Hadleigh Road cemetery, Ipswich, first excavated by Nina Layard in 1906–7 (Plunkett 1994).

It will not be possible to understand fully the impact of this new information until it has all been published. Nevertheless, it is worth advancing some preliminary hypotheses, if only to act as a foil for future research. The first area of speculation concerns the twin relationships between Snape and Sutton Hoo and between Snape and the other Anglo-Saxon cemeteries of the area. To begin with the former, it has been apparent since 1938, when Mrs Pretty's chauffeur drove Basil Brown to view the Snape rivets in Aldeburgh Museum (Bruce-Mitford 1974, 150), that there must be a link between Snape and Sutton Hoo. The principal initial aim of the Snape Project was to provide data which could be directly compared with that generated by the Sutton Hoo Project (above, p. 1) and this aim was largely realised, for it is now possible to make direct comparisons between the two sites, and to reveal both similarities and differences.

To begin with the similarities, there is that of location. Both sites are similarly situated, on marginal heathland overlooking a major river estuary. It will be recalled that, before the recent plantations, the Snape cemetery would have been clearly visible from the river Alde, in the same way that Sutton Hoo is visible from the river Deben (above, p. 1). Both sites survived into the 19th century as visible barrow cemeteries.

There is a similarity too in the apparently deliberate use of existing (prehistoric) earthworks. The 'swamping' of a Bronze Age barrow by the builders of the grave 1 ship burial can be directly compared with the fact that, at Sutton Hoo, every attempt seems to have been made to place mounds astride the linear banks and ditches which criss-cross the site (Carver 1990a, fig. 5).

The most obvious similarity between the two sites, however, is the shared rite of high status ship burial. It was argued above that the presence of a seal ring in the 1862 ship burial from Snape (grave 1) implies that the man buried in the ship was of the highest (arguably royal) status.

This similarity is far deeper than just ship burial; it extends to the whole panoply of pagan Anglo-Saxon burial rite evident at the two sites. As at Snape, so at Sutton Hoo, variety is a striking feature, with almost as many methods of burial as there are excavated mounds. Carver's inventory (1993, 17–19) lists:

Inhumation in ship (Mound 1)
Inhumation under ship (Mound 2)
Inhumation in ?tray or ?dugout under mound (Mound 3)
Inhumation burial in coffin with horse (Mound 17)
Cremation burial in bronze bowl (Mounds 4, 5, 6, 18)
'Deviant burials', including human sacrifice, associated with mound (Mound 5) or in isolation (Group 1, east of the barrow cemetery)

It is striking that every single one of these methods of burial can be paralleled at Snape:

Inhumation in ship (Grave 1)
Inhumation under part of a boat (Grave 10)
Inhumation in a dugout (Graves 4, 47 and ?3)
Coffin burial (Grave 17)
Horse burial (associated with Grave 47)
Cremation burial in bronze bowl (Grave 68)
Deviant burials associated with another body (Grave 19, upper body)
Deviant burial associated with a mound (?Grave 44)

If these shared methods of burial are the most obvious link between the two sites, they also reflect one of the most significant differences, that of the scale of the burials. Carver has argued that the burials at Sutton Hoo are either those of the elite or of those bound to them, burials at both ends of the scale but not in the middle of it. At Snape, by contrast, there are burials of all types, from the splendour of the ?royal ship burial in grave 1, through the majority 'average' Anglo-Saxon graves to the 'deviant burials' of graves 44 and 19. The parallel use of particular types of burial rite indicates that the same messages were being given at both sites; at Sutton Hoo there seems to have been a need to put much greater emphasis upon them. The significance of this fact is considered below.

The second difference between Snape and Sutton Hoo is one of date. Despite the difficulties of accurate dating at both sites (see above, pp. 234–6 for Snape) it is clear that Snape is the earlier of the two. As Snape comes to an end in the late 6th or early 7th centuries, so Sutton Hoo starts, with the bulk of the excavated graves being put into the 'late 6th/early 7th century' or later (Carver 1993, 17–19).

A final difference is the length of time that the two sites were in use. Snape, as discussed above, may have had a period of use of in excess of 100 years. Sutton Hoo by contrast seems to have had only a brief burst of intense activity.

It is intriguing that it is precisely those features separating Snape from Sutton Hoo which link it to other Anglo-Saxon cemeteries. In terms of its size, date, length of use and the scale of the graves, Snape is a 'typical' Anglo-Saxon cemetery. A similar range of burial rite (including the use of a dugout boat), for example, has been observed at the Buttermarket cemetery in Ipswich (K. Wade, pers. comm.).

It is immediately clear, therefore, that Snape forms a link between the 'elitist' cemetery of Sutton Hoo, and the mass of pagan Anglo-Saxon cemeteries, which Martin

Carver has called 'folk cemeteries'. It is possible to go further and to consider more carefully the nature of this link.

In the first place, one can define more subtly the features which the Snape cemetery shares with other 'folk cemeteries'. It is notable that, if looking for the closest parallel to Snape in terms of size, grave density, and mixture of inhumation and cremation, one is inevitably drawn, not to the classic East Anglian cemeteries of Spong Hill and Morning Thorpe, but south to the East Saxon cemeteries such as Mucking II (*Current Archaeology* 1975). This apparent bias towards the south is reinforced by other features. Briscoe (above, p. 231) has commented on the fact that the pottery stamps relate more to sites in Essex and the Thames Estuary than to the more inland East Anglian sites. In view of the presence of a characteristically Saxon cremation pyre (above, pp. 252–5), this latter fact should come as no surprise. Indeed this Anglo-Saxon link between the Sandlings and Essex should be seen as no more than the continuation of a tradition which stretches back at least to the Iron Age, when this area of south-east Suffolk looked south to the Catuvellauni rather than north to the Iceni (Martin 1988, 68–72). If anything it would have been strengthened in the early medieval period by the relative ease of sea communications between the regularly spaced and deeply penetrating estuaries of south-east Suffolk and Essex, compared with both the lack of such estuaries to the north and to the slow and cumbersome nature of land communication (Carver 1990b, 122 and fig. 15.3). Indeed, in a curious way, it continues today: far more boat owners on the Alde and Deben have sailed south to Hamford Water and the river Blackwater, even to the Thames, than have ever ventured north of Orford Ness.

The fact that in archaeological terms the links both of Snape specifically, and the Sandlings generally, were with Essex to the south rather than with East Anglia to the north is intriguing; the written evidence gives a different perspective. For we know that, by AD 664 at the latest, this part of Suffolk lay within the kingdom of East Anglia. The source of this information is of course Bede's by-the-by statement in *HE* iii, 22, that the East Saxon king Swidhelm 'had been baptised by Cedd in the province of the East Angles at the king's *vicus regius* of Rendlesham [...] his godfather was Æthelwald, king of the East Angles, brother of king Anna'. Æthelwald was king from 655–664.

It is necessary therefore to explain why, despite its similarities with Saxon Essex, the Sandlings at an early date became part of the East Anglian kingdom. The (or, perhaps more modestly, an) answer may be found by a more careful analysis of the link between Sutton Hoo, Snape and the other Sandling cemeteries. The discussion above shows that the variety of burial ritual identified by Carver as a distinguishing character of Sutton Hoo is in fact equally a characteristic of Snape and, arguably, of the Sandling cemeteries in general.[2]

This shared variety of burial rite can only mean that the people buried at Sutton Hoo have their origins in the Sandlings area. As was discussed above, in the context of Snape, the choice of burial rite was one of a number of ways of signalling ethnic origin. In choosing to use ships and logboats as a distinctive part of the burial rite at Sutton Hoo, those organising the funerals were signalling not just a Scandinavian but also a Sandling origin. Any suggestion, therefore, that the Sutton Hoo burials are those of invading outsiders from Essex or anywhere else must be dismissed (see for example Parker Pearson *et al* 1993).

In his discussion of Sutton Hoo, Carver has interpreted the elite nature of the cemetery, and the lack of 'normal' Anglo-Saxon burials, as demonstrating archaeologically the moment at which a newly emerging Anglo-Saxon royal dynasty (by implication the Wuffingas) was able to break free of a local tribal base, and to base its power on a firmer standing (Carver 1989, 141–58). Carver has suggested that this firmer standing was taxation, though a kingship based on tribute gained from large-scale raiding used to maintain a warrior elite in the type of heroic society portrayed by *Beowulf* is equally plausible. Newton's suggestion for the poem's composition in East Anglia at about this time could thus gain additional relevance (Newton 1993). Whatever the precise nature of the foundations for this newly enlarged kingship, however, Carver's overall interpretation remains persuasive. If it is correct, then two conclusions follow.

The first is that the Snape cemetery, with its ship burial (and other mounds) among 'folk graves', represents the immediately preceding stage in this process, when a local Sandling elite had developed but had not yet managed to break free from its local ties. The relative chronology of the Snape and Sutton Hoo cemeteries (above, p. 265) fits this pattern perfectly. The fact that the 1862 ship burial from Snape (grave 1) appears to have swamped a pre-existing mound also gains in relevance. Although we know that mound to have been Bronze Age, the Anglo-Saxons (as Bradley 1987 has demonstrated) would have had no such concept. They are likely to have seen it as the mound of an earlier, ancestral ruler. The deliberate swamping of this mound by the 1862 ship burial indicates the assertion of power by a new elite, anxious to stake its claim as superior to the 'ancestors'.

The second conclusion of Carver's analysis of Sutton Hoo combined with the foregoing analysis of Snape is that the Wuffinga kings of East Anglia had their origins in the Sandlings, an area peripheral to, perhaps even ethnically distinct from, the kingdom which they made their own. Why they expanded to the Anglian north and west, rather than to the Saxon south, must remain a matter of mystery, though it may be quite simply because the kingdom of the East Saxons was already firmly established by the time that the Wuffingas were ready to expand.

The evidence from Snape, taken in conjunction with the emerging evidence for Sutton Hoo and the other Sandling sites, provides perfect archaeological support for the 'knock-out' model of the emergence of Anglo-Saxon kingdoms put forward by Bassett (1989, 26–7), whereby the smaller kingdoms were gradually subsumed into larger units, often by conquest, until the seven major kingdoms of the 8th century emerged. Snape adds detail to this model by illuminating the earlier phase in which local leaders sought to demonstrate their growing power within a local tribal base. It also demonstrates the random nature of the process of the formation of an Anglo-Saxon kingdom, whereby a local elite from the very edge could successfully lay claim to the kingdom as a whole.

IV. Postscript: the Later Use of the Cemetery
by William Filmer-Sankey

The surviving barrows of the Snape cemetery were a striking sight in the 19th century and it is inconceivable that they did not figure in the lives of the medieval inhabitants of the village. We are fortunate to have a rare and intriguing glimpse of a use to which they may have been put. In the late 13th and 14th centuries there was a family in Snape which held land along the parish boundary with Friston (*i.e.* in the area of the cemetery) by the name of Thingelow. The name Thingelow is clearly derived from the OE *Thing* (meeting) and OE *hlaw* (mound); a direct parallel is to be found in the West Suffolk Hundred of Thingoe, which took its name from the meeting place of the Hundred Court. This parallel with the known meeting place of a hundred court is intriguing. The Snape cemetery lies in the Hundred of Plomesgate, for the court site of which there is no documentary evidence.

Endnotes
1. For a popular summary of the current approach to cemeteries and their contents, see Welch 1992, 71–87. See especially p. 72: *'Cemetery analysis is undertaken with the aim of firstly establishing the sequence of development of the burial ground and its organization [...]. It then goes on to attempt to assess the relative status within that community of the individuals buried in each generation'*. A very different view of 'Anglo-Saxon' cemeteries is given by Lucy (1995).
2. Proof of this hypothesis must await publication of the Buttermarket and Boss Hall cemeteries. Even at this stage, however, a general similarity in burial rites has been observed (K. Wade, pers. comm.).

Bibliography

Anon, 1966
Orford Ness: A Selection of Maps, Mainly by John Norden, Presented to James Alfred Steers, (Cambridge)

Anthony, D.W. and Brown, D.R., 1991
'The Origins of Horseback Riding', *Antiquity* 65, 22–38

Arbman, H., 1939
Birka: Sveriges äldsta handelstad, (Stockholm)

Arnott, W., 1955
Suffolk Estuary: The Story of the River Deben, 2nd ed. (Ipswich)

Arnott, W., 1961
Alde Estuary: The Story of a Suffolk River, (Ipswich)

Arnold, C., 1980
'Wealth and Social Structure: A Matter of Life and Death' in Rahtz P., Dickinson T. and Watts L. (eds), *Anglo-Saxon Cemeteries 1979,* Brit. Archaeol. Rep. Brit. Ser. 82, 81–142

Arwidsson, G., 1977
Die Gräberfunde von Valsgärde III: Valsgärde 7, Acta Musei Antiquitatum Septentrionalium, (Uppsala)

Ashwin, T. and Bates, S., 2000
Excavations on the Norwich Southern Bypass 1989–91 Part I: Excavations at Bixley, Caistor St Edmund and Trowse, E. Anglian Archaeol. 91

Bantelman, N., 1988
Suderbrarup: ein Gräberfeld der römischen Kaserzeit und Völkerwanderungszeit in Angeln, (Offa NF 63, Neumünster)

Barfield, L. and Hodder, M., 1987
'Burnt Mounds as Saunas and the Prehistory of Bathing', *Antiquity* 61, 370–379

Barfoot, J.F. and Price-Williams, D., 1976
'The Saxon Barrow at Gally Hills, Banstead Down, Surrey', *Res. Vol. Surrey Archaeol. Soc.* 3, 59–76

Bassett, S., 1989
The Origins of Anglo-Saxon Kingdoms, (Leicester)

Bateman, N.C.W., 1997
'The Early 11th to Mid 12th Century Graveyard at Guildhall, City of London' in de Boe, G. and Verhaeghe, F. (eds), *Death and Burial in Medieval Europe,* Papers of the Medieval Europe Brugge 1997 Conference 2 (Zellik), 115–120

Bede, *HE,*
Historia Ecclesiastica Gentis Anglorum, transl. Colgrave B. and Mynors R.A.B. 1969, (Oxford Medieval Texts, Oxford)

Bethell, P.H. and Carver, M.O.H., 1987
'Detection and Enhancement of Decayed Inhumations at Sutton Hoo', in Boddington, A., Garland A.N. and Janaway R.C. (eds), *Death, Decay and Reconstruction,* 10–21, (Manchester)

Bethell, P.H. and Smith, J.U., 1989
'Trace-element Analysis of an Inhumation from Sutton Hoo, Using Inductively Coupled Plasma Emission Spectrometry: An Evaluation of the Technique Applied to Analysis of Organic Residues', *J. Archaeol. Sci.* 16 (1), 47–55

Beowulf, transl. Gordon, R.
Anglo-Saxon Poetry, (London)

Bidder, H.F., 1906
'Excavations in an Anglo-Saxon Burial Ground at Mitcham, Surrey', *Archaeologia* 60, 49–63

Biek, L., 1963
Archaeology and the Microscope, (London)

Blair, J., 1995
'Anglo-Saxon Pagan Shrines and their Prototypes', *Anglo-Saxon Stud. Archaeol. Hist.* 8, 1–28

Bond, J., 1993
'The Cremated Animal Bone' in Timby, J. 'Sancton I Anglo-Saxon Cemetery. Excavations Carried Out Between 1976 and 1980', *Archaeol. J.* 150, 243–365

Bond, J., 1994
'The Cremated Animal Bone' in McKinley, J., *The Anglo-Saxon Cemetery at Spong Hill, North Elmham, Part VIII: The Cremations,* E. Anglian Archaeol. 69, 121–134

Bradley, R., 1987
'Time Regained — The Creation of Continuity', *J. Brit. Archaeol. Ass.* 140, 1–17

Brown, G.B., 1915
The Arts in Early England, IV: Saxon Art and Industry in the Pagan Period, (London)

Bruce-Mitford, R.L.S., 1952
'The Snape Boat Grave', *Proc. Suffolk Inst. Archaeol. Hist.* 26, 1–26

Bruce-Mitford, R.L.S., 1974
Aspects of Anglo-Saxon Archaeology, (London)

Bruce-Mitford, R.L.S., 1975
The Sutton Hoo Ship Burial Vol. 1, (London)

Bruce-Mitford, R.L.S., 1978
The Sutton Hoo Ship Burial Vol. 2, (London)

Bruce-Mitford, R.L.S., 1983
The Sutton Hoo Ship Burial Vol. 3, (London)

Bruce-Mitford, R.L.S. and Bruce-Mitford, M., 1970
'The Sutton Hoo Lyre, *Beowulf* and the Origins of the Frame-Harp', *Antiquity* 64, 7–13

Bruce-Mitford, R.L.S. and Bruce-Mitford, M., 1983
'The Lyre' in Bruce-Mitford, R. (ed.), *The Sutton Hoo Ship Burial* Vol. 3, 611–731, (London)

Brunello, F., 1973
The Art of Dyeing in the History of Mankind, (Vicenza)

Brush, K., 1993
Adorning the Dead: The Social Significance of Early Anglo-Saxon Funerary Dress in England (Fifth to Sixth Centuries AD) 2 vols, (unpubl. PhD thesis, Univ. of Cambridge)

Buckley, D., 1995
'Quernstones and Quern Rubbers' in Rickett, R., *Spong Hill Pt. VII: The Iron Age, Roman and Early Saxon Settlement,* E. Anglian Archaeol. 73, 86–87

Cameron, E. and Filmer-Sankey, W., 1993
'A Sword Hilt of Horn from the Snape Anglo-Saxon Cemetery, Suffolk', *Anglo-Saxon Stud. Archaeol. Hist.* 6, 103–105

Cardon, D. and du Chatenet, G., 1990
Guide des Teintures Naturelles, (Paris-Lausanne)

Carnegie, S.A. and Filmer-Sankey, W., 1993
'A Saxon Cremation Pyre from the Snape Anglo-Saxon Cemetery, Suffolk', *Anglo-Saxon Stud. Archaeol. Hist.* 6, 107–112

Carver, M.O.H., 1986
'Research Design', *Bull. Sutton Hoo Research Comm.* 4, 1–89

Carver, M.O.H., 1989
'Kingship and Material Culture in Early Anglo-Saxon East Anglia' in Bassett, S. (ed.), *The Origins of Anglo-Saxon Kingdoms,* 141–158, (Leicester)

267

Carver, M.O.H., 1990a — 'Interim Conclusions for the Anglo-Saxon Period', *Bull. Sutton Hoo Research Comm.* 7, 17–19

Carver, M.O.H., 1990b — 'Pre-Viking Traffic in the North Sea' in McGrail, S. (ed.), *Maritime Celts, Frisians and Saxons,* Counc. Brit. Archaeol. Res. Rep. 71, 117–125

Carver, M.O.H., 1992 — 'The Anglo-Saxon Cemetery at Sutton Hoo: an Interim Report' in Carver, M. (ed.), *The Age of Sutton Hoo,* 343–371, (Woodbridge)

Carver, M.O.H., 1993 — 'The Anglo-Saxon Cemetery: An Interim Report', *Bull. Sutton Hoo Research Comm.* 8, 11–19

Chadwick, S.E., 1958 — 'The Anglo-Saxon Cemetery at Finglesham, Kent', *Medieval Archaeol.* 2, 1–71

Chiflet, J., 1655 — *Anastasis Childerici Francorum Regis sive Thesaurus sepulchralis Tornaci Nerviorum effossus et Commentario illustratus auctore Ioanne Iacobs Chifletis, Equite, Regio Archiatrorum Comite et Archiducali Medico primario,* (Antwerp)

Christlein, R., 1973 — 'Besitzabstufungen zur Merowingerzeit in Spiegel reicher Grabfunde aus West- und Süddeutschland', *Jahrbuch des Römisch-Germanischen Zentralmuseums Mainz* 20, 147–180

Christlein, R., 1974 — 'Merowingerzeitlicher Grabfunde unter der Pfarrkirche St Dionysus zu Dettingen, Kreis Tübingen, und verwandte Denkmale in Süddeutschland', *Fundberichte aus Baden-Wurttemberg* 1, 573–596

Clarke, D., 1991 — 'Brightlingsea', *Current Archaeol.* 126, 272–273

Coles, J., 1979 — *Experimental Archaeology,* (London)

Cook, A.M. and Dacre, M.W., 1985 — *Excavations at Portway, Andover 1973–75,* Oxford Univ. Comm. Archaeol. Monogr. 4

Cooper, J.C., 1978 — *An Illustrated Encyclopedia of Traditional Symbols,* (London)

Cosack, E., 1982 — *Das sächsiche Gräberfeld bei Liebenau, Kr. Nienburg (Weser)* Teil 1, (Berlin)

Cox, P.W. and Hearne, C.M., 1991 — *Redeemed from the Heath: The Archaeology of the Wytch Farm Oilfield (1987–90),* Dorset Natur. Hist. Archaeol. Soc. Monogr. Ser. 9

Crowfoot, E., 1973 — 'The Textiles' in West, S. and Owles, E., 'Anglo-Saxon Cremation Burials from Snape', *Proc. Suffolk Inst. Archaeol. Hist.* 33, 53–54

Crowfoot, E., 1983 — 'The Textiles' in Bruce-Mitford, R., *The Sutton Hoo Ship Burial* vol. 3, 409–479, (London)

Crowfoot, E., 1987 — 'Textiles' in Green, B., Rogerson, A. and White, S., *The Anglo-Saxon Cemetery at Morning Thorpe, Norfolk,* E. Anglian Archaeol. 36, 171–188

Crowfoot, E., 1989 — 'Textiles', in Speake, G. *A Saxon Bed Burial on Swallowcliffe Down. Excavations by F. de M. Vatcher,* Engl. Heritage Archaeol. Rep. 10, 116–17

Crowfoot, E., 1990 — 'Textile Fragments from "Relic-Boxes" in Anglo-Saxon Graves' in Walton, P. and Wild, J.-P. (eds), *Textiles in Northern Archaeology (NESAT III: Textile Symposium in York),* 47–56, (London)

Crowfoot, E., 1998 — 'Textiles associated with metalwork' in Malim, T. and Hines, J., *The Anglo-Saxon Cemetery at Edix Hill (Barrington A), Cambridgeshire,* Counc. Brit. Archaeol. Res. Rep. 112, 235–246

Crowfoot, E., forthcoming — 'The Textiles', in Hirst, S.M. and Clark, D. *Excavations at Mucking Volume 3: The Anglo-Saxon Cemeteries,* Engl. Heritage Archaeol. Rep.

Crowfoot, E. and Appleyard, H., 1985 — 'The Textiles' in Hirst, S.M., *An Anglo-Saxon Cemetery at Sewerby, East Yorkshire,* York Univ. Archaeol. Publ. 4, 48–55

Crowfoot, G.M., 1951 — 'Textiles of the Saxon Period in the Museum of Archaeology and Ethnology', *Proc. Cambridge Antiq. Soc.* 44, 26–32

Crowfoot, G.M., 1952 — 'Anglo-Saxon Tablet-Weaving', *Antiq. J.* 32, 189–191

Crowfoot, G.M., 1956 — 'The Braids' in Battiscombe, C.F. (ed.), *The Relics of Saint Cuthbert at Durham,* 433–463, (Oxford)

Crumlin-Pedersen, O., 1991 — 'Bådgrave og Gravbåde' in Andersen, S.H., Lind, B. and Crumlin-Pedersen, O., *Slusegårdgravpladsen III: Gravformer og Gravskikke, Bådgravene,* 93–263, (Aarhus)

Current Archaeology, 1975 — 'Mucking: The Saxon Cemeteries', *Current Archaeol.* 50, 73–80

Davis, S.J.M., 1987 — 'The Dentition of an Iron Age Pony' in Ashbee, P., 'Hook, Warsash, Hampshire Excavations, 1954', *Proc. Hampshire Fld. Club Archaeol. Soc.* 43, 21–62

Davison, A., Green, B. and Milligan, W., 1993 — *Illington: A Study of a Breckland Parish and its Anglo-Saxon Cemetery,* E. Anglian Archaeol. 63

Davidson, H.R.E., 1964 — *Gods and Myths of Northern Europe,* (Harmondsworth)

Davidson, H.R.E., 1992 — 'Human Sacrifice in the Late Pagan Period in North-Western Europe' in Carver, M.O.H. (ed.), *The Age of Sutton Hoo,* 331–340, (Woodbridge)

Davidson, H.R.E. and Webster, L., 1967 — 'The Anglo-Saxon Burial at Coombe (Woodnesborough), Kent', *Medieval Archaeol.* 11, 1–41

Davidson, S., 1863 — 'Snape', *Proc. Soc. Antiq.* 2nd ser. 2, 177–182

Dean, M.J. and Kinsley, A.G., 1993 — *Broughton Lodge,* Nottingham Archaeol. Monogr. 4

Dickinson, T. and Härke, H., 1992 — Early Anglo-Saxon Shields, *Archaeologia* 110

Dickinson, T. and Speake, G., 1992 — 'The Seventh-Century Cremation Burial in Asthall Barrow, Oxfordshire: A Reassessment' in Carver M.O.H. (ed.), *The Age of Sutton Hoo,* 95–130, (Woodbridge),

Down, A. and Welch, M., 1990 — *Chichester Excavations 7: Apple Down and the Mardens,* (Chichester)

Ekwall, E., 1960 — *The Concise Oxford Dictionary of English Place-Names,* (Oxford)

Evison, V., 1982 — 'Anglo-Saxon Glass Claw-Beakers', *Archaeologia* 107, 43–76

Evison, V.I., 1987 — *Dover: The Buckland Anglo-Saxon Cemetery,* English Heritage Archaeol. Rep 3

Evison, V.I., 1994 — *An Anglo-Saxon Cemetery at Great Chesterford, Essex,* Counc. Brit. Archaeol. Res. Rep. 91

Farwell, D.E. and Molleson, T.L., 1993 — *Excavations at Poundbury 1966–80 Volume II: The Cemeteries,* Dorset Natur. Hist. Archaeol. Soc. Monogr. Ser 11

Faulkes, A., 1987 — Snorri Sturluson's *Edda,* (London)

Faull, M., 1977   'British Survival in Anglo-Saxon Northumbria' in Laing, L. (ed.), *Studies in Celtic Survival,* Brit. Archaeol. Rep. Brit. Ser. 37, 1–56

Fell, V. (ed.), 1996   *The Anglo-Saxon Cemetery at Snape, Suffolk: Scientific Analyses of the Artefacts and Other Materials,* Ancient Monuments Laboratory Report 9/96

Field, N. and Leahy, K., 1993   'Prehistoric and Anglo-Saxon Remains at Nettleton Top, Nettleton', *Lincolnshire Hist. Archaeol.* 28, 9–38

Filmer-Sankey, W., 1984   'The Snape Anglo-Saxon Cemetery and Ship Burial: The Current State of Knowledge', *Bull. Sutton Hoo Research Comm.* 2, 13–15

Filmer-Sankey, W., 1990a   'A New Boat Burial from the Snape Anglo-Saxon Cemetery, Suffolk' in McGrail, S. (ed.), *Maritime Celts, Frisians and Saxons,* Counc. Brit. Archaeol. Res. Rep. 71, 126–134

Filmer-Sankey, W., 1990b   *On the Function and Status of Finger-rings in the Early Medieval Germanic World, c.450–700,* (unpubl. D.Phil thesis, Univ. of Oxford)

Filmer-Sankey, W., 1992   'The Snape Anglo-Saxon Cemetery: The Current State of Knowledge' in Carver, M.O.H. (ed.), *The Age of Sutton Hoo,* 39–51, (Woodbridge)

Filmer-Sankey, W., 1996   'The Roman Emperor in the Sutton Hoo Ship Burial', *J. Brit. Archaeol. Ass.* 149, 1–9

Filmer-Sankey, W., n.d.   *Forty Tons of Lime Later,* (unpubl. report in excavation archive)

Fisher, G., 1979   *Finger-rings of the Early Anglo-Saxon Period,* (unpubl. M.Phil thesis, Univ. of Oxford)

Francis, F., 1863a   in *The Field, the Country Gentleman's Magazine,* January and March, 61–62 and 74–75

Francis, F., 1863b   in *Archaeol. J.* 20, 373–374

Fremersdorf, F., 1943   'Zwei wichtige Frankengräber aus Köln', *Jahrbuch für Prähistorische und Ethnographische Kunst,* 1941–2, 124–139

Fryer, V. and Murphy, P., 1992   *SNP 007: Assessment of Charcoals and Soil Samples,* (unpubl. report in excavation archive)

Geake, H., 1992   'Burial Practices in Seventh- and Eighth-Century England' in Carver M.O.H. (ed.), *The Age of Sutton Hoo,* 83–94, (Woodbridge)

Genito, B., 1992   'The Horse Burials of Central Asiatic Type from Molise, Southern Central Italy', *Medieval Europe Conference 1992 Pre-printed Papers IV: Death and Burial,* 47–54

Genrich, A., 1981a   'A Remarkable Inhumation Grave from Liebenau, Nienburg, Germany' in Evison V.I. (ed.), *Angles, Saxons and Jutes: Essays Presented to J.N.L. Myres,* 59–71, (Oxford)

Genrich, A., 1981b   *Die Altsachsen,* (Hildesheim)

Grainger, G., 1986   Review of Hirst, S.M. *Sewerby* in *J. Brit. Archaeol. Ass.* 139, 160–162

Green, B. and Rogerson, A., 1978   *The Anglo-Saxon Cemetery at Bergh Apton, Norfolk,* E. Anglian Archaeol. 7

Green, B., Rogerson, A. and White, S., 1987   *The Anglo-Saxon Cemetery at Morning Thorpe, Norfolk,* E. Anglian Archaeol. 36

Hald, M., 1950   *Olddanske Tekstiler,* (Copenhagen) (reprinted 1980 in English edition as *Ancient Danish Textiles from Bogs and Burials*)

Hall, R., 1984   *The Viking Dig: The Excavations at York,* (London)

Halstead, D., 1963   *Coleoptera Histeroidea,* Royal Entomological Society Handbook for the Identification of British Insects 4(10)

Härke, H., 1989   'Early Saxon Weapon Burials: Frequencies, Distributions, Weapon Combination' in Hawkes, S. (ed.), *Weapons and Warfare in Anglo-Saxon England,* 49–61, (Oxford)

Häßler, H.-J., 1983   *Das sächsische Gräberfeld bei Liebenau, Kr. Nienburg (Weser)* Teil 2, (Hildesheim)

Häßler, H.-J., 1990   *Das sächsische Gräberfeld bei Liebenau, Kr. Nienburg (Weser)* Teil 4 (Hildesheim)

Hawkes, S., 1976   'Orientation at Finglesham: Sunrise Dating of Death and Burial in an Anglo-Saxon Cemetery in East Kent', *Archaeol. Cantiana* 92, 33–51

Hele, N., 1870   *Notes or Jottings About Aldeburgh,* (London)

Henderson, J., 1989   'Pagan Saxon Cemeteries: A Study of the Problem of Sexing by Grave-Goods and Bones' in Roberts, C.A., Lee, F. and Bintliff, J. (eds), *Burial Archaeology: Current Research, Methods and Developments,* Brit. Archaeol. Rep. Brit. Ser. 211, 77–83

Henderson, J., Janaway, R. and Richards, J., 1987   'A Curious Clinker', *J. Archaeol. Sci.* 14, 353–365

Hills, C.M., 1977   'A Chamber Grave from Spong Hill, North Elmham, Norfolk', *Medieval Archaeol.* 21, 167–76

Hills, C.M., Penn, K. and Rickett, R., 1984   *The Anglo-Saxon Cemetery at Spong Hill, North Elmham. Part III: Catalogue of Inhumations,* E. Anglian Archaeol. 21

Hills, C.M. and Wade-Martins, P., 1976   *The Anglo-Saxon Cemetery at the Paddocks, Swaffham,* E. Anglian Archaeol. 2, 1–44

Hines, J., 1984   *The Scandinavian Character of Anglian England in the Pre-Viking Period,* Brit. Archaeol. Rep. Brit. Ser. 124

Hines, J., 1993   *Clasps, Hektespenner, Agraffen. Anglo-Scandinavian Clasps of Classes A–C of the 3rd to 6th Centuries AD: Typology, Diffusion and Function,* (Stockholm)

Hines, J., 1997   *A New Corpus of Anglo-Saxon Great Square-Headed Brooches,* (Woodbridge)

Hirst, S.M., 1985   *An Anglo-Saxon Inhumation Cemetery at Sewerby, East Yorkshire,* York Univ. Archaeol. Publ. 4

Hirst, S.M., 1993   'Death and the Archaeologist' in Carver, M.O.H. (ed.), *In Search of Cult: Archaeological Investigations in Honour of Philip Rahtz,* 41–43, (Woodbridge)

Hirst, S.M. and Clark, D., forthcoming   *Excavations at Mucking Volume 3: The Anglo-Saxon Cemeteries,* Engl. Heritage Archaeol. Rep.

Hogarth, A.C., 1973   'Structural Features in Anglo-Saxon Graves', *Archaeol. J.* 130, 104–119

Hope-Taylor, B., 1977   *Yeavering: An Anglo-British Centre of Early Northumbria,* Dept. Envir. Archaeol. Rep. 7

Hoppitt, R., 1985   'Sutton Hoo 1860', *Proc. Suffolk Inst. Archaeol. Hist.* 36, 41–42

269

Humphreys, J., Ryland, J.W., Barnard, E.A.B., Wellstood, F.C. and Barnett, G., 1923   'An Anglo-Saxon Cemetery at Bidford-on-Avon Warwickshire', *Archaeologia* 73, 89–116

Hundt, H.-J., 1984   'Die Textilreste aus dem Reihengräberfeld von Niedernburg', *Aschaffener Jahrbuch* 8, 123–144

Hutchinson, P., 1966   'The Anglo-Saxon Cemetery at Little Eriswell, Suffolk,' *Proc. Cambridge Antiq. Soc.* 59, 1–32

Ingle, C.J., 1989   *The Characterisation and Distribution of Beehive Querns in Eastern England,* (unpubl. PhD thesis, Univ. of Southampton)

James, E., 1979   'Cemeteries and the Problems of Frankish Settlement in Gaul' in Sawyer, P.H. (ed.), *Names, Words, and Graves: Early Medieval Settlement,* 55–89, (Leeds)

Johnson, W., 1912   *Byways in British Archaeology,* (Cambridge)

Jones, M.H. and Jones, W.T., 1975   'The Crop-Mark Sites at Mucking, Essex, England' in Bruce-Mitford, R.L.S. (ed.), *Recent Archaeological Excavations in Europe,* 133–187, (London)

Keepax, C., 1974   *Danebury Tile Kilns,* Ancient Monuments Laboratory Report 1735

Kennett, D., 1971   'Graves with Swords at Little Wilbraham and Linton Heath', *Proc. Cambridge Antiq. Soc.* 63, 9–26

Klindt-Jensen, O., 1978   *Slusegårdgravpladsen* 2 vols, (Copenhagen)

Lambrick, G., 1985   'Further Excavations on the Second Site of the Dominican Priory, Oxford', *Oxoniensia* 50, 131–208

Lawson, A.J. with Bown, J.E., Healy, F., Le Hegarat, R. and Petersen, F., 1986   *Barrow Excavations in Norfolk 1950–82,* E. Anglian Archaeol. 29

Lawson, A.J., Martin, E.A. and Priddy, D., 1981   *The Barrows of East Anglia,* E. Anglian Archaeol. 12

Lawson, G., 1978   'The Lyre from Grave 22' in Green, B. and Rogerson, A., *The Anglo-Saxon Cemetery at Bergh Apton, Norfolk,* E. Anglian Archaeol. 7, 87–97

Lawson, G., 1980   *Stringed Musical Instruments, Artefacts in the Archaeology of Western Europe, 500 BC to AD 1200,* (unpubl. PhD thesis, Univ. of Cambridge)

Lawson, G., 1984   'Zwei Saiteninstrumente aus Haithabu' *Berichte über die Ausgrabungen in Haithabu* 19, 151–159, (Neumünster)

Lawson, G., 1987   'Report on the Lyre Remains from Grave 97' in Green, B., Rogerson, A. and White, S., *The Anglo-Saxon Cemetery at Morning Thorpe, Norfolk,* E. Anglian Archaeol. 36, 166–171

Leeds, E.T. and Harden, D.B., 1936   *The Anglo-Saxon Cemetery at Abingdon, Berkshire,* (Oxford)

Leeds, E.T. and Pocock, M., 1971   'A Survey of Anglo-Saxon Cruciform Brooches of Florid Type', *Medieval Archaeol.* 15, 13–36

Lethbridge, T.C., 1926   'The Anglo-Saxon Cemetery, Burwell, Cambs' in *Proc. Cambridge Antiq. Soc.* 27, 72–79

Lethbridge, T.C., 1931   *Recent Excavations in Anglo-Saxon Cemeteries in Cambridgeshire and Suffolk,* Cambridge Antiq. Soc. Quarto Publ. n.s., 3

Lethbridge, T.C., 1933   'Anglo-Saxon Burials at Soham, Cambridgeshire', *Proc. Cambridge Antiq. Soc.* 33, 152–63

Levine, M.A., 1982   'The Use of Crown Height Measurements and Eruption-Wear Sequences to Age Horse Teeth' in Wilson, B., Grigson, C. and Payne, S. (eds), *Ageing and Sexing Animal Bones from Archaeological Sites,* Brit. Archaeol. Rep. Brit. Ser. 109, 223–250

Liddle, P., 1979   'An Anglo-Saxon Cemetery at Wanlip, Leicestershire', *Trans. Leicestershire Archaeol. Hist. Soc.* 55, 11–21

Lucas, A.T., 1960   *Furze — A Survey and History of its Uses in Ireland,* (National Museum of Ireland Stationery Office)

Lucy, S., 1995   *The Anglo-Saxon Cemeteries of East Yorkshire,* (Unpubl. PhD thesis, Univ. of Cambridge)

Malim, T. and Hines, J., 1998   *The Anglo-Saxon Cemetery at Edix Hill (Barrington A), Cambridgeshire,* Counc. Brit. Archaeol. Res. Rep. 112

Martin, E., 1988   *Burgh: The Iron Age and Roman Enclosure,* E. Anglian Archaeol. 40

Mayr-Harting, H., 1972   *The Coming of Christianity to Anglo-Saxon England,* (London)

Mays, S.A., 1992   *Anglo-Saxon Human Remains from Mucking, Essex,* (Ancient Monuments Laboratory Report 18/92)

McGrail, S., 1978   *Logboats of England and Wales* 2 vols, Brit. Archaeol. Rep. Brit. Ser. 51

McGrail, S., 1987   *Ancient Boats in Northwest Europe,* (London)

McKinley, J., 1989a   'Cremations: Expectations, Methodologies and Realities' in Roberts, C.A., Lee, F. and Bintliff, J. (eds), *Burial Archaeology: Current Research, Methods and Developments,* Brit. Archaeol. Rep. Brit. Ser. 211, 65–76

McKinley, J., 1989b   'Spong Hill Anglo-Saxon Cemetery' in Roberts, C.A., Lee, F. and Bintliff, J. (eds), *Burial Archaeology: Current Research, Methods and Developments,* Brit. Archaeol. Rep. Brit. Ser. 211, 241–248

McKinley, J., 1994   *The Anglo-Saxon Cemetery at Spong Hill, North Elmham. Part VIII: The Cremations,* E. Anglian Archaeol. 69

Meaney, A.L., 1964   *A Gazetteer of Early Anglo-Saxon Burial Sites,* (London)

Merrifield, R., 1987   *The Archaeology of Ritual and Magic,* (London)

Mortimer, C., 1990   *Some Aspects of Early Medieval Copper-alloy Technology, as Illustrated by the Anglian Cruciform Brooch,* (unpubl. D.Phil thesis, Univ. of Oxford)

Müller-Wille, M., 1970   'Bestattung im Boot. Studien zu einer nordeuropäischen Grabsitte' *Offa* 25/26 for 1968/69, (Neumünster)

Müller-Wille, M., 1970/1   'Pferdegrab und Pferdeopfer im frühen Mittelalter', *Berichten van de Rijksdienst voor het Oudeidkundige Bodenmonderzoek* 20–1, 119–247

Myres, J.N.L., 1977 — *A Corpus of Anglo-Saxon Pottery of the Pagan Period* 2 vols, (Cambridge)

Myres, J.N.L. and Southern, W.H., 1973 — *The Anglo-Saxon Cremation Cemetery at Sancton, East Yorkshire,* Hull Museum Publ. 218

Nerman, B., 1949 — 'Sutton Hoo — en svensk kunga — eller hövdinggrav?', *Forvännen*

Newman, J., 1992 — 'The Late Roman and Anglo-Saxon Settlement Pattern in the Sandlings of Suffolk' in Carver, M.O.H. (ed.), *The Age of Sutton Hoo*, 25–38, (Woodbridge)

Newman, J., 1993 — 'The Anglo-Saxon Cemetery at Boss Hall, Ipswich', *Bull. Sutton Hoo Research Comm.* 8, 33–35

Newton, S., 1993 — *The Origins of Beowulf and the Pre-Viking Kingdom of East Anglia,* (Woodbridge)

Nockert, M., 1991 — *The Högom Find and Other Migration Period Textiles and Costumes in Scandinavia,* Archaeology and Environment 9 Högom Pt. II, (Umeå)

Oexle, J., 1992 — *Studien zu merowingerzeitlichem Pferdegeschirr am Beispiel der Trensen,* Germanische Denkmäler der Völkerwanderungszeit Serie A, Band XVI, 2 vols, (Mainz)

O'Connor, T., 1994 — 'A Horse Skeleton from Sutton Hoo, Suffolk, UK', *Archaeozoologia* 7(1), 29–37

O'Kelly, M.J., 1954 — 'Excavations and Experiments in Ancient Irish Cooking Places', *J. Roy. Soc. Antiq. Ir.* 84, 105–55

Ólsen, B.M., 1909 — 'Om Ordet Sedoir' *Aarbøger for Nordisk Oldkyndighed Og Historie*, II Raekke, 24 Bind, 317–331

Olsen, O., 1966 — 'Hørg, Hov og Kirke', *Aarbøger for Nordisk Oldkyndighed Og Historie 1965*

Owen-Crocker, G.R., 1986 — *Dress in Anglo-Saxon England*, (Manchester)

Owles, E., 1970 — 'Archaeology in Suffolk', *Proc. Suffolk Inst. Archaeol. Hist.* 32, 92–107

Parker-Pearson, M., Van de Noort, R. and Woolf, A., 1993 — 'Three Men and a Boat: Sutton Hoo and the East Saxon Kingdom', *Anglo-Saxon England* 22, 27–50

Payne, G., 1893 — *Collectanea Cantiana,* (London)

Pearson, T., 1988–89 — 'The Anglo-Saxon Pottery' in Adams, B. and Jackson, D. (ed. Badenoch, L.), 'The Anglo-Saxon Cemetery at Wakerley, Northamptonshire. Excavations by Mr D Jackson 1968–69', *Northamptonshire Archaeol.* 22, 69–183

Peers, C.R. and Radford, C.A.R., 1943 — 'The Saxon Monastery at Whitby', *Archaeologia* 89, 27–88

Penn, K., 2000 — *Excavations on the Norwich Southern Bypass 1989–91 Part II: The Anglo-Saxon Cemetery at Harford Farm,* E. Anglian Archaeol. 92

Perizonius, W.R.K., 1984 — 'Closing and Non-closing Sutures in 256 Crania of Known Age and Sex from Amsterdam (AD 1883–1909)', *J. Human Evolution* 13, 201–216

Piggot, S., 1992 — *Wagon, Chariot and Carriage. Symbols and Status in the History of Transport,* (London)

Pirling, R., 1974 — *Das Römische-fränkische Gräberfeld von Krefeld-Gellep 1960–1963 Serie B, Vol. 8, Text,* (Berlin)

Pirling, R., 1986 — *Römer und Franken am Niederrhein,* (Mainz)

Plunkett, S., 1994 — 'Nina Layard, Hadleigh Road and Ipswich Museum, 1905–8', *Proc. Suffolk Inst. Archaeol. Hist.* 38, 164–192

Posse, O., 1909 — *Die Siegel der deutschen Kaiser und Könige von 751 bis 1806* Vol. 1, (Dresden)

Powlesland, D., Haughton, C. and Hanson, J., 1987 — 'Excavations at Heslerton, North Yorkshire 1978–82', *Archaeol. J.* 143, 53–173

Prigg, H., 1888 — 'The Anglo-Saxon Graves, Warren Hill, Mildenhall', *Proc. Suffolk Inst. Archaeol. Hist.* 6, 57–72

Proc. at Meetings, 1863 — 'Proceedings at Meetings of the Archaeological Institute', *Archaeol. J* 20, 373–4

Prummel, W., 1992 — 'Early Medieval Dog Burials', *Helinium* 32, 132–194

Rackham, O., 1986 — *The History of the Countryside,* (London)

Rackham, O., 1990 — *Trees and Woodland in the British Landscape,* (London)

Rahtz, P., 1978 — 'Grave Orientation', *Archaeol. J.* 135, 1–14

Reichstein, J., 1975 — *Die kreuzförmige Fibel,* Offa-Bücher Bd 34, (Neumünster)

Reimers, C., 1980 — 'Stallet från Broa i Halla', *Riksinveteringens Rapport,* Kungl. Musikaliska Akad. 25, 10–22, (Stockholm)

Reynolds, A., 1996 — 'Anglo-Saxon Human Sacrifice at Cuddeston and Sutton Hoo?', *Pap. Inst. Archaeol.* 7, 23–30

Reynolds, A., 1997 — 'The Definition and Ideology of Anglo-Saxon Execution Sites and Cemeteries' in de Boe, G. and Verhaeghe, F. (eds), *Death and Burial in Medieval Europe,* Papers of the Medieval Europe Brugge 1997 Conference Vol.2 (Zellik), 33–41

Richards, J.D., 1987 — *The Significance of Form and Function of Anglo-Saxon Cremation Urns,* Brit. Archaeol. Rep. Brit. Ser. 166

Richards, J.D., 1992 — 'Anglo-Saxon Symbolism' in Carver, M.O.H. (ed.), *The Age of Sutton Hoo*, 131–147, (Woodbridge)

Rodwell, K., 1993 — 'Post-Roman Burials' in Darling, M.J. with Gurney, D., *Caister on Sea: Excavations by Charles Green 1951–55,* E. Anglian Archaeol. 60, 45–61

Rodwell, W., 1981 — *The Archaeology of the English Church,* (London)

Roffia, E. (ed.), 1986 — *La Necropoli Longobarda di Trezzo sull'Adda,* (Firenze)

Roth, H. and Wamers, E. (eds), 1984 — *Hessen im Frühmittelalter: Archäologie und Kunst,* (Sigmaringen)

Rowell, S.C., 1994 — *Lithuania Ascending. A Pagan Empire Within East-Central Europe 1295–1345,* Cambridge Stud. Medieval Life and Thought 4th ser. 25

Saggau, H.E., 1985 — *Bordesholm: der Urnenfriedhof am Brautberg bei Bordesholm in Holstein* 2 vols, (Neumünster)

271

Salin, B., 1922 'Fyndet från Broa i Halla, Gotland', *Fornvännen* 17, 189–206

Salin, B., 1952 *La Civilisation Mérovingienne*, (Paris)

Samhylová, A., 1993 'Dyes from the Shrine of St Maurus'. Unpublished lecture given to 12th *Dyes in History and Archaeology* meeting, Koninklijk Instituut voor het Kunstpatrimonium, Brussels, 25–26 November 1993

Scarfe, N., 1972 *The Suffolk Landscape*, (London)

Schiek, S., 1992 *Das Gräberfeld der Merowingerzeit bei Oberflacht*, (PLACE)

Schön, M.D., 1999 *Feddersen Wierde, Fallward, Flögeln, Archäologie im Museum Burg Bederkesa*, (Bad Bederkesa)

Schönbäck, B., 1983 'The Custom of Burial in Boats' in Lamm, J.P. and Nordström, H.-A. (eds), *Vendel Period Studies*, Statens Historiska Museum Studies 2, 123–132, (Stockholm)

Schulze, M., 1976 'Einflüsse byzantinischer Prunkgewänder auf die fränkische Frauentracht', *Archäologisches Korrespondenzblatt* 6, 149–161

Scull, C., forthcoming *Anglo-Saxon Cemeteries at Boss Hall and St Stephen's Lane/Butter Market, Ipswich*, Engl. Heritage Archaeol. Rep.

Serjeantson, D., 1994 'The Animal Bones' in Evison, V., *An Anglo-Saxon Cemetery at Great Chesterford, Essex*. Counc. Brit.Archaeol. Res. Rep. 91, 66–70

Shephard, J., 1979 'The Social Identity of the Individual in Isolated Barrows and Barrow Cemeteries in Anglo-Saxon England' in Burnham, B. and Kingsbury, J. (eds), *Space, Hierarchy and Society*, Brit. Archaeol. Rep. Int. Ser. 59, 47–79

Sherlock, S.J. and Welch, M.G., 1992 *An Anglo-Saxon Cemetery at Norton, Cleveland*, Counc. Brit. Archaeol. Res. Rep. 82

Shipman, P., Foster, G. and Schoeninger, M., 1984 'Burnt Bones and Teeth: An Experimental Study of Color, Morphology, Crystal Structure and Shrinkage', *J. Archaeol. Sci.* 11, 307–325

Sjosvard, L., Vretemark, M. and Gustavson, H., 1983 'A Vendel Warrior from Vallentuna' in Lamm, J.P. and Nordstrom, H.-A. (eds), *Vendel Period Studies* Statens Historiska Museum Studies 2, 133–150, (Stockholm)

Sjøvold, T., 1984 'A Report on the Heritability of Some Cranial Measurements and Non-Metric Traits' in van Vark, G. and Howells, W.W. (eds), *Multivariate Statistical Methods in Physical Anthropology*, 223–246, (Groningen)

Smith, H.E., 1884 'An Ancient Cemetery at Saffron Walden', *Trans. Essex Archaeol. Soc.* n.s. 2, 311–334

Smith, K.G.V., 1973 'Forensic Entomology' in Smith, K.G.V. (ed.), *Insects and Other Anthropods of Medical Importance*, 483–6, (London)

Smith, K.G.V., 1986 *A Manual of forensic Entomology*, (London)

Smith, K.G.V., 1989 *An Introduction to the Immature Stages of British Flies*, Royal Entomological Society Handbook for the Identification of British Insects 10(14)

Speake, G., 1989 *A Saxon Bed Burial on Swallowcliffe Down. Excavations by F. de M. Vatcher*, Engl. Heritage Archaeol. Rep. 10

Stuart-Macadam, P., 1989 'Porotic Hyperostosis: Relationship Between Orbital and Vault Lesions', *American J. Physical Anthropol.* 80, 187–193

Stuart-Macadam, P., 1991 'Porotic Hyperostosis: Changing Interpretations' in Ortner, D.J. and Aufderheide, A.C. (eds), *Human Paleopathology*, 36–39, (Washington)

Stuiver, M. and Pearson, G.W., 1986 'High-Precision Calibration of the Radiocarbon Time Scale, AD 1950–500BC', *Radiocarbon* 28, 805–838

Stuiver, M. and Reimer, P.J., 1986 'A Computer Program for Radiocarbon Age Calculation', *Radiocarbon* 28, 1022–1030

Swanton, M.J., 1973 *The Spearheads of the Anglo-Saxon Settlements*, (London)

Swinburne, A.J., n.d. *Memories of a School Inspector*, (privately printed, Snape)

Tacitus *Germania: the Agricola and the Germania*, transl. Mattingly, H. with revisions by Handford, S.A. 1970, (Harmondsworth)

Taylor, G.W., 1990 'Reds and Purples: From the Classical World to Pre-Conquest Britain' in Walton, P. and Wild, J.-P. (eds), *Textiles in Northern Archaeology (NESAT III: Textile Symposium in York)*, 37–46, (London)

Taylor, G.W. and Walton, P., 1983 'Lichen Purples', *Dyes Hist. Archaeol. Textiles* 2, 14–19

Thomson, R.H., 1957 *Naturally Occurring Quinones* 1st ed, (London)

Thrane, H., 1987 'The Ladby Ship Revisited', *Antiquity* 61, 41–49

Todd, M., 1987 *The Northern Barbarians 100 BC – AD 300* 2nd ed, (Oxford)

Tutin, T.G. *et al*, 1964–80 *Flora Europaea* 5 vols, (Cambridge)

Van de Noort, R., 1993 'The Context of Early Medieval Barrows in Western Europe', *Antiquity* 67, 66–73

Vierck, H. von, 1970–1 'Pferdegräber im Angelsächsischen England' in Müller-Wille, M. 'Pferdegrab und pferdeopfer im frühen Mittelalter', *Berichten van de Rijksdienst voor het Oudheidkundige Bodermonderzoek* 20–1, 189–198

Wahl, J., 1982 'Leichenbränduntersuchungen: Ein Überblick über die Bearbeitungs- und Aussagemöglichkeiten von Brandgräbern', *Praehistorische Zeitschrift* 57(I), 1–125

Walton, P., 1988 'Dyes of the Viking Age: A Summary of Recent Work', *Dyes Hist. Archaeol* 7, 14–20

Walton, P. and Taylor G.W., 1991 'The Characterisation of Dyes in Textiles from Archaeological Excavations', *Chromatography and Analysis* 17, 5–7

Walton Rogers, P., 1999 'Farbstoffanalysen an Proben aus Eberdingen-Hochdorf und dem Hohmichele', in Banck-Burgess, J., *Hochdorf IV: Die Textilfunde aus dem Fürstengrab von Eberdingen-Hochdorf (Kreis Ludwigsburg) und weitere Grabtextilien aus halstatt- und Latènezeitlichen Kulturgruppen*, Forschungen und Berichte zur vor- und frühgeschichte in Baden-Württenberg 70, 240–245

Walton Rogers, P., forthcoming 'Textile and Dress from the Anglo-Saxon Cemetery at West Heslerton, North Yorkshire' in Powlesland, D. and Haughton, C., forthcoming, *The Anglo-Saxon Cemetery at West Heslerton*

Watson, J., 1994   'Wood Usage in Anglo-Saxon Shields', *Anglo-Saxon Stud. Archaeol. Hist.* 7, 35–48

Welch, M., 1983   *Early Anglo-Saxon Sussex,* Brit. Archaeol. Rep. Brit. Ser. 112

Welch, M., 1992   *Anglo-Saxon England*, (London)

Wells, C., 1960   'A Study of Cremation', *Antiquity* 34, 29–37

Wells, C., 1973   'Appendix B: The Human Cremations' in West, S.E. and Owles, E., 'Anglo-Saxon Cremation Burials from Snape', *Proc. Suffolk Inst. Archaeol. Hist.* 33, 56–57

Werner, J., 1971   'Zur Zeitstellung des Bootgrabes von Snape', *Actes du VII Congrès International des Sciences Préhistoriques et Protohistoriques, Prague 1966* Vol.2, 997–998, (Prague)

Werner, J., 1986   'Nachlese zum Schiffsgrab von Sutton Hoo. Bemerkungen, Überlegungen und Vorschläge zu Sutton Hoo Band 3 (1983)', *Germania* 64(2), 463–497

Werner, J., 1992   'A Review of the Sutton Hoo Ship Burial Volume 3. Some Remarks, Thoughts and Proposals', *Anglo-Saxon Stud. Archaeol. Hist.* 5, 1–24

West, S., 1988   *The Anglo-Saxon Cemetery at Westgarth Gardens, Bury St Edmunds, Suffolk*, E. Anglian Archaeol. 38

West, S.E., 1990   *West Stow, The Prehistoric and Romano-British Occupations,* E. Anglian Archaeol. 40

West, S.E., 1998   *A Corpus of Anglo-Saxon Material from East Anglia: Part I Suffolk*, E. Anglian Archaeol. 84

West, S. and Owles, E., 1973   'Anglo-Saxon Cremation Burials from Snape', *Proc. Suffolk Inst. Archaeol. Hist.* 33, 47–57

White, R., 1988   *Roman and Celtic Objects from Anglo-Saxon Graves*, Brit. Archaeol. Rep. Brit. Ser. 191

Whitelock, D., 1954   *The Beginnings of English Society* 2nd ed., (Harmondsworth)

Whiting, M.C., 1983   'Appendix 2: Dye Analysis' in Crowfoot, E., 'The Textiles' in Bruce-Mitford, R. (ed.), *The Sutton Hoo Ship Burial* Vol. 3, 465, (London)

Williams, D.F., 1992   *Neolithic and Bronze Age Saddle Querns and Rubbers from Goldington, Bedford, Bedfordshire,* Ancient Monuments Laboratory Report 35/92

Williamson, C., 1977   *The Old English Riddles of the Exeter Book,* (Chapel Hill, North Carolina)

Wilson, D.M., 1956   'The Initial Excavation of an Anglo-Saxon Cemetery at Melbourne, Cambridgeshire', *Proc. Cambridge Antiq. Soc.* 49, 29–41

Wilson, D., 1992   *Anglo-Saxon Paganism,* (London)

Wróblewski, W., 1992   'The Magic Power of the Rowan Tree. Analysis of Finds from Grodzisk, Poland', *Medieval Europe Conference 1992 Pre-printed Papers VI: Religion and Belief,* 183–188

Wymer, J.J., 1996   *Barrow Excavations in Norfolk, 1984–88,* E. Anglian Archaeol. 77

Index

Illustrations are indicated by page numbers in *italics*. The letter n after a page number denotes that the reference will be found in a note.

274

East Anglian Archaeology

is a serial publication sponsored by the Scole Archaeological Committee. Norfolk, Suffolk and Essex Archaeology Services, the Norwich Survey and the Fenland Project all contribute volumes to the series. It is the main vehicle for publishing final reports on archaeological excavations and surveys in the region. For information about titles in the series, visit **www.eaareports.org.uk**. Reports can be obtained from:

Phil McMichael, Essex County Council Archaeology Section
Fairfield Court, Fairfield Road, Braintree, Essex CM7 3YQ

or directly from the organisation publishing a particular volume.